KING ALFRED'S COLLEGE
WINCHESTER
Library: 01962 827306

SEVEN DAY LOAN ITEM
To be returned on or before the day
marked below, subject to recall

0 7 MAY 2002

0 4 OCT 2004

3 NOV 2004

- 8 NOV 2004

*THE SHAKESPEARIAN
PLAYING COMPANIES*

The Shakespearian Playing Companies

ANDREW GURR

CLARENDON PRESS · OXFORD

Oxford University Press, Great Clarendon Street, Oxford OX2 6DP

Oxford New York

Athens Auckland Bangkok Bogota Bombay
Buenos Aires Calcutta Cape Town Dar es Salaam
Delhi Florence Hong Kong Istanbul Karachi
Kuala Lumpur Madras Madrid Melbourne
Mexico City Nairobi Paris Singapore
Taipei Tokyo Toronto Warsaw

and associated companies in
Berlin Ibadan

Oxford is a trade mark of Oxford University Press

Published in the United States
by Oxford University Press Inc., New York

© Andrew Gurr 1996
First published 1996

British Library Cataloguing in Publication Data
Data available

Library of Congress Cataloging in Publication Data
Gurr, Andrew.
The Shakespearian playing companies/ Andrew Gurr.
Includes bibliographical references and index.
1. Shakespeare, William, 1564–1616—Stage history—To 1625.
2. Theatrical companies—England—History—16th century.
3. Theatrical companies—England—History—17th century.
4. Theater—England—History—16th century. 5. Theater—England—
History—17th century. I. Title.
PR3095.G869 1995
792'.094209031—dc20 95-3653
ISBN 0-19-812977-7

3 5 7 9 10 8 6 4 2

Printed in Great Britain
on acid-free paper by
Ipswich Book Co.
Ipswich, Suffolk

Preface

Histories are almost always revisions of previous histories. There has, however, never been a history of the early London playing companies directed to a general coverage of the subject. There are histories of individual companies, and there are the two great compendia of largely factual material, E. K. Chambers's *The Elizabethan Stage*, which devotes 294 pages of its four volumes to the histories of the companies up to 1616, and its successor, G. E. Bentley's *The Jacobean and Caroline Stage*, which records the later companies on 342 pages in the first of its seven volumes. Both works, invaluable though they are for their scrupulous transcription and interpretation of masses of factual evidence, do read a little like *Hamlet* without the prince. They give minimal attention to the plays and the distinctive repertory traditions that led the different companies to stage them. They indicate the major historical changes of the time only incidentally. This book, besides supplying a longer historical perspective, some corrections of fact, and a large input of new material, shifts the focus back to the plays and to their highly mobile social and political contexts.

In general the evidence is transcribed in mildly adjusted versions of the original unmodernized forms. Quotations are given in the original spelling but adopt the modern typographical forms, replacing initial *i* with *j* and modernizing initial *v* and medial *u* where appropriate. Prices are given in the old forms of pounds (£), shillings (*s*), and pence (*d*), when twenty shillings made a pound and twelve pence made a shilling. Modern dating, with the year starting in January, replaces the old year-start in March. Where the financial year started at Michaelmas, as it did in most of the provincial records, the adjustment of dates is indicated.

Versions of several chapters in the first part of this book have already appeared as articles. For permission to reprint I should like to offer my grateful thanks to the editors of *Elizabethan Theatre* 13, *Shakespeare Quarterly*, *Shakespeare Survey*, *Studies in the Literary Imagination*, *Theatre Notebook*, and *Theatre Research International*. These are only some of the surface manifestations of the massive debts I owe to friends and colleagues with whom I have discussed these matters. My special debt to all the workers in the *Records of English Drama* beehive at Toronto are listed in detail in Chapter 9. Seminars at the Folger and at UCLA in 1989 and 1990 brought me many benefits, particularly from Anne Armentrout, Jill Biemdiek, Ed Brubacker, John D. Cox, Nina Greeley, Victoria Hayne, Margaret Rose Jaster, Arthur Kinney, Kristin Leuschner, Mike Neumann, Line Pouchard, Julie Salomon, Bruce R. Smith, Pat Tatsbaugh, and Joann Thomas. To the Folger Library at large I owe an unpayable debt for so generously providing resources both scholarly and financial that have helped this work along. For their more localized and specific responses, and the very tangible benefits I have gained from them, I should like to give my warmest thanks to John Astington, Mary Blackstone, Susan Cerasano, Richard Dutton, Reg Foakes, Christopher Hardman, Franklin Hildy, C. Walter Hodges, Roslyn L. Knutson, Scott McMillin, John Orrell, Stanley Wells, and Glynne Wickham. The errors, which in a work with pretensions to being a resource for some kinds of reference must be an especially sharp mark of incompetence, are, I fear, all mine own.

A.G.

Contents

List of Abbreviations

CSP	*Calendar of State Papers*
ELR	*English Literary Renaissance*
ES	E. K. Chambers, *The Elizabethan Stage* (4 vols.; Oxford, 1923)
HLQ	*Huntingdon Library Quarterly*
JEGP	*Journal of English and Germanic Philology*
JCS	G. E. Bentley, *The Jacobean and Caroline Stage* (7 vols.; Oxford, 1941–68)
MLR	*Modern Language Review*
MP	*Modern Philology*
MRDE	*Medieval and Renaissance Drama in England*
MSC	*Malone Society Collections*
NQ	*Notes and Queries*
PMLA	*Publications of the Modern Language Association*
REED	*Records of Early English Drama*
RES	*Review of English Studies*
SEL	*Studies in English Literature*
SP	*Studies in Philology*
SQ	*Shakespeare Quarterly*
ShS	*Shakespeare Survey*
TN	*Theatre Notebook*
TRI	*Theatre Research International*
YES	*Yearbook of English Studies*

PART I

A History of the London Companies
from the 1560s to 1642

1   An Introduction

Historians make their pictures from fragments, like a mosaic. Mosaics only make sense when the fragments are put into recognizable relationships with one another, which is not easy when most of the pieces available have fuzzy edges, like a soft jigsaw. The resulting construct suffers from the jigsaw enthusiast's desire to make a complete picture out of the fragments, inventing linkages to make them fit what guesswork suggests ought to be there.[1] This history is like a soft mosaic or a fragmentary jigsaw puzzle, with the one saving grace that its external borders are reasonably distinct. Within those borders the multitude of fragments can be arranged in too wide a variety of ways for comfort, and no simple picture can be made from them. This book is just one possible assemblage of the fragments.

It is also, like all histories, a moving picture. Any freeze-frame of the kind that is used here, for instance in the fifth chapter of this book, can only be useful as a temporary capture for the purpose of closer study of something that in its nature is perpetually mobile. And, to extend the analogy, we need to acknowledge the camera's position and the reasons why it is focused on some components and not on others. Varying camera angles can change the look of these soft fragments. Historians in any case are not cameras. Writing history is a field game played in fog by untested rules.

Most attempts at writing a history fall between two stools. The recognition that the work is one of interpretation or even fiction conflicts with the anchorage that has to be found for the fiction in accepted fact. Consequently most books fall between openly setting out a thesis and hopefully building a work of reference. This book makes enough of an attempt to look like a work of reference for its theses to appear necessarily rather smaller and more segmental than they really are. The book generally is meant to serve as an aid to travel through time, but while it tries to anchor itself in the kind of tangible and exemplary anecdote that has made elements of the new historicism so enriching, the gaps in its factual base all too often make it ride like a hovercraft on a downdraft of 'possibly's, 'probably's, and 'most likely's. The result is like a hovercraft pretending to be a camera, made of soft-edged jigsaw pieces.

The borders to the territory are set, however arbitrarily, by the principal fragments that we have, the surviving plays from the period that threw up Shakespeare and his contemporary playwrights. The seven hundred or so play-texts that were printed or that survive in manuscript from their use on the professional stages of the late sixteenth and early seventeenth centuries in England, the few written

---

[1] For a relevant exchange about the problems of fragmentation in history, see Theresa Coletti, '"Fragmentation and Redemption": Dramatic Records, History, and the Dream of Wholeness', *Envoi*, 3 (1991), 1–13, a review article on the latest *Records of Early English Drama* (hereafter *REED*) volume, and the reply by Peter H. Greenfield, 14–23.

remains from a massively complex set of social inventions, are the ultimate justification for this history's focus. All the major written texts belong to London. So the borderline is set first by the record of the performances given by the professional companies in London. The immediate criterion for choosing which companies to include in the history is the record of their presence at the professional London playing venues. It is not quite an arbitrary boundary, since the processes that brought the playing companies to focus their activities in London are much the same as those that developed the records of their activities, the plays. The two kinds of record, one the surviving play-texts, the other the surviving records of the companies' presence in London, are chiefly found lodged in the official notes which register performances at court, and both of them reflect the peculiar privilege and the distinctive character that the drama acquired in these years.

It is impossible to separate the social privilege that such records reflect from the events, political and dramatic, which brought them into existence. The final boundary of time to the period, for instance, is the Act of Parliament of September 1642 which issued the instruction that all playhouses should be closed until the currently 'disordered time' should pass. That proclamation and the eighteen years without any authorized playing that followed make the most distinct terminus that any historian could wish for. The earlier time boundary, the start of London playing, is far less distinct. The traditional date of 1576, when James Burbage, a player leading a company known as Leicester's Servants, built the Theatre in Shoreditch, comes relatively late in the beginnings of the story. His brother-in-law had paid for a building with a scaffolding of galleries and a stage for plays in Whitechapel as much as nine years before. Plays by adult travelling companies and boy groups had been a stock provision for court entertainment since long before the 1560s. The first placement of London-based companies was a very gradual process. The professional playing companies emerged out of anonymous travelling groups to become celebrated troupes holding a regular foothold in London; but the foothold was slippery, and it was a long time before it became secure. Only slowly did the companies develop an ambition to hold it. The first of the major companies belonging to great lords that began to offer their plays at court and in London with any regularity first appear in the early 1560s, and that is as firm a commencement date as can be established.

The borders are also defined by the phenomenon of London itself. London was the only really large market for the peculiarly portable commodity that the playing companies had to sell. Like most markets, from the outset the status and the prosperity of the companies depended on the regularity of their visits to their customers. Gradually, following the ambition that lurks in most owners of market stalls, the visiting companies shifted to more durable premises. After a long interim period when they used temporary footholds, either city inns or innyards or the specially built amphitheatres for their (usually brief) stays, the leading companies finally secured their own purpose-built premises for their exclusive use in the 1590s. The Globe in 1599 and the Fortune in 1600 are unique as the first playhouses supplied to and for the sole use of a London company whose residence was officially approved. No other city in England ever offered this kind of security and status to travelling players. In 1604, in Bristol, an innkeeper converted his inn into a small playhouse, and York and a village in Lancashire briefly had places for playing, but no other town followed suit before the 1660s.

The rising strength of playing that got the London playhouses built was matched by the rising strength of playwriting and the growing security and durability that it achieved with print. Like the consistent and familiar repertories that regular use of the London playhouses now allowed the companies to offer, the propagation of plays through print was also a phenomenon unique to London. The companies' improving status in London was most clearly marked by these twin tangible achievements. They belonged to the London market alone, durable playhouses and plays recorded even more durably in print. In London's own terms it was never a large industry. There can never have been more than about two hundred people directly employed in the play-making business, and less than four hundred making money from it even in the peak years of the 1630s. But the character of their business gave them a uniquely high profile in the public eye. They were a famous novelty, and although from 1594 they were officially fixed off-centre in the London suburbs, thanks to their reputation and their periodic travels their influence covered the whole country.

One of the more striking things that this success obscures is the way it came to separate London from the rest of the country. By the 1630s playing in London had the court's protection. It flourished there in isolation. Almost every other large town came routinely to show a broad-based hostility, made explicit in the way that almost all the municipal authorities banned visits by the playing companies or turned them away without playing. In that last decade companies travelled with the privilege of royal licences; but, increasingly, they found themselves rejected by the towns which they had been regularly visiting to play in for nearly a century. Playgoing in London through the 1630s becomes a peculiarly isolated phenomenon when set in the context of the country as a whole. The anti-theatrical prejudice in the country, which sustained itself throughout all the growth in playgoing and which finally destroyed the theatres in 1642, is one of the strongest means to measure both what the leading companies did achieve in London and the fragility of their new status.[2]

London's city authorities were far from being the only enemies that the professional playing companies had to face. The city of Chester, one of the last to maintain local performances of the Corpus Christi plays by the local amateurs of the craftsman guilds, was entirely consistent in its refusal of admission or payment at any time to the professional visiting companies that from the 1570s tried to

---

[2] An exhaustive study of the history of this attitude, which had a range of manifestations both overt (in the various authorities' prohibitions) and subconscious, can be found in Jonas Barish, *The Anti-Theatrical Prejudice* (Berkeley, Calif., 1981). A much more recent manifestation of it is Harry Berger, Jr., *Imaginary Audition: Shakespeare on Page and Stage* (Berkeley, Calif., 1989).

replace the local products. The only gratuities given to professional travelling companies that appear in the Chester records were made by the Dean and Chapter of the Cathedral, not by the city corporation, and even they only gave access to Queen Elizabeth's company. When Chester's local lord, the earl of Derby, wrote to the city's mayor in 1606 asking if Hertford's company, which had been entertaining him at his house at Lathom and was due to return there for Christmas, could play in the meantime at the Chester town hall, his request was noted but ignored. The corporation passed regulations in 1596 and again in 1615 banning any performance within its jurisdiction by professional companies.

Norwich, equally hostile to players, did the same at regular intervals from 1589 onwards. In April 1624 the Norwich authorities, having received a letter from the Privy Council that expressed sympathy for their bans on public playing, used it as their ground to forbid the next company that arrived carrying a royal warrant from playing in the city. They had enough courage, bolstered by their conviction that playing corrupted the poor, to actually argue that the Privy Council's letter supporting their position overruled the king's signet on his licence to the company. Predictably, the outcome was stormy, though entirely local. The Norwich records state that

This day Francis Wambus brought into this Court A Bill signed with his Majesties hand . . . whereupon there was shewed forth unto him the Letters directed from the Lords of his majesties most honorable privie Counsell Dated the 27th of May 1623 . . . whereupon the said wambus peremtorily affirmed that he would play in this City & would lay in prison here this Twelvemoneth but he would try whether the kinges Command or the Counselles be the greater . . . the said wambus was according to the Counselles order Comanded to forbeare to play within the liberties of this City And he netheles answered that he would make tryall what he might doe by the kinges authority for he said he would play.[3]

Norwich used the Privy Council's authority to counter the king's. Wambus and his Lady Elizabeth's company made an attempt to test which was the stronger on that same day, 24 April, by setting up a playbill saying that a play called *The Spanish Contract*[4] would be played at the White Horse in the city. The Norwich authorities promptly imprisoned Wambus, who admitted to the court that he had written the playbill himself. The mayor subsequently released him on a bond paid by Wambus's co-leader, Townsend. Wambus returned to Norwich that September with Townsend carrying a letter from the Master of the Revels, Henry Herbert, which said that he had been freed from his imprisonment on the Lord Chamberlain's authority. This letter Wambus used to demand the repayment of Townsend's bond. The Norwich court stood its ground and refused to give the money back.[5]

[3] Transcribed in *REED, Norwich*, 180.
[4] The play has been lost. Its title suggests that it was written to ride on the same wave of anti-Spanish feeling that produced *A Game at Chess* a few months later.
[5] See *REED, Norwich*, 180–3. Six years went by after this confrontation before the Lady Elizabeth's eventually returned to play at Norwich.

Such hostility to playing on the part of local authorities was widespread and rarely wavered, even though few seem to have gone to the length that Chester did of refusing the visitors any gratuity at all. To judge by the municipal records across the country, the strength of the hostility in most local authorities, including London, to professional playing was notably greater than it was to other crowd-pulling enterprises such as bear- or bull-baiting, or even to the smaller groups of entertainers like tumblers and acrobats. It was not just a matter of local religious hostility to the kind of public leisure pursuits thought to do the devil's work. Nor was it just a matter of the riots and affrays which the authorities expected to take place whenever large crowds gathered. Something more basic, a prejudice that was in complex ways rooted in the idea that people who paid money to witness the counterfeits and con-tricks which happened when men and boys pretended to be what they were not were at risk, sits somewhere under this broadly felt animus. What really inspired it is about as extricable as taking the religious motives out of the political in 1642. In some respects the animus did have a religious basis, since the towns which made the most intense efforts either to preserve or to suppress the local Corpus Christi plays were often the same towns which showed most hostility to the professional players. But it is equally possible that the growth of hostility under the Stuarts can be related to the growth of political hostility to the crown. There is no clear way to identify such broad and collective motivation.

This animus against professional playing lasted throughout the period, for all the popular appeal of the Shakespearian plays, and for all the royal and noble backing that they had from the outset. The enemies of playgoing finally took control only when Parliament took power from the king. In that sense the companies were allied to their masters, the nobles and royals who stood as their patrons, and to that faction on the Privy Council which consistently supported the professional companies for their usefulness in providing entertainments at court. The first patron to give the companies firm backing was Charles Howard, Elizabeth's Lord Admiral, along with his father-in-law and successor as Lord Chamberlain, Henry Carey. The two of them combined on the Privy Council to set up their companies in 1594 at the suburban playhouses. There, unlike in the city itself, Howard had direct power over the local magistrates. In 1603 it was James himself who upheld the companies, and finally under the early Stuarts they were backed by the two Pembroke brothers, both in turn Lords Chamberlain. These figures stand out as the leaders of a curious alliance between the few grandees who actively promoted the companies and the mass of people who showed the popular appetite for plays, both working in the interests of a form of public entertainment that was unique to England at the time.[6] It was a peculiar struggle, unique for any time in the incongruity of the alliances that it evoked, peculiarly

[6] Philip Herbert, the 4th earl, appears to have changed his attitude to playing after 1642. In 1647 when the House of Lords voted for a new six-month ban on playing, he was one of 6 lords who urged a perpetual ban. See Leslie Hotson, *The Commonwealth and Restoration Stage* (Cambridge, Mass., 1928), 25. Attitudes polarized after 1642, and Pembroke was on the more puritanical side.

revealing about the schizophrenic state of English thinking up to the battles of the 1640s.

The provincial records are more revealing here than London's own struggles. As the Stuart system of control for the companies developed and the Master of the Revels began issuing annual licences for the travelling companies to carry with them, increasingly local mayors turned them away. In essence, the London experience, where the professional playing companies received protection from royalty and royalty's closest supporters on the Privy Council against the uniform hostility of the City of London authorities, was repeated throughout the country. The difference was that, outside those suburbs in Middlesex and Surrey which catered for London's playgoing demands, it was usually the local authorities that won. Their hostility was quite specifically aimed at the professional companies. Chester's mayor in 1575, Sir John Savage, took the long journey to London in an attempt to preserve the Chester guilds' Whitsun plays against orders forbidding them that had been sent him by the Archbishop of York and the earl of Huntingdon.[7] Such a strenuous attempt to preserve local performances had a religious motive, and it did lead to Savage being promptly replaced as mayor for upholding 'ye popish plaies of Chester'. But it is a clear mark of the prejudice that most civic dignitaries always had, and of the fact that this prejudice was set not so much against plays in themselves as against commercial and professional playing. Later mayors had no evident religious basis for giving their support to local performances while banning those by visiting professionals.[8]

The main differences in the kinds of company that flourished in this period make curiously potent signifers for what they did and what they stood for. At one extreme stands the Shakespearian company, a group of between eight and twelve adult players working as a team and taking collective responsibility for all decisions. It was professional and democratic, sharing the investments in time, skill, and resources, and sharing the profits accordingly. At the other extreme were the impresario-led companies. The first of these were groups of boys led and managed by schoolmasters or choirmasters. After 1600 the boy groups became openly commercial, their leaders financiers who invested in them and managed them for their own profit. That practice was modified as the boy groups grew older and the boy companies grew further and further from their choir-school origins. After 1609 they formed companies of 'youths', with up to five or six adult players as their controllers. The impresarios who ran such companies usually owned or leased their playhouses, since the theatres were a key element in any company's financing. The King's and Queen's Revels Children of the second decade of the seventeenth century, the Caroline 'young' company that opened the Salisbury Court hall play-

---

[7] *REED, Chester,* 109.

[8] The Chester court in 1596, while banning all plays, did authorize compensatory payments to be made to the travellers, 20s. to the Queen's company and 6s. 8d. to any nobleman's group. On the other hand there is no record of any such payments ever being made, although professional companies did visit Chester. See *REED, Chester,* pp. lviii, 184.

house in 1629, and 'Beeston's Boys' who reopened the Cockpit after the 1636–7 plague closure were all of this kind.

There was a quite fundamental difference between the two kinds of company in their financial and social organization. The sharer system was a strikingly democratic system in a deeply patriarchal and authoritarian age. The impresario system was an autocratic form of rule imposed on a profession which had grown into being by means of a long tradition of collaborative and democratic practices. Some of the companies fell between the extremes. Usually they were adult companies dependent on a financier and theatre-owner, such as the companies who worked in the later years for Henslowe and Christopher Beeston. Beeston's decision at the end of his life to abandon the adult companies he had worked in and for through the previous forty years, in favour of a company of youths with adult helpers, is an indication that the impresarios found it easier to work with players who were more dependent on their financier than the adult sharers. That makes it all the more striking that the King's Men, the most successful and the longest-running of all the professional companies, maintained its system of collective government throughout. But there are many other issues at stake here, and it is important not to let the commercial and economic factors swallow other considerations.

The authorities were frightened of the companies of players. Their travelling habits made them comparable to vagabonds. Their freedom to roam the country was menacing. They might carry infection from the outside world in ideas as well as the plague. They attracted large crowds, and their insistence on being paid for their work of 'play' made them dangerous as well as seductive. Behind all those threats there was the strangeness of their counterfeiting, their imitations of reality. Somewhere beneath the obvious grounds for authority's suspicion of adult players lie other motives, a fear that may help to explain such odd features of the constraints they laid on the companies as the total ban against women appearing on stage, a restriction unique to England, and the readiness to tolerate boy players more than adults. The Shakespearian sharer-led company was anomalous for its time in its democratic social and political organization. It was a threat to order and authority. That gives a sharp edge to the prime paradox in all this history, that the survival and the growing prosperity of such companies, the King's Men above all, was due almost entirely to the support and consistent protection given them by the highest authority in the land.

The story of the professional playing companies, whether they were made up of mature adults or children, can be used as a symptom that identifies not just the one prejudicial set of feelings about playing, but a multitude of changes through the reigns of Elizabeth, James, and Charles. Elizabeth herself was a showman of considerable skill. During one of her progresses in 1574 to Worcester she responded to the crowd, who were throwing their caps up in the air in the stock gesture of public celebration, by throwing her own up too.[9] Since women, unlike men, never doffed

---

[9] See Simon Adams, 'Eliza Enthroned? The Court and its Politics', in *The Reign of Elizabeth I*, ed. Christopher Haigh (London, 1984), 55–77, n. 12.

their headgear, it made a vividly androgynous and theatrical gesture of fellowship. Elizabeth's populism stands in sharp contrast to her successor, James, whose enthusiasm for the country was confined to hunting, and to his son, Charles, who insulated himself with a court culture that kept him remote from the affairs either of city or country. Under the Stuarts the court became a society to itself.

A closely similar pattern appears in the history of the playing companies. The two or three adult companies that first established themselves with a base in London in the 1590s appealed equally to the entire spectrum of London's population. By contrast, the five companies of the 1630s divided their attentions, aiming at different social levels and appetites which were largely determined by the prices their clientele paid for seats at a hall playhouse or to stand in an amphitheatre. The King's Men were taken over in the mid-1630s by a group of courtier poets who commandeered the company's repertory even for the more populist summer seasons at the Globe.[10]

The chief difficulty in a study of this kind is that, more commonly than most histories, it has an extrinsic motive behind it. That of course might be counted redemptive, since it allows the author's prejudice to become overt. My ultimate justification here is not the companies' history as an end in itself, but that of supplying a fuller context for the plays. This reliance on the records of the play-texts in their written forms abets the falsifications that follow from the unavoidable need to assume that all the other records that happen to survive in written form are the best materials from which to compose this soft mosaic. They are certainly the most detailed and specific extant records, but whether they give an accurate or sufficient outline of the general picture is open to serious question. In large part the study's focus on London and on the few companies that the court considered to be the best of their time, and beyond that on the companies that put the most of their repertory into print, is a consequence of the limited availability of evidence. Like a slag-heap, it takes its shape as the most natural form for the surviving debris from that original process of mining which produced the plays in performance. The difficulty is in relating the shape of the debris to the original events.

There are, however, a few metaphors rather more attractive than slag-heaps. History is linear in time, and slag-heaps are self-evidently deposits in space more than in time. History's time-line is never straight, of course. It is made intricate by the infinite diversity of the forces that work on the changes which give the line its direction. The different lines, we might say, make a fabric, a complex weave of interlocking and interacting forces. The easiest histories are narratives of single threads running through that broad weave. The emphasis in this kind of study, on the other hand, has to be an assemblage of all the lines, and the more obvious pattern or patterns that they appear to make when traced through the whole fabric.

---

[10] Davenant's comments on the Globe audiences, reaffirmed in Shirley's *The Doubtful Heir*, have to be read in this context. See Gurr, *Playgoing in Shakespeare's London* (Cambridge, 1987), 179–82, 187–90.

Ultimately this study is about some of the processes and the companies which helped to produce Shakespeare, the maculate bearers of Shakespearian conceptions.[11] It is not, though, a study of single lives or single lines, nor even of individuals, but rather of a complex interaction of people working together in tangible groups or teams in the larger grouping of English society. The groupings that made the playing companies into teams usually worked individualistically, in competition with one another. Their individualism, like their professionalism, was driven by the common need for money.[12] They were a peculiar, unique, new phenomenon in London and in the country at large. Even their place in society was anomalous, since they functioned as workers in time of carnival. While they always worked as groups under the name of a 'company', that title in provincial records often meant not the travelling players but the audience attending their performances. The players were companies outside the company of the societies they visited. It is impossible to trace such tricky and elusive group activities by following single lines.

The usual metaphors for historical process are either a river, a social mechanism which is always flowing but never seems to alter, or else organic and evolutionary, the image of a growing plant, sometimes Darwinian. Neither fits this history. It does deal with what appears to be an organism, a social feature that grew, ripened, and was suddenly killed when the environment changed. It deals with a flow of individual molecules governed by quasi-physical laws that can be identified, however dimly. But no metaphor makes a perfect fit for something so viscous and transient as this phenomenon. Different images, like Shakespeare as the iceberg tip, can fit at moments, but not in a flow, even of the glacier that breaks off into icebergs. The currently popular image of history as theatre (used effectively by Paul Carter[13] and others), has some appeal, if an incestuous one. But even the concept of the reader as a relatively innocent spectator of events meaningfully staged by the calculating historian has its limits. It may avoid either the mechanistic or the organic metaphors, but it falls too easily into the individualistic.

In large part, like all histories, a study such as this has to be a record of an attempt at retrieval. It tries not to be too judgemental, and indeed tries to emphasize the imperfection and the partiality of the written records which generated the search, even those records which preserved a version of Shakespeare's plays for posterity. Without finding much use for the concept of a flock of mute inglorious Miltons lying unheard and unseen across the landscape because their musings were never recorded in writing, it does try to give priority to the sociable and the collective over the individual. Its focus is not on the written texts but the social events of which the texts are a partial record, an outcropping. In particular it looks at that flock of events, the actual performances of the plays in their own time which, because they

[11] I signal that bias blatantly by using the adjective 'Shakespearian' rather than the historians' currently fashionable but regrettably vague term for the period, 'early modern'.

[12] Douglas Bruster, in *Drama and the Market in the Age of Shakespeare* (Cambridge, 1992), sets out the narrowly mercantile context for the companies. I have tried to broaden the frame of reference in which the companies operated beyond Bruster's materialist approach to commodification.

[13] See e.g. Paul Carter, *The Road to Botany Bay: An Essay in Spatial History* (London, 1987), xix.

were never recorded as texts, have been lost from cultural circulation. That, ultimately, is what makes the theatrical metaphor inappropriate. Each event, and
especially each theatrical or performance event, is unique to its moment. It cannot
be recuperated. So this history must be not a story of texts, even of lost texts, but
of the contexts for the events which generated some of the texts, a battered Chinese
box.

For all the concern with the social context and the collective processes of social
change that generated that context, the individual has to loom large too. Each play
generated by the social processes of London and England under the Tudors and
Stuarts had to be individual, different from its predecessors in a calculated way.
Gratifying though familiar pleasures are, all the London companies were ruled by
the constant demand for novelty that they served. Throughout their first eighty
years the playing companies used their familiar tools in the manufacture of novel-
ties. This need to be innovatory, set in a production process that was firmly
traditional and reluctant to change, is another of the multitude of paradoxes that a
history such as this has to work within.

This history is also ambivalent in the double scale it uses. The first part deals
with the general context of the plays and the historical process in which they were
originally set. That is general history, largely deterministic, social, sub-marxist,
concerned with historical process, the economics and politics of change. It works
against the idea of the individual as a social force, despite the fact that the plays
themselves were largely products of individual inspiration. The second part, by
contrast, deals with the individual histories, the separate development of the different companies and the influence that individual players, patrons, impresarios, and
writers had in their progress. Other anomalies follow from this, in that most of the
evidence determining this focus on the most populist phenomenon of the time, the
public stages of London, comes from the court and its noble and royal patrons. A
fresh focus on the power of the courtly patrons and the way they separated the
playing companies from the feeling of the rest of the country is, in fact, a major
discovery of this history.

And there are many other paradoxes. The carnival spirit of playgoing stands
against the pressure on the professional players to make money, creating the
paradox which worried the civic authorities, that play for some made work for
others. Almost all of the surviving records about the companies other than the
scripts of the plays are financial in one sense or another. The national holidays
which brought most revenue to the players were their own prime working days.
The paradoxical thinking that grew as the municipal performances of Mystery
plays on religious festivals were banned and holy days were turned into holidays is
nothing beside the paradox of visiting professionals working to make profit from
workers' holidays.

Carnival is the word chosen by new historicists to identify Bakhtin's concept
of that form of opposition to established values which celebrates freedom from

authority, in holiday and the activities of holiday.[14] A flexible concept, it stands against work as 'play', in whatever form the local customs of any society might allow. Tudor playing ranged from the variable kinds of May festivals in the country areas to the scheduled days off urban work approved by the city fathers, such as the Shrove Tuesday holidays, when apprentices commonly ran riot. Tudor and Stuart 'play' in London became anomalous with the arrival of the professional companies, when the leading spirits of the holiday worked and were paid for giving pleasure to others. That anomaly probably has a lot to do with the heavy prejudice shown at Chester against professional playing.

The other great anomaly about English playing, the recurrent preference for using boys to play adults, probably also reflects some of the feeling that it was peculiar for professionals to work at 'play'. Even the earliest boy companies, who had the respectable cachet of education to support them, supplemented their academic 'pronunciation' of solemn tragedies by using an extremely broad and bawdy kind of knockabout in comedies such as *Mother Bombie*. The commercial boy companies that resurfaced in 1600 offered plays crammed with sex jokes that were at least equal in raunchiness to anything the adult companies offered. In some way the boy companies, along with the 'young' companies of 1610–13 and the so-called Beeston's Boys of the 1630s, had an appeal designed to exploit the feeling of licence that went with what Heywood called their 'juniority'. Professional players were not real people, a view endorsed in many pulpits. Boys playing adults were more evidently unreal than adults playing adults. For both kinds, their role in carnival was an inversion of the realities that carnival itself sought to invert.

When carnival shifts from a participation sport to a spectator sport its character changes radically. When play becomes work the composition of the carnival element becomes more calculated, more fixed, and subversive in quite new ways. It also, largely by the accident of available technology, becomes better recorded. Those two features of professional 'play' in Tudor and Stuart London, the calculated nature of its carnival elements and the precision with which its records have survived, give modern students of this period of English history an odd perspective. We see some of the products that for the first time were being developed professionally and commercially to entertain as fixed and calculated versions of the subversive joys of carnival. We evaluate the records of such fixtures in the light of the modern experience that all entertainment ought to be professional if it is any 'good'. That is where capitalism takes over from carnival. Durable entertainment is that which has proved commercially successful. It has attracted enough spectators to achieve fixity, and to be recorded in print for future generations. As such, it is inherently hostile to the concept of carnival as subversion. That paradox underlies and undermines much of the evidence available for studies such as this.

[14] See, with some reservations, Michael D. Bristol, *Carnival and Theater: Plebeian Culture and the Structure of Authority in Renaissance England* (New York, 1985).

A rather better concept than carnival as a means of making sense of this new phenomenon, which set itself out for the first time in the sixteenth century as London's regular alternative to work, is the sale of sex. William Prynne, in *Histrio-mastix*, his massively exhaustive account of the damage that playing did to Londoners, emphasized the proximity of the first playhouses to London's most famous brothel districts. 'Our Theaters', he wrote, 'if they are not Bawdy-houses, (as they may easily be, since many Players, *if reports be true, are common Panders,*) yet they are Cosin-germanes, at *leastwise neighbours to them*: Witnesse the *Cock-pit*, and *Drury-lane*: *Black-friers Play-house*, and *Duke-humfries*; the *Red-bull*, and *Turnball-street*: the *Globe*, and *Bank-side Brothel-houses*, with others of this nature.'[15] The comparison has its point if the playing companies are seen in essence as providers of public pleasure for their own personal profit. Certainly the London authorities saw them that way. Brothel-keepers and playing companies alike suffered periodic assaults not only by the city's lawmen, but by mobs of self-righteous apprentices. In *Holland's Leaguer*, a Salisbury Court play making comic use of the recent siege of a Southwark brothel, one of the characters describes the brothel as 'a province by itself, a privileged place, | A strong corporation, and has factions | In court and city'.[16] That fairly summarizes the position both of brothels and of playhouses. The chief difference was that the playing companies claimed to serve the court, and the court openly, if intermittently, protected and fostered them. In practice people from all sections of London's community paid to enjoy both kinds of pleasure. The main difference between the brothels and the playhouses was that brothels were provided only for men, whereas the playhouses catered very distinctly for women too. Being more often than men illiterate and only educated to hear and see instead of to read, they could gain relatively more benefit than men from playgoing.

Both kinds of paid-for pleasure in fact enjoyed a good deal of covert and often hypocritical support, whether to feed the flocks of the Bishop of Winchester's geese, or to give the Privy Council a reason to protect the players on the grounds that the monarch must be entertained over Christmas. Privy-Council support for the players was much more overt than support for the brothels, of course, but the basic thinking behind both kinds of unlawful licence was much the same: that the only alternative was to geld all the youth of the city. The Duke's problem at the outset of *Measure for Measure*, which sets out at large the double metaphor of 'liberty' meaning freedom within the law and the licentiousness of sexual freedom, is a paradigm for how the general issue presented itself in London. That play's ultimate answer was the social and comedic resolution of marriage, sex under the licence of law. No such formal licence ever existed for the brothels, but it did develop in the suburbs of London for the playhouses. The suburbs, where the justices of Middlesex and Surrey were under the control of playgoing Privy Coun-

---

[15]   William Prynne, *Histrio-mastix* (1633), Ddd3v–Ddd4.

[16]   *Holland's Leaguer* (1632), IV. v. Another character in IV. i says, equally aptly, ' 'Tis barren, I confess, yet wholly given | To the deeds of fructification'.

cillors like Charles Howard, were the region for licensed carnival. The city of London always resisted both kinds of shameful pleasure. The Privy Council's licensing of a few companies to play around London's fringes was a marriage of sorts. It required the court to override, though only tactically and tentatively, the constant and strenuous enmity of the city. That enmity cannot be underestimated. It kept all the playhouses except for the one peculiar case of the Blackfriars[17] out of the orbit where the city ruled, and is the sole reason why the players stayed encamped in the freer suburbs and 'liberties' of the city.

History as narrative, and as dramatic fiction, is a well-established current definition.[18] Here, when the central facts are so elusive, and especially when the central target is so transient, the chronic ambivalence between referential fact and history-as-fiction is given a deeper dimension. Theatre is always invented for an occasion. It is an 'event'. It does not belong naturally in print. Each new performance of a play that has established itself in a repertory and achieved fixity through print is a new occasion. The history of professional theatre is crammed with plays that died on their first performance and were resurrected successfully a generation or more later. The printed texts of playscripts work against that feature of a play in performance as a transient event or occasion. That is the chief justification for writing a history of the context in which the playtexts first appeared. We already have histories of the theatres that the different companies used, studies of the staging practices, biographies of individual players, and even histories of some individual companies. This study is an attempt at the largest context, a comprehensive history of the companies which generated the London plays and first put them on stage.

It is certainly not a history of individual achievement. The companies worked collectively, as teams, making joint decisions about everything from the plays in the repertory to the direction of their tours. They had no stars and little need of an inspirational leader. Plays in performance are the product of teamwork, and all the companies' operations were done as a team. The nineteenth-century tradition of famous actors taking companies round the world on the strength of their own name as a drawcard is a misleading guide to the ways the companies worked in Shakespeare's time. Almost all the official records, whether they were written by the accountants in Norwich or Coventry, by the Revels Office naming the payees for performances at court, by the Privy Council summoning the companies to a hearing, or by Philip Henslowe working as his company's banker, routinely named at least two men as the agents of each company. The men named were its representatives, not its leaders.

---

[17] James Burbage built the Blackfriars playhouse in a liberty in 1596. Ironically, in the same year that the King's Men acquired it, 1608, it came under the city's jurisdiction. Apart from the anomaly of Paul's playhouse which sheltered literally under a wing of the cathedral in the centre of the city, this was the only victory the players ever had over the city fathers.

[18] I acknowledge some allegiance to Hayden White's metaphysics of history as narrative, in *Tropics of Discourse: Essays in Cultural Criticism* (Baltimore, 1979), and especially to Jean Howard's outline of methodologies in 'The New Historicism in Renaissance Studies', *ELR* 16 (1986), 13–43.

Those individuals whose names do emerge were entrepreneurs rather than players, individualists in commerce, not stars in the teamwork of performing. The chief individual names were impresarios such as Henslowe, Christopher Beeston, Richard Gunnell, or Richard Heton. Apart from the famous clowns like Tarlton and Kemp, who were individual stars even in their own companies, Edward Alleyn was the nearest to a star player that any company had, and the only player in the entire period who seems to have behaved like one.[19] Even he would be far less notable now if he had not allied himself in 1592 to the Henslowe enterprises and become doubly famous as an impresario, founding a college which preserved the records of his impresario activities. Richard Burbage's career is more characteristic of the average player mentality. He had access, like Alleyn, to family resources in playhouse buildings, but he never made himself into an impresario and his company's landlord in the way that Alleyn did. Burbage in fact did the opposite, allocating half the shares in the playhouse property he inherited to other players in his own company. He remained quite precisely and consistently no more than a sharer in his playing company and its properties.[20]

This study concentrates on a collection of play-team groupings which have a wide range of different histories. The leading companies had lives lasting more than two generations. The Chamberlain's/King's Men, Shakespeare's company, ran continuously from 1594 to 1642, forty-eight years in all. The company that started as Worcester's in 1577, became Queen Anne's in 1603, and ended as the Revels company at the Red Bull and other playhouses, had an even longer continuous life. The first rivals to Shakespeare's company, the Admiral's, later Prince Henry's and later still the County Palatine's Servants, ran from 1576 to 1625. Some companies had distinctive roles to play in the process of getting a foothold in London, notably Leicester's and Queen Elizabeth's in the sixteenth century, and the companies of the King and of Queen Anne in the seventeenth. After 1594, when the two approved companies first became settled at fixed playhouses, the companies that followed them started to develop their own distinctive repertories. These ranged from the scandalous 'railing' satires run by the Blackfriars Boys and based on verbal wit to spectacles of athleticism, including what Jasper Mayne called 'Red-Bull' wars',[21] the drum-and-trumpet plays of what came to be called the citizen playhouses of the 1630s. Repertories ranged from the King's Men's arcadian pastoral plays, staged for Queen Henrietta in the 1630s, to the plays set in fashionable outer-London venues by the other hall companies in that decade, like *Tottenham Court* and *Covent Garden*.

---

[19] Alleyn became exceptional in 1591, when he retained the Lord Admiral's livery while playing in another patron's company. His subsequent alliance with Henslowe was part of the same independent thinking. See below, Ch. 4.

[20] For an account of the Burbage shares in the Globe and the Blackfriars, see Chs. 6 and 16.

[21] Mayne wrote a memorial for Ben Jonson in 1638, praising his plays for never descending to the level where sieges were laid to the stage balcony's music room. The relevant passage is quoted in E. K. Chambers, *The Elizabethan Stage* (4 vols.; Oxford, 1923) (hereafter *ES*), iii. 96.

What energized it all was the dynamics of competition, the constant pressure to rival and to imitate the success of the other teams. Good work and innovation were rewarded at one end by performances at court and at the other by a settled life in a London playhouse, not to mention a decent level of income and personal prosperity. Failure meant the break-up of the team. The lives of the companies were often brutal, and usually short. Nearly forty companies are studied here, only five of which were still active in 1642.

As in any study of historical process, the principal concern in this study is change and the processes that determined change. Part I follows the London companies through all the more general transformations, while Part II looks at the history of the individual companies. Part I begins with the first companies settling to play in London as an enriching supplement to their usual travels. That led to the establishment of the Queen's Men in 1583, with the consequence of its uniquely large size on its cast-lists and their effect on the poets who wrote for it. That led to the growth of other 'large' companies up to 1594, and in that year the Privy Council's approval of fixed playing-places for only two companies in London, which settled Shakespeare's place in the process. In 1603 the application of royal patronage increased the two approved companies to three and later to five, plus the resurgent boy companies. Royal patronage helped the King's Company to start performing at the Blackfriars'-hall-playhouse in 1609, the final step in the leading companies' slow progress up to a firmly established and privileged place in London.

The thirty years that followed, up to the English revolution and the close-down of playing in 1642, saw greater use of the more expensive city venues and a widening gap between the upper and lower social reaches that the playing companies catered for. This aggregation of settled companies and familiar repertories created a new situation. Companies competing for the same market share of audiences became rivals. Rivalry created differences between the repertories; and these differences grew into distinct cultural identities for the leading companies. The survival of so many of the plays written in this later period makes it possible to recognize some of the complex interactions that took place between company repertories and audience expectations, and the ways in which audience prejudice was acknowledged by the commissioning companies and the knowing writers. Part II starts with the earliest London companies, and follows their overlapping careers and the individual vectors that their repertories took. In the process it gives rather more detail about some of the turning-points in the general history than is given in Part I.

It was a broad and gradual process of change. No one individual and no one company took a controlling or even a particularly interventionist part in the changes. We might pick out a few individuals such as Charles Howard, the Lord Admiral, a patron who intervened at the highest levels from the early 1580s to secure good conditions for the first London playing companies. He, if anyone, seems to have deliberately worked to promote their interests. In the 1590s Philip

Henslowe, starting as a playhouse landlord and ending as an impresario, evolved a managerial system that was imitated widely in London and spread into the rest of Europe. By contrast, Shakespeare's company in 1599 more or less fortuitously set up a secure system of control and playhouse ownership different from Henslowe's, that other companies subsequently tried hard to imitate, though with limited success. But no single individual or company did much entirely on their own to shape the major changes that this history of the companies and their products reveals. It is a story without heroes.

It is also a story that will eventually need some rewriting. Most of the fragments of the mosaic identified so far have a place here, but new pieces are turning up all the time, whether in parish records, from the archaeology of the playhouse foundations, or in the records of the companies on their travels outside London. And each new piece prompts a small shift in the ruling idea of what the total picture might be. It will be at least another twenty years before the provincial records in the *Records of Early English Drama* series can make any claim to a reasonably thorough coverage of town and country records about playing and playing companies. It will probably be even longer before the priority given to the written forms of record is displaced in favour of the necessarily more ephemeral notes about transient 'events', those occasions which written scripts so inadequately report. All that this history can claim is to be making a reasonably coherent and certainly a fresh kind of pattern, different in focus and in priorities from its predecessors, out of the soft fragments that can be applied to the whole mosaic's plastic setting.

2   *The First London Companies*

The attraction of playing in London was by far the strongest influence on the playing companies, and the strongest factor determining their development between 1574 and 1642. It gave them bigger audiences and a much bigger income. It allowed the Lord Chamberlain and his deputy, the Master of the Revels, to vet them for performance at court, which in terms of social standing was the ultimate audience. London was different from the rest of England, not just as the seat of the court and government and the country's major port for trade, but in its size and the attendant resources it commanded. Its own exceptionally rapid population growth through the period when the companies settled there made it a magnet for everything the country held dear. London doubled in size twice between 1550 and 1650, when its 400,000 people made it the largest and probably the richest city in Europe. Certainly no other city in England could match it. Norwich, Bristol, Coventry, and the other major cities that were regularly visited by the travelling companies never had more than 20,000 in their urban parishes. No other place had the resource in population, let alone wealth, to let players offer their plays there on a regular daily basis. It had by far the best resources, in audience, in playing accommodation, and in writers, to support its progress. It was quite literally the biggest market in the world for playing.

London also had the cream of society, the richest playgoing clientele, and the particularly sweet topping of the royal court. Practising to perform at court for the monarch's entertainment was the only officially accepted excuse the playing companies could give for playing regularly in London. And they had to employ that excuse all too often, given the strength and consistency of the opposition that London's citizens put up against plays. The city fathers were far from unique amongst the governors of large towns in England in opposing professional playing, but London itself was a unique place. Only London was large enough in population to make it advantageous for the companies to stay any length of time. Norwich or Leicester might allow a visiting company to perform three or four times before moving on, if they did not pay the players to leave without performing.[1] Only in London was there enough population to justify a really lengthy stay; and it was this which drew the city's hostility. The performance of plays for money daily was a great temptation to the young, the apprentices who worked for the London citizenry and the law students who kept their terms in London, far greater than

---

[1] At Ipswich in 1608 the town authorities ordered that 'Noe freeman or their servants or apprentises shall resort to any Playes to be holden within this Town under perill of Forfaiture for every offence 12d, to be levied by distress by the Chamberlins' (*Malone Society Collections*, xi, 183). That was a fine equal to two days' wages for the infrequent chance of backsliding when a visiting company came to town. London's temptations were constant. In 1614 Ipswich banned visiting professional players from using the moot hall, a mark of disapproval echoed in most of the larger towns.

anything that the occasional brief runs of a travelling company could offer. So the history of the playing companies in the sixteenth century, the years when they got their first distinct footholds in London, was a constant battle to secure a place in the capital. The court gave them help intermittently, the city hindered them as much as it could. In the short run the court won all it wanted. In the long run the city's long-held opposition to playing prevailed, speaking with finality in Parliament's closure edict of September 1642.[2]

The eighty years of companies playing in London that ended in 1642 make an intricate paradigm for the social forces and social processes, monarchic and independent, religious and intellectual, public and private, that grew into conflict through these years and finally brought the government down. Even if Shakespeare had not floated like an iceberg-tip through the running waters as a part of that process, the companies, their political, social, and religious allegiances, their patrons and protectors, their enemies, their motives, even the few non-monetary considerations that they were governed by, made a formidable contribution to the history of England and most specifically to the history of London.

Eventually London did allow the travelling companies some fixed and custom-built theatres to perform in. The city remained consistently hostile, but the court gave the companies enough protection to allow them to use the city's suburbs, where the magistrates of Middlesex and Surrey were more lax in their disapproval of playgoing, and where powerful nobles such as Charles Howard, who ran companies wearing their lord's liveries, were among the authorities. The size of that new market quickly transformed its suppliers. Access to London audiences laid demands on the companies to produce new plays at a uniquely rapid pace. Habitual playgoers, a phenomenon unique to London, soon grew familiar with each company's repertoire of plays and demanded new versions of the same product. The Privy Council acknowledged these pressures in 1594, establishing a system of patronage and privilege for the two leading companies that set a pattern for the next fifty years, as London developed more and more of a distinctively urban culture, and as even the greatest lords came to believe that London was the centre of their lives instead of remaining monarchs of all they surveyed on their country estates.

As the seventeenth century went on, plays developed a new social cachet. Regular playgoing became for the first time a firmly established and socially reputable habit. In the late 1630s the companies revised their old repertory system, which was based on the travelling habit of offering a new play each day, and introduced what is now the standard urban practice of running the same play on successive days. With five playhouses available the same plays could run for a week or longer at the same playhouse. That last decade saw the beginnings of many of the modern

[2] Steve Rappaport, *Worlds with Worlds: Structures of Life in Sixteenth-Century London* (Cambridge, 1989), 8, notes that it could not really have been the riots at playhouses that troubled the city authorities. None are recorded after 1581, apart from a mob which attacked the Cockpit in 1617 and the pursuit and killing of Dr Lambe from the Fortune in 1628. There was a football riot in Cheapside in 1591, and many other riots not associated with playhouses. London was an orderly city compared with its rivals in other countries.

practices in playgoing. The next four chapters of this book deal with the ways developments such as this affected the companies. It has to start with the form of working life in which the playing companies themselves learned their work, the long tradition of travelling companies. It ends with the transformation of those practices into the basis of the modern repertory system. The first real question is when these changes began and when the travelling companies began to feel that they belonged in London.

The apparent dates are easy, the social realities more complex. In March 1583, when the queen agreed to make herself patron of a company, the government's protection for her company against the city was assured. Eleven years later, in May 1594, two Privy Councillors, the Lord Chamberlain and his son-in-law the Lord Admiral, set up a pair of monopolistic companies to replace the disintegrating Queen's Men, and gave each of the new companies a fixed and clearly designated playhouse in the London suburbs to play in. Those were the crucial footholds. The causes and effects of these two actions by the Privy Council, the reasoning that set things up for the players in this way and still more the effects of the process on the plays themselves, are the most revealing pieces in this whole puzzle.

A letter from the theatre-owner Philip Henslowe in London, written in September 1593 to his son-in-law, the player Edward Alleyn, then travelling with Strange's Company near Bristol, supplied him with news from London about another of the companies, Pembroke's, whose history ties in oddly with Alleyn's and the first important patrons.[3] Forced to tour like Alleyn's group during that year's long prohibition on playing because of the plague, Pembroke's Company had run out of money and given up. Henslowe wrote to Alleyn on 28 September mainly on domestic matters, but also with his answer to a question from Alleyn which was probably about a matter of their shared business, though some readers have heard a note of glee over a rival's failure in what Henslowe had to report. Henslowe wrote 'as for my lorde a penbrockes wch you desier to knowe wheare they be they are all at home and hauffe ben this v or sixe weackes for they cane not save ther carges wth travell as I heare & weare fayne to pane ther parell for ther carge'.[4] Pawning their playing costumes was the last resort for any company. Pembroke's was in dire straits. But gloating or not, the most intriguing note in this sad account is Henslowe's casual phrase that tells what he thought was the broken company's base. For all the long stints of travelling that every company still practised because of the epidemics of plague and the Lord Mayor's hostility to playing, and in spite of the fact that the Lord Chamberlain had not yet designated any of the suburban playhouses for the approved companies to use, what Henslowe knew was that by 1593 the leading companies thought of London as 'at home'.

When did London become 'home' for the players under Elizabeth? Fifteen years after Henslowe's comment, in 1608, Heywood in his *Apology for Actors* could hail 'my good friends and fellowes the Citty Actors' as a group of workers permanently resident in London. That, though, was some time after James had given royal patronage to all three of the leading companies. The practice of one company staying at a single London playhouse to work for long periods of time had certainly not become long-established by 1593.[5] In the 1580s even a company as pre-eminent as the Queen's Men used a wide variety of playing-places in London. In their prime they are on record as using at least three inns and three different playhouses in London, every one of the known venues, in fact, for playing.[6] Stays at London playhouses were usually short-lived up to 1594. Strange's Company played at Henslowe's Rose from the beginning of 1592, when they first established themselves there, for barely six months in all, up to August 1593, in spite of the fact that their leading player, Alleyn, married Henslowe's step-daughter in October 1592.[7] Pembroke's had probably been using the Theatre across the river through the same period, which could hardly have been long enough to give either playhouse a firm identity as the players' home. The fact that most players for whom records have been found were resident in the London parishes closest to the playhouses, Shoreditch, Bishopsgate, and Southwark, is not a substantial confirmation that they were 'at home' there, because no searches have yet been made to identify whether any players lived in other towns. Most of the records about players that have turned up come from the later years, when residence in London had become a practical necessity for all the leading players.

It is true that many of the players in the large companies from the 1570s onwards had families based in London. So far as we can tell from the limited records that survive, a substantial majority had wives and children, and hence presumably regular housing, in the city. The records that exist, of course, are mainly of the most familiar names, whose interests must have based them in London more readily than any of the other towns that their companies regularly visited. Early players from before 1600 with wives and children living in London besides Edward Alleyn include: Richard Allen, Christopher Beeston, William Bird, both of the Robert Brownes, George Bryan, James Burbage, Alexander Cooke, Richard Cowley, Richard Darlowe, Thomas Downton, John Duke, Edward Dutton, John Dutton, Lawrence Dutton, Lawrence Fletcher, John Garland, Thomas Goodale, Robert Gough, Thomas Greene, John Harrison, John Heminges, Francis Henslowe, Thomas Heywood, Antony Jeffes, Humphrey Jeffes, William Johnson, Richard Jones, Ben Jonson, Edward Juby, Richard Juby, William Knell, Tobias

---

[5] For the question of how quickly the companies can been seen from outside as becoming London-based, see also William Ingram, *The Business of Playing. The Beginnings of the Adult Professional Theater in Elizabethan London* (Ithaca, NY, 1992), 14.

[6] On 28 Nov. 1583 a city permit allowed them to perform 'at the sygnes of the Bull in Bushoppesgate streete, and the sygne of the Bell in Gratioustreete and nowheare els within this Cyttye' (*ES* iv. 296). The Bull as a venue is confirmed in *Tarlton's Jests*. They were also playing at the Theatre in about 1584 (*Pierce Penilesse*, i. 197, about Harvey's *Saturn and Jupiter*, 1583: 'Tarlton at the Theator made jests of him'), and at the Bel Savage in 1588 (again on the evidence of *Tarlton's Jests*). They also played at the Curtain (*Tarlton's Jests*: 'one in mockage threw him in this theame, he playing then at the Curtaine'). They played at the Rose in 1594.

[7] Late Jan. to June 1592, and Jan. to early Feb. 1593.

Myles, John Nill, Robert Pallant, Augustine Phillips, Robert Shaw, Martin Slater,[8] Richard Tarlton, and Robert Wilson. No player from the years and the companies when London was the obvious centre of action, whose identity is well-known and whose name can be found in parish or other records, has a residence listed any-where but in the city or its suburbs.

It is likely that many of the players belonging to the 'large' companies that tried to secure a foothold in London in the 1590s would only have taken London lodgings while working there, as Shakespeare did. Will Kemp is recorded as living in 'Samson's Rents' in Southwark in 1595, 1596, 1598, and 1599, and in Langley's New Rents in 1602. These records probably mean that he stayed in lodgings while he had employment in London. There is no mention of a wife and children. A similar history applies to Thomas Pope and Gabriel Spencer. Other parish records identify some 'base-born' children whose fathers were players, suggesting that they were not family men. These include Will Sly and Edmund Shakespeare. But by the 1590s a clear majority of the players did have families, and their families all seem to have been based permanently in London. When Joan Alleyn re-used her step-father's term, writing to her husband on 21 October 1603 to say that all the companies were now 'Come hoame . . . at theyr owne houses',[9] it was a normative statement. But it was not one that would have been made even twenty years earlier.

A rather greater enigma than Henslowe's report that Pembroke's headed for their homes in London when the company's finances collapsed lies in the term that Henslowe used for the company crisis which caused them to return to the city. Pembroke's sale of their properties meant that they had no money. They were suffering the equivalent, in modern terminology, of going bankrupt: the curiously matching word of the time for what happened was that they 'broke'. When the Queen's Men failed in London, in June 1595, Henslowe's phrase was that they 'brocke & went into the contrey to playe'.[10] It was a dismissive word to use. Fynes Moryson, twenty years later, meant much the same thing when he called the groups of English players travelling in Europe 'stragling broken Companyes'.[11] Just what the term meant, either in financial, organizational, or social terms is not really clear. It may imply equally well that they were made to renew their travels as divided fragments of former groupings, or less likely as one group smaller in numbers than a full company. It might also have been, at least in part, a comment on their finances. Being 'broke' was beginning to emerge as a financial term, the equivalent

---

[8] Slater may be a special case. He was a chronic traveller, who played in places as far distant as Edinburgh in 1599, and was noted in five different towns between 1605 and 1625. None the less, it was said in 1609 that he had a family in London consisting of ten dependants. This does suggest that even the most travelled players felt at home in the metropolis. Slater's records are cited in Mark Eccles, 'Elizabethan Actors iv: S to End', *NQ* 238 (1993), 165–76, p. 171.

[9] *Henslowe's Diary*, 297.

[10] Ibid. 7.

[11] *Shakespeare's Europe: Unpublished Chapters of Fynes Moryson's Itinerary, Being a Survey of the Conditions in Europe at the End of the 16th Century*, ed. Charles Hughes (6 vols.; London, 1907–36), iv. 304.

of a modern bankruptcy, though it did not yet have many of the distinctively modern associations.[12]

The possibility that such companies 'broke' by splitting into smaller groups ought to be considered, at least for the period after the 1580s. Evidence from the years following 1583, when the Queen's Men were set up with a larger number of sharers than previous companies, suggests that 'large' plays written for casts of fifteen and more started to appear well before the end of the 1580s. And that raises the question of whether the companies who played in London with those 'large' plays travelled the country with the same number of players that they employed in London. A single 'large' company, if it had to 'break' and was forced to stop playing in London, might have split into two groups for the country. There are certainly records of groups travelling with a duplicate of the one authorized company's licence, as some of the London companies commonly did in the seventeenth century. The question about this is whether the newly divided companies made their numbers up to the full London complement for travelling. Alternatively, a broken company might have broken up altogether, with individual players looking for employment in other, more durable companies. All we can be sure of is that the terminology of a playing company being 'at home' or 'breaking' signals the centrality of the role that London had now begun to hold in the companies' and their associates' own vision of their aims and their progress.

Fixing the main playing-places in the suburbs of London was a crucial development. In one way it marginalized them, because it ousted them from the inns inside the city. In others, though, it stabilized them. It gave them much better security, the best access to resources in playwriting, new players and hangers-on, a much better income, and eventually the chance of running in long tenures at a single venue. That in turn enabled the companies, especially those who found a single, settled place in London to store their resources, to build up a far more substantial backing for their performance then the slim stock of playbooks, costumes, and properties that they could carry on their tours.

The regular availability of playing in the suburbs must also have generated a new disposition in the London audiences. Once the companies started playing in the suburbs every day of the week, audiences got into the habit of expecting to see a fresh play every day, and the playwrights had to start writing for an audience that had been weaned on varied kinds of play and was constantly demanding novelty. Those were the conditions that through the 1580s and 1590s stimulated the intense growth in playwriting of which Shakespeare became both the chief promoter and the chief beneficiary. The first step in this was the building of specially designed playing-places, the Red Lion amphitheatre in 1567, the Paul's hall theatre and the first of the Blackfriars hall theatres in 1575 and 1576, and the Theatre and Curtain in 1576 and 1577. The second and more crucial step was the official acknowledge-

---

[12] In *Richard II* II. i. 257 it was used as a specifically financial simile: 'The king grown bankrupt like a broken man'. A few years later, in *As You Like It* II. i. 57, the two words are merged in the description of 'that poor and broken bankrupt'. The terms are analogous, but not identical.

ment in 1594 that the Rose and the Theatre should be homes for the two officially approved companies. That was followed in 1599 and 1600 by the construction of the first theatres designed specifically for a resident company, the Globe and the Fortune.

In the earlier years, before London began to realize its distinctive urban identity, many different kinds of professional entertainment could supplement the local participatory sports. Besides the small travelling groups of the 1560s, usually comprising not more than five or six players, who offered their plays or 'interludes', the archives surviving in the cities such as Norwich and Bristol indicate that regular payments were made not only to the local players but to smaller groups of performers and single travellers, jesters, jugglers, acrobats, rope-dancers, different sorts of musician, bear-wards, and presenters of other kinds of 'show', few of whom have left much sign of what they had to offer. The spoken word was easier to record than the skills of the performers in this variety of national and local skills. And distinctive skills were prized, even between one region and another. A mid-sixteenth-century skit boasting about the particular skills of Herefordshire men gives an idea of the range:

The courts of kings for stately measures: the Citie for light-heeles, and nimble footing: the Country for shuffling dances: Westerne-men for gambouls: Middlesex-men for tricks above ground: Essex-men for the Hey: Lancashire for Horne-pypes: Worcester-shire for Bagpypes: but Hereford-shire for a Morris-daunce.[13]

Almost no evidence about these visual shows survives, since the written word was the only record available, and only the surviving scripts for a few of the civic presentations that incorporated speeches give much idea of what was said. Spoken presentations were distinctive in the sixteenth century precisely because they were the only kind easily recorded. They employed the kind of skill that, by the end of the century, culminated in Shakespeare's plays; but the success of this form of show, the 'large' two- or three-hour play as we know it now, ought not to make us think the less of the variety of skills that may have been on offer in the less recordable kinds of public entertainment. These other entertainments persisted long after written drama had secured its foothold in the theatres of London and left its mark in the durable record of print.

Shakespeare was the tip of an iceberg of almost immeasurable size. The fact that the written word until fairly recently has been the only durable means to record

[13] 'Old Meg of Herefordshire', REED, Herefordshire/Worcestershire, 125. This boast endorses the view that each county had a sense of its local community and culture which intensified the general consciousness of regional contrasts and the radical differences that existed and were sustained between the counties and London. See John Morrill, The Revolt of the Provinces: Conservatives and Radicals in the English Civil War, 1630–1650 (London, 1976). From a different perspective François Laroque, Shakespeare's Festive World (Cambridge, 1991), 10, confirms this view. London itself was an aggregate of the various communities that are found in any large conurbation. For a survey of one such in London, see James Knowles, 'The Spectacle of the Realm: Civic Consciousness, Rhetoric and Ritual in Early Modern London', in Theatre and Government under the Early Stuarts, ed. J. R. Mulryne and Margaret Shewring (Cambridge, 1993), 157–89.

events and performances has given an air of substance to the written word that it certainly never possessed in Tudor and Stuart times. The survival in written form of what we now think of as Renaissance drama texts is largely fortuitous. It distorts the social realities from which they came. The realities of quotidian life, the multitude of verbal and visual experiences it offered, whether in human gossip and labour or in the different forms of community recreation, can be retrieved only in sadly distorted form in written records. To read a Shakespearian playscript gives us little more of the social reality that the original performances entailed than a look through the raw filmscripts can tell us of the impact that *Citizen Kane* or *Casablanca* had on their first audiences. In one sense, the tip of the Shakespearian iceberg is not even made of ice. It is more like a banner, a flag which by the accident of its written form has proved more durable than the ice it first drew attention to.

There are few records of Tudor bear-baitings or tumbling to compare with the written scripts that survive from the drama. Even the play-texts survive only in a few of the spikes and peaks that rose above the everyday levels of the daily perform- ances. Of the 175 play-titles recorded by Philip Henslowe as played at the Rose theatre between 1592 and 1602, no more than thirty-seven scripts survive.[14] From the total period of London performing that this history is concerned with, roughly five hundred playscripts survive, out of a probable total of more than three thou- sand. The survivors are very likely to be the best or at least the most popular of the many original scripts, of course. Of Shakespeare's thirty-eight known plays only *Cardenio* has been lost. Little beside Jonson's *Isle of Dogs* is known to have disap- peared from his long *œuvre*. But that 'best' and 'most popular' depends on the local and immediate valuations, not on modern ones. The distribution of the survivors is very uneven. Very few of the scripts that were made for performance have survived in manuscript or print from the early years up to the 1590s. The rush into print only began when the first 'large' companies had firmly established themselves at home in London. It grew hugely in later years, when the printing of a play-text became the second accolade for a play after its 'first publication' on stage.[15] Even that, though, produces another form of distortion. It was more often the author who saw his play into print than the company that owned it. And authors give tacit priority to the words in the script over whatever spectacle was supplied to it on the stage, a priority which few of the playgoers of the time would have recognized, and probably none of the players. Jonson's reiterated claim that his plays as printed contain more lines than were performed on the stage has ominous implications for attempts to retrieve the original performance scripts.

The record of plays performed on the public stages in London is extremely patchy. Harbage[16] gives titles for 1,056 plays known to have been performed by the

[14] See *Henslowe's Diary*. My count is based on the daily performance records and notes of payments to the writers, 16–38, 47–8, 54–60, 96–107, 121–38, 164, 166–71, 175–87, 199–208, and 213–26.

[15] Print as a second form of publication after the original staging was a concept that Francis Beaumont voiced in his verses for the printing of Fletcher's *The Faithful Shepherdess* in 1610.

[16] Alfred B. Harbage, *Annals of English Drama, 975–1700* (Philadelphia, 1940); rev. S. Schoenbaum, 1964, 1970; 3rd edn. by Sylvia S. Wagenheim (New York, 1988), from which these figures are taken.

playing companies between 1560 and 1642. Of these, some form of text for just over 500 survives either in manuscript or print, or in summary in manuscript 'plots'. The totals (give or take a few conjectures) run: 1560–70, 32 titles and 18 surviving texts; 1571–80, 79 titles and 6 texts; 1581–90, 59 titles and 37 texts; 1591–1600, 266 titles and 78 texts; 1601–10, 183 titles and 103 texts; 1611–20, 120 titles and 74 texts; 1621–30, 148 titles and 74 texts; 1631–42, 169 titles and 125 texts. These figures reflect various changes. Most notably there are first the enormous growth in the number of plays along with the new habit of printing them that started in the 1590s, and secondly a slow decline in the production of new plays through the 1630s, along with increasing readiness to publish them. That is why close to 25 per cent of all the surviving texts were written in the last twelve years of this eighty-year period. The figures themselves are of limited value, because the sources for the information are so incomplete. The bulk of the evidence about play-titles in fact comes from the records of court performances, highly selective and patchy though they are, plus Henslowe's day-by-day records for the 1590s. No other records for a company or a playhouse's repertory survive, and the parish and town records of the visits by London companies hardly ever bother to say what plays they performed. This is the iceberg's tip again. The total number of playscripts written between 1560 and 1642 was probably at least three times the thousand or so titles that survive and at least six times the number of surviving texts.

Playgoing as a distinctive, though relatively expensive, form of public entertainment was popular at all levels of society in Tudor England. The touring companies fed the appetite that helped them grow, as they commanded more and more resources and more income from the towns and great houses that they visited. This must have helped them in the 1570s and 1580s to secure royal favour. In 1578 the Master of the Revels, for many years the chief organizer of court entertainments, was at last given official status[17] and a budget for the long winter season of staged entertainments at court. It did not take the first appointee, Edmund Tilney, long to realize that the existing court tradition of staging masques at Christmas, set-piece shows with elaborate scenery, music, dancing, and verse, was far more expensive than importing companies of professional players with their ready-made plays.[18] From then on the playing companies were protected by the Master and the Privy Councillors that he worked for, as necessary adjuncts to the royal pleasure, and their long-term prosperity and growth were assured. In a Minute of 3 December 1581 the Privy Council announced that its priorities included, after the need to protect the country against plague, the further need to safeguard the royal pleasure against the opposition of the city fathers to public playing:

Whereas certayne companyes of players hertofore usinge thier common excercise of playing within and aboute the Cittie of London have of late in respect of the generall infection within the Cittie ben restrayned by their Lordships' commaundement from playing, the said

[17] See W. R. Streitberger (ed.), *Jacobean and Caroline Revels Accounts, 1603–1642* (Malone Soc. Collections xiii, Oxford, 1986), x.

[18] Ibid. xviii.

players this daye exhibited a peticion unto their Lordships, humbly desiring that as well in respecte of their pore estates, having noe other meanes to sustayne them, their wyves and children but their exercise of playing, and were only brought up from their youthe in the practise and profession of musicke and playeng, as for that the sicknes within the Cittie was well slaked, so as noe danger of infection could follow by the assemblyes of people at their playes, yt would please their Lordships therfore to grante them licence to use their sayd exercise of playeng as heretofore they had don; their Lordships their upon for the consyderations aforesaid as also for that they are to present certayne playes before the Quenes Majestie for her solace in the Christmas tyme now following, were contented to yeld unto their said humble peticion, and ordered that the Lord Mayor of the Cittie of London should suffer and permitt them to use and exercise their trade of playing in and about the Cittie as they have hertofore accustomed upon the weeke dayes only, being holy dayes or other dayes, so as they doe forbeare wholye to playe on the Sabothe Daye, either in the forenone or afternone, which to doe they are by this their Lordships' order expressly denyed and forbidden.[19]

The city's opposition to playing started a long battle between the Privy Council and the Lord Mayor which did not really end until 1642. The city won a victory of sorts in 1594, when the Council closed the city inns to playing, but the same deal allowed the Privy Council to protect the Rose and the Theatre in the suburbs. When James gave the leading companies royal patrons even the city had to accept a theatre inside its walls, though it only ever allowed the one, and that with recurrent protests. The Jacobean and Caroline armistice only ended when royalty itself lost its power in 1642.

Fixing the main playing-places in London, a process that started in the 1560s and became firm when the first custom-built playhouses appeared in the suburbs in the 1570s, was the key that unlocked many doors for the companies. It gave the players the idea that a capacious, open-air, permanent playing-place might have advantages over the smaller and transient venues they were practised at playing in, at country guildhalls and inns as much as at court. For the first time they had a say in the design of the places they played in. The companies could build up far more substantial resources for performance when they were based at a fixed London venue than they could carry on their tours. And London generated a new kind of audience. Once regular playgoing became routine, and the London audiences got into the habit of seeing a fresh play every day, the first Marlowes and Peeles appeared to cater for audiences weaned on varied kinds of play and constantly demanding novelty.[20] Those were the conditions that through the 1580s and 1590s stimulated an intense growth in playwriting. Marlowe, Kyd, and Shakespeare were the chief promoters and the chief beneficiaries of these new conditions.

The other giant factor that affected playing was the creation of the Queen's Men in 1583. Its twelve sharers made a bigger company than ever before. Within a few

---

[19] *Acts of the Privy Council of England*, ed. J. R. Dasent (32 vols.; London, 1890–1907), xiii. 269.
[20] Steven Mullaney, *The Place of the Stage: License, Play, and Power in Renaissance England* (Chicago, Ill., 1988), lays emphasis on the unique 'liberty' of companies performing in the suburbs and 'liberties' of London. This view has some truth only for the years up to 1608.

years plays were being written for exceptionally large casts, though they shrank again a little after 1594. Other companies began to imitate them. The earl of Leicester took with him into the Netherlands in 1586 a company of fifteen players, by then the new standard size. But there were difficulties too. The greater size did mean greater resources, but it also meant greater costs. Running a company with bigger numbers and bigger costs meant working at a much higher risk-level. The new 'large' plays could only be mounted by the large companies, so a version of Matthew's Law came into operation.[21] The biggest companies succeeded while the smaller groups fell further and further behind. Only those companies with all the resources necessary to mount the large plays could hope to gain a foothold in the new market that London created. The eleven years between the first large company in 1583 and the first firm foothold with a fixed playing-place in London in 1594 saw radical changes for the few leading companies. They started the massive shift from habitual travelling to habitual residence in London.

The practice of travelling was endemic under Elizabeth. No lord or esquire who took the trouble to give a group of players his patronage wanted them on hand all the time. Travel gave them an income, and also the great economy of constantly changing audiences, so that the same limited repertoire of plays might last them for a whole year's tour. It was a marginal life, in almost all respects. On tour companies were often refused leave to play by the mayor and corporation of the towns they came to. Quite apart from the chronic suspicion of professional players, a conscientious mayor might worry that large gatherings of his people would run the risk of infections such as the plague, and mayors always feared the disruptions caused by crowds who gave attention to the dubious morality of low and possibly licentious shows. Playing companies always ran the risk of being unwelcome, though they usually got something for their trouble. Even in these years, while a mayor would normally pay the players to entertain the townspeople he might equally well pay them not to perform. Either way, they had money for their pains.

This precarious existence had a strong effect on the evolution of the companies. Mayors were commonly swayed in their willingness to sanction performances by the status of the company's patron. Elizabeth's Proclamation of 16 May 1559 had ordered all mayors to judge the fitness of any play before allowing it to be performed. Under the terms of the 1572 Statute against vagabonds the companies had to show the mayor their lord's licence authorising them to play. It was a strong-minded mayor who would refuse leave to my Lord of Leicester's players, or later to the Queen's Men, while he might feel much freer in deciding whether or not to admit Sir Robert Lane's company.[22] A careful study of the records seems to suggest

---

[21] Matthew 13: 12 (AV): 'For whosoever hath, to him shall be given, and he shall have more abundance; but whosoever hath not, from him shall be taken away even that he hath'.

[22] A company of players under licence from Lane was at Bristol in Aug. 1570, and played at court in the 1571–2 season. They appear subsequently to have become Lincoln's Men, as a result, Chambers suggests, of the tightening of patronage and its confinement to barons or nobles of higher rank in the 1572 Act. See *ES* ii. 97. The groups supported by the lower gentry were usually minstrels or tumblers, e.g. Sir George Throckmorton, Sheriff of Warwick in the 1530s, kept a group of minstrels.

that payments from the civic accounts to such companies usually reflected the status of the patron even more than the quality of the players.

But the rudimentary character of the records in civic accounts do not make it easy to see just how strong the influence of the patron's name might have been. Between 1583 and 1590 the Queen's Men regularly received twice as much as other companies. In general, the lower the social standing of a patron the less his players might expect; but it does not seem always to have worked like that. When Alleyn left the Admiral's Men for Strange's in 1591, the remaining Admiral's company that was on tour through these years generally received far less in payment than Strange's. It is recorded at Bath and Folkestone in 1591–2, Norwich, Faversham, and Folkestone in 1592–3, and Lydd in 1593–4. Faversham records the Admiral's in 1590, and Strange's in 1591–2, and again in 1592–3. In the latter year, Strange's were paid 20s. while the Admiral's, on a separate visit, were only paid 10s. Lydd in 1593–4 did rather better by the Admiral's, with 6s. 8d., calling it 'the Townes benevolence'. As the lesser company, never called to perform at court through these years, the Admiral's were not highly regarded and less well-rewarded. Quality of playing must have had some share in the process by which the leading companies managed to get a foothold in the most lucrative market-place of all, London.

In London, though, the companies could have no expectation of civic generosity. Mayors of London were consistently hostile to playing, for reasons partly moral and partly commercial. As the players' foothold in London became more secure under royal protection, successive lord mayors regularly complained to the Privy Council about the trouble they caused. The first considerable notice that the city's aldermen took about the problem of the crowds attracted by players inside their jurisdiction was an Act of the Court of Common Council of 6 December 1574. It was probably prompted by a pained enquiry from the Privy Council sent to the Lord Mayor on 22 March, asking 'what causes he hath to restrain plaies'.[23] Anticipating the function later to be given to the Master of the Revels, and obeying the 1559 Proclamation, the city's Act insisted that any play-text to be performed at any inn inside the city liberties must first have the mayor's approval. It also insisted that the players make donations to the poor of each ward in the city. The Act does seem to signal what William Ingram has called 'a change of strategy' for the city,[24] a withdrawal from total disapproval and instead a clear determination to insist that the terms of the new royal patent should be precisely observed. It was noticeably conciliatory in giving its consent to the 'Lawfull honest and commely use of plays', especially when they were performed in private houses, over which the city had no control.

This was not a position the city maintained with much consistency in subsequent years. Sometimes, particularly in the years after the first theatres were established,

---

[23] An extensive study of this and related papers from 1574 is in William Ingram, *The Business of Playing*, 121–35.
[24] Ibid. 136.

1576–84, the Lord Mayor may have financed pamphleteers like the former play-wright Stephen Gosson to attack the irreligious iniquities of playgoing. The more puritanical adherents of the Church of England deplored the viewing of idle spectacles as much as they deplored the theatrical icons and rituals of the Catholic Church. Shows incited people to lechery and other kinds of sin, most notably idleness. And idleness in particular gave the Lord Mayor an incentive to refuse the players any place in London. Plays were necessarily performed in daylight, through the afternoons of the working week. Holidays, which always drew the largest crowds to plays, were too infrequent to sustain the companies. Audiences therefore had either to be idle to start with or to take time off work to see the play. Since the mayor and his corporation were all citizen-employers in the great guilds that controlled all the workers of London, they had a vested interest in closing down shows that drew their employees away from their work.

The first result of the city's opposition to playgoing was that the players built their theatres in the suburbs, outside the Lord Mayor's jurisdiction. Theatres appeared to the north of the city in Shoreditch, to the east in Stepney, and to the south across the river in Southwark. Use by players of the city itself was dependent on bending the rules. City innyards, and sometimes rooms inside inns, especially in winter and bad weather, were used for plays until 1594, when the Privy Council at last backed the Lord Mayor and ordered them closed to players. Companies of boy choristers performed plays at Paul's and in the liberty of the Blackfriars from the 1570s to 1590, and from 1599 to 1608. But the Lord Mayor's hostility was consist-ent and potent. No player or impresario dared build a theatre inside the city, even in the Stuart years when the leading companies had royal patronage. Apart from a few inns like the Bel Savage near St Paul's and the Bull and the Cross Keys in Gracechurch Street, which were never recognized officially as playhouses, and the tiny theatre built for the Paul's Boys abutting the cathedral, no playhouse was in regular use within the city's bounds until 1608.

In that year, in return for a large loan from the citizenry, James allowed the liberties to come under city jurisdiction. The Blackfriars liberty, a prime residential neighbourhood, had acquired a playhouse in 1596, intended for Shakespeare's company. They were barred from using it in November 1596 because the residents of Blackfriars did not want a 'common playhouse' in their midst, and successfully petitioned the Privy Council to stop it from opening. As a means of retrieving some income from it late in 1599 the owners leased it to a boy company, who were not so noisy and performed only once a week. They made it, at least ostensibly, a 'private' playhouse, immune at first from the regulations that controlled the public per-formers. Shakespeare's company did not secure it for their own use for another nine years. Ironically, by the time they did secure it in 1608 the Blackfriars had come under the city's control. But by then Shakespeare's company was the King's Men, and safe from the Lord Mayor.

The steps that took the best of the travelling companies into residence in London provide the clearest indication of the factors influencing that progress. They show the market forces that enabled the companies to build their base in London, and the constraints that shaped their functioning there. In such a broad process it is much easier to identify general patterns of change than the individual decisions that might have influenced them. Some personalities do emerge, though. The evidence for companies being present in London and being accepted as of good quality lie almost entirely in the court records of the Revels Office. The Master himself became a potent force from the 1580s onwards, rewarding or depriving the companies who offered themselves to him each autumn with their entertainments for the court. Behind and above him stood the nobles who made themselves patrons of travelling companies. Some features of this influence on the rising companies will be dealt with in Chapter 4. A word needs to be said first, though, in this more general survey, about the part these noble eminences played in helping their 'servants' to work as companies of players in the years before the Stuarts took over the patronage of the London groups.

Very little direct evidence survives about the attitudes of patrons to their companies. Hints have to be picked out of a morass of incidental stories and small details. We can tell that the earl of Leicester saw his company as one of his political tools and that he worked to protect it and to use it. This is evidenced by his intervention to secure their patent after the 1572 Act imposed its restrictions on players and the professional companies.[25] Leicester's brother, the earl of Warwick, certainly saw the treatment of his company as a reflection on his own status, to judge by his sharp reaction in 1580 to the Lord Mayor of London when he blocked Warwick's player from performing for a fencing prize. In a similar exchange of letters of about the same time, we can see that Lord Berkeley felt that he was personally responsible for his players, and wanted them treated fairly.[26] Charles Howard, the Lord Admiral, and his father-in-law Henry Carey, the Lord Chamberlain, seem to have been more distant, but that might be expected of Privy Councillors responsible for the government of the state. It is difficult to separate their personal views about their livery-wearers from their political views as government officers responsible for the playing companies generally.[27] Thomas Nashe's testimony in 1596 after Carey died, that his company felt 'their state setled' while working for him,[28] can be read in two ways, either as a declaration that he valued them highly or as a statement that he had given them the official support of the Lord Chamberlain's office. Howard seems to have been more remote from the leaders of the Lord Admiral's Men. In an exchange over their getting the appointment of a new royal bear-master, Henslowe and Alleyn make it quite clear in the letters they wrote about it in 1598 that they expected to get little direct help from

---

[25] For an assessment of the likelihood that Leicester used his company to press his political views, see Paul Whitfield White, *Theatre and Reformation: Protestantism, Patronage and Playing in Tudor England* (Cambridge, 1993), esp. 163–74.

[26] For a more detailed account of these exchanges see Ch. 10.

[27] See Ch. 4.

[28] Nashe, *Works*, ed. R. B. McKerrow (5 vols.; London, 1904–10), v. 194.

their patron.[29] On the other hand, the case for Howard's active support of his own players and his placing them in a secure position in London can be made very positively.

Such hints are elusive and imprecise. They give no indication of any direct intervention by patrons with the players who wore their livery over what they might play in their repertory, for instance, which is one of the most tempting questions to speculate about. That Leicester should have expected his company to support his political positions, whether in the form of anti-Catholic plays or with pro-war propaganda in the later years, is an easy supposition; but there is not a shred of tangible evidence to support it. It is equally easy to assume that any company which was used to living off the privileges accorded it when it showed its master's livery and licence to the mayor of every town it visited would never have offered any plays that it thought its lord would not favour. Such assumptions are easy to make, but difficult to sustain. For the opening of the 1606 Christmas festivities, on St Stephen's Night, 26 December, while the king was pressing Parliament to pass a law uniting his two kingdoms of England and Scotland, the King's Servants presented a play at court about 'the division of the kingdoms' of ancient Britain. In the presence of the king's two sons, Henry and Charles, of whom Henry had the title Prince of Wales and Duke of Cornwall, while his younger brother had recently been made Duke of Albany, the play's first scene divided the kingdom of ancient Britain between the Dukes of Albany and Cornwall. Nobody at court that night could have failed to make the connection, and its application to the disunited modern kingdoms of England and Scotland. It is difficult not to assume from this that the Master of the Revels could only have approved *King Lear* for a performance at court because he had thought the play supported the king's position over the question of uniting the kingdoms.[30] It is equally difficult not to assume that the company knew what it was doing. The very wearing of a patron's livery was a constant reminder where the servant's loyalty belonged.

By 1606, of course, the three leading companies had royal patronage. From 1603 onwards all the London companies wore the livery of one or other member of the royal family. That made a different game of the question of personal loyalty to a patron's personal or political allegiances. Before that, and most particularly in the early years up to 1594 when the companies expected to be travellers rather than 'at home' in London, the relations of the remote patron to his touring players must have been quite different. With royal patronage after 1603 the companies had laid on them both a general and a localized allegiance to their patron. The Prince's Men, for instance, played at court before the prince and his siblings much more frequently than they played before the king himself. For the earlier years under

---

[29] *Henslowe's Diary*, 299. In a letter to Alleyn, Henslowe says of his quest for the Mastership of the royal bears and bulls that he has asked for Howard's support, but 'I am sure my lord admeralle will do nothinge'. In the event he did not secure the appointment until 1604.

[30] See Leah Marcus, *Puzzling Shakespeare: Local Reading and its Discontents* (Berkeley, Calif., 1988), 148–59.

Elizabeth, though, when the leading companies had noble and even non-courtier patrons, the evidence is tenuous in the extreme. Except for a few hints in the earl of Leicester's papers,[31] we do not know when or even whether a company would expect to play before its own patron. We might well think that at the least a royal visit to a patron's house would require the players to take their part in the royal entertainments. But apart from the implication that Elizabeth, after seeing the shows at Elvetham in 1591, brought Hertford's Men to court for their unique appearance a few months later, nothing mentioning professional players at such entertainments has survived.

Perhaps the strongest sign that players and their patrons were intimately connected shows in what happened when a patron died. A playing licence automatically lost its validity once its signatory was dead. The company then had to find another signatory, another name, another livery. There are a few indications from the changes that took place in a company when its patron died that the loyalty was fairly personal. In the crisis year of 1594, when the 'large' companies were under unique strain from the long closure, and the patrons of both Sussex's and Strange's/Derby's Men died, the reshuffling of company membership was considerable. The new earl of Sussex and the new earl of Derby started wholly fresh companies which ran in the country for several years afterwards. The leading players from both of the old companies joined the two companies of the duopoly with its Privy Council patrons that the Lord Chamberlain set up in May of that year. How far Carey and Howard were ruthlessly picking out all the leading men from the two defunct companies for their own new groups on the precedent of the 1583 creation of the Queen's Men, or how far their motive was an act of charity to the remains of their relatives' companies, we cannot know. The starting-up of new companies of Derby's and Sussex's Men makes the former more likely.[32] But it does not deny that a company might be identified very closely as personal servants of its patron. Leicester's, Rich's, Oxford's, Berkeley's, Pembroke's, as well as Sussex's and Strange's, all disintegrated when their lord died. The way the Chamberlain's Men passed from Henry Carey to his son George on his death in 1596 is fairly anomalous, and was probably linked to the creation of the duopoly and the brief change of Lord Chamberlain from a Carey to a Cobham.

A substantial part of this question about the possible relations between patrons and their companies belongs as much to religion as to politics. Ferdinando, Lord Strange, who ran the best of the early companies at the Rose in the early 1590s, was a Catholic based in Lancashire, a county which had a peculiarly intense record for pursuing recusants, and a lot of great-family recusants to pursue. Munday's deliberate choice of the most sympathetic sources for his dramatized life of Thomas

---

[31] Sally-Beth MacLean, 'The Politics of Patronage: Dramatic Records in Robert Dudley's Household Books', *SQ* 44 (1993), 175–82, and 'Players on Tour: New Evidence From Records of Early English Drama', *Elizabethan Theatre*, 10, ed. C. E. McGee (Port Credit, 1988), 155–72.

[32] See Ch. 4 and Scott McMillin, 'Sussex's Men in 1594: The Evidence of *Titus Andronicus* and *The Jew of Malta*', *Theatre Survey*, 32 (1991), 214–23.

More when he wrote it for Strange's company may have been influenced by what he knew about the company patron's religious allegiance.

How much a covert loyalty to the old faith in their patron might have affected the playmakers and their plays is a difficult question partly because the whole business of theatrical display relates more closely to Catholic rituals than to Protestant. Antipathy to Catholic ritual and to playing went together. The point about the affinity between the two kinds of theatre was made on many occasions by the Puritan critics of playgoing. In some degree religious allegiance does seem to have gone with the attitude to plays. Recusants of varying degrees of openness are known to have been involved in playmaking or playgoing throughout the period. Sebastian Westcott, the choirmaster who ran the Paul's Boys in the 1570s, was an open Catholic. Christopher Beeston's wife was twice charged with recusancy by her local court in the second decade of the seventeenth century, and his son William was thought to be a Catholic. Toby Matthew, the notoriously exhibitionistic recusant son of the Archbishop of York, was a regular playgoer. London's secret Catholic priests were warned in the 1620s by their chief to beware of their enthusiasm for playgoing. Richard Gunnell, manager of the Fortune and the Salisbury Court, was called 'a Papist' in Richard Kendall's account of the companies in 1634.[33] James Shirley became a clergyman in 1618, but left the Church and turned to playwriting on being converted to Catholicism in 1625. None the less, there is not much external evidence to suggest that either in religion or in politics the fraught condition of most people's minds over religion was consistently a consideration with the players. Most of the plays that show strong polemical impulses belong to occasions when a particular incident prompted satire or similar expressions of opinion.

The early moralistic plays certainly worked as propaganda. The early Tudor companies, such as the one for which Skelton wrote his *Magnificence*, gave the kind of performance their great patrons wanted.[34] John Bale ran a company that toured all England in the 1540s with his *King Johann* and its fervently anti-papal line.[35] How much that practice persisted in later years, when moral interludes had lost favour, when playing companies became more distant from their patrons, and the new London repertories were established, is open to doubt. No plays performed under royal patrons expressed openly republican views, though plays about unjust rulers and about killing kings were always popular. From the familiar histories, whether of Rome, England, France, or Spain, the poets took far more stories about evil monarchs and court assassinations than stories of just or all-conquering rulers. The mightiest conqueror shown on London's stages was 'that atheist Tamburlaine', no model for any Christian king.

---

[33] G. E. Bentley, *The Jacobean and Caroline Stage* (7 vols.; Oxford, 1940–68), (hereafter *JCS*), ii. 688. See also Jerzy Limon, 'An Allusion to the Alleged Catholicism of some Jacobean Players in John Gee's *New Shreds from the Old Snare* (1624)', *NQ* 230 (1985), 488–9.

[34] See Suzanne R. Westfall, *Patrons and Performance: Early Tudor Household Revels* (Oxford, 1990).

[35] See Greg Walker, *Plays of Persuasion: Drama and Politics at the Court of Henry VIII* (Cambridge, 1990).

3 *Travelling*

Most of the companies that performed through the sixteenth century have disappeared leaving little record of their passing. For the city of Leicester alone in the sixteenth and seventeenth centuries there are notes of more than fifty companies that came to perform before the citizens. And that was at a time when the borough records are far from complete and only register the more conspicuous events. After 1560 the number and frequency of visits grew hugely.[1] Along with this growth in the number of travelling companies the size of the playing groups grew too, till the creation of the Queen's Men in 1583 set a ceiling figure for the number of sharers that no later company ever exceeded. In the long tradition of professional playing in England the Tudor century was the heyday for travelling players, and travelling was the Tudor norm. London playing did not really begin to dictate standards until a little before Elizabeth died in 1603.

Travelling dictated all the early playing practices. The habits that went with it lasted through much of the early Stuart period when London playing became secure. Company organization, the teamwork of sharing and using few extras beside the boy 'apprentices', the essential resources of playbooks and costumes, the plays themselves seen as things that could be carried from one place to another, and the related expectation that performances could be mounted at new venues at short notice, these were all features of early company life that never lost their place in company thinking. Playing as an urban and settled phenomenon took a long time to develop.[2] So it is important to identify the habits that companies learned from travelling as the basic underpinning for all of their London activities.

The chief statute that the government employed to control players was the Act for the Punishment of Vagabonds of 1572. Aimed more directly at masterless men than was the old Act of Retainers, it specified that, without the right to wear the livery of a great man as their patron, all players must be counted as vagabonds. The '*Acte for the punishement of Vacabondes and for Relief of the Poore & Impotent*' (*14 Eliz*, c.5) stated that:

All & every person and persons whatsoever they bee, being above thage of fourtene yeres . . . & all Fencers Bearewardes Comon Players in Enterludes & Ministrels, not belonging to any Baron of this Realme or towardes any other honorable Personage of greater Degree; all Juglers Pedlars Tynkers and Petye Chapmen; which seid Fencers Bearewardes

---

[1] Alice B. Hamilton, *REED Newsletter*, 1 (1979), 18.

[2] François Laroque, *Shakespeare's Festive World: Elizabethan Seasonal Entertainment and the Professional Stage* provides a thorough survey of the transition from the essentially rural and provincial seasonal patterns of self-generated entertainment to the more passive reception of professional playing in London and the rest of England. For a critique of Laroque's views and others, see Thomas Pettit, 'The Seasons of the Globe: Two New Studies of Elizabethan Drama and Festival', *Connotations*, 2 (1992), 234–56.

Comon Players in Enterludes Mynstrels Juglers Pedlers Tynkers & Petye Chapmen, shall wander abroade and have not Lycense of two Justices of the Peace at the leaste, whereof one to be of the Quorum, when and in what Shier they shall happen to wander . . . shalbee taken and adjudged and deemed Roges Vacaboundes and Sturdy Beggers.[3]

Earlier statutes had given the right to authorize a company of players to people with the status of esquires or above, or else two justices or senior burgesses of a county.[4] The 1572 statute narrowed that restriction to the more senior nobility, and the right to be a patron narrowed still more as the century went on. In the wake of the 1572 statute, in May 1574, the earl of Leicester took his own steps to legitimize his company of players. He set up the notable innovation of a royal patent which authorized his company to play throughout the country. The 'Proclamation for the Execution of the Laws made against Unlawful Retainers' of 3 January 1572 had demanded enforcement of the old statutes about retainers, particularly 3. *Hen. VII* (1487), c.12, which forbade the giving of livery by a lord to any but menials and lawyers. Leicester's players had written to him in January 1572 appealing for a written licence with his name on it in consequence of this proclamation. The patent that he secured for them in 1574 clarified the position of liveried companies of players, and introduced a novel form of licence. Companies would now have to carry their patents with them on their travels, ready to show the mayor of each town they came to as their licence to play there and their right to wear their patron's livery. It was one of the government's more effective forms of regulation, though it could still be easily circumvented. Until the Lord Chamberlain started circulating letters about forged patents in 1616, few local authorities questioned the authority of a patent. Before that, the records sometimes show mayors getting confused when two companies using the same patent appeared within a few weeks of each other. Norwich, for instance, had visits in September 1591 from two companies in close succession, each claiming to be the legitimate Chandos's players.[5] Some tightening of the system of regulation came in 1598, when the Lord Chamberlain confirmed the position of the duopoly established in 1594 by confining the right to be patron of any company to men of baronial or higher status.[6] It loosened again once the

[3] *ES* iv. 269–70.

[4] The early proclamation issued in Elizabeth's first year, on 16 May 1559 (509), renewed and sharpened earlier attempts at regulation by specifying that 'The Quenes Majestie doth straightly forbyd all maner Interludes to be playde eyther openly or privately, except the same be notified before hande, and licenced within any Citie or towne corporate, by the Maior or other chiefe officers of the same, and within any shyre, by suche as shalbe Lieuetenauntes for the Quenes Majestie in the same shyre, or by two of the Justices of peax inhabyting within that part of the shire where any shalbe played . . . And further her majestie gyveth speciall charge to her nobilitie and gentilmen, as they professe to obey and regarde her majestie, to take good order in thys behalfe wyth their servauntes being players, that this her majesties commaundement may be dulye kepte and obeyed'. Quoted in *ES* iv. 263–4. This gave mayors and Justices of the Peace the power to approve or dismiss companies which they only began to lose after 1616.

[5] For other such mishaps, see *REED, Norwich*, xxxiii–xxxiv.

[6] The 'Acte for punyshment of Rogues Vagabondes and Sturdy Beggars' of 9 Feb. 1598 (39 *Eliz.* c. 4) stated that 'All Fencers Bearewardes common Players of Enterludes and Minstrelles wandring abroade (other than Players of Enterludes belonging to any Baron of this Realme, or any other honorable

Revels Office started issuing annual licences, and the patronage system weakened under Charles.

Once the London companies were firmly settled under the Stuarts, forging patents became a fairly standard means of getting a form of authority for travelling. Whether these 'duplicates' or 'exemplifications' of the London patents were made to allow the London groups to divide and multiply, one group sticking to London while another toured, or whether they were simply designed to rip off the privileged London authorizations, it is difficult to tell. Certainly some of the London companies seem to have run duplicate travelling groups. On the other hand some of the players who were named in the 'exemplifications' seem to have shifted their designation from one company name to another at different times, which suggests they may have been travelling on forged warrants. After about 1616, and especially under Charles, the Master of the Revels issued annual licences to the travelling companies. This seems to have marked the final dismissal of local power to authorize companies to play that was granted in the 1559 Proclamation.

In the later years, especially under Charles, the evidence for travelling fades away. The London companies on the whole travelled less frequently than they did under Elizabeth, and some of the London groups seem to have sponsored duplicate companies to travel for them. And civic disapproval of playing seems to have grown. Several towns noted only that they turned the professional companies away. The difficulty in sifting through the *REED* evidence for the last twenty years is that the travellers were left to fend for themselves. Usually they did not have to secure the mayor's approval to play. The old 1559 Proclamation no longer had any force. The Master of the Revels licensed them to travel, and they did so freely on his authority. They may have simply gone straight to the familiar inns, put up their bills, and played. As a result, the civic records list visits by playing companies more and more infrequently. The puzzle is to determine how much the disappearance of the records stemmed from civic disapproval of professional playing and how much from a relaxation of civic control. It seems likely that the Puritanical hatred of playing was stronger and showed itself earlier outside London, where the court had less sway. Few civic mayors would have regretted the 1642 closure.

The other form of government control was censorship. This was a different matter for travelling companies than it was for the companies which settled in London. Officially the Master of the Revels had to approve all playscripts before any play could be performed. The London companies were ostensibly as subject to his constraints on their travels as when they performed in the suburbs of London or at court. In practice, of course, he had little real say over what they chose to offer outside London. A letter from Tilney recorded at Leicester in 1583 says he insists that only plays containing his signature could be performed, but it has a despairing note. In the rest of England it was for the local authorities to exercise their own

Personage of greater Degree, to be auctoryzed to play, under the Hand and Seale of Armes of such Baron or Personage) . . . shalbe taken adjudged and deemed Rogues Vagabondes and Sturdy Beggers'. Quoted in *ES* iv. 324–5.

constraints. A wise company would arrive at the guildhall wearing its livery and showing its licence. The Queen's Men visiting York in 1587 'cam in hir majestes Lyvereys & plaid in the common hall'.[7] In Bristol an Ordinance of the Common Council in November 1585 laid it down that the mayor should censor all plays brought by visiting companies. Following the 1559 Proclamation, no play could be performed without his licence: 'noe Maior of this Cytie shall Licence or permitt anye players whatsoever to playe in the Guildhall of Bristoll att anye tyme here-after, uppon . . . payne of xl s. to be payd by the Maior . . . unlesse such plaiers doe playe there before the Mayor and his brethren'.[8] This was standard, though it was not consistently enforced. Bristol renewed the order in December 1595, after a decade in which two or three visits and performances a year had been tolerated. Frequent changes of mayor did not give much consistency to the enforcement, and the will to see plays was always likely to override official constraints, as the Cambridge University authorities found in their thirty-year struggle to prevent students from attending public performances. Still, most towns were small enough for the mayor's edict to hold some force.

From 1559 plays had either to be licensed directly by the mayor, or seen in performance by the whole corporation. The authorities used their presence as a tacit form of constraint on the companies. The standard procedure for a company on arrival in a new town is given in the celebrated account by R. Willis of his childhood visit to a play at Gloucester:

In the City of Gloucester the manner is (as I think it is in other like corporations) that when Players of Enterludes come to towne, they first attend the Mayor to enforme him what noble-mans servants they are, and so to get licence for their publike playing; and if the Mayor like the Actors, or would shew respect to their Lord and Master, he appoints them to play their first play before himself and the Aldermen and common Counsell of the City; and that is called the Mayors play, where every one that will comes in without money, the Mayor giving the players a reward as hee thinks fit to shew respect unto them.[9]

This procedure is confirmed by a ruling of 1582 in the York rolls, that 'players of Interludes now come, and comyng from hencforth to this cittie shall play but twise in the comon hall of this cyttie viz. once before the Lord maior and aldermen &c. and thother before the commons'.[10] What Francis Wambus's company tried to do at Norwich in 1624 confirms that this procedure remained the standard practice. The York restriction to two performances in all is an early hint of what was to come in all the cities once the Master of the Revels started issuing annual licences for the London companies to travel, and the municipalities hardened against this impo-sition of royal and London authority on them.[11] There was always a strong feeling that the visiting companies were an alien nuisance.

[7] REED, York, i. 430.   [8] REED, Bristol, forthcoming.
[9] REED, Cumberland/Westmorland/Gloucestershire, 362–3.   [10] REED, York, i. 399.
[11] We should not make too much of the wording in the Exeter accounts for 1630–1: 'Paid for oppressing the Players per mr maiors order £0 /10s./ od.' (REED, Devon, 196).

There was also a potent side-effect of the 1559 Proclamation, and the access it gave the professionals to playing in town halls. In all towns the largest indoor venue for playing was the town hall or guildhall. Where early Tudor players offered their wares on outdoor scaffolds in marketplaces, in the last third of the century plays went indoors.[12] If the town hall was not available an inn would be used. An indoor venue had the distinct advantage for the players of giving them better control over their audiences and their purses than an open market-place. To a great extent the switch from open places to guildhalls and inns in the lesser cities around England anticipated London's more gradual shift from amphitheatres to roofed hall-theatres.

The history of the first London companies starts with them as travellers. Most of them went on travelling until 1642, however fixed their workplaces in London became. This practice survived the establishment of the first 'large' company in 1583 which swelled the number of sharers from eight to twelve, and created more mouths that needed to be fed from the same income. It survived the establishment of fixed and approved places to play in London in 1594, and it survived the leading companies' elevation to become servants of royalty in 1603. Even the King's Servants toured during the years when they were supreme and supremely privileged under the early Stuarts. This tradition was amazingly durable. Some players, odd though it may seem to today's householders, appear to have actively chosen a life of travelling in preference to living and working in London. The retention of the tradition of companies travelling with plays is due to a great many more factors than the one usually cited, the periodic closures of London's playing-places because of the plague. At such times the plague was usually spreading through the country too, and local authorities were often suspicious that the players might themselves be carrying the plague.[13] How and why the tradition of travelling lasted through all the changes between 1583 and 1642 needs careful scrutiny. It underpinned most of the companies, and the practices that went with it help to explain some of the London policies.

It has almost always been assumed that because travel was strenuous the London-based companies made economies in their resources when they had to travel. They cut the numbers of players in the group, it is assumed, and they cut their playbooks so that the smaller number of players on tour could offer the country cut-down versions of their London plays. That, I believe, is a mistaken view. Economies were possible when travelling, of course. By far the biggest one was the number of plays the company had to keep in its repertoire. Donald Lupton said in his short and cynical *London and the Countrey Carbonadoed* (1632, printed in duodecimo) that players used to leave London for the country, not because of the

---

[12] See Robert Tittler, *Architecture and Power: The Town Hall and the English Urban Community c. 1500–1640* (Oxford, 1991), 140.

[13] While preparing for Queen Anne's visit to the city in 1613, the Bristol authorities decreed that 'noe Stage players shalbe permitted to play in the Cytie this St James tyde In regarde of the infection of the plague at Aburgavenney and other places in Wales, and the daunger thereof nowe greatlye feared in Bristol'. *REED, Bristol*, forthcoming.

reasons that rich men left, but under the kinds of pressure that, beside the plague closures, modern scholars have come to see as the standard reason for players travelling generally. 'Sometimes they fly into the Countrey; but its a suspicion, that they are either poore, or want cloaths, or else Company, or a new Play: Or do as some wandring Sermonists, make one Sermon travaile and serve twenty Churches.'[14] Travelling, by this easy assumption, was the cheap option. One play could serve twenty towns. Travelling required far fewer costumes and playbooks, and probably fewer players, than London called for.

It cannot have been so simple. In the later years some of the London companies hardly travelled at all. Others kept two groups, one which travelled and one which remained based firmly in London. Some Stuart players regularly named in the provincial records, notably Martin Slater, Thomas Swinnerton, Nicholas Long, Gilbert Reason, Robert Kempston, Nicholas Hanson, William Perry, William Daniell, and Elias Guest, seem to have led permanent touring groups using duplicates, not always authorized, of the London companies' warrants. From the beginning of his career as Master of the Revels, Henry Herbert began to license the travelling companies annually. Renewable licences were almost the only means that government had to control and censor the non-London companies.[15] Other groups or members of groups, some of them senior sharers in the King's Men, stuck to London and rarely, if ever, travelled. Christopher Beeston was markedly reluctant to let his companies travel. It may have been he who initiated the system whereby a secondary group travelled permanently using a duplicate of the London group's patent.

These alternative roles, travelling or sticking 'at home' in London, which grew into habits under James, were marked by the way the companies handled their material possessions. It was a question of group priorities whether a company thought of itself as based in London, and so took only a proportion of its resources with it on tour, leaving the major assets safely stowed, or whether it took everything on tour because it had no sense that London was 'home'. Richard Kendall, wardrobe-keeper to the King's Revels at Salisbury Court in 1634, said that his company came to Oxford 'furnished with 14 playes'.[16] That number was just about their entire current repertoire. That they carried so many of their resources with them is a reflection that they did not feel at all confident of their London base. They were in fact just transferring from the Fortune to the Salisbury Court, and may well have felt that their future in London was insecure.

It is also a nice question whether travelling, besides saving money on new playbooks and costumes, allowed the cutting of the plays themselves to be another cheap option. A company permanently on its travels might be expected to adjust its

---

[14] *London and the Countrey Carbonadoed* (1632), Gɪv.

[15] Norwich noted in May 1623 that the Palsgrave's company at the Fortune in 1623 had protested that William Daniell had 'injuriously gotten their Letters Patentes'. *REED, Norwich*, 176. The Norwich authorities, generally hostile to playing, scrupulously recorded each visiting company's licence to play.

[16] *JCS*, ii. 688–9.

playbooks to suit its necessarily mobile and reduced resources, but whether the London-based companies also took the trouble to trim their playbooks is a much more dubious proposition. And once the London companies had all the licences for playing, we have to ask whether they employed two kinds of text, a full one for London and another one cut for the country.

Much ink has been spilt over the so-called 'bad' quartos of the earlier play-texts. The six or seven surviving examples are usually thought to be shortened texts made up by players from their memory of the scripts of plays in the repertory.[17] The assumption that touring meant shorter texts has been employed most strongly to identify these quartoes as deriving from travellers' playbooks. It is a view that does not stand up to close inspection.[18]

The evidence that any company ever used to cut its playing numbers to make travelling cheaper is equally open to question. David Bradley in *From Text to Performance in the Elizabethan Theatre* spends a chapter (58–74) challenging what he wryly calls 'an unshakeable myth of theatre history', that the personnel of a company were always reduced for travelling. He adduces several reasons for them not cutting their numbers before they went on tour. First is the evidence that the 'bad' quartos are made up from texts supposedly cut for touring. None of these texts, least of all the quarto and the 'plot' of *The Battle of Alcazar*, which he subjects to a particularly close scrutiny, shows any sign that their cuts and changes were made to allow fewer players to perform them.[19]

Secondly Bradley argues that the companies would have needed to re-license their playbooks if they altered the approved copies (72–3). The Master of the Revels signed the books he read and approved for performance for London and for the country as a whole, and would not allow changes to be made. Local authorities checked a company's authority to play, but left censoring the playscripts to the Master. At Leicester in 1583 a clerk questioning the credentials of Worcester's company three days after a group with a forged licence from Worcester had passed through noted that '*No play is to bee played, but such as is allowed by the sayd Edmund* [Tilney], *& his hand at the latter end of the saide booke they doe play.*'[20] He was quoting Tilney's patent, a copy of which was sent to all local authorities. Henry Herbert's papers have no record that he ever approved any texts that had been revised specifically for touring.

The third argument against smaller companies touring with shorter plays is that the playing-time for plays in the provincial towns was generally the same as for

---

[17] They include the early quartos of *2* and *3 Henry VI*, Q1 *Hamlet*, Q1 *Henry V*, Q1 *Merry Wives*, possibly Q1 *Romeo and Juliet*, and the A text of *Faustus*.

[18] See e.g. Paul Werstine, 'Narratives About Printed Shakespearean Texts: "Foul Papers" and "Bad" Quartos', *SQ* 41 (1990), 65–86; and Kathleen M. Irace, 'Reconstruction and Adaptation in Q *Henry V*', *SB* 44 (1991), 228–53.

[19] There is plenty of supporting evidence for this view; e.g. T. J. King, in *Casting Shakespeare's Plays: London Actors and their Roles, 1590–1642* (Cambridge, 1992), 73, dismisses Gary Taylor's claim that the quarto of *Henry V* was adapted for a reduced cast.

[20] J. T. Murray, *English Dramatic Companies, 1558–1642* (2 vols.; London, 1910), ii. 320.

London. Some local authorities did lay down a limit on how far into the night playing might go, but that was infrequent, and did not restrict the actual length of time available for the plays. This is a rather shadowy case, since the evidence about playing times and the length of plays was as variable as the plays.[21]

The fourth and by some way the most substantial argument is the point that the occasional records giving the numbers of a visiting company indicate similar sizes to the London figures and to the casts called for by the printed plays. Bradley cites a few such numbers, and there are many more that he omits. Sussex's had only six men in the company at Ludlow in 1569–70, and Clinton's had six in 1576.[22] But that was before the rapid escalation in numbers that the establishment of the twelve-sharer Queen's Men precipitated, and when plays were still being written for small companies. There were twelve players altogether in Leicester's Company at Southampton as early as 1577, eleven in Bath's, and ten in Worcester's. Worcester's also had ten at Norwich and Leicester in 1583, the year that the Queen's was given its twelve sharers. Southampton's records also note smaller companies (six in Clinton's, six in Berkeley's) in the 1570s, presumably running only with older plays for smaller casts. In the 1580s the numbers in all the major companies rose sharply. Leicester's took fifteen to the Low Countries in 1585.[23]

Once the Queen's Men had established a higher limit for players and new plays began to be written for the larger casts, all the major touring companies seem to have contained the same number of players as those who performed in London. Thomas Platter counted fifteen actors playing *Julius Caesar* at the Globe in London in 1599, by which time the fashion for 'large' plays had diminished somewhat.[24] Provincial records confirm this number. In 1617–18 the Lady Elizabeth's had twenty players at Plymouth. Elias Guest led thirteen of Queen Henrietta's Men to Norwich in February 1627, saying that others were to follow from Thetford. William Daniell took himself and sixteen others of a 'Revels' company to Coventry in 1635. Even the group that Martin Slater led with a licence from the late Queen Elizabeth's players had fifteen players when it called on the Cliffords of Yorkshire in 1619.[25] The King's Revels Company, when they visited Norwich in 1635, were travelling with twenty-eight players.[26] The inclination to take large numbers on

---

[21] See Ch. 5.   [22] Murray, *Dramatic Companies*, ii. 324.

[23] See Sally-Beth MacLean, 'The Politics of Patronage: Dramatic Records in Robert Dudley's Household Books', *SQ* 44 (1993), 175–82, 181, and 'Leicester and the Evelyns: New Evidence for the Continental Tour of Leicester's Men', *RES* 39 (1988), 487–93.

[24] See Gurr, 'The Chimera of Amalgamation', *TRI* 18 (1993), 85–93, esp. 85–6.

[25] Murray, *Dramatic Companies*, ii. 255.

[26] Ibid. ii. 358. G. E. Bentley, *The Profession of Player in Shakespeare's Time, 1590–1642* (Princeton, 1984), 184–8, uses these figures to argue that the numbers must have been reduced for travelling. To support his assumption of larger London casts he cites the fact that the King's Men in 1624 and 1625 had thirty-five men altogether, plus the boys. This ignores the number who were stage hands and assistants, not players. It also ignores the evidence from Norwich of a group of players, Prince Charles's (II) company, then at the Red Bull, who numbered 28 in 1635, which Bentley thinks must have been two companies, and the fact that at Worcester in 1632 the King's was in two groups: 'the kings majesties

tour was such that Herbert imposed a limit of twenty on William Perry's travelling group in 1624, and fifteen on William Daniell's group in 1634.[27] Such numbers were ample for the London stages and the London plays. It was the non-performing helpers, stage hands, gatherers, and others who were shaken off when a company left London to go on tour.[28]

Travelling, and the readiness to plant a performance in whatever venue offered itself at a day's notice, whether a London playhouse, a scaffolded hall at court, a private house in the Strand, the hall of a country house, or a market-place, inn, or guildhall in a country town, was the guiding principle until 1594 and after.[29] Not until the Privy Council named the Rose and the Theatre in London as the approved places for the two approved companies was any playing group able to develop the feeling of security and durability that a settled place for playing gives. If we except the special case of Burbage's Blackfriars hall, the Globe and the Fortune share the distinction of being the first playhouses ever built for specific companies to use on a permanent basis. It was several years after that, when the Jacobean royal patrons were in place, that the division in company character took place, and some companies became permanent Londoners while others took to constant travel. After 1603 the need for the leading company to travel diminished, since James started paying the King's Servants sums of money to compensate them for the plague closures. At the end of the long closure for plague in 1603–4 he made an exceptional payment of £30 to help them maintain their resources while they could not play. This payment became a standard award to the company to compensate for the longer closures. In 1609 they received £40, in 1625 £67 (100 marks), in 1630 Charles gave them £100, and in 1637 they had a bounty of £1 for each week of the closure. No other company received such a payment, though. The King's Men were unique in not having to travel during plague closures. Yet they did, and regularly, even if in the later years they delegated much of their travel to groups of younger players.

Travelling must have generated a specific mentality, perhaps not unlike the mindset indicated by the current use of the word as a euphemism for communities living in caravans. Travellers did not stay long in any one place. A Whitehall letter of April 1618 confirming the patent issued to John Daniel for his Bristol company of youths specified that they should not perform in one place for 'above Fowreteene

players beinge two Companies'. Companies kept their players when on tour but shed their backstage staff and assistants. The Norwich records twice note affrays involving a company's gatherer, one in 1583 and one in 1627. On the second occasion the gatherer was one of the players.

[27] The first order was dated 9 Apr. 1624 in the Exeter records (copied 31 May: *REED, Devon*, 192–3), the second 28 Nov. 1634 in the Norwich records (copied 3 Sept. 1635: *REED, Norwich*, 220). Daniell is recorded at Coventry in 1635 as travelling with sixteen others in his company (*REED, Coventry*, 437).

[28] Sometimes the whole company did travel. The Revels group who visited Oxford in 1634 with their fourteen plays included the book-keeper and the wardrobe keeper. As noted above, it may have been a mark of its uncertain future in London that it carried everything with it.

[29] It is not easy to see how consistently the laws of hospitality to travellers were extended to playing companies. Some of the conditioning factors are noted by Daryl W. Palmer, *Hospitable Performances: Dramatic Genre and Cultural Practices in Early Modern England* (West Lafayette, Ind., 1992).

daies together'.[30] Travelling meant what its name said. It meant living out of a waggon, and presumably fairly often in it. A company waggon was a basic feature of this existence. At Faversham in 1597–8 a fine of fifteen shillings and ninepence was imposed on 'certen persons' who were caught in a 'misdemeanoure done in the Towne uppon misusage of a wagon or coache of the Lo. Bartlettes players'.[31] To call it a coach, even as a synonym, suggests that it must have been at the least a covered waggon. Protection for the costumes and playbooks, let alone the players themselves, against the weather was vital. The welfare of the company's properties meant saving costly fabrics from getting bleached in the sun or rotting in the rain, quite apart from the effect that water had on the ink of the playbooks. A covered waggon also gave shelter and accommodation at night on the longer journeys.

England's roads in the sixteenth century were quite heavily used, and generally of a reasonable all-weather standard for the numbers of travellers and industrial loads that had to use them. The huge appetite and rapid growth of the metropolis, which dominated the country, and which in 1600 held one-twentieth of England's otherwise largely farming population, meant that most roads led to London. No part of the country was more than two weeks' travel from the seat of government, and coastal shipping made regular and simple connections between the coastal towns and the great docks on the Thames. There were inns with accommodation and food for travellers along every highway. For companies to travel with bags and baggage was standard practice. The chief hazard, as with most lengthy journeyings, was the lack of paper authority. Every local mayoralty insisted on the travellers showing their papers authorizing the company to play and to prove that its players were not vagabonds and sturdy beggars.

The companies generally covered one region as thoroughly as possible before moving on.[32] The Lady Elizabeth's in 1613 is recorded in East Anglia at Norwich on 19 April, before moving to Kent at Faversham on 6 June, at Canterbury on 4 July, and at Dover on 12 July. Their next recorded appearance was in the Midlands at Leicester on 13 October. They were also at some date between Michaelmas 1613 and October 1614 playing at Leominster on the Welsh Marches. Similarly Essex's Servants in 1573 were at Bath on 15 May, at Bristol for the beginning of June, and then went up to Nottingham on 25 July. A report in the Bristol city records in 1633 marks the track of a minor company, between towns surprisingly remote from one another, which included visits to several private houses, a feature of travelling practices that has been somewhat camouflaged by the predominance of the civic

---

[30] *REED, Bristol*, forthcoming.

[31] Murray, *Dramatic Companies*, ii. 274. The will of Simon Jewell in 1592 identifies as part of his contribution to his company's costs 'horses waggen and apparrell newe boughte' (*Playhouse Wills 1558–1642: An Edition of Wills by Shakespeare and his Contemporaries in the London Theatre*, ed. E. A. J. Honigmann and Susan Brock (Manchester, 1993), 59). A Coventry letter of 31 Mar. 1615 naming the 7 adults and 7 boys of Lady Elizabeth's also lists '5 Horses in the Company' (*REED, Coventry*, 394). Presumably some of the adult players managed to ride on horseback instead of in the waggon.

[32] A preliminary study of the routes the companies followed is Sally-Beth MacLean's 'Tour Routes: "Provincial Wanderings" or Traditional Circuits?', *MRDE* 7 (1993), 1–14. It suggests that each company followed broadly the same route each year.

records. The places named for the company's travels over six months cite 'Lecester: Stratford; Meriden, Silloll att Sir William Spencers, Sir Thomas Lucyes . . . last they came to Keinton in Warwickshire and theire they played three dayes'.[33]

Despite the evidence that the companies would visit all the towns in one region at a time, the records also consistently show that when need be (though for no visible reason) they could cover long distances at a surprisingly high speed. Queen Anne's went from York on 23 September 1607 via Ipswich in early October to Dunwich in Suffolk by 14 October. That looks like a southward drive to get within reach of London and the Master of the Revels's testing of plays for the court in good time for the Christmas season. Other rapid shifts are less explicable, and may equally well indicate either prior commitments or inaccurate datings in the records. But if enough of the datings given in the provincial records are even approximately correct,[34] it seems that it was quite practicable for Queen Anne's Men, for instance, to travel from Leicester where they performed on 16 March 1613 to Hythe in Kent where they had played by 3 April, a journey of more than two hundred and thirty miles in eighteen days, presumably with some days spent playing at towns on the way in between. The Queen's Men are a more difficult proposition to pin down, since they ran as two companies for some years, but it appears that the same group played at Norwich on 25 June 1594 and at Coventry on 4 July, a distance of a hundred and thirty miles in eight days by the main Tudor roads.[35]

There is no record of the companies using any other form of transport, but one does wonder whether they did not often travel round the coast by sea. The number of times they are recorded at a port such as Plymouth or Bridgwater and soon after turn up in the north or at Dover or Southampton is ground for speculation that can only be settled when much more comprehensive listings of the provincial records have been made. Travels in Wales seem always to start at the Bristol Channel ports. The Queen's Men travelled more than 150 miles from Ipswich on 17 December 1588 to perform at Dover by Christmas 1588, a journey most easily made by water down the North Sea coast. Several companies show a notable rapidity of transit between Dover and Norwich, or Plymouth and Dover. A visit to a port is a regular prelude to the next recorded visit appearing a hundred or more miles away, often

---

[33] REED, Bristol, forthcoming.

[34] There is reason to doubt the accuracy of some dates in the records and the days to which they refer. Generally, companies would have to be paid on the spot, while they were still in town. So we might believe the New Romney register of the Queen's Men being paid for a play on 13 Feb. 1589 and then their playing at nearby Lydd on 15 Feb. But the recorders made their entries at different times, without always noting the exact days of performance. The King's Men are reported at Lydd on 9 July 1623 and at New Romney on the same day (MSC vii, 112, 143). Queen Anne's company is recorded at both Dover and Lydd on 18 March 1620 (MSC vii, 51, 111). The Dover entry appears to have been made retrospectively. A further note in the Dover records about a visit by the Prince's players dated 20 Apr. 1622 says vaguely that the money was 'geven to the princes players about 3 weekes past' (MSC vii, 51).

[35] It is unlikely to have been the same company at Leicester on 20 May 1589 and then at Ipswich two days later. The Ipswich records for 1591 note payments on 15 May 'unto the Quenes players', and on 28 May 'unto Another company of the Quenes players'.

in another port. Shipping was the most comfortable way to transport properties and large numbers of people. But this is speculative. There is not a jot of evidence to suggest that the companies ever used anything except horse power to help them on their travels.

Not that travelling by any form of transport was likely to be a very prosperous way of making a living. The explicit contempt that London residents such as John Marston felt for the poverty of travelling companies comes out strongly in *Histrio-mastix*. A much later play in the repertory of Queen Henrietta's Servants, a company that hardly ever travelled, boasts that its players 'make no yearely Progresse with the *Anatomy* of a Sumpter-horse, laden with the sweepings of *Long-lane* in a dead Vacation, and purchas'd at the exchange of their owne whole Wardrobes. They buy not their Ordinary for the Copie of a *Prologue*; nor insinuate themselves into the acquaintance of an admiring *Nigle*, who for his free comming in, is at the expence of a Tavern supper, and rinses their bawling throats with Canarye'.[36] The image of bedraggled players buying their food by selling copies of their texts and charming stage-struck locals is unkind but all too recognizable.

Taking a long perspective, it becomes clear that the early companies thought of themselves as travelling players who occasionally had the good luck to secure a period when they could play in London and replenish their stocks of new plays to travel with. By contrast, once the leading companies knew they were securely 'at home' in London, with royal patents and playhouses which some companies part-owned, travelling for some of them became the exception rather than the rule. The records for the Admiral's Men and the Chamberlain's Men travelling between 1594 and 1603 are strikingly thinner than for any of the companies before 1594. And yet when Shakespeare's company became the King's Men it appears to have maintained some tradition of touring whether the plague was a presence in London or not.

Traditions must have died hard for all the companies. The shift from thinking of themselves as travellers first and Londoners after to the opposite view certainly started with the 1594 approval of the two London playhouses, but other factors came into play too. In effect thinking of themselves 'at home' in London was a device for making economies, since the establishment of the Queen's Men in 1583 with its exceptionally large number of sharers had prompted the composition of new 'large' plays. By the 1590s there were four companies able to stage these 'large' plays. These companies had to pay a price for their size when they travelled. That must be the reason why Strange's in 1593 made a unique appeal to the Privy Council for rescue from the plague closure. They pleaded with the Privy Council, most likely during the long 1593 closure, asking for leave to reopen at the Rose, 'Forasmuch (righte honorable) oure Companie is greate, and thearebie our chardge intollerable, in travellinge the Countrie, and the Contynuaunce thereof wilbe a

---

[36] Thomas Nabbes, *Covent Garden* (1638), I. i. Alan Somerset, 'Provincial Playing, Playing Places and the King's Men', *ShS* 47 (1994), challenges the easier assumptions about the travelling companies that are based on their portrayal in plays such as Marston's.

meane to bringe us to division and seperacion, whearebie wee shall not onelie be undone, but alsoe unreadie to serve her majestie, when it shall please her highenes to commaund us'.[37] They also pleaded for the impoverished watermen, who were suffering from the absence of customers going by ferry to the plays. The fifteen-plus size of the major companies now made travelling less easy and less cheap than it had been formerly with many companies each of five or eight players. And the fixture of the London playing-places now made a choice between staying in London and travelling possible.

One effect began to show in the Admiral's repertory by the end of the century. Roslyn Knutson's analysis of the Henslowe records suggests that this can be seen in their actions with new plays after the Privy Council's closure order of July 1597 expired and the breakaway Pembroke's group began to return to them:

On 27 October 1597, the Admiral's returned to the Rose after having closed the previous July (on the eighteenth). They opened the fall season with a repertory of old plays, both continuations and revivals of very recent productions. They did not introduce a new play until 4 December. But for the two months thereafter, they introduced a new play (or a play new to them) nearly every week. These entries imply that a company alternating frequently between London and provincial performances might keep a number of old plays in produc-tion, both for the tour itself and as a filler in the London schedule while the players rehearsed new material. Thus reinforcing each other in effects on the repertory, playhouse closure and touring may have served to reduce the number of new plays needed by a company in a given year and to increase the number of old plays kept at ready.[38]

This points up the compensations of travelling, and perhaps helps to isolate the Strange's Company's appeal to the Privy Council about its costs. That appeal, if it was made in 1593, was evoked at the height of the 'large play' phase. The slight reduction in the size of casts subsequently may be one sign that travelling was seen as more than just a last resort and a costly encumbrance. The plague made it a constant possibility, of course. It had to remain as an integral part of any company's plans each year. But part of the compensation that travelling brought for the loss of London revenues was that so long as a London closure lasted it saved the company from buying new plays. Travelling also kept the company working as a unit.

That situation changed after 1603. Individual and company preferences over travelling were clearly variable, and while some companies maintained the practice after 1603, whether or not impelled by the plague, others took another course. One player who was consistent for forty years in his dislike of travelling was Christopher Beeston. The company that he ran for the longest stint any company ever had at his Cockpit, Queen Henrietta's Men, travelled less frequently than any other company of comparable stature and durability. Beeston's first company, Queen's Anne's Men, once they were settled at the Red Bull in 1605, appear to have launched a new practice to reconcile working in London with travelling. They divided their forces,

---

[37] *ES* iv. 311–12.

[38] Roslyn Lander Knutson, *The Repertory of Shakespeare's Company 1594–1613* (Fayetteville, Ark. 1991), 106.

leaving travelling to a secondary group which took a copy of the same licence. Thomas Swinnerton, instrumental in setting the company up at the Red Bull, for which he later held part of the lease, appears in provincial records subsequently as the leader of a second Queen Anne's group using a duplicate or 'exemplification' of the London patent. For all that from 1604 he seems to have held a share in a London playhouse[39] he is on record certainly from 1616 and probably long before as the leader of a country company. He went on travelling with duplicate warrants until as late as 1628 and after, while the main company stayed in London using the original. Tudor and Stuart regulation of the playing companies was wholly dependent on the efficiency of the local administrators upholding it. The distance between London and the country in the later years can be measured in more than miles, and poor communications gave the less scrupulous players ample scope to pretend to rights they did not really have.

Once company patronage was taken on by the royal family after 1603 the possession of a patent became a more vital asset than it had been with the barons and earls of Elizabeth's time. A royal patent with the Great Seal on it was more than just the prerequisite for a company to be allowed to play in any large town. The result, under James, was a set of copies of the original patents which secondary companies took round the country while the real patent stayed in London. Usually called duplicates or exemplifications in the provincial records, this practice was stamped on at least twice, under rather peculiar circumstances. In 1616 William Herbert, the Lord Chamberlain, sent the player Joseph Moore around the country with an official letter naming various players who were using fake patents. Moore was a leader of the Lady Elizabeth's which had recently folded in London and started travelling. The letter Moore carried for the Chamberlain, presumably based on good information, identified the chief culprits and the companies they claimed to run. It reads:

wheras Thomas Swynaerton and Martin Slaughter beinge two of the Queens Majestes Company of playors havinge separated themselves from their said Company, have each of them taken forth a severall exemplification or duplicate of his Majestes Letters patentes graunted to the whole Company and by vertue therof they severally in two Companies with vagabondes and such like idle persons, have and doe use and exercise the quallitie of playinge in diverse places of this Realme to the geat abuse and wronge of his Majestes Subjectes in generall and contrary to the true intent and meaninge of his Majestie to the said Company And whereas William Perrie havinge likewise gotten a warrant whereby he and a Certaine Company of idle persons with him doe traviall and play under the name and title of the Children of hir Majestes Revels . . . And wheras also Gilberte Reason one of the prince his highnes Playors having likewise separated himself from his Company hath also taken forth another exemplification or duplicate of the patent granted . . . And likewise one Charles Marshall, Humfry Jeffes and William Parr: thereof Prince Palatynes Company of Playors

---

[39] A petition in 1605 states how Martin Slater and Aaron Holland 'hath altered some stables and other roomes, beinge before a square Court in an Inne to turne them into galleries', and make the Red Bull. The petition was a plea to the Privy Council to let it go forward. Holland later sold a 1/7 share to Swinnerton. See Mark Eccles, 'Elizabethan Actors iv: S to End', *NQ* 238 (1993), 165–76, 170–1.

havinge also taken forthe an exemplification. . . . These are therfore to pray, and nevertheless in his Majestes name to will and require you upon notice given of anie of the said persons by the bearer herof Joseph More whome I have speciallye directed for that purpose that you Call the said parties offendors before you and thereupon take ther said severall exemplifications or duplicates or other ther warrantes by which they use ther saide quallitie from them, And forthwith to send the same to me.[40]

The named players were to give bonds that they would go immediately to White-hall and answer to the Lord Chamberlain for their offences. Moore was the thief set to catch the thieves. He was also, perhaps less than voluntarily, working to protect the monopolistic status of the authorized London companies against rivals.

The Chamberlain repeated this circular seven years later, in 1624. This time, instead of using Moore from the Lady Elizabeth's, which had just resumed playing in London, he used Gilbert Reason, one of the 'vagabondes' named in the 1616 letter. On 29 January 1625 Reason showed the Norwich authorities a printed warrant from the Lord Chamberlain to 'all Maiors Sheiriffes Justices of peace Baliffs Constables & other his Majesties officers', noting how many

grantes Comissions & lycences which they have by secret meanes procured both from the kinges Majestie & also from diverse noblemen by vertue whereof they doe abusively Clayme unto themselves a kinde of licentious fredome to travell aswell to shew play & exercise in eminent Cities & Corporacions within this kingdome as also from place to place without the knowledge & approbacion of his Majesties office of the Reveles & by that meanes doe take upon them at their own pleasure to act & sett forth in many places of this kingdome diverse & sundry playes & shewes which for the most part are full of scandall & offence both against the Church & State.[41]

The state felt the need to reassert its control through censorship. This time the letter named no names, but insisted that no company could travel without authorization from the Master of the Revels. From then on the Master appears to have followed the practice that George Buc started in the second decade of the century, issuing annual licences to travel.

In fact Swinnerton and Slater went on travelling under various licences for another decade. Duplicates of the London company patents, particularly those of Queen Anne's, Prince Charles's, and the Lady Elizabeth's, were not uncommon. Judging from the provincial records, in fact, all three of these companies ran a duplicate company outside London while the main group worked inside it. Thomas Swinnerton ran a touring company using a copy of the old Queen Anne's company patent until at least 1628. He teamed up with Robert Lee, also a Queen Anne's patentee who, like Swinnerton, was given cloth for Anne's funeral but seems never to have worked in London. Like Swinnerton, Lee had interests in London theatre property, buying a share in the Fortune in 1623. Swinnerton, named with Lee in

[40] The Norwich authorities, who had originally caught Swinnerton out in Mar. 1616, made a transcript of the Chamberlain's letter on 4 June 1617, given in *REED, Norwich*, 151–2.
[41] Ibid. 188.

the Chamberlain's letter of 1616, had bought a share in the Queen Anne's Red Bull in 1605. In 1622 Lee organized a travelling group made from a few of the former Queen Anne's men and some children, under the name of the Children of the Revels. The Master of the Revels still counted him as a Red Bull player in 1622.[42]

Swinnerton and Slater, for all their London connections with the companies, as playhouse owners and as London-based family men, are the clearest examples of players who preferred to lead travelling groups rather than stay at the one playhouse in London. Martin Slater seems the most obviously dishonest of this set of travellers who 'thieved' their papers of authorization. He may have used his talent as a forger to set up the first duplicate Queen Anne's warrant for himself as early as 1608. The Leicester records for that year mention the visit of two different Queen Anne's companies, and Slater was in the Queen's at that time. That the travels of the two groups should coincide at the same town suggests that they were not in very close communication with one another, and that the London-based official Queen Anne's may not have known that Slater was using the same name. The Leicester records report a recurrence in 1616, the year when Swinnerton was caught by the Norwich authorities. That imposition of order may have led Slater to change his papers. By 1619 he seems to have replaced his Queen Anne's patent with an old warrant for Queen Elizabeth's players which, sixteen years out of date, obviously needed replacement. At Leicester in October 1625, when the old system of company patents with royal patrons and the royal seal had been replaced with the annual warrants from the Master of the Revels, he claimed to be a King's man.[43]

Gilbert Reason was another permanent traveller. He was named on the patent for the Duke of York's players in 1610, and kept some contact with their later formation as the first Prince Charles's group. He received cloth from Charles for James's funeral in 1625. On the evidence, he seems to have led a duplicate Prince Charles's company in the country through all the years when it was officially based in London. Elias Guest did the same for the Lady Elizabeth's, along with William Perry. He started as a member of the Lady Elizabeth's in 1612 or earlier, but later ran a provincial group that was probably made up from remnant members of the Queen's Revels and King's Revels merger into the Lady Elizabeth's, and possibly the merger of Lady Elizabeth's with Prince Charles's of 1616. Nicholas Long was another traveller. He was linked with Philip Rosseter, William Perry, and Robert Lee at Norwich in 1618. Like Guest and Perry, he progressed from the Queen's Revels Children into the Lady Elizabeth's and then into their travelling branch.

William Daniell is a more shadowy and possibly more dodgy figure who does not seem to have had any real London patent to duplicate. He claimed to be a 'Revells

---

[42] See *JCS* ii. 496–7, 588–9.

[43] It is rarely possible to be sure about this kind of evidence, because the local recorders did not always get the company's titles exactly right. When the Great Seal was the authorization on a patent, all companies were in a sense licensed in the king's name, and might be called the king's servants. Perry at Reading in 1629 claimed to have the king's warrant, but the entry notes more accurately that the players were 'all of the Red Bull company'. Similar confusions occurred over Elias Guest's group and the Lady Elizabeth's.

Company' player at Coventry in 1622 and a King's Servant at Canterbury in the same year. In May 1623 the Fortune players protested that he was using a copy of their patent. In the 1630s he appears with Townsend from the Lady Elizabeth's, now the King and Queen of Bohemia's Company, and also as a King's Revels player. Another shadow is Richard Errington. He appears in the Norwich records in 1627, where he testified about an affray that occurred while he was acting as gatherer for the King's Men. Like other players who did the gathering for the company on their provincial tours, he was chiefly a player, a leader of travelling companies. His name appears linked with Elias Guest at Reading in 1631 and then with William Daniell at Coventry in 1636.

The system of issuing patents to the approved companies became intermittent and more or less lapsed under Charles. The King's Men got a new patent in 1625, but despite the thorough shake-up of companies that followed James's death none of the others did. The King and Queen of Bohemia's got one in 1628, possibly more as a reinforcement of their powers when touring than as a fresh form of authority. Instead, licensing of the companies seems to have joined the licensing of playhouses and playbooks for performance and print as a duty of the new Master of the Revels, Henry Herbert. He started to issue annual licences, with the royal signet, durable for only a year at a time. The functions of the Privy Council in government shrank in these years, and the Councillors took a smaller and smaller interest in playing. Whether the delegation of authority for licensing to the Master was a part of this general shift of power, or whether the royal patents were seen as a less effective means of controlling the companies than Herbert's annual licences, is not entirely clear. The new system does not seem to have affected the company practices that started under James very greatly. The 'Revels' licences mean that the number of 'Revels' companies in provincial records multiplied under Charles, as the abandonment of the patronage system made it more difficult to identify a company by its patron's name. But by then most of the London companies seem to have chosen to stay put all the year round, and to have left most of the travelling to duplicate companies with duplicate licences.

One rather underrated piece of evidence from the provincial records is the role of plague epidemics in determining the companies' travels. Some municipalities blocked companies from playing because they were expected, if not to bring infection with them, then to promote it by drawing large crowds. Worcester allocated an annual sum from 1631 to prevent playing companies from entering the city.[44] Given the invariable practice of the Privy Council and the London authorities in closing the playhouses whenever the death roll began to climb high, we must expect travelling to be best recorded through the years of the longest closures, in 1593, 1603, 1609, 1625, and 1636. There is, however, remarkably little sign of any major variation in the travelling pattern for any of the major companies, and very little sign of any sudden influx into the country by the companies when plague came.

---

[44] *REED, Herefordshire/Worcestershire*, 303.

Their appearances in the provincial records across the years are far more frequent than they would be if the only motive that led the London companies to travel was the epidemics of plague.

In London plague certainly closed the theatres,[45] but there is surprisingly little correlation between the plague closures and the records of touring. The evidence is rather two-faced as well as incomplete. Queen Henrietta's, for instance, rarely appear in the records as a travelling company, yet at Reading in 1629, at Doncaster in 1632, and Norwich in 1633 they arrived when there was no plague closure. Elias Guest's name as the company's leader for the 1629 appearance at Norwich, how-ever, suggests that these visits may have been by a second group, not the main London company. The only visit recorded that might have been in plague time and might have been by the main company was at Coventry in 1636. By then Beeston had discarded them so, lacking a London playhouse, they may have been turning their hand to a new activity and conceivably even joining up with Elias Guest's travelling group. Plague closures did have an effect on the companies that did not like travelling, though even then they may well have chosen to divide themselves between the players who would travel and those who chose not to. For the large companies like the King's and Queen Anne's, and later the Jacobean Prince Charles's and the Red Bull company, which seem to have had permanent travelling components, such a division was not difficult. For the others touring was a large decision, and probably one better treated as a routine break, usually but by no means always in the summer, rather than as a coerced response to closures.

Leeds Barroll's book on Shakespeare's company and the plague has an appen-dix[46] which asks some pertinent questions. He challenges the assumption made by the New Oxford Shakespeare editors[47] that Shakespeare's company routinely went on tour between June and September each year. More substantially, he questions the assumption that there was a regular summer break in which the companies all avoided the hot-weather spread of plague by touring along their traditional routes.[48] As evidence Barroll cites the run of Admiral's Men's performances in the summers of 1594 to 1602 that are recorded in Henslowe's *Diary*, and assumes, not unreason-ably, that Shakespeare's company would have followed a similar schedule. In 1594 there were plays in London from 3 June to 30 September. In 1595 they ran from 3 till 26 June, and from 25 August to September. In 1596 they ran for seven weeks from 1 June, and for more than seven weeks in 1597, until the Privy Council's ban because of the *Isle of Dogs* incident at the Swan. In 1598 they played from 3 June to

[45] For the extant records of plague closures, see Ch. 5.

[46] J. Leeds Barroll, *Politics, Plague, and Shakespeare's Theater: The Stuart Years* (New York, 1991), App. 3: 'The Playing Season at the London Theaters'.

[47] *A Textual Companion to the New Oxford Shakespeare* (Oxford, 1987), 90.

[48] *Politics, Plague, and Shakespeare's Theater*, 227. He might have added that the plague's outbreaks through the country must have frequently reshaped the direction of these tours. When the plague was rampant in southern England in 1603, for instance, the King's Men could be found to the west in Bath, northwards to Coventry and still further north in Shrewsbury. The Admiral's also went to Bath and Coventry, and on north to Leicester and York.

29 September, for a similar period in 1599, and from 3 June to 12 September in 1600. In 1601 they played from 30 June to 5 September, and in 1602 from 12 June to 10 September. For the Admiral's, an experienced though after 1594 a reluctant touring group, travelling was certainly not a regular and seasonal warm-weather activity. Nor could it have been for the Chamberlain's, their only peer at that time.

For the two approved companies of 1594 an intermittent and irregular resorting to the road was their practice up to 1603, when the royal patrons took over. A few hints from the later years after the London base was firmly established do exist about the new company practices in times of plague. We know, for instance, that two senior members of the King's Servants bought 'country houses' near London, and that the company sometimes assembled there when the London playhouses were closed. In 1604 Augustine Phillips had a house in Mortlake not far from Richmond Palace. One item paid to the company during the plague closure of 1603–4 was for the cost of their travel from Mortlake to perform at Wilton.[49] Evidently the company had based itself during the plague closure at Phillips's house. Whether they did so to escape the plague in the city, or to hold themselves in readiness for the sort of call that eventually came to them, it was a logical retreat. Henry Condell had a house in Fulham, outside the city, by 1625.[50] It may well be that in these later years a subsidiary group, the younger players, kept themselves in practice by going on tour, while the leading sharers stayed at home, clinging to the rural outskirts of London. The Shakespeares among them might have used the London closures for a visit to their homes in the country. Otherwise the only holiday the players could ever have was the fewer than forty days of the closures through Lent.

The London year was a series of different seasons, and not just seasons of varying weather. Michaelmas, at the end of September, was the start of the law term, and the time for the Master of the Revels to begin his four-month season of work at court testing plays and preparing places to play for the Christmas festivities. That required the presence or at least the proximity of the adult companies to London's Revels Office and the court. Sometimes the court had the companies give plays in November, and sometimes in the summer if a major visitor arrived, like the Queen's brother, Christian of Denmark, in 1606. The Christmas season always started on St Stephen's night, Boxing Day, 26 December. Under Elizabeth it ran until Twelfth Night, 6 January. Under the Stuarts it ran on until Lent, and the closing performance was always on Shrove Tuesday, the night before the start of Lent. But it was not impossible for a company to be summoned at short notice. I suspect that the house in Mortlake and its successors would have been a fairly regular resort for the leading sharers of the King's Servants when plague was in town, wherever the company's patent got to on the road.

---

[49] Chamber accounts, 2 Dec. 1604. Leeds Barroll has suggested that the Mortlake house was being used as a rehearsal place in *Politics, Plague and Shakespeare's Theater*, 12.

[50] A pamphlet dated 1 Aug. 1625 exists in the form of a letter addressed to 'Mr. H. Condall, at his country-house in Fulham'. It is quoted in *JCS* i. 19.

4 Lording it Over the Players

The main instruments of change in the years when the companies were first securing a foothold in London were the companies themselves, with their determination to establish a grip on the financial resources that the thousands of London's paying customers offered them daily. The significant agents of change were the great lords of the Privy Council who gave them patronage. Until the companies acceded to royal patronage in 1603, three or four leading patrons led the fight against the city authorities' opposition to playing. One figure looms particularly large in the story of how they secured their London foothold: Charles Howard, Lord Effingham, later Lord Admiral and later still the earl of Nottingham. Before looking at his actions in these years, though, it is appropriate to consider the first of the official controllers of companies, a man who was Howard's kin and whom Howard patronized, Edmund Tilney.[1]

The Privy Council as a whole, though in the early years it did contain several councillors such as Howard and Carey who were supporters of playing, as well as the official controller, the Lord Chamberlain, never allowed any motive for supporting the professional companies to show other than a recurrently expressed concern to maintain the resources for entertaining the Queen over Christmas. That was the concern registered in Tilney's initial appointment in 1578. This reason for directly protecting players against the city in order that they could perform at court was expressed in a letter dated 24 December 1578 from the Privy Council to the Lord Mayor, listing the companies approved for use at court. The Council's minute notes:

A letter to the Lord Maiour, &c, requiring him to suffer the Children of her Majesties Chappell, the servauntes of the Lord Chamberlaine, therle of Warwicke, the Erle of Leicester, the Erle of Essex and the Children of Powles, and no companies els, to exercise playeng within the Cittie, whome their Lordships have onlie allowed thereunto by reason that the companies aforenamed are appointed to playe this tyme of Christmas before her Majestie.[2]

This was a short-term order, giving authority for the Master to run in London four companies of adult players, Sussex's (the Lord Chamberlain's), the two Dudleys', and Essex's, together with the two London choir-school companies. In essence it supplied, for that season, six companies of known worth, all of which were used to performing at court.

That was perhaps the initial need, but Tilney's appointment was soon recognized as an opportunity to secure more direct control over the playing companies

---

[1] A careful account of the work of the successive Masters of the Revels starting with Tilney is given by Richard Dutton, *Mastering the Revels: The Regulation and Censorship of English Renaissance Drama* (Basingstoke, 1991).

[2] *Acts of the Privy Council of England*, xi. 73.

and their products. The need to bridle the growing power of plays as a form of self-expression is registered in a patent of 1581, which confirmed his duty to license and censor all playbooks. This patent, dated 24 December when the court's mind was on its Christmas pleasures, regularized his role first as controller of the royal entertainments, and secondly, in a large segment of that role, as an authority over all the playing companies.

And furthermore also we have and doe by these presentes aucthorise and commaunde our said Servant Edmunde Tilney Maister of our said Revells by himselfe or his sufficient deputie or deputies to warne commaunde and appointe in all places within this our Realme of England, aswell within franchese and liberties as without, all and every plaier or plaiers with their playmakers, either belonginge to any noble man or otherwise, bearing the name or names of usinge the facultie of playmakers or plaiers of Comedies, Tragedies, or showes as they shall have in readines or meane to sett forth, and them to present and recite before our said Servant or his sufficient deputie, whom wee ordeyne appointe and aucthorise by these presentes of all suche showes, plaies, plaiers and playmakers, together with their playing places, to order and reforme, auctorise and put downe, as shalbe thought meete or unmeete unto himselfe or his said deputie in that behalfe.[3]

With such an authority Tilney needed no list of approved companies to guide him. His control was, however, still limited in some respects. A loophole in the regulations which appeared later was to make the last years of Tilney's tenure in office under James up to 1610 distinctly uncomfortable. The letter of 1578 specified two choir-school companies who had regularly performed at court along with the leading adult companies. At the beginning of the next century, when two boy companies were revived after a ten-year absence, their management was not in the hands of the schoolmasters but held by entrepreneurs more concerned with profit than education. At least one of these boy companies appears to have wriggled out of the Master's control by claiming not to be public or common players. The boy companies, as groups offering what appeared to be only 'private' performances as part of their education, and not ostensibly or officially opening their shows to the public, could claim to be exempt from the interests of the Master, whose duty was to control and censor only the 'public' shows. This definition of the Master's scope was never made clear, and it was not until the Blackfriars Boys throughout 1605 and 1606 created public scandals with their plays that the Master took them in hand.[4]

The question of the 'private' companies is the most awkward single aspect of the steady advance of the Master's authority over playing. The greyest area of his

[3] Albert Feuillerat, *Documents relating to the Office of the Revels in the Time of Queen Elizabeth, Materialen zur Kunde des alteren Englischen Dramas* (Louvain, 1908), xxi. 51, *ES* iv. 285–7.

[4] Paul's Boys had *The Old Joiner of Aldgate* licensed for them by Tilney in 1603 (Dutton, *Mastering the Revels*, 131), but the Blackfriars Boys, besides being under Daniel's control instead of Tilney's in 1603–4, made no evident use of the Master until after two of their plays had to be censored in 1605 and 1606. There were changes in the Revels Office in 1606 because Tilney's successor, George Buc, took on the new function of licensing plays for printing in that year. This was probably in the main a compensation to him for his long wait for dead man's shoes, but it may also mark some tightening as well as extending of the Office's control, evidently needed for the Blackfriars Boys.

control from the start was the line between 'public' performances, by licensed players on licensed stages, and performances that might be designated 'private', whether done by boys at their school, students at the university, or household servants in a great house in the country, where a more local censorship, such as Claudius expected Hamlet to exercise over the Mousetrap, could prevail.[5] For the Master to insist on reading and approving texts sent to him by teachers and students, let alone by a remote household in Lancashire or Cornwall, was ludicrously impractical. The 1581 patent insisted that his right covered all performances, but it clearly applied in reality only to London. Originally it specified not that he should read the playbooks but that the companies must take all their 'plaies, Tragedies, Comedies or showes as they shall have in readines or meane to sett forth, and them to presente and recite before our said Servant or his sufficient deputie'.[6] This was censorship in rehearsal. All the Council was really concerned with was to have a check on performances before they came to the court; but it also made sense, however impractical, to assert the Master's authority over any performance anywhere in the realm. Tilney himself made the point in a letter transcribed into the Leicester records in 1583, where he declared that no mayor could allow a play to be staged in his town unless it had the Master's signature on it. How thoroughly that order was applied we do not know.

His originally narrow responsibility for the court broadened as Tilney's work grew. First he added the right to license playhouses as well as companies. Henslowe paid him a regular fee for the Rose. In about 1606 Tilney added the right to license playbooks for printing. This, probably conceived at first as a means of fobbing off his successor, George Buc, who was impatient to start making money from the office, came at an awkward time. By 1606 the Blackfriars Boys had staged two plays that caught the royal and courtly notice because of their satirical content. Neither of them had been licensed by the Master, who was probably still unsure of his role in the wake of Daniel being made censor and Master of the Blackfriars boys when they became 'the Children of her Majesty's Revels' in 1604. Daniel soon lost that unique eminence with his catastrophe over *Philotas*, but either Tilney or the boy company's managers or both seem to have remained unsure whether he should now replace Daniel as the boys' censor. It was a fiction that the boy companies played 'privately' and were freer than the 'public' players from official control, but the Blackfriars Boys clung to that freedom for the profits of scandalmaking until 1608.

The adult companies could never assume such a freedom. The Privy Council's directives in the 1572 Act against vagabonds, the 1574 patent for Leicester's Men, and Tilney's own patent of 1581 were aimed precisely at them. Tilney was the government's voice and its agent in their London activities. He acted for them directly only two years after his patent was issued, in 1583, when Francis

---

[5] 'Have you heard the argument? Is there no offence in 't?' (*Hamlet*, III. ii. 221) is the question a king would put to his chamberlain and censor.

[6] Feuillerat, *Documents*, 51.

Walsingham as Secretary to the Privy Council ordered the creation of a new company with royal patronage, the Queen's Men. The circumstances of this company's formation are described more fully in Chapter 12. What needs emphasis here is Tilney's function in executing the Privy Council's order, and the effects on London playing at large of this new company, plus the interventions of Tilney's patron Charles Howard with London's mayor to uphold the new regime.

Tilney was the man who knew all the players best, and he must have been instrumental in choosing who was drawn from which company to form the new group. The Revels Accounts have a note dated 10 March 1583 ordering the Master 'To choose out a companie of players for her majestie'.[7] He chose some of Leicester's Servants, for instance, but excluded their truculent leader James Burbage. He was impartial in taking a similar number, no more than two or three players, from each of the existing companies who had a foothold in London. He also chose to set up a bigger company than had existed hitherto, with twelve of the most outstanding players from all the major groups. After doing that, though, he left the subsequent and consequential negotiations to secure playing-places for the new company in London to his seniors.[8]

That took a little time, since no Lord Chamberlain was appointed for six months after Radcliffe, the earl of Sussex, died in June 1583. The Privy Council woke up to the problem when the next Christmas season loomed. Burghley, Bromley, Bedford, Knollys, Hunsdon, Hatton, and Walsingham wrote to the Lord Mayor on 26 November. They said:

Forasmuch as (God be thanked) there is no suche infection within that citie at this presente, but that hir majesties playeres may be suffered to playe within the liberties as heretofore they have done, especially seeing they are shortly to present some of their doeinges before hir majestie, we have thought good at this present to pray your Lp. to geve order, that the said players may be licenced so to doe within the Citie and liberties betwene this and shroftyde next; so as the same be not done upon sondaies, but upon some other weke daies, at convenient times.[9]

The job of treating with the Lord Mayor over letting the Queen's Company perform freely in London rightly fell to the new Lord Chamberlain. Charles Howard, appointed to succeed Sussex as Chamberlain on the first day of 1584, undertook that duty adroitly. In essence his plan implemented the Privy Council's basic scheme, which was to secure playing in London for one great company that had the immunity of royal patronage. The other main step had already been taken with the large number of players allotted to the Queen's.

In the seventy years from the writing of Skelton's *Magnificence* to Marlowe's *Tamburlaine*, the prescription for the cast of a play stageable by an adult travelling company changed substantially. Up to 1583, the standard size of a company was

    [7] *ES* ii. 104.
    [8] Ludlow, Leicester, and Bath in 1583–4 record visits by a company using Tilney's own name. Conceivably he tried to set up a shadow Queen's group.
    [9] *ES* iv. 295–6, *MSC* i. 66.

rarely more than eight men.[10] *Magnificence*, written for five men to play, one player in the title role and the other four quick-changing into a total of seventeen other roles, had a tight and economical design. John Bale's *King Johann*, scripted and re-scripted for his travelling company in the 1540s, needed six men to play the nineteen roles. The slow growth in playing numbers meant that new and larger groups could perform the older plays while taking on new ones designed for their increasing capacity. Of the plays written in the 1560s and 1570s, *Cambises* (1561) needed eight players, and *Clyomon and Clamydes* (1570) needed ten. It was a one-way process, since smaller-sized companies could not take on the plays written for larger companies. And there had to be a peak in size and efficiency beyond which companies could not go. The Queen's company of 1583 reached it.

Establishing a company of twelve men and an undefined number of boys set a new parameter for the poets. It was a great leap forward to shift from writing for a maximum of eight adult players to writing for twelve. The effect on the plays is evident by 1590, when the first texts of the 'large' plays requiring casts of fifteen or more speaking parts began to appear in print. By 1594 at least four companies could mount such plays. David Bradley and T. J. King, in their studies of the casts needed to perform the plays of this time, produce some tables which are in substantial agreement over the total numbers needed.[11] Bradley's tables identify eight plays which, as originally composed, seem to call for more than the usual minimum of fifteen adult players and four boys, even with rigorous doubling. They are: *The Wounds of Civil War* (24+), *Edward I* (19+), *Edward II* (20), *Edward III* (20), *1 Henry VI* (23), *2 Henry VI* (22, or as *The Contention* 24+), *3 Henry VI* (17, or as *The True Tragedy of Richard Duke of York* 22), and *Sir Thomas More* (20+, or 16+ in its revised form). *Titus Andronicus* requires a minimum of sixteen and the plot of *2 Seven Deadly Sins* requires at least fifteen. King's tables, making no allowances for doubling, always a speculative question, are rather more generous, giving *1 Henry VI* twenty-eight men and two boys, *2 Henry VI* twenty-four men and five boys (for both versions), *3 Henry VI* twenty-four men and five boys (two men less for *The True Tragedy of York*), and *Titus* twenty-three men and four boys, while *Sir Thomas More* needs nineteen men and six boys. Calculating the possible doubling as tightly as Bradley does, these figures match up well.

Scott McMillin[12] has calculated the cast-lists on a rather different basis, taking note of the number of speakers required for the first 500 lines of each play. This also gives him eight plays from the period up to 1594, plus *More*. Of these only *1 Henry VI*, *The Contention*, and *More* correspond with Bradley's list. McMillin's list omits the three *Edward* plays and *Titus*, but does include *2 Seven Deadly Sins*. To these it adds *The True Tragedy of Richard III*, *The Famous Victories*, *Friar Bacon and*

[10] See David M. Bevington, *From 'Mankind' to Marlowe: Growth of Structure in the Popular Drama of Tudor England* (Cambridge, Mass., 1962), 71–2.

[11] David Bradley, *From Text to Performance in the Elizabethan Theatre: Preparing the Play for the Stage*; T. J. King, *Casting Shakespeare's Plays*.

[12] *The Elizabethan Theatre and the Book of Sir Thomas More* (Ithaca, NY, 1987), 57.

Friar Bungay, The Massacre at Paris, and *The Taming of the Shrew*. Allowing for different readings of the numbers needed, fourteen plays in all come into the 'large' category between 1588 and 1594.

All of these plays call for larger casts than the surviving plays written before this time and almost all of the plays written subsequently. Why they came into being then, and why they disappeared after 1594, is a matter for speculation. Mostly they were history plays, and the fashion for large-scale histories did pass with time, although not until after 1600. Shakespeare's second tetralogy of English history plays, written between 1595 and 1599, lays smaller demands on company numbers than the first tetralogy. The initial growth must have been chiefly the result of ambitions swelling once the London foothold seemed secure, and shrinking again after the 1594 settlement.

The writing of such plays up to 1594 was not an activity commissioned by only one company. From what we know of the companies for whom these plays were composed, it seems that over the six years from 1588 the companies capable of mounting them were the early Admiral's (*Wounds*), Strange's (*2 Seven Deadly Sins*, *1 Henry VI*, *More*), and Pembroke's (*2* and *3 Henry VI*, *Edward II*, *The Shrew*, *Titus*), as well as the later Admiral's. The Queen's must have too, if we can accept Scott McMillin's calculations. *Edward I* appeared with either the Queen's or the early Admiral's. *Edward III's* company is unknown, though since it was written in about 1590 it must have been one of the large-capacity groups. From McMillin's list we might add two Queen's plays, two Strange's, and one Pembroke's. Adding McMillin's plays to Bradley's lets us allocate one and possibly two to the early Admiral's, two and probably three to the Queen's, five to Strange's and five to Pembroke's. It seems clear from these figures that however we calculate the size of the company needed to perform the large plays, at least three and later four were prepared to handle them. The writing of these new large plays by 1590 shows how grandly the ambitions and aspirations of the playing companies were swelling. And it was clearly a widespread London-based infection.

The period following the establishment of the Queen's company in 1583 was a time of drastic change for poets and for players. The effect on the poets can be seen in the appearance of plays such as *The Spanish Tragedy* and *Tamburlaine*. The effect on the companies was less recognizable but equally drastic. As the popular plays demanded larger resources to stage them, so the companies became more costly and therefore more vulnerable to financial disaster. The large number of the companies that 'broke' in the early 1590s was not just a consequence of a uniquely long period of closure for the plague. That was a problem chiefly confined to London. Longer closures happened at other times, when fewer companies broke. The crisis of 1592–4 came about chiefly because the larger plays which demanded larger casts in imitation of the Queen's Men created a structure where more players were dependent on the company's income. The repertoire of large-cast plays made travelling more costly, and the travellers' income failed to match the new costs. Towns did not increase their payments because the companies were now bigger. Such large groups made travelling less rewarding, with its reduced revenues compared to London. That, more than the spread of plague through the country, caused Pembroke's Men to break in 1593, and Strange's Men to appeal to the Privy Council at about the same time over the financial strain of travelling that the larger numbers in the company now brought them. The new size stimulated the rapid turnover of the London companies in these years.

Along with the turnover of companies in the 1580s and 1590s went an almost equally rapid turnover of patrons. Three of these were in turn Lords Chamberlain, and the story of the London companies in these years ties in surprisingly closely with the history of the successive Chamberlains. Thomas Radcliffe, third earl of Sussex, Charles Howard, first Lord Effingham, later Lord Admiral and earl of Nottingham, and Henry Carey, first Lord Hunsdon, all favoured playing, and used distinct policies to help the professional companies. All of them Privy Councillors, they worked together while implementing different policies. Howard served as Radcliffe's deputy when he was ill, and Carey deputized for Howard before succeeding to the office himself. Each of them ran his own playing company. In office, though, their attitude to their own companies differed markedly. The two most significant changes in policy, both involving the creation of new companies, were implemented in 1583 while Sussex was dying, and in 1594.

The Lord Chamberlain's principal duty was to provide the court's programme of entertainments for the long Christmas season. Under the earl of Sussex up to 1583 this duty was exercised rather differently from the way Howard and Carey ran it. The changes came partly because of the creation of the Queen's Men, partly because conditions were altering in any case, and partly because plays were themselves changing and becoming more popular. They were also a lot cheaper to stage at court. After 1578 the Master of the Revels acting as the Chamberlain's executive soon grasped the simple economic fact that the price of employing a company of public players for the royal pleasure was only a quarter what it cost to stage a masque.[13] From then on the companies played at court much more frequently. Sussex himself kept a company that performed at Court every winter from 1576 to 1583. After his death his group vanished for some years. Howard, who served as Deputy Chamberlain in 1575–7, maintained a contrary policy so far as his own players were concerned. He never brought his own company to court while in the Chamberlain's office. Up to 1594 Carey did the same. During the entire time that these two men held the office up to 1594 no players who wore their livery were ever summoned to perform at court apart from one joint appearance by a combined group of their two companies on 6 January 1586.[14] Both men, when Chamberlain, maintained a policy favouring the Queen's Men against all the others.[15] That ran until May 1594, when the two men set up their replacements.

[13] *MSC* xiii. p. xviii.   [14] *ES* ii. 193.
[15] See Richard Dutton, *Mastering the Revels*, 49–55; chs. 2 and 4 set out the broad context for these interventions. See Scott McMillin's sharp study, 'The Queen's Men and the London Theatre of 1583', *Elizabethan Theatre*, 10 (1988), 10.

Thomas Radcliffe, the third earl of Sussex, was Lord Chamberlain from 1572 until his death in June 1583.[16] Elizabeth had already laid down the policy, affirmed in the document of 3 January 1572, that determined the Chamberlain's control over professional players. The Statute of Retainers defined the limitations the players had to work under. It also set out the basic requirement that the Chamberlain's office organize the annual court entertainments. Radcliffe favoured his own company in his first winter as Chamberlain with a performance at court, and it returned for almost every festive season thereafter. That company seems to have been called the Chamberlain's Men in provincial records up to 1583.[17] When he died it passed to his brother Henry. It did not return to court until 1592.

Before Sussex died in June 1583 someone had already intervened to amplify the new and cheaper policy of favouring playing companies for the royal entertainments with a monopolistic royal company. Sussex's final illness may have supplied the opportunity to modify the policy he had followed through his eleven years in charge of the revels. This change, the creation of the Queen's own company, which Walsingham as Secretary to the Privy Council set in train, may be part of the reason why the office of Chamberlain remained vacant for six months after Sussex's death in June. Then on New Year's Day 1584, in the middle of the Christmas festivities, it passed to Charles Howard.

Howard's wife, Lord Hunsdon's eldest daughter Katherine Carey, was Queen Elizabeth's own closest blood relative, though as a Boleyn she had no claim to the succession. She was one of the queen's most intimate and reliable friends from the time of her arrival at court as maid of honour at the beginning of the 1560s. This relationship made her husband an obvious choice for such a quasi-domestic court office as the Chamberlainship.[18] The fact that he had deputized for Sussex during his illness and was therefore his obvious successor makes the delay in his appointment a mark of how delicate negotiations over the office must have been. Katherine Carey's father, Henry, also shared the familial closeness to Elizabeth. A man with a distinctively frank personality, he was loyal to his queen, personally unambitious, and provided a regular ally for his son-in-law once he joined the Privy Council as Chamberlain. Robert Naunton described the first baron Hunsdon as

a fast man to his prince and firm to his friends and servants, and though he might speak big and therein would be borne out, yet was he not the more dreadful but less harmful and far from the practice of my Lord of Leicester's instructions, for his was downright. And I have

[16] Thomas Radcliffe was one of the chief opponents to the Leicester circle. Robert Naunton's retrospect on Elizabeth's court reported that 'there was such an antipathy in his nature to that of Leicester's that being together in court and both in high employments, they grew to a direct feud and both in continual oppositions, the one setting the watch and the other the sentinel, each on other's actions and motions'. (Robert Naunton, *Fragmenta Regalia*, ed. John S. Cerovski (Washington DC, 1985), 53). The antipathy between Sussex and Leicester and Sussex's favouring his company for court performances helps to explain Leicester's interventions to help his players while Sussex was Chamberlain.

[17] *ES* ii. 93.

[18] For an account of Elizabeth's court, see Simon Adams, 'Eliza Enthroned? The Court and its Politics', in *The Reign of Elizabeth*, ed. Christopher Haigh (London, 1984), 55–77.

heard those that both knew him well and had interest in him say merrily of him that his Latin and dissimulation were both alike and that his custom of swearing and obscenity in speaking made him seem a worse Christian than he was.[19]

For all the cutting edge in that account, Carey's record as a patron was quietly distinguished. He housed Sir Robert Cotton, for instance, who formed the Society of Antiquaries with his former teacher Camden, and created the study group which Jonson called 'a kind of university'.[20] Both Howard and Carey gave Elizabeth good reason to regard them as her most loyal servants.

After less than two years as Chamberlain, though, Howard moved on to become Lord Admiral. That released the office to his father-in-law, who had already started work as his deputy. Carey took office in July 1585. As Chamberlain, Howard had presided over a commission on the navy, and the appointment as Chamberlain may have been envisaged as no more than the way to get him a place on the Privy Council as a stepping-stone to the higher office.[21] Conceivably his father-in-law, already a Councillor, always expected the Chamberlainship to revert to himself. Judging from a Council paper of 1584 quoted below, he seems to have been assumed to be, if not actually in post as, the designated Vice-Chamberlain while Howard was Chamberlain.

However transient his tenure, in his two years as Chamberlain Howard fulfilled his duties in the office by setting up a new agreement with the Lord Mayor over the professional companies' access to playing-places in London. In 1584 he fended off the latest city request for the suppression of playing, with backing in the Privy Council from Christopher Hatton. Unlike his cousin Sussex, his policy remained as it had been when he deputized for Sussex in the 1570s, supporting the companies, but now chiefly the Queen's Men rather than any of the others, including his own. That seems to have been a positive choice. His own company was evidently not below standard. After he relinquished the deputy-Chamberlainship in 1575 they played at Court twice in the 1576–7 season, and again in the following year. They did not perform while he was Lord Chamberlain in 1584–5, but they returned in the 1586–7 season and regularly thereafter. His father-in-law and successor similarly did not allow his own company to perform at Court while he was Chamberlain. The sole anomaly in his adoption of that rule, apart from the joint court performance of 1586, is that before the Chamberlainship passed to Carey from Howard he appears to have given his livery to James Burbage, formerly a Leicester's player, who was then running the Theatre in Shoreditch. That, too, may have had something to do with the Chamberlain's 1584 negotiations with the Lord Mayor.

As Chamberlains, Howard and Carey worked closely together. In June 1584, following a fracas in Shoreditch outside the Theatre and the Curtain, William

---

[19] *Fragmenta Regalia*, 69–70.

[20] See Kevin Sharpe, *Sir Robert Cotton 1558–1631: History and Politics in Early Modern England* (Oxford, 1979), 203.

[21] See Robert W. Kenny, *Elizabeth's Admiral* (Baltimore, Ma., 1970), 28.

Fleetwood reported to Lord Burghley what the Privy Councillors had done about it. Fleetwood wrote:

Uppon Sonndaye my Lo.[Mayor] sent ij Aldermen to the Court for the suppressing and pulling downe of the Theatre and Curten. All the LL. agreed thereunto, saving my Lord Chamberlen and mr. Viz-chamberlen, but we obteyned a lettre to suppresse theym all. Upon the same night I sent for the quenes players and my Lo. of Arundel his players, and they all willinglie obeyed the LL. lettres. The chiefestes of her highnes players advised me to send for the owner of the Theater, who was a stubburne fellow, and to bynd hym. I dyd so; he sent me word that he was my Lo. of Hunsdons man, and that he wold not come at me, but he wold in the mornyng ride to my lord.[22]

Burbage, a belligerent defender of his property and resources, was quick to invoke Carey's support. Fleetwood's account implies that he at first refused to believe that his patron as a Privy Councillor would have signed such an order. Only on witnessing the signature and being warned about the consequences of disobedience did he back off. Carey, having joined Howard in openly disagreeing with the decision, may then have done some work behind the scenes to preserve Burbage's playhouse, because the order to pull the theatres down was not carried out.

It was shortly before this fracas that Howard took action to protect the Queen's Men as the monopolistic holders of royal authority to play in London. The court *Remembrancia* from March 1584 to January 1587 are missing, but the Lansdowne papers have a partial record. They include a petition that the Queen's Men sent to the Privy Council appealing against pressure laid on them by the city fathers, together with the responses to it from the Lord Mayor and from Howard as Chamberlain. Howard's 'remedies' for the city's grievances included setting specific limits on the times for playing, and most specifically declaring 'That the Quenes players only be tolerated, and of them their number and certaine names to be notified in your Lps. lettres to the L. Maior and to the Justices of Middlesex and Surrey. And those her players not to divide themselves into several companies'.[23] The city inns where the Queen's Men would be allowed to play were specified. In order to maintain such a firmly announced policy in subsequent years he had to disadvantage the company that he himself patronized.

For his first nine years as Chamberlain, Carey followed the same broad policy as Howard. He protected the companies against the mayor of London, favoured the Queen's Men, and with the one exception did not allow his own company to perform at court. He evidently worked closely with his son-in-law, whose company in fact rose through the late 1580s to become one of the most frequent performers at court. Their joining with Carey's own men for the 1586 entertainments may be evidence of collaboration between the two patrons rather than the players. It is this long early history of co-operation between the two men that makes sense of the decision they made years later, in May 1594, to sponsor two new London companies, the Lord Admiral's and the Lord Chamberlain's Servants.

[22] *ES* iv. 297–8.   [23] *ES* iv. 302.

It is usually said that what precipitated the creation of Carey's company in 1594 was the difficulties the London companies had been suffering because of the long plague prohibitions through the preceding years. This possibly overstates the case and the evidence for Carey being sympathetic to the companies. His main motive was not the good of the players but his Privy Council duty to maintain the annual provision of court entertainments, which were endangered by the players' difficulties. At the beginning of December in 1592 Lord Burghley had actually written from the Privy Council to the vice-chancellors of Oxford and Cambridge, asking them to supply plays by their students for the court 'by reason that her Majesties owne servantes, in this time of infection, may not disport her Highnes with theire wonted and ordinary pastimes'.[24] Neither university felt that it could satisfy the Privy Councillor's request, and that season at court saw three plays by Strange's and two by Pembroke's to none by the Queen's. By the following Christmas Lord Strange had died and Pembroke's had broken. Only the one performance by a Queen's group was staged that year. For the Lord Chamberlain to fulfill his primary duty each Christmas it was clearly essential to set up a new regime with strong companies.

The model behind the new policy is not far to seek. What Carey and Howard set up in May 1594 was a duopoly imitating the original Queen's Men's monopoly of eleven years before. That precedent is evidenced most clearly by subsequent attempts that the Privy Council made to maintain the special privileges given to these two companies to the exclusion of all others. Privy Council Orders set out in 1598 and 1600 by the next Chamberlain, Carey's son, affirmed the Chamberlain's and Admiral's exclusive rights to play in London. These orders renewed the Howard deal with the Lord Mayor of 1584 giving sole rights to the Queen's Men. The 1594 innovation was essentially a renewal of the 1583 scheme, with the added precaution that it doubled the number of privileged companies.

This scheme was not laid out as to some extent the earlier one was, to quell the competitive exhibitionism of the great lords at court who patronized the better companies. This time it was designed solely to make more feasible the Chamberlain's first duty of providing good Christmas festivities. Carey had to create more stability and more durability among the leading companies that could entertain at court than there had been recently. From the Privy Council's perspective, the new scheme renewed the rights of the old Queen's Men with the better insurance of having two strong companies rather than one.

It had other effects too, not least satisfying the Lord Mayor's demand to exclude playing entirely from the city at last, and instead securing a guarantee of fixed suburban playhouses for the two companies. The most intriguing aspect of this rearrangement is how far in choosing the new companies the 1594 plan renewed the original and radical scheme of 1583, which systematically creamed off the best players from each of the nobly-patronized companies around London. It is clear

[24] *REED, Cambridge*, i. 346.

that both companies were in effect new creations. Whether, as before, it was Tilney who chose the membership for each of the new groupings, or whether the two patrons made their own decisions this time, is a question worth looking into.

One particularly curious aspect of the question is the fact that Edward Alleyn worked consistently as an Admiral's servant for three years with Strange's while the rest of the players who wore the Admiral's livery played as a separate company. When he left them for Strange's they kept on touring in the Admiral's livery, while Alleyn used his own suit as an Admiral's man to play for Strange's. Wearing another lord's livery showed a conspicuously faint loyalty to the patron of his new company. Town authorities insisted on seeing the players' patents before giving them leave to play. That the guildhall scribes so scrupulously named each company by its patron confirms that the players were indeed thought of chiefly as their master's servants. Alleyn is unlikely to have felt, as it has been conjectured, that retaining a personal patent from Howard with its right to wear his livery was just an insurance so that he could run his own separate company at some time in the future. As a Strange's man in 1592 he was already in the strongest company, with its own supportive patron. His choice must have been chiefly a show of personal allegiance, an old loyalty which happened also (though incidentally) to give him a licence for working separately if need be. It was a unique arrangement, and certainly suggests an awkward kind of allegiance to the lord under whose patent he now travelled. In the event what keeping his old master's livery did give him was the right to take up once again the Lord Admiral's playing licence when Lord Strange died, and later to bring some of his former fellows and their Marlowe plays into his new company when it was formed in May 1594. He and his patron together are the most likely sponsors of the 1594 plan.

The 1594 innovation certainly gave the Chamberlain and his son-in-law two strong groups, and with them a means to limit the competition amongst the other companies. The Rose and the Theatre were made into the two allowed playhouses in London, and their resident companies the allowed performers. The new arrangement was an advance on Howard's deal in 1584, when the Queen's were given access to playing in the city in return for a ban on the other companies. Now the Lord Mayor was appeased by an undertaking not to permit any playing at all in the city's inns. Later in 1594 Carey had to make a special plea to get permission for his own company to play at one inn for the winter months. He wrote to the Lord Mayor on 8 October to ask if his 'nowe companie' might be allowed to use the Cross Keys inn.[25] That, if it was allowed, was the last occasion that the city inns were ever used for playing. Banning playing at the city inns and confining it to the suburbs of Middlesex and Surrey where Howard had control (he was Lord Lieutenant of Surrey, where the Rose and later the Globe were located, and he was on the commission of magistrates for Middlesex, where the Theatre and Curtain and later the Fortune were) was a large part of the duopolizing deal. Thereafter Howard's

[25] *ES* iv. 316.

father-in-law so actively kept to the plan and its conditions that Nashe's comment after his death that his company 'in there old Lords tyme . . . thought there state setled'[26] has the ring of hard truth.

In effect, from May 1594 onwards the Admiral's and Lord Chamberlain's companies knew themselves to be based in London as a part of the government's policy, with accompanying privileges. The policy worked well for both parties at the court festivities. In the first season, 1594–5, only the Chamberlain's and the Admiral's performed, playing three times each. In 1595–6 the Chamberlain's played four times to the Admiral's three, with one joint performance. In 1596–7, when Carey had died and Cobham was Chamberlain, only the Carey company played, six times in all. With a new Carey as Chamberlain from early 1597, the Chamberlain's played four times in the 1597–8 season and the Admiral's two. No company besides these two performed at court at all between 1594 and 5 February 1600, when Derby's were given one performance, and 1601 when two boy companies returned.

That settled state, of course, had strict limits. Carey's priority was to establish and maintain the new order, not just to support two new companies of players. His heir's signature in November 1596 on the petition to stop Burbage from using his new Blackfriars playhouse reflects the firmness with which the Careys held to that design, even when the Chamberlainship had moved out of the family.[27] Burbage built the Blackfriars in a liberty to offset the loss of the city inns as winter playing-places. Such a renewed intrusion into the city was no part of the deal made between the Lord Chamberlain and the Lord Mayor. The inhibition placed on Langley's Swan in July 1597 was part of the same policy.

The deliberate lines of this Chamberlain's policy can be seen in the official pronouncements about playing through the following years. A Privy Council order of 19 July 1598 stated that 'licence hath bin graunted unto two companies of stage players retayned unto us, the Lord Admyral and Lord Chamberlain, to use and practise stage playes'.[28] The order was to suppress a third company, Pembroke's, which had been trying to establish itself in Southwark. Another order of 22 June 1600 tried to check new inroads by specifying not only the two companies, but the two new playhouses that had replaced the Rose and the Theatre, the Fortune and the Globe, as the only players and playing-places authorized for London performances.[29] The boy companies, both of which appeared at court in the 1600–1601 season, seem not to have been part of the Lord Chamberlain's concerns at this time.

[26] A letter to William Cotton, a client of Carey's, printed in *Works*, ed. R. B. McKerrow (London, 1904–10), v. 194.

[27] After Carey's death in July 1596 the post went first to Lord Cobham, with some awkward consequences for Shakespeare's portrayal of Sir John Oldcastle, Cobham's ancestor. But Cobham died in Mar. 1597, and the Chamberlainship was promptly transferred to Carey's son George, then aged 50. There were several court struggles over the post at this time, and George Carey may have been lucky to secure his father's former eminence. He had been in dispute with Pembroke, another powerful Privy Councillor. Robert Sidney, Pembroke's nephew, was a keen candidate for the possible office of vice-chamberlain, along with many others including Raleigh and Sir John Stanhope (Millicent V. Hay, *The Life of Robert Sidney* (Washington DC, 1984), 160).

[28] *ES* iv. 325.   [29] *ES* iv. 329–31.

The Privy Council's policy over playing appears most clearly in a full statement made after Howard intervened in 1600 to secure the new Fortune for his company. The Council on 22 June that year set out the whole policy on which the duopoly was based. As a statement of what, in the event, turned out to be Howard's last significant contribution to the control of playing under Elizabeth, it is worth quoting at length. It was an Order 'for the restrainte of the imoderate use and companye of playhowses and players':

Whereas divers Complaintes have bin heretofore made unto the Lordes and others of hir Majesties privie Counsaile of the mainfold abuses and disorders that have growen and doe Continew by occasion of many howses erected & emploied in and aboute the Cittie of London for common Stage Plaies. And nowe verie latelie, by reason of some Complainte exhibited by sondrie persons against the buildinge of the like house in or nere Golding Lane by one Edward Allen, a servant of the right honorable the Lo: Admirall, the matter aswell in generalities touchinge all the said houses for Stage Plaies and the use of playenge, as in particular concerninge the said house now in hand to be builte in or neere Goldinge Lane, hath bin brought into question & Consultacion amonge their LL. Forasmuch as yt is manifestlie knowne and graunted that the multitude of the said houses and the misgoverment of them hath bin made and is dailie occasion of the idle riotous and dissolute livinge of great numbers of people, that leavinge all such honest and painefull Course of life, as they should followe, doe meete and assemble there, and of maine particular abuses and disorders that doe there uppon ensue. And yet neverthelesse yt is Considered that the use and exercise of such plaies, not being evill in yt self, may with a good order and moderacion be suffered in a well governed estate, and that hir Majestie beinge pleased at some times to take delighte and recreacion in the sight and hearinge of them, some order is fitt to be taken for the allowance and mainteinance of suche persons, as are thoughte meetest in that kinde to yeald hir Majestie recreacion and delight, & consequentlie of the howses that must serve for publique playenge to keepe them in exercise. To the end therefore, that bothe the greatest abuses of the plaies and plaienge houses maye be redressed, and the use and moderacion of them retained, The Lordes and the rest of hir Majesties privie Councell, withe one and full Consent, have ordered in manner and forme as followeth.

First, that there shall bee about the Cittie two howses and noe more allowed to serve for the use of the Common Stage plaies, of the which howses one shalbe in Surrey in that place which is Commonlie called the banckside or there abouts, and the other in Midlesex. And foras muche as there Lordshippes have bin enformed by Edmond Tylney Esquire, hir Majesties servant and Master of the Revells, that the howse now in hand to be builte by the said Edward Allen is not intended to encrease the number of the Plaiehowses, but to be in steed of an other, namelie the Curtaine, Which is either to be ruined and plucked downe or to be putt to some other good use, as also that the scituation thereof is meete and Convenient for that purpose. Yt is likewise ordered that the said howse of Allen shall be allowed to be one of the two howses, and namelie for the house to be alowed in Middlesex, soe as the house Called the Curtaine be (as yt is pretended) either ruinated or applied to some other good use. And for the other allowed to be on Surrey side, whereas [there Lordshipps are pleased to permitt] to the Companie of players that shall plaie there to make there owne Choice which they will have, Choosinge one of them and noe more, [And the said Companie of Plaiers, being the Servantes of the L. Chamberlen, that are to plaie there have made choise of the house called the Globe, yt is ordered that the said house and none other shall be there allowed]. And especiallie yt is forbidden that anie stage plaies shalbe plaied (as sometimes they have bin) in any Common Inn for publique assemblie in or neare about the Cittie.

Secondlie, forasmuche as these stage plaies, by the multitude of houses and Companie of players, have bin too frequent, not serving for recreacion but inviting and Callinge the people daily from there trad and worke to mispend there time. It is likewise ordered that the two severall Companies of Plaiers assigned unto the two howses allowed maie play each of them in there severall howse twice a weeke and noe oftener, and especially that they shall refraine to play on the Sabboth daie, uppon paine of imprisonment and further penaltie, and that they shall forbeare altogether in the time of Lent, and likewise at such time and times as anie extraordinarie sicknes or infeccion of disease shall appeare to be in and about the Cittie.[30]

This was the last attempt made by Howard and the Council to renew the terms for playing in London that he and Carey agreed with the Lord Mayor in 1594. Philip Henslowe's records of the Admiral's repertory become irregular at about this time, but there is nothing to suggest that the two companies followed the restriction noted here to playing twice a week instead of the six days that Henslowe records them performing up to this.

The positive policy aspects here in the management of playing seem clear. The question that remains is how active a part the two patrons took in the formation of their new companies in 1594. It was not so wholesale a decimation of the best from the existing companies as in 1583, but the sweep was still quite broad. The Admiral's was formed around Alleyn with his old Howard livery, based on his father-in-law Henslowe and the Rose. The Chamberlain's was based on James Burbage's Theatre and his son Richard. Otherwise both companies were made up from a mixture of players from the old Admiral's, together with Strange's and Sussex's, both of which had recently lost their patrons,[31] a few of the defunct Pembroke's (possibly coming via the now-patronless Sussex's), and the Queen's. James Tunstall came to the new Admiral's from the old Admiral's, which had been travelling since 1591 with the *Tamburlaine* plays and *Faustus*. The reappearance of these famous playbooks in the Rose repertory with the post-1594 Admiral's indicates that the leaders of the old Admiral's touring group and their playbooks, long familiar to Alleyn, went into the new company as part of the new deal.

The only alternative explanation for the belated appearance of these Marlowe plays in the Rose records from 1594 onwards is that Alleyn kept his most valuable playbooks to himself for nearly three years, unused, while he was playing for Strange's. That is a possibility, though I think it unlikely. At the Rose the Strange's company had its own resources, including two other Marlowe plays, *The Jew of Malta*, and *The Massacre at Paris*, along with Talbot in *1 Henry VI* and *Titus Andronicus*. These 'large' plays might have given Strange's enough resources to warrant Alleyn withholding his most famous roles from them between 1592 and

---

[30] *Acts of the Privy Council of England*, xxx. 395; *MSC* i. 80–3, *ES* iv. 329–31.
[31] Sussex died on 14 Dec. 1593. Strange, the short-lived 5th earl of Derby, died on 16 Apr. 1594.

1594. But I suspect that the two *Tamburlaines* and *Faustus* remained in the old Admiral's Men's possession and travelled the country with them. If so, Alleyn took advantage of the reshuffle of May 1594 to draw the old Admiral's players into the new group, perhaps with the thought in mind that he could now renew his former roles in the early Marlowe plays. They were certainly the roles he became most famous for in the great years that followed.

Tunstall certainly came from the old Admiral's into the new grouping, most probably bringing his company's Marlowe plays with him. Richard Jones, a former Admiral's Man who had been travelling on the Continent in 1592–3, may have returned to rejoin the old Admiral's before 1594. He also now joined the new Admiral's. Five of Alleyn's former fellows in Strange's, now Derby's, went to form the core of the new Chamberlain's, but a sixth, Thomas Downton, left them for the new Admiral's. Duke, Goodale, and Pallant, all named in the early Strange's manuscripts and later associated with the Henslowe companies, may have gone from Strange's to the Admiral's at the Rose in the 1594 shake-up too. The clown John Singer most likely came to the new Admiral's from the Queen's, of which he had been a founder member in 1583 and which he was still with in 1588. Richard Allen, also in the Admiral's by 1597, was probably another Queen's man in 1594.[32] Another arrival in the new Admiral's, Edward Dutton, may also have been a Queen's player, like his namesake, Laurence. Of the other post-1594 Admiral's Men, Edward Juby, Martin Slater, and Thomas Towne, no previous records exist.

Whether Alleyn had much say in the composition of the new company is rather doubtful. Singer's presence suggests strongly that the two Privy Councillors were doing what Walsingham had done with the Queen's, selecting a few men from each of several different groups. Alleyn might have been consulted, but he lacked the authority to select players from other companies for himself. Both companies were a thorough mix of other groupings. Alleyn certainly would not have contributed directly to the equally wide-ranging selection of Carey's new company.

The Chamberlain's and his relative's initiative in setting up two new companies makes the choice of players who joined Carey's company a puzzle, if they were not just a selection of the best from what was currently available in London. For its core the answer was easy, and family links again come into it. Ferdinando Stanley, formerly Lord Strange and now the Earl of Derby, died on 16 April 1594. His widow was sister to George Carey's wife. George Carey was Henry Carey's son. Derby's widow certainly took an interest in her husband's players, because they are recorded at Winchester on 16 May 1594 under her name. From these Strange's/ Derby's Men, whose credentials include a period when they dominated court performances and a longish history of playing alongside Alleyn at Henslowe's Rose,

---

[32] Evidence about the players is taken from *ES*, and E. Nungezer, *A. Dictionary of Actors and Other Persons Associated with the Public Representation of Plays in England Before 1642* (New Haven, Conn., 1929); S. P. Cerasano, 'New Renaissance Players' Wills', *MP* 82 (1985), 299–304; and Mark Eccles, 'Elizabethan Actors i. A-D', *NQ* 236 (1991), 38–49, 'Elizabethan Actors ii. E-J', *NQ* 236 (1991), 454–61, 'Elizabethan Actors iii. K-R', *NQ* 237 (1992), 293–303, and 'Elizabethan Actors iv. S to End', *NQ* 238 (1993), 165–76.

the new Chamberlain's company drew five of its sharers, George Bryan, John Heminges, Will Kemp, Augustine Phillips, and Thomas Pope, along with some others. They did not, however, make up the numbers for a full company. Downton, and probably others from Strange's/Derby's, split from their fellows and went with Alleyn into the Admiral's. Carey seems to have deliberately left room in his new grouping for other players drawn from other companies. The most notable of those were Richard Burbage and William Shakespeare. Where they came from is a question that brings in a short-lived and much-disputed company, the second to be patronized by the second earl of Pembroke.

Near the beginning of the 1590s player's names in the plots of 2 *The Seven Deadly Sins* and *The Dead Men's Fortune*, manuscripts prepared for Strange's Men probably before 1592,[33] show that Strange's then included a 'Mr' George Bryan, Richard Burbage, Richard Cowley, John Duke, Thomas Goodale, John Holland, Robert Pallant, 'Mr' Augustine Phillips, 'Mr' Thomas Pope, Will Sly, and John Sincler, plus a Harry, Kitt, and Vincent, and several other boys. Those with 'Mr' in front of their names are thought to have been sharers. 'Harry' may have been Henry Condell, and 'Kitt' may have been Christopher Beeston, both later to appear in the Chamberlain's Men. Some of these players left the company at some time during 1591–3, most likely when Alleyn quarrelled with James Burbage and left the Theatre in May 1591. Sincler and Holland are named in the extant Pembroke's plays. Richard Burbage, too, was not a member of Strange's in the years while Pembroke's was active. In all, seven and possibly nine of the players named in these early Strange's manuscripts eventually joined the new Chamberlain's. All but five of them, however, played under some other patronage in the intervening years.

The Pembroke's of 1592–3, successful at court, did not survive the plague closure of 1593. Where their leading players went after they 'broke' is not known for certain. Several companies besides Pembroke's had strong players to offer in 1594, and one of them had probably taken on the ex-Pembroke's players. Sussex's and one group of the Queen's were available in London, playing first separately and then jointly at the Rose between December 1593 and April 1594. The Queen's Men had broken in two before 1590, and by 1594 were evidently ripe for reallocation. Sussex's is the mystery company. It was evidently staffed well enough in 1594 to play *Titus Andronicus*, which they inherited from Pembroke's (according to the quarto title-page) since it is a play demanding as many as twenty-six players for the opening scene.[34] Sussex's had played jointly with Laneham's section of the Queen's

---

[33] The most accessible transcription from these manuscripts is in *Henslowe's Diary*, 327–8. An account questioning the standard reading of the evidence is Scott McMillin, 'Building Stories: Greg, Fleay, and the Plot of 2 *Seven Deadly Sins*', *Medieval & Renaissance Drama in England*, 3 (1988), 53–89. I find its scepticism overstated.

[34] *Titus* and its 1594 title-page has occasioned a lot of discussion. Paul E. Bennett, 'The Word "Goths" in "A Knack to Know a Knave" ', *NQ*, 200 (1955), 462–3, suggested that the play dates from 1593, and that its title-page simply lists the three companies who shared its performance, but there is no other title-page that lists a group of the companies who performed the play in this form, whereas there are several which list a sequence of performing companies. A strong claim for Sussex's making a

in 1590 and 1591. Possibly the same Queen's group augmented Sussex's numbers in their initial run at the Rose in December and January, although it is at least equally likely that the two companies shared the playhouse, playing there on alternate days. Otherwise the fact that Sussex's joined up with the Queen's three months later must indicate some drastic loss of manpower in the interim. Henslowe did not link the two companies by name in December and January as he did in April, but the later naming may merely indicate that he had by then become more familiar with the arrangements of the joint company and the name on its licence. It is also possible that members of Pembroke's, broken by August 1593, had joined Sussex's. That would explain the transfer of *Titus*.

Just who were the players who composed the Pembroke's which started in late 1591 or 1592 and died in 1593 has caused a lot of debate.[35] It became prominent in London surprisingly quickly for a company of wholly new players. Besides performing several of Shakespeare's plays and having Marlowe's *Edward II* written for them, they were evidently good enough to nearly match Strange's at court in the season of 1592–3, with two performances to Strange's three. They broke up in August 1593. Their collapse that summer helps to explain the flow of their playbooks into print in 1593 and 1594.

The new Chamberlain's certainly took up several players who had been in Pembroke's at one time. They included John Sincler, a Strange's man in *2 Seven Deadly Sins*, who is cited by name at III. i. 1 in *3 Henry VI*, which (like *Richard Duke of York*) was a Pembroke's play by 1593.[36] John Holland, also named in a Strange's manuscript earlier, is named there as a Pembroke's player along with him. Sincler's name also recurs in *The Shrew's* Induction, most likely from its time as a Pembroke's play.[37] What these two players did after Pembroke's collapsed in

contribution to the new Chamberlain's is Scott McMillin's 'Sussex's Men in 1594: The Evidence of *Titus Andronicus* and *The Jew of Malta*', *Theatre Survey*, 32 (1991), 214–23.

[35] Chambers and Dover Wilson thought that Pembroke's was an offshoot of what they took to be an amalgamation between Strange's and the Admiral's (see *ES* ii. 123, and Gurr, 'The Chimera of Amalgamation', *TRI* 18 (1993), 85–93). David George accepts Chambers's view, and assumes that the amalgamation's other playbooks reverted to Strange's ('Shakespeare and Pembroke's Men', *SQ* 32 (1981), 305–23, 307). But that leaves the Admiral's out of account, and ignores what happened to *Titus*. There is nothing in Henslowe's letter to Alleyn about Pembroke's to indicate that they had any direct connection. Henslowe was reporting business and social gossip to Alleyn, not matters of direct financial interest.

[36] A notably small and skinny player, Sincler has been identified through several of the plays written later for the Chamberlain's. Parts written for him include Nym, Slender, Aguecheek (a 'manikin'), possibly Thersites ('toadstool', 'cob-loaf', and 'fragment'), and probably Robert Faulconbridge, the Bastard's brother, in *King John*, where at I. i. 140–3 he is described in similar terms. There is no evidence of any part being written especially for a thin man in the later *Henry VI* plays, for all that Sincler's name appears in one of them, or in *Titus*, *Richard III*, or the early comedies. The note of his name in the Pembroke text may indicate that he joined that company late. *King John* does have a part for him, but its disputed dating, variously ascribed to 1590 or 1595, makes it no help in fixing a date for Sincler's arrival in the company.

[37] The naming of players in playscripts is a vexed question that depends heavily on what sort of manuscript is identified as the source for the printed text, and when the names were inserted in the manuscript. See Scott McMillin, 'Casting for Pembroke's Men: The *Henry VI* Quartos and *The Taming of A Shrew*', *SQ* 23 (1972), 141–59. Some weight has to be attached to the evidence that the two *Henry*

1593 is conjectural, though there is one strong clue in the track of Shakespeare's plays recorded on the title-page of the 1594 quarto of *Titus Andronicus*, which went from Strange's to Pembroke's to Sussex's. Sincler and Holland certainly went from Strange's to Pembroke's, and may have gone from there to Sussex's. Sussex's is recorded by Henslowe as performing *Titus* at the Rose early in 1594. When Pembroke's collapsed Sincler and Holland might have accompanied the play to Sussex's, whence they were taken up for the Chamberlain's. Conceivably Richard Burbage took the same path. And Shakespeare himself? When Pembroke's collapsed he was writing epyllia for the earl of Southampton. *The Rape of Lucrece* was entered for printing on 9 May 1594, less than four weeks before the run of combined performances by the new Chamberlain's and Admiral's Men that Henslowe records. Shakespeare must have had some interest in Sussex's since they acquired *Titus*. The transfer of his entire early corpus of plays to the new Chamberlain's suggests that he was in the habit of keeping ownership of the plays in his own hands while they shifted from one company to another, whether or not he also acted in them. Either that, or someone knew what he was doing rounding up the playbook-owning sharers for the new company. It seems likely that Sincler, Holland, and probably Burbage stayed with the Shakespeare corpus on its travels, whether or not their author did so as well, until the Lord Chamberlain descended on them for his new company.

Very likely it was Carey's original policy of not giving his name to any company while he was Chamberlain that drove James Burbage to Pembroke in late 1591 when he needed a new patron. Burbage wore Carey's livery in 1584, but after he became Lord Chamberlain in that year Carey's reading of his duties would have stopped him from patronizing a new company. So after Burbage quarrelled with Alleyn, and his Theatre lost Alleyn and Strange's Men to the Rose after May 1591, he may have arranged to form a new company, using Richard Burbage as its leader, by applying to Pembroke to sponsor them. Pembroke had been intimate with Burbage's old master, the earl of Leicester.

Pembroke and Leicester shared many activities through the 1570s and 1580s. Pembroke's marriage to Mary Sidney in 1577 made Leicester's sister into his mother-in-law. Leicester visited Wilton in 1577, and Pembroke and Leicester took the Buxton waters together later that year. In September 1578 Pembroke was present at Leicester's house in Wanstead when Francis Knollys came to settle the marriage of his daughter, who was pregnant by Leicester. Leicester used Baynard's Castle, Pembroke's London base, for his discussions with Pembroke and Philip Sidney over Elizabeth's proposed Alençon marriage in 1579. Leicester and his brother Warwick kept companies, but Pembroke did not, after his patronage of an

VI quartos were Pembroke's plays, printed when Pembroke's broke up and would have sold their playbooks. That supports the case made by textual scholars who claim that the two quartos are reported texts deriving from versions of the manuscripts eventually used to print the Folio text. With some help from the evidently memorial character of much of the transcription in the two quartos, not to mention their uncomprehending versions of the Latin tags, I am inclined to accept that reading of the evidence.

apparently short-lived travelling group in 1575–6. Yet he and Leicester liked plays. They saw Gager's play *Meleager* at Oxford together in 1585.

Burbage had been a Leicester's man up to 1583. Pembroke may well have been present at one or more of the times when Leicester's, led by Burbage, played before their patron. Pembroke was the most likely choice for an ex-Leicester's player to turn to as a new patron. He was a senior noble not then patronizing any company. And there are other possible incentives for Burbage to have gone in that direction in 1591. After Leicester's death in 1588 the Leicester circle had migrated to the Countess of Pembroke. She herself was writing plays in 1591–2. Burbage might have seen an appeal to her as his best way to secure the noblest level of patronage for the new company. Whether Mary Herbert did intervene with her husband to make him its patron and add the new company to her already long list of literary patronage there is just not enough evidence to say. Among the many guesses about Mary Sidney's interest in reforming the drama there are a few which have proposed that she must have prompted her husband to become the patron of a new company in 1592[38] Pembroke himself was not often to be found in London; he was in fact beginning the long decline in health that brought his death in 1601. There is a letter dating from 1595 in which he writes that he dreams of death and desires it.[39] Yet late in 1591 or early in 1592 he chose to change his long-held practice by giving his name as patron to a new London company. His wife's intervention cannot be discounted, although it is at least equally possible that he was approached directly by the impresario of the Theatre. If we go by the connections of patrons alone, no other great lord would have been more likely as the patron of a new Burbage company in 1591 or 1592.

Pembroke's name, plus the other circumstantial evidence, strongly supports the theory that Richard Burbage, after a start playing as a junior member of Strange's in 1590 and 1591, separated from Strange's when Alleyn quarrelled with his father, and helped to set up the new Pembroke's as a company to occupy the Theatre when Alleyn and Strange's moved to the Rose. Only a year or so younger than Alleyn,[40] he lacked Alleyn's stature in 1591. But he had comparable family connections. After Pembroke's collapsed in the autumn of 1593 he may have gone to the Rose

---

[38] Mary Ellen Lamb, 'The Myth of the Countess of Pembroke: The Dramatic Circle', *Yearbook of English Studies*, 11 (1981), 194–202, demolished the view that she helped a circle of playwrights to introduce French and Senecan drama in an attempt to purify the common English style. David Bergeron, 'Women as Patrons of English Renaissance Drama', in *Patronage in the Renaissance*, ed. Guy Fitch and Stephen Orgel (Washington DC, 1981), 274–90, is more positive, noting that more books were dedicated to her than to any woman but Lucy Bedford and Queen Elizabeth. The company did not participate in the Ramsbury 'Astraea' for Elizabeth's visit on 27–9 Aug. 1592, but Simon Jewell, a player, does mention Mary Herbert as a patron in his will. To J. A. B. Somerset, 'The Lords President, Their Activities and Companies: Evidence from Shropshire', *Elizabethan Theatre*, 10 (1988), 93–111, that makes her the sponsor of Pembroke's (109). Margaret P. Hannay, *Philip's Phoenix: Mary Sidney, Countess of Pembroke* (New York, 1990), sees her very likely patronizing players. Gary Waller, *The Sidney Family Romance* (Detroit, 1993), 224–5, is even more positive.

[39] Michael Brennan, *Literary Patronage in the English Renaissance: The Pembroke Family* (London, 1988), 101.

[40] Alleyn was born in 1566, Burbage in 1567. See Eccles, 'Elizabethan Actors i: A–D', 43.

with Sussex's for a few months before setting up as the leader of the new Chamberlain's back at his father's Theatre in 1594. Both Alleyn and Burbage used parental property as the London base for their two companies from 1594 onwards. Very possibly Richard Burbage's track from as early as 1591 was similar to Alleyn's, and as a player possibly also the same as Shakespeare's.

The plays that Henslowe recorded in his *Diary* in the first half of 1594 give some indication of the repertoire that the pre-1594 'large' companies ran, and (at the risk of some circular argument) also hint at the plays of their two successors.[41] In its run between 27 December 1593 and 6 February 1594 Sussex's performed nine plays that only appear in the *Diary* for that run, including *George a Greene*, which was printed in 1599 as a Sussex's play, and *Friar Francis*, which Heywood in his *Apology* reported as belonging to Sussex's. *Titus Andronicus* also appeared for the first time, if, as I believe, the earlier 'Titus' that Henslowe records in the entries preceding those for the Sussex company was *Titus and Vespasian*. The *Fair Maid of Italy* also appears in Henslowe's records for the first time, as a Sussex's play. Only *The Jew of Malta*, a regular in the *Diary* since the first Strange's entries at the beginning of 1592, seems not to have been a new title introduced by Sussex's.

During the brief conjoint run when Sussex's allied themselves with the Queen's Men at Easter 1594, the two companies are noted with five titles. Two, *The Jew* and *Friar Bacon and Friar Rungay*, were old Henslowe stock. One, *The Fair Maid*, was a Sussex's title, and one other, *King Leir*, must have come from the other side of the paired appearances, since it later appeared in print as a Queen's Men's play. Another previously unknown play, *The Ranger's Comedy*, also made its first appearance now. It was later to reappear in the Admiral's repertory, so it may have been a new play recently purchased by Henslowe rather than another of the Queen's Men's imports. Alternatively, its presence in the resources of the later company may indicate the transfer of some Sussex's or Queen's players along with the *Ranger's* playbook into Alleyn's group.

Tracking these titles through the later records gives us a firm indication of what was at stake when the new companies were formed in May 1594. For their three-day run between 14 and 16 May the Admiral's offered one play that was definitely Henslowe's, *The Jew*, plus one play that was probably his, *The Ranger's Comedy*, and a new title, *Cutlack*, which Everard Guilpin was later to identify as a role played by Alleyn in 1598, and which must therefore have come either from his own or from Henslowe's personal stock.[42] The most intriguing and possibly most revealing list of plays is the one that records joint or alternate performances by the new Admiral's Men and the Chamberlain's for their brief run in tandem at the same

[41] Henslowe's play-lists for 1594 are recorded in *Henslowe's Diary*, 20–2.
[42] Scott McMillin, 'Sussex's Men in 1594: The Evidence of *Titus Andronicus* and *The Jew of Malta*', considers that *The Jew* was Alleyn's, not Henslowe's. This is possible, though it does not explain how the script could be played at the one playhouse by so many different companies in succession, including at least one that Alleyn never belonged to.

playhouse.[43] It is, in fact, the only evidence that survives to indicate what may have been in the original playstock of the Chamberlain's Men. Between them the two companies offered seven plays from 3 to 13 June 1594. Predictably the seven included Henslowe's *The Jew of Malta*, probably current then because of the Lopez trial.[44] But the others came from elsewhere, almost certainly from the companies where Carey and Howard had found the players to set up their new groups. Besides Alleyn's *Cutlack*, *Titus Andronicus* reappeared, presumably with the help of some players from Sussex's, who had been playing it at the beginning of the year. Four new plays appear, *Hester and Ahasuerus, Bellendon, Hamlet*, and *The Taming of A Shrew*. The last of these had once been a Pembroke's play, like *Titus*. Where the *Hamlet* came from is uncertain. References to a play of that name had been appearing since 1589, which means that it belonged to one of the older companies then in London, most likely the Queen's.

It is possible to guess more closely about that from the later history of the seven titles. *Bellendon, Cutlack*, and *The Jew of Malta* appear subsequently in the Admiral's lists with Henslowe. *Titus* and *The Shrew* (assuming it was related to *A Shrew*) were part of the Chamberlain's playstock, to judge from their reappearance in the First Folio. *Hamlet* and *Hester* may have been too, since they never reappear in the Admiral's lists. Possibly this *Hamlet*, like *King Leir, The Troublesome Raigne of King John*, and *The Famous Victories of Henry V*, was originally a Queen's Men's play that now passed to the Chamberlain's, to be rewritten some time later by their resident playwright. The two approved companies did get into the habit of matching their plays, Falstaff with Oldcastle, *Richard III* with *Richard Crookback, The Jew of Malta* with *The Merchant of Venice*, and others.[45] Henslowe's addition of a play about Henry V to his list in November 1595 conceivably was meant to match the Chamberlain's Men's use of the older Queen's Men's play. For Shakespeare's *King John* the favoured date of composition, or perhaps of revision, in 1595 would make sense if the company had recently acquired the old play and wanted a quick rewrite for its fresh repertoire. Rewriting *The Famous Victories*, which covers most of the ground Shakespeare retilled with the two *Henry IV* plays and *Henry V*, had to wait till after the first play of the second Henriad, *Richard II*, in 1595. Rewriting *Hamlet* and *King Leir* took longer still. Apart from the ascriptions to the Queen's on their title-pages, and Henslowe's acquisition of a play about Henry V in 1595, there is no evidence that any of these old plays ever reappeared in their original form on the stage after 1594. But these remnants from the old Queen's Men in the Chamberlain's do call for some explanation. From the tracking of playbooks it

[43] Carol Chillington Rutter (ed.), *Documents of the Rose Playhouse* (Manchester, 1984), 83, reckons that since *Bellendon* appeared in the Admiral's list shortly after the joint performances, each play must have been performed separately by each company.

[44] Lopez was at risk from Feb. to July 1594, when he was beheaded. Revivals of *The Jew of Malta* coincided with his two trials. See Margaret Hotine, 'The Politics of Anti-Semitism: *The Jew of Malta* and *The Merchant of Venice*', *NQ* 236 (1991), 35–7.

[45] Roslyn Lander Knutson, 'Evidence for the Assignment of Plays to the Repertory of Shakespeare's Company', *MRDE* 4 (1989), 75–89, 83.

seems that some players from the Queen's and Pembroke's, the latter arriving via Sussex's if the title-page of the 1594 *Titus* is to be believed, went along with their plays to the new Chamberlain's company.

Based with Alleyn's father-in-law, Henslowe, at the Rose, the new Admiral's had a good repertoire. To the Rose's staples, like *The Jew of Malta* and *Friar Bacon*, they could add Alleyn's own stock, which now included *Tamburlaine, Faustus*, and *Cutlack*. They used some plays once performed at the Rose by Strange's and some by the Queen's. Since these plays passed through several companies, I think they must all have been Henslowe's own property. On the other hand, none of the Sussex's plays that appeared in Henslowe's lists early in 1594 and none of the Queen's Men plays brought to their amalgamation with Sussex's in 1594 reappear in the *Diary* after May of that year. Nor does 'harey the vj'. Most likely these were all taken by the new Chamberlain's. The evidence supplied by Henslowe's play-lists about the short run of the joined companies upholds the view that to the five-man core of Strange's/Derby's Men Carey added some of the old Pembroke's, who had possibly later gone into Sussex's, and a share of the Queen's. Redisposing the Queen's Men would have helped to endorse his decision to replace the old monopoly with a duopoly.

After the Queen's Men were established in 1583 Charles Howard went to some lengths to secure exclusive rights for them to play in London. The mistake then was in licensing one company but not one playhouse. Other companies still occupied all the venues they could, and the Queen's company had to move from one to another as they became available. Howard and Carey evidently learned from that early experience. In 1594 they prescribed the two playhouses for their own two companies, and closed all other venues by finally granting the long-standing request of the Lord Mayor to prohibit playing in any of the city inns. That satisfied everybody except the unsuccessful companies and the landlords of the other playing-places.

It was five years before a third company began to gain a grip on playing in London, and for all Francis Langley's bold venture with the Swan it was a similar length of time before a third playhouse became available to the aspirant companies. Langley's Swan in 1595 and Burbage's Blackfriars in 1596 were both investments in new playhouses prompted by the 1594 clampdown, attempts to fill the gap left by the closing of the inns. The troubles that they underwent are a measure of the rigour with which the two Privy Councillors implemented their new policy.

5 Settled Practices

The Privy Council's settlement of two approved companies in two approved playhouses in 1594 was the first permanent foothold for the companies in London. It created a new sense of security, guaranteed the two companies prosperity beyond anything possible before, and laid unprecedented demands on their personnel and their writers. Uniquely, the financial records of one of the two companies in this first period of secure London tenure have survived. The years from 1594 to 1603 laid down new patterns, which only altered very slowly in the decades that followed. It seems appropriate, therefore, to use this period as a baseline to identify the characteristic practices that the London companies developed and made standard when they were at their best. A number of different aspects of their working, such as the times and conditions of performance, licensing, the effects of the plague bills, and the sharer system and company finances are considered in this chapter. The main practices are looked at under separate sub-headings.

Given the variety of playing through time and space, the number of different playhouses and playing companies, the seventy-five-year span of performances, changing tastes among playgoers and playwrights, and the inevitability of change, development, and even evolution in theatre traditions, we do it wrong to use it so homogeneously, as if it was a single, invariable practice. Given such variety, too, many of the questions that stand up about the London theatres of Shakespeare's time get answers for which the evidence is all too imprecise. But this is a chapter for the sort of generalizations which reflect the basic similarity in the various playing groups, the teams, the competing companies that flourished through the eighty years of this history.

The Times of Day for Performances

On 8 October 1594 the Lord Chamberlain wrote a letter to the Lord Mayor about his newly formed company. It seems to have been partly prompted by an agreement that the two authorities had reached between them, that they would ban playing at inns in the city, because it asks as a special concession that the Chamberlain's Servants should be allowed to play at the Cross Keys through that winter. From 1595 onwards, no adult company was allowed to perform at a city inn. As part of this proposed modification to the agreement, no formal record of which has survived, the Lord Chamberlain agreed that his new company had conceded 'that where heretofore they began not their Plaies til towardes Fower a clock, they will now begin at two and have done betwene fower and five'.[1] That was written in the

---

[1] *ES* iv. 316. It was not only in London that plays caused trouble through ending late. The Exeter City Council Chamber Book for 14 Sept. 1609, in an order about the troubles that visiting players

autumn, as the nights closed in. It may reflect the seasonal shift in daylight hours from summer, when 4 p.m. was entirely feasible as a starting time, into the winter when a 2 p.m. start made more sense. Thomas Platter saw *Julius Caesar* at the Globe on 21 September 1599 'after lunch, about two o'clock'.[2] That being only ten days after the autumn equinox, it gives little help to the idea of different seasonal times, though it does suggest that the start-time of 2 p.m. agreed in 1595 was maintained. Platter goes on to say that 2 p.m. starts were normal. On the other hand, Henslowe's contract drawn up with Robert Dawes of Lady Elizabeth's Men, dated 7 April 1614,[3] says that Dawes had to be present and 'ready apparrelled . . . to begyn the play at the hower of three of the clock in the afternoone'. This was drawn up after the spring equinox, so it could simply reflect the arrival of longer daylight hours. But the articles of the contract themselves were certainly not designed to apply only to the summer months. A 3 p.m. start must therefore have been standard at the Fortune by 1614.

The 1594 agreement sounds like a new deal. The early start was possibly introduced only for the one season, to appease the Lord Mayor. The general trend may have been towards a later start, whether the 3 p.m. of Lady Elizabeth's Men in 1614 or the 4 p.m. of the Chamberlain's Men before 1594, which the Lord Chamberlain's undertaking sought to correct. On the other hand, in 1619 the officials of the Blackfriars precinct complained that the crowds for winter performances blocked the district 'from one or twoe of the clock till sixe att night'.[4] When the Globe's *A Game at Chess* was enjoying its notorious nine-day run in August 1624, John Chamberlain complained that it was so popular that 'we must have ben there before one a clocke at farthest to find any roome'.[5] These two testimonies indicate that a 2 p.m. start remained customary for the King's Men for thirty years, and was followed both at the winter Blackfriars and the summer Globe. On that basis, if no other, it may be best to conclude that the different companies had different starting-times, and that the Globe company's normal starting-time was 2 p.m.

There is other evidence indicating that this pattern for the King's Men applied at the Blackfriars as much as at the Globe. In November 1610 Jonson supplied the King's Men with a play that exhibited the classical unities of time and place to a level of perfection that suggests a burlesque of the traditions Jonson was generally so loud in upholding. The first of what Harry Levin has linked together as 'two magian comedies',[6] *The Alchemist*, was located firmly 'here in the friers', where the playhouse stood, and the times for each step in the plot were signalled in the text through the hours of natural daylight, from before 9 a.m. till about 5 p.m. That

caused, laid it down that all plays must end 'att the Hower of Fyve in the afternoe' (*REED, Devon*, 183). Plays that ran after dark were often cited as occasions for disorders.
[2] *Thomas Platter's Travels in England 1599*, trans. Clare Williams (London, 1937), 166.
[3] *ES* ii. 256.   [4] *MSC* i. 1: 92
[5] *The Letters of John Chamberlain*, ed. N. E. McClure (2 vols., Philadelphia, 1939), ii. 577–8.
[6] Harry Levin, 'Two Magian Comedies: *The Tempest* and *The Alchemist*', *ShS* 22 (1971), 47–58.

was Jonson's game with the classical unities. The revelation lies in an extended burlesque of Jonson's precision in the other play, Shakespeare's *Tempest*, which was almost certainly written while *The Alchemist* was in rehearsal. It seems to parody Jonson's timing by matching the time of the plot immaculately not just to the time of a day, but to the time of the performance. At I. ii. 239 Prospero asks Ariel 'What is the time o'th'day?', to which Ariel replies 'past the mid-season'. Prospero makes this more specific: 'At least two glasses', that is, 2 p.m., and underlines the point by going on to say 'The time 'twixt six and now | Must by us both be spent most preciously'. By the fifth act Prospero asks his timekeeper 'How's the day?' and is told 'On the sixth hour' (V. i. 2), meaning 5 p.m. This timing is affirmed by the Boatswain when he is awoken and brought to the company, where he describes 'our ship | Which but three glasses since we gave out split'. If a 'glass' was an hourglass, in 1610 *The Tempest* was evidently expected to run for three hours' traffic of the Blackfriars stage, starting at 2 p.m. Both plays were written for afternoon performance at the Blackfriars.

Playing-times at the Hall Playhouses as Compared with the Amphitheatres

The indoor playhouses used candles to light the stage and auditorium, while the open-air playhouses used natural daylight. In the halls, therefore, there was not the same need to use the daylight hours. The King's Men do, however, appear to have followed a similar pattern of playing times at the Blackfriars to those they needed at the Globe. Night performances at the Blackfriars were, of course, as feasible there as they were at court, where plays were always given at night. Queen Henrietta Maria went to see plays at the Blackfriars four times. On 13 May 1634 she saw the King's Men perform *The Tragedy of Cleander*. In 1635 she was reported as seeing Lodowick Carlell's *2 Arviragus and Philicia*, a play performed at court in the next winter season. On 6 May 1636 she saw *Alphonso*, and on 23 April 1638 she saw Davenant's *The Unfortunate Lovers*. Bentley[7] reckons that all of these performances were 'probably given at night when the theatre was chartered', basing his reading on the fact that the payment for *The Unfortunate Lovers* was listed along with others performed at court. This is possible, though I think it unlikely in all of the cases. Either way, night performances at the Blackfriars were special occasions. Generally the same time of day seems to have been used for hall-theatre performances as for the amphitheatres. Afternoon performances were well suited to the hall theatres' chief clientele, the idle 'afternoon's men'. In fact, to judge from Dekker's reference to the shutters being closed for a dark tragedy at a hall playhouse[8] normally even the indoor theatres were expected to be lit by the sun as well as by candles.

---

[7] *JCS* iii. 221.
[8] Thomas Dekker, in *The Seven Deadly Sins* (1606): 'All the Citty lookt like a private Play-house, when the windowes are clapt downe, as if some *Nocturnall*, or dismal *Tragedy* were presently to be acted.' *The Non-Dramatic Works*, ed. A. B. Grosart (5 vols.; London, 1884–6), ii. 41.

There may also have been some local variations among the boys' companies for their performance times. One reference to lighting candles in a hall playhouse is in a context which seems to suggest that the gentry did not much like their fine attire being smirched for too long with candle-smoke. The induction to Middleton's *Michaelmas Term*, written for Paul's Boys, says that 'we dispatch you in two hours without demur; your suits hang not long here after candles be lighted'. This limitation seems to confirm the point made by William Percy in his 'note to the Master of Children of Powles', that there were external constraints on the children 'not to begin before foure, after prayers, and the gates of Powles shutting at six'.[9] Clocks striking the canonical hours still ruled the cathedral's commercial offshoot. Similar constraints may in time have come to apply also at the adult halls. In Fletcher's *Love's Pilgrimage* at the Blackfriars in 1615, the Prologue starts by renewing his welcome to the audience, 'To this place Gentlemen, full many a day | We have bid ye welcome; and to many a Play'. He goes on 'This night | No mighty matter, nor no light, | We must intreat you look for: A good tale, | Told in two hours, we will not fail | If we be perfect, to rehearse ye'. The halls could evidently run till after dark more readily than the amphitheatres, as we might expect with the King's Men playing there only in winter.

The Length of Performances

As early as 1574 Geoffrey Fenton, in a pamphlet based on French sources but written for London, complained of 'those twoo or three howres that those playes endure'.[10] John Northbrooke's pamphlet attacking dicing, dancing, and playgoing also speaks of those who 'can tarie at a vayne playe two or three houres, when as they will not abide scarce one houre at a sermon'.[11] Both of these statements were made when plays and interludes were shorter than they became in the 1580s and 1590s. But throughout the whole period, claims about the time needed even for the longer plays either remained the same or shrank. A Marprelate counterblast in 1589 produced the statement that at the Theatre or Curtain a player might 'play the foole but two houres together'.[12] Shakespeare declared that the stage time for *Romeo and Juliet* was only 'two hours' traffic' for its 3,185 lines. Jonson claimed 'two short howers' for *The Alchemist* at the Blackfriars in 1610. 'Two hours travel' is noted in *Two Noble Kinsmen*, and 'two poor hours' in *Hengist*, also a King's Men's play.[13] As late as 1636, when the extra time taken by the concluding jig had been replaced by a preliminary overture by the musicians, Shirley declared that his 3,000-line *The Duke's Mistress* also took 'but two howers'. Ben Jonson specified for the exceptionally long *Bartholomew Fair*, a play even longer than the 3,904 lines of the Folio *Hamlet*, 'the space of two houres and a half, and somewhat more', which

[9] A. Hart, 'The Time Allotted for Representation of Elizabethan and Jacobean Plays', *RES* 8 (1932), 395–413, 399–400.
[10] *ES* iv. 195.   [11] *ES* iv. 198.   [12] *ES* iv. 230.   [13] A. Hart, 397.

is not out of keeping with the length of performance time allotted by the Lord Chamberlain in his declaration, quoted above, that his company's performances would 'begin at two and have done betwene fower and five'. These claims cannot easily be reconciled with the practice of the King's Men at the Blackfriars, who from 1609 allowed their musicians to start the afternoon with a concert lasting as much as an hour. And if *The Tempest's* 2,341 lines was expected to take three hours, even with its scenic banquet and masque, the longer plays can hardly have taken less time. Was the common statement of 'but two hours' a defensive cliché?

In contrast to the customary claims for plays to take only two hours there is Dekker's account of 'three houres for two pence' in *The Raven's Almanack* of 1608, and 'three howres of mirth' in *If It Be Not Good* at the Red Bull in 1611.[14] Against that, Christopher Beeston, who was then running the Queen's Men at the Red Bull, held it as 'two hours well spent' in his verses prefixing Heywood's *Apology* in 1611 or 1612. It may be that the two-hour claim was made with the official constraints on the length of time thought proper for plays in mind, while Dekker was maximizing the length of pleasurable time available at the theatres in his two statements. That would suggest there was a fairly uniform amount of time for most performances, and that they lasted somewhere between two and three hours in all.

According to Hart, the average length of a play, measured in the total number of lines in the plays that were staged by the five major companies through the years 1590–1616, was 2,532 lines.[15] A text of more than 3,000 lines was rare except for some of Jonson's plays, which were published with advertisements claiming that their printed texts contained more than was set down for performance, and some of Shakespeare's earlier plays. The published texts of Jonson's plays, including those like *Every Man Out* which were said to contain 'more than hath been Publikely Spoken or Acted', average 3,580 lines. Deducting the ten English history plays from Shakespeare's totals, his average length comes to 2,671 lines. Altogether sixty-two plays of the King's Men average out at 2,644 lines.

Hart[16] claimed that the optimum speaking rate is 22 lines or 176 words per minute, which from current practice seems a reasonable estimate. Without adding the modern practice of intervals, it would make the two hours' traffic quite feasible. The Shendandoah Shakespeare Express, for instance, a company working under the stimulus of Ralph Cohen and his concept of original Shakespearian performances, does its Shakespeares largely uncut and without many signs of express haste. They use a few of the obvious features from the original theatre: no intervals, full auditorium lighting so that actors can address the audience directly, recognizable doubling of parts, and minimal props. Their *Comedy of Errors* takes about one and

---

[14] The extreme case is a satirical German poem of 1615, quoted by Jerzy Limon, *Gentlemen of a Company: English Players in Central and Eastern Europe, 1590–1660* (Cambridge, 1985), 29. It speaks of people preferring to stand and hear an English play for 'four hours' rather than spend one in a church.

[15] A. Hart, 'The Length of Elizabethan and Jacobean Plays', *RES* 8 (1932), 139–54, 153–4.

[16] 'Time Allotted', 404.

a half hours, their *Merchant of Venice* a little under two, cutting less than 400 lines of the full 2,737-line text in the process.

The Accuracy of Elizabethan Timekeeping

J. U. Nef, in his Wiles lectures in 1956, identified the late sixteenth century in Europe as the first historical period when it was found necessary to establish precisely fixed quantities, whether of time or space.[17] For the man in the London street in that century, though, precise measurements of time were still inaccessible. Hours were fixed by church clocks, and personal timepieces were a rare luxury. Henry VIII gave a watch of sorts to Catherine Howard, his fifth wife, in 1540, but portable timepieces were not at all common until the end of the seventeenth century. Jonson's Pennyboy junior in *A Staple of News* (1626) was conspicuously profligate in buying a watch. Pepys never possessed a watch of his own through all his years as a civil servant. The word 'clock', like the French 'cloche', originally meant a bell. Shakespeare's Londoners would have told the hour from church bells, and in a few locations the quarter-hours as well. The first mechanical clocks arrived in church towers in the fourteenth century, as a costly but labour-saving device to mark the canonical hours for prayer. Salisbury Cathedral has the oldest surviving clock in England, dating from about 1386. It strikes only the hours, and not very accurately. The arrival of mechanical clocks to strike church bells did introduce the sixty-minute division for the hour to England, but most clocks marked only the hours.[18] In London, while some clocks may have struck on the quarter-hour, such times for meetings as have survived on record all go by the full hour. Jonson's 'two hours and a half and somewhat more' for *Bartholomew Fair* is impractically if characteristically over-precise.

Changes in Play-runs in the Shakespearian Repertory

Henslowe's records show a remarkable pattern of play performances in his records for the 1590s of the companies that performed at the Rose. Each day had a different play, and the nearest thing to a run was the performance of both parts of two-part plays such as *Tamburlaine* on successive days. No other day-by-day playhouse records survive. It is generally assumed that this incredibly high-speed repertory system lasted until the closure in 1642. Given such a strenuous system, with the massive demands it laid on resources, the number of plays themselves, the exceptional memory-capacity the players needed if they were to retain so many scripts in their heads with so little time for rehearsal, and the quantity of properties and

---

[17] J. U. Nef, *Cultural Foundations of Industrial Civilizations* (Cambridge, 1958), 17.
[18] See G. J. Whitrow, *Time in History: The Evolution of our General Awareness of Time and Temporal Perspective* (Oxford, 1988), ch. 7, esp. 104–13.

costumes that so many changes of play called for, we ought to ask how long such a system could have survived. The system with daily changes of play that was needed in the 1590s, when there were hardly more than two playhouses offering plays, would have less value from 1616 onwards when there were five or six playhouses. So we should consider the possibility of changes being made to repertory practices through these years.

In the 1590s the small number of playhouses and the need to offer something fresh every day was clearly a primary consideration. In January 1596, when they put on 26 performances, the Admiral's Men staged 14 different plays in the one month.[19] Six of these plays were given only once. The shortest interval between two performances of the same play was three days. In Henslowe's records generally, the only reasonably reliable prediction you could make about the next day's offering was that if on one afternoon it had been *1 Tamburlaine*, it would probably (but not always) be *2 Tamburlaine* on the next day. This speed of turnover is evidenced for all the Henslowe companies throughout the period of his *Diary*.

There is some indication that between 1590s and the 1630s the pattern of daily change itself slowly changed. We know, for instance, that in the 1630s a new system of payments to playwrights began. Instead of just offering a lump sum to purchase a playscript, impresarios started adding the second or the third day's takings. It was a neat system, and one which proved surprisingly durable through the succeeding century. It favoured the impresario, of course, since if a play was booed off the stage on the first afternoon the author got nothing. It seems to have been invented some time in the 1630s by one of the Caroline theatre's impresarios.[20] He would not have done so if it had not by then become standard practice to run a play for much more than the one day at a time. That was easier once there was a wider range of plays on offer daily than the two shown daily at the Rose and the Theatre in 1596. Once plays were being staged daily by more than the 'four companys' that existed at the beginning of the 1620s, and the companies were relying more on old favourites than on novelty, a run of three days or more would have become quite practicable. But when did it start?

The earliest recorded long run is the nine day's wonder of *A Game at Chess* in August 1624 at the Globe. Other sensational plays were given long runs later, the first of these to be proclaimed being the six days for *Holland's Leaguer* in 1631.[21] That play was a rather special case. It slotted in a few scenes about a local scandal, where a notorious brothel in Southwark was allegedly besieged by the local-authority officers for several days. The fact that it took its title from the siege suggests

[19] *Henslowe's Diary*, 33 4.
[20] See G. E. Bentley, *The Profession of Dramatist in Shakespeare's Time, 1590–1642* (Princeton, NJ, 1971), 128–34.
[21] *The Dramatic Records of Sir Henry Herbert, Master of the Revels, 1623–1673*, ed. Joseph Quincy Adams, (*Herbert Dramatic Records*, New Haven, Conn., 1917), 45. The so-called Record Book itself has vanished, and its contents only survive in notes made from it by Malone and Chalmers at the end of the 18th cent., and used in their editions. J. Q. Adams drew all these notes together in his 1917 edn., but they still make a very inadequate patchwork of small items from the original volume.

that the small Salisbury Court company was working hard to cash in on the scandal. There was a similar notoriety about the story behind the next long run, when a group of people concerned in a northern witch-hunt were brought to London to be questioned. In a letter to his patron written on 16 August 1634, Nathaniel Tomkyns described his attendance at a performance at the Globe of Brome and Heywood's *The Late Lancashire Witches*.[22] He reported that it had been 'acted by reason of ye great concourse of people 3 dayes togither'. This was evidently still an exceptional run. Presumably the expectation was still that unless a play proved unusually popular, it would only have the one performance at a time.

Soon after, though, evidence from a contract made with one of the play's authors for a different company suggests that at least one of the hall playhouses had begun to operate a different system. The information is from a playwright's contract of the late 1630s that allows part of the payment to the author to come from a 'benefit performance'. Richard Brome's contract of 1638 with the Salisbury Court play-house strongly implies, in fact, that a hall play might be expected to run for a good deal more than ten days, since he was allowed to choose any day for his benefit from the first ten.[23] This is a radical shift from 1596, when plays changed daily. In 1638, at least at some hall playhouses, they were expected to run for weeks unchanged. Between those dates, apart from the anomalous case of *A Game at Chess*, which ran for nine days, the only evidence is for the shorter runs of *Holland's Leaguer* and *The Late Lancashire Witches*, two other anomalous sensations. But Brome's contract is difficult to argue against.

By 1639 longer runs must have become standard. Contemporary accounts of two plays which seem to have made use of recent sensations with a political edge claim a five-day run in 1639 for *The Valiant Scot*, and it was also claimed that *The Rebellion* of the same year was 'acted nine dayes together'. *The Knave in Grain New Vampt* at the Fortune and *The Whore New Vampt* at the Red Bull were also acted 'many dayes together' according to their title-pages. In 1640 Thomas Jordan claimed a record run of nineteen days for his *Walks of Islington and Hogsdon*.[24] Moreover, the King's Men and possibly other companies had by this time got into the habit of giving the Master of the Revels a benefit day, a change which also presumes longer runs. Henry Herbert was paid by the King's Men with a 'benefit performance' from the profits of the second day of a revival. This would only have been possible as a result of introducing long runs into repertory practices.

Revivals

There is not a great deal of evidence about how frequently the more famous plays, those in print and on sale, might have been revived. Even *Richard II*, out in three quartos in 1597 and 1598, was dismissed in February 1601 by one of its players as

---

[22] See Herbert Berry, 'The Globe Bewitched and *El Hombre Fiel*', *MRDE* 1 (1984), 211–30, 212.
[23] Bentley, *The Profession of Dramatist*, 129.   [24] Bentley, *JCS* i. 13, n. 2.

'so old and so long out of use that they should have small or no company at it', if we can believe Augustine Phillips's protestations of innocence to the judges of the Essex conspiracy. The printing of two quartos subsequently would seem to contradict the player's testimony, of course, and their reappearance in print may be signs of further revivals. The records of court performances do suggest that revivals grew in numbers as the years went on. From 1625 and even before complaints were laid, especially by the writers, that repertories were ruled by a taste for the old plays. That applied both to the King's Men, with their Shakespeares and Beaumont and Fletchers, and to the other amphitheatre companies. From contemporary comment we know that *Faustus* and *Tamburlaine* were regularly revived at the two northern amphitheatres. Falstaff and Hamlet were celebrated for the last forty years that the Shakespeare company was in existence. Plays were rewritten for revival throughout the period. Dekker did so for Henslowe routinely, and Jonson reworked *The Spanish Tragedy* for him in 1602. Heywood revamped his Red Bull plays for Beeston's Cockpit in the 1620s. Fletcher wrote a sequel to *The Taming of the Shrew* in the same decade, simultaneously affirming his own novelty and the old play's durability. The hall companies of the 1630s bought more new plays than the amphitheatre companies, but the Beestons' actions in holding on to the best titles in their company repertories show that they also relied heavily on old favourites.

Playing on Sundays and in Lent

Playgoing was a direct rival to churchgoing. Since the other happenings that drew large crowds in the great centres like London were relatively infrequent events, such as executions or animal baitings, plays were the only regular occurrence to rival the Sunday and Wednesday church services. So the official restraints on playing always took account of the demands of the church on people's time. It was a complex question. Church festivals and holy days were the only release that paid workmen in the cities had from their work. The holidays established over the centuries by the Catholic Church were traditional carnival time, recognized as the opposite to working days. Commercial playgoing, the new urban habit of paying to attend a play by professional players, was an innovation and an intrusion into this traditional division of people's time. The authorities, especially in London, which was the only city where serious questions of control and regulation arose, always resisted it. The church itself gave them reason to protect Sundays and certain holidays from playing, but they could hardly resist it on other holidays, at least those which were not so much holy as free.

   In practice, the authorities fought most strongly to protect Sundays and the forty days of Lent running from Ash Wednesday until Easter against the intrusions of playing. Sundays were easiest to preserve; the chief troubles came over the other holidays. Lent was a problem because of its length. The players were under constant commercial pressure to perform regardless of officialdom, the same pressure that made them fight the plague closures. If they could not perform, they made no money. So the players treated Lent as a moveable anti-feast, intruding into it as often and as far as they could.

The Establishment view about days for playing was expressed most clearly during the struggle to fix a space for the Queen's Men to perform in London. In his letter written as Secretary of the Privy Council to the Lord Mayor on 1 December 1583, Francis Walsingham set down what he saw as a necessary clarification of the terms for playing. It hints at some cynicism about the arguments his colleagues on the Council had put forward ('in their grave wisdoms'), but it amounts to a forceful injunction laid on the city:

Understanding that upon the receipte of my Lordships letters written lately unto yow in the behalf of hir majesties players, your Lordship interpreteth the licence geven them therin to extend onely to holy daies and not to weke daies I have therefore thought good being partly privie to their Lordships meaning signified in their letters to explane more plainely their pleasures herein to your Lordship, whoe considering in their grave wisdomes that without frequent exercise of such plaies as are to be presented before hir majestie, her servantes cannot conveniently satisfie her recreation, and their owne duties were therefore pleased to directe their letters unto yow, that upon the weke daies and worke daies at convenient times your Lordship wold geve order that they might be licenced betwene this and Shrovetide to exercise their playes and enterludes (sondaies onely excepted) and such other daies wherein sermons and lectures are comonly used.[25]

This was the last of a series of exchanges about playing. The Privy Council's commitment to these 'free days' was periodically renewed in subsequent dealings between the Council and the city for the next fifty years.

Playing in Time of Plague

The English government concerned itself early and closely with attempts to control the epidemics of bubonic plague that swept the country every summer.[26] The towns, and especially the city of London, became its main instruments to control the spread of plague, because the plague showed itself most strongly in large conurbations. London was also not only the seat of government but the place where the administrative resources for recording and control were most readily available. The machinery in place was a collaboration between the city authorities and the Privy Council.

From the mid-sixteenth century the Privy Council laid down regulations based on information provided by the city that enabled it to do something about the risk

[25] *MSC* i. 1. 67.
[26] Bubonic plague was transmitted by the rat flea, which operated best in warmer temperatures. For a concise summary of Tudor attitudes, see F. P. Wilson, *The Plague in Shakespeare's London* (Oxford, 1927), 1–13. For a detailed account of the medical parameters, see J. Leeds Barroll, *Politics, Plague and Shakespeare's Theater*, 73–89.

of infection that always seemed to accompany people gathering in crowds. Each Thursday the London parishes had to draw up bills of the week's mortalities. These lists, put together to provide statistics to cover the whole city, included a separate list numbering the deaths that could be attributed to the plague. Under the Privy Council's supervision, when what John Donne called 'the plaguy bill'[27] for the central London parishes reached a certain number in the weekly totals, most gatherings of people in large numbers were banned. It was a popular edict. The weekly bills were published, and everyone knew what the totals were.[28] When they rose ominously high the law terms were postponed or transferred elsewhere, beggars (but not regular churchgoers) were ordered to keep out of the churches in time of service, and of course all public performances of plays were halted, until the Council could rule that the weekly numbers of plague dead had fallen again to an acceptable level.[29]

God's hand was seen in the epidemics, and that assumption showed in the kind of orders issued to control them. Gatherings at church services could never be halted. Protection was offered by the right to exclude non-local figures and others prone to infection such as beggars. Playgoing, thought to be evidence of profanity in the populace and therefore by some as a cause of the plague's visitations, was always stopped. Many Londoners voted with their feet when the plague figures rose, leaving London if they could afford to, and avoiding crowds so far as they could, including those gathering at playhouses.

In London since the fifteenth century the city authorities had drawn up a collective total of plague deaths from the returns sent in every Thursday by the more than 100 parishes within its direct control, and published the totals. The number of parishes making returns to the Mayor of London in 1593 was increased to include Westminster and the riverside parishes of St Katherine's and St Giles, plus the playhouse suburbs of Southwark and Shoreditch. In 1603 another 11 parishes were added, and a twelfth in 1606, making a total of 121 parishes in all, although many of the more populous flanking areas, including Newington and Stepney, both of which had been the sites of playhouses, were still not included. Nor were burials in St Paul's, Westminster Abbey, or the chapels of the Inns of Court and most of the hospitals.[30] The awkward division of authority between the city and the surrounding counties of Middlesex and Surrey did not make this task easy, and the listings for the city and the suburban areas seem to have been kept separate.[31] Determining the size that the death list should be to justify a closure was not made any easier by these shifts in the basis for calculating them, nor the exclusions. It was one reason why the Privy Council kept to itself the authority to

[27] 'The Canonisation', l. 15, in *The Complete English Poems*, ed. A. J. Smith (Harmondsworth, 1971), 47.
[28] John Chamberlain and his correspondent Dudley Carleton regularly reported the London plague totals to one another. Foreign ambassadors justified their escapes from London to their masters by citing them.
[29] Wilson, *The Plague*, 50.   [30] Ibid. 195.   [31] *ES* iv. 346.

order closures: it was the only body with overarching power over all the districts in and around London.

The first of the city of London's many embargoes on public playing because of the risk of plague appeared on 12 February 1564.[32] Edmund Grindal, the Bishop of London, a rigorous opponent of playgoing, wrote to Burghley on 22 February that plays were a daily cause of trouble, and especially on public holidays, 'wherunto the youthe resorteth excessively, & ther taketh infection'.[33] In different forms, that became a standard complaint. On 3 May 1583, as summer increased the rate of infection, the Lord Mayor voiced it in a letter to the Secretary of the Privy Council, Walsingham. He appealed to godliness, and inserted a grumble about the limits of his jurisdiction, arguing that

the assemblie of people to playes beare bayting fencers and prophane spectacles at the Theatre and Curtaine and other like places to which doe resorte great multitudes of the basist sort of people; and many enfected with sores runing on them being out of our jurisdiction and some whome we cannot discerne by any diligence; and which be otherwise perilous for contagion biside the withdrawing from Gods service, the peril of ruines of so weake byldinges, and the avancement of incontiencie and most ungodly confederacies, the terrible occasion of gods wrathe and heavy striking with plages. It availeth not to restraine them in London unlesse the like orders be in those places adjoyning to the liberties.[34]

This, more than the other complaints, led to a debate about how large the number of plague deaths had to be before the Privy Council's embargo on assemblies should be introduced. The Queen's Men had just been set up, and this kind of issue lay close to the centre of the negotiations between the Council and the mayor. Charles Howard's negotiations in 1584 to secure special privileges for the new company had to include an acknowledgement of this question. A total of fifty was proposed, but the city objected, reasonably enough, that the number of deaths was only the peak of a much larger number of infections. The normal death rate in the central parishes was between forty and fifty, and they proposed a restraint whenever the number rose above normal. The Council held this figure in mind, but for the next twenty years it worked pragmatically, ordering closures whenever the danger seemed urgent enough. It kept control in its own hands, issuing letters and proclamations ordering closures when it thought them necessary, without any precise figure being specified to trigger them.

Under James a more standardized system appeared, at least for the bans on playing. The patents to the three companies with royal patrons drawn up in 1603-4 specified that thirty weekly deaths from plague was the cut-off point. That total may have been raised to forty by 1608, probably because of the extra parishes that were added to the catchment area in 1603 and 1606. The actual total is a matter for some dispute, not helped by the fact that the Privy Council papers for the

[32] Ibid. 52.   [33] *MSC* i. 2: 148.   [34] *MSC* i. 1: 63-4.

period from 1602 which would have reported the dates of the restraints were lost in a fire at Whitehall in 1619. A figure that varied from thirty to fifty appears to have been the number of deaths used for the rest of the early Stuart period.[35] The exact size of the figure was important, because the levels often ran at between thirty and fifty a week, and the choice of the number that brought down closures made a huge difference to the opportunities the companies had for playing in London. How willingly the companies went on their travels when the plague levels rose is a nice question. They did pay for their loss of profit with a lower risk of infection.

Travelling and the plague is a subject to itself, and one for which, because it depends on personal and no doubt usually unvoiced fears, there is little direct evidence. The towns outside London were always alert to the danger of plague being brought in by visitors, and the outflow from London when the plague bill rose was a constant reminder of the risks. Some richer London players in later years kept houses outside the city, which suggests that the players knew the risks as well as anyone. Those players who tried to flout the Privy Council's restraints on playing were at risk from angry Londoners as well as the infection. A note by the Court of Aldermen during the long closure of 1608–9 reports sending two players to prison for it. Dated 17 November 1608, it reads:

William Pollard and Rice Gwynn were by this Court comitted to the goale of Newgate there to remayne during the pleasure of this Court, for that they yestardaye last suffered a stage playe to be publiquely acted in the white fryers during the tyme of the present infection contrarye to his majesties late proclamation.[36]

There was a new playhouse in Whitefriars at this time, used by the Blackfriars Boys for a while once they lost their Blackfriars playhouse to the King's Men. Who the two men were we do not know. That they 'suffered a stage playe' to be performed suggests that they were not professional adult players, but would-be impresarios using a boy company.

A straightforward table listing the dates when the playhouses were closed is not easy to draw up, since the forms of order to restrain playing varied, and they are missing altogether between 1603 and 1619. Nor are the precise dates of their enforcement and withdrawal always clearly identifiable. From Henslowe's records it can be seen that the starting and conclusion of the restraints did not always correspond with the dates when the orders were issued. The table of the dates of plague closures that follows is based mainly on four studies, amended where more recent information has justified alteration. E. K. Chambers, *The Elizabethan Stage*, summarized the evidence up to 1616. He treated the actual plague bills where they

---

[35] J. Leeds Barroll, *Politics, Plague, and Shakespeare's Theater*, 97–100, questions F. P. Wilson's assumption that 40 was the weekly total. I find his case a little over insistent. He gives too little credit, for instance, to the profit motive that drove the players. When set against the Privy Council's orders for restraints on playing, Henslowe's records of the days when the companies stopped playing indicate a lot of slippage, as they do over the observance of Lent.

[36] *MSC* ii. 3: 318–19.

survive with rather more respect than the generally reliable figures given in Stowe's *Annales*. *Henslowe's Diary* has been used as primary evidence to check Chambers's conclusions. G. E. Bentley, in *The Jacobean and Caroline Stage*, prints plague tables from *London's Remembrancer* (1665) and other contemporary lists for each year from 1615. J. Leeds Barroll has a sceptical chapter on the dates of the plague closures, arguing that closures were more drastic and longer than claimed in earlier studies such as F. P. Wilson's *The Plague in Shakespeare's London* (1927). Barroll includes a table of closures by his estimates for the years 1603–1613 (173). He also gives a list of weekly totals for the period 1603–1610, with a note of his additional sources of information (Appendix 2, 217–26). For all Barroll's doubts, I think Wilson's book still offers a reliable trawl of earlier studies of the plague in

TABLE 1. *Dates of Playhouse Closures for Plague, 1563–1642*

Year or year extent	Month or season	Kind of closure
1563–4	30 Sept.–Jan.	
1569	31 May–30 Sept.	
1572	?a	
1574–5	15 Nov.–Easter	
1577	1 Aug.–31 Oct.	
1578	10 Nov.–23 Dec.	
1580	17 Apr.–31 Oct.	
1581	10 July–18 Nov.	
1582	summer–autumn	
1583	summer–26 Nov.	
1584	?summer	
1586	11 May	precautionary restraint
1587	7 May	precautionary restraint
1592	23 June–29 Dec.	
1593	1 Feb.–26 Dec.b	
1594	3 Feb.–1 Apr.	
1596	22 July–27 Oct.	
1603	19 Mar.–29 Apr., 1–12 May	[Mar.–Apr.; June–]c
1604	12 May–9 Apr.d	[–Apr., June–Sept.]

Notes:

a Indicates indirect or imprecise evidence, e.g. based on Harrison's *Description of England*, or Stowe.

b A heavy year for plague: over 15,000 identified plague deaths, more than half the total mortality for the year, continuing through 1594.

c Lists in square brackets from Barroll, *Politics, Plague, and Shakespeare's Theater*, Appendix 2, 217–26.

d This closure began on 19 Mar. 1603 when Elizabeth entered her final illness; in Apr. it continued as a closure for plague. *Henslowe's Diary* (209, 225) indicates some playing in May, but then none until after Lent 1604. Stowe indicates 30,000 plague deaths during the year; none the less, that winter the court had its plays. Possibly playing resumed before Lent; but restraint was withdrawn in Apr. 1604.

TABLE 1. *Continued*

Year or year extent	Month or season	Kind of closure
1605	5 Oct.–15 Dec.ᵉ	[Mar.; Oct.–Dec.]
1606	? July–? Nov.	[Mar.–Apr.; July–Dec.]
1607	? Julyᶠ–? Nov.	[Jan.–Mar.; May–Dec.]ᵍ
1608	? July–	[Jan.–Mar.; Aug.–••]
1609	–? Dec.ʰ	
1610		[–Jan.; Mar.; July–Nov.]
1611		[Feb.–Mar.]
1612		[Mar.–Apr.; Nov.–Dec.]
1613		[Feb.–Mar.; July–Dec.]
1625	12 May–24 Nov.ⁱ	
1630	8 July–28 Nov.	
1636	12 May–	
1637	–2 Oct.	
1640	23 July–29 Oct.	
1641	15 July–9 Dec.	

ᵉ Order of the Privy Council, BL Add. MS 11402, f. 107, 109; printed in *MSC* i. 4–5: 371–2.

ᶠ The Lord Mayor asked the Council to stop plays in a letter, 12 Apr. 1607 (*MSC*, i. 1: 87–8). The plague bill by the end of Apr. was 43; it then fell until July.

ᵍ Barroll considers (I think wrongly) that the cold weather which froze the Thames Dec.–Feb. would have stopped playing.

ʰ Plague deaths were heavy: 2,262 in 1608; 4,240 in 1609; the epidemic persisted into 1610. See Dekker, *Work for Armourers* (1609, *Non-Dramatic Works*, iv. 96).

ⁱ The year of James's death and of greatest plague mortality on record, with 35,417 deaths.

Sources:
E. K. Chambers, *The Elizabethan Stage*, App. E (*ES* iv. 345–51).
R. A. Foakes and R. T. Rickert (ed.), *Henslowe's Diary* (Cambridge, 1961).
G. E. Bentley, *The Jacobean and Caroline Stage* (7 vols.; Oxford, 1941–68), ii. 667–72.
J. Leeds Barroll, *Politics, Plague and Shakespeare's Theater*.

London, and has valuable sections about its effects on the companies between 1564 and 1642.

For the earlier years there is not always any direct confirmation that the length of the plague bill caused the playhouses to be closed. Only direct evidence for closure is used here. It should also be noted that the dates of the orders do not always correspond precisely to the stoppages. Henslowe's records, for instance, show that the order of 3 February 1594 was not enforced at the Rose till after a performance on 6 February. Plague epidemics continued, with the great plague of 1665 followed by the great fire of London in 1666, until the brown rat, which carried the rat flea, lost its ecological niche to the black rat, which did not.

The Admiral's Servants, 1594–1600: Henslowe's Records

Henslowe's Diary, inconsistent and incomplete though it is, tells us far more than any other source possibly could about the patterns of playing which the companies followed in the 1590s and after. Henslowe's detailed accounts are the most reliable basis for this kind of assessment that we have. Almost all the other evidence appears from testimonies made in lawsuits. These, being based on memory rather than figures written down at the time, are far less reliable. The *Diary* covers the time when the Admiral's Men were at their peak, the early years when they were half of the great duopoly that had official backing to rule the boards through the formative years from 1594 to 1603. Its detail, and the consequential insights it provides into the routine activities of a major London company in its heyday, are unique. How far these insights are typical of all the companies from 1594 to 1642 is open to question. In the absence of any strong counter-indications, though, this record of the diurnal activities of one company does stand up as the nearest indication there is of typical practice.[37]

Company Finances

So far as it is possible to interpret the evidence of the average takings at the Rose from Henslowe's figures, it appears that attendance at Rose plays between 1592 and 1600 normally ran at between 1,000 and 2,000 people. It has been calculated that on 25 August 1594, for instance, 1,212 people paid for a seat in the galleries, plus an unknown but probably smaller number, despite the summer season, who stood in the yard.[38] The receipts taken from that number of playgoers at the outer door, for entry to the yard, which all went to the company, would have brought them on average £6–£7 a day. To that they could usually add half the receipts from the half or more of the audience who went on to sit in the galleries, which might have doubled the takings. The other half of these gallery receipts went to the landlord as rent for the playhouse. Both players and landlord had reason to favour playing in the rain, since presumably a higher proportion of the audience would then head for the costlier but sheltered seating on the gallery benches, though it must also have reduced the total numbers in the audience. The landlord, who presumably employed his own gatherers at the entrances to the galleries, took his half of the gallery receipts from his gatherers, and took his repayments for his loans to the company from the other half, the balance of which went to the company. For both beneficiaries the regularity of this income, of course, depended on the freedom to play in London. Henslowe offers no evidence about the income and expenditure from travelling.

[37] Neil Carson, *A Companion to Henslowe's Diary* (Cambridge, 1988), 55, thinks the working practices of the Admiral's were typical of the major companies. Roslyn Knutson, *The Repertory of Shakespeare's Company 1594–1613*, 19, takes the same view.

[38] Knutson, ibid., 24.

The figures for expenditure are a little more reliable than the income figures. In the period when Henslowe acted as banker to the Admiral's Men, their outlay on properties, including costumes, and playbooks was heavy. The totals in Henslowe amount to £32 in the spring and summer of 1596, after two years of good times. In the latter half of 1598, with the Pembroke's crisis well past, they took from Henslowe £142 in loans for properties and payments to writers.[39] These figures may be a better indicator of the financial health of a company at a given time than the takings, since the sharers must have judged the wisdom of investment in either playbooks or costumes by the current state of their finances as much as by their prospects for a prosperous future.

The most striking and potentially the most confusing aspect of the finances was the value that was given to a company share. A sharer had to buy his way into a company, and the price he paid for doing so amounted to the company's own subjective valuation of its worth, in resources and status. The value of a Queen's Men's share in 1592 appears to have been £80, to judge from the will of one of its players, Simon Jewell.[40] A Chamberlain's Men's share in 1596 was probably the same as the Admiral's, at £50. By the 1630s it must have been considerably higher, since the return by then on a King's Men's share could be as high as £180 each year. Values fluctuated drastically. Francis Henslowe borrowed £15 from his uncle in 1593 to help him buy a share in the Queen's Men. When Richard Jones and Robert Shaw left the Admiral's in 1602 the Henslowe papers record a payment to them of £50, which suggests that the company's valuation was then £25. In 1612 Queen Anne's Men paid £80 to a departing sharer, and in 1613 the Admiral's successors, the Prince's Men, paid £70. William Bankes paid £100 to become a sharer in Prince Charles's (II) Company in the 1630s.[41]

Company Management

The most obvious limit to the information that can be taken from the Henslowe papers is that principally they record only the financial transactions. Moreover, the essential 'Diary' is a record of the transactions relating only to the Rose, not the Fortune, although papers belonging to the later period do appear amongst Alleyn's relics at Dulwich College. The information available from these papers is also restricted by the change, or changes, that took place in Henslowe's functions in relation to the companies occupying his playhouses. From 1592 till the new arrangement of 1594 he operated solely as landlord to the different companies that used the Rose. From 1594 to 1597 he continued in that function with the one company that now had secure tenure there. He also extended his money lending

[39] Carson, *Companion*, 102–17, gives a complete table of the Admiral's Men's production expenses from 1596 to 1601.

[40] See Mary Edmond, 'Pembroke's Men', *RES* (n.s.), 25 (1974), 129–36; and Scott McMillin, 'Simon Jewell and the Queen's Men', *RES* 27 (1976), 174–7.

[41] G. E. Bentley, *The Profession of Player in Shakespeare's Time*, 29.

activities to them. Then, after complications that followed the breakaway of some Admiral's Men to Pembroke's in the summer of that year, the mode of operation between Henslowe and the Admiral's sharers changed. From the autumn of 1597 Henslowe worked with the Admiral's much less in the role of landlord and much more as their banker or bank manager.[42] The long and stable tenure of the Admiral's at the Rose brought a much closer relationship between Henslowe and the players than had been evident before in his dealings, apart from Alleyn's marriage to his stepdaughter. His grief at Gabriel Spencer's death by Ben Jonson's hand in 1598, his possible involvement in the commissioning of new plays,[43] and his interest-free loans to individual players as well as to the sharers, are points about his intimacy with the players that offset the complaints of a later group of players, voiced in the notorious 'articles of grievance' which the Lady Elizabeth's Men laid down against him in 1614.

Henslowe had invested heavily in his playhouse in 1587. No information about the companies that used it before 1592 exists, and indeed there is only one hint that it actually was used at all through those years before the enlargement that followed the arrival of Alleyn and Strange's Men in February 1592.[44] Its early use was probably intermittent, if the evidence about the major companies such as the Queen's shifting from one inn or playhouse to another up to 1594 carries much weight. Until the Privy Council designated specific playhouses for the leading companies, as they appear to have done for the first time in 1594, no playhouse owner could have acted as much more than a landlord to the itinerant companies who occupied their playhouses so transiently. Henslowe's main additional function, so far as it can be deduced from the tantalizingly unclear hints in the *Diary*, was the possession of a set of playbooks which he loaned along with his playhouse to the visiting companies. Unfortunately despite the precision of his financial records there is nothing to say whether he rented such playbooks out or whether they were freely available with the playhouse.[45]

No note of any special payments for such loans of plays appears in the *Diary*, so we can only infer that the recurrence of the same play when it was performed by different companies was as a loan from the landlord, and the absence of any note of

[42] For different interpretations of the dealings recorded in the *Diary*, see *Henslowe's Diary*, xxiv–xl; Carol Chillington Rutter (ed.), *Documents of the Rose Playhouse* 101, 122–3; Carson, *Companion*, 6–8, 15–18.

[43] The sole hint I have found to suggest that Henslowe was himself a keen playgoer is the reference to 'perce of exstone' in 1598 (*Diary*, 88), subject for a play that seems never to have been written. It could have made a subject for a play to rival Shakespeare's *Richard II* in the other company's repertoire. See Gurr, 'Intertextuality in Henslowe', *SQ* 39 (1988), 394–8.

[44] There is no mention at all of the first Rose being used except for a Privy Council order of 29 Oct. 1587, and it only notes that plays were being performed on Sundays in Southwark. It does not specify the Rose, then the only playhouse on the Bankside, although since the inns used for playing were in the city the complaint must have fitted either the Rose or its more southerly companion the Newington Butts playhouse.

[45] Scott McMillin considers that Henslowe owned no playbooks, and that *The Jew of Malta* and others recurring in his records with different companies were the property of his son-in-law. ('Sussex's Men in 1594: The Evidence of *Titus Andronicus* and *The Jew of Malta*', *Theatre Survey*, 32 (1991), 214–23; and see Ch. 4, n. 42).

payment must make that doubtful. Henslowe instituted a system of recording loans after 1597 which makes the absence of any notes about lending his plays before 1594 all the more suspect. Apart from the inference from recurring play-titles, the main hint is in a list of playbooks in the Admiral's Men's stock, made in 1598, that survives only in a copy made at the end of the eighteenth century.[46] The list may be of Alleyn's or possibly the company's own possessions rather than Henslowe's. Besides seventeen titles bought for the company, it includes plays acquired from the short-lived Pembroke's in 1597, five bought as a block from Martin Slater, and some unknown titles. It omits such regulars as *Faustus* and Chapman's 'comedy of umors', (*An Humorous Day's Mirth*), and quite a few of the recent purchases. Ownership of the playbooks that a company might perform was evidently not a simple matter. What makes it difficult to interpret with any confidence is the absence of any indication in the *Diary* that the various owners, including the playhouse landlord if he was one, ever received any payment in return for the use of their playbooks. The *Diary* is most baffling in the things it fails to record.

The latter period of the different phases it deals with, 1597–1600, offers the best evidence for the management system that evolved when playing was stabilized and fixed at specific playhouses after 1594. How widely it can be seen as representing a standard working relationship between the sharers of a company and their financier is impossible to say, because there is hardly any other evidence about company management except for fragments of evidence from lawsuits, which are rarely impartial in their accounts of the traditional practices. The evidence from Henslowe's middle period, when he shifted from the role of landlord to that of bank manager, is distinctive in its systematic record of a successful and enduring system. Given the influence of the Henslowe-Alleyn partnership on at least two of the three later adult companies in Jacobean times and after, it does not seem unreasonable to use it as a basic model for the whole period after 1594.

Before Henslowe, the sharers managed all the company's affairs. After his time, landlords and managers such as the ex-players Christopher Beeston and Richard Gunnell took on the more directly managerial role that seems to have been evolving in Henslowe's last years, to judge by his conflict with the Lady Elizabeth's Men. But the process of change was gradual and piecemeal. Some Caroline companies appear to have maintained a version of the old collective-sharing principle, some allowed their leading players to become their managers and controllers, while others submitted themselves to the control of a Beeston or Gunnell.[47] Henslowe's middle-period position, backed by the day-by-day record of his activities, has features that mark both the older system of sharer control and the subsequent growth of landlord-impresario control.

Henslowe's records show that through this middle period in routine matters of company work, almost all of them manifested in authorizations for payments, he

---

[46] The copy was made by Malone, and published in his 1790 Shakespeare edn. For an analysis of the list, see Carson, *Companion*, 49.

[47] An account of the leading 'managers' is in Bentley, *The Profession of Player*, 147–76.

took orders from two of the principal sharers. In 1597, when Alleyn retired from playing and therefore from his sharership, they were Robert Shaw (Shaa), one of the Pembroke refugees, and Thomas Downton. In 1599 Samuel Rowley replaced Downton. He had only become a sharer in 1597 after the Pembroke fracas, having been a hired man before that. As a player and writer he had a strong influence on company policy in these years. Subsequently, when the Fortune came into operation, Alleyn returned and became chief authorizer along with Downton. It was standard to have two sharers giving authorization, a practice the neglect of which caused the same company trouble in its later years as Queen Anne's Men. One feature of the lawsuit that Susan Greene, a sharer's widow, brought against them in 1623 was the way Christopher Beeston had taken over sole control of company finances, apparently more to his personal profit than the company's.[48] The players deposed that they had 'put the managing of their whole businesses and affaires belonging unto them jointly as they were players in trust' into Beeston's hands, a policy they now regretted.[49]

The System of Sharing

The system of shares and sharers in a playhouse company was complex, and inevitably it altered as time went on. The main changes appear to have been in the numbers of sharers, the decision-making processes that grew in a collaborative system where a group of eight or ten men shared the workload, the costs of investments and production, and the profits. Changes came about chiefly as the practice of playing in London stabilized. The major change came after the Privy Council fixed certain companies at certain playhouses. This strengthened the position of the landlords at the designated playhouses, but it also created an incentive for strong companies to acquire playhouses of their own.[50] The question of sharer control and finance in several companies in later years is complicated by the innovation the Chamberlain's Men introduced in 1599, when several sharers became part-owners of the company's playhouse. Other companies imitated them in later years, but the later records are made difficult to analyze by uncertainty as to whether a particular 'share' was the traditional piece of company capital or part-ownership of a playhouse. A playhouse share was tangible, of reasonably fixed value, and could be bequeathed or sold like any other property. A company share was less tangible, simultaneously an investment expecting a recurrent dividend and part of the collective goodwill that made the company work successfully. A player

[48] For details of the lawsuit, see C. J. Sisson, 'Notes on Early Stuart Stage History', *MLR* 37 (1942), 25–36, esp. 30–6.

[49] Ibid. 34.

[50] Susan Cerasano's, 'The Business of Shareholding, the Fortune Playhouses, and Francis Grace's Will', *MRDE* 2 (1985), 231–52, while it is sensibly sceptical of the assumption that sharing was a uniform practice based on a mercantile model, does not make the necessary distinction between company and playhouse shares.

who was a sharer might expect to recoup his investment if he left the company amicably, and his widow when he died might expect to get his capital returned to her. A share in a playhouse could be held outside the company. It could be inherited, or broken into part-shares. The two kinds of share had their resemblances, but they ran to different rules. Confusion is easy when it was a player who had both kinds of share.

Henslowe's notes suggest that the sharers in a company generally worked together, without any firm or consistent division of labour or finances.[51] Some players owned their own costumes, for instance, while others were company property. Individual players had their own boys working as apprentices. But company policy over the purchase of costumes and properties, acceptance of finished playbooks, and presumably the sequence of plays chosen for performance, was decided collectively. All the authorizations for payment came from the company as a whole, whoever supplied the actual signatures. The sharers as a group never acknowledged any single player as their leader, even Alleyn. How widely this system of operation and co-operative management was spread is difficult to see. It must have varied widely with the individual chemistry of each group. Some companies, possibly most of them, delegated control of their finances to one sharer, as the King's Men eventually did to John Heminges. Other company functions were less easily isolated from the collective processes of decision-making and co-operation within the group.

The number of sharers in a company varied over the years, growing from as few as six in the 1560s to twelve in 1583 for the Queen's, a number that other companies came to match in subsequent years. The splitting of shares into halves and quarters increased the number of playing sharers without increasing the company's capitalization. Ten or twelve was the number of shares in the leading companies under James. In the prime years of Henslowe's *Diary*, the years of the 'large' company plays, the Admiral's Men had ten sharers. All ten signed a promissory note to Henslowe in 1598: they were William Bird, Thomas Downton, Humphrey Jeffes, Richard Jones, Charles Massey, Samuel Rowley, Robert Shaw, John Singer, Gabriel Spencer, and Thomas Towne.[52] Since a share was technically an investment in the company's finances, it was possible to buy a half-share, or even a quarter-share. Humphrey Jeffes stepped up from hired-man status to become a half-sharer in the Admiral's in January 1598. He became a full sharer some time later.

The managerial work of the sharers must have been deeply committed to day-by-day organization: making sure enough new plays were moving through the pipeline, getting rehearsals under way, preparing the week's schedule of plays to be

---

[51] A fairly comprehensive survey of the information about sharers is in Bentley, *The Profession of Player*, 25–63.

[52] *Henslowe's Diary*, 87. It has been thought that the designation 'mr' in the *Diary* and in the surviving 'plots' signifies a sharer. If so, either Henslowe was inconsistent in awarding the title or the sharers changed their shares much more rapidly than the evidence says.

performed, the playbills written and posted up, and ensuring that the costumes and properties were on hand, as well as checking the staging details for that day's play in each morning's rehearsal period. Writers usually submitted their script in piecemeal form, and it is not clear exactly at what stage in the delivery process the company signified its acceptance. The sharers decided on a script's worth as a group. Henslowe notes five shillings on the company's account to cover costs at the Sun inn in New Fish Street on 13 March 1598, 'for to spend at the Readynge of that boocke', a script by Drayton, Dekker, and Chettle of a play about Henry I.[53] From acceptance to performance involved a lot of collective decisions. Judging from the book-keeper's 'plots' that have survived in the Henslowe papers the sharers themselves did not automatically take all the leading speaking roles, so the work of allocating parts and controlling the work of the hired men must have been another regular duty.

One document preserved in the Dulwich College archives gives a graphic picture of the constraints on the sharers' and hired men's conduct of their business. As he took on a more directly managerial and controlling role under James, Henslowe began to draw up contracts that he required new players to sign. The paper of an 'agreement' with Robert Dawes, signed on 7 April 1614, is one such. It was to run for three years, with Dawes as holder of one full share in the Lady Elizabeth's company. He was required to attend all rehearsals, which would have been announced the previous night, on a penalty of a shilling (payable to Henslowe) for late arrival and two for each rehearsal he missed. He should be dressed and ready to perform each playing afternoon unless licensed to the contrary by six other sharers, on a penalty of three shillings. If he was judged to be drunk at playing time in the opinion of four sharers, he would pay a fine of ten shillings. If he failed to turn up at all for a performance without either a licence from the sharers or the excuse of illness he would pay a pound and also forfeit to Henslowe his share of the gallery takings. He was also forbidden to wear any of the company's apparel outside the playhouse, on a penalty of £40.[54] Performing needed teamwork, and every sharer shared the responsibility for the team's success.

The amount of income which sharers might expect to receive for their work inevitably varied widely. A hired man could expect a fixed wage, but the sharer's profit depended on the company's success both at maintaining a long run of uninterrupted performances and in attracting large numbers to the plays. A hired man's weekly takings usually ran at between five and ten shillings a week.[55] In 1598, judging by Henslowe's figures, those of an Admiral's Company sharer varied from seven to twenty-six.[56] As a measure of comparison we might take Dekker's income in his first years as a writer for Henslowe, when he secured roughly £20 a year. It

[53] Ibid. 88.

[54] The complete contract, which is in the Henslowe papers, not the *Diary*, is quoted in *ES* ii. 255–7.

[55] Bentley, *The Profession of Player*, 106–12, cites the evidence for hired men's wages, concluding that they fluctuated along with the company's financial health.

[56] Carson, *Companion*, 42.

was hardly a generous rate of pay, though it was a living wage. The sharers generally did rather better than the writers.

One other function that some sharers took on needs a comment. The boys used for special roles including women and children seem always to have been contracted to specific players, in bonds involving some form of contract rather like that of a trade apprenticeship.[57] It was not the kind of regulated seven-year contract that the guild companies operated, though it did have a rough parallel in that a successful boy player, like an apprentice turning journeyman, might expect eventually to graduate into the profession as an adult player. The laws for trade apprenticeships did not admit apprentices at the age the companies needed for their boys. The average starting age for a London apprentice in the livery companies was 17.7 years.[58] The Statute of 1563 fixed the minimum age for completing an apprenticeship at 24. Neither the starting nor the completing ages suited the players, who required younger boys with unbroken voices. So the playing-company needs called for a system that in no way conformed to the livery-companies' regular apprenticeships. Still, most of the players known to have taken on apprentices were members of one or other of the livery companies. James Burbage was a member of the Carpenters, John Heminges a member of the Grocers, John Shank a Weaver, Thomas Downton a Vintner, Robert Armin and John Lowin Goldsmiths. They may have exploited their trade membership to justify their playing contracts with their boys. A will made by Elizabeth Holland in 1631 left forty shillings to 'Arthur Savill Apprentize unto Mr Cayne Gooldsmyth'.[59] Both Savill and Cane had parts in *Holland's Leaguer* at the Salisbury Court playhouse that year, but Mrs Holland identified Cane as a goldsmith, not a player.

The difficulty with the theory that livery-company membership was used to authorize the playing apprenticeships is that some players who certainly had apprentices, notably Augustine Phillips, are not known to have been members of any company. Henslowe's payments given to the employer-players for their apprentices' services to the company seem to support a reading of the regrettably sketchy evidence that indicates an attempt to make the apprentice system look respectable by relating it to the formal city apprenticeships. By no means all sharers had boys. Those who did presumably offered their services training their boys for playing as a distinctive and individual contribution to the company's affairs.

The Repertory System

Henslowe's notes about the companies that stayed any length of time at the Rose show similar patterns in their operations. They played when possible for six afternoons each week, Sundays only excepted, and staged a different play each

[57] The main evidence for this is gathered in Bentley, *The Profession of Player*, 113–26.
[58] S. Rappaport, *Worlds within Worlds: Structures of Life in Sixteenth-Century London*, 295, Table 8. 2.
[59] Quoted in *Playhouse Wills 1558–1642*, 3.

afternoon. The best money came from performing on holidays, although generally Sundays and Lent were accepted as times that were embargoed for playing, the only breaks from playing the players had in the entire year. It was a uniquely demanding schedule. The most popular plays had runs which at most brought them on stage once a week. Two-part plays would run on successive days. Sequels and spin-offs were a regular feature in most repertories, whether it was *2 Henry IV* following *1 Henry IV* or *Every Man Out* following *Every Man In*; and the sequels usually had to be played along with repeats of the original play.[60] Every two weeks or so a new play would appear. These, at higher admission prices, almost always brought higher takings than did repeat performances, so that the players were constantly under pressure to offer new plays. Not many plays stayed in the repertory very far beyond their first year.[61] Strange's and the other companies playing at the Rose between 1592 and 1594 mostly brought their own plays, but enough titles of popular plays (*The Jew of Malta, Friar Bacon, Orlando Furioso*) recur with different companies to suggest that Henslowe himself held the best plays. Possession of playbooks, and access to new playbooks, was a major priority for the sharers.

The most extraordinary feature of the repertory was its huge appetite. Quite apart from the provision of six different plays each week, the rate at which new plays were introduced suggests that the need for novelty dominated everything. In the first nine months of their operations in 1594–5 the Admiral's Men staged seventeen new plays, at a rate of roughly one a fortnight. In 1595–6 they produced seven new plays in fifteen weeks. In 1596–7 it was five in eleven weeks. This, of course, was at a peak in company growth and operations. For the first time they had Privy-Council backing and a fixed London playhouse, and for six or more years they had an outstandingly profitable run of performances. There was progress still to come: royal patronage, four approved companies instead of two (though that might not have been seen as progress by the individual companies), better playhouses, and a return to the city with hall playhouses. But this was the first period when it seemed possible to satisfy London's appetite for new plays, so the playwriting teams were kept hard at work. This was the time when the richest resources of playbooks were being built up. Later companies were able to live much more off revivals and the old favourites that first began to establish themselves in this initial period. By the 1630s even the King's Men were not buying more than three or four new plays a year, compared with the twenty or more of the 1590s.

The speed of the whole operation of mounting a new play is graphically demonstrated in Henslowe's records. Pre-rehearsal preparations might run for no more than two or three weeks, which would include the reading and formal acceptance of a text, casting the roles and annotating the playbook and getting it licensed by the

[60] See Knutson, *The Repertory of Shakespeare's Company*, 51–2, 73.
[61] Knutson, *The Repertory of Shakespeare's Company*, in a generally cogent summary of Henslowe's evidence for repertory playing (26–55), notes that only 5 out of 52 plays stood in the repertory for more than 12 months (33).

Master of the Revels, transcribing all the 'parts', getting costumes and special properties ready, and running through the play itself in rehearsal.[62] It rarely took much more than three weeks from acceptance of a new script to its first performance. Most of the company's rehearsal time seems to have gone into the new plays. Judging by the 'plots' old plays, even when they were revised, simply came back in the shape of the original working-through of the play into performance.

The Writers

The pressures that were laid on the company and its 'bank manager'[63] by the demand for new plays show up most strongly in the period after 1596, when Henslowe established his new system of loans and repayments for the two principal capital investments that the company needed, costumes and playbooks. Playwriting was chiefly a collective exercise. In 1598 82 per cent of the plays bought for the company were written in collaboration.[64] Altogether, only 34 plays of the 89 that Henslowe paid for in full on behalf of the Admiral's were by single authors.[65] The standard price for a play was £6. The amount paid to writers came to roughly half the value of the costumes acquired in the same period. The writers themselves came from all directions. Some, like Jonson and Thomas Heywood, began as players before they started writing. Old stalwarts like Munday were joined by vigorous younger men like Dekker and Chettle, and occasionally older writers who had previously been chiefly concerned to write poetry now turned their hands to the stage, like Chapman. Dropouts from the Inns of Court like John Day also came into collaborative work. Collaboration involved teams of as many as four writers, dividing the work by acts or scenes once the basic story-line was agreed with the sharers. All the writers must have been driven to write quickly by the urgent need for new plays. First the chief collaborator produced a 'plot' or outline of the story, then sections of the script were assigned to individual writers, and finally the 'book' would be delivered to the sharers for a reading.[66] Payment went in stages according to the delivery of the 'plot' and each act.

The Properties and Other Assets

Besides the goodwill registered in the price of a share, the two assets every company had to have were their stock of playbooks and their wardrobe. On the evidence of the inventories in the Henslowe papers the basic costumes and apparel, hats,

---

[62] For instances of specific rehearsal schedules, see Carson, *Companion*, 74
[63] The term is Rutter's, *Documents*, 102.   [64] Carson, *Companion*, 57.
[65] Rutter, *Documents*, 128.
[66] The closest study of the collaborative process as evidenced in the *Diary* is in Carson, *Companion*, 58–66.

jerkins, doublet and hose, seem to have been the players' own. There are a few pieces of ordinary daily wear noted in the inventories, but certainly not enough to equip a whole company of players for a performance. The stock of special costumes in Henslowe's records and the purchases made between 1597 and 1600 seem to have been provided only for special plays and special effects. There are more women's gowns, for instance, than men's cloaks or doublets, and there are costumes for specific roles such as churchmen or Robin Hood's men ('vj grene cottes'), or Henry VIII's clown, Will Summers. Most of the items relate to specific plays. There is even one intriguing costume recorded as 'Eves bodeyes'.

The amounts that Henslowe disbursed on behalf of the Admiral's during his bank-managership period, 1597–1600, varied in the totals between playbooks and apparel. In the summer of 1598 he paid £37 for eight plays, and £45 for special costumes of different kinds. At this time the amount for costumes was roughly twice the amount for plays.[67] In 1599 the amount for plays exceeded that for costumes, though the balance was restored in 1600.

Licensing

One of the more puzzling sets of records in Henslowe's papers is his payments to the Master of the Revels. They start at the beginning, in 1592, when he paid Tilney five shillings a week, a sum which rose gradually through that year. Then the payments vanish until 1595, when there are some cryptic entries about things 'lycensed', but no indication of or for what. At the end of February 1596 a note reports 'the master of the Revelles payd untell this time al wch I owe hime'. The main difficulty is in working out what these payments were for. The weekly payments in 1592 would most likely have been for the playhouse to be licensed, and the 1595–6 payments may have been for the same purpose. If so, they were landlord's entries, not the company's banker kind which appear from 1597 onwards. But no note of any payments to the Revels Office appear in this later period, either for the playhouse or the licensing of playbooks. The absence of these records seems to indicate that presumably they were matters for the sharers and did not involve sums large enough to need loans from Henslowe.

It is certainly easiest to see this item of Henslowe evidence as showing only playhouse licensing, which involved sums varying from five to ten shillings for each week when the Rose was in use.[68] These charges only appeared in the periods when plays were running. When plague took the companies out of London no fees were paid. This early system is perhaps a reflection of the uncertain length of tenure and continuity that the companies had at the various playhouses up to 1594. After the Rose became an officially approved playhouse Henslowe made payments covering longer periods, fortnightly or monthly. In October 1598 he paid £6 to cover a

[67] Rutter, *Documents*, 152.   [68] See Carson, *Companion*, 17–18.

three-month period. This was not slackness, but confidence in the licensing process and the status of the Rose as an approved playing-place. Other playhouse owners were a good deal less scrupulous in paying their fees than was Henslowe. In 1606 Tilney took Cuthbert and Richard Burbage to court to secure an arrears of £100 dating back to 1595 for his charges in licensing their company's playhouses.[69]

The *Diary* also records a fee of seven shillings for licensing new plays for performance. This source of income for the Master of the Revels was enlarged in later years. It went up to a standard £1 from the 1620s under Henry Herbert, and in 1632 to £2 for a new play or £1 for a revival. In about 1606 George Buc, waiting for the dead man's shoes of the Mastership to revert to him, added a licence for permitting plays to be printed to the existing licensing for performance.[70] After the Restoration, when there was nothing to stop him making inflated claims, Herbert reckoned that the annual company fees alone had brought him £400 a year. Against this should be set the £20 a year that we know he gained from 1633 onwards from the King's Men, paid in two instalments at Christmas and midsummer.

[69] I am grateful to Mary Edmond for drawing my attention to a lawsuit in the Court of Common Pleas (CP40/1749, mem. 735), in which Tilney sued the Burbages for non-payment.

[70] See N. W. Bawcutt, 'New Revels Documents of Sir George Buc and Sir Henry Herbert, 1619–1662', *RES* 35 (1984), 316–31; and Dutton, *Mastering the Revels*, 193. Dutton gives further consideration to the evidence for the Blackfriars Boys being unlicensed in 'Ben Jonson and the Master of the Revels', in *Theatre and Government Under the Early Stuarts*, ed. J. R. Mulryne and Margaret Shewring (Cambridge, 1993), 57–86, 71.

6 The Changes of 1603

Amongst the inferences that it seems reasonable to make from the hints thrown out by the Privy Council in the years after the great settlement of 1594, one of the most potent for the players is the new policy over playing-places in the London area. Up to 1594 the companies that were 'at home' in London had to use a multitude of venues for their performances. The Queen's Men are known to have played at different times at all the city inns that were used for plays and at every one of the amphitheatres, the Theatre, the Curtain, and the Rose.[1] At one time or another they used every venue available in London. There is nothing to tell what governed this spread of activity, except the fact of the playhouses being built in the suburbs outside the direct jurisdiction of the city, the location of the inns inside that jurisdiction, and the evident preference of the companies to play inside the city whenever they could, rather than in the suburbs.[2] It also took time for the expectation of travelling to give place to the expectation of playing in only one venue indefinitely.

It does appear that the players preferred to use the inns (especially those which offered not galleried open-air yards like the amphitheatres but rooms with roofs) and did so as much as they could, especially in winter, just because of the seasonal changes in the weather and the hours of available daylight, and that the large-capacity suburban playhouses were their fall-back. The events of 1594–6 and James Burbage's attempt in the latter year to replace his old Theatre with a city hall to play in seem to confirm the idea that in their early years of playing in London the companies had acquired such a preference. The agreement drawn up in 1594 between the Privy Councillors and the Lord Mayor prescribed specific playhouses for the two approved companies and banned any further use of inns inside the city, as if both authorities knew where the players would go if they were left free to do so. James Burbage's response was to build a new playhouse inside the city in a liberty. It was an attempt to restore access to roofed playing-places in the city without actually breaking the terms of the new agreement. That tactical preference was no doubt influenced by the fact that players had been used to indoor venues outside London for decades. When guildhalls were not available in towns like Bristol or Leicester for playing they used inns. A Bristol inn was converted into a playhouse in 1604, and others had been changed earlier in York and Lancashire. The trend was strongly in the one indoor direction; to a considerable degree the building of the Globe and Fortune might have been seen by the companies as a retrograde step.

[1] See Ch. 2, n. 6.
[2] For some debatable comments on the link between the marginality of playing and of playing-places in London, see Stephen Mullaney, *The Place of the Stage: License, Play, and Power in Renaissance England.*

The most obvious reason for Burbage to build a new playhouse was that his lease of the Theatre's land was shortly to expire. The landlord was refusing any extension of the lease, and a new playhouse would be necessary. What was most challenging about Burbage's choice was that instead of building another suburban amphitheatre he built a hall theatre, and set it inside the city like the inns that had just been taken away from the players. The neighbours of the new Blackfriars playhouse forced the postponement of that grand plan for another thirteen years, but it remained as a dream, an improved version of the old life. When in 1608 the company led by the Burbage sons repossessed the Blackfriars playhouse, they set up a system of operation which in effect renewed the old tradition. For the King's Servants to play in summer at their open amphitheatre and in winter at their roofed venue from 1609 enacted an ideal version of what they had been used to before 1594. It was ideal (and extravagant) in that they were now actual owners of both kinds of venue, and could have unrestricted access to both.

The full story of the Chamberlain's and King's Men's commitment to the Blackfriars hall-playhouse belongs in the chapter on the Chamberlain's Men. A summary of the story is appropriate here, however, for the light it throws on this step in the progress the two approved companies were making after 1594 towards a firm place in London. James Burbage first hatched his plan in 1596, as his lease of the Theatre's land drew to its end. Possibly he drew up the plan with Henry Carey's connivance. A new playhouse in the Blackfriars liberty would not technically flout Carey's agreement with the Lord Mayor to forbid playing inside the mayor's territory. But Carey died in July 1596, and any support he might have offered for Burbage's plan was not matched by the new Lord Chamberlain, Cobham, nor by Carey's son who became the company's new patron when his father died, nor (probably) by Howard, who was still concerned to implement the policy that had created the duopoly. The new Chamberlain was in fact called on as a Blackfriars resident who would be harmed by the new playhouse, in a petition of protest which the neighbours drew up in November 1596. The petition was directed to the Lord Chamberlain and the Privy Council, and it was signed by a Blackfriars resident, George Carey, who was the company's new patron. The Privy Council, with Charles Howard there to uphold the old policy, was not to be moved. Its apparently anomalous action in July 1597, a year after George Carey had been made Chamberlain, when it ordered all playhouses to be pulled down, must be seen as a further sign, however oblique its signalling, that it was determined to maintain its new policy.

The Privy Council order of 28 July 1597 banning playing and ordering the closure and demolition of all the playhouses has caused much debate.[3] Its apparent lack of consistency with Carey's and Howard's already well-implemented policy is one question. Its relation to the Pembroke's company's trouble over *The Isle of Dogs*

---

[3] See Glynne Wickham, *Early English Stages 1300–1660*, ii. 2: 9–29; William Ingram, 'The Closing of the Theaters in 1597: A Dissenting View', *MP* 69 (1971–2), 105–15; Rutter, *Documents of the Rose Playhouse*, 118–25.

that same July is another. The third is the rather odd record of Henslowe's doings in his *Diary* in relation to the ban and to the Pembroke's company. Henslowe, the Burbage heirs, and the Privy Councillors of course all had a vested interest to defend, Henslowe even more than Burbage, because Langley's Swan, where the Pembroke's men set up to play, was on the Rose's doorstep. The Burbage sons were in no position to do anything, since both of their own playhouses were closed and their inherited capital was locked up in their father's abortive attempt to create the new hall. I suspect that the main opposition to Langley came from Henslowe, and the Privy Council's action in 1597 was either a ham-fisted response to his appeals for help, or else an exceptionally ingenious manœuvre which he knew about in advance. The Privy Councillors had the power, and we can only assume that they got what they really wanted, whatever the ostensible aim of the order. All that we can be sure of is the bare sequence of events, and their consequences.

So far as Henslowe was concerned the story started in February 1597. In that month Langley made an agreement with Pembroke's that they would play at the Swan. Five Pembroke's men gave Langley a surety of £100 each to guarantee that they would play at his playhouse for twelve months. The Pembroke's players were not by any means new to London. Four of the five guarantors had until recently been along the lane at the Rose as Admiral's men, a loss which explains why for three weeks from 12 February the Admiral's did not play. Robert Shaw, William Bird, Richard Jones, and Thomas Downton were the four who left Henslowe and Alleyn's company for Pembroke's, where they joined up with Humphrey Jeffes and Gabriel Spencer. Those two had probably been members of the original Pembroke's in 1592 (a 'Gabriel' was in the Pembroke's *2 Henry VI*, and a 'Humfrey' in *3 Henry VI*). Spencer, with the four ex-Admiral's Men, put up the five sureties for Langley. Pembroke's Men then started playing at the Swan. After four years of travelling and the loss of their 1593 plays they obviously needed new material to satisfy London's appetite, and one of their new offerings soon got them into trouble.

The Isle of Dogs, written by the brilliantly notorious 'English Aretino', Thomas Nashe, and a then-unknown player in the company, Ben Jonson, brought their downfall for its 'seditious' contents at the Privy Council's intervention. It may not, however, have been the immediate occasion for the general ban. That seems rather to have been prompted by a letter from the Lord Mayor, making the standard complaint, and written on the same day as the Council's order, 28 July. It argued that plays are 'neither in politie nor in religion . . . to be suffered in a Christian Commonwealth', and asked for 'the present staie & fynall suppressinge of the saide Stage playes, aswell at the Theatre, Curten and banckside, as in all other places in and abowt the Citie'. The Council issued their order to the justices of Middlesex and Surrey in a form of words that seem to make use of the Lord Mayor's complaint. It banned playing until October ('Allhalloutide next') and specified that the Curtain and the Theatre in Shoreditch, and 'the playhouses in the Banckside, in Southwarke or elswhere in the said county within iij miles of London' should be destroyed.[4] The order was quite specific. The Justices were to 'plucke downe quite the stages, gallories and roomes that are made for people to stand in, and so to deface the same as they may not be ymploied agayne to suche use'. It has been suggested that the Council, which that day met at Greenwich, could not have received the Lord Mayor's letter, written in the city on the same day, but the wording is similar and the coincidence is remarkable. I think the Council knew what it was doing. The only question is how far they expected the order to be obeyed, and how closely it really focused on Langley and the Swan, intruders on the Council's policy of running only two companies at two playhouses. The plural 'playhouses' specified on the Bankside firmly identifies the Swan as well as the Rose.

At the Greenwich meeting eight Councillors were present: the Secretary, Robert Cecil, the Lord Keeper, the Lord Treasurer, Lord North, Lord Buckhurst, and the Comptroller, together with Howard and George Carey, Lord Admiral and Lord Chamberlain. Two of these councillors had set up the deal of 1594 with the then Lord Mayor. The promptness of the Council's reaction on 28 July may be a sign of their anger at the breach in this accord that the Lord Mayor's letter signalled. What is less clear is how wide the salvo was meant to spread. Cecil already had Langley in his sights for his dealings over a large diamond that had been landed as part of a privateer's haul of loot from the Spanish, and which Cecil was trying to retrieve for the crown. George Carey and Howard had no brief for Langley either, since he had broken the agreement over the two companies. And yet the order is precise in demanding that the Theatre and the Rose be demolished as well as the Swan. Here we can only guess how much the two patrons knew about the current state of their companies' affairs, because the Theatre had been out of use for three months by 28 July.[5] The Burbages might have thought the order to destroy their old amphitheatre would be a way to secure the use of their new hall theatre, which the Council had forbidden them in November of the previous year. Henslowe might have thought the loss of his four players and their reinstatement as nearby competitors needed a drastic solution.

In the event, *The Isle of Dogs* did that for him. In a notorious act of censorship (Day's *Isle of Gulls*, written nine years later for the Blackfriars Boys, explicitly alludes to the play and its well-known troubles) the Council called the play 'lewd', and 'contanynge very seditious and sclanderous matter', and used that characterization as the reason for their subsequent action of 15 August. This ordered the Pembroke's players to be imprisoned and got the spymaster Richard Topcliffe to scrutinize Nashe's papers, which the Council secured from his lodgings. Two of the players, Gabriel Spencer and Robert Shaw, were imprisoned, along with Jonson. Nashe escaped. The other players promptly returned to Henslowe, as if they knew they were safer there. He immediately made them sign new contracts of service with him. Spencer and Shaw were also signed up on their release from

---

[4] Quoted in *ES* iv. 321–3.   [5] See Ch. 16.

prison on 3 October. Henslowe did not even observe the ban of 28 July for its full run, because the Admiral's was back at the Rose with *The Spanish Tragedy* and 'the comodey of umers' by 11 October, three weeks before Hallowe'en, when he notes 'be gane my lord admerals & my lord of penbrockes men to playe at my howsse'.[6]

More than anything else what must have bound up the muscle-power behind these blunt instruments was the difference between ordering playing to stop and getting playhouses destroyed. The companies were vulnerable since they had to be licensed, but the buildings themselves were tangible pieces of property, and their destruction raised problems of legal title and compensation that the authorities never actually got round to testing. Henslowe may have been aware of the pitfalls, because he made good use of the July order and the *Isle of Dogs* trouble. They enabled him to put down his competitor, while nothing was done about any of the playhouses. The early resumption of playing at the Rose probably indicates that he thought the job had been thoroughly done, as much to the Council's satisfaction as his own.

The contracts that he forced the new arrivals from Pembroke's (Spencer and Jeffes) and the former Admiral's players (Bird, Downton, Jones, and Shaw) to sign were a precautionary measure, possibly stimulated by his knowledge of the bonds that Langley had taken from them for playing at the Swan. He certainly knew about the bonds later, because he records payments that he made over the lawsuits that Langley took out against the players. Conceivably he was aware that there was such a risk, and that was his reason for at first identifying his new company as a joint venture of the Admiral's and Pembroke's. Possibly he was also trying to secure a second playing licence for a reserve company. After only two entries including the Pembroke's name he reverted to calling them one company, the Admiral's. That a Pembroke's company reappeared soon after in the provincial records shows that the company's licence to play survived, but presumably not in Henslowe's hands.

The 1594 establishment of the two authorized companies and their playing-places took some time to make its effect felt on the companies themselves. Understandably they both wanted to protect their joint monopoly against intruders such as the 1597 Pembroke's Men. Since that company played at the Swan and included a number of players who had deserted the Admiral's at the nearby Rose, the brunt of the intrusion was felt by and acted on by Henslowe rather than the Burbages, who had troubles of their own with their playing-place at that time. Understandably too, the rivalry between the company using the Theatre and its temporary successor, the Curtain, in the north and the company using the Rose on Bankside made them poach on each other's successes, and try to match their repertories. These activities are reasonably well documented. What is much less apparent is the effect that this new security had on their thinking, and the consequent shifts in their practices.

---

[6] *Henslowe's Diary*, 60.

The secure tenure of an officially assigned playhouse was some compensation for the loss of the city inns in winter, and the accompanying hazard of mayoral wrath that went with such uses, although James Burbage went to considerable expense in his attempt to resurrect the practice. For its part the Privy Council certainly held on to its policy of two companies consistently into the last years of Elizabeth's reign. On 22 June 1600 it issued an order 'to restrain the excessive number of Plaie howses & the imoderate use of Stage plaies in & about the Cittye'. The order explicitly authorized the two companies' new playhouses, the Chamberlain's Globe and the Admiral's Fortune. It specified:

First, that there shall bee about the Cittie two howses and noe more allowed to serve for the use of the Common Stage plaies, of the which howses one shalbe in Surrey in that place which is Commonlie called the banckside or there abouts, and the other in Midlesex. And foras muche as there Lordshippes have bin enformed by Edmond Tylney Esquire, hir Majesties servant and Master of the Revells, that the howse now in hand to be builte by the said Edward Allen is not intended to encrease the number of the Plaiehowses, but to be in steed of an other, namelie the Curtaine, Which is either to be ruined and plucked downe or to be putt to some other good use, as also that the scituation thereof is meete and Convenient for that purpose. Yt is likewise ordered that the said howse of Allen shall be allowed to be one of the two howses, and namelie for the house to be alowed in Middlesex, soe as the house Called the Curtaine be (as yt is pretended) either ruinated or applied to some other good use. And for the other allowed to be on Surrey side, whereas [there Lordshipps are pleased to permitt] to the Companie of players that shall plaie there to make there owne Choice which they will have, Choosinge one of them and one more, [And the said Companie of Plaiers, being the Servantes of the L. Chamberlen, that are to plaie there have made choise of the house called the Globe, yt is ordered that the said house and none other shall be there allowed]. And especiallie yt is forbidden that anie stage plaies shalbe plaied (as sometimes they have bin) in any Common Inn for publique assemblie in or neare about the Cittie.

Secondlie, forasmuche as these stage plaies, by the multitude of houses and Companie of players, have bin too frequent, not serving for recreacion but inviting and Callinge the people daily from there trad and worke to mispend there time. It is likewise ordered that the two severall Companies of Plaiers assigned unto the two howses allowed maie play each of them in there severall howse twice a weeke and noe oftener, and especially that they shall refraine to play on the Sabboth daie, upon paine of imprisonment and further penaltie, and that they shall forbeare altogether in the time of Lent, and likewise at such time and times as anie extraordinarie sicknes or infeccion of disease shall appeare to be in and about the Cittie.[7]

This was largely a formal reaffirmation of the previous edicts, inserting the new playhouse names and reaffirming that the limit was two companies. The Council was ignoring the admission of Derby's and the two new boy companies to perform

[7] *Acts of the Privy Council of England*, xxx. 395; *MSC* i. 80; *ES* iv. 329–31. Jonson, in *Poetaster*, for the Blackfriars boy company in 1600, mocked the monopoly held by the two adult companies. A pair of adult players, Aesop, a 'politician', and Histrio, who in III. iv. 201 are linked with 'your *Globes*, and your *Triumphs*', in V. iii. 123–5 are rewarded with 'a *monopoly* of playing, confirm'd to thee and thy covey, under the Emperours broad seale, for this service', not a kindly reference. Quotations from Jonson's plays are taken from *Ben Jonson*, ed. C. H. Herford and P. and E. Simpson (11 vols.; Oxford, 1925–52).

at court the previous Christmas. The Curtain and the Rose in fact remained in use, the Rose for a brief stint by a third company before it was demolished, the Curtain on and off for another twenty-five years.

The times for daily playing may have shifted a little, if the Lord Chamberlain's undertaking to the Mayor in 1594 is anything to go by. Other practices, such as the traditional embargoes on playing on Sundays and Lent (and the companies' less-than-rigorous observation of the forty days of Lent) did not alter. The main changes came as the result more of economic forces than of governmental ones. Company sizes remained the same, although the number of ambitiously 'large' plays in the repertories shrank. Among playgoers the appetite for new plays grew. Only two things seem to have changed greatly under the post-1594 system. One, predictably, was the larger role that the company landlord was able to take now that he had the security of a single approved company's tenure of his property. Henslowe's shift from landlord to company banker is the best evidence for that, although Langley at the Swan with his bonds seems to have tried much the same thing, and the history of James Burbage's entrepreneurial financing of the companies is a long one copied in oblique ways by his sons. The other change began a much larger and more durable shift of priorities, though its signs are barely apparent in these first years: the attitude to travelling outside London, dealt with in Chapter 3.

The next changes that took place in the wake of the new policy of 1594 came in at least two separate steps. By far the larger was the transfer of the three leading companies into royal patronage in 1603. That process itself contains several enigmas but, as usual with the large policy decisions of this time, no record survives to indicate the thinking that prompted them. Within a month of James's arrival in London the Chamberlain's Men were awarded a patent as the King's Men. This was in May 1603, long before they might expect to be called on for the Christmas festivities. The other two adult companies were not chosen for royal patronage until the Christmas revels were actually under way, and the Blackfriars boy company was not taken up by Queen Anne until the end of the Christmas season. In the absence of explicit testimony, the only recourse now is to judge the reasons for these choices by assessing the situation before and after.

From the London angle the 1603 changes are at least partly explicable by the status of the four companies to whom royal patrons were allocated. The unknown factor is what knowledge the king himself brought to the situation from Edinburgh, and how active a part he might have taken himself in the decisions. In the 1602–3 Christmas season at court the Chamberlain's Men had taken prime position with the first performance of the season on St Stephen's Night, followed the next night by the Admiral's. Paul's Boys had taken the New Year's Day slot, then Hertford's had their one and only court appearance.[8] In the weeks up to Ash Wednesday the Admiral's performed twice more and the Chamberlain's once, altogether giving the

[8] See Ch. 17.

Admiral's three to the Chamberlain's two. The Blackfriars Boys did not perform at all. Nor did Worcester's, now moving into place as the third London company, and already affirmed as the third company with a right to play at the Boar's Head by a Privy Council order of 31 March 1602. Assuming that the Christmas 1603 choice of the companies to perform can be used as evidence for the Revels Office valuations, it seems that other factors were at work in the first Stuart king's choice of where to apply royal patronage.

If the court performances before Elizabeth's death mark the opinion of the Master of the Revels about each company's standing, it was clearly not he who advised James about what professional company the king might patronize in May 1603. By his valuation, the Admiral's was equal to and perhaps a little ahead of the Chamberlain's. The Chamberlain's gained prime position on St Stephen's Night, but the Admiral's probably had more new plays. The two companies that Queen Anne eventually took to herself, Worcester's and the Blackfriars Boys, were no-where. Hertford's, the third adult company to perform at court that Christmas, never gained a foothold in London, and the Paul's Boys remained as the cathedral group. Paul's were in a slightly anomalous position, distinguished for those with long memories by their long tradition, but uncomfortable in the new situation. In the event they did not manage to secure the status that went to the other four companies, and only ran for three more years.

One of the outside factors influencing the choice of the four might have been the status and interests of the old patrons of the three adult companies, but again the choices made do not closely match the standing that the three men had in 1603. Charles Howard and Worcester were the most powerful men, after Cecil, on the Privy Council. Howard retained his Lord Admiralship in the new court, and the newer figure, Worcester, Master of the Horse, also kept his Elizabethan post and strengthened his standing considerably. By contrast, George Carey had stopped attending Privy Council meetings through the previous year because of his poor health, and was to die later in 1603. He lost the Chamberlainship automatically when Elizabeth died, and his place as Chamberlain was given to Thomas Howard, soon to become earl of Suffolk. It is just conceivable that James took the company with the absentee patron for himself in order not to offend the other patrons who were still powerful. That, however, was not James's way in the excitements of 1603. It would be more plausible to read the evidence the other way: that the delay in giving the other two companies to the Prince and the Queen was because their powerful patrons, unlike Carey, clung on to them.

In the event the Chamberlain's Men were honoured uniquely in being given their new patent on 19 May 1603. However much it might appear on the surface to be a simple renewal of Elizabeth's act in 1583 of taking a company under her own patronage, what happened in May 1603 was unique both in its timing among the great flurry of activities that attended James's accession, and in the history of company patronage. Who prompted the patent to be issued so early in James's frenetic round of decision-making and new appointments it is impossible to say. It can hardly have been Tilney, so the matter must have been surprisingly high on the agenda either of James himself or of one of his senior advisers at the English court. The patent added a new name, Lawrence Fletcher, to the familiar names of the Chamberlain's sharers, which may be a token of Edinburgh thinking. Fletcher had led a company of English players to Scotland for James's wedding to Anne of Denmark, and had performed with Martin Slater in Edinburgh in 1599 and in other towns in Scotland for some years up to 1603. His inclusion in the company, the only record of which is his name in the patent and a gift to him in Augustine Phillips's will, does hint that James took a personal interest in giving the company his patronage and insisted that the only player he knew personally should be included in it.[9]

On the other hand, advice from London could have argued that for the new king the ex-Chamberlain's company was the obvious one, since its patron was dying and the other contenders had strong and useful Privy Councillors as their patrons. I think it rather more likely that James arrived with an enthusiasm for English players that required little prompting than that some *éminence grise* at court advised him to choose that one company for his patronage.[10] The fact that the choice was made so quickly, and so out of season in the annual cycle of court entertainments, supports the view that it was as much James's own decision as anyone's. He had just issued a proclamation about his first love, hunting, on 16 May. The decision to give his patronage to a professional playing company would have gone with that first indication of his preferences. The real mystery is why he should choose this company rather than either of the others. It must have been their reputation rather than their repertory, since he had not yet seen any of them perform.

The patent that set up the King's Men was dated 19 May 1603, two months after Elizabeth's death and one month after James's arrival in London. It does not follow the form of previous company licences exactly. In particular it names more names than usual, probably supplying a complete roll-call of the company's sharers, starting with James's own addition, Lawrence Fletcher. In full it reads

James by the grace of god &c. To all Justices, Maiors, Sheriffes, Constables, hedborowes, and other our Officers and lovinge Subjectes greetinge. Knowe yee that Wee of our speciall grace, certeine knowledge, & mere motion have licenced and aucthorized and by theise presentes doe licence and aucthorize theise our Servauntes Lawrence Fletcher, William Shakespeare, Richard Burbage, Augustyne Phillippes, John Heninges, Henrie Condell, William Sly, Robert Armyn, Richard Cowly, and the rest of their Assosiates freely to use and exercise the Arte and faculty of playinge Comedies, Tragedies, histories, Enterludes,

---

[9] Fletcher was named as a legatee and called a 'fellow' along with Armin and others in Phillips's will in May 1605. This suggests either that he did stay with the company for a while, or (less likely) that he was an old friend of Phillips from earlier in their playing days. There is no record of Fletcher's later presence anywhere.

[10] J. Leeds Barroll, *Politics, Plague, and Shakespeare's Theater: The Stuart Years* (New York, 1991), says 'the early patenting of the King's Servants bespeaks an interest in the company by an unknown figure at court who effected the patent through special influence'. He picks young William Herbert, 3rd earl of Pembroke, as the *éminence grise* and friend at court (48–9, 114, 181).

moralls, pastoralls, Stageplaies, and Suche others like as theie have alreadie studied or hereafter shall use or studie, aswell for the recreation of our lovinge Subjectes, as for our Solace and pleasure when wee shall thincke good to see them, duringe our pleasure. And the said Commedies, tragedies, histories, Enterludes, Morralles, Pastoralls, Stageplays, and suche like to shewe and exercise publiquely to their best Commoditie, when the infection of the plague shall decrease, aswell within their nowe usual howse called the Globe within our County of Surrey, as alsoe within anie towne halls or Moute halls or other conveniente places within the liberties and freedome of anie other Cittie, universitie, towne or Boroughe whatsoever within our said Realmes and domynions.[11]

The manuscript copy that has been preserved includes a marginal note 'Commissio specialis pro Laurencio Fletcher & Willelmo Shackespeare et aliis'. Putting Fletcher's name at the head both of the company names and of the marginal note is another indication that the wish being enacted may have been voiced by James himself.

The other two London companies at first continued to run under their old patrons' licences. On 17 November the Coventry accounts report payments of forty shillings to the King's Men and half that amount to the other two, who were recorded as Nottingham's (the Lord Admiral was now the earl of Nottingham), and Worcester's. Leicester also gave them their old names. The Court warrants for the 1603–4 Christmas season, dated 19 February 1604, give them their new names as the Prince's and the Queen's Men for the first time. A slightly earlier one of 4 February changed the Blackfriars Boys into the Queen's private company, with Samuel Daniel as their Master and censor.

What Anne's reasons for adopting the boy company as well as the third of the adult companies might have been are open to entertaining speculation, fuelled by some of the contemporary comments.[12] An enigmatic note by Dudley Carleton, written to John Chamberlain on 15 January 1604,[13] says that the Queen and Prince Henry were better friends to the players than James, and subsequently took them 'to their protection'. Quite what that means, unless it implies that Anne and Henry took a separate initiative to make themselves patrons of their companies during the Christmas revels, is unclear.[14] James's new company was given pride of place in the court revels, giving the first six performances without any competition up to 1 January, and altogether eight performances through the season. Those eight com-

---

[11] P. R. 1 Jac. I, pars 2, membr. 4, repr. in MSC i. 264, ES ii. 208.

[12] For some context about the anomalous boy company, see Ch. 20, esp. the letter by the French ambassador Beaumont quoted at 350–1. Anne showed enthusiasm for boy companies throughout her life as queen of England. After her visit to Bristol in June 1613 she secured a patent from the Master of the Revels allowing John Daniel to run a boy company there. See REED, Bristol, forthcoming.

[13] 'The first holy days we had every night a public play in the great hall, at which the king was ever present and liked or disliked as he saw cause, but it seems he takes no extraordinary pleasure in them. The queen and prince were more the players' friends, for on other nights they had them privately and have since taken them to their protection.' Dudley Carleton to John Chamberlain 1603–1624: Jacobean Letters, ed. Maurice Lee, Jr., (New Brunswick, NJ, 1972), 53.

[14] Heywood, always loyal to Worcester, wrote a dedicatory epistle addressed to him in Gunaikeion in 1624 which says that 'amongst other of your servants, you bestowed me upon the excellent Princess Queen Anne'. This is not evidence that Worcester freely handed the company over to its new patron.

pare with five by the Prince's, two by the Queen's, one by the Queen's Boys and one by Paul's Boys. James did attend the plays in some excitement through this season, making loud comments on the pleasures and disappointments of what he saw. It may have been that his noisy comments led courtiers such as Carleton to think him a more hostile critic than his wife or son were. He may, of course, have been disappointed by what he saw his new company perform in December. That, in its way, would reinforce the view that he must have originally taken the initiative himself to seize the company in May 1603.

The story of the companies in the first years under James is really one of consolidation. It could not have appeared like that at the time, particularly given the highly provocative role that the Blackfriars Boys adopted with their railing satires, a new phenomenon that gave the Master of the Revels much to do. That story is given in more detail in Chapter 20. Up to 1608 the little eyases made a powerful impression on the adult companies, in their repertories and in their audiences. After their early attempts to revive favourites from the time that they had last been in London ten years before, which brought them some derision, the boy companies, particularly the Blackfriars Boys, by some way the more flauntingly outrageous of the two, soon developed a kind of repertory which the adult companies could not ignore. On the whole, the adults reacted by going in conspicuously different directions. Shakespeare's company, for all the notorious reference to the eaglet boy companies in *Hamlet*, chose to pay relatively little attention to the new fashions. Their non-Shakespearian plays clung tightly to the older traditions.[15] Their main rivals chose to be innovatory in a way that ran even more distinctly contrary to the satirical fashion at the Blackfriars. They emphasized the traditional values in stage fashion, 'theatre of enchantment', in preference to the boy companies' 'theatre of estrangement', and exploited the current nostalgia for Elizabeth's time and the political virtues of Protestant history as set down in Foxe's Book of Martyrs.[16]

The second major step in the process of company change after 1594 came much later, in 1608–9, but its causes can be found in earlier history. Its consequences only applied directly to the King's company, but the pre-eminence they had gained by then was to make them models for the others through the later years. They became the benchmarks for success under the Stuarts. Their reorganization during the long closure of 1608–9 proved to be the last and certainly the most successful affirmation of player-power over impresario-power. In the short term, financially, it was quixotic. In the longer term it helped more than anything besides Shakespeare's own plays to secure the company's enduring prosperity.

Richard Burbage, financier of sorts and leading sharer in the King's Men, allied with his older brother Cuthbert, a non-playing manager of sorts and investor in the company, found themselves with an important new choice to make in 1608. In

[15] See Knutson, *The Repertory of Shakespeare's Company*, esp. ch. 4.
[16] The best study of the boy company repertory is Michael Shapiro's *Children of the Revels* (New York, 1977). The development of alternative kinds of theatre in these years is described by Neil Carson, 'John Webster: The Apprentice Years', in *Elizabethan Theatre*, 6 (1978), 76–87.

1599, when they despaired of getting the use of their Blackfriars playhouse and could not budge the owner of the Theatre into renewing their lease, they had purloined the Theatre's timbers to make the frame for a new amphitheatre on Bankside. From their own finances, drained by the Blackfriars fiasco, they put up only fifty per cent of the cost of this new playhouse themselves, and brought in five of the senior players in the company to get the other fifty per cent. That for the first time made a substantial number of the sharers in a playing company into landlords for their own tenant company. Players acting as impresarios had built playhouses before, including James Burbage from Leicester's in Shoreditch and Jerome Savage from Warwick's at Newington Butts. Players or ex-players had an interest in the Curtain. The 1599 deal, though, was new.

The shortage of cash that made the Burbage sons bring five of the company sharers in to help pay for the new Globe was certainly a spur-of-the-moment innovation. At the time it had little to do with the long-term interests of the company. In 1599 they had been in existence only five years, quite a long time by standard company histories up to then, but still a brief period in any company's financial fortunes. The innovation was a fortuitous and probably a desperate decision forced on the Burbages by their chronic shortage of cash thanks to their father's miscalculated investment in the new hall playhouse in the Blackfriars liberty.

Nine years later the 1599 innovation of making company sharers into sharing playhouse-holders, tenants who were their own landlords, had become so evident a success that the Burbages renewed and extended it. With the king as their patron and another eleven of Shakespeare's plays in their repertory by then they had little to fear financially. Moreover, the troubles of the last surviving boy company in 1608, added to another plague closure, gave them the opportunity for making a further innovation to extend the idea. In August of that year Henry Evans, the impresario who had been running the Blackfriars Boys for the last nine years at the Burbages' hall-playhouse, finally surrendered his lease to them. It was the brothers' own playhouse at last, and the company was now strong enough for them to think of playing in it without the risk of local opposition that had stopped them in 1596. But what the Burbages opted to do was again distinctly eccentric.

The two Burbages, owners of the whole of the Blackfriars playhouse, could now become impresarios to the company. The company could abandon the Globe and move into the hall playhouse that had originally been built for them three years before the Globe. But they would have to do so at the price of becoming tenants to a playhouse landlord again, even if one of the landlords was their leading player. Alternatively the company might have continued playing at the Globe while the Burbages let out the new playhouse to another company, as they had been doing for the last ten years. What the company and the Burbages chose instead was the extravagant but ultimately rewarding course of occupying both playhouses themselves in alternate seasons of each year.

In effect what the Burbages and the company chose to do was renew their old habit of playing in a large-capacity suburban amphitheatre through the summer months and transfer to a smaller roofed venue for the winter. It fulfilled at least a part of old Burbage's design to replace the city inns traditionally used in winter with a roofed city playhouse. They originally tried to renew that system in October 1594 when they got Henry Carey to ask the Lord Mayor if they could use the Cross Keys in winter. At that time, though, renewing the players' access to city inns ran counter to the deal the Chamberlain and the mayor had set up, and the request was never repeated. Nostalgia for that old tradition, plus a degree of concern for personal comfort, must have dictated this choice by the Burbages in 1608 rather than any financial consideration, since it meant leaving one playhouse barren and unrented for half of each year. There is no evidence that either the Burbages or the members of the company who were householders ever tried to rent the playhouse that the company was not using to any other company.

The two Burbages were certainly ruled by a kind of quixotic nostalgia, because they extended the landlord-sharing deal that they first introduced for the Globe in 1599 to the Blackfriars in 1608. It was not a deal made for their personal profit. They ceded half of their new acquisition, their inheritance, to the sharers who already co-owned the Globe. Clearly this collective landlordism, using the Globe with the company as both landlord and tenant, had been a thorough success. The arrangement with the Blackfriars, completed in August 1608, affirmed and perpetuated the system originally applied at the Globe. After the boy company's impresario surrendered the lease, on 9 August, the Burbages and a financier called Thomas Evans joined with Shakespeare, Heminges, Condell, and Sly, the four main shareholders in the Globe along with the Burbages, to become co-owners of the Blackfriars. This consortium, five of the company's sharers plus the leading sharer's brother and one outside financier, took possession of the two playhouses. At the time the long closure for plague prevented any early implementation of the company's new plan to try the old system of playing at one in summer and the other in winter, but it was clearly what they all had in mind as soon as the Blackfriars lease was surrendered.

There was a substantial amount of nostalgia, too, in the group's decision to retain the Globe. James Burbage had built the Blackfriars intending it to be a complete replacement for the old Theatre. He planned to change the company's centre of gravity from suburban amphitheatres, which even in 1596 he saw as too marginal for his ambitions, to a much richer place inside a city 'liberty'. The younger Burbages ignored that design. Whether it was entirely their own preference and their own initiative or a collective inspiration with the other sharers in the company it is impossible to say. Probably they all made a collective decision that the Globe, built as a second-best substitute for the Blackfriars out of second-hand materials, and proved such a success that it was worth keeping on, whatever the cost of leaving one of the two playhouses vacant. Conceivably the decision to give the sharers who were Globe 'housekeepers' shares in the Blackfriars was in part a pay-off for keeping the Globe. The new Blackfriars shares gave the Burbages some extra capital, and they would get the same level of income from the two playhouses as they had been used to from the Globe on its own. What it cost them was the doubled rents they would have obtained if either playhouse had been let to another company. Nostalgia had a high price.

It was to lay an even higher price on the Burbages and the company housekeepers four years later, when the original saving they made by roofing the Globe's galleries with thatch instead of the more expensive tiles proved a false economy and the thatch burned the theatre down. That gave the housekeepers a chance to rethink their choice of 1608. By the summer of 1613 they had already been performing happily at the Blackfriars through three winter seasons. After the fire that July they had to return unseasonably to the hall playhouse, and play on there in the summer. They were then at last in a position to implement the plan that James Burbage had originally hatched eighteen years before. The only difference was that the Blackfriars precinct was no longer a 'liberty'. But they were the King's Men, and had already been playing at the Blackfriars regularly since 1609.

The choice was simple. They could easily have stayed at the Blackfriars all the year round and surrendered the lease on the Globe's land, becoming players only for the rich gentry instead of the broader social span of the Globe's audiences. That option they ignored. Instead the company's player-housekeepers each donated hundreds of pounds to have the Globe rebuilt more splendidly than before. It was certainly much more an investment in nostalgia than an investment for profit, since their income would have remained much the same from playing at the Blackfriars all the year round as it would from the two playhouses used seasonally. In fact, by 1613 they must have known that the Blackfriars could bring in consistently higher returns than the Globe. Despite that, between them they put up the total cost of rebuilding the Globe, which was said to be in total more than was spent on any other playhouse throughout the whole period. All the cost of rebuilding came from the housekeeper-players themselves. It was an entirely unnecessary extravagance.

These two decisions, the first in 1608 to run two playhouses instead of one, and the second in 1613 to renew that system at a high cost in capital and some cost in revenue, were both cause and effect of the leading company's position under James. What both decisions indicate most clearly is that the players' sense of traditional values prevailed over commercial wisdom. The system introduced more or less accidentally in 1599, of making the chief playing sharers into housekeepers, had worked well. At a time when Henslowe and Christopher Beeston were evolving into authoritative company landlords, managers, and impresarios, the King's players went in the opposite direction. It was an elaboration of the sharer system, the only real alternative to the impresario system of company management. In the following years other companies viewed it with envy.

The King's sharers' decision in 1608 to use two playhouses, one for the gentry in the winter and one for the whole populace through the summer, also turned out to be a success. How far these management decisions were what determined the company's standing at this time and long after, or alternatively how far it was their incomparable repertory of memorable plays that gave them the luxury of making such a choice, it is not easy to say. The status they achieved certainly made them a model for the time. The various effects of these choices on their imitators is a matter for the next chapters.

On 29 March 1615 the Privy Council summoned the leading representatives of the London companies to present themselves before it. It named two players from each of four groups that it wanted to speak to. From the King's Men it asked for John Heminges and Richard Burbage; from Queen Anne's, Christopher Beeston and Robert Lee; from the Palsgrave's (formerly the Prince's), William Rowley and John Newton; from Prince Charles's (I) Company, Thomas Downton and Humphrey Jeffes.[1] With the disappearance of the last of the boy companies and the recent merger of the two companies that were patronized by James's younger children into one, four had become the set number of approved playing companies by 1615.

The number of London companies had risen to as many as six in the preceding years. It reached that total by 1611, once James's second son, the young Duke of Albany and York, and his sister, the Lady Elizabeth, had started their own companies, with a sixth in the form of the former Blackfriars Boys so long as they kept their London foothold as a company of youths. The Duke of York's was formally patented on 30 March 1610. The Lady Elizabeth's company's patent, a year later, made it the sixth to be officially tolerated in London, after the King's, Queen's, Prince Henry's (now the Palsgrave's), and York's, plus the Blackfriars Boys, now once again calling themselves the Children of the Queen's Revels. But the events of the next years indicate that in the commercial marketplace six was too large a number of companies for London to sustain comfortably. Even at the height of their social standing under Charles London could not accommodate easily more than five companies. So by 1615 the former boy company had merged with the Lady Elizabeth's, and that merged group had in turn joined up with the Duke of York's to take the duke's new title as Prince Charles's company. That left the four groups whose leaders the Privy Council summoned in 1615. Apart from a few rather short-lived incursions by outside groups, four became the normal number of London companies through the next twelve years and even after.[2] Although no record exists of any formal declaration being made about the allowed total, it evidently became the agreed figure. On 29 January 1618, for instance, the Master of the Revels made a note about a payment received from Heminges of the King's 'in the name of the four companyes'.[3]

---

[1] *Acts of the Privy Council of England, 1615–1616* (London, 1925), 86.

[2] From 1629, when Richard Gunnell built the 3rd hall playhouse, Salisbury Court, there were five companies normally playing in London.

[3] *Herbert Dramatic Records*, 48. Besides the number that the Master, George Buc, specified in 1618, Henry Herbert makes two later references to four companies as the authorized number, in 1623 and 1636 (*Herbert Dramatic Records*, 25, 65). This seems to have continued to be Herbert's preferred number of London companies, despite the rise to five in Caroline times, since he still named only four in 1636. But that was at the outset of a long closure; five companies did get restarted in 1638.

The shrinkage from six to four between 1613 and 1615 was due to more factors than the economic pressure of the attempt to increase the supply of plays to the same-sized market of playgoers. It was also a question of the places available to play in. By 1615 there were barely four playhouses even for the four companies that were then in operation in London, and the city was not going to relent in its hostility to the building of new playhouses. The King's Men kept to themselves the luxury of playing at their Globe and Blackfriars alternately. They even rubbed their superiority in by rebuilding the Globe as their spare playhouse in 1614. The Queen Anne's played at the Red Bull. The Palsgrave's had the Fortune. In 1615 the fourth company, the merger of Prince Charles's with the Lady Elizabeth's, used the Hope. That playhouse had been disliked by the Lady Elizabeth's when they opened it in 1614 because it also served for bear-baiting. The only other venue available to the newly-merged company was the old Curtain. The Swan was still in existence, but for various reasons had never been used very much for playing, and hardly ever by a resident company. There was a serious shortage. The Hope stank. The Curtain, built in 1577, was not much better, because it was now by a long way the oldest amphitheatre in London.[4] It was also the one with distinctly the lowest reputation.[5] So long as the King's kept their two playhouses for their own exclusive use, the other three companies of 1615 had not enough good playhouses available to them.

A new playhouse was urgently needed, but besides the predictable opposition of the city, the Privy Council was also less than co-operative. On 26 September 1615 it issued instructions to block a venture by Philip Rosseter, musician and former manager of a boy company, who allied himself with Edward Alleyn and others to build a new playhouse at Porter's Hall designed to match the Blackfriars.[6] In the event the Porter's Hall playhouse enjoyed only a single performance, if that, before the Privy Council closed it down.[7] The impresarios and financiers, and very likely the players too by now, did not want another amphitheatre. The Hope was undesirable according to the players, and the Curtain was too old. What the companies and their financiers all wanted was a new hall playhouse to rival the success of the King's at Blackfriars. That was what the short-lived Porter's Hall in the city was designed for. A subsequent and, in the end, much more successful enterprise, Christopher Beeston's adaptation of a cockpit outside the city in Drury Lane into a playhouse, was directed by the same inspiration. By 1615 the familiar presence of one leading company of adult players performing daily in a hall playhouse was

[4] Still in use in 1622, it had the longest life of any unreconstructed playhouse in London, more than the forty-three years of the two Globes together, or the forty-two of the two Fortunes.

[5] See John Orrell, 'The London Stage in the Florentine Correspondence, 1604–1618', *TRI* 3 (1977–8), 155–81, 171.

[6] The order is quoted in *ES* iv. 343. Another Privy Council minute of 27 Jan. 1617 instructed the Lord Mayor that 'certaine persons that goe about to sett up a Play howse in the Black Fryaers neere unto his Majesties wardrobe, and for that purpose have lately erected and made fitt a Building, which is almost if not fully finished', that they were doing so contrary to several prohibitions, and that the king that day had given instructions to pull the building down. *MSC* i. 4 and 5, 374.

[7] S. P. Cerasano, 'Competition for the King's Men? Alleyn's Blackfriars Venture', *MRDE* 4 (1989), 173–86.

crying out for imitation. So the Hope stands in history as the last and shortest-lived amphitheatre playhouse in London. Thanks in large part to the evident value the Blackfriars had for the King's Men, probably endorsed by the widely-known fact that a hall playhouse could bring in larger revenues than an amphitheatre, for all the splendid rebuilding of the Globe in 1614, from this time on the only new playhouses were halls.

There are widespread implications in this upward shift of company ambitions. It suggests that all the London companies now saw what James Burbage had envisaged first in 1596, that the future lay in enclosed theatres. It may also indicate that, for all the divisions inside the Privy Council, the companies were beginning to feel more secure with the social élite than with the groundlings. Behind that thought is the certainty that the court and the great patrons were the best protection the companies had against the repressiveness of city officialdom. It leaves less clear the least tangible of all of these considerations, the question of the companies' continuing loyalty to their basic clientele, the traditional London populace. From this time on audiences began to divide according to the kind of playhouse they could afford. How comprehensively and how early the Fortune and Red Bull became the 'citizen' playhouses while the Blackfriars and Cockpit became gentrified is the most complex question of this period. In one sense the change must have been immediate, because the halls cost so much more for admission than the amphitheatres. On the other hand, changes in repertory plays and practices to fit these new target audiences went much more slowly.

How company policies changed is part of the argument about the separation of the 'great' (or canonical) cultural tradition from the 'little' tradition of populist culture.[8] Did different companies ever owe consistent allegiance to different levels of Stuart society? It is a question almost impossible to answer confidently because of the lack of evidence from the populist side. There is, for instance, a distinct paucity of printed texts other than those that featured in the canonical tradition. As a result, there is no easy way to distinguish the real cultural allegiances on either side, if indeed there ever was a clearly distinguishable divide between them.

In this complex process of change the most likely and certainly the most easily identifiable of all the possible motives that guided the players themselves is, of course, the commercial one. The shifts in company placements at the different kinds of playhouse indicate that they were most strongly motivated by the financial advantage of the wealthier clientele who went to the hall playhouses. Against that is the fact that the companies found it quite easy to switch themselves and their plays in both directions between halls and amphitheatres even in the 1630s. There is no ready way to identify whether the initiative lay with the playgoers at particular playhouses or with the companies who served them.

It was not an easy process to open new halls. The embargo that the Privy Council laid on Porter's Hall in 1615 made it clear that, despite the privilege given the

---

[8] Alexander Leggatt's section on 'Popular Culture' has some cogent points to make about the theatrical traditions in *Jacobean Public Theatre* (London, 1992), 32–9.

King's to play at Blackfriars, the Council still remembered its undertaking of 1594 to the city to keep playhouses out of the city's territory. The city's own opposition to playing inside its walls had certainly not diminished. Christopher Beeston, the only one to succeed in opening a hall playhouse in this decade, was a good deal more tactful than the Rosseter-Alleyn consortium when he made the second attempt to imitate the success of the King's Men at the Blackfriars with his Cockpit; but even he ran into major troubles over it. He avoided the Privy Council's and the city's disapproval by finding a site that stood outside the city in the West End, not too far from the Blackfriars. An old circular hall used for public displays of cock-fighting, it was located in Drury Lane. That put it near the rapidly growing, wealthy suburbs of Westminster, and equally close to the Inns of Court which provided a large proportion of the more affluent audiences, but left it free (like the suburban amphitheatres) from the threat of city restraint that now hung over even the Blackfriars. For all the ostensible protection that the Privy Council gave to playing against the city's hostility, the two administrations seem to have worked together in restricting entrepreneurs from speculating with new hall playhouses.[9] Beeston chose the best place he could. It is only mildly ironical that the huge growth of London since then has made his choice of suburban lane for his new playhouse into London's most famous theatre locality.

Built shortly after the Porter's Hall theatre opened and was promptly closed, towards the end of 1616, Beeston's Cockpit was even smaller than Burbage's Blackfriars. Its design may have been hampered by official constraints on new buildings in the West End, which allowed new constructions only in the form of enlargements to existing structures, and that by not more than one-third. If the plans that Inigo Jones, the royal surveyor, drew up for an unnamed hall playhouse in about 1616 were commissioned by Beeston, they met this restraint very neatly. Jones as the king's surveyor would have had first-hand knowledge of the constraints on new building.[10] The plans made use of the existing circular auditorium of the old cockpit, cutting into the circle with a square stage and flanking boxes, and a rectangular tiring house behind it. Auditorium capacity in the round cockpit was augmented with the boxes flanking the stage, and ranks of benches or 'degrees' on either side of the music room above the stage. Its total audience capacity was probably less than five hundred, but the much higher prices that could be charged at this superior kind of venue evidently still made it a good investment in Beeston's eyes.

Indirectly it was the high prices for admission rather than the Privy Council that gave Beeston his main trouble with the new playhouse. The basic story behind the

[9] The city took over control of the liberties in 1608 in return for raising a large grant of money for crown expenses, which by then were well out of control. In the subsequent years the city seems to have accepted the status quo and allowed the King's Servants to continue playing in the Blackfriars, but that quiescence remained a unique privilege. Neither the Privy Council nor the city allowed any other playhouse to open in London before 1660.

[10] For a detailed account of Jones's plans and the likelihood that they were made for Beeston's Cockpit, see John Orrell, *The Theatres of Inigo Jones and John Webb* (Cambridge, 1985), ch. 3.

attack by a gang of apprentices on the new playhouse on the Shrove Tuesday holiday in March 1617 has been told before.[11] It gives the first clear indication that playgoing was highly prized by the poorer people among London audiences, and it reveals a problem over the use of hall playhouses that Beeston, for all his cautious manœuvres to circumvent the various obstacles that officialdom might have put in his way, evidently never anticipated.

The boy companies who had always played in halls and the King's Men who followed them at Blackfriars did not suffer any of the difficulties that Beeston found with his Cockpit. The boy companies were a small-scale alternative to the predominant adult companies at the amphitheatres. The King's Men took themselves off to the Blackfriars for only half the year, and used the Globe for the other half. Only when Beeston took his company from its usual playhouse, the Red Bull, to the new Cockpit did the problem of financially segregated audiences come into the open for the first time. Beeston took the Red Bull players and their plays away from the amphitheatre, where the apprentices could see them for a penny, to the Cockpit where they would have to pay six times as much. Their objection to paying that price cost Beeston dearly.

Only two years before, the King's Men's had decided that they must rebuild the Globe when it burned down and left them with only a hall playhouse. In retrospect Beeston's experience shows that to have been a tactful as well as an expensive decision. Queen Anne's Men at the Red Bull had a solid repertory based on Heywood and Rowley's plays, a resource not dissimilar to the fare on offer with Dekker's plays at the nearby Fortune. Taking this repertory off to Drury Lane and out of the reach of their pockets enraged the city's apprentices. On their traditional holiday at the beginning of Lent a gang of more than a thousand marched to the Cockpit and broke in on the players. There was a fierce fight, one of the players killing an apprentice with a pistol shot in the head. The attackers were too many for the players, and they smashed or burned everything they could get their hands on. An official report says that they

wounded divers of the players, broke open their trunckes, & whatt apparell, bookes, or other things they found, they burnt & cutt in peeces; & not content herewith, gott on the top of the house, & untiled it, & had not the Justices of the Peace & Sherife levied an aide, & hindred their purpose, they would have laid that house likewise even with the grownd.[12]

It was an invasion, cultural and social. Drury Lane was a long way from apprentice territory. Their grievance was precisely with the players who had left their old Red Bull home and its audiences and gone off into the alien West End.

Beeston's new playhouse venture made this loss to the apprentices of their familiar entertainment into a smouldering grievance. After their first Shrove Tuesday attack they made a plan to renew their attack on the following Shrove

[11] See Gurr, 'Money or Audiences: The Impact of Shakespeare's Globe', *TN* 42 (1988), 3–14, 10–12, and ch. 18.
[12] Quoted in *JCS* vi. 238.

Tuesday early in 1618, directing their anger on this occasion at both of the offending playhouses. This time, though, the Privy Council got wind of the plan. It wrote
to the Middlesex magistrates, under whose aegis came both the Cockpit and the
Red Bull, warning them to be prepared for more trouble.

It is well knowne unto yow what disorder and tumulte was comitted the last Shrove Tuesday
in divers partes aboute the Cittie by Apprentices. . . . And though divers of the offenders
were comitted to Newgate, and proceeded withall at the Sessions accordinge to lawe: Yet
they are soe farr from beinge warned by that example as they rather take occasion thereby,
in regarde that some of their Fellowes were in dainger and punished the last yeare, to cast
sedicious lybells into Playhouses in the name of some London Fellowe Apprentices, to
Summon others in the Skirtes and Confynes, to meete at the Fortune, and after that to goe
to the Playhouses the Redd Bull, and the Cock Pitt, which they have designed to rase, and
pull downe.[13]

The ringleaders were clearly targeting the Cockpit and Red Bull and their
companies, not playhouses indiscriminately, since their plan was to meet at the
Fortune before attacking the nearby amphitheatre and the more distant new hall.
This time they were stopped, and there is no evidence to say what further troubles
Beeston may have had with his audiences at either playhouse. It was his first major
step as an impresario and playhouse-owner rather than company manager. The
troubles and their cost did not deter him. In the long run he won through, and his
career as impresario grew stronger and stronger from then on.

In the short term, though, it was a setback from an unexpected quarter. The
Cockpit was put out of action for several months while Beeston repaired it, and
besides the cost of the repairs he lost the income from his investment during the
closure. What playbooks were also lost by the attack and the burning of the more
flammable company resources we do not know. Nor do we know in any detail
how Beeston reallocated his plays and his players in the interim while the new
playhouse was closed. The Queen's Company would most likely have had to return
to the Red Bull for a while, postponing the amphitheatre's tenure by the waiting
Prince Charles's Men for several months. The Privy Council's letter about
the threat of a renewed attack suggests only that it was designed as a revenge
for the previous defeat, but the addition of the Red Bull itself to the Cockpit as a
target also raises the likelihood that the apprentices were now aggrieved by the
whole Beeston enterprise, not just over the prices charged at the new hall. The
companies themselves were certainly drawn into the fight. The apprentices' grievance is made more understandable by the unavoidable toing and froing of the
companies and their plays between the playhouses—which the apprentices had
prolonged—at this time.

Some time before the Cockpit's troubles the Lady Elizabeth's Men gave up the
Hope and merged with Prince Charles's. Faced with using the old Curtain, the
merged group asked Alleyn to help them find a new venue. That did not get them

---

[13] Ibid. vi. 56–7.

far. Alleyn, having lost his investment in the new hall playhouse at Porter's Hall and now beginning to turn his attention and his finances to the foundation of Dulwich College, which was to immortalize him, could not have been keen in 1616 to invest large sums in yet another new playhouse. Indeed, he appears to have tried in 1617–18 to set up a co-ownership deal with some of the sharers from the company using his Fortune that seems to have been an imitation of the King's Men's set-up at the Globe and Blackfriars.[14] That may have been a sign either of a new reluctance to invest much in playing or of the beginnings of his withdrawal from what was still regarded as a less than respectable kind of business. He was still the businessman and the respected entrepreneur of playing and bear-baiting, as is evident from the number of times the companies approached him for help of one sort or another. But the man who was setting up the College of God's Gift and was shortly to take as his third wife a daughter of the Dean of St Paul's was no longer a venturesome impresario.

Beeston must have gone through some elaborate negotiations with Alleyn in 1616 and 1617 over the various tenant companies, both as company manager and as a would-be playhouse owner. In the event the solution lay with Beeston himself. Beeston's own Queen Anne's Men were set to move into the Cockpit before the end of 1616, and the merged Prince Charles's, still using the Curtain but desperate for a better playhouse, were ready to replace them at the Red Bull. The damaged Cockpit must have delayed these transfers for a while, or else made each new tenure short-lived, which could itself have been an irritant to the frustrated regulars at the Red Bull. It is not clear whether in February 1618 the apprentices planned to attack two different companies, the old and the new tenants of the Red Bull, or whether they were after the Queen Anne's Men alone. As a mob, their rancour may have been fairly indiscriminate, but they did start with a clear plan to attack both playhouses from their starting-point at Alleyn's Fortune.

Unfortunately it is not possible to tell from the provenance of the plays staged at the Red Bull at this time whether Beeston made any attempt to appease the apprentices by leaving some of the old Queen Anne's plays behind to be played by the Red Bull's new tenants. He certainly took a lot of the Red Bull plays to his new Cockpit. The troubles may have prompted him to introduce a new procedure of selection which becomes much more apparent later, and which may have already started with the King's Men. The hall playhouses had a quite different character from the amphitheatres. The stage area at the halls was half the size of the amphitheatre platforms, and space there was even more cramped by the practice of allowing up to fifteen gallants to take stools from the tiring house and sit on the stage itself. That made scenes calling for large casts on stage and rapid movement, as in battle scenes, far less practicable in the halls than in the open amphitheatres. Even small-scale duels like Hamlet's might make the gallants' stools precarious places to watch from. Nor were the indoor halls so convenient as the open-air

---

[14] See Ch. 16.

amphitheatres at dispersing noise and smells, so that fireworks and cannonfire were far less desirable. These differences eventually came to influence the choice of plays for staging at the halls. The practice of discriminating between plays thought suitable for hall performances and those more suited to the target and broadsword 'drum-and-trumpet' mould that prevailed at the amphitheatres might well have been started by Beeston as a result of the troubles he had moving plays from the Red Bull to the Cockpit.[15] The King's Men's practices were not so straightforwardly imitable as Beeston originally thought.

One feature of the life of the four companies towards the end of the second decade that reflected the move of the gentry indoors to watch their plays is in Sir George Buc's increasing preference for inviting to the court revels the companies and their plays from the hall playhouses rather than the amphitheatre companies. From 1616 the King's Men at Blackfriars, and Queen Anne's company and its successors at the Cockpit, were drawn on more and more for the Christmas and other festivities. Through its last ten years from 1615 onwards the Palsgrave's at the Fortune was never once called on to perform at court. The Red Bull company was never called on to play at court after 1617. The Fortune company appeared a few times in the 1630s, but that was when it kept switching between the amphitheatre and Salisbury Court's hall-playhouse. Amongst the gentry and with successive Masters of the Revels the view was evidently now gaining force that only the hall companies could provide plays for the court, and the amphitheatre fare was only for citizens. Whether that caused or reflected the loss of interest in court and gentry affairs by the amphitheatre companies that helped to separate the canonical tradition from the populist is a matter for conjecture.

Renamed the Phoenix, for obvious reasons, when it reopened, it took a long time for the Cockpit to match the Blackfriars in esteem. The more gentrified spectators in London showed some readiness to follow a particular company and its repertory in the following years rather than just go by the discriminatory cost of admission. In the 1630s Humphrey Mildmay, grandson of the founder of Emmanuel College, Cambridge, and one of a family of regularly playgoing brothers and wives, recorded in his diary eighteen visits to the King's Men at the Blackfriars but also four to the same company at the Globe. He made another four visits to the Cockpit. He names no other playhouse for the fifty-seven visits that he made in all to see plays through this period. There is no doubt that Rosseter, Alleyn, and Beeston were right in 1616 to see the future lying in hall playhouses, but the quality of each company and its repertoire of plays had a large say too. Beeston's Cockpit did not really come to rival the King's Men's Blackfriars until after 1625, when the long closure for James's death and the plague allowed him to set up an outstanding new company which ran unchanged there for ten years. He never let his earlier companies last for more than three, and in ways for which there is no tangible record their standing with the London public suffered.

---

[15] See Gurr, 'Playing in Halls and Playing in Amphitheatres', *Elizabethan Theatre*, 13 (1994), 27–62.

For all the evidence of mergers and of troubles with playhouses in the second decade of the century, there is plenty of other evidence that the companies were developing a settled way of life. Travelling took on a rather new character, for instance, as duplicates of the London company patents began to proliferate. The merger between the Lady Elizabeth's and Prince Charles's which freed one licence for travelling may have been a stimulus to that, though there are signs that Queen Anne's had been running a double company, one in town and one in the country, for some time already. The Lord Chamberlain's belated clampdown on duplicates of company patents in 1616 led to some reshuffles, too. Robert Lee, who was caught at Norwich in 1617 with a duplicate of the Queen Anne's patent, reappeared on 29 August 1618 in a new group led by himself along with Philip Rosseter, William Perry, and Nicholas Long.[16] Rosseter had evidently given up his plans to build a playhouse in London for his boy company. Perry and Long had been with the Lady Elizabeth's as boys in 1615. Perry was to have a lengthy provincial career as leader of a company under various names. Nicholas Long by 1619 was leading a company of Revels Children along with Rosseter.

The company that arrived in Norwich in August 1618 was not identified by any patron's name, but it had a licence dated 31 October 1617 'to play Comedyes &c by the space of Fourten dayes in any Citty &c'.[17] Whether that included London is not stated, though the same terms were used in the Lady Elizabeth's licence of 20 March 1617. It seems that, probably as a result of the calling-in of the duplicate patents of the London companies in 1616 and the shake-up amongst the various London groups including Beeston's, the Lord Chamberlain issued a set of new licences in 1617 designed explicitly for the non-London travellers. To judge from the dates cited in some of the Norwich records, from the early 1620s the Master then developed the practice of renewing these licences each year. In May 1623 a group led by Perry with Lee and Rosseter showed the Norwich authorities a licence as the late Queen Anne's players, along with 'A Confirmacion under the hand of Sir Frances Markham Deputy to the Maister of the Revelles bearinge date in Aprill last which confirmeth the kinges authority for a yeare'.[18] These annually renewed licences became the standard form of authority for playing by the travelling companies in the next reign.

---

[16] This may be the company which led the mayor of Exeter to complain to the king's secretary in June 1618 that while the visiting group's patent was for a company of 'children and youthes' it had only five youths and 'the rest ar men som about 30 and 40 and 50 yeares' (*REED, Devon*, 188). The three men had associations with boy or youth companies for the whole decade, and may have retained the old 'Revels Children' patent of 1610 for use until at least 1619.

[17] *REED, Norwich*, 157. Norwich also records a letter from the Privy Council to them, dated 27 May 1623, which acknowledged a Norwich alderman's complaint about the visiting companies, and reiterated the general ban on playing by 'that sort of vagrant and Licentious Rabble by whose means & devises the purses of pore servantes and apprentizes and of the meaner sort of people are drayed and emtied' (177–8). Norwich became consistently hostile to playing under the Stuarts, and on one occasion used this sympathetic letter from the Privy Council to overset the king's licence to the players. See Ch. 1 and Ch. 22.

[18] Ibid. 175.

When Anne died in 1619 and the Queen's Men had to find another patron there were more switches and more duplications. By then the four companies had their four playhouses, the Globe allied with the Blackfriars, the Cockpit, the Fortune, and the Red Bull. This settled number of playing places made it easier for the Master of the Revels to hold things steady. The fire that destroyed the Fortune in 1622 was only a temporary setback, since Alleyn was quick to make up a consortium consisting of a few players and a lot of financiers to rebuild it. Its company used the old Curtain while it was rebuilding. The speed and the richness of its reconstruction testifies to the stability and the financial security that investment in playhouses now clearly offered.

It might seem from the story of Beeston's struggle to open the Cockpit that the upward mobility of playing, its reach into the gentry's pockets and culture, was a strong feature of life for the four companies from 1616 on. That would be misleading. It was not until after 1629, when the Salisbury Court hall was added to the available playhouses, that the social gulf between the amphitheatres and the halls, with their different clienteles, really began to yawn. Up to 1625 there were few major upheavals and no large changes in the regulation of the playing companies, and few signs even of subterranean changes. Plays and playgoing were now standard daily activities, and were slowly becoming more socially respectable.

The most conspicuous of the major shifts appear in the content of the plays. In particular they show a growing readiness in some of the writers to flout the old restraints over topics of current and political concern. In his last years James's own ban on any public discussion of matters of state was predictably provocative, but long before he issued that Canute-like edict the stage was taking itself seriously enough to deploy not only the kind of issues that are now meat for the daily press, but more fundamental questions of proper human conduct. Given the strict layering of English society, and the explicitly different forms of conduct expected at each level, that was a divisive feature of playwriting and playgoing that affected the companies irreversibly.

One of the main shifts in company repertories was away from the old country interests. Near the end of Elizabeth's reign Chettle and Munday had written for the Admiral's a series of Robin Hood plays, making urbanized versions out of the country May-game festive plays. That company and its successors had also celebrated citizens and apprentices with plays like *The Shoemaker's Holiday* and *George a Greene* which, like other Admiral's plays, also featured Robin Hood, and Heywood's perennial Red Bull play *The Four Prentices of London*. The amphitheatres still revived these, along with the noisy drum-and-trumpet plays, but the Blackfriars and Cockpit now had to promote plays about courts and courtiers. The court and its scandals had always been a focus of attention, but its presentation on stage changed radically between 1606 and 1620. Public attention to corruption at James's court in the early years around 1606 was a subject dominated by direct presentation, local and immediate satire of individual quirks and idiosyncrasies, down to the satirical exploitation of the two court accents, English and Scots, used in the staging of *The Isle of Gulls*. The more general kind of corruption thought characteristic of courts was a larger branch of the topic that had to wait for the Italian stories that were broached with *The Revenger's Tragedy* and the plays of the later Jacobean period. *The Duchess of Malfi*, first staged at the Blackfriars in 1614, mixed its moralistic 'fly the courts of princes' motif with pruriently self-indulgent shows of poison and torture. The distance from that to the unabashed cynicism with which the moral degeneracy of the court was shown in *Women Beware Women* and *The Changeling* in the early 1620s is a measure of how the emphasis shifted in these years. David Lindley gives this a context by his account of the contemporary reactions to Frances Howard's divorce from the earl of Essex, her marriage to the earl of Somerset, and their subsequent trial for the Overbury murder.[19] The whole story was a sensation that must have generated a new kind of 'application' from life to the stage and back again. Sensationalist accounts of Frances Howard's Borgian attempts to rid herself of an unwanted husband by poison and necromancy, Overbury's murder, possibly by poison, in the Tower, the divorce, and the subsequent trial of Howard and her new husband, James's favourite, cannot have been quite as exotic then as they seem now. The drama of the previous decade gave that kind of reading of the story much of its currency and its plausibility. It became a circular exercise. Such readings of the evidence about Frances Howard's assumed devilry offered a justification for the Italianate dramas that preceded and followed them.

The changes that were becoming manifest in the company repertories through the Jacobean period reflect in odd ways the changes in London that came in James's wake. James, for all his love of hunting and his fear of crowds, found his society in London. The court and the great courtiers became Londoners, where under Elizabeth they had been landowners and builders of great houses. Audley End, completed in 1616, was the last of the really grandiose country houses. New money went into the great mansions that were being built in and around London. Now more than ever the great began to spend their money and most of their lives there. They rode in coaches, and crammed their houses with house servants, who swelled the number of the idle afternoon's men who were the most regular frequenters of plays. Court culture became more urban, and more exclusive.[20] The different social strata became more divided, as the great followed James's own example and kept themselves out of the reach of commoners. From 1616 and the opening of the Cockpit, the playhouses and to a lesser extent the companies, began to divide themselves into different social niches.

[19] David Lindley, *The Trials of Frances Howard: Fact and Fiction at the Court of King James* (Basingstoke, 1993).

[20] For a general survey of changes in court behaviour under the early Stuarts, see R. Malcolm Smuts, *Court Culture and the Origins of a Royalist Tradition in Early Stuart England* (Philadelphia, 1987). His generalization (286) that 'Elizabethan court culture was flamboyant and theatrical, whereas that of the Caroline period was more subdued, reserved, and exclusive' matches the evidence of company history in its own growing exclusiveness and the intensity of its focus in London.

Once the King's Men settled into the use of two quite different types of play-house, and consequently acquired two financially distinct types of clientele, there rose the question of catering for them with different kinds of play. Until then the companies had maintained their flexible practice of adapting themselves to the different kinds of venue, taking plays to perform at one kind of place or another without anything but a few on-the-spot adjustments. Their long training through travelling made that a habitually familiar practice. Even for the greatest of companies, performing at the Globe or the Blackfriars in the afternoon was routinely followed by an evening performance at court or at a great house in the Strand. That flexibility they never lost. But playing for long seasons at a hall and at an amphi-theatre was different. The hall playhouse's stage was less than half the size of the Globe's, and besides the gentry sitting in the boxes flanking the stage it had the young gallants perched on stools on the stage floor itself. Crowd scenes, and especially crowd scenes calling for violent action such as the finale of *Hamlet* with its six bouts of duelling, were more of a strain in the smaller place.

The drum-and-trumpet repertoire was most at risk in the close confines of the Blackfriars auditorium. When the boy company which first used the Blackfriars needed military fanfares or similarly loud music it replaced the brass of trumpet or hunting horn with the quieter cornet and other woodwinds.[21] Jonson's *Epicene, or the Silent Woman* is the only play written for the boys at Blackfriars that used a brass hunting horn; of course, it had a special reason for using brass there to torment the hyperacusic Morose. Otherwise the similarly noise-sensitive audiences in the confines of the Blackfriars were kept free from Morose's torment. The same consideration applied to fireworks, not just for their noise but their stink. The 'sulphurous breath' which helps to identify the deity descending from heaven on his eagle in *Cymbeline* as Jupiter, and which invariably accompanied devils arriving on stage from the other extreme, was not welcome in the hall playhouses. At some fairly early phase in their use of the Blackfriars the King's Company had to start sorting out their repertoire. Before Charles came to the throne they were beginning to relegate the plays unsuitable for the smaller enclosed venue to the summer season at the Globe.

This new practice, staging different plays at the different venues, was a problem that also faced Christopher Beeston when he took the Red Bull company to the Cockpit. Between 1616 and 1627 four sets of players from the Red Bull moved to the Cockpit to play. It evidently proved easy for Beeston to transfer the Red Bull companies. How easy it was to transfer the amphitheatre plays as well is a question that embraces the King's Men's problem too.

In the prologue to *The Unfortunate Lovers*, written for the King's Men in 1638, William Davenant mocked the old-fashioned tastes of twenty years before. Then, he wrote, the predominant taste was for 'a Jigg, or Target-fight, | A furious tale of *Troy* which they ne'r thought | Was weakly writ, if it were strongly fought.' Such

---

[21] See Gurr, 'Playing in Amphitheatres and Playing in Hall Theatres'.

appetites he identified in the present audience's 'homely ancestors', wearers of the 'high-crowned hats' of the citizenry.[22] By 1638 the gulf between hall and amphi-theatre preferences was deep, and it was continually being redug by courtier and gentry poets like Davenant. It was an entrenchment of the separation not only of hall from amphitheatre but of old from new. Davenant was right to see it growing through the twenty years that followed the opening of the Cockpit in 1616–17.

There is evidence that Beeston chose the plays he took from the Red Bull to the Cockpit with some care. He copied Webster's example, for instance. In 1614 Webster had voted with his feet by taking *The Duchess of Malfi* to the Blackfriars, after his *White Devil* flopped at the Red Bull. Beeston transferred *The White Devil* to his hall playhouse long before its 1631 quarto proclaimed it as a Cockpit play, probably some time before 1625. He also transferred *The Jew of Malta* (though no other Marlowe plays), Heywood's *Rape of Lucrece*, and Dekker's 1604 Red Bull play *If You Know not Me* along with his much later *Match Me in London*. The last of these Dekker composed after his release from debtor's prison in 1621. It was exactly right for the hall playhouse, although it started at the Red Bull, according to its 1631 title-page, which declares that it played 'First, at the *Bull* in St-Johns-street; and lately, at the Private-house in Drury-Lane, called the Phoenix'. It has no fights, and is a rewrite of the Borgian *Women Beware Women* in the form of a Fletcherian tragicomedy, where all the poisons turn out to be sleeping pills. That, in exemplary form, indicates Dekker's reading of the new trends.[23]

Along with these plays, Beeston also took the Middleton and Rowley pair *A Fair Quarrel* and *All's Lost by Lust*. It is notable that despite the smaller stage space several of these plays include duels, which may mean that the King's Men also felt it possible to stage *Hamlet* at the Blackfriars. But none had massed battles with drum and trumpet-calls,[24] sword-brandishing, and target-bashing, and none had devils with fireworks. Thomas Nabbes, writing *Hannibal and Scipio* for the Cockpit in 1635, felt that he had to reassure his audience that for all the twenty years of famous Italian battles that were the setting for his play, 'Nor need you Ladies fear the horrid sight: | And the more horrid noise of target fight | By the blue-coated Stage-keepers'. Instead his prologue asks the audience to 'conceive his battailes done . . . Betwixt the acts'. The Cockpit provided for the gentry and their ladies, who wanted neither battles nor noise, let alone blood.

So far as the evidence goes about the plays the King's Men ran at their two playhouses, they followed Beeston's practice. When the poets writing for the Blackfriars started mocking amphitheatre preferences, they used the same terms. According to Davenant the Blackfriars had 'Art, or Witt', while the Globe had

---

[22] *The Shorter Poems*, ed. A. M. Gibbs (Oxford, 1972), 67.

[23] Kathleen McLuskie, *Dekker and Heywood, Professional Dramatists* (Basingstoke, 1994), sees *Match Me* as a revelation of 'the difficulties of locating the professional dramatists in an opposition between élite and popular culture' (174).

[24] Military practice was to issue commands on the battlefield by drum for infantry and by trumpet for cavalry. The 'drum and trumpet' epithet refers to the whole business of massing extras on stage, and the standard issuing of orders for battle scenes, as much as to the noise they generated.

'shewes, Dancing, and Buckler fights'.[25] According to Shirley, by 1640 the Globe's plays were characterized by 'Target fighting', 'Bawd'ry', 'Ballads', a 'Clown', 'squibs', and 'Divells' in contrast to those at the Blackfriars.[26] The poets were marking the division that was now firmly fixed in the repertories between the gentrified halls and the plebeian amphitheatres. However much the playgoers may have stayed locked in their preferences for old-fashioned battles, or have looked for swordplay rather than wit-play, the writers insisted to the difference.

One other substantial change that had taken place by 1620 was the use of plays for a larger scale of political comment than is evident earlier. Studies of the relations between the Master of the Revels and the companies usually concentrate on his acts of censorship. The last Master of the Revels, Henry Herbert, had a problem that neither Tilney nor Buc, his predecessors, had to face to such an extent or with such political muscle in them. Like most censors, Tilney read his texts in a rather literal-minded way, and was probably right to do so. The 'application' of stories shown on stage to current issues had, according to Jonson, grown into 'a trade' by 1607, but that was more a matter for the appliers than the players. Part of the reason why the Chamberlain's Men got away with staging *Richard II* for the Essex conspirators was because it had been the conspirators' choice, not the players', to 'apply' the play's story to Elizabeth and Essex. The play was already there. Responsibility for applying it lay with the conspirators. By 1620, though, plays had become substantial enough as a presence in London's society to warrant their being used for propaganda, to register political sentiment and give serious publicity to the issues and to opinions about the issues.

To verify such a claim it is distinctly easier to turn to the commentators of the time rather than to look for specific instances in the plays themselves. John Chamberlain, always a reliable reporter of London's gossip, wrote to Carleton in 1620 that 'our pulpits ring continually of the insolence and impudence of women: and to helpe the matter forward the players have likewise taken them to taske, and so to the ballades and ballad singers, so that they can come no where but theyre eares tingle'.[27] This outcry seems to have been largely prompted by the troubles that followed the earl of Suffolk's disgrace as Lord Treasurer, and some of the aftershocks from the Frances Howard affair involving Lady Roos and others. It may be feasible to see in the plays of this period dramatizations of this gossipy concern for the conduct of court ladies. The difficulty is to make any direct connection. The virginity test in *The Changeling* was a more direct reflection of the Howard trial than Vittoria's willingness to use poison in *The White Devil*, but subsequent application was possible even though Webster's play preceded the Howard scandal by some years. Both reflect a basic concern about female conduct. What Chamberlain's comment indicates is that in 1620 playgoers developed a sharpened focus of interest

[25] William Davenant, *News from Plymouth* (1635), Prologue.
[26] James Shirley, Prologue to *The Doubtful Heir*, in *Poems* (1646), D4v–5.
[27] Chamberlain, *Letters* ii. 289. See the earlier letter (25 Jan. 1620), which notes that the Bishop of London had told the clergy that the king had ordered them to attack extravagances of dress in women.

in the conduct of great ladies at court and in their marriages, and that the companies catered to this interest.

The fact that this developed at a time when James was becoming less and less willing to tolerate open discussion made the whole business of staging plays that focused on morality or politics into a still more covert exercise, a more intricate game of juggling with the complex hermeneutics of censorship, than it had ever been. From well before 1619 plays were being written to advertise popular sentiments about current issues.[28] The practice which culminated in the scandal of *A Game at Chess* in 1624 started a good few years earlier. The gradual rise in the social status of plays and the shift of 'application' from personal satire to allegorical and political moralizing made the post of Master of the Revels as censor of plays a much hotter seat than it had been when only the single lines or scenes of *Sir Thomas More* were at issue.

Sir John van Olden Barnavelt was an early venture by the King's Men into the melodramatic politics of the Low Countries, and the war against the Spanish forces who had been such a long-standing colonizing and military presence there. As they had done with previous attempts to stage versions of currently newsworthy sensations, people in high places came to recognize *Barnavelt* rather belatedly as a dangerously current story, and one unlikely to please the Spanish embassy in London, the most feared as well as the most hated locus for international interests. According to letters preserved in the State Papers, the King's Men were ready to stage the play in early August 1619 when they 'at th' instant were prohibited by my Lord of London'. This was a distinctly non-routine and urgent act of censorship.

The Bishop of London, who usually intervened as a censor only on the basis of specific complaints, may have wished to handle this matter himself instead of leaving it to the Master of the Revels, George Buc, who was near the end of his career and suffering fits of the insanity that finally killed him. The surviving manuscript, however, shows no evidence of the bishop's intervention and clear signs of Buc's censorship. The bishop evidently gave his approval to the result, because a second letter of 27 August reported that the players 'have fownd the meanes to goe through with the play of Barnevelt, and it hath had many spectators and receaved applause'.[29] Although it was staged in the same holiday month of the year as *A Game at Chess*, the text as it stands in the manuscript censored by Buc does not show many signs of the overtly political propaganda that the same company plunged into with Middleton's play five years later. The bishop's intervention may be an early sign that the King's company was beginning to engage in the politics of the time, but evidence from the surviving manuscript of the play indi-

---

[28] Margot Heinemann, 'Drama and opinion in the 1620s: Middleton and Massinger', in *Theatre and Government under the Early Stuarts*, ed. J. R. Mulryne and Margaret Shewring (Cambridge, 1993), 237–65, gives a succinct account of the chief political interests at this time, although she conceivably overstates more than a little the number of plays involved.

[29] *Calendar of State Papers, domestic series, of the reigns of Edward VI, Mary, Elizabeth and James I* (London, 1856–1935) (*CSP Dom.*), 1619–23, 71–3. On *Barnavelt* as a censored text, see Kathleen McLuskie, in *The Revels History of Drama in English* iv. 131–2.

cates a far less direct kind of interventionism than was to appear in Middleton's play. What gave the bishop concern seems to belong rather more with the kind of newsworthy staging that put Francis Vere and Robert Sidney on stage in battle at the Curtain in 1601. The fact that the bishop did allow a play about a recent sensation to be staged is noteworthy, however much the censor may have watered it down. It does indicate an acknowledgement of the growing urge to stage serious political comment, if only in the form of a depiction of the sensational events themselves.

Thomas Drue's *The Duchess of Suffolk*, written in 1623 for the Palsgrave's at the new Fortune, was a different though not wholly dissimilar matter. Henry Herbert, from July the new Master of the Revels, censored it heavily. The story came, like several of the plays written for the Fortune at the beginning of the century, from Foxe's 'Book of Martyrs', and its portrait of a persecuted Protestant martyr appealed to the same anti-Spanish and anti-Catholic sentiments that Middleton was to call on a year later. It was not the currency of the story that brought the censor down on this play, but its implicit criticism of the Spanish. Like *Barnavelt*, the censored text that survives shows little of what Herbert thought to be 'full of dangerous matter'.[30] The play itself harks back to the nostalgia for Elizabethan times that often showed up when the stories from Foxe about Protestant martyrs were used. This kind of nostalgia appeared in the Fortune repertory in the first years of James's rule, and again when Prince Henry was seen to be promising England a better future. Its particularly religious form, a kind of affirmation of a better world, makes it a corollary to the anti-Spanish feeling so often evident on the stages.[31]

After the trouble with *Barnavelt* in 1619 Margot Heinemann identifies a strong clampdown on censorable matter, despite which she also finds what she calls 'a wave of anti-tyrant plays'.[32] The plays she regards as part of this wave are mostly known only by their titles, which is not very reassuring, and elsewhere she acknowledges that there was little open criticism or subversion in the period 1620–3 between *Barnavelt* and the return of Charles and Buckingham from Spain, which precipitated a wave of feeling that she thinks led directly to the staging of *A Game at Chess* in 1624.[33] It would be more to the point to locate the period of maximum repression in the three years after James decided to dissolve Parliament in November 1621 because it had petitioned him over his pro-Spanish policy. This set up a time of greater repression on the public discussion of matters of state than England had yet known. By this time the machinery for controlling the public voice, whether in print, in the pulpit, or on the stage, had become more efficient than it had ever been. Buckingham boasted to the Spanish ambassador, Gondomar, in

[30] *Herbert Dramatic Records*, 18, 27.
[31] This nostalgia for Elizabeth recurred under Charles. See Anne Barton, 'Harking back to Elizabeth: Ben Jonson and Caroline nostalgia', *ELH* 48 (1981), 706–31.
[32] 'Drama and opinion in the 1620s: Middleton and Massinger', 240.
[33] Ibid. 248. The background to the story of *A Game at Chess*'s staging is given in Ch. 8.

1622, that 'no man can now mutter a word in the Pulpit, but he is presently catched and set in straight prison'.[34] The playing companies felt this pressure as much as anyone in the public eye. In particular it showed itself when the zealous Henry Herbert moved into the Mastership of the Revels in 1623. He certainly felt himself to be a more rigorous censor than his predecessors. In later years he even insisted on re-reading plays that had been licensed before. 'All ould plays ought to bee brought to the Master of the Revells, and have his allowance for them, for which he should have his fee, since they may be full of offensive things against church and state; ye rather that in former time the poetts tooke greater liberty than is allowed them by mee.'[35] Whatever the ordinary human reaction to repression might be, the absence for the three years from 1621 to 1624 of any platform in Parliament inevitably meant that the playing companies came under pressure as an alternative venue to give the vigorous chorus of critical voices their say.

The rigour of the machinery of control makes the hermeneutics of censorship a tricky subject when looking at the plays of this time. Just when a play was written and staged could affect its content profoundly. Margot Heinemann, for instance, makes a neat contrast between Massinger's *Maid of Honour*, written for the Cockpit company in 1621–2, and *The Bondman*, which was staged at court for Charles after his return from Spain in December 1623, when he started to espouse the militant cause.[36] The second play, she notes, has none of the ambivalence of the first, urging military strength when foreign invasion threatens. This comparison is as useful for what it says about the poet's and the company's sense of discretion in 1621 as its subsequent bravado when preaching to the converted in 1623.

A similar kind of discretion is evident in the same poet's *A New Way to Pay Old Debts*, which pilloried Giles Mompesson as the villainous Overreach. Mompesson's activities had excited the gossips of London in 1621. Massinger waited until he was dead before characterizing him in his pungent rewrite of *A Trick to Catch the Old One*. None the less, however tactful, these plays do show a new sense that plays could and should voice opinions about serious matters of state that deserved to be heard. The drama had become a natural part of the Establishment's culture, whatever limits the government tried to impose on it.

[34] Quoted by Thomas Cogswell, 'England and the Spanish Match', in *Conflict in Early Stuart England*, ed. Richard Cust and Ann Hughes (London, 1989), 117.
[35] *Herbert Dramatic Records*, 21. This was written in Oct. 1633, in his letter to the King's Men clarifying his practices and justifying his ban on Fletcher's reprise of *The Taming of the Shrew*, *The Woman's Prize*, which he had to purge 'of oaths, prophaness, and ribaldrye' before he would allow it to be staged. It was in fact performed at court a month later.
[36] 'Drama and opinion in the 1620s: Middleton and Massinger', 240–1.

8   *From 1625 to 1642: Before the Revolution*

The Caroline control of playing differed from the control system exercised by the Lord Chamberlain and the Master of the Revels under James in a number of ways, not all of which can be ascribed to a specific reason or motive. The smaller number of members of the royal family available to act as patrons might explain why two of the five companies that ran in London after 1629 never had any patron, for instance. From the restart after the plague closure of 1625–6 the King's players gained the new king as their patron, but the others were a mix of new patrons and new groupings without patrons. Beeston set up Queen Henrietta's in place of his former Cockpit company. The Fortune company seems to have retained the Palsgrave as its patron, now the exiled king of Bohemia, but it combined with the former Lady Elizabeth's and took its new name from both the king and queen of Bohemia. The Red Bull company and the later Salisbury Court company never had a patron. The only sign they gave of any need for a special title was the term 'Revels', which both companies used when on tour. That came from the licences issued by the Office of the Revels, now fully the instrument of control for company activities of every kind.

Under Charles the special patents that put a royal signature on the authority of the companies patronized by the Jacobean royal family gradually fell into abeyance. Instead the Master of the Revels issued a more or less annual licence to the London companies, authorizing them to play and to travel. Probably it was thought that this system of control was tight enough, and that the position of the leading companies was secure enough, so that there was no longer any need to give them direct royal or noble authorization. If so, it shows how remote court thinking was from the rest of the country. The use by the city authorities of Norwich in 1624 of a Privy Council letter to overrule the royal signature authorizing the Lady Elizabeth's Men to play shows how narrowly the court was now exercising its power, and how firmly the king's own control now replaced the former functions of the Privy Council. The players challenged the Norwich decision in the king's name, and the matter was referred to the Lord Chamberlain, but it did not bring any compensation to the players.[1] That was one small price they paid for the closeness of the court's grip on the companies.

Except for the King's Men the Caroline companies were a shifting set of groups. As in the later Jacobean period, there were four companies who resumed playing in 1626. They used the four sets of playhouses then available. A fifth company started up when a new hall-playhouse opened in 1629. The King's kept their binary system going with the Blackfriars and the Globe. Beeston kept his Cockpit, and took some interest in the Red Bull. The other impresario, Richard Gunnell, Alleyn's suc-

---

[1] See Ch. 1 and Ch. 22.

cessor and like Alleyn a former Fortune player, augmented his Fortune amphitheatre with a new hall venture, Salisbury Court, in 1629. It is not easy to say how much the new changes were set in motion by the impresarios and how much by the companies themselves. Nor is it easy to find a simple explanation of how completely the impresarios now controlled the companies who used their playhouses, what determined the shifts of company between one kind of playhouse and another, and what prompted the periodic regroupings of company membership. Several companies switched their playhouses, either between amphitheatre and amphitheatre or between amphitheatre and hall playhouse, for reasons that often seem tortuous and individual.

The clearest way to set these rather complicated shifts of playhouse out is in a table. The King's Men never changed their pair of playhouses. All the other companies, identified here in abbreviated form, shifted at roughly the traditional three-year intervals.

TABLE 2. *Occupancy of Caroline playhouses, by years of change*

Year	1626–	1629–	1631–	1634–	1637–	1640–
Cockpit	QH	QH	QH	QH	BB	BB
Salisbury Court	—	KR	PC2	KR	QH	QH
Fortune	Boh	Boh	KR	Rev	Rev	PC2
Red Bull	Rev	Rev	Rev	PC2	PC2	Rev

QH = Queen Henrietta's / BB = Beeston's Boys / KR = King's Revels / PC2 = Prince Charles's (II) / Boh = King and Queen of Bohemia's / Rev = Red Bull (Revels).

It can be seen that no single cause could have ruled these shifts from place to place. The Prince Charles's company, set up shortly after his birth in 1631, used three playhouses in its twelve years of playing: one hall and two amphitheatres. All of the other companies played at two, except for the relatively short-lived King and Queen of Bohemia's, dispersed in 1631 to help form the new Prince Charles's which lodged in a different playhouse, and Beeston's Boys. It does seem that the playhouses were not nearly so strong a factor in giving the companies their identity as has been assumed.

It is certainly true that the distinction between the hall and the amphitheatre companies was not so great in relation to their playhouses as it was, presumably, to their repertories. Henry Herbert was consistent in using the hall companies for court performances and ignoring the amphitheatre groups, except for one three-year period when the third hall company transferred to an amphitheatre. Through that period his knowledge of company membership, status, and repertory seems to have overruled his usual relegation of the amphitheatre groups. The implications of these questions, and their likely answers, will be considered further below.

Under Charles playgoing became socially more respectable than it had ever been, and as a result the different playing companies found their social and cultural allegiances diverging from one another further than ever. More plays were being taken for performance at court, in a winter festive season that grew longer and longer. On the evidence of Herbert's and the court's treatment of the different companies, if nothing else, the companies in the hall playhouses worked more and more distinctly for the gentry and the court, while the amphitheatre companies worked exclusively for the citizenry.

Of all the signs of change in this period, Ben Jonson's sense of his own quality as a writer, which made him produce his plays in a large folio edition, four years in the printing, in 1616, and which gained him widespread respect as a playhouse poet under Charles, is one of the clearest. The Jonson Folio was a harbinger for the new status that printed playbooks now acquired. Plays generally became valued sufficiently seriously to be bought and read privately as well as shared in the playhouses. Thomas Bodley chose to ban common play quartos from his new library at Oxford, but when the Lord Chamberlain and the king himself were readers of play-texts, his seems the more eccentric choice. Inns of Court students were said to prefer Jonson's 'book of playes' to their lawbooks.[2] And when the literate and the politically eminent began to pay serious attention to plays, it was inevitable that matters both of state and cultural policy should enter them more strongly. The old game of 'application' stopped being a covert exercise of personal allusion. It came in the later 1620s to be treated more and more as a serious exercise in moralizing. The older kind of topical allusions gave way to broader moral applications and allegorizations. With respectability plays and their applications became serious, even solemn. As Kathleen McLuskie puts it, 'what the later Stuart drama reveals above all is the triumph of romance over satire'.[3] The plays advertised questions of honour and love, and the difficulties of loyalty in both. These were the moral issues that courtiers and gentry took to be the keys to their culture and their conduct.

It was a period of radical shifts in the more conspicuous features of English culture, especially at the highest social levels. As R. Malcolm Smuts puts it,

During these years, the court became more firmly anchored in London, more distinct from provincial landed society in its outlook, and more sympathetic to the Baroque cultures of Europe. The Crown's great servants stopped keeping military retinues, participating in tournaments, and building prodigy houses on their country estates and began to attend the theater and amass large collections of European art. In virtually every area of cultural life, a revolution in taste occurred.[4]

This shift affected playing and the companies in a variety of ways. At the top level, court interests profoundly influenced the King's Men, and to a lesser extent the Cockpit companies. Whether subservient or subversive, the focus of their repertory

[2] Francis Lenton, *The Young Gallants Whirligig* (1629), C3r.
[3] *The Revels History of Drama* iv. 257.
[4] Smuts, *Court Culture and the Origins of a Royalist Tradition in Early Stuart England*, 1. Smuts also notes (54) how strongly this new culture came to focus on London to the exclusion of the rest of the country.

was on subjects that chiefly concerned the court, gentlemanly conduct, and the morality of government. The Fortune and Red Bull companies catered for a different social and cultural level. While they kept the old repertory of drum-and-trumpet plays, more and more they followed city interests, not excluding the basic issue of proper stances on religion and politics. Their art of 'application' was older too, dealing with the more localized scandals in the city of London, and upholding an anti-Arminian religious stance.

Charles kept his own library of plays, both in print and in manuscript. His high valuation of the drama, and its influence on his thinking that was affirmed so ludicrously by his Fletcherian and quixotic ride incognito across France in 1623 to capture the Spanish Infanta's heart, gave a licence to plays to become a prime topic for talk at court. He read them like a critic, writing marginalia in the text and voicing comments which on occasions he gave to the Master of the Revels as judgements to help his work as censor. Nobles such as the Lord Chamberlain Philip Herbert, the fourth earl of Pembroke, had libraries of playbooks too. Like Charles, Pembroke read and made notes in them. He had the 1625 edition of Chapman's *Conspiracy and Tragedy of Byron*, for instance, which he re-read in the 1630s marking the analogies between Byron's history at the French court and his own time.[5]

For courtiers to be reading plays made the business of staging them more respectable, and it may have made their 'application' less amenable to censorship.[6] But it also made the choice of plays to be staged more conservative. In the first scene of Massinger's *The Roman Actor* the player complains of the 'sowre censurer who's apt to say | No one in these times can produce a Play | Worthy his reading since of late, 'tis true | The old accepted are more than the new'. So far as the poets were concerned the companies were now burdened with their inheritance of long-running successes. It is doubtful, though, if the companies themselves viewed it quite so sourly.

For the companies, and in particular those patronized by the court, it was a difficult time. The court itself was schismatic, and different grandees wanted the stage to show different things. Loyalty to the patron became a complex issue when the patron was royal, and even more so when he was the king. The King's Men were disloyal to James in 1624 with *A Game at Chess*, when they adopted the court party line favoured by William Herbert, Lord Chamberlain and third earl of Pembroke. Ten years later they worked for his brother Philip, who succeeded him as Lord Chamberlain, when they staged a play that appears to have been designed to boost his opposition in the Privy Council to the king's chief agent on the Council,

<hr />

[5] A. H. Tricomi, 'Philip, Earl of Pembroke, and the Analogical Way of Reading Political Tragedy', *JEGP* 85 (1986), 332–45.

[6] There were in any case discrepancies between censorship of plays in performance and in print. Usually the Master of the Revels proved the more rigorous controller. Herbert ordered Jonson's satire against Inigo Jones as Vitru Hoop to be deleted from the 1633 performances of *A Tale of A Tub*, but the printed text had In-and-In Medlay, an '*Architectonicus professor*' who stages the concluding shadow-play with ludicrous banality.

Archbishop Laud.[7] Philip Herbert after 1642 joined the Parliamentary side against Charles.

The Herberts had a loyal ally in Henry Herbert, brother of the poet, a man from a cadet line of the family who acted as Master of the Revels under both earls of Pembroke. It is reasonable to assume that Henry Herbert's appointment was sponsored by the Pembrokes, not least because in 1623 he took the post from the man to whom its reversion had been promised for some time.[8] The losing candidate, John Astley, was a Buckingham man, and the Pembrokes were devout enemies of the unpopular Duke. Heminges's and Condell's dedication of the Shakespeare First Folio to the brothers in 1623 was only one of several indications of where the leading company's closest allegiance lay at court.

It was not an easy time to be Master of the Revels and censor of plays. As their rising status began to promote them into reading texts, the temptation to 'apply' them grew in scope far beyond the kind of concern that earlier Masters such as Tilney had to be watchful for. When Jonson wrote his prologue in sonnet form for the court performance of *A Staple of News* in 1626, he offered his excuses framed specifically as an appeal for discreet licence from the more studied appliers. Disavowing the thought that the play really was about news, he wrote:

> We yet adventure here to tell you none,
> But show you common follies, and so known
> That though they are not truths, th'innocent Muse
> Hath made so like, as fant'sy could them state
> Or poetry, without scandal, imitate.[9]

This defence of censorable matter is doubly defensive: to the libeller's claim that he tells only the raw truth is added the satirist's claim to offer recognizable truth with the further disclaimer that these are like, but are not actually, truths. The noteworthy feature of this familiar line is its appeal to the courtier audience for faith in the truth of poetry. Previous defences had not dared to give plays the credential of having the same literary status as poetry.

Henry Herbert's work as Master of the Revels looms large in the King's Men's great sensation of August 1624, *A Game at Chess*. The anti-Spanish faction at court must have backed the play, and protected Herbert as well as the company from its consequences. It was not a wholly radical choice of sides. After his return with Buckingham from his abortive Spanish romance Charles himself had joined the anti-Spanish party. The story of the play's staging implies a lot about the King's

---

[7] See Ch. 21.

[8] See Dutton, *Mastering the Revels*, ch. 9, and N. W. Bawcutt, 'Evidence and Conjecture in Literary Scholarship: The Case of Sir John Astley Reconsidered', *ELR* 22 (1992), 333–46.

[9] *A Staple of News*, in *Ben Jonson*, vi. 283. It has been claimed that Jonson upheld the ban on public discussion of foreign policy in *Staple*, and in his masque, *News from the New World*. See Sarah Pearl, 'Sounding to Present Occasion: Jonson's Masques of 1620–5', in *The Court Masque*, ed. David Lindley (Manchester, 1984), 60–77, esp. 60–3.

Company's status by this time, particularly its willingness to oppose their patron and his current prohibition on any public discussion of matters of state.[10]

Obviously staging Middleton's play aligned the players with the anti-Spanish party and its hugely populist antagonism to the former Spanish ambassador in London, Gondomar. The ambassador knew the value of players as symptoms of popular feeling. He took a large party to the Fortune in 1621, and the players gave him a banquet in the adjoining garden afterwards. Since the Fortune company's patron then was the king of Bohemia, husband to James's daughter and the proclaimed leader of the Protestant forces opposing the Catholics in Europe, it was a rather heavy-handed piece of Spanish diplomacy. There is no record of what play the company showed him. In 1624 when Gondomar's English enemies set up the King's Men to perform a play against him he was out of the country and Carlos Coloma had replaced him in London. But the memory lingered on. The company went to great lengths to make their satire specific. According to John Chamberlain they even secured for use on stage the special chair made for him to accommodate his fistula. Chamberlain's letter reports that the players 'counterfeited his person to the life, with all his graces and faces, and had gotten, they say, a cast sute of his apparell for the purpose, and his Lytter'.[11]

More to our point, though, are the negotiations that went on in the background over the play's staging. Henry Herbert licensed it on 12 June, and although he could not have known that the players would go to such lengths in representing Gondomar himself on the stage, he must have seen the political application of the play at large, and, besides its characterizations of the royal family, the personal application of its references to De Dominis, the renegade bishop of Spalato, and Toby Matthew, Catholic son of the Archbishop of York. Herbert's connivance is suggested first by the long wait between the date when he licensed the play and its actual staging, which began on Friday 6 August, and secondly by the absence of any evidence that he was severely reproved for issuing the licence. Staging the play in August meant waiting until the court was on its travels through Norfolk, Northamptonshire, and Derby, a distance sufficient to delay the king's reaction for some days. Gondomar had finally left England in June, to public demonstrations of joy. The plot was well-prepared.

It was a demonstration of less than personal allegiance to the company's royal patron in one striking way. James, visiting Buckingham at his house at Burghley on 2 August, ordered Secretary Conway to summon the 'King's Servants . . . according to His Majesty's good pleasure'.[12] It was a good two days' ride from Burghley to the Bankside, so the letter must have reached the players just as they started their play's run. Such a summons presented them with a direct conflict of interest. Their choice was not what would be expected of the king's loyal servants.

[10] The background of political tension over James's plan for a Spanish alliance is well described by Thomas Cogswell, 'England and the Spanish Match', in *Conflict in Early Stuart England*, ed. Richard Cust and Ann Hughes (London, 1989), 107–33.

[11] *Letters* ii. 577–8. The letter is dated 21 Aug. 1624.   [12] *CSP Dom. 1623–1625*, 320.

The English courtiers attending the king on his travels kept quiet about what they heard of the play's sensational success in London, and it was the Spanish ambassador himself who finally laid a complaint on 11 August. James grumbled that none of his ministers had cared to report it to him.[13] There was certainly connivance at a high level over the staging, and the main figures responsible are not far to seek. Henry Herbert had licensed the play. He worked directly under William Herbert, the third earl of Pembroke and Lord Chamberlain. William Herbert had known the King's Men for many years.[14] After Burbage's death he refused to see a play on the grounds that he was mourning for Burbage who had been his 'old acquaintance'. The Shakespeare First Folio in 1623 was dedicated to him and his brother Philip. The King's Men were the obvious company to stage Middleton's play, if only because they were the least likely of all the companies to suffer real damage from the punishments that would inevitably follow. As Lord Chamberlain, William Herbert was perfectly placed to defend the company and his agent, the Master of the Revels, before the Privy Council.[15]

Threats of punishment came quickly from the king. The Spanish ambassador, Carlos Coloma, who had taken over from Gondomar in 1622, reported the event in scandalized tones to Madrid, and put his complaint to James in similar terms. On 12 August the king's secretary, Edward Conway, wrote to the Privy Council ordering them to 'certifie his Majestie what you find that comedie to bee, by whom it was made, by whom lycenced, and what course you thinke fittest to bee held for the exemplarie, and severe punishment of the present offendors'.[16] Middleton, the author, Herbert, the Master of the Revels and licenser, and the players were all

[13] 'The King is informed by the Spanish Ambassador, that a scandalous comedy, in which his Majesty the King of Spain, Count Gondomar, and the Archbishop of Spalato are personified, has been performed by his players. There being a prohibition against representing modern Kings on the stage, he wonders at their boldness, and that none of his own ministers, who must have heard of it, have reported it to him.' *CSP (Dom.) James I, 1623–1625*, 325. The main documents in the case are quoted by Bentley, *JCS* i. 10–13, and v. 871–7. For the political allegiances behind the story, see Margot Heinemann, 'Drama and Opinion in the 1620s: Middleton and Massinger', in *Theatre and Government under the Early Stuarts*, 237–65. The section on *A Game at Chess* is on 241–8. T. H. Howard-Hill's article, 'Political Interpretations of Middleton's *A Game at Chess* (1624)', in *The Yearbook of English Studies*, 21 (1991), 274–85, is directed at the question of who sponsored the play. Howard-Hill concludes that it was not a direct instrument of state policy.

[14] Besides the conjecture that he could have been the 'Mr. W. H.' of Shakespeare's sonnets, J. Leeds Barroll has suggested that Pembroke was the *éminence grise* who prompted James to make himself the company's patron in 1603. In any case, as Lord Chamberlain he had ample reason and occasion for regular contact with the major companies.

[15] William Herbert was firmly identified as a leader of the anti-Spanish faction. His former chaplain, Thomas Scott, wrote a series of attacks on the Spanish ambassador, Gondomar, and James's pro-Spanish policy. The first was published anonymously as *Vox Populi* in 1620 and printed abroad. The second *Vox Populi* pamphlet was subtitled '*Gondomar appearing in the likenes of Matchiavell in a Spanish Parliament, wherein are discovered his treacherous & subtile Practises*'. Middleton used both for his play. For this and the general context, besides the essay by Margot Heinemann cited in n. 12, see Jerzy Limon, *Dangerous Matter: English Drama and Politics in 1623/24*, 6–16, and Albert H. Tricomi, *Anticourt Drama in England 1603–1642* (Charlottesville, Va., 1989). A very strong case against any direct court role in the play's production is made by Thomas Cogswell, 'Thomas Middleton and the Court, 1624: *A Game at Chess* in Context', *HLQ* 42 (1984), 273–88.

[16] *CSP (Dom.) James I*, 171 no. 39, 325.

specified as targets for punishment. In the event Middleton went to ground, the play's run was stopped on 17 August, and the players were then restrained from playing for about ten days. Nothing exists to show that Henry Herbert suffered any punishment.

That suggests that he was being protected from on high. Initially, though, the investigation focused most closely on his role. A letter of 21 August from five members of the Council led by the Archbishop of Canterbury, to Secretary Conway, reported on their enquiries in a way that directed attention almost entirely to the role of the Master of the Revels in letting it reach the stage.

touching the suppressing of a scandalous comedie acted by the King's players we have called before us some of the principall actors and demanded of them by what lycence and authorities they have presumed to act the same, in answere whereunto they produced a booke being an originall and perfect coppie thereof (as they affirmed) seene and allowed by sir Henry Herbert, knight, master of the revelles, under his owne hand and subscribed in the last page of the said booke; we demanding further whether there were no other partes or passages represented on the stage then those expressly contayned in the booke, they confidently protested they added or varied from the same nothing at all. The poett, they tell us, is one Middleton, who shifting out of the way and not attending the Board with the rest, as was expected, we have given warrant to a messenger for the apprehending of him.

The Board gave the players 'a round and sharpe reprooff', and directed the next set of enquiries towards Herbert:

As for our certifying to his Majestie (as was intimated by your letters) what passages in the said comedie we should fynd to be offensive and scandalous; we have thought it our duties for his Majesties clearer informacion to send herewithall the booke itself subscribed as aforesaid by the master of the revelles that soe ither yourself or some other whom his Majestie shall appoint to peruse the same may see the passages themselves out of the orriginall and call Sir Henry Herbert before you to know the reason of his lycensing thereof.[17]

Surprisingly, given the emphasis that his report laid on Herbert as the responsible body, the players were the only culprits actually to suffer any punishment. As the lowest in social standing and therefore the most vulnerable this was perhaps predictable. But how Herbert got away with it, and why the players in the event also got off so lightly, was a matter that suggests some powerful protection was available for both parties in the affair. Sorting out the factors that left the players with such a small penalty is a question of how much the whole concept of the play was initiated in league with figures at court. The prior involvement of Henry Herbert and perhaps his master the Lord Chamberlain along with other Privy Councillors is the only practical explanation why it was all carried off so painlessly. A clear light on this scandal would say a lot about the company's status at court and the risks they were prepared to take, whether for political advantage or for the money such a long run before such crowds brought them. On paper, of course, the only extant

---

[17] *Acts of the Privy Council of England 1623–1625*, 305.

form of evidence, nobody was willing to admit that they had been directly involved in the plot.

The company had to give a bond for £300, a huge amount for any company, while their case was examined. Herbert was summoned to answer the Council over his own involvement, but in the event his share in the scandal was never examined, possibly because it involved names in even higher places than his. Revealingly, Pembroke wrote to the Privy Council on 27 August saying that

his Majesty nowe conceives ye punishment if not satisfactory for all their Insolency, yet such, as since it stopps ye current of their poore livelyhood and maintenance without much prejudice they cannot longer undergo. In commiseracion therefore of those his poore serv-ants, his Majesty would have their Lordships connive at any common play lycensed by authority, that they shall act as before.[18]

They were not to play *A Game at Chess* again, and enquiries to find who was actually responsible, the poet or the players, were to continue. Pembroke's letter quietly excluded Henry Herbert from this further enquiry.[19]

In the event the Council took a testimony from the absent Middleton's son Edward on 30 August and then did nothing more. There was too much support for the play's anti-Spanish sentiments and too much secret glee at the malicious portrayal of Gondomar for the Spanish complaint to carry any durable weight with complicit courtiers. James in any case had really ceded the war party's position over the Spanish back in June, when he issued a proclamation against the Jesuits and accepted military intervention across the Channel. Charles and Buckingham had tacitly joined the war party after their return from Spain in October 1623, and James's pacifist position in effect became untenable from then on. His own outrage was not just because he heard that his favoured policy had been flouted in public. He always reacted in the same way to an ambassadorial complaint. But even he cannot have taken the ambassador's grievance quite as seriously as the Spanish did.

The company itself made the most of the fame the play brought them. They knew they had been let off lightly, and they knew that they had not only made money but friends by it. The prologue to *Rule a Wife and Have a Wife*, which they staged in the following October, boldly asks 'doe not your looks let fall, | Nor to remembrance our late errors call, | Because this day w'are *Spaniards* all againe, | The story of our Play, and our Sceane *Spaine*: | The errors too, doe not for this cause hate, | Now we present their wit and not their state'. As the enemy Spain was an easy prey for the players.

Two months after that, though, in December, Henry Herbert showed that his teeth were still sharp by forcing the King's company to apologize to him over a lost play, *The Spanish Viceroy*. Whether it dealt only with Spanish wit, like *Rule a Wife and Have a Wife*, or with affairs of the Spanish state, we cannot tell, but the

---

[18] BL Egerton MS. 2023, f. 28.
[19] Almost all students of this incident recognize responsibility in high places. The most sceptical is Richard Dutton, *Mastering the Revels*, 245, who calls it 'an unnecessary conjecture'.

company had omitted to get Herbert's licence for it. Eleven members of the company had to sign a letter, dated 20 December 1624, at the height of preparations for the Christmas season at court, apologizing for the offence and promising 'that wee will not act any play without your hand or substituts hereafter, nor doe any thinge that may prejudice the authority of your office'.[20] Herbert, who copied the letter into his office book in 1633 as a further reminder to the King's Men of his authority, evidently felt that the events of the last few months of 1624 had put his position at risk, and wanted to flex his muscles.

Just how deeply Pembroke's hand was plunged into the setting up of *A Game at Chess* is never likely to be made clear. Even if he had committed his mind to paper, many of the family papers were subsequently lost in a fire at Wilton. He certainly protected the players afterwards, and he almost certainly gave protection to his kinsman and client Henry Herbert. That he knew of the play in advance of the scandal is a more likely theory than that he simply befriended the company in its wake for their courage in staging such a politically sharp satire on the Spanish. That supposition is supported by another case from ten years later, which shows that the Pembroke family was by then well aware of how useful the King's Men could be in mounting populist political propaganda. The story behind *The Late Lancashire Witches* reveals manœuvres by Privy Councillors that drew the King's Men's into the activities of one faction on the Council against another. Again, it is highly likely that it was a Pembroke hand which set the King's Men on to mount the play that was intended to influence public opinion. Using the company for Middleton's propaganda in 1624 made staging plays a far more substantial device in court politics than the Essex conspirators' attempt to use *Richard II* in 1601. From 1625 King Charles, the one king in English history who held plays and playgoing in high esteem, gave the London companies in general and his own players in particular a status that English theatre has never enjoyed before or since. The courtiers followed suit.

The Late Lancashire Witches of 1634 is a fairly clear instance of the King's Men conniving with a Pembroke in high places. A play written to be performed at the Globe in the same holiday month of August as *A Game at Chess*, it repeats the story of Middleton's play of ten years previously on a much smaller scale. As before, it appears that the Lord Chamberlain, now William Herbert's brother Philip, used the leading London company to rouse popular support for his own political position. The play, written to order in July and August 1634, might be seen as a company pay-off for the warrant to take up players from other companies that the same Chamberlain had issued to Lowin and Taylor a year before, in May 1633.

As with *A Game at Chess*, the Pembroke role in the Brome and Heywood play's inception has to be inferred from the circumstances. The so-called witches had been charged in 1633 on the testimony of a young boy, Edmund Robinson, and his father.[21] Twenty-one people from the Pendle area were tried, and twenty were

[20] *Herbert Dramatic Records*, 21.
[21] See Herbert Berry, 'The Globe Bewitched and *El Hombre Fiel*', *MRDE* 1 (1984), 211–30.

found guilty of witchcraft at the Lancashire assizes in March 1634. The judges were worried by the case, which carried an automatic death penalty, and referred it to the Privy Council. In June four accused women and the two Robinsons were sent to London with their depositions. The women were examined by surgeons, and further depositions were taken from the Robinsons. The boy then confessed that the accusations were 'a meere fiction of his owne', but no immediate judgement was made on the case. The six remained in custody in London from 16 July awaiting a Privy Council decision. It was that decision which Heywood and Brome's play was probably commissioned to influence.

Witchcraft became a topical issue. On 20 July the King's Men petitioned the Lord Chamberlain to protect their intended play against competition from the Salisbury Court company, which, they complained, was 'intermingleing some passages of witches in old playes'. This would prejudice the King's Men's 'designed Comedy of the Lancashire witches'. They asked the Lord Chamberlain to stop it 'till theirs bee allowed & Acted'. The Chamberlain duly got the Master of the Revels to do so. The players must have expected him to help them, because their play must have been written with his connivance. The script that Heywood and Brome were writing was based in part on copies of the two most condemnatory depositions in the case laid before the Privy Council. These depositions, along with four others which in fact convincingly refuted the first two, were confidential, and only Privy Councillors had access to them. Pembroke himself was one of the very few people in a position to take out the documents which condemned the witches and supply them to the company.

Pembroke also had a motive. The most ready reason for him to pass on to the writers the testimonies which damned the witches and to withhold those which exonerated them was not that he believed in witchcraft but that he hated Archbishop Laud. Laud was the most powerful man on the Privy Council, and had been openly sceptical of the charges of witchcraft from the outset. Dismissing the charges would strengthen his position on the Council, while convicting them might help to weaken him. As with *A Game at Chess*, the play was commissioned to arouse public opinion and by so doing to influence the Council's decision.

There is no suggestion from the text of the play itself or the surviving account of it on stage by an alert and sceptical witness, Nathaniel Tomkyns, who saw it in mid-August, that the writers took their task very seriously. The players enjoyed themselves with a series of magic tricks and wizardry loosely based on the original Robinson testimony, showing a bridegroom made impotent by witchcraft, a magic banquet with food flown in by pulling on a cord, witches dressed as cats, one of whom loses a hand, and so on. Audiences flocked to see it for three days on end in a minor re-run of Middleton's notorious success. It lacked the political edge of *A Game at Chess*, of course, but witchcraft was high in public interest.

One sidelong feature of this less-than-dignified story about the King's Men is whether part of that lack may not reflect the declining status of the Globe in the 1630s. The play was a far cruder piece of knockabout theatre than Middleton's

Game at Chess. It lacked any kind of satire, unless the very breadth of the comedy was an oblique comment on Pembroke's commission, a refusal either by Heywood and Brome or by the company to take it at all seriously. It certainly includes many of the features that restricted certain of the older plays to the amphitheatres, notably devils and their fireworks. It was an amphitheatre play designed for the summer months when the court and the lawyers were out of town and the most of the gentry going to plays were visitors up from the country on business, like the play's eyewitness, Nathaniel Tomkyns.

Censorship is a huge and complex subject. In its outward manifestations in the work of Henry Herbert, the line that officialdom drew is quite clear through these years.[22] Self-censorship is another question. That the writers of plays had opinions, usually strong ones, about affairs of life and state there can be no doubt. How openly they felt able to express these opinions, and how often the opinions stood at the heart of any play, is a much-debated question. Taking a long perspective, it is possible to find evidence of considerable changes from the 'railing' plays with their local and satirical allusions that the Blackfriars boy company made so much use of in the first years under James, which are mainly jibes with individual applications to real people or types of the time, to the more broadly allegorical parallels used in the plays of the Caroline period. The rise in status of plays and playgoing made thematic stories with obvious applications, either local or general, into a respected and an expected feature of playwriting. Poets like Massinger and Shirley were expected to build recognizable equivalences into their plays. Using thematic parallels rather than direct local allusions of the kind Jonson and Marston made against the Scots in *Eastward Ho!* also made self-censorship much easier. A broad parallel or a hypothetical moral dilemma was a much more discreet device for 'application' than an openly satirical crack. In 1639 the Red Bull company was made to suffer for its reversion to the topical crack.[23]

The characteristic mode of playwriting that developed under Charles, at least for the hall playhouse companies, can be illustrated from a play that Henry Herbert picked out as a model for the time, Shirley's *The Young Admiral*. Licensed on 3 July 1633 for Queen Henrietta's at the Cockpit, and later presented to the king and queen at court on 19 November, Charles's birthday, it gave Herbert an opportunity to be forgiving. Seven months previously he had sharply reproved Shirley and the Queen's Men for a play in which 'ther were divers personated so naturally, both of lords and others of the court, that I took it ill'.[24] This was too much like the old-style satirical games. The company's impresario, Christopher Beeston, had to promise that he would cut the scenes and reprove the poet. He was, as always, effective in his tactful dealings with Herbert, so the play, *The Ball*, eventually was licensed for performance. By contrast, and possibly with some consolatory motive, Herbert

---

[22] Richard Dutton, 'Ben Jonson and the Master of the Revels', in *Theatre and Government Under the Early Stuarts*, has some sound comments on Herbert's notorious interventions with Massinger and Shirley, 75–6.
[23] See Ch. 24.   [24] *Herbert Dramatic Records*, 19.

expressed his admiration for Shirley's next play, *The Young Admiral*, not just because it was free from offensive language, another recurrent worry to Herbert, but because he enjoyed the story. In his *Dramatic Records* he wrote

The comedy called *The Yonge Admirall*, being free from oaths, prophaness, or obsceanes, hath given mee much delight and satisfaction in the readinge, and may serve for a patterne to other poetts, not only for the bettring of maners and language, but for the improvement of the quality, which hath received some brushings of late.[25]

The play did offer a model for 'the bettring of maners' according to courtly interests. Shirley took his story from Lope de Vega's *Don Lope de Cardona*, stream-lining it so that he could focus on a central moral dilemma. He added some broad comic characters, but the main thrust was the moral problem presented to the noble subjects of an outrageous prince who had to be obeyed. The play sets up tests for the loyalty of the hero to his ruler, in a context which applies pressures from different loves, of wife and of country, love for the wife conflicting with love for the father, and in the father love for the son conflicting with love for the ruler. These conflicts were Shirley's addition to his Spanish source.[26] Tests of love and honour in the face of monstrous behaviour by the prince were not ready subjects for censorship in the way that foul language or caricatures of local figures were.

This model for the 1630s was of course aimed only at the courtly end of the social spectrum. Under Charles, playgoing and the playhouses apportioned themselves fairly evenly across this spectrum. In 1629 Richard Gunnell, formerly an associate of Alleyn's at the Fortune, built himself a third hall-playhouse in Whitefriars to compete with the Blackfriars and the Cockpit. From then on the number of companies that Henry Herbert tolerated rose to five, although in 1636 a note seems to indicate that he kept to the official line of tolerating only four. He himself took a financial interest in the third of the hall playhouses, the Salisbury Court. That made five playhouses available for playing, and five companies used them from then on. Two of the companies played in the two amphitheatres, the Red Bull and the rebuilt Fortune. The fact that they twice exchanged playhouses seems to indicate that there was some degree of interchangeability in their repertory and their audiences. The equivalence, though, was not only between amphitheatres, since the new hall-playhouse in 1629 stiffened its young company with several players from one of the Red Bull companies, and the company itself later spent three years playing at the Fortune. The apportioning of playhouses across the social spectrum was quite even. Like the two companies at the amphitheatres, two companies played in halls, the Cockpit and Gunnell's new Salisbury Court playhouse. The Cockpit impresario had an interest in the Red Bull, and the Salisbury Court impresario had an interest in the Fortune. The King's Servants went on using both kinds of playhouse in season.

---

[25] Ibid.

[26] See John Loftis, 'English Renaissance Plays from the Spanish Comedia', *ELR* 14 (1984), 230–48, esp. 241–2.

There was thus a rough balance in the division between the amphitheatres with their thousands of customers and the hall theatres with their hundreds, marked out chiefly by the different levels of affluence of their clientele. In summer, when the Globe was in use, the amphitheatres had a capacity approaching nine thousand places a day, while the two halls then running had less than one thousand. In winter the King's Men's transfer to the Blackfriars raised the halls' capacity to about fifteen hundred while the amphitheatre capacity shrank to six thousand. But for all the difference numerically, each kind of playhouse and the social slice it catered for could offer half of the plays available in London at any time.

The different repertories began to divide socially under Charles much more clearly than was apparent under James. Even the poets writing for the theatre show evidence of an upward movement socially. Massinger and Shirley, both professionals, were caught up in 1630 in a conflict mounted by the amateur poets of the court, William Davenant, Thomas Carew, and their friends, who fought for and eventually took over the Blackfriars for their own plays. Shirley, Massinger, and Ford retreated to Beeston's Cockpit. Shirley, the youngest of this group, did make a bid for preferment with the Queen, for whose company he wrote in the 1630s, but by then he had already been shouldered out by younger poets of higher social stature.

None the less, it was not in any way a simple division. The playgoers divided themselves much more distinctly than some of the companies and their repertories did. The players continued the practice of switching between hall and amphitheatre as readily as they had done in Beeston's first years at the Cockpit. That one company could switch between the Fortune and the Salisbury Court, for instance, has a heavy bearing on the question of the gulf between the select audiences at the halls and the populace at the amphitheatres. It suggests that while the playgoers stuck to the playhouses they were used to or could afford, there was a much less evident gulf between the companies that catered to them. The companies seem to have made rather less of where they played than we are inclined to now.

Mainly working on the basis of the different repertories, Martin Butler has identified three social levels in the audiences at this time: the courtly, the élite, and the popular.[27] By that division the King's Men and to a much lesser extent the Cockpit companies provided for the courtly audiences. The popular plays were at the Fortune and Red Bull. The élite gentry kept themselves to the halls, but not in company with the courtly. Such a three-level social division is difficult to see clearly because it overrides the simple two-level split in the kinds of playhouse and their pricing. It finds the middle level, the non-courtly élite, at the halls, and has to divide the courtly at the Blackfriars and the Cockpit from the élite at the same playhouses and the Salisbury Court. Given the ease with which the companies switched from one kind of playhouse to the other, identifying two kinds of playgoer at the halls is a dubious approach. By Butler's categories the three halls between

[27] Martin Butler, *Theatre and Crisis* (Cambridge, 1984), 282. See esp. chs. 3 and 4, on court drama and the courtier plays about lovers and tyrants. See also Alexander Leggatt, *Jacobean Public Theatre*, 28–39.

them had to provide for the 'élite' (on the simple grounds that the 'populace' could not afford their prices) and also for the courtly. It is inevitable that divisions of some kind should be found in such audiences. But whether the courtiers can be separated so easily from the élite among the gentry is possibly to make too much use of the hindsight that can be taken from the post-1640 political divisions.

According to the threefold division, the Cockpit and Salisbury Court hall companies avoided the old-fashioned 'drum-and-trumpet' repertoire of the amphitheatre companies, but they also avoided the courtly affiliations of court drama, the pastoral and the plays of the courtier poets that the King's Men staged at the Blackfriars. Butler gives an insightful section in chapter 7 of his book about the city comedies that appealed variously to courtiers and the gentry. This division does seem to make a rather uncomfortable reformulation of the obvious gulf between halls and amphitheatres. There was certainly a marked division of values between the different social groupings, but whether on the one hand it is right to extend the obvious twofold division into three, or whether the threefold grouping should not itself be seen as a dangerous over-simplification of the multitude of individual attitudes that developed in these years, it is not easy to say. We might, for instance, question Butler's demotic and heroic elevation of Brome's *A Jovial Crew, or the Merry Beggars*, staged by Beeston's Boys at the Cockpit in 1641, to the status of 'a truly national play written at a turning-point in the history of the English stage and the English nation',[28] a potent reaction to political crisis. It may be such an iconic text, though we should note that Pepys saw it twice in 1661, and called it 'the most innocent play that ever I saw'.[29] Innocence is not the most obvious mark of a rising national consciousness.

It took some years for the courtly fashion to impose itself at any level of the general London public. Most of the evidence about the start of this innovation comes not from the plays in themselves but from a dispute that was advertised on stage at the Blackfriars in 1630, and has sometimes been called the second poets' war. It generated a strong rivalry between the new Blackfriars poets and those at Beeston's Cockpit, but perhaps more weightily it also marked a fight between playgoing factions at the Blackfriars itself, between supporters of the new courtier poets and those of the old guard of professional writers such as Massinger, and the Inns of Court resident and long-time collaborative playwright, John Ford, who were still writing for the King's Men.

The dispute started in 1629, when Davenant wrote a play, *The Just Italian*, for the King's Men at the Blackfriars. The play was not well received, so to accompany its publication in 1630 Carew wrote a poem attacking the plays and the audience's preference for the rival and currently more popular repertory at the Cockpit. He started by noting how generous Davenant himself was to weaker poets: 'I have

---

[28] *Theatre and Crisis*, 275. The play is discussed at length, 269–79. Butler's discussion of the shift through the last years in playwriting from popular to political, 228–36, is particularly cogent. He sees *The Court Beggar* (1640) as 'the tip of an iceberg of popular political drama' (232), almost all of which has melted away. Beeston's Boys staged *The Court Beggar* at the Cockpit in 1639–40.

[29] *JCS* iii. 70.

beheld, when pearched on the smooth brow | Of a fayre modest troope, thou didst allow | Applause to slighter workes'. But now, Carew complained, the noisy mob have taken over, and this is working against the Davenant mode: 'he is taxed for drowth | Of wit, that with the crie, spends not his mouth'. Noisy playgoers in their numbers will 'slight | All that exceeds Red Bull, or Cockepit flight', while they leave the Blackfriars empty, for all its great traditions: 'the true brood of Actors, that alone | Keepe naturall unstrayn'd Action in her throne[30] | Behold their benches bare, though they rehearse | The tearser *Beaumonts*, or great *Johnsons* verse'.[31]

Carew was declaring several allegiances here. In part he was evoking Lyly's and Sidney's preference expressed back in the 1580s for soft smiling over loud laughter in the theatre, and the subtler form of wit that provokes the quiet smile. Audiences given to guffaws and 'ignorance' he now finds at the Cockpit, the reason for which he ascribes to the long-standing link between the Cockpit plays and those of the Red Bull, some of which Beeston had been redeploying at the Cockpit. The Blackfriars, complains Carew, maintains the great tradition of witty poetry marked by Jonson and Beaumont, and has small audiences as a result. In the past, he says, the 'weake | Spectator gave the knowing leave to speake', but now only noise in the volume more suited to amphitheatres than to halls prevails with modern playgoers.

Carew's attack on the Cockpit repertory brought a prompt response, and not only from the Cockpit poets. Shirley was the writer-in-residence at the Cockpit, and his *The Grateful Servant* was rushed into print in the same year with verses that responded to Carew's attack. Thomas Craford dismissed Carew's verses as 'a discourse of cock and bull'. Thomas Randolph, one of the Sons of Ben,[32] acknowledged the Cockpit's takeover of the Red Bull's martial tradition, writing of Shirley's verse that 'I heare the muses birds with full delight | Sing where the birds of mars were wont to fight'.

Shirley himself wrote a dignified address to his readers objecting to Carew's attack on the Cockpit players and, more personally, on its stage poetry. Carew had characterized the Cockpit as an 'adulterate stage, where not a tong | Of th'untun'd Kennell, can a line repeat | Of serious sence, but like lips, meet like meat'. Carew's

---

[30] This claim that only the King's Men could act well in 1630 has to be set against Jonson's complaint about his *New Inn*, which he printed in 1631 with a title-page that said, 'As it was never acted, but most negligently play'd, by some, the Kings Servants. And more squeamishly beheld, and censured by others, the Kings Subjects. 1629'.

[31] Verses prefixed to Davenant, *The Just Italian*, 1630. A longer account of this dispute and its context, and the way it drove Ford to write for Beeston instead of the King's Men, is in Gurr, 'Singing through the Chatter: Ford and Contemporary Theatrical Fashion', in Michael Neill (ed.), *John Ford: Critical Re-Visions* (Cambridge, 1988), 81–96.

[32] The Jonson allegiance in these years is an odd feature of the poetic groupings in Charles's time. Early 'Sons of Ben' like Beaumont and Fletcher had followed his path from writing for the boy companies to writing for the King's Men, but the Caroline group, identified formally as the 'Sons', included, besides Randolph, Carew himself, Lucius Cary, James Howell, Joseph Rutter, William Cartwright, Jasper Mayne, Thomas May, and Herrick. As writers of plays for the different companies of the time their loyalties appear to have been spread surprisingly indiscriminately.

attack bit deep and wide. Shirley was not the only stage poet to be stung by the claim that his Cockpit verse was 'untun'd'. So was Heywood, then writing for the Cockpit, and much more strikingly, so was Massinger, the resident poet of the time at the Blackfriars. It was a quarrel about what kind of stage poetry should be the ruling fashion. Shirley's defenders upheld his 'So smooth, so sweet' verse against Davenant's 'mighty rimes, | Audacious metaphors'. Massinger, a more local and immediately vulnerable target than Shirley, was attacked by the Carew side for writing 'flat | dull dialogues frought with insipit chatt' in contrast with Carew's own 'sweet Muse, which sings | ditties fit only for the eares of Kings'.[33] It was, at least ostensibly, a question of different tastes in poetic style. Literary criticism had at last reached the playhouses. Davenant's next play for the King's Men, *The Wits* (1633), applauded the division of the Blackfriars audience into two factions. He could do so because he knew his own faction was winning.

Shirley's troubles indicate some of the pressures that helped to introduce this shift of values to the hall-playhouse companies after 1630. In 1632, possibly because he was the resident poet of the Queen's own playing company, he was appointed to a post in Henrietta Maria's household.[34] For two years he served her loyally. In 1633, calling himself 'Servant to her Majesty', he mockingly dedicated his new play, *The Bird in a Cage*, to the by then caged William Prynne, in prison for *Histrio-mastix*, his giant book against playing. Written over at least the five years before 1633, *Histrio-mastix* had the bad luck to come from the press with its attack on the offensiveness of women who chose to appear on stage just after Henrietta Maria had herself appeared in a play at court.[35] Prynne's attack was massively intense and personal. He had enjoyed going to plays as a youngster, but had repented. In 1633 he rehearsed all the old arguments against playing with new vigour and new applications. In effect, *Histrio-mastix* was a political document. It implicitly attacked the court for its devotion to theatre, in ways that emphasized the distance of court from country. Charles and his queen were divorced from the spirit and the morality of society as Prynne upheld it. Marvell's later description of Charles in his *Horatian Ode* as 'the royal actor . . . upon that memorable scene' was a delicate reformulation of the point that Prynne tried so laboriously to make. The Star Chamber punished Prynne by taking his money and his academic degrees, putting him in the pillory and cropping his ears, and leaving him in the Tower for life. How much that was done in defence of playing and how much for the personal affront to Henrietta it is not easy to say. If the former, it was the sternest defence

[33] Quoted by Peter Beal, 'Massinger at Bay: Unpublished Verses in a War of the Theatres', *YES* 10 (1980), 190–203.

[34] For a general account of Shirley's short-lived career as Valet to the Chamber of Queen Henrietta Maria, see Marvin Morillo, 'Shirley's "Preferment" and the Court of Charles I', *SEL* I (1961), 101–7.

[35] The animosity of most preachers towards playing should not be underestimated. It influenced the civic authorities outside London to ban players, and it influenced Parliament when it closed the playhouses in 1642. Nor was animosity towards the Catholic queen confined to the pulpits. In the 1630s church bells always rang to celebrate the anniversary of Queen Elizabeth's accession, after remaining conspicuously silent the day before, which was Henrietta Maria's birthday. See Jonson, *Underwoods* lxvii (1630).

that government ever made of playing.[36] Shirley was certainly on the court's and Henrietta's side as a defender of playgoing in this matter.

His alliance with the queen's court faction was, however, short-lived. He was chosen to supply the libretto for a masque at court, *The Triumph of Peace*, in 1633, and in the 1633–4 Christmas season the king judged *The Gamester*, according to Herbert, to be 'the best play he had seen for seven years'.[37] But in 1636, when the playhouses were closed by plague, he left London for a four-year stint in Dublin. Davenant, not Shirley, got the laureateship in 1638. As a follower of the queen Shirley was in direct competition with Davenant and the imitators of *The Arcadia* and the pastoral mode, a role that did not suit him well. The fashion for platonic love and the *précieuse* concern for Arcadian pastoralism that Henrietta Maria brought from France suited Carew, Suckling, and Lovelace much better.[38]

In fact it was the King's company who offered more pastorals than the Cockpit company at this time. Walter Montague's seven-hour *The Shepherd's Paradise*, which was staged at court on 9 January 1633, and in which Henrietta Maria acted, not only gave the king occasion to punish Prynne for his condemnation of women who demeaned their womanhood by acting, but provided a guarantee for the King's Men's subsequent success when they revived Fletcher's distinctly briefer *The Faithful Shepherdess* for the court in 1634.[39] Pastorals, along with stories of pure and platonic love, the extreme of virtue free from sex that stood at one end of Fletcher's gamut of the different kinds of shepherd love, became the fashion that predominated at court.[40] It was evidently not much to Shirley's taste.

How much it may have been to the taste of the general public, let alone Butler's élite, is difficult to say, since the plague closure of 1636 imposed drastic changes on the playing companies and those changes to some extent upset all the trends of the preceding years. The King's Men stayed in position, continuing to cater loyally to the king and queen at court and at the Blackfriars. But Beeston replaced Queen Henrietta's company at the Cockpit during the closure with a new group of younger players, keeping the Cockpit's existing repertoire of plays popular with the gentry and maintaining the firmly middle-of-the-road policy that had sustained the Queen Henrietta's company over the preceding decade. Whether he kept that policy and that kind of play out of choice, in order to differentiate his company's

[36] Philip Edwards has some acute comments on Prynne's book in *The Revels History of Drama in English*, vol. iv. *1613–1660*, 63–5. Butler gives 15 pages (ch. 5) to a commentary on him and what he stood for in *Theatre and Crisis*.

[37] *Herbert Dramatic Records*, 55.

[38] It has been argued that Shirley wrote a dramatization of *The Arcadia* in 1632 as part of his new allegiance. See, however, Alfred Harbage, 'The Authorship of the Dramatic *Arcadia*', *MP* 35 (1938), 233–7.

[39] See Gurr, *Playgoing in Shakespeare's London*, 181–2. Henrietta Maria's devotion to Neoplatonic love and its pastoral forms, and the plays written for it, started in or before 1633. Davenant's *Love and Honour* (1634) was an early attempt at the genre. See Mary Edmond, *Rare Sir William Davenant* (Manchester, 1987), 56, and Anne Barton, *Ben Jonson, Dramatist* (Cambridge, 1984), 264.

[40] For a concise summary of the cult of Neoplatonism, see James Bulman, 'Caroline Drama', in *The Cambridge Companion to English Renaissance Drama*, ed. A. R. Braunmuller and Michael Hattaway (Cambridge, 1990), 375–8.

repertory from his rival's, or whether he simply held to what he knew had good commercial value, we cannot say. Once a long repertoire of viable plays popular with London's audiences had been built up, as Massinger acknowledged in 1625 in *The Roman Actor*, it would never be easy for any company to switch its policy very radically, even if they had wanted to. The Beeston position only slipped in the last two years, when Christopher's son William tried to mount a satire by Brome about recent royalist activities on the Cockpit's stage and incurred official censure and a political reversal by losing his post to the courtier poet Davenant. But I think it unlikely that Henry Herbert, when he imposed that punishment on the younger Beeston, was opting in any deliberate way for the Blackfriars repertory against the Cockpit's.

The plethora of comments that come from the poets and the more aspiring gentry in this last decade condemning old-fashioned audience preferences is one mark of the way the repertories were separating and different playhouses catering to more clearly distinguishable appetites. The 'Praeludium', written for the 1638 revival at the Cockpit of Thomas Goffe's nineteen-year-old contribution to the current fashion for pastorals, *The Careless Shepherdess*, has a gentleman from the Inns of Court condemning the raw audiences who 'did nothing understand but fools and fighting'. His opposites, a country gentleman and a citizen, both make it clear that he is dismissing what they prefer, and the citizen leaves for 'the Bull or Fortune' where he can see a play for much less, and 'a Jig to boot'. Not even Jonson, the first critic to cast audiences in the role of judges, saw the range of audience tastes as having the social and aesthetic breadth that was proclaimed in the 1630s.

It was a wide gap between the courtly focus of the King's Men's pastoral plays that followed Montague's *The Shepherd's Paradise* on the one hand, and the mockery of royalty and the court in *The Court Beggar*, Richard Brome's wittily satirical piece written for the Cockpit in 1640, on the other. Brome's play appears to have been the one which was banned for its political satire and especially its 'passages of the K.s journey into the Northe'.[41] One of the reasons Herbert reacted so strongly to it was probably not just its satire but the hostility it displayed to the courtier poets Suckling and Davenant. Satire against personalities was again raising its head. Brome had already shown a particular animus against the courtier poets in his open contempt for the cost of mounting Suckling's *Aglaura*, which was said to have cost the poet over £300. He may well have nursed his animus since 1634, when he stopped writing for the King's Men in favour of Davenant. But the complex of individual motives that lay behind the choice of the different repertories is never clearly identifiable. Following the royal enthusiasm for pastorals must have seemed to be a necessary part of the King's Men's duty. That they took on Davenant,

---

[41] *Herbert Dramatic Records*, 66. See also *JCS* iii. 61–5, and Butler, *Theatre and Crisis*, 220–9. Besides mocking the incompetent expedition to suppress the Scots, the play burlesques Suckling, a friend and ally of Davenant, who led a troop of soldiers in the northern army. Davenant also figured in the burlesque. He reaped a large if short-lived reward from Beeston's difficulties.

Suckling, and the others was part of that choice. That other writers were excluded was one of its consequences.

Loyalty to the courtier poets' enemies cost the Cockpit a lot. Staging Brome's play without Herbert's licence proved to be a rash political act which lost William Beeston his position as Cockpit manager and handed the garland to Davenant. How tightly all these repertory choices were tied to what the companies and their impresarios felt their public wanted is never easy to settle. What happened in the very last years, with Davenant moving up from poet to impresario, and the Cockpit, the Fortune, and the Red Bull all staging political satires as the train of national events moved out of the king's control, should probably be held separate from the pattern that had settled into place in the previous years up to 1636.

There were significant changes in the composition of the two hall companies after the long plague closure of 1636–7. Both Beeston at the Cockpit and Heton at the Salisbury Court set up new companies consisting of youths with a core of not more than four older players, who may not actually have done much performing. It was an impresario's change. Boys had much smaller maintenance costs than a company of adults, and were more biddable, more easily held under managerial control than a company led by adult sharers. Beeston had followed Henslowe and Alleyn in becoming an impresario twenty years before after a long run as a player. Richard Heton came into the business purely as a financier. I suspect that the chief motive for the changes of 1636–7 was managerial, though it did mean a reversion to something like the old Blackfriars and Whitefriars companies of 1608–11. But it was not in any obvious way a revival of the appetite for the raunchy and outrageous work of boy players licensed by their juniority that had made the early Blackfriars Boys so tasty.

The most colourful part of the end of the story really belongs with William Davenant's rise and fall. He had fought to get a grip on the King's Men's repertoire of plays at the Blackfriars from the start of the 1630s. First he succeeded in displacing Massinger and Shirley from their places as the resident professionals, and probably Brome too. Then, along with friends like Carew, he set his cap firmly at Henrietta Maria and her court, his 'witty' plays strengthening the King's Men's commitment to her tastes. He beat Shirley to a royal poet-laureateship in 1638, a mark of high success and status that may have persuaded him in 1639 that he could move into the theatre business on his own as a playhouse owner and therefore one of the new controllers, an impresario. In March he got a warrant from the king to build a grandiose new playhouse in Fleet Street, by some way the largest and most ambitious theatre-building project that London had ever seen.[42] It would transfer the grandeur of court staging to the public at large. It was to show not only plays but 'musical presentments, Scenes, Dancing, and the like'.[43] Staging with scenery, which Suckling had introduced at a considerable and notorious expense for his

[42] John Freehafer, 'Brome, Suckling and Davenant's Theatre Project of 1639', *Texas Studies in Literature and Language*, 10 (1968), 367–83; and see Mary Edmond, *Rare Sir William Davenant*, 75–6.

[43] Quoted in Freehafer, 'Brome, Suckling and Davenant's Theatre Project', 373.

Aglaura at the Blackfriars a year before, to Brome's derision, was a feature hitherto almost entirely confined to court staging. But Davenant's ambitions were out of scale, and he ran into such opposition that six months later he had to renounce the permission he was given in the king's warrant.

The source of the opposition to his grand scheme is not known completely, but Heton, manager of the Salisbury Court, and his landlord the earl of Dorset both took a part. Since a new theatre in Fleet Street would have been a direct challenge to the neighbouring Salisbury Court and also to the nearby Beeston enterprises, the opposition very likely came from a combination of the two hall-impresarios and their backers at court. Henry Herbert, who had a share in the Salisbury Court, most likely also joined the fight against Davenant. Within six months the poet laureate had to announce that he would withdraw his scheme. A year later he got his revenge and his impresario role at last by taking the management of Beeston's Boys at the Cockpit from Christopher Beeston's son, when Henry Herbert punished him for staging Brome's play. Brome fled to the Salisbury Court.

But Davenant's new venture did not last long either. It is easy to admire his ambitions, which amounted to the kind of theatre innovation that he eventually brought into being in the Restoration.[44] But his practical activities as an entrepreneur and politician are less impressive, particularly given his deep involvement in the abortive Army Plot of May 1641 that cost him all he had worked for up to then. William Beeston retrieved the management of his father's Cockpit for another fifteen months, until Parliament closed all the playhouses. Brome's *A Jovial Crew* was written during these last days.

When the Long Parliament ordered that 'while these sad Causes and set times of Humiliation doe continue, publike Stage-Playes shall cease, and bee forborne',[45] on 2 September 1642, the companies quickly disintegrated. Martin Butler has argued that the closure was not intended to be of the long duration that it eventually became, and that the 1642 proclamation was no more than the usual tactic of closing public meeting-places whenever there was a serious danger of riotous assemblies.[46] G. E. Bentley has pointed out that the number of plague deaths had climbed into the forties through the previous August, which may also have been a reason for the closure.[47] Whatever the reasons, it is not insignificant that for the first time the close-down was done by an edict of Parliament, and not the usual order of the Privy Council. The consistent running down of Privy-Council authority under James and Charles is not a sufficient explanation for that innovation. Parliament had never before intervened over playing. And authority always determined the range of freedoms the companies had to work at their play. Deep in the heaving mass of

[44] Freehafer suggests that Davenant's hostility to Brome extended into the Restoration, since he never staged any of Brome's 20 plays in his theatres, although he could have. Three of them were staged by other companies. See 'Brome, Suckling and Davenant', 382.

[45] *JCS* ii. 690.

[46] Martin Butler, 'Two Playgoers, and the Closing of the London Theatres, 1642', *TRI* 9 (1984), 93–9.

[47] *JCS* i. 69, n. 1.

continual change that shaped the activities of the playing companies, it can be seen that the gradual shift of power from Elizabeth's Council to the king's bedchamber-lords, and most challengeably to Charles himself, and finally its total takeover by Parliament, was in the end the main change that destroyed the companies.

PART II

The Company Histories

This section of the book gives to each chapter a detailed history of one or more of the individual companies known to have performed in London between about 1560 and 1642. To the end of each history is attached a list of the plays, the players, and other known helpers, the company's playing-places in London, a record of its appearances in different parts of the country on tour, and its appearances at court. This last item is the factor that largely determines the inclusion of the company in these chapters, since none of the commercial companies is known to have presented a play at court unless it had been performing in London at some point in the preceding autumn, and its play had been approved then by the Master of the Revels.

The major sources for information about the companies, their organization, the government's measures of control, and such special features of their activities as their travels, are diverse and far from comprehensive. The records that Chambers and Bentley set out in their eleven volumes, for instance, are quite comprehensive for the state of knowledge as it stood in, respectively, 1922 and 1940/1968. Neither, however, takes much account of the playing conditions, and neither takes any account of the distinctive repertoire of plays that each company ran, so far as that could be known. It is in this latter area that the greatest advances have been made in recent years, in the work of scholars such as Scott McMillin, Roslyn L. Knutson, Reavley Gair, Paul Whitfield White, and Albert H. Tricomi.

For this section the chief records of the performances at court have been transcribed and printed from the original records in different volumes of the Malone Society's *Collections*. Records from the Declared Accounts of the Treasurer of the Chamber, giving the specific entries relating to dramatic events between 1558 and 1642, are printed in the Malone Society's *Collections* (*MSC*) vi. 1962, edited by David Cook and F. P. Wilson, under the title *Dramatic Records in the Declared Accounts of the Treasurer of the Chamber, 1558–1642*. A summary taken from the raw accounts is in *ES* iv. 80–118. *MSC* i. 3 (1909), prepared by E. K. Chambers and W. W. Greg, under the title 'Dramatic Records from the Patent Rolls: Company Licences', includes (160–84) the procedure for obtaining a company patent and transcripts of fourteen patents. The Revels Office 'Declared Accounts' for the post-Elizabethan period are in *Jacobean and Caroline Revels Accounts, 1603–1642*, which constitute *MSC* xiii. (1986). The editor, W. R. Streitberger, presents a summary of the accounts with additions and corrections made by recent scholarship, particularly from the diplomatic correspondence for the period.

The Revels Office accounts for the Elizabethan period were transcribed by Albert Feuillerat as *Documents relating to the Office of the Revels in the Time of Queen Elizabeth*, and printed in *Materialen zur Kunde des Älteren Englischen Dramas*, xxi.

(Louvain, 1908). N. W. Bawcutt has identified the 'Craven Ord Transcripts' of a number of the records made by a later Master of the Revels, Henry Herbert. Herbert's own records of his doings from the 1620s survive only in transcripts made by Malone and Chalmers, most of them printed by Malone in his 1790 edition. They were subsequently regrouped by J. Q. Adams and published as *The Dramatic Records of Sir Henry Herbert* (New Haven, Conn., 1917), from which the extracts printed in this book are taken.

Records of the companies performing outside London were first gathered by John Tucker Murray, *English Dramatic Companies 1558–1642* (2 vols.; London, 1910). The first volume deals with the information about London performances, and is largely out of date. The second deals with provincial records. This has not yet been adequately replaced. Murray's listings are selective and often inaccurately transcribed, but up to now they have been only partially checked and revised. In 1931 the Malone Society initiated a set of more careful transcriptions from specific localities with its *Collections* ii. 3., edited by E. K. Chambers as 'Players at Ipswich', 258–84. It lists the entries that can be related to playing, including musicians and tumblers, that appear in the Ipswich Town Council Accounts from 1553 till 1625. In *Collections* vii. (1965) Giles E. Dawson supplied the 'Records of Plays and Players in Kent, 1450–1642', listing them on a similar basis under thirteen towns, each town's records entered separately, with an Appendix identifying the companies by their patron and place of origin. *Collections* viii. (1974) supplied the 'Records of Plays and Players in Lincolnshire, 1300–1585', edited by Stanley J. Kahrl, on the same principles. In *Collections* xi. (1980) David Galloway and John Wasson transcribed the 'Records of Plays and Players in Norfolk and Suffolk, 1330–1642', again town by town, with appendices altered in several ways from the pattern initiated by Giles E. Dawson.

The Malone Society procedures were augmented and developed in the first volumes of the *Records of Early English Drama* (*REED*), issued from Toronto under the direction of Alexandra Johnston, who with Margaret Rogerson edited the volumes for the first town, York, in 1979, and the executive editorship of Sally-Beth MacLean. For the same series David Galloway supplemented his work on Norfolk with a volume for Norwich from 1540. Volumes on the larger cities, Cambridge, Chester, Coventry, and Newcastle followed, and more are in the process of being published. They were augmented by the first volumes that covered whole counties: Cumberland and Westmorland, Hereford and Worcestershire, Gloucestershire, Devon, Lancashire, and Shropshire. In alphabetical order, the eleven *REED* volumes available at the time of publication of this book were: *Cambridge*, ed. Alan H. Nelson (2 vols.; 1989); *Chester*, ed. Lawrence M. Clapper (1979); *Coventry*, ed. R. W. Ingram (1981); *Cumberland / Westmorland / Gloucestershire*, ed. Audrey C. Douglas and Peter Greenfield (1986); *Devon*, ed. John Wasson (1986); *Herefordshire / Worcestershire*, ed. David N. Klausner (1990); *Lancashire*, ed. David George (1991); *Newcastle*, ed. J. J. Anderson (1982); *Norwich 1540–1642*, ed. David Galloway (1984); *Shropshire*, ed. Alan Somerset (1994); and *York*, ed. Alexandra F. Johnston and Margaret Rogerson (2 vols.; 1979). In addition, the records for Berkeley Castle (Peter Greenfield, ed.), Berkshire (Alexandra Johnston, ed.), Bristol (Mark Pilkinton, ed.), Buckinghamshire (Alexandra Johnston, ed.), the Clifford family (John Wasson, ed.), Cornwall (Sally Joyce and Evelyn Newlyn, eds.), Derbyshire (John Wasson, ed.), Dorset (Rosalind Hays and C. E. McGee, eds.), Hampshire (Peter Greenfield, ed.), Kent (James Gibson, ed.), Leicestershire (the late Alice Hamilton, ed.), Nottinghamshire (John Coldewey, ed.), Sussex (Cameron Louis, ed.), Oxford town (Marianne Briscoe and Alexandra Johnston, eds.), Oxford University (John Elliot, ed.), Somerset (James Stokes, ed.) Bath (Robert Alexander, ed.), Wales (David Klausner, ed.), and Dublin (Alan Fletcher, ed.), were consulted at the *REED* office in Toronto. To all these scholars I express my most grateful thanks. I owe a particularly special debt of thanks to the general editorial team of the *REED* project, Alexandra Johnston, Sally-Beth MacLean, and Bill Cooke, for their wonderfully generous help with this rather anticipatory trawl of the current evidence.

The records of the London companies on their travels are necessarily extremely limited. The *REED* documentation has so far covered barely half of the country, with its main materials drawn from the largest towns. As we might expect, given the patronage system, the professional companies mixed visits to towns with visits to the great country houses, very few of whose records for such visits have yet been found. Of the published *REED* volumes, only *Lancashire* and *Shropshire* have so far made very deep inroads into this kind of evidence. Even the municipal records are very far from complete. One town might record the names of the visiting companies in detail, another only under a general entry for all visits over the year. Leominster, for instance, in the *REED* volume for Herefordshire and Worcestershire, entered each company by its name, date, and payment, while the nearby Hereford, most likely the next stop for the same companies, gave only a general note about payments, for instance a curt 'solutis diversis lusoribus hoc Anno xx s' for 1587–8.[1] Worcester similarly lumped all such payments under the one unrevealing heading. Mostly, too, these entries record only a part of the companies' total takings from a visit, that of the municipal payments that were routinely made as a gratuity to each visiting company. Most of the municipal records enter their contribution as a fee paid in addition to whatever the companies took at the door. Such payments were, as the scribes in Leicester commonly put it, 'more than was gathered'. This was sometimes an act of routine generosity, sometimes a form of compensation for refusing to allow the company to play. On occasions it was more or less openly reported as a bribe to the company to go away and not perform. In the earlier years it might be a special payment for the initial performance in front of the mayor and corporation, who viewed the play in the role of censors before the company could be allowed to let its offerings loose on the paying populace.

These are all minimal hints about the general picture. In some towns the recorders chose to ignore the companies altogether. Chester has no records of orders

---

[1] *REED, Herefordshire/Worcestershire*, 123.

about playing at all, either to ban players or of payments made, except for a single entry in 1596 authorizing one level of payment for visits by the royal company and a lower level for noblemen's companies. Cambridge town has a few notes, mostly of bans, but some of protests over the companies who chose to defy the ban and perform in outlying villages such as Chesterton, a neat reproduction of the tactic the companies were familiar with in their use of the London suburbs. How often they resorted to such tactics when banned by the municipalities there is little evidence.

As the government system for the control of the professional companies changed, so do the records. The richest haul of information generally comes in the Elizabethan period, following the proclamation of 1559 which required all travelling companies to first present themselves to the local mayor and perform before him in order to secure approval for 'common' performances. This at the least meant that the mayor would give something from the town coffers to the players for their presentation, and it would therefore normally be entered in the civic accounts. Usually the company's name was specified along with the amount of the town's gift. Except when the gift was to the company to go away without performing, these entries tell us little about the financial side of travelling. They often acknowledge that the town's 'reward' was an addition to what was 'gathered'.

That was the Tudor system. Once the leading companies were granted royal patrons, it decayed, and entries became fewer. The practice of the Master of the Revels issuing travelling licences might prompt an entry, often simply to record that the company was sent away without performing, or to protest against the way the companies behaved in the king's name. But we know that they did perform throughout this period, usually at local inns, mostly without bothering to report to the local authorities. Thomas Crosfield reported in his diary that two aptly-named inns, the King's Head and the King's Arms, were being used for plays at Oxford in July 1635, but there is nothing in the city records in that year about any companies visiting.[2]

The situation at Oxford and Cambridge is revealing. As playgoing became more and more popular, both universities tried to stop students from going to plays. The earl of Leicester as Chancellor of Oxford confirmed the university's ban on 'common stage players' in 1584, saying in a letter than he thought 'the prohibicion of common stage players very requisite', though he would not like to see academic plays by students themselves banned. This ban was renewed in 1593, in the form of a letter from the Privy Council to the Vice-Chancellor and Masters of the colleges. It was signed by both Cecils and others, including Essex and Charles Howard. The message was to be passed on to the mayor of Oxford to ensure that the ban held for a five-mile radius around Oxford.[3] Cambridge did the same. And yet the boasts on the title-pages of Q1 *Hamlet* (1603), *Volpone* (1607), and other plays that they had been applauded at both universities are certainly correct. The

² See Ch. 21, 381.   ³ *REED, Oxford University*, John Elliott, ed., forthcoming.

King's Men played in the town regularly through that decade. They were at Oxford in 1609–10, when they produced the performance of *Othello* that led a don to praise its acting. Robert Armin dedicated *A Nest of Ninnies* (1608) to the 'Gentlemen' of Oxford, Cambridge, and the Inns of Court. He wrote, paraphrasing Justice Shallow, 'I have seene the stars at midnight in your societies . . . I was admitted in Oxford to be of Christs Church, while they of Al-soules gave ayme, such as knew me remember my meaning'. Even allowing for Armin's heavy-handed puns on religion, this suggests a level of informal contact between the company and students that makes nonsense of the official ban. The King's Men are on record as visiting Oxford in 1603–4, in October 1605, and in 1609–10. That they continued to visit fairly often in the succeeding decades there is no doubt, but Oxford has almost no evidence about the companies that visited. Gilbert Burnett in his *Life of Matthew Hale* (1682) reports (4) that while Hale was at Oxford University between 1626 and 1629, he was 'so much corrupted' by 'the Stage Players coming thither' that 'he almost wholly forsook his Studies'. On going to London he resolved never to see a play again. There is no record to say which dangerous companies were the ones that seduced him from his books.

The lists of information supplied here from the cull of provincial records for each company about its travels are even more piecemeal, and in many ways more frustrating in what they omit, than the information about the London activities. The plays the companies performed are hardly ever mentioned even by title. How they lived on their travels can only be deduced by inference from such patches of information as the repair of the Berkeley's Men's covered waggon, or the five horses listed as part of the Sussex's retinue. And these professional companies were the peak of what we know was a mountain range of playing, which started in the foothills with local and town groups, and grew into innumerable small groups retained by the country gentry even after the Privy Council restricted the power to patronize a company to the dozen or so great lords who wanted to. The *REED* records are an essential contribution to the national picture in their trawl of notes about the myriad and anonymous acting groups from the local towns touring their counties, and the flow of jugglers, musicians, bear-wards, and trumpeters who the townsfolk were able to enjoy far more often than the professional companies. But the civic records are, to put it mildly, spasmodic. As the seventeenth century goes on they turn into distinctly infrequent twitches.

Where possible, the records at the end of each of the following chapters give prices in the original form, in pounds, shillings, and pence (twenty shillings to a pound, twelve pennies to a shilling). The years given follow the modern form. Where a date covers two years, as in 1595–6, it marks an undated entry for the town's financial year, which normally ran from Michaelmas (30 September) in the first year to Michaelmas (29 September) in the second. Those towns which used a different accounting year, often starting from Lady Day (the beginning of the old year, 26 March) or from some other date, have their datings noted with the month when their year started.

In this section the lists of the professional companies' players and other helpers are taken from a range of sources. An initial listing of players was made by E. Nungezer, *A Dictionary of Actors and Other Persons Associated with the Public Representation of Plays in England before 1642* (New Haven, Conn., 1929). Bentley improved on this in his listings in the second volume of *The Jacobean and Caroline Stage* (*JCS*), 1940. His records are supplemented here by a variety of other evidence, including the discoveries by scholars such as Mary Edmond and Susan Ceresano. Evidence drawn particularly from London parish records has been gathered together by Mark Eccles in his series of articles about players in *Notes and Queries* 236–8 (1991–3). The lists of court performances are based on Chambers (*The Elizabethan Stage*, iv. 78–130), and Bentley (*The Jacobean and Caroline Stage*, i. 94–100, 173, 194, 213, 249, 299, 322, 336), checked against the *MSC* entries and other transcripts of the Revels Office records. The records of each professional company's travels are based initially on the second volume of Murray, corrected and supplemented by the *MSC* records for Kent (including Canterbury and Dover), Lincolnshire, and Norfolk and Suffolk including Ipswich, then by the eleven *REED* volumes available up to the time of publication, and finally by the further records in the *REED* offices but not yet in print. Altogether, twenty-one counties and most of the major towns in England and Wales have been included in this trawl, rather more than two-thirds of the total area covered by the professional companies in their travels. Even though these records are bound to be supplemented by future discoveries, including the new volumes from the *REED* series, I can only offer the hope that the picture painted here is unlikely to be seriously distorted by any future additions.

The lists of entries from the provincial records about the companies on their travels that appear at the end of each chapter are given here in the most concise form practicable. The lists are organised by companies, and they appear in the sequence of dating for each company's travels that seems to make the best fit of the regions and the travel-times. The dating is based on each town's records and is often imprecise, so that the sequencing of the entries is necessarily conjectural. The dates are given in standardised form. The payment totals are also standardised into a modern version of the old pounds, shillings and pence. Where an entry gives any exceptional information, it is supplied in quotation marks. The need for consistency in the form of each record conceals the many local variations in the records. Like all scholars working in this kind of teritory, I am deeply grateful to the editors of the REED volumes, and most especially to the editors of the materials so far unpublished, who have helped, some of them actively checking my listings, in the long process of making up this compilation. All of the inevitable errors, both in transcription and interpretation, are my own.

The basic criterion for inclusion here, an appearance at court in the 1570s, gives a near-guarantee that the company chosen to perform had been making its presence felt in London. It is, however, clearly inadequate. There is no evidence to say what other and less-noted professional companies might have included London in their peregrinations through the early years but were never called to court, either because of the transience of their visit or because their patron was not sufficiently prominent. The role of the patron, and the extent to which he might push himself by promoting the activities of his company, is only the largest of a variety of unknown factors. The 'lesser' companies justify that adjective more by the absence of information about them than by their real status.

In the twenty years up to the formation of the Queen's Men in 1583 a total of eleven adult companies performed at court. They ranged in patron status from the Lord Chamberlain's own group, Sussex's Men, to Sir Robert Lane's. For almost none of the eleven do we have any play-texts, nor even the names of the men who played in them. For the three plays given at court in 1563–4 we do not even have the company's name. Of the eleven companies that we know performed at court in that twenty years, three of them, Howard's, Hunsdon's, and Derby's, proved to be durable well past the cut-off point when the Queen's Men took their leaders. They have been dealt with in other chapters. A fourth, Leicester's, has also been given a chapter to itself. The other seven, along with one extra group for which a chance conflict has left evidence telling us that it played in London but not at court, are all dealt with in this chapter.

Leicester's Men dominated the festivities through the 20 court seasons from 1563 to 1582. They performed altogether 19 times in 11 of the 20 court seasons. Sussex's Men were their chief rivals, appearing 15 times in a similar number of years. Leicester's brother Warwick's company appeared 12 times over a span of 14 years.[1] Of the 6 companies besides Sussex's and Warwick's that are dealt with in this Chapter, Rich's Men performed 4 plays at court in 3 successive years through 1567 till 1570, and Clinton's Men 3 in 2 successive years, 1573–5. The smallest number of appearances was by Lane's Men, who performed twice in the 1571–2 season, Lincoln's, once in 1572–3, and Lady Essex's, once in 1577–8. Howard's Men, later to become the Lord Admiral's, appeared once in 1576–7 and once in 1577–8. Derby's Men appeared once in each of the three seasons from 1579 to 1583. Hunsdon's, which later fell dormant and was to be reactivated in 1594 as the

---

[1] These figures are chiefly based on the 'Court Calendar' in *ES* iv. 80–99.

Lord Chamberlain's Men, appeared once, in the season immediately preceding the formation of the Queen's Men, 1582–3. The sixth company considered in this chapter, Berkeley's Men, were a long-lasting touring group. They evidently played in London in July 1581, though they were never called to play at court.

Berkeley's Men illuminate the frayed border of this fringe territory where the presence of companies in London led to occasional appearances at court and so into this history. Lord Berkeley had come into his baronage in 1553. He married a Howard, daughter of the earl of Surrey, and his daughter married the son of George Carey in 1596, shortly before Carey became Lord Chamberlain. This Berkeley kept a company which appeared intermittently in provincial records from 1578 until shortly before his death in 1611. He is noteworthy largely because, besides having a company in London that was never called to perform at court, he is almost the only early patron of a company who gave them active support, and whose correspondence about the trouble they got into in London has survived. Addressed to the Lord Mayor, his letter is a courteous response to one of several incidents of the early 1580s when students from the Inns of Court made trouble for the professional players. Provoking fights at plays seems to have been a student fashion of sorts at this time, and even the city's own record in this case appears for once to exonerate the players.

Still, Berkeley's players were caught up by the law. After the incident, in July 1581, they were held in the Counter pending further investigation of the case. Dated 11 July, the city's own note about the trouble says:

Parr Stafferton gentleman of Grayes Inne for that he that daye brought a dysordered companye of gentlemen of the Innes of Courte & others, to assalte Arrthur Kynge, Thomas Goodale, and others, servauntes to the Lord Barkley, & players of Enterludes within the Cyttye, was by this Courte committed to the Compter in Wood streete, and the said players lykewyse. And aswell the sayd players as the sayd Parre Stafferton, weare by this Courte commanded to set downe in wrytinge the maner how the same quarell began.

Lord Berkeley wrote promptly to ask for his men's release. He was clearly well-informed, not only about the incident but about the Lord Mayor's attitude to playing in general, however true his claim to know little about the actual clash. Whether he also knew that the Privy Council had only the day before issued one of its periodic bans on playing in London because of the plague we cannot be sure. His plea to have his men released so that they could leave London and play in the country 'to avoide querrell' may be an innocent offer. Certainly it must have been his players who notified him about their side of the story and appealed for his help to get them out of prison. He was, conveniently for the players, in London at the time of the affray.

However courteous his approach to the subject, Berkeley's letter takes a quietly firm line over the wrongful nature of the players' imprisonment, and gives them a strong testimonial.

To the right honorable the Lord Maior of the Citie of London.
My very good Lord, ther is lately fallen owt some broile betwixt certaine of my men and

some of the Innes of the Courte, sought onely by them. The matter, as I ame advertised, is better knowen to your Lordship then to my self. Whereupon ther is some of my men comitted to warde. If by their misdemeanour they shold deserve imprisonment, I am most willing they shold abide it: Otherwise behaving them selves honestly in every respecte, as I cannot learne the contrary, saving that they played on the sabothe daie contrary to your order & comaundement unknowen to them, in respecte of that I yelde them faultie and they them selves crave pardon. So ame I now to desier your Lordship to sett them at libertie, whoe are upon going into the Countrie to avoide querrell or other inconvenience that mought follow. And thereupon I geve my word that at any time hereafter, if further question shall arise hereby, they shalbe fourthcoming to answere it, and so I leave your good Lordship to the Almightie. From my lodging at Strand this present Tuesdaie. 1581.[2]

There is no indication here what caused the original affray. The law students are unlikely to have been objecting seriously to the company playing on a Sunday. Parr Stafferton quarrelled with some of the players on a matter not mentioned in the report, and then brought his friends to the play to fight them. The plea that the players did not know about the ban over playing on the Sabbath is highly improbable, and their willingness to go into the country was disingenuous if they already knew about the plague ban. What is most evident is Berkeley's regard for his players, and his willingness to intervene to protect them from the law. The company seems to have been a capable one, since Thomas Goodale ten years later was a player in Strange's through its great years. Berkeley's Men's failure to be called to play at court only makes the company marginal by the restrictive criteria used for this book.

If we can call it that without misrepresentation, the least conspicuous of all the professional companies' appearances at court was the one by the Countess of Essex's Men on 11 February 1578. They were called in then at the queen's command to perform instead of Leicester's Men, for no reason that has been identified clearly. It might have been an insult to Leicester, who was not in great favour at the time. It could have been meant as a form of sympathetic gesture to the Countess over the death of her husband the Earl, although by then he had been dead for fifteen months. The Chamber accounts for payments to players simply note a payment to 'The Countess of Essex players . . . for presentinge a playe before her majestie on Shrove Tewesdaye at nighte', and also one to 'the Earle of Leicesters players . . . for makinge their repaire to the Courte with their whole company and furniture to presente a playe before her majestie uppon Shrovetuesdaye at nighte in consideracion of their chardgies for that purpose althoughe the plaie by her majesties comaundement was supplyed by others'.[3] It was either a distinctly last-minute substitution, or a failure of communication by the Revels Office, which should have notified Leicester's of the change of plan. If the queen herself did order it, that would explain the last-minute switch of companies. On the other hand, if the Chamber accounts are wrong and it was not the queen herself who ordered the switch, Leicester himself might have been the one to order it as a gallant gesture to the countess, since he married her secretly the following September.

[2] The city's note and Berkeley's letter are transcribed in *ES* iv. 282.   [3] *MSC* vi. 13–14.

The Essex's company had been in existence since the early 1570s. It first appears under the first earl's name in the records for Nottinghamshire and the west, Bath, Bristol, and Gloucester, in 1573. It is recorded under the countess's name through 1578–80, after which the revelation of her remarriage to Leicester probably helped to make it vanish from the records. It is possible that this company had at least some of the same personnel as the second earl's company, which started appearing in the records from 1581. Given the dates, it is at least possible that the second earl took over his mother's company. Neither company seems ever to have acquired the status to warrant regular appearances at court, although Essex's was the company that went with the Queen's to play in Dublin in 1589 on what was probably at least a semi-official visit. The second earl, Robert Devereux, although he made himself protégé, rival and, from 1588, successor to Leicester, never ran such a strong company as did Leicester, and despite his rapid rise in status at court and his readiness to accept book-dedications from just about every writer of the 1590s, he himself evidently took no trouble to have his company appear at court.

Richard Rich, the first baron Rich, who was Lord Chancellor for three years under Edward VI, was nearly seventy by the time his company first appears in the provincial records. Their run of performances at court in three successive years, plus a performance at Lincoln's Inn three nights before their final court appearance,[4] none the less shows his company's quality. It did not reappear in any civic records through the next decade, although Gabriel Harvey made a reference to the company as late as 1579,[5] two years before Rich's death in 1581. His death would have terminated its activities as a company under his name. Unfortunately, not knowing the names of any of its players, we cannot tell whether they reappeared as a group or individually under another patron's title in the following years. Several of the 'lesser' companies of the 1570s and 1580s seem to exist in this evanescent form for the same reason.

Sir Robert Lane was a Northamptonshire landowner, in his fifties when the first record of his company turns up in August 1570 at Bristol. The only other record of their existence is for their two court appearances in the one season, on 27 December 1571 and 17 February 1572. Lane's company's appearances at court may be not so much an example of patron power as an early instance of self-promotion by the players. The ambitious Laurence Dutton, soon to show up in other companies, may have made his first mark through Lane, who presumably gave his patronage up when the 1572 Act against vagabonds restricted the power of giving their name as patrons to barons and those of higher rank. Dutton and his brother were distinctly restless, transferring from one company to another, through at least four in all, in the 1570s. Whether it was the 1572 Act or their own ambition that drove them to

---

[4] *ES* ii. 92.

[5] *The Letter-book of Gabriel Harvey, A.D. 1573–1580*, ed. E. J. L. Scott (Camden Soc., London, 1884), 67. Harvey's note also refers to Leicester's and Warwick's Men, along with another group, Lord Vaux's. Although on the evidence of Harvey's note the Vaux company also performed in London, it was never summoned to perform at court.

make the first of their transfers out of Rich's Men it is impossible to know. The Duttons reappeared with the next company, Lincoln's, very likely as a part of one large group which made the transfer together. That would suggest that the Act was a deciding factor.

Lincoln's Servants may have been the same as his son Lord Clinton's, though the connection is chiefly apparent through the name of the highly mobile Laurence Dutton, who appeared in both. The earl of Lincoln, Elizabeth's Lord Admiral up to his death in 1585, had a company touring in 1566–7, although the only appearances of a Lincoln's company in provincial records under that name are for one using a later earl's name which started in 1599 and ran for the next ten years. This almost unique absence from travelling by a company good enough to perform at court suggests strongly that it ran under a different name in the country, most likely Clinton's. Laurence Dutton was Lincoln's leader when it performed at court in 1572–3, and he was leading Clinton's when it appeared at court in the following season. He had been with Lane's Men at court in 1571–2, and subsequently performed at court in 1575–6 with Warwick's. E. K. Chambers believes that Lane's Men changed their patron after the 1572 Act, becoming Lincoln's Men, and that Lincoln passed the same group to his son in 1573.[6] It is not possible to be confident about this. A company calling itself Clinton's reappears in the provincial records up to 1577, so they did not dissolve entirely when Dutton moved on to Warwick's, nor did they move as a group with him. Lincoln's disappears from the records until they were resurrected in 1599 for a long run, but they never came within reach of a peformance at court in these later years.

Warwick's Men had a more substantial existence than any of these groups. They also had the strong backing at court and in the country that came from wearing their master's livery, backing that did not greatly differ from that accorded the earl's brother's company, Leicester's. At roughly the same time as James Burbage from his position as leader of Leicester's was building the Theatre, Jerome Savage as leader of Warwick's built the playhouse at Newington Butts.[7] The two companies had comparable ambitions. The location of Savage's playhouse south of the Thames was markedly less advantageous than the Theatre's in Shoreditch on the northern side, being a good mile, or rather a muddy and difficult mile, from London Bridge and nearly that distance from the settled quarters of London. In later years when Henslowe ran it the problem of its smallness and the mud on the route proved a serious drawback to its use. The Red Lion, built in Stepney in 1567, had already shown the difficulties of building a playhouse too far outside the city walls where what thought of itself as London's population lived, the people the playbills spoke to. But the formative concept was similar, and Savage's enterprise sets Warwick's Men up alongside Leicester's in this brief first phase of intensive

[6] ES ii. 97. William Ingram, *The Business of Playing*, 140–1, also suggests that Laurence Dutton had his brother John with him when he led Lane's Men, and that it was the 1572 statute that made them all transfer to Lincoln's.

[7] A full account of Savage's activities is given in William Ingram, *The Business of Playing*, 163–81.

capital investment in playhouses, 1575–6.[8] Again, some collusion between the two brothers as patrons may be inferred, although it is at least equally likely here that Burbage and Savage were taking their chances on their own initiative in equal competition, on the basis of the security that Leicester's Men's had been given by their 1574 patent and the city's Act of Common Council of December 1574. The opening of five playhouses in three years suggests that the five entrepreneurs were infected by something rather more tangible, and most likely more profitable, than a simple copycat impulse.

A company of Warwick's Men had been running through the 1560s, very much on the same pattern as Leicester's, though markedly less frequent in its appearances in the civic records. It played at court in the 1564–5 season, but is then absent from the records through the early 1570s. Savage may even have had to re-establish them in 1574 as part of a general enterprise to compete with Leicester's. They were touring in Devon and the Midlands in 1574–5, and appeared again at court on 14 February 1575. The Duttons had only left Clinton's Men at some point in 1574 (Laurence was payee for them at court on 3 January 1574[9]), which suggests there was a change of membership, if not a wholly new company setting itself up in that year. Warwick's played at court each year from the 1574–5 season until 1580, being eminent enough to present the opening St Stephen's Day play in 1575, 1576, and 1578 (in the other years the opening performance was by Leicester's). Gabriel Harvey named them with Leicester's as one of four celebrated 'London' companies in the summer of 1579.[10]

Their subsequent disappearance is probably explained, however incompletely, by a set of satirical verses written in about 1580. The verses certainly indicate some hostility among playgoers to the Duttons, and possibly also to their new patron, the seventeenth earl of Oxford. The manuscript in which these verses have survived is prefaced by a note alleging that '*The Duttons and theyr fellow-players forsakyng the Erle of Warwycke theyr mayster, became followers of the Erle of Oxford, and wrot themselves his COMOEDIANS, which certayne Gentlemen altered and made CAMOELIANS.*'[11] This made the fourth identifiable switch of companies in nine years for the Duttons, or five if Lincoln's was a different company from his son's, in a period when most players were or were expected to be loyal and long-serving servants of their lords, so there seems to be some point in the jibe. The shift of personnel along with the Duttons certainly seems to have foreclosed on the Warwick's company. Ambrose Dudley himself made no effort to improve the quality of his residual company for himself, which may be a comment on how remote most of the patrons were from their playing servants. The further question, whether the new Oxford's Men of 1580 and onwards was made from a wholesale transfer of

---

[8] Besides the Theatre and the Newington Butts playhouse, the first hall theatre at Blackfriars opened in 1576, and the Curtain opened 200 yards from the Theatre in 1577. Paul's had acquired their own hall playhouse by the Cathedral in 1575.

[9] *MSC* vi. 7.   [10] See n. 5.

[11] The full text is quoted from an MS copy (*Harl.* MS. 7392 f. 97), printed in *ES* ii. 98–9.

players out of Warwick's, is considered elsewhere, in the section on Oxford's in Chapter 17.[12]

In fact, the withdrawal of some of Warwick's players into Oxford's did not result in the Ambrose Dudley company's total disappearance. They, or more likely a revived company, are recorded in Ipswich and Winchester in 1581–2. They finally went into abeyance a few years later when the Queen's Men disrupted five or more of the leading groups by decapitating them in March 1583. Up to then Warwick was as ready as his brother to help his players, and in 1582 his support is evidenced in a clash he had with the mayor of London. Their exchange of letters is the second set of documents showing how willing some of the noble patrons were in these years to support their players against the city. The relevant documents in the London *Remembrancia* begin with an outburst by Warwick, dated 23 July 1582, over the mayor banning a 'prise', a fencing bout, which a player of Warwick's had advertised in a playbill.[13] His letter starts 'My Lord Maior I cannot thinke my self frendely delt with to have my servante put to such publike disgrace.' Warwick's grievance was that the mayor had given his leave but then banned his man from playing the prize at the playing-place in the city that he had advertised on his bills. Warwick went on to complain that 'to repulse him and to forbid the place appointed, after allowance & publicacion of his Bills (wherein my name was also used) and my servante hereby greatly charged, wanteth some part of that good and frendely consideracion, which in curtesie and common humanitie, I might looke for'. The player had run up costs and his lord's public image had been wounded by the cancellation. Warwick was prepared to take that as a personal insult rather than as a reminder of London's policy over playing. 'Yf yow be resolved that it standeth most behovefull for the good goverment of the Citie to have those exercises utterly put downe and none allowed hereafter to deale in these kinde of prises, my man shall rest him selfe without further sute, (albeit the first and last to whome disgrace hath ben offered in this sorte:) But if others be suffered to proceade as heretofore, and they not restrained, aswell as my man; I must nedes juge it no frendely, nor indifferent maner of dealing.' Warwick's real complaint was the insult to his name. It must have been his player-servant who suggested that he should make the quasi-legalistic claim that this was the first time such a ban had ever been imposed.

Impressively, in the face of such emphatic language and the leverage that the Dudleys had at court, the mayor stood his ground. 'The truthe is', he replied on 24 July, 'that I did not expulse your servant from playeng his prise, but for your sake I did geve him licence. Onely I did restraine him from playeng in an Inne, which was somewhat to close for infection and appointed him to playe in an open place of the leaden hall more fre from danger and more for his Comoditie.' That was the mayor's first step. But then a fortnight later the number of plague deaths had increased, so the player was sent out to play his match in the open fields. The mayor

---

[12] Some rather speculative notes on Warwick's Men, including the role of Jerome Savage in its activities, are included in William Ingram, *The Business of Playing*, 171–4.

[13] The correspondence is transcribed in *MSC* i. 1.56–8, 'The Remembrancia'.

closed his letter with an assurance that 'I have herein yet further done for your servante what I may, that is that if he obteine lawefully to playe at the Theater or other open place out of the Citie, he hath and shall have my permition with his companie drumes and shewe to passe openly through the Citie being not upon the sondaye, which is asmuche as I maye justefie in this season'. There was more than one official likely to heave a sigh of relief when, in the wake of the Queen's Men's arrival on the scene, the Lord Chamberlain negotiated a new set of ground rules with the Lord Mayor to license playing in London.

The last of these early companies not given a Chapter to itself, Sussex's, was the greatest and the longest-lived of all the Elizabethan companies except for the three that gained royal patronage in 1603. It ran as one company from 1569 until at least 1594, when some of its players may have joined the new Chamberlain's Men, and provincial records continue to note the Sussex livery well into the second decade under James. Three earls in succession kept it going, though it is not easy to tell from the patchy records of its players how continuous it was in membership and repertory as a single company.

The basic policy regarding playing companies followed by Thomas Radcliffe, the first patron of Sussex's Servants, through his years as Lord Chamberlain, has been looked at already.[14] His company first appeared as a six-man group in the provincial records in 1569, three years before he became Lord Chamberlain. Once he acquired that office his company played at court in February 1573, but then lost out to Leicester's, Warwick's, and the Lincoln's/Clinton's players until 1575–6 and 1576–7. In the season of 1574–5 they prepared two plays for the court but did not perform them. The Chamber accounts do not record that any payment was given them for this preparation, and it may be that they were judged inadequate as performers for that season. Those were the years when Radcliffe's illness made him withdraw from the court, and Charles Howard ran the Chamberlain's office in his place.

The company went back to the court when its patron returned in 1578. In that year Sussex's Men were included in a Privy Council warning to the Lord Mayor to give the companies who had been scheduled to play at court that Christmas leave to practise: 'the Children of her Majesties Chappell, the servauntes of the Lord Chamberlaine, therle of Warwicke, the Erle of Leicester, the Erle of Essex and the Children of Powles'.[15] It was through these years that Sussex's had the services of Richard Tarlton, who evidently played as one of their stars until he was taken for the Queen's Men in 1583.[16] His presence may be the reason why there was such a crush for their play *The Red Knight*, performed before the mayor and his corporation and the citizens in the mayoral hall at Bristol in August 1575. The crush was so great that afterwards the hall's doors had to be repaired. It may of course have

---

[14] See Ch. 4.   [15] *Acts of the Privy Council of England*, xi. 73.
[16] A fragment of *Tarleton's Tragical Treatises* in 1578 says that he was in Sussex's service. See Mark Eccles, 'Elizabethan Actors iv: S to End', *NQ* 238 (1993), 165–76, 173.

been routine for people to crowd in for the 'common' performance of a play after the opening one for the officials. At Bristol the mayor only entertained two or three visits by professional companies a year, so each visit had some rarity value. The same doors had to be repaired again after a performance by Leicester's just over two years later, in October 1577. On the other hand, in between these two visits four other companies had played at the guildhall without wrenching the door off its hinges, and many more performed after the Leicester's visit without any further damage being reported. It does seem likely that Sussex's and Leicester's shared the highest reputation in the country at this time, and were a good draw in Bristol, at least in comparison with Lord Compton's, Essex's, Clinton's, and the earl of Bath's companies, who were the four recorded as performing in the intervening years.

From 1578 the Sussex company with Tarlton performed at court each year until the quiet season of 1581–2, and the one following, just before the Queen's Men were set up in 1583. In the town records outside London the company was often called the Lord Chamberlain's Men, presumably in acknowledgement of the wording on the company's official licence. That title does seem to have given them a cachet of some sort. It certainly tended to get them better levels of payment than the other companies of the time. But in 1583 it suffered the same losses as every other major company. John Adams and Richard Tarlton, its leading players, were drawn into the Queen's Men. That loss took it out of London and also out of the provincial records for nearly two years, until the beginning of 1585. The death of their patron in June 1583 meant their automatic dissolution, and it took his heir some time to assemble a new company. Sussex's reappeared in Kent and Gloucester in that year, and grew stronger as the years went on. They returned for a performance at court in the 1591–2 season, and for a run at Henslowe's Rose in December 1593. Between 27 December 1593 and 6 February 1594 they gave thirty performances of twelve plays at the Rose, including a profitable 'ne' production of *Titus Andronicus* on 24 January. They then linked up with the Queen's Men, probably playing on alternate afternoons at the same playhouse, for a run of another eight performances, adding three more titles to their list.[17] After that they were replaced at the Rose by the Admiral's.

What else was taken from them after that has been discussed in Chapter 4 above. As before in 1583, their leaders and their best playbooks were probably sequestered in May 1594 to form part of the two new companies. Certainly *Titus Andronicus* left their hands at around this time and went into the Chamberlain's Men's repertoire. Their departure from the Rose also deprived them of *The Jew of Malta* after its

---

[17] *The Ranger's Comedy* and *King Leir*, two of the plays not performed in the previous run, were the Queen's Men's, and may have been performed by them separately. *Friar Bacon and Friar Bungay*, another of the new plays, was printed in 1594 as a Queen's Men's play. But it had previously been played at the Rose by Strange's so, like *The Jew of Malta*, it may have been a Henslowe property. This union of the two companies in Henslowe's *Diary* is likely to have been a book-keeper's merger rather than a real one between the two groups. See Ch. 4.

three performances.[18] The company then dissolved completely, its patron having died in December 1593, because it does not appear in country records at all between 1594 and the financial year that started in October 1602. Probably the fourth earl raised a new company when James came to the throne. This group is recorded outside London until at least 1618.

There is little evidence about the plays in the Sussex's repertory between 1578 and 1594, apart from the few that Henslowe records, some of which were probably his own stock. Shakespeare's *Titus*, which the 1594 title-page says was at first Strange's and then Pembroke's before it passed to Sussex's, is their chief credential. Heywood's *Apology* reports them as also having played *Friar Francis* at King's Lynn:

At *Lin* in *Norfolke*, the then Earle of *Sussex* players acting the old History of Fryer *Francis*, & presenting a womane, who insatiately doting on a yong gentleman, had (the more securely to enjoy his affection) mischievously and seceretly murdered her husband, whose ghost haunted her, and at divers times in her most solitary and private contemplations, in most horrid and fearefull shapes, appeared, and stood before her. As this was acted, a townes-woman (till then of good estimation and report) finding her conscience (at this presentment) extremely troubled, suddenly skritched and cryd out Oh my husband, my husband! I see the ghost of my husband fiercely threatning and menacing me. At which shrill and unexpected out-cry, the people about her, moov'd to a strange amazement, inquired the reason of her clamour, when presently un-urged, she told them, that seven yeares ago, she, to be possest of such a Gentleman (meaning him) had poysoned her husband, whose fearefull image personated it selfe in the shape of that ghost: whereupon the murdresse was apprehended, before the Justices further examined, & by her voluntary confession after condemned. That this is true, as well by the report of the Actors as the records of the Towne, there are many eye-witnesses of this accident yet living, vocally to confirme it.[19]

This is made to seem like a story dating back to long before 1594. Unfortunately, there is nothing now in the records for King's Lynn to confirm any link between a visit by Sussex's Men and the conviction of a murderer. Through 1580 to 1605[20] the records for King's Lynn are exclusively concerned with a local company of waits, except for a series of visits by the Queen's Men in 1586, 1587, 1588–9, 20 June 1591, 21 July 1595, and again in 1596, one by 'the Lorde Chamberlynes plaiers'[21] in the year up to November 1586, a visit by Essex's Men in 1591, and one by Pembroke's in 1592–3, plus payments to Derby's and Morley's not to play on 20 September 1594, and to Worcester's not to play in 1598–9. Sussex's made only one appearance under that name, in 1592–3, when they were paid the same amount as Pembroke's. This may be the origin of the story, and *Friar Francis*, which is one of

---

[18] For an alternative reading of the early history of *Titus* and *The Jew of Malta*, see Scott McMillin, 'Sussex's Men in 1594: The Evidence of *Titus Andronicus* and *The Jew of Malta*', *Theatre Survey*, 32 (1991), 214–23.

[19] Thomas Heywood, *An Apology for Actors* (1612), G1v–G2.   [20] *MSC* xi. 61–9.

[21] The Lord Chamberlain in 1586 was Henry Carey, whose policy was to run no company of his own while acting as Chamberlain. The company might have been running under the name of his predecessor Sussex, though he had been dead 3 years by then.

the titles that appears only a year later in Henslowe's lists as an Admiral's play, may have descended to Henslowe from the Sussex's stay at the Rose in 1593–4. But I can find no evidence of any woman being convicted for murder in King's Lynn either in 1592–3 or in 1586 when the 'Lorde Chamberlynes' company played there. Heywood may just be repeating hearsay. The record of the Sussex's company's visit does at least make it seem a little more than a total invention.

John Adams is noted in the Chamber accounts as the company's payee in 1576. Unfortunately his and Tarlton's are the only names that can definitely be ascribed to the company through any of these years. Both were taken, possibly along with a third player from amongst their fellows, for the Queen's Men in 1583. The court records name most of the plays they performed there up to 1583, but none of the texts has survived. Some of the texts as well as the titles from the run of twelve plays with Henslowe have survived, but none of the players' names. The rest, after 1594, is silence.

BERKELEY'S PLAYERS, 1577–1611

Plays
What Mischief Worketh in the Mind of Man (lost) (Bristol July 1578).

Playing Sharers
Thomas Goodale, Arthur King.

London Playhouses
Curtain? Theatre in 1581?

At Court
never.

Travelling records
Gloucester 1577–8, 14s. 6d. / Coventry 1578, 5s. / Bath 11 July 1578, 4s. 3d. / Bristol July 1578 'the matter was what mischeif workith in the mynd of man', 10s. / Gloucester 1578–9, 6s. 8d. / Abingdon 1578–9, 5s. / Coventry 1579, 6s. 8d. / Bath early 1579, 7s. 2d. / Bristol Nov. 1579, 13s. 4d. / Gloucester 1579–80, 13s. 4d. / Coventry 1580, 6s. 8d. / Gloucester 1580–1, 6s. 8d. / Bath June 1580–1, 7s. 4d. / Stratford-on-Avon 1580–1 / Maldon 1581 / Coventry 1581, 10s. / Gloucester 1581–2, 13s. 4d. / Bath June 1581–2 / Coventry 1582, 10s. / Ludlow 11 Sept. 1582, 6s. 8d. / Gloucester 30 Nov. 1582, 13s. 4d. / Exeter Dec. 1582, 'to me Lord Bertletts players', 13s. 4d. / Bath June 1582–3, 9s. 1d. / Stratford-on-Avon 1582–3 / Coventry 1583 'the Lo Barkeles players & musicions', 13s. 4d. / Bridgwater, Somerset Dec. 1583 'at the comen haulle', 13s. 4d. / Barnstaple, Devon 1583–4 'to the Lord Bartlettes men beynge Enterlude players', 5s. / Bath June 1583–4, 10s. / Fordwich, Kent 1583–4 'my lorde Bartleys players', 6s. 8d. / Dover 4 July 1584, 5s. / Coventry 1584, 10s. / Nottingham 7 Oct. 1584, 5s. / Wollaton Hall, Nottinghamshire (Willoughby household accounts) Oct. 1584 'my Lord bartleis players', 10s. / Bath June 1584–5, 13s. 4d. / Gloucester 1584–5, 10s. /

Bridgwater, Somerset 9 Dec. 1584, 10s. / Totnes, Devon 1584–5, 6s. / Dover May 1585, 10s. / Hythe, Kent 1586 'my lord bartlettes players', 3s. 4d. / Bath 1586–7, 9s. 10d. / Nottingham 1591–2, 2s. 6d. / Ludlow 11 June 1592, 6s. 8d. / Faversham, Kent 1597–8, £1. / Coventry Dec. acct. 1598, 10s. / Leicester 1598, 10s. / Saffron Walden 1598–9 / Leominster, Herefordshire 1600–1, 10s. / Faversham, Kent 1602–3 'my Lo: Bartlett players', 10s. / Coventry Nov. acct. 1604, 10s. / York Churchwardens' Accounts 1605, 20s. / Bridgwater, Somerset May–July 1605, 20s. / Coventry Nov. acct. 1607, 20s. / Coventry Nov. acct. 1608, 13s. 4d. / Canterbury 1608–9 'to ye lorde Bartely his players for that they shoulde not playe here in the citye by reason that the sicknes beynge her', 20s. / Coventry 13 June 1609, 10s. / Norwich 3 May 1610 'unto the lord Abnes his men xl s and unto the Lord Bartletts men xx s in regard that they should not play', £3. / Canterbury Nov. 1610 'for that they should not playe by reason of the sicknes' 10s. / Coventry 25 Nov. 1612 'Paid unto the lord Barkeleys men xxij s when Maister Maior and his Bretheren Did Dyne at Callowden', 22s.

ESSEX'S PLAYERS, 1572–1596

At Court
11 Feb. 1578.

Travelling
Wollaton Hall, Nottinghamshire (Willoughby household accounts) July 1572 'to therle of Essex his players for playing twyce before my mr', 30s. / Hengrave, Suffolk 1573, 6s. / Bath May 1573, 5s. / Bristol June 1573, 13s. 4d. / Gloucester 10 July 1573, 13s. 4d.; 'Allsoe spent uppon them', 4s. 6d. / Leicester 1573–4 'to my Lorde of Darbie his Bearwarde and to my Lorde of Essex menne', 19s. 9d. / Nottingham 25 July 1574 / Coventry 29 Aug. 1574 (Chamberlains), 20s. / Coventry 1574 (Wardens), 6s. 8d. / Dover 15 Oct. 1574, 14s. / Folkestone 1574–5, 5s. / Gloucester 1574–5, 13s.; 'and more in wine bestowed', 5s. / Coventry Nov. acct. 1575, 6s. 8d. / Leicester 1575–6, 10s. / Nottingham 20 Sept. 1576 'the Erle of Essexe plears', 6s. 8d. / Coventry Nov. acct. 1576 'to the Counties of Essex players', 10s. / York Minster Accounts 1576, 20s. / Oxford town 1576–7 'to the Counties of Essex players in money and a bankett', 16s. / Bristol Sept. 1577, 13s. 4d. / Coventry Nov. acct. 1578, 3s. / Beverley 12 Sept. 1578, 16s. 8d. / Gloucester 1578–9 'to the Countes of Essex players', 20s. / Oxford town 1578–9, 10s. / Coventry 1579 'to the Countesse of Essex players', 6s. 8d. / Ipswich 1579–80, £1. / Oxford town 1579–80 'to the Countice of Essex players', 10s. / Stratford 1580, 'Countess of Essex' / Exeter 1581–2, 10s. / Coventry Nov. acct. 1582, 2s. / Nottingham 1582–3, 6s. 8d. / Coventry Nov. acct. 1583, 10s. / York City Books Mar. 1583, 20s. / Gloucester 5 Oct. 1583, 6s. 8d. / Ipswich 1583–4, 20s. / Leicester 1583–4 'more than was gaythered', 4s. / Shrewsbury 1583–4 'in the aple market place', 15s. / Coventry Nov. acct. 1584, 10s. / Bath June 1584–5, 7s. 4d. / Bristol Sept. 1584, 20s. / Ludlow July 1584, 13s. 4d. / Faversham, Kent 3 Nov. 1584, 5s. / Dover

Nov. 1584, 13s. 4d. / Gloucester 1584–5, 13s. 4d. / Norwich 12 June 1585, 10s.; 26 June 1585 'This daye it is ordered that forasmocheas the Erle of Essex players wer forbidden to playe and notwithstonding they did playe at Thorpp after they had the cities reward yf they shall hereafter com to this citie they shall never have reward of this citie' / Leicester 1585–6 'being not suffered to play at the hall', 20s. / Dover 1585–6, 10s. / Hythe, Kent 1586, 5s. / Gloucester 1585–6, 5s. / Southampton 23 Mar. 1586, 20s. / Bristol Mar.-Apr. 1586, 26s. 8d. / Ludlow 'in apryll' 1586, 16s. / Ipswich 1586, 20s. / Coventry Nov. acct. 1586, 2s. 6d. / Stratford 1586–7 / Gloucester 1586–7, 13s. 4d. / Shrewsbury 1586–7, 20s. / Kendal 1586–7 'to ye plaiers of my lord of sussex & my lord of essex', 2s. / York City Books 27 Feb. 1587, 30s. / Leicester 16 July 1587 'more than was gaythered', 10s. / Nottingham 24 Oct. 1587 'musicyons & players', 6s. 8d., 12d. / Fordwich, Kent 1587–8, 6s. 8d. / Hythe, Kent 1587, 6s. 8d. / Faversham, Kent 1587–8, 6s. 8d. / Maidstone 1587–8, 10s. / New Romney, Kent 1587–8, 13s. 4d. / Leicester 25 Jan. 1588 'more then was gaythered', 10s. / Ipswich 1588, 13s. 4d. / Coventry Dec. acct. 1588, 20s. / Dover Sept. 1588, 20s. / Hythe, Kent 1588, 6s. 8d. / Rye, Sussex Oct. 1588, 13s. 4d. / New Romney, Kent 1588–9, 8s. / Lydd, Kent 1588–9, 6s. / Reading 1588–9, 10s. / Bath June 1588–9, 10s. 9d. / Coventry Nov. acct. 1589 'to lake the Erle of Essex man', 2s. / Dublin summer 1589 'making Sporte to the mayor aldermen', 10s.[22] / Knowsley, Lancashire (Derby Household Book) 7–13 Sept. 1589 'the quenes players played in the afyter none & my Lord Essix at nyght' / Ipswich 31 Oct. 1589, £1. / Norwich 1589–90, 20s. / Hythe, Kent 1589, 15s. / Maidstone 17 Nov. 1589, 10s. / Lydd, Kent 1589–90, 10s. / Faversham, Kent 21 Nov. 1589, 10s. / Faversham, Kent 4 Jan. 1590 'to the Queen's Players and to the Earl of Essexe Players', 20s. / Bristol July 1590, 30s. / Coventry Nov. acct. 1590, 10s. / King's Lynn 22 Apr. 1591, 20s. / Ipswich 21 May 1592, 10s. / Smithills, Lancashire (Household accounts of Sir Richard Shuttleworth) 31 Aug. 1594 'to my Lord off Essex players which came hither to Smythills', 2s. / Hardwick, Derbyshire (Cavendish household accounts) 10 Nov. 1595 'unto certaine of the Lord of Essex his men', 5s. / Faversham, Kent 8 Mar. 1596, 10s. / Ludlow Apr. 1596, 16s.; 'Mor for that thei played one the next daye' 4s. / Oxford town 1596–7 6s. 8d.

RICH'S PLAYERS

At Court
Christmas 1567 twice, 26 Dec. 1568.

Travelling
Cambridge town 1563–4, 5s.; 'at another tyme', 10s. / Ipswich 3 May 1564, 6s. 8d. / York 6 Apr. 1565, 6s. 8d. / Beverley 1565 'to the Lord Riche players', 15s., 'gyven more in reward to them at William Wryghtes' 2s. 6d. / Ipswich 31 July 1567

---

[22] This visit to Dublin was associated with the Queen's Men's visit at the same time, though Essex's were paid a lot less. Their link with the Queen's at Knowsley in Sept. may be part of the same association, a joint tour.

13*s*. / Ipswich 1567–8 'for playeng upon the hall', 8*s*. / Bristol May 1568 'paid to my Lord Riches players in the yeld hall at thend of their play', 13*s*. 4*d*. / Cambridge town 1569–70, 13*s*. 4*d*. / Canterbury 1569–70, 13*s*. 4*d*. / Dover. 1569–70, 13*s*. 4*d*. / Rye, Sussex June–Sept. 1570 'in the court hall', 6*s*. 8*d*. / Lydd, Kent 1570–1, 10*s*. / Cambridge 1587–9.

LANE'S PLAYERS

Plays
Cloridon and Radiamanta (lost), *Lady Barbara* (lost).

Players
Laurence Dutton, Thomas Gough, John Greaves (Chamber accounts, 1571–2, etc.).

At Court
27 Dec. 1571, 17 Feb. 1572.

Travelling
Bristol May 1570 'to Sir Robert Lanes players in the yeld hall at thend of their play', 10*s*.

LINCOLN'S PLAYERS, 1566–1609

At Court
1–3 Feb. 1573.

Travelling
York City Books 1599, 20*s*. / Leicester Oct. 1599 'more than was gaythered', 10*s*. / Ipswich 15 Oct. 1599, 6*s*. 8*d*. / Coventry 4 Jan. 1600, 10*s*. / Newcastle Mar. 1600 'to the Earle of Lincolne & my Lorde Dudleys ther players', 40*s*. / Coventry Dec. acct. 1601, 10*s*. / Leicester 1601–2 'more then was gaythered', 14*s*. 6*d*. / Norwich 1601–2, 20*s*. / Ipswich 23 Apr. 1602, 10*s*./ Coventry Dec. acct. 1602, 14*s*. 6*d*. / York City Books 3 Oct. 1602 'which played not before my Lord maiour', 20*s*. / Coventry Nov. acct. 1603, 5*s*. / Coventry Nov. acct. 1604, 6*s*. 8*d*. / Norwich 1608– 9, 20*s*. / Kendal June–July 1609, 2*s*. 6*d*. / Carlisle 24 July 1609, 20*s*.

CLINTON'S PLAYERS

Plays
Herpetulus the Blue Knight and Perobia (lost), *Pretestus* (lost).

At Court
3 Jan. 1574 (*Pretestus?*),[23] 2 Jan. 1575 [Revels accounts 27 Dec. 1574 'The hier of a wagon to carry a Lode of stuf to the Coorte for the Duttons playe'].

[23] A note in the Revels accounts dated 20 Dec. 1574 lists Clinton's *Pretestus* and two other plays (Feuillerat, *Revels Accounts*, 238).

Travelling
Beverley, 5*s*. / Southampton 24 June 1577 'to sixe of my Lorde Clintons players', 10*s*. / Bristol July 1577, 13*s*. 4*d*. / Coventry Nov. acct. 1577, 10*s*.

WARWICK'S PLAYERS, 1559–1582
[See also Oxford's Men.]

Plays
[*The Painter's Daughter, The Irish Knight* at court 1576–7, *The Three Sisters of Mantua, The Knight in the Burning Rock* 1578–9, *The Four Sons of Fabius* 1579–80 —all lost].

Playing Sharers
John Dutton, Laurence Dutton, Jerome Savage [Court payees 1576] [Verse 1580 about *'The Duttons and theyr fellow-players forsakyng the Erle of Warwycke theyr mayster, became followers of the Erle of Oxford' ES* ii, 98–9], John David [letters by Warwick to Mayor of London, July 1582, asking for permission to play at the Bull. *ES* iv. 289–90].

Playhouses
Newington Butts' theatre 1576–80, Bull 1582.

At Court
1564–5 (twice), 14 Feb. 1575, 26 Dec. 1575, 1 Jan. 1576, 5 Mar. 1576, 26 Dec. 1576, 18 Feb. 1577, 28 Dec. 1577, 6 Jan. 1578, 9 Feb. 1578, 26 Dec. 1578, 1 Mar. 1579, 1 Jan. 1580.

Travelling
Gloucester 1559–60 'to the Lord ambrose duleies plaiers by the commaundement of mr mayre playeng openly in the bothall', 6*s*. 8*d*. / Cambridge town 31 Oct. 1560 'my lord ambrose dudleys players on all hallowe daie', 10*s*. / Canterbury 1560–1, 6*s*. 8*d*. / Norwich 1560–1, 10*s*. / Winchester 1560–1, 9*s*. 4*d*. / Beverley 1561 'my Lord Ambrose players', 13*s*. 4*d*. / Canterbury 1561–2, 10*s*. / Oxford town 8 June 1562 'when they playd in the guyld hall', 6*s*. 8*d*.; 'spent upon them the same tyme' 16*d*. / Gloucester 1561–2, 10*s*.; 'Also payed for a bankett made to the seid players & for makynge of a Scaffold in the bothall', 4*s*. 2*d*. / Bristol June–July 1562 'for playinge in the yeld hall', 10*s*. / Bridgwater, Somerset 1562, 8*s*.; 'of Candelles for the said players', 7½*d*. / Cambridge town 1562–3 'to thearle of warwycke his players', 5*s*. / Canterbury 1562–3, 10*s*. / Lydd, Kent 1562–3, 15*s*. / Dover 1562–3, 11*s*. / Southampton 19 Mar. 1563, 13*s*. 4*d*. / Exeter 29 May 1563, 13*s*. 4*d*. / Plymouth 9 June 1563, 13*s*. 4*d*. / Bridgwater, Somerset June–July 1563, 10*s*. / Southampton 25 Oct. 1563, 13*s*. 4*d*. / Norwich 1563–4 'to my Lord Ambrose Dudley his Servauntes for playeing A game in the freechamber', 20*s*. / Gloucester 1563–4, 10*s*.; 'Also upon the same playores at the wine taverne', 3*s*. / Rye, Sussex 1564–5, 10*s*. / Canterbury [1564–5?] / Tavistock, Devon St Eustace's Church-

wardens' Accounts 1572–3 'more payed unto the Earle of Warwyckes servants for a playe', 13s. 10d. / Coventry 1574, 6s. 8d. / Leicester 1574–5 'more then was gaythered', 5s. / Lichfield 1575, 8s. 8d. / Coventry Nov. acct. 1575, 6s. 8d. / Stratford 1576 / Leicester 1576–7 'more then was geythered', 24s. / Nottingham 1 Sept. 1577, 10s. / Nottingham 12 Oct. 1577, 'musyssyons and plears', 10s. / Ipswich 1580–1, 15s. / Winchester 1581–2, 9s. 4d. / Ipswich 30 Mar. 1592, 13s. 4d.

SUSSEX'S PLAYERS, 1572–1594 [ALSO KNOWN AS CHAMBERLAIN'S, 1572–1583]

[Joined with Queen's, travelling 1591, and at Rose 26 Dec. 1593–6 Feb. 1594].

Plays
[at court 1573–4 *The Red Knight* (lost) [Bristol 1576], 1574–5 *Phedrastus, Phigon and Lucia* (both lost), 1576–7 *The Cynocephali* (lost), 1578–9 *The Cruelty of a Stepmother, The Rape of the Second Helen, Murderous Michael* (all lost), 1579–80 *The Duke of Milan, Portio and Demorantes, Sarpedon* (all lost), 1582–3 *Ferrar* (lost),] *Friar Francis* (lost), *George a Greene, The Jew of Malta* (old), *Titus Andronicus* (old); from *Henslowe's Diary: Abraham and Lot, Buckingham, The Fair Maid of Italy, God Speed the Plough, Huon of Bordeaux, Richard the Confessor, William the Conqueror* (all lost), *King Leir* (old), *The Ranger's Comedy* (lost), *Friar Bacon and Friar Bungay* (old).

Playing Sharers
John Adams [payee at Court 2 Feb. 1576], Richard Tarlton.

London Playhouses
Rose 1593–4.

At Court
1572–3, 2 Feb. 1577, 2 Feb. 1578, 28 Dec. 1578, 6 Jan. 1579, 3 March 1579, 26 Dec. 1579, 2 Feb. 1580, 16 Feb. 1580, 27 Dec. 1580, 2 Feb. 1581, 6 Jan. 1583, 2 Jan. 1592.

Travelling Records
Canterbury 1568–9, 5s. / Cambridge town 1568–9, 13s. 4d. / Nottingham 16 Mar. 1569, 6s. 8d. / Dover 1568–9 'my lord of sowthesex players', 11s. 10d. / Gloucester 1569–70 'to theirle of suxsex plaiers plainge before Mr Maior', 10s.; 'Allsoe spent on them' 2s. 6d. / Bristol Aug. 1570, 13s. 4d. / Ipswich 24 Oct. 1570, 10s. / Winchester 1570–1 'the players of the Lord Chamberlain', 20s. / Beverley 1570–1, 6s. 8d. / Cambridge town 1570–1, 10s. / Canterbury 1 Nov. 1570, 10s. / Dover 1570–1, 10s. / Faversham, Kent 1570–1, 2s. 6d. / Folkestone 1570–1, 20d. / Ipswich 1571–2, 10s. / Wollaton Hall, Nottinghamshire (Willoughby household accounts) Sept. 1572, 10s. / Southampton 27 Nov. 1572, 10s. / Cambridge town 1572–3, 13s. 4d. / Gloucester 3 Apr. 1573, 13s. 4d.; 'Allsoe spent upon them at that time' 5s. / Bristol April 1573, 13s. 4d. / Bath May 1573, 4s. 2d. / Leicester July 1573 'for that they Did not pley', 5s. / Nottingham 4 Sept. 1573, 10s. / Beverley

1573, 26s. 8d. / Ipswich 7 Oct. 1573, 20s. / Leicester 1573–4 'my Lorde of Sussex Playors more than was gathered', 11s. 8d. / Canterbury 1573–4 'the l. chamberleyn his players', 13s. 4d. / Fordwich, Kent 12 Jan. 1574, 6s. / Rye, Sussex Jan.–Apr. 1574, 6s. 8d. / Sudbury, Suffolk 1573–4, 3s. 4d. / Hengrave, Suffolk 1574, 6s. / Ipswich 3 Aug. 1574, 13s. 4d. / Coventry 1574, 20s., 10s. / Nottingham 14 Sept. 1574, 10s. / Sudbury, Suffolk 1574–5, 2s. 9d. / Bristol Nov. 1574 'my Lord Chamberleyns players', 20s. / Gloucester 1574–5, 13s. 4d.; 'and more to them in wine and makinge a skaffolde', 18s. 8d. / Cambridge town 1574–5, 13s. 4d. / Leicester 1574–5 'more then was gaythered', 5s. 4d. / Ipswich 18 May 1575 'my lorde Chamberleynes players', 15s. / Nottingham 10 Sept. 1575, 20s. / Oxford town 1575–6, 10s. / Bristol Aug. 1576 'my Lord Chamberlayns players at thend of their play called the red Knight before master mayer and thaldermen in the yeld hall'[24], 20s. / Gloucester 1575–6, 20s. / Ipswich 1575–6 'the Lorde Chamberleynes players', 13s. 4d. / Abingdon 'upon St James Daye' [25 July] 1576, 10s. / Ipswich 1576–7 'my Lord Chamberlyn's players', 20s. / Beverley 1576–7, 26s. 8d. /Bath June 1576–7 'My Lorde Chamberlains players', 13s. 4d. / Ipswich 30 May 1577, 20s. / Nottingham 31 Aug. 1577, 13s. 4d. / Coventry 1577, 10s. / Faversham, Kent 1577–8, 13s. 4d. / Bath June 1577–8 'my lorde of sussex players', 5s. / Bristol Tuesday 27 Oct. 1578 'my Lord Chamberleyns players', 20s. / Bath June 1578–9, 5s. 2d. / Rye, Sussex Sept. 1578, 10s. / Norwich 1580–1 'the L. Chamberleynes Players', 40s.; Dean and Chapter Receivers acct. 20s. / York 1 Sept. 1581 'my Lord of Sussex men being players of Interludes shall play this after none at the Comon hall at two of the clocke' / Nottingham 14 Sept. 1581, 10s. / Southampton 1582 'my Lorde Chamberlaynes players', 10s. / Ipswich 1581–2 'the Lord Chamblens players', 13s. 4d., 20s. / Norwich Dean and Chapter Receivers acct. 1581–2, 10s. / Coventry 1582, 6s. 8d. / Coventry Nov. acct. 1583, 10s. / Maidstone 1584–5 'my Lord chamberlenes playeres', £1 / Dover 15 May 1585, 6s. 8d. / Gloucester 1584–5, 13s. 4d. / Bath 22 July 1585, 7s. 8d. / Nottingham 1585–6 'musycyons and players', 6s. 8d. / Southampton 5 Mar. 1586, 20s. / Gloucester 1585–6, 5s. / Dover 19 Feb. 1586, 6s. 8d. / Nottingham 1585–6 'at our townes hall to the Erle of sussex musicians & players', 20s. / Bath May 1586, 6s. 9d. / King's Lynn 1586 'to the Quenes plaiers & the Lorde Chamberlynes plaiers', £3. 10s. / Coventry Nov. acct. 1586, 6s. 8d., 10s. / Leicester 1586–7 'the Countys of Sussexe playors', 20s. / Canterbury 1586–7, 10s. / Southampton 1586–7, 20s. / Exeter 1586–7, 20s. / Kendal 1586–7 'to ye plaiers of my lord of sussex & my lord of essex', 2s. / York 1587, 30s. / Ipswich 23 Sept. 1587, 10s. / Coventry 'in september' 1587, 13s. 4d. / Southampton 1587–8, 40s. / Bristol Sept. 1587, 20s. / Bath June 1587–8, 10s. 10d. / Nottingham 1588–9 'musicyons & players', 6s. 8d. / Ipswich 18 Apr. 1588, 13s. 4d. / York 20 June 1588, 26s. 8d. / Gloucester 17 Sept. 1588, 6s. 8d. / Coventry

---

[24] For this performance the Bristol accounts also have an entry about a sixpenny payment for repairs to the guildhall door '& for mending the cramp of Iren which shutteth the barre, which cramp was stretchid with the presse of people at the play of my lord Chamberleyns Servantes in the yeld hall'. *REED, Bristol*, Mark Pilkinton, ed., forthcoming.

Dec. acct. 1588, 10s. / Hythe, Kent 1588, 5s. / Canterbury 5 Dec. 1588, 13s. 4d. / Nottingham 1588–9, 5s., 3s. 4d. / Exeter 1588–9, 13s. 4d. / Leicester 17 Feb. 1589 'who were not suffered to playe', 20s. / Ipswich 1 Mar. 1589 / Norwich 8 Mar. 1589, 20s. / Gloucester 2 Sept. 1589, 20s. / Faversham, Kent 5 Oct. 1589, 10s. / Lydd, Kent 1589–90, 6s. / New Romney, Kent 1589–90, 6s. 8d. / Leicester 19 Nov. 1589 'in Reward, not playinge', 10s. / Ipswich 17 Feb. 1590, 10s. / Norwich 28 Feb. 1590, 20s. / Exeter 1590–1, 13s. / Gloucester 1590–1 'To the Queenes and the earle of Sussex players', 20s. / Southampton 'Shrove Sunday' 1591 'the Queenes majestie & the Earle of Sussex players', 30s. / Ipswich 17 Feb. 1591, £1. / Coventry 24 Mar. 1591 'to the Quenes players & the Earle of Sussex players', 15s. / Norwich 5 June 1591, 20s. / Leicester 11 Aug. 1591, 33s. 4d. / Nottingham 1591–2, 5s. / Ipswich 1592–3, 13s. 4d. / Sudbury, Suffolk 1592–3, 2s. 6d. / King's Lynn 1592–3, 20s. / York Aug. 1593, 40s. / Newcastle Sept. 1593, 40s., 'in full paymente of iij l. for playing a free play commanded by mr maiore', 20s.[25] / Winchester 7 Dec. 1593–4, 10s. / Coventry Nov. acct. 1603, 5s. / Dover Oct. 1606 'in Reward for not suffering them to play', 5s. / Canterbury 1607–8, 20s. / Norwich 1608–9, 20s. / Bristol Dec. 1608–Feb. 1609, 20s. / Leicester 31 Aug. 1615, 30s. / Kendal 12 Nov. 1617, 5s. / Carlisle 1617–18, 13s. 4d.

[25] i.e., to supplement the original sum of £2 and make the total payment £3.

A lord as successful and as flamboyant as Leicester might have been expected to mount a company of players, as much to advertise his power as for his own entertainment. When, however, the practice of self-advertisement by using one's company to entertain the court became an established practice in the 1570s Leicester's Men ran into some difficulties. The chief reason was that among the more outspoken of Leicester's enemies was the Lord Chamberlain, the earl of Sussex. It was probably this enmity that prompted Leicester to take exceptional steps in strengthening the position of his players through the 1570s. The security he obtained for them with the patent of 1574 gave his leading player, James Burbage, enough confidence to build the Theatre in Shoreditch in 1576. So to some degree Leicester can be seen as the noble who enabled the playing companies to get their first real foothold 'at home' in London.

Leicester was an early starter as an active patron of players under Elizabeth. A company known as 'Lord Dudley's' players can be found in provincial records from the late 1550s.[1] Leicester himself wrote in June 1559 to the Lord President of the North asking his permission for them to play in Yorkshire. He undertook that they 'shall plaie none other matters (I trust); but tollerable and convenient, whereof some of them have bene herde here alredie before diverse of my lordis'.[2] The royal Proclamation dated 16 May 1559 had called for all performances of 'Interludes' to be licensed. Specifically 'her majestie gyveth speciall charge to her nobilitie and gentilmen, as they professe to obey and regarde her majestie, to take good order in thys behalfe wyth their servauntes being players'.[3] Leicester was quick to obey his mistress's voice. Whether or not as a reward for their patron's punctilio, the company performed at court the following Christmas, and for the two after that.[4]

As Leicester's players they appear only in the provincial records through the next decade, a period when the court was entertained mainly by the boy companies and masques. Despite the fact that Leicester's appear more frequently in provincial records than any other company, those chosen to play at court were Leicester's brother Warwick's players in 1564–5, Rich's Men for three years starting in 1567–8, and Lane's Men after them in 1571–2. These years of relatively unimportant functioning for Leicester's company, and the status that they imply, may have been in part what led them to write to him in 1572 asking for more explicit support.

---

[1] Sally-Beth MacLean, 'The Politics of Patronage: Dramatic Records in Robert Dudley's Household Books', *SQ* 44 (1993), 175–82, 177, has found a note of their existence in the Leicester household account book shortly after he was made Master of the Horse. An entry just after Easter 1559 records a payment of 20*s.* to 'your L players'.

[2] Lambeth MS 3196, quoted by Sally-Beth MacLean, 'The Politics of Patronage', 178.

[3] *Tudor Royal Proclamations*, ed. P. L. Hughes and J. F. Larkin, 3 vols., New Haven, Conn., 1964–9, ii. 115–16. See also *ES* iv. 263.

[4] *MSC* vi. 1–2.

There was also a more immediate cause. The statute 'for the punishement of Vacabondes', issued in a Proclamation on 3 January, because it reinforced the law about players without patrons being 'sturdy vagabonds', was certainly the threat that prompted the playing sharers of his company to write to him asking for his protection. The letter is redolent with anxiety about the new enforcement, and seems to feel that Leicester's recollection of his company's needs might need some nudging. It begins by noting that 'there is a certayne Proclamation out for the reviving of a Statute as touchinge retayners', and goes on as his 'humble Servants and daylye Oratours' to ask if 'you will now vouchsaffe to reteyne us at this present as your houshold Servaunts and daylie wayters',

not that we meane to crave any further stipend or benefite at your Lordshippes hands but our lyveries as we have had, and also your honors License to certifye that we are your houshold Servaunts when we shall have occasion to travayle amongst our frendes as we do usuallye once a yere, and as other noble-mens Players have done in tyme past, wherebie we maye enjoye our facultie in your Lordshippes name as we have done hertofore.[5]

The letter ends with a rhyming quatrain wishing that with health and wealth Leicester will live twice as long as Nestor. It was signed by 'James Burbage, John Perkinne, John Laneham, William Johnson, Robert Wilson, Thomas Clarke'.

These six men were presumably the sharers in the company. Eleven years later three of the six were to be taken up for the Queen's Men, and Burbage, probably the writer of the letter if not the company leader, to judge from the place his name occupied, gave up Leicester and took Henry Carey's livery to work as an impresario at the Theatre. Apart from Burbage the most noteworthy figure in this 1572 list is Robert Wilson, clown and playwright, who was hailed by Howes in Stowe's *Annales* for his 'quicke, delicate, refined, extemporall witt'.[6] Laneham, taken like Wilson for the Queen's in 1583, became a leader of one of the Queen's companies when they split in 1589. In the meantime, between 1572 and 1583, Leicester's proved itself a durable group of talented players.

There is no record of any immediate response from Leicester to the company's letter. It is an intriguing document, not so much for the evidence it supplies of the independence with which the players ran their activities at a distance from their patron, but for the claim that the only time they needed to bring themselves to their patron's notice was so that he could give them their licence and livery for travelling once a year. They clearly never expected to intrude on him for the rest of each year. Provincial records give a fairly consistent list of places they stopped at on their tours, which seem to have run along similar routes year by year. The occasional appearance of precise datings for their many stops suggests, contrary to what the letter implies, that travel was a constant feature of the way they made their living.

It was an all-round occupation, in time and geographically. Each year they traversed East Anglia and the university towns, the south-eastern counties of Kent and Sussex, the south-western towns and counties of Bristol, Dartmouth, and

---

[5] *ES* ii. 86.   [6] Edmond Howes, additions to John Stowe, *Annales* (1615), 697.

Plymouth, Somerset and Devon, and made the long trek through the Midlands via Coventry, Leicester, and Nottingham to the north, Cheshire, Lancashire, and Yorkshire and beyond. They served their patron by carrying his livery and his name throughout the country. He paid them intermittently, most likely for the few actual performances they gave before him, with a total of £7 4s. in the fifteen months from December 1559 to April 1561.[7] None of the household accounts for 1558–61 note payments made for performances in the presence of Leicester himself.

For the next ten years the company followed the same pattern of travelling and taking his livery and his name around the country, with little return for their allegiance except the welcomes they were accorded by local authorities because of their master's eminence. Only at Bristol in April 1587 is there any sign that the players were associated directly with their patron. In that month the city gave an official welcome to Leicester and his brother Warwick as their country's general in the Spanish war, and paid Leicester's Men to perform for the occasion. That was probably at the city's initiative, though it is unlikely to have been an utter coincidence that the players were in the vicinity at just the right time.

Whether it was the 1572 statute, or whether Leicester felt that his players did need some specific protection against his enemy the Lord Chamberlain, he eventually used his privilege as royal favourite two years after their pleading letter to secure them a royal patent. Issued on 10 May 1574, this was the first written patent for a playing company ever to be allocated by the government.[8] It was an invaluable piece of paper. When Tilney was appointed Master of the Revels four years later such patents became standard, but Leicester's was by some way the first. The initiative for such an innovation must have been Leicester's own: only he could have interceded with the queen to secure such a unique licence. Radcliffe, the Lord Chamberlain, might have done it, but he would have wanted it for his own company, not his enemy's. In part at least it gave them protection against the Chamberlain, as well as a means to bring the company to the royal notice. In the next Christmas festivities, 1574–5, Leicester's Men performed for the first time for ten years, playing three times as compared with twice by Clinton's and once each by three boy groups. Sussex's and Lincoln's had performed once each in February 1573, but not in the 1573–4 or 1574–5 seasons, when Leicester's and Clinton's were the only adult companies to perform. The Sussex company's patron was sick and away from the court in 1574–5.

They evidently made a good impression on their return to play at court. For the next few years they performed there more frequently than any other company. Sussex's overtook them in the number of their performances by 1578–9, but despite Sussex's hostility to their patron they continued to secure appearances every year until the barren season of 1581–2, which saw only three plays, all by

---

[7] Sally-Beth MacLean, 'The Politics of Patronage', 179.

[8] The full patent is in *MSC* i. 3, 262–3. It names five of the six players who signed the 1572 letter: Burbage, Perkin, Laneham, Johnson, and Wilson.

children, and a night of tumbling 'activities' by Strange's Men. That season seems to have begun the run-up to the establishment of the Queen's Men at the end of the next Christmas period, the innovation which removed three of Leicester's best men. What happened in those manœuvrings can only be inferred, but the resources and status that the Leicester's company had acquired in its strongest years through the mid-1570s must have been a potent factor in the decision to cut them down.

Like all the other major adult companies through these years, they maintained a constant circuit of travel, much more than the regular summer tour which has sometimes been read into their record on the basis of the 1572 letter.[9] Their status, or more likely the name they carried on their licence, gave them ready access to most of the large boroughs and towns, and Leicester's name brought them rewards that helped to augment that status. London was just one stop on that constant round. They appear to have performed even less frequently for their patron himself than they did for the queen. According to the surviving records Leicester actually paid musicians more generously than his players. London performances were a step towards being chosen for a court performance, but otherwise little different from a visit to any other large town, at least until 1576.

Their progress through the 1570s is the clearest indicator of company development at this time. Through 1574–5, the first years after the Leicester's patent was issued, the Lord Chamberlain was ill and stayed away from the court. His official deputy, Charles Howard, Lord Effingham, was not yet a Privy Councillor, and would do little to oppose Leicester. And in 1576 the players took their own initiative. Burbage was the chief author of the letter that prompted Leicester's original intervention in 1572, and it may have been he who asked Leicester to give them the security of the patent in 1574. The new patent was marked with his name, 'pro Iacobo Burbage & aliis de licencia speciali'. In 1576 he used these securities, with the powerful extra motive of a base in London which would help the company maintain access to performances at court, to justify his risky venture of building the Theatre in the suburb of Shoreditch.

Burbage, a freeman of the city through his enrolment in the carpenters' guild, had been involved once before, at least by association, in the building of a theatre in the London suburbs. His wife's brother, John Brayne, had built the Red Lion playhouse in Stepney in 1567.[10] We do not know what happened to the Red Lion after its construction, but the protections that Burbage secured for Leicester's Men before he went on to build his own theatre suggest that the early project had run into trouble. What is least clear about the building of the Theatre is how far Burbage conceived it as a home for his company or how much it was simply a new venture into property-owning and the consequent impresario functions in London

---

[9] See Sally-Beth MacLean, 'The Politics of Patronage', 175–82.

[10] For Burbage's origins, see William Ingram, 'The Early Career of James Burbage', *Elizabethan Theatre*, 10 (1988) 18–36. Ingram's book, *The Business of Playing*, has a chapter (92–113) on John Brayne and the Red Lion project.

that the building enabled Burbage to maintain in the next years. The absence of his name from the later lists of Leicester's players suggests that, whatever connections he chose to maintain with the travelling company of his earlier career, he himself lodged in London from 1576 and served the companies at large as landlord to whichever group wanted to use his playhouse. His attempt to write into the lease of the land where he built the Theatre a proviso that he would be allowed to dismantle it and use its timbers elsewhere shows his sense of caution about the venture.

None of the early playing companies appear to have developed any concept of a single settled place to play in. That only happened after 1594 when the duopoly had playhouses designated for them by the Lord Chamberlain and Lord Admiral. The habit of travelling was not just a reaction to the annual visitations of the plague in London. Alleyn may have expected a long tenure with Strange's Men at the Rose when he married his impresario's step-daughter, and he did secure a long run there, but it was innovatory, and did not last even a year. The Queen's Men, as secure a group as there was in the 1580s, on one visit or another used every place available to them in London. Up to 1594 the companies seem to have actively preferred irregular access to the inns inside the city rather than long runs at the suburban places, however much more safe and advantageous the custom-built amphitheatres in the suburbs may have been. That is only an inference, of course, since there is almost no evidence about frequency of use for any of the different venues. The Lord Chamberlain's securing of the city inns for the Queen's Men in 1584 was a matter confined to the city venues because they were all that stood inside the Lord Mayor's jurisdiction.

So Burbage's venture in 1576 is rather more likely to have been a commercial enterprise of his own than part of a Leicester's-company venture to secure a regular foothold in London. His choice of a Roman name and the circular design suggests that he may have had grandiose ambitions to provide London with a copy of one of Rome's great inventions. Its name affirms that it was not just another converted innyard like the Bel Savage. But even with the company's patent to back them, Burbage cannot have expected it to provide Leicester's Men or any other company with a permanent home. That the Theatre became the company's venue from 1576 onwards is a hopeful presumption unsupported by any evidence, like the presumption that Leicester's Men must have performed for Elizabeth in the famous visit to Kenilworth in 1575. The closest link between the company and Burbage's play-house in these years is in a letter written by Gabriel Harvey to Edmund Spenser in the summer of 1579. It relates Robert Wilson and 'Lycesters' Men along with Warwick's, Rich's, and Vaux's Men to the 'Theater, or sum other paintid stage',[11] hardly a precise linkage. Moreover, when the establishment of the Queen's Men put Leicester's into eclipse in 1583 there is nothing to say that Burbage was still playing with them. Certainly by 1584 he had obtained the livery of Henry Carey in

---

[11] *The Letter-book of Gabriel Harvey, AD 1573–1580*, 67.

place of Leicester. It is most likely that from 1576 on he remained in London as impresario at large with his Theatre in Shoreditch.

The manœuvres at court that led to the setting-up of the Queen's Men have to be inferred in part from the changes in the playing groups who were called to perform at the court in the two seasons 1581–2 and 1582–3. In 1581–2 Paul's children launched the festivities on the traditional night, 26 December, and the Chapel children played on 31 December, with Strange's feats in between. This was in spite of the fact that the French Duc d'Alençon, the queen's suitor, her dear 'frog', was a visitor to the court and might have expected some entertainment. There were no plays or shows at all through January, and the next month was largely taken up with the queen's 'progress' through Kent to see Alençon off. The Chapel children played before the court again on 27 February, to close a season remarkable for being the first in eleven years when no adult company gave a performance. And that in spite of the high standards that Leicester's, Sussex's, and other companies had established.

There is a good case for seeing this absence of the adult companies in 1581–2 as a first reaction to their use for self-aggrandizement by their patrons. Leicester's must have been at the forefront of that practice. Scott McMillin may be right in seeing Tilney, a relative of the Lord Chamberlain, taking a large part in that struggle and favouring Sussex's Men and the companies of Derby and Strange, to whose family he was also related, above those of the two Dudleys, Leicester and his brother Warwick.[12] If so, the Christmas events of 1582–3 appear to have included some counter-attack. The 1582–3 season saw a boy's play at each end, but between 27 December and 10 February four adult companies gave one play each: Hunsdon's, Derby's, Sussex's, and Leicester's, besides another night of activities by Strange's tumblers. It may be a coincidence that Tilney, Master of these Revels for five years by now, had family associations with all of the chief company patrons except Leicester. Certainly his choice of the twelve Queen's Men at the end of this season plundered Leicester's even more deeply than the others.

Tilney took three of the leading Leicester's players for the Queen's. Burbage was a fourth loss from the six sharers of the early 1570s, so it is not surprising that the residual company seems to have taken some time to regroup after the 1583 cuts. They are not in fact recorded as touring again till 1584–5, when they returned once more to their now-traditional circuits. Leicester himself paid them £5 for a performance at Leicester House in London on 5 May 1585, with an extra 10 shillings for the clown Will Kemp.[13] They then resumed their travels through East Anglia and the Midlands. Leicester again drew on their numbers that autumn when he landed in Flushing as commander of the English forces against the Spanish rulers of the Low Countries. The surviving account-books for these years show that his

[12] For an analysis of the manœuvres between the great lords at this time, including a table of court performances, see Scott McMillin, 'The Queen's Men and the London Theatre of 1583', *Elizabethan Theatre*, 10 (1988), 10–14.

[13] Sally-Beth MacLean, 'The Politics of Patronage', 180.

entourage included several musicians and fifteen players, a good-sized company, amongst his quasi-regal train of courtiers and entertainers.

These fifteen players may not all have been the old group. With them across the North Sea in December 1585 they also took Robert Wilson, formerly a fellow but now a Queen's Servant, and Robert Browne from Worcester's, besides Will Kemp. Philip Sidney wrote to Walsingham from Utrecht on 24 March 1586 complaining that his previous letter, which was carried from Holland by 'Will, my lord of Lester's jesting plaier' enclosed in a letter to Sidney's wife, had not reached Walsingham because the player had delivered the papers instead to Leicester's wife. The erring player was almost certainly Kemp, who was in Calais in November 1585, and at the Danish court a year later.

Five other players, including George Bryan and Thomas Pope, later to join Kemp in the 1594 Chamberlain's Men, are named in the Danish records. Whether they were or ever had been working as Leicester's servants is not definitely known. As Lord Governor in the Low Countries he did write a recommendation for a company of comedians to the king of Denmark in that year. But a different company under Leicester's name also continued to travel in England through these years. The writ that allowed a lord to patronize only one company did not apply overseas. It may well be that Leicester put together a special group, including men already experienced at travelling on the Continent such as Browne, and others such as Wilson who were especially eminent, leaving the others to reconstitute themselves as a remnant group. Leicester's sojourn in the Low Countries was a bonus for the players, since it allowed the company to double itself while retaining Leicester's livery, provided that one of the groups remained overseas. The Lord Admiral's Men divided into one local and one overseas group similarly in 1592.[14]

Leicester's Men did return to play at court for a last time on 27 December 1586, in a season when the Queen's gave four plays and Paul's Boys one. This one performance is a good indication that they were still strong enough despite the split, and that they were playing in the vicinity of London once again. Mostly, though, they toured as before throughout their last years. They were at Exeter in March 1587, at Bristol to perform at the city's welcome for Leicester and his brother Warwick in April, through Kent as usual, and at Gloucester, Abingdon, Marlborough, and north to Coventry and York through the next year. They were ready to stand up for their livery and their patron at Norwich on 4 September 1588, when they had a cobbler committed to prison 'for lewd words uttered against the ragged staff'.[15] But Leicester died on 4 September, and the company's patent died with him.

In the absence of any names for the group who stayed in England after 1585, there is no trace of what livery the former members of the company put on after his death in 1588. The appearance in Strange's of Bryan and Pope in 1590 and of Kemp from 1592 may indicate where the core of both of the Leicester's groups

[14] See Ch. 14.   [15] *REED, Norwich*, 90.

went. The strength of Strange's after 1588 may well be a sign that they made new acquisitions from Leicester's at that time.

Like the other companies of these early years, Leicester's Men have left few strong traces of their thinking, apart from the one demonstration of loyalty to their lord at Norwich in 1588 when the cobbler insulted Leicester's emblem. Leicester's prominent role on the Privy Council, his leadership with Walsingham of the more zealous anti-Catholics, his standing as political leader of the Puritan movement, and his consistent support for the 'war party' on the Council have left few visible marks on his playing company. But it would be wrong to see Leicester's devotion to playgoing as something kept exclusively for his idle moments. Attempts have been made to see the repertoire of adult plays in these years, and particularly the plays of Leicester's Men, as upholding a rigorously Protestant dogma. As leader of the more puritanical wing of the establishment Leicester might be expected to foster his loyalties in the men who wore his livery around the country. Unfortunately these attempts are undermined by the absence of any reliable texts or even titles for the plays they performed.

It seems plausible, if no more than that, to claim as Paul Whitfield White does that 'after an initial period of outrage and resistance, many Protestant leaders in the church and in the civil government came around to accepting playgoing as suitable recreation and recognising once again its power as a medium of shaping public opinion'.[16] Leicester as the outstanding leader of the activists against the threat from Catholic Spain throughout the 1570s and 1580s, when Phillip II looked likely to insist on his right as Mary's husband and a lineal descendant from John of Gaunt to claim the throne of England from Elizabeth, may have used his players to reinforce his case and his position. In any case it is almost inconceivable that the players themselves would not have known what their patron stood for, and supported it in their plays. That is wholly plausible, but the dearth of play-texts leaves it no more than an inference.

LEICESTER'S PLAYERS, *c.*1560–1588

Plays
[*Predor and Lucia, Mamillia, Philemon and Philecia* at court 1573–4, *Panecia* 1574–5, *The Collier* 1576–7, *A Greek Maid* 1578–9, *Delight* 1580–1, *Telemo* 1582–3, all lost], '*Myngo*' [Bristol 1577–8, lost], *The Story of Samson* [lost],[17] *The Three Ladies of London.*

---

[16] Paul Whitfield White, *Theatre and Reformation: Protestantism, Patronage, and Playing in Tudor England*, 173. White makes his case in the chapter entitled 'Changing Reformation Attitudes Towards Theatre', 163–74.
[17] The Red Lion scaffold and stage were constructed at Mile End in 1567 by John Brayne, James Burbage's brother-in-law, for a performance of 'the storye of Sampson'. There is no evidence that the company waiting to do the performance was Burbage's, but the odds are on it. See William Ingram, *The Business of Playing*, 103–12.

Playing Sharers

'Laurens' [1559],[18] James Burbage, William Johnson, John Laneham, John Perkin, Robert Wilson [named in 1574 patent], Thomas Clarke [in letter to Leicester 1572].[19]

London Playhouses

Red Lion? Theatre?

At Court

1560, 1561, 1562, 1572–3 (three times), 26 Dec. 1573 (*Predor and Lucia*), 28 Dec. (*Mamillia*), 21 Feb. 1574 (*Philemon and Philecia*), 26 Dec., 1 Jan. 1575 (*Panecia?*), 28 Dec., 4 Mar. 1576, 30 Dec. (*The Collier*), 26 Dec. 1577, 11 Feb. 1578 (replaced by Lady Essex's), 4 Jan. 1579 (*A Greek Maid*), 28 Dec. (not performed), 6 Jan. 1580, 26 Dec. (*Delight*), 7 Feb. 1581, 10 Feb. 1583 (*Telomo*), 27 Dec. 1586.

Travelling

Oxford town 1557–8, 6s. 8d., 'bestowed upon the said players at mr Cogans house' / Norwich 'to my Lorde Robarte Dudleye his players' 1558–9, 20s. / Nottingham 1558–9, 13s. 4d. / Plymouth 1559–60 'to my lord Robert dodleis players which pled in the churche', 20s. / Canterbury 1559–60, 6s. 8d. / Lydd, Kent 1559–60 'ye lorde Dudlees players', 6s. 8d. / Rye, Sussex Mar. 1560 'to my Lord Dudlyes players . . . in the name of the hole Towne', 10s. / Dover 26 Mar. 1560, 10s. / Bridgwater, Somerset 20 July 1560, 13s. 4d. / Bristol July 1560, 10s. / Norwich 1560–1, 20s. / Cambridge town 1560–1, 10s. / Rye, Sussex 1560–1 'to the quenes plaiers and Sir Robert Doodleys plaiers', 20s. / Lydd, Kent 1560–1, 13s. 4d. / Canterbury 17 Mar. 1561, 7s. / Dover 29 Mar. 1561, 10s. / Gloucester 1560–1 'the lord Robert dudleyes playores', 6s. 8d. / Southampton 4 Oct. 1561, 13s. 4d. / New Romney, Kent 1561–2; 'for dryncke', 6d. / Lydd, Kent 1561–2, 11s. / Beverley 1561 'my Lord Robert players', 26s. 8d. / Ipswich 1561–2 'For my lorde Roberts plaiers', 10s. / Oxford town 1561–2, 6s. 8d. / Gloucester 1561–2, 13s. 4d.; 'Also spente upon the seid players at the taverne and for makynge of the scaffold in the bothall', 4s. 8d. / Cambridge town 18 Mar. 1562, 10s. / Canterbury 5 May 1562, 10s. / Dover 27 June 1562, 10s. / Bristol Sept. 1562 'to my lord dudley is players for playing in the yeld hall', 13s. 4d. / Norwich 1562–3, 26s. 8d. / Ipswich 1562–3 'Unto my Lorde Robart players', 6s. / Beverley 1563 'in reward and spent upon them in wyne', 27s. / Leicester 12 Nov. 1563 'more then was gatherd', 6s. / Ipswich 18 Nov. 1563, 10s. / Canterbury 1563–4, 10s. / Lydd, Kent 1563–4, 15s. / Norwich 1562–4, 26s. 8d. / Ipswich 2 Jan. 1564, 6s. 8d.; 3 Jan. 20d. / Hengrave, Suffolk 30 Jan. 1564, 'Sondaye', 10s. / Dover 22 Apr. 1564, 10s. / Rye, Sussex 27 Apr. 1564, 6s. 8d. / Leicester 1 July 1564, 10s. / Beverley 1564 'to therle of Lacester players', 20s. / Cambridge town 1564–5, 10s. / Norwich 1564–5, 20s.; 'for brede and Drynke', 6d. / Ipswich 21 Feb. 1565, 10s. / York 6 Apr. 1565, 13s. 4d. / Long

---

[18] Sally-Beth MacLean, 'The Politics of Patronage', 177–8.

[19] The company's number was 12 in 1577, according to the Southampton records.

Sutton, Lincs. 1565–6 'the lorde Robertes players did play here' / Norwich 1565–
6, 20s.; 'for breade and Drynke at the same tyme', 8d. / Canterbury 1566-7, 10s. /
New Romney, Kent 7 Apr. 1569, 6s. 8d. / Nottingham 11 Aug. 1569 'to the erle of
lesyter and to the erle of Worster plears', 20s. / Beverley 1569, 20s. / Abingdon
1569–70, 10s. 3d. / Gloucester 1569–70 'to therle of lecesters players playing
before Mr Maior', 13s. 4d. / Southampton 1569–70 'the second tyme they played
when that sir henry Wallope and his Ladie was there', 6s. 8d. / Dover 1569–70, 13s.
4d.; 'a stope of sacke to the pleyers', 12d. / Canterbury 1569–70, 13d. 4d. /
Faversham, Kent 1569–70, 3s. 4d. / Lydd, Kent 1569–70, 8s. 10d. / Totnes,
Devon 1569–70 'Soluti lusoribus Comitis de leycetter', 20s. / Barnstaple, Devon
1569–70, 12d. / Plymouth 1569–70, 20s. / Bristol Jan. 1570, 13s. 4d. / Rye, Sussex
Mar. 1570, 10s. / Oxford town 4 May 1570, 6s. 8d. / Dartmouth 30 July 1570 'unto
my Lorde of Leasters men the plaid at church', £1. / Ipswich 25 Oct. 1570 'Lord
Robarts players', 13s. 4d. / Leicester 1570–1 'more than was geythered', 8s. 6d. /
Saffron Walden 1570–1, 2s. 6d. / Maidstone 1570–1, 10s. / Gloucester 30 Apr.
1571, 13s. 4d.; 'Alsoe spente upon them at the Taverne', 3s. 8d. / Beverley 1571,
20s. / Boston, Lincs. 6 Aug. 1571, 10s. / Cambridge town 1571–2, 10s. / Leicester
1571–2, 8s. / Ipswich 15 July 1572 'the Lord of Leycetors players', 13s. 4d. /
Nottingham 20 Aug. 1572, 10s. / Beverley 7 June 1573, 20s. / Beverley 8 Aug.
1573, 30s. / Stratford 1573 / Bristol Oct. 1573, 20s., 'paid for taking down the table
in the mayors courte and setting yt up agayne after the said players werre gonne',
20d. / Ludlow 20 Oct. 1573, 20s. / Oxford town 1573–4, 10s.; 'more of them', 3s.
1d. / Leicester 1573–4 'more than was gathered', 11s. 8d. / Bewdley, Worcs. 1573–
4, 8s. / Hengrave, Suffolk 1574, 5s. / Ipswich 18 June 1574, 15s. / Doncaster 1574,
20s. / Nottingham 1 Sept. 1574, 20s. / Coventry 1574, 26s. 8d. / Southampton
1574–5, 20s. / Canterbury 3 Dec. 1574 'for playeng before Mr Mayer & his
bretherne at the Courte halle', 18s.; 'for Candells & torches then spent', 16d. (20s.)
/ Rye, Sussex Sept.–Dec. 1575, 10s. / Sandwich, Kent 26 Sept. 1575, 10s. / New
Romney, Kent 26 Dec. 1575, 10s. / Ipswich 1575–6 'my Lorde Robertes players',
10s. / Coventry early 1576, 26s. 8d. / Thetford, Norfolk 1576, 5s. / Exeter 1576–
7, 13s. 4d. / Canterbury 1576–7, 20s. / Faversham, Kent 1576–7, 13s. 4d. / New
Romney, Kent 1577, 20s. / Sandwich, Kent 24 Aug. 1577, 20s. / Stratford 1577 /
Rye, Sussex Sept. 1577, 20s. / Southampton 22 Sept. 1577 'to my Lorde of
Leycesters plaiers xii of them', 20s. / Exeter Oct. 1577, 30s. / Bristol Oct. 1577
'and for lyngkes to geve light in the evenyng the play was called Myngo',[20] 22s. /
Bath June 1577–8, 14s. / Norwich, Dean and Chapter Receivers acct. 1577–8, 20s.
/ Ipswich 10 Sept. 1578, 20s. / Canterbury Dean and Chapter 1578–9, 30s. /
Dover 1578–9, 5s. / Kertling, Suffolk 3–4 Nov. c.1579, 40s. / Canterbury 1579–
80, 20s. / Faversham, Kent 1579–80, 10s. / Fordwich, Kent 1579–80, 5s. / Ipswich

---

[20] This performance damaged the guildhall door, as an earlier visit by Sussex's had done. A
further entry in the mayor's accounts notes a payment of 3s. 6d. for 'mending the borde in the yeld
hall and dores there, after my Lord of Leycesters players who had leave to play there'. *REED, Bristol*,
Mark Pilkinton, ed., forthcoming.

1579–80, £1. / Cambridge 21 June 1580 [letter from Vice-Chancellor to Lord Burghley: 'it hath pleased your honour to commende unto me and the headdes of the universitye my Lorde of Oxenforde his players . . . consydering & ponderinge, that the seede, the cause and the feare of the pestilence is not yet vanished & gone, this hote tyme of ye yeare . . . ye commencment tyme at hande, which requireth rather diligence in stodie then dissolutenesse in playes; and also yat of late wee denyed ye lyke to ye right Honorable ye Lord of Leiceter his servantes' / Kertling, Suffolk 15–17 May 1580, 25s. / Norwich 1580–1 Chamberlains' acct., 40s.; Dean and Chapter Receivers' acct., 20s. / Coventry Nov. acct. 1580, 30s. / Fordwich, Kent 1580–1, 7s. / New Romney, Kent 13 Mar. 1581, 20s. / Newcastle Sept. 1580, 50s. / Shrewsbury 1581–2, 6s. 8d. / Ipswich 1581–2, 20s. / Winchester 1581–2, 10s. / Southampton 1582, 13s. 4d. / Coventry 1582, 20s. / Gloucester 1584–5, 20s. / Norwich 1584–5, 'to thentent they should not playe in the Citie', 40s. / Sudbury, Suffolk 2 June 1585, 6s. 8d. / Ipswich 4 June 1585, 20s. / Bath Aug. 1585, 14s. / Leicester 1585 'more than was gathered', 24s. / Coventry 1585, 30s. / Exeter 24 Mar. 1586, 10s. / Abingdon 1585–6, 15s. / Gloucester 1586–7, 20s. / Marlborough 1586–7, 5s. / Nottingham 1586–7 'musicions and players', 10s. / Norwich 1586–7, 40s. / Southampton 1586–7, 30s. / Exeter 1586–7, 20s. / Fordwich, Kent 1586–7, 6s. 8d. / Canterbury 1586–7, 10s. / Maidstone 23 Jan. 1587, 6s. 8d. / Dover 4 Mar. 1587, 20s. / Rye, Sussex Mar. 1587, 10s. / Bristol Apr. 1587, 26s. 8d. [plus costs for receiving the earls of Leicester and Warwick] / Bath June 1586–7, 23s. 8d. [at Leicester's and his brother's visit to Bath in Apr. 1587] / Leicester 1586–7 'more than was gaythered', 17s. 4d. / Lathom House, Lancs. (Derby Household Book) 2–8 July 1587 'on thorsday mr stanley departed, & the same daye my Lord of Leysesters plaiers plaied on fryday they plaied againe' / Coventry 'in July' 1587, 20s.; 'Lamas day Last' [1 Aug.] 30s. / Nottingham 1587–8, 10s. / Norwich 1587–8, 40s. / Exeter 1587–8, 20s. / Oxford town 11 Dec. 1587, 6s. 8d. / Reading 1587–8, 10s. / Bath June 1587–8, 20s. / Dover 1587–8, 13s. 4d. / Hythe, Kent 1587–8, 10s. / Lydd, Kent 1587–8, 10s. / New Romney, Kent 1587–8, 20s. / Faversham, Kent 1587–8, 13s. 4d. / Folkestone 1587–8, 5s. / Rye, Sussex Feb. 1588, 13s. 4d. / Plymouth 15 May 1588, 10s. / Gloucester 17 June 1588, 20s. / Coventry Dec. acct. 1588, 40s. / Bristol June 1588 'paid by master Mayor and thalldermens appoyntementte unto the Earle of Leicesters players whome played before them & the Common Counsell in the Guild hall', 26s. 8d. / York City Books 13 July 1588, 30s. / Norwich 4 Sept. 1588 'So as they play not above ii tymes and then depart which they have promysed to doo', 40s.; 7 Sept. 1588 'This daye upon compleynt made by the Erle of Leicesters men ageynst William Storage a Cobler for leawd woordes utteryd ageynst the raggyd staff is commyted to pryson' / Ipswich 14 Sept. 1588, £1 /

A company known in civic listings as the Queen's players is frequently recorded performing around the country in the 1560s and 1570s. It was never called on to play at court, however, and that gives some reason either to doubt its credentials as a play-acting company or else to see it as a special kind of playing group. The queen's bear-ward appears regularly in the provincial records, and her early 'players' may have been tumblers or performers of 'activities' of the sort that did not demand written playscripts. They may have been a company of boys, though if so it is the more strange that they offered no plays at court through these early years. It is, none the less, a possibility. At Ipswich in July 1587, in the heyday of the known company of Queen's players, a visit by 'the Queanes players' was closely followed by another from 'the Quenes players being the Childeren'.[1] Companies of children did sometimes go on tour with plays, and it may be that up to 1583 chorister groups from the Chapel Royal or from Windsor claimed the royal title when travelling. Apart from the payments made to the early Queen's groups that appear periodically in the records of travelling, nothing is known either about the membership of these travelling companies or about their repertory, if it did include plays. They certainly had none of the impact on company history that the special company set up in 1583 was to have. Stowe's account of the establishment of the 1583 company goes so far as to say that until then Elizabeth had no professional company of her own.

There is no tangible evidence about what prompted the queen, or her agent, the Privy Council's secretary Francis Walsingham, to set up a new and monopolistic company with her patronage on 10 March 1583. There had been prominent royal companies before, notably under her father, Henry VIII. But the 1583 development is likely to have been the result of more local and immediate concerns. Leeds Barroll and Scott McMillin have suggested that setting up the new company was a means to emasculate the companies who had started to compete for performances at court, sponsored by their patrons, and this rivalry between the great lords was becoming an embarrassment.[2] The illness and imminent death of the Lord Chamberlain, Sussex, was no doubt also a factor. Equally urgent must have been the weight of the City's hostility to playing, and the need, now that adult-company playing had become the favoured form of Christmas entertainment, for the court to give some protection to the leading players, or at least enough to permit them to play in London and so fulfil their duties in the Christmas revels.

---

[1] *MSC* ii. 3, 274.

[2] See J. Leeds Barroll, 'Drama and the Court', *The Revels History of Drama in English* iii (1975), 4–27, and Scott McMillin, 'The Queen's Men and the London Theatre of 1583', *Elizabethan Theatre*, 10 (1988), 1–17, esp. 8–13.

The negotiations that the new Lord Chamberlain took in hand with the Lord Mayor in 1584 over accommodation for the Queen's company in London indicate that this last motive was at least as strong as the others. The claim that support for the leading companies was necessary in order to ensure the annual supply of plays to the court now became the Privy Council's standard argument in defence of playing. The pressure on the Privy Council to find a means of giving the players some space was strengthened by an outcry from the pulpits over the collapse of the scaffold frame which caused eight deaths at a bear-baiting at Paris Garden on 13 January 1583. Because it happened on a Sunday, the clergy said that it was an act of God against idolatrous playgoers. Some regulation was called for, and the Queen's Men were part of the response. In any case, to Privy Council thinking a single and uniquely privileged company was more easy to control than a gaggle of competing groups working for different great nobles.

For all the urgent precipitating factors that turned up together in the court's Christmas season of 1582–3—Sussex's illness, the Christmas competition amongst the nobles to promote their companies, the pulpit outcry against plays—I strongly suspect that the order from the Privy Council to set up a new playing company patronized by the queen was far from an unpremeditated act. Walsingham, who executed the order, was one of the two principal secretaries to the Council, and acted as their executive officer. He never showed much interest in players, though, and is unlikely to have been the one who initiated the idea. He is usually credited with authorizing the Master of the Revels to establish the new company on the basis of Howes's addition to Stowe's *Annales*, which says that 'at the request of Sir Francis Walsingham, they were sworn the queens servants, and were allowed wages and liveries as grooms of the chamber'.[3] Technically, for Walsingham to issue the order made it a formal enactment authorized by the full Privy Council. As an innovation, though, it is unlikely to have been his own initiative, or even the queen's.[4] It was a positive act with the far from insubstantial advantage to the Privy Council of solving a range of its current problems. Someone more alert to these problems and more sympathetic to the idea of playing than the Privy Council's secretary must have been behind the move.

Walsingham had joined the Privy Council in 1573, after a stint as England's ambassador to Paris, a post Burghley had acquired for him. Once he gained a position on the Council, however, he became Leicester's closest supporter against the faction that backed Burghley. In 1578 the Spanish Ambassador wrote home saying that Walsingham was Leicester's 'spirit'.[5] By the 1580s the Council had more or less settled into two factions. On Burghley's side were the earl of Sussex,

---

[3] John Stowe, *Annales* (1615), 697.

[4] Mary A. Blackstone, 'Patrons and Elizabethan Dramatic Companies', *Elizabethan Theatre*, 10 (1988), 112–14, offers a sceptical assessment of the role of Elizabeth herself as a possible initiator of theatre patronage in 1583.

[5] The classic account of the Council's power-play through the 1570s and 1580s is by Conyers Read, 'Walsingham and Burghley in Queen Elizabeth's Privy Council', *English Historical Review*, 28 (1913), 34–58. Mendoza's letter is quoted on 38. Later views have found a more complex set of interactions and

Thomas Radcliffe, who openly hated Leicester,[6] the earl of Lincoln, Henry Carey (Lord Hunsdon), and several others. Besides Walsingham Leicester's supporters included his brother Warwick, the earl of Bedford, and Francis Knollys, who like Walsingham but unlike Burghley had gone into exile under Mary. He was a more radical Protestant than Burghley and the others who had stayed in England under Mary and conformed. The factions were chiefly divided over religious policy and the related question of war against Spain that had gone along with it since 1570. It was not, however, a clean factional divide, like two-party government. Individual members of the Council might change sides on specific issues. Charles Howard, for instance, who worked closely with Burghley from his appointment at the beginning of 1584, also worked closely once he was made Lord Admiral with the Leicester and Walsingham group, a key alliance so long as the war against Spain was at issue. Almost all the Councillors on both sides were closely connected, either by blood or marriage.

I strongly suspect that the idea of setting up a royal company may have started with a man who in 1583 had not yet acquired a seat on the Privy Council, but who came on after Radcliffe's death, and eventually was appointed to follow him as Lord Chamberlain. Charles Howard, later to take over from Lincoln as the Lord Admiral, always had a close ally on the Burghley side of the Council in his father-in-law, Henry Carey. Carey, in general an ally of Sussex against Leicester, may have worked on Howard's behalf with the Council to plant the idea of a new company in the minds of the Councillors. Howard's closeness to the queen herself through his wife, and the fact that he, like Carey, had a company of his own, would have made him the most likely man to propose that she should become a patron of players.

Carey must certainly have been instrumental in pushing Howard's subsequent appointment to the Council, because almost all the other appointees in those years were supporters of Walsingham and Leicester. Carey was not a subtle man— Walsingham drafted a letter in 1584 in which he wrote that Burghley 'doth use Hunsdon as a counterpoise against Leicester, though God wot he be but a weak one'[7]—but he became a consistent supporter of Howard subsequently in matters relating to playing, and indeed followed his policies once he in turn became Lord Chamberlain. Howard was the most obvious candidate to succeed Radcliffe as Lord Chamberlain, since he had deputized for him in the seventies during one of Radcliffe's previous illnesses. Moreover, the agent who set the new company up, Edmund Tilney, Master of the Revels for the last five years, was not only Howard's cousin but indebted to him because Howard had originally secured him the Mastership.[8] It was most likely Tilney who conceived the precise form of the new plan, and put it to his patron.

overlapping loyalties than the consistent two-party rule of the Burghley group and the Leicester group that Read identified.

[6] Some consequences for the playing companies of the hostility between Leicester and Sussex as Lord Chamberlain are described in Ch. 4.

[7] CSP Scotland, 35, no. 55.

[8] See Richard Dutton, Mastering the Revels, 44–5. In 1616 Charles Howard's son claimed that it was his father who originally secured the office for Tilney.

So long as the old Lord Chamberlain was still in charge Howard could do nothing directly. But by March 1583 he knew that Radcliffe was dying. He presumably hoped that the Chamberlainship would revert to him, since his father had been Lord Chamberlain (and Lord Admiral) before him, and he had deputized for Sussex already. The Chamberlainship was a valuable prize to Howard largely because it secured him a place on the Privy Council. He had reason to prompt the innovation now, but also to stay in the background, waiting for Sussex to die. In the meantime Walsingham as Privy-Council secretary took the enabling step that gave Tilney the authority to set up the new company. It is probably a measure of the delicacy of the games being played between the great patrons and their companies and Howard's position as a non-supporter of Leicester that his place on the Privy Council and his succession to the Chamberlainship were not formally confirmed until the middle of the next Christmas season, all of six months after Radcliffe died. To go into the Christmas season without a Lord Chamberlain to control the entertainments was dangerous, indeed unique in the history of Elizabeth's court.

Howard's interventionism over the London playing companies has generally been underestimated. He gave the undertakings to the Lord Mayor on behalf of the Queen's Men in 1584 that launched the set of compromises over playing-times and locations for the major companies, which became the basis for the durable if uneasy settlement between Guildhall and the Council over London playing that lasted for the next eleven years. His undertakings did not especially favour the companies, not even the new company, though it got unique privileges over all the others. But it did get them better access to playing inside the city than any company ever had in the later years. And on several occasions subsequently Howard intervened in the players' interests. In February 1592, when London was closed for playing, he personally issued a passport as Lord Admiral for his company to tour in the Low Countries.[9] Before that he had let Edward Alleyn retain his personal livery when he left the Lord Admiral's company for Strange's, and in 1594 he was quite as active as his father-in-law, who followed him in the post of Lord Chamberlain, in setting up the duopoly that replaced the Queen's Men, with Alleyn as one of the two company leaders.[10] In 1600 Howard actively interceded with the Privy Council to get the Fortune built for his half of the duopoly.[11] His record as a governmental supporter of the best companies is consistent and unequalled.

It is quite possible that the idea of setting up a company under the Queen's name had been in Howard's mind for some time before the combination of Radcliffe's last illness and the Paris Garden accident gave him his chance. In the season of court shows that ended in March 1583 four adult companies, Hunsdon's, Derby's, Sussex's, and Leicester's gave plays, and Strange's Men offered 'activities', whereas the previous Christmas the only entertainment that an adult company

[9] Jerzy Limon, *Gentlemen of a Company: English Players in Central and Eastern Europe 1590–1660* (Cambridge, 1985), 3.

[10] See Gurr, 'The Chimera of Amalgamation', *TRI* 18 (1993), 85–93, and 'Three Reluctant Patrons', *SQ* 44 (1993), 159–74.

[11] See the letter from the Privy Council to the Justices of Middlesex, 8 Apr. 1600, signed by Cecil, Howard, and Hunsdon, quoted in *ES* iv. 328–9.

offered was Strange's 'activities'.[12] In any case, by 1583 Tilney had been in post for five years and was well-prepared for the job of selecting the best players. He drew the new company together from his experience each year of inspecting the companies and their performances to select what should be shown at court for Christmas.

In the event he took rather more men than those who were immediately available to him in London from the five companies who performed at court in the season just ending. Oxford's, for instance (formerly Warwick's), from which he took John Dutton, had not been at court since 1580. Tilney must have made his selection on the basis of his full five years of experience. From Leicester's he took three men, William Johnson, John Laneham, and Robert Wilson. He did not take their former leading player, James Burbage, though we can only speculate why this should be. Burbage may have already committed himself to staying in London in order to manage his playhouse. Certainly he did not stay with the residual company of Leicester's Men after its decapitation, because in 1584 he claimed that he was a servant to Carey, the Vice-Chamberlain, at a time when Carey had no playing company.[13] Burbage's alternative career as theatre-owner and impresario may have been in Tilney's mind in making his selections for the new company in 1583. He might equally have thought that Burbage's charisma as a leader and innovator was dangerous. Jerome Savage, doing a similar job for Warwick's, was also left out of the Warwick's cull. There was evidently no thought in the government's minds at this stage in their plans for playing that it would be a good idea to secure the Theatre as a permanent base for the new company. On the evidence of Howard's negotiations with London in 1584, indeed, it was rather places in the city itself that they expected the players to use. Even though Howard had authority in the county of Middlesex, where the playhouses were located, at this point he did not consider the suburban authorities worth drawing into his new plans.

Whatever the underlying motives, culling the best players from the other companies for its sharers immediately made the Queen's Men into the cream of London companies. With twelve sharers it also became by some distance the largest company.[14] There is good reason to believe that it was the enlarged size and scope of the Queen's Men that soon prompted the production of a new kind of play. The first of the 'large' plays demanding casts of fifteen or more of men and boys were appearing in print at the end of the decade, by when at least four companies had resources in numbers comparable to the Queen's. There is no doubt that the size of the Queen's Men through their great years from 1583 till 1588 raised company standards to a new level of achievement.

[12] These unidentified actions probably consisted mainly of tumbling and other forms of non-verbal entertainment. Strange's Men, whether players or tumblers, were favoured by Tilney in these years, probably because of his close connections with the Derby and Strange family. See Scott McMillin, 'The Queen's Men and the London Theatre of 1583', 11–12.

[13] See Ch. 4.

[14] See Gurr, 'The Chimera of Amalgamation', 85–6.

Tilney, of course, made the Queen's Men into the best company not just by the quantity of players he acquired for it but by their quality. While special skills such as Robert Wilson's in playwriting and those of the known players of tragic or clown roles were required for the new team, the choice was restricted by the expectation that only a few would be taken from each company. Still, they were being taken for the queen's service, and Tilney must have enjoyed the task. Unfortunately we do not know the previous affiliations for half of the new sharers. Three we know came from Leicester's, one from Oxford's, and two, the famous clown Richard Tarlton and John Adams, came from the Lord Chamberlain Sussex's Men. John Bentley, the new company's leading tragedian, Wilson, and the other four named players all came from unknown companies. It is not unlikely that most of them came from the two other playing companies who had performed at court that Christmas, Carey's (Hunsdon's), and Derby's.

The new company received unique privileges at the court's next season, 1583–4. The Queen's Men gave three performances, along with two by boy companies (the Chapel Children and Oxford's Boys), between St Stephen's Night and 3 March. In the following Christmas season they gave five plays (actually four performances, one play being prepared but not shown). The only other presentations that season were one play by Oxford's Boys and an evening of 'activities' by Oxford's Men. In the meantime Charles Howard as Lord Chamberlain had negotiated unique rights with the Lord Mayor for them to play in the city. The right to wear the royal livery's red coats also gave them strong support and a better income when they went on tour through the country. At this time no mayor would risk being called disloyal by turning away the Queen's own players. At Bristol, Gloucester, Cambridge, Dover and other parts of Kent, Nottingham, and Shrewsbury over the next few years they were usually paid twice as much as other companies. This may reflect their greater size. It certainly reflected their pre-eminent name and greater prestige.

The Privy Council's prescripts for the new company included a specification of where they could play inside the city. This did not bother to include either of the Middlesex amphitheatres, Burbage's Theatre and the Curtain. The negotiations were only with the city, for permission to play at the venues inside the city walls. A consequent order of November 1583 from the Guildhall granted permission for them to play 'at the Sygnes of the Bull in Busshoppesgatestreete, and the sygne of the Bell in gratiousstreete and nowheare els within this Cyttye'.[15] The Bull in Bishopsgate Street was an inn like the Bel Savage, with a square of galleries open to the sky. The Bell in Gracechurch Street, by contrast, seems to have been an inn with a large indoor hall available for playing. Specifying the two allowed the company a large good-weather and a smaller bad-weather venue, both of them inside the city. Howard confirmed that this concession by the city would be unique to the new company in 1584.

---

[15] From a licence of the Court of Aldermen, 28 Nov. 1583. Printed in the *MSC* ii. 3 (1931), 314.

Where or even whether they also played regularly at the custom-built playhouses such as Burbage's Theatre we do not know, since the Middlesex justices issued no comparable orders. Playing in the suburbs was presumably a free add-on. There were still plenty of constraints in the new deal. The same Guildhall order gave the Queen's company leave to play only on holidays, Wednesdays, and Saturdays, which left ample time in the week for the company to offer other performances at the suburban playhouses.[16] Stories of the Queen's Men in the 1580s, mostly anecdotes about Tarlton, indicate that they did play at both the Theatre and the Curtain, as well as at the Bull and the Bel Savage in the city.[17] In 1594 their last appearances in London were at the Rose. Evidently, though, in 1583 and 1584 the purpose-built theatres had not yet assumed the precedence that they were to gain ten years later. The city was where the companies wanted to play most. It may well be that the suburban amphitheatres only gained their eminence subsequently as a second-best option once the 1594 deal finally met the Lord Mayor's demands and the Chamberlain agreed that the companies must stop using the city venues.

Membership of the Queen's company changed only slightly in its first five great years. Bentley and Tobias Mylles died in 1585,[18] and William Knell came into the company in that year, presumably as a replacement for Bentley. John Dutton had brought in his brother Laurence before 1588. Tarlton died, on 3 September 1588. Knell was killed by a fellow-player, John Towne, in the same summer, and John Symons, a tumbler who had been in Strange's presumably as a principal in its 'activities', joined the company. It was still a stable group. A list dated 30 June 1588 of royal household subsidies names Laneham, Johnson, Towne, Adams, Garland, Dutton, Singer, and Cooke, eight of the original twelve, two of them having died. The company's unique privileges evidently meant that the company's members did not readily see any reason to give up the royal livery.

If the provincial records are reliable, their first five years from their original establishment in 1583 were hugely active. They were paid more and given more respect in towns around the country than any other company in the century. From 1583 to 1588 they appear in the provincial records far more frequently than any other company in any other period. So often do they appear in different parts of the country on similar dates, in fact, that just as London found reason to complain in 1584 that every company was now claiming to be the Queen's Servants, so the country towns probably should have questioned the authority of the name on their licence more often than they usually did. Unfortunately the terseness of civic records and the imprecision of their dating give no clear indication how many companies claiming to be the Queen's Men might have been on tour in these years.

---

[16] They none the less protested at this restriction, appealing to their protectors. Three days later Walsingham wrote to the Lord Mayor declaring that the Privy Council had meant that the players should be allowed to play on working days in the week, 'at convenient times . . . (sondaies onely excepted) and such other daies wherein sermons and lectures are commonlie used'. *MSC* i. 1, 67.
[17] See Ch. 4.
[18] Bentley's will is reproduced in *Playhouse Wills 1558–1642*, 57.

The earliest and in some ways the most thorough piece of evidence for their early travels comes from Norwich in the summer of 1583. John Bentley and John Singer on 19 June were committed to prison there while the city authorities investigated an affray at the door of the Red Lion inn, where the Queen's company was then playing after its guildhall performance. A local man, named in the legal testimonies only as 'George', was killed in the fight. The records, which also name Tarlton as a participant in the fray, include a testimony from one of the local participants, Henry Brown, a servant to Sir William Paston. He reported that

this examynate beinge at the play this Afternone word was brought into the play that one of her majesties servauntes was abused at the gate whereupon this examynate with others went owt and one in a blew cote Cast Stones at Bentley and brocke his heade being one of her majesties servauntes whereupon this examynate sayed villan wilt thowe murder the quenes man and the fellowe called this examynate villan agayne and thereupon this examynate stroke hym with his Sworde and hyt hym on the legg.[19]

The fight had started as a struggle with the company's gatherer at the entry-way by locals trying to gain access. Some of the players left the stage to join in. As Brown's testimony went on to say,

Beinge examined how manye of the players went from of the Stage on Satturdaye to Stryke the man wyche was Slayne he sayeth there were but two of the players wich went viz Bentley and one other in a black dublyt called Singer and Tareton also was going but he was stayed by the way.

Other testimonies confirm this account. Singer subsequently used his sword on the man hit by Brown, who declared that Bentley 'thrust at hym twice with his naked Raper the one thrust was about thee knee but hee knoweth not where the other thrust was'. That was before Brown made his own hit on his leg. Another witness, a weaver called William Kilby of Pockthorpe, said he saw three players leave the stage with swords in scabbards in their hands. Another said that he saw one of the players break a man's head with his sword hilt. In a rather different version another witness said that Bentley overtook the man in the blue coat, who was running away, and thrust him in the leg, whereupon the man cried 'oh you have mayned me' and threw a stone at Bentley's head, drawing blood, whereupon Henry Brown struck him on the leg. That appears to have been the crucial blow, from which the victim bled to death.

The man who first started the trouble, whose name is given in the testimonies only as Winsdon, wanted to get in to see the play before he was prepared to pay for it. It must have been one of the last instances of customer suspicion over plays, the kind of reluctance to pay before the entertainment had been delivered that used to be normal when performances were in open market-places and payment was secured by the players going hat in hand round the crowd. As the man pushed forward he knocked the gatekeeper's takings out of his hand. The affray grew from

[19] The documents are transcribed fully in *REED, Norwich*, 66–76.

there. The man who died was said to have been Winsdon's servant fifteen or sixteen years before. He was entered in the burial register under the solitary name of George. How seriously Henry Brown was trying to stand up for the Queen's servants is not easy to determine. The players were certainly concerned at first only to protect their takings. The city gave them forty shillings that year.

It may have been in about 1588 that the company's official membership split into two parts. If the dates in the provincial records are any guide, there had been duplicate Queen's companies as early as 1584, the year when London complained that every company was claiming to be the Queen's. A Queen's company was paid on 26 August 1584 at Faversham in Kent, and also at Leicester in the Midlands in September. One of these must have been a travelling company using a forgery or copy of the royal licence. The same doubling may have happened in September 1586 when one Queen's company was at Bridgwater in Somerset and another at Lydd in Kent on 21 September and at Canterbury on 27 September. One company was at Nottingham on 13 August 1586 and at Faversham in Kent on 22 August. It was possible to get from Bridgwater, Somerset's chief port, to Dover in Kent by sea quite quickly, but the fact that other places reported a Queen's company appearing in Kent that month suggests that two companies were abroad. It would not have been possible, and certainly not very cheap and practical, for the same company to travel the two hundred miles from Nottingham to Faversham in a little over a week. One of these two companies must have been travelling on a fake licence and in false livery.

By 1588, though, and probably as early as 1587, the real Queen's Men seem to have started travelling as two more-or-less-officially separate groups, one led by the Duttons and one by Lancham and Symonds. A Queen's company with musicians is recorded at Nottingham, a town which welcomed musicians more than players, on 20 August 1587, only four days after a Queen's company with tumblers was recorded at Bristol. Meanwhile, another Queen's company had been recorded at New Romney in Kent on 13 August. Ipswich in East Anglia recorded a Queen's company visiting on 3 July 1587, while Gloucester and Bath recorded one on 12 and 13 July, and Bristol with tumblers on 16 August. That summer, it seems, one company was touring the eastern counties while the other covered the west, and a third was in Kent. The three had become two in 1589, when one company was at Reading on 2 September while the other was at Knowsley in Lancashire in the same month.

And they went further abroad. This was the season when Dublin records two companies visiting, a Queen's and Essex's. The gratitude expressed in the entry in the Dublin books (recorded below) implies that the visit was by invitation, but for what occasion is not said. The fee was hardly generous enough to have covered the costs of the sea trip to Dublin, so the company must have augmented its income with some public performances, the only ones on record in Dublin for this entire period. It is one of the more tantalizing local records, since it says so little about the occasion, unique though it was. The excursion could hardly have been a long one, since the records through that summer even for only two Queen's companies are quite frequent and well-dispersed.

One of the two Queen's companies that had the original players certainly had a group of acrobats or tumblers in its numbers, and may have offered 'activities' as a supplement to their plays. The Queen's company which stopped at Nottingham in August 1587 may have picked up their instrumentalists along the way, knowing Nottingham's weakness for waits and fiddlers. They were chiefly concerned to market their plays. It is difficult to see which sort of entertainment the group calling at Bristol on 16 August 1587, and identified as 'the Queenes Majesties Players & Tomlaiers', would have offered to the mayor and corporation. Tumbling and acrobatics were not likely to have been the sole entertainment. It was a year later, in 1588–9, that Nottingham was able to differentiate between the group led by 'Symons' and another group led by 'the two Duttons'. This gives us a date when the formal split was in operation, together with an entry which identifies the personalities leading the two halves of the original company. Whether or not one of the two included musicians, the other certainly included tumblers, though there is some doubt as to which it was. Symons, who was the queen's tumbler, had left them for the Admiral's by the court season of 1588–9. Some shifts in personnel in addition to the split must have happened even before Tarlton and Knell died in 1588. Speculation about the Duttons as a pair of strongly entrepreneurial independents is tempting.

The Queen's Men who had the tumblers were evidently well worth the exceptional fees they received. A schoolteacher called Taylor, writing a local history of Shrewsbury in the last years of the century, recorded his own experience of the Queen's tumblers after their visit in July 1589. It was an event of which, he wrote, 'the lick was never seene in shrewsburie before'. In Taylor's account the 'Turk' noted in several provincial records as appearing with the Queen's at Norwich, Bristol, and Coventry in 1590, a master of tight-rope dancing, becomes a Hungarian (then still a part of the Turkish empire). I have added some necessary punctuation to Taylor's story:

they wold turne them selves twise bothe backward and forward without towchinge any grownde in lightinge or fallinge upon their feete. Som of them also wold apeare in a bagge upright in the same beinge tieed fast at the mowthe above his head and wold beinge in the sayde bagge turne bothe foreward and backward without towchinge any grownde in falling upright upon his feete in the sayde bagge, marvellous to the beholders. Also a litill from the sayde stadge there was a gable roape tighted and drawen strayte uppon poales erectid against master pursers place in the sayde corne market uppon the whiche roape the sayde hongarian did assende and goe uppon withe his bare feete having a longe poale in his handes over his headd and wold fall stridlinges uppon the sayde roap and mowntinge up again upon the same withe hys feete.[20]

[20] The text of 'Dr Taylor's history' recording this visit is given in *REED, Shropshire*, 247.

It is worth noting from this account that the main performance was done on a stage of the kind that the companies normally set up for plays in the Shrewsbury cornmarket. Acrobatics and tight-rope walking may have been a separate entertainment, but they were more likely to have been an accompaniment to the plays. Conceivably both of the divided Queen's companies had acrobats in their number, though only one had the celebrated rope-dancing 'Turk'.

The division of the company with its one official licence into two separate touring groups is one of the questions where the evidence in the provincial records seems to suggest practices which are at odds with the London records of the company. We do not know which of the two groups, if not both, played in London and bought Greene's *Orlando Furioso*, for instance. Both the Dutton and the Laneham group played at court. But other evidence is sketchy. There can be no doubt that the multiple records of more than one Queen's company touring outside London through the later years of the 1580s are basically reliable. The named licencees divided into two separate touring groups at some time roughly four or five years after their first formation. What that had to do with their gradual decline in the late 1580s, and whether it was cause or effect, apart from other factors like the death of their leading clown, is not any easier to identify than what may have first caused the split. The split itself must have affected the quality of both the two separated companies; their repertoire of plays would be halved for one thing.

The division of their repertory is one of the factors which might be identified as either a cause or a result of their decline. Several notable Queen's Men's plays from the late 1580s got into print in the first surge of play-publication between 1590 and 1594. None of them have the radical new qualities of the Admiral's *Tamburlaines* published in 1590, nor of *The Spanish Tragedy*, which was clearly not a Queen's play. The loss of player-quality and of play-quality to the other rising 'large' companies such as Worcester's, the Admiral's, and Strange's may be among the causes of their gradual descent.

Other factors, including their eminence as the royal company, may have affected them too. After 1588 the Laneham-led company did get itself involved in the Marprelate controversy (Lyly and Nashe both refer to 'old Lanam' lashing Martin with his rhymes), although that was hardly more than a loyal royal company might have been expected to do. After the Dublin expedition, which must have been prompted by the company being the royal one, one of the two went in September 1589 to Scotland from Cumberland, again presumably as a royal embassy, to play before King James at his marriage to Anne of Denmark, though delays to the wedding by storms at sea prevented it.[21] These are hints about official use of the royally-patronized company that become frustratingly enigmatic when we know that more than one company was using the royal name.

It seems to have been somewhere round about late 1588 that the split into two separate companies seems to have become permanent and officially

---

[21] *CSP (Scotland)*, 1509–1603, (London, 1858), x. 178–9.

approved.[22] Tilney's annual re-valuation of the companies for performances at court must also have helped the steady down-grading of the Queen's. The season of 1588–9 saw the first appearance at court since 1583 of a second adult company besides the royal company, the Admiral's Men. Each company gave two of the seven plays performed (Lyly's Paul's Boys gave the other three). A permanent division, with possibly both companies allowed to carry the royal authorization, appears to have been accepted after that.

Tilney certainly accepted the separate existence of the two companies. In the following court season of 1590–1, after the Scottish excursion, the Dutton brothers were paid £40 for four performances while Laneham received a £10 payment for a separate performance. From here on the civic records certainly relate to the separate groupings of the Dutton company and the Laneham company. Two separate groups of Queen's Men played at Ipswich on 15 and 28 May 1590. In January 1591 one group performed twice at court while another set of 'Queen's Men' were appearing in Maidstone. These do appear to be records of the original company, now divided. The royal patent stayed in use for a remarkably long time, even after Elizabeth's death. It reappeared as late as 1623 when the Norwich authorities caught Martin Slater with a twenty-year-old patent as a Queen Elizabeth's man. But there is no note in the Privy Council papers from this time of any patent authorizing a second royal company.

It is quite likely that the split happened as a simple consequence of incompatibility between some of the original players. 'Old' Laneham may have resented the Dutton brothers, the same pushy pair who were called chameleons for their frequent switches of company in the 1580s. Or it may equally have been a division to give more players employment and to maximize profit. From the beginning of the 1590s the notes made by several towns that one of the groups had a Turkish acrobat suggests that the two groups were making themselves recognizably different in what they offered. Some diversification from acting plays there certainly was. I do not think it likely, as has been suggested on the basis of a reference at Bath to the 'quenes men that were tumblers', that one of the two companies continued to offer plays while the other was solely acrobatic, because the leaders of both groups, Laneham and the Duttons, were chiefly players.[23]

Whatever caused it, the split might have brought difficulties for the two units to mount separately the large-cast plays that had been written for the original

[22] G. M. Pinciss, 'The Queen's Men, 1583–1592', *Theatre Survey*, 11 (1970), 50–65, 64 n. 38, questions the evidence for a split. Chambers relied for his view that there was one on Murray's argument about a Queen's company recorded as playing at court on 1 and 3 Jan. 1591, but also performing at Maidstone on 2 Jan. The other evidence cited here makes it almost certain that a split did occur. Bradley (*From Text to Performance*, 253 n. 19), says it is probable that Symons and Laneham led a group of actors while Dutton led tumblers. Chambers reckons the reverse. Yet Laneham was certainly a player and rhymer, while Symons was a notable tumbler. It is most likely that both companies could offer plays along with other 'activities'.

[23] The Bristol records do have an entry for 'the Queens Players which tumbled before the [mayor and aldermen] at the Free schole where was tumblinge shewen also by a Turcke upon a Robe. with runninge on the same'. Tightrope-walking and acrobatics did evidently comprise a complete show in this case.

twelve-man company. That may be the main reason why one of the two Queen's companies subsequently solved the problem by joining forces with another group. A Queen's Men's company is recorded as playing in 1590–1 at Southampton, Bristol, Gloucester, and Coventry in a partnership with Sussex's Men. Gloucester and Coventry also record visits by a Queen's Company without Sussex's, though the civic records do not indicate whether it was the same or a different set of Queen's Men. Usually it was the solo group which had the Turk and his ropes. Southampton names a Dutton as payee for the visit without Sussex's on 29 June 1590, the month when a Queen's group without Sussex's also performed at Winchester. The group linked with Sussex's had already played at Southampton in March of that year. Since Dutton was named in the solo group, presumably it was therefore the Laneham-led group that chose to unite with Sussex's in 1591. There is nothing to say which of the two groups played in London in 1590 and 1591, though it could be argued that it would have been the same group that played in consort with Sussex's later, in early 1594, presumably Laneham's.

There are no records from touring through the following years to suggest that the link of a Queen's Men group with Sussex's was sustained for very long. Dutton's group is recorded at Cambridge on its own in September 1591. Of the other group there is no certain trace, though the records do confirm that two separate groups calling themselves the Queen's Men were continuing to travel through the following years. We cannot tell which group was at Bristol in July 1592 and which at York in the same month, when the city paid them £3 6s. 8d. and the Minster on 24 July 20s., but the Wardens' accounts for Coventry in 1592 record separate payments to 'the Queenes players' and to 'mr duttons players'. The former received forty shillings and the latter only five.[24] Identifying one company by its chief player's name and not by its patron suggests that a distinction was now being made between the two groups that had emerged from the split and which still claimed the same patron.

There is no firm evidence that more than one of the two groups kept going into 1594, when Henslowe records the renewal at the Rose of the old alliance between a Queen's group and Sussex's. Since Laneham's was judged by Coventry to be worth eight times as much as Dutton's group, that seems to support the idea that Laneham's was the group that played in London and which periodically linked with Sussex's.

After the five plays given by the two Queen's groups at court in the 1590–1 season only one gave a single court performance in the 1591–2 season, compared with six by Strange's and one each by Sussex's and Hertford's. We do not know which of the two groups gave this court performance, though again if provincial payments relate to quality of performance it is more likely to have been the Laneham group which had been given forty shillings at Coventry than the Dutton group. Neither Queen's company appeared at court in 1592–3. The Laneham group were the only company to appear at court in the next season, after a disastrous year for plague, performing just once, on 6 January 1594. Then, at Easter 1594, Henslowe records a stay at the Rose of the Queen's and Sussex's, performing five plays. These performances appear to have been by a joint company, rather than by the two playing on alternate afternoons, as happened at the Rose later in 1594 with the new Admiral's and Chamberlain's. These five performances were the last recorded appearance of a Queen's company in London.

To judge by the appearance of their plays in the repertory of the new Chamberlain's Men later in 1594, some of the Queen's members were culled, along with their playbooks, for the two companies that the Privy Councillors set up to replace the former Queen's monopoly. On 8 May Henslowe made a loan of £15 to his nephew, Francis Henslowe, for a share in the Queen's Men once they, in his usual phrase, 'brocke & went into the contrey to playe'.[25] It was witnessed by John Towne, who had been a Queen's Man since 1583. Towne, like Francis Henslowe, was evidently not wanted for the duopoly that replaced the Queen's Men, although his brother Thomas subsequently appears in the Admiral's.[26] The company's 'break' from London, following the close of their short season at the Rose on 8 April, meant a life of touring from then on. The Admiral's half of the duopoly was formed early in May and started playing at the Rose on 14 May 1594.

A residual Queen's company, most likely only the one, can be traced around the country for several more years. The records for York in 1598 name John Garland, William Smith, and John Cowper as members. Among these men Garland was the only survivor from 1583. Roslyn Knutson believes that the company might have played at the Swan in 1595–6, near the Rose, prompting the Chamberlain's Men to mount their *King John* to stand against the Queen's Men's *Troublesome Raigne*, and prompting the Admiral's to mount their *Henry V* against the Queen's Men's *Famous Victories*. I think that the alternative reading, which gives both of the old Queen's plays to the Chamberlain's to be rewritten later by Shakespeare, holds rather more water than this theory. If the Queen's Men did play at the new Swan, they were running against the 1594 establishment of the duopoly, which relegated the Queen's Men out of London.[27] The history of the 1597 Pembroke's shows how difficult a ploy that was. The Queen's had, of course, been dispossessed by the establishment of the new Lord Chamberlain's and Lord Admiral's companies, and they may have sought to set up in competition against them. They would be less likely to do so if, as I suspect, some of their members and playscripts had gone to the new companies.

---

[25] *Henslowe's Diary*, 7.

[26] Speculation about the post-1590 membership of one group of the Queen's Men has been stirred by Mary Edmond's discovery of the will of Simon Jewell. The will mentions a 'Mr Smithe' who may be the Queen's William Smith, and 'Mr Cooke' who might be Lionel Cooke. See Mary Edmond, 'Pembroke's Men', *RES* n.s. 25 (1974), 129–3, together with Scott McMillin, 'Simon Jewell and the Queen's Men', *RES* 27 (1976), 174–7, and David George, 'Shakespeare and Pembroke's Men', *SQ* 32 (1981), 308–10.

[27] Roslyn Lander Knutson, *The Repertory of Shakespeare's Company*, 169.

There is no positive evidence that the Queen's ever again played in London, although the Swan must have been used by some company in 1596, since Johannes De Witt said he visited it then, and presumably he did so in order to see a play there. His sketch of the playhouse certainly shows players acting on the Swan's stage. If Roslyn Knutson is right, it is faintly conceivable that his friend Van Buchell's copy of De Witt's drawing shows the remnant Queen's Men making one of their last London appearances.

Quite apart from the vexed question of whether in its first years the royal company was expected to use its position to promote the royal interests, there is no doubt that its uniquely large size must have exercised the playwrights to produce new work especially for it. Unfortunately, as is usual for this early period, very few of the earliest texts for this new 'large' company survive. The idea of producing printed texts of plays other than quasi-academic works like Newton's translations of Seneca was still a fairly novel one at this time. No more than ten extant plays can be positively ascribed to the Queen's Men's repertory from the years of its greatest prestige. Nine of the ten did not appear until the years following their collapse, 1594 and 1595. Of these, *Three Lords and Three Ladies of London*, a sequel to the *Three Ladies of London* originally written by Robert Wilson for Leicester's Men, contains a lament for Tarlton, which dates it precisely to 1588. The other eight all name the Queen's Men on their title-pages. They probably come from different periods in the company's life, though there is not much in any of the texts to indicate which period or which players were expected to perform them. The eight are: *The Famous Victories of Henry V, Friar Bacon and Friar Bungay, King Leir, The Troublesome Reign of King John, The Old Wives Tale, Selimus, Sir Clyomon and Sir Clamydes*, and *The True Tragedy of Richard III*. A tenth, *Valentine and Orson*, was entered in the Stationers' Register in 1595 but has not survived. Besides these, three others, *A Looking Glass for London and England, James IV*, and *Orlando Furioso*, have also been ascribed to the company on a variety of different grounds.[28] Four other titles of lost plays, two of them omnibus titles for short pieces (*Five Plays in One, Three Plays in One*), also survive in the records of the 1584–5 court season. And Tarlton wrote a play of his own, *The Seven Deadly Sins*, of which little other than the title survives, unless the 'plot' of the second part of *The Seven Deadly Sins* in the Henslowe papers was made up from Tarlton's script.

The 'Seven Deadly Sins' play was evidently a primary feature of the travelling repertoire. Gabriel Harvey tells us in *Foure Letters* (1592) that he had been 'verie gently invited thereunto at Oxford, by Tarleton himselfe.' The Queen's Men were playing in Oxford town in 1585, and did not visit there again until the financial year 1588–9, by when Tarlton had most likely died. Harvey's account calls the play

---

[28] See G. M. Pinciss, 'Thomas Creede and the Repertory of the Queen's Men 1583–1592', *MP* 67 (1970), 321–30. Scott McMillin, 'The Queen's Men in 1594: A Study of "Good" and "Bad" Quartos', *ELR* 14 (1984), 55–69, analyzes the texts and casts of *Bacon and Bungay, Selimus,* and *The True Tragedy of Richard III,* concluding that all three needed a cast of 11 men and 3 boys to play their most crowded scenes. He also notes (58) that *The Coblers Prophecy* calls for a cast of 14, while *A Looking Glass* needs 12, and *Orlando Furioso* 16.

'famous', and adds 'which most dea[d]ly, but most lively playe, I might have seene in London'.[29] He was invited to see it instead by the author himself in Oxford, and did so. Harvey, a Cambridge resident, was a frequent traveller to London, much less so to Oxford. But there is no particular reason why he should specify Oxford as the venue if it were not what really happened.

To some extent this short list from what must have been a much larger repertoire of plays does reflect the developments in playwriting through the 1580s. The interlude tradition, represented here by *Sir Clyomon and Sir Clamydes*, the allegorical figures in *The Three Lords*, and probably (to judge from their titles) by the four lost plays performed at court in 1584–5, stand in contrast to the new modes that entered at the end of the 1580s. Marlowe never wrote for the Queen's Men, but some of the company's later plays show his influence. *Friar Bacon* deals with a legendary English magician, in the fashion made famous by Marlowe's *Faustus*. *Selimus* deals with Turkish history in the mode of *Tamburlaine*. Most notably in this list the 'large play' fashion is also represented by four history plays. One of them celebrated what the Tudors regarded as England's finest hour, Agincourt. A play about ancient Britain, *King Leir*, stands with a play about the last Scottish king to be defeated in battle by the English. A fourth play, about King John, written in the wake of the Armada scare, was strongly anti-Catholic. Moral and political conformism, and even patriotism, shines out from this list.

THE QUEEN'S MEN 1583–1594

Plays
Sir Clyomon and Sir Clamydes, *The Famous Victories of Henry V*, *Felix and Philiomena* (lost), *Five Plays in One* (lost), *Friar Bacon and Friar Bungay* (old?), *James IV*, *King Leir*, *A Looking Glass for London and England*, *Orlando Furioso*, *Phyllida and Corin* (lost), *Three Lords and Three Ladies of London*, *Three Plays in One* (lost), *The Troublesome Reign of King John*.

Playing Sharers
[twelve according to Stow] John Adams (Sussex's 1576), John Bentley (d. 1585), Lionel Cooke, John Dutton (ex Oxford's), Laurence Dutton (brother of John, named at Nottingham in 1588–9, payee with brother for court performances 1590–1), John Garland,[30] William Johnson (ex Leicester's), William Knell (killed by sword by fellow player John Towne, 13 June 1587), John Laneham (ex Leicester's), Tobias Mylles (d. 1585), John Singer, John Symons (joined after Tarlton's death: a tumbler in Strange's before and after, named in Nottingham accounts 1588–9), Richard Tarlton (ex Sussex's, died 3 Sept. 1588), John Towne, Robert Wilson (ex Leicester's).

---

[29] Gabriel Harvey, *Foure Letters and Certaine Sermons* (1592), 28–9.
[30] Garland did not die until 1624, so he must have been a relatively young player in 1583. Beside appearing in the York list of 1598, he was in Lennox's in 1605, and the Duke of York's/Prince Charles's in 1611.

Royal Household list 30 June 1588: Laneham, Johnson, Towne, Adams, Garland, Dutton, Singer, Cooke. After 1594: Francis Henslowe (?), George Attewell (?), Robert Nicholls, William Smyght (?), John Shank.
Nottingham 1597 'John Towne'.
York 1598 'William Smyth John garland & John Cowper'.

London Playhouses
28 Nov. 1583 city permit 'at the Synges of the Bull in Busshoppesgatestreete, and the sygne of the Bell in gratioustreete and nowheare els', Theatre *c.*1584 (*Pierce Penilesse*, i. 197, on Harvey's *Saturn and Jupiter*, 1583), Bel Savage (1588, *Tarlton's Jests*), Curtain (*Tarlton's Jests*), Rose 1594.

At Court
26 Dec. 1583, 29 Dec. 1583, 3 Mar. 1584, 4 plays 1584–5, 3 plays 1585–6, 4 plays 1586–7, 3 plays 1587–8, 2 plays 1588–9, 2 plays 1589–90, 4 plays 1590–91 [when split], 29 Dec. 1591, 1 play 1593–4.

Travelling
Nottingham 1582–3, 20s. / Ipswich 1582–3, 40s. / Norwich, June 1583, 40s. / Shrewsbury 1582–3, 40s. 6d. / Abingdon 1582–3, 20s., 'in wine' 16d. / Leicester 1582–3 'more then was gathered,' 38s. 4d. / Gloucester 1582–3 / Dover 1582–3, 40s. / Canterbury 1582–3, 40s. / Hythe, Kent 1583–4, 20s. / Rye, Sussex Sept. 1583, 20s. / Cambridge town 1583–4 'forbiddinge theim to playe in the towne & so to ridd theim cleane away', 50s. / Bristol July 1583, 40s. / Gloucester 1583–4 'To the players of the Master of the Revelles of the Queenes majestes howse', 13s. 4d. / Lydd, Kent 1583–4, 20s. / Bath June 1583–4, 20s. 7½ d. / Southampton 1583–4, £2. / Cambridge town 9 July 1584, 20s. / York City Books Aug. 1584, £3. 6s. 8d. York Minster Accounts, 40s. / Faversham, Kent 26 Aug. 1584, 20s. / Hythe, Kent 1584–5, 10s., 1584–5, 20s. / Lydd, Kent 1584–5, 20s. / Rye, Sussex Sept. 1584, 20s. / Leicester 30 Sept. 1584, 'more than was gathered', 15s. 8d. / Cambridge 1584–5, 26s. 8d. / Dover 1584–5, 40s., 'bestowed upon a breakefast for them' 3s. / Folkestone 1584–5, 10s. / Norwich 1584–5, 30s. / Oxford town 1585–6, 10s.[31] / Abingdon 1585–6, 20s. / Norwich 1585–6, 40s. / Leicester 1585–6 'more then was gathered', 24s. / Exeter 1585–6, 53s. 4d. / Bristol July 1586 'for that they played ₍not₎ before Mr Mayor and his Bretheren and others of the Cominaltie', 20s. / Maidstone 1585–6 '& in wyne', 23s. 4d. / Dover 1586, 40s., 'Bestowed then for a drinckinge to welcome them to towne and for their breakefast at their departure', 10s. 8d. / Faversham, Kent 22 Aug. 1586, £1. / Hythe, Kent 1586–7, 20s. / Lydd, Kent, 21 Sept. 1586, 20s. / Canterbury 27 Sept. 1586, 30s. / Rye, Sussex 29 Sept. 1586, 20s. / Bridgwater, Somerset Sept. 1586, 30s. / Ipswich 25 Oct. 1586, 26s. 8d./ King's Lynn 1586 'to the Quenes plaiers & the Lorde Chamberlynes

---

[31] Either this visit or the one in 1588–9 if that was before Tarlton's death in 1588 must have included a performance of Tarlton's *Seven Deadly Sins*. See above, 210.

plaiers',[32] £3. 10s. / Nottingham 13 Aug. 1586, 40s. / Coventry 1586, 40s. / Bath June 1586–7, 19s. 4d. 'and was to make it up 26s. 8d. that was gathered at the benche' / Stratford 1586–7 / Leicester 1586–7 'more than was gaythered', 24s. / Norwich 1586–7, 36s. 8d. / Canterbury 1586–7, 20s. / Gloucester 1586–7, 30s. / Worcester 1586–7, 10s. / Abingdon 1586–7, 20s., 'to the glaser . . . to mend the yeld hall window . . . aftir the quenes plairs were gone' / King's Lynn 1587, 40s. / Ipswich 3 July 1587, 26s. 8d. / Gloucester 12 July 1587, 33s. 6d. / Bath 13 July 1587, 'beside the gatheringe' 15s. / Southampton 25 July 1587, 40s. / Dover Aug. 1587, 40s., 'spent then uppon them at their goynge away' 5s. 2d. / Hythe, Kent 1587–8, 20s. / New Romney, Kent 13 Aug. 1587, 20s. / Rye, Sussex Aug. 1587, 20s. / Nottingham 20 Aug. 1587 'musicions & players', 13s. 4d. / York City Books 9 Sept. 1587 'to the quenes majestes players which cam in hir majestes Lyvereys & plaid in the common hall', £3. 6s. 8d. / Beverley 1587 'to the quenes majesties plaiers & others upon a bill dated the iiij of September', 59s. 2d. / Coventry 'in september' 1587, 40s., 'more in september', 20s. / Coventry Dec. acct. 1587, 40s. / Exeter 1587–8, 20s. / Plymouth 1587–8, 10s. / Worcester 1587–8 'Rewardes to the Quenes players & others, expences at the Trynytie Hall' / Nottingham 1587–8 'given in Reward to the Quenes players, the two duttons & others', 20s. / Lydd, Kent 1587–8, 10s.; 10s. / Maidstone 1587–8, 20s. / Faversham, Kent 1587–8, 12s. 2d. / Canterbury 27 Mar. 1588, 20s. / Rye, Sussex Apr. 1588, 20s. / Dover Apr. 1588, 10s. / Gloucester 12 July 1588, 33s. 6d. / Bath 19 July 1588, 23s. / Bristol 20 July 1588, £2. / Bath 14 Aug. 1588, 17s., 'more given by mr mayor to the quenes men that were tumblers', 10s. / Bristol 16 Aug. 1588 'to the Queenes Majesties Players & Tomlaiers' 26s. 8d. / Faversham, Kent 1588–9, £1. / Hythe, Kent 1588–9, 10s. / Dover 1588 'at their last beynge heere', 40s. / New Park, Lancashire (Derby Household Book) 6–12 Oct. 1588 'the Qwenes players on frydaye mr dutton . . . on satterday they went' / Leicester 6 Nov. 1588 'to certen of her Majestes playars more then was gaythered', 10s./ Norwich 10 Dec. 1588, £2. / Ipswich 17 Dec. 1588, 20s. / Dover 'at Christmas laste' 1588, 20s. / Nottingham 1588–9 'given in Reward to Symons and his Companie beinge the Quenes players', 20s. / King's Lynn 1588–9 'geven to the Quenes players & ij messengers', 26s. 8d. / New Romney, Kent 1588–9, 20s. / Maidstone 1588–9, 13s. 4d. / Folkestone 1588–9, 5s. / Canterbury 1588–9, 30s. / Faversham, Kent 30 Jan. 1589, 20s. / Canterbury 'about candlemas [2 Feb.] 1589', 20s. / New Romney, Kent 14 Feb. 1589, 10s. / Lydd, Kent 15 Feb. 1589, 20s. / Rye, Sussex Feb. 1589, 20s. / Winchester 10 Mar. 1589, 20s. / Oxford town 1588–9, 10s. / Gloucester 17 Apr. 1589, 20s. / Leicester 20 May 1589 'payed to others moe of her Mayestyes playars more than was gaythered', 10s. 8d. / Ipswich 22 May 1589, 30s. / Norwich 3 June

---

[32] This is more likely to have been the old Sussex's than the Admiral's or Henry Carey's, even though Carey became Lord Chamberlain in 1586. This visit may not have been the actual union of the two companies that is evidenced in the provincial records a few years later. Such a large sum from a small town suggests separate payments for separate performances.

1589, £2 / Dublin summer 1589 'payed to the Quenes players coming to this Cittie, as a requittal of there good wylls in showing there Sporte', £3.[33] / Shrewsbury 24 July 1589[34] / Maidstone 2 Aug. 1589, 20s. / Rye, Sussex Aug. 1589, 20s. / Coventry Nov. acct. 1589, 20s. / Lathom, Lancashire (Derby Household Book) 6–10 July 1589 'the Qwenes plaiers plaied ij severall nyghtes' / Knowsley, Lancashire (Derby Household Book) 31 Aug.–6 Sept. 1589 'the quenes players came & played at nyght' / Reading 2 Sept. 1589, 20s. / Knowsley, Lancashire (Derby Household Book) 7–13 Sept. 1589 'Sondaie mr Leigh preached the quenes players played in the after none & my Lord off Essix at nyght' / Carlisle 20 Sept. 1589 letter of Henry Scrope 'upon a letre receyved from Mr Roger Asheton, Signifying unto me that yt was the kinges earnest desire for to have hir Majestes players for to repayer into Scotlande to his grace I dyd furthwith dispatche a servant of my owen unto them where they were in the furthest parte of Langkeshier, wherupon they made their returne heather to Carliell, wher they are, and have stayed for the space of ten dayes, wherof, I thought good to gyve yow notice in respect of the great desyre that the king had to have the same, to Come unto his grace: And withall to praye yoe to gyve knowledg therof to his Majestie' / Chester Dean and Chapter Oct.–Nov. 1589, 20s. / Bristol Oct. 1589, £2. / Bath Nov. 1589, 15s. / Gloucester 1589–90 'geven to the Queenes players which played in the Colledge Churche yarde', 30s. / Exeter 1589–90, 26s. 8d. / Oxford town 1589–90, 10s. / Nottingham 1589–90, 20s. / Folkestone 1589–90, 10s. / New Romney, Kent 1589–90, 16s. / Hythe, Kent 1589–90, 20s. / Faversham, Kent 1589–90, 20s. / Lydd, Kent 1589–90, 20s. / Faversham, Kent 4 Jan. 1590 'to the Queenes players & the erle of Essexe players to gether', 20s. / Winchester 1589–90, 20s. / Norwich 22 April 1590 'to the Quenes men when the Turke wente upponn Roppes at newhall', 40s. / Ipswich 28 May 1590 'unto Another company of the Queenes players', 30s. / Knowsley, Lancashire (Derby Household Book) 21–27 June 1590 'mr dutton & the Qwiens playes came' / Ludlow July 1590, 10s., 'a gifte of whyte wyne and Sugar at there departinge' 12d. / Marlborough July 1590, 10s. / Bristol 2–8 Aug. 1590 'paid by mr Mayor and Thaldermans appoyntementt unto the Queens Players which tumbled before them at the Free schole where was tumblinge shewen also by a Turcke upon a Robe. with runninge on the same', 30s., 'et for wyne drancke there by mr Mayor' 2s. / Canterbury 10 Aug. 1590, 20s. / New Romney, Kent 20 Aug. 1590, 20s. / Coventry Dec. acct. 1590 '& the turk', 40s. / Leicester 30 Oct. 1590 'at the hall dore' 10s., 'by the appoyntment of Mr Mayor and his bretherne' 40s. / Bridgnorth, Shropshire 1590–1 'at the dauncinge on the Rop', 10s. / Shrewsbury 1590–1, 40s. / Chester Dean and Chapter Oct.–Nov. 1590, 20s. 0d. / Oxford town 1590–1, 13s. 4d. / Faversham, Kent 1590–1, 10s. / Canterbury 1590–1 'the Quenes players, and my

[33] The dating for this overseas visit is not precise. Nor is it clear which of the two Queen's companies made the visit, which appears from the wording to have been by invitation.
[34] A local historian cites the acrobatic wonders done by the Queen's players on this visit, acted at 'a scaffold put up in the cornemarket in salop'. His account is quoted in part above, and in full in *REED, Somerset*, 247.

Lord Admiralls players', 30s. / Maidstone 2 Jan. 1591, 20s. / Canterbury 11 Jan. 1591, 20s. / Dover 23 Jan. 1591, 10s. / Folkestone 1590–1, 10s.; 5s. / Lydd, Kent 1590–1, 20s., 13s. 4d. / Bristol Mar. 1591 'unto the Queenes Majesties Plaiers and the Earle of Sussex', 26s. 8d. / Weymouth, Dorset 1591, 10s. / Southampton 'Shrove Sunday' 1591 'to the Queenes majestie & the Earle of Sussex players', 20s. / Coventry 24 Mar. 1591 'to the Quenes players & the Erle of Sussex players', 15s. / Newark, Nottinghamshire 1591, 20s. / Maidstone 28 May 1591, 10s. / Gloucester 1590–1 'to the Queenes players xxx s. To the Queenes and the earle of Sussex players xxx s.' / Ipswich 15 May 1591, 20s. / Ipswich 28 May 1591, 30s. / King's Lynn 20 June 1591 '& att an other tyme', £4. / Norwich 23 June 1591, 40s. / Winchester June 1591, 20s. / Southampton 29 June 1591 'to Mr Dutton fore the Queenes players', 20s. / Bath June 1591–2, 15s. 6d. 'besides that which was given by the companie' [i.e., the audience] / Bristol Aug.–Sept. 1591, 30s. / Coventry 24 Aug. 1591 30s. / Newcastle Sept. 1591, £5. / Chester Dean and Chapter Oct.– Nov. 1591, 40s. / Coventry 20 Oct. 1591, 20s. / Nottingham 1591–2, 20s. / Winchester 1591–2, 20s. / Gloucester 1591–2, 30s. 'Payed for a breakfast for them at Mrs Powelles', 9s. 5d. / Bath June 1591–2, 40s. / Worcester 1591–2 'uppon the quenes Trompeters & players', £4. / Cambridge town 1591–2, 10s. / Cambridge University 10 June 1592 'beinge debarred from playinge', 20s.[35] / Stratford 1592 / Leicester 20 June 1592 'more than was gaythered', 40s. / Coventry Nov. acct. 1592, 40s.; 'to mr duttons players', 5s. / New Romney, Kent 1591–2, 10s. / Fordwich, Kent 1591–2, 20s., 'more for theyr horsemete and beer', 16d. / Maidstone 1591–2, 30s. / Faversham, Kent 1591–2 'at twyse', 40s. / Folkestone 1591–2, 7s. / Lydd, Kent 1591–2, 20s. / Oxford town 25 Feb. 1592, 10s. / Canterbury 30 Mar. 1592, 20s. / Ipswich 1 May 1592, 33s. 4d. / Norwich 27 May 1593[2][36] 'although they played not', 40s. / Bath June 1592 'besides that which was given by the companie', 15s. 6d.; 10s. / Bristol July 1592, £2. / York City Books July 1592, £3. 6s. 8d.; York Minster 24 July 1592, 20s. / Southampton 3 Aug. 1592, 40s. / Bath 22 Aug. 1592 14s. 9d. / Cambridge Sept. 1592 / Rochester 1592, 20s. / Maidstone 1592–3, 20s. / New Romney, Kent 1592–3, 10s. / Canterbury Nov. 1592, 10s., 'for the dynner of the Quenes players then wch were there with Musyck', 3s. / Faversham, Kent 1592–3, 20s. / Reading 1592–3, 20s., 'to Mr Maior which he gave to the Quenes men 3s. 4d.' / Barnstaple, Devon 1592–3, 10s., 'and paid for amendynge the Seelynge in the Guildhall that the Enterlude playeres had broken downe there this yere', 6d. / Plymouth 1592–3, 9s. / Exeter 1592–3, 36s. 8d. / Ipswich 1592–3, 26s.

[35] In September 1592 the University authorities objected to a company playing at nearby Chesterton when plague was threatening. The company was evidently the Queen's, 'whereof one Dutton is A principale'. Determined to defy the ban and play outside the university, they set up 'theire bills . . . upon our Colledge gates' (REED, Cambridge, i. 338–43). The university vice-chancellor wrote to Lord Burghley early in December responding to a request for a play to be staged at court by student actors to replace the Queen's Company's, which was suppressed because of the plague. Like Oxford University, they said they had trouble with the short notice and over choosing between one in English or Latin, and begged to be let off.

[36] The entry specifies 'the xxvijth of maye 1593', but the account is in the Chamberlains' books for 1591–2.

8*d.* / Kendal 1592–3 'yis somer', 20*s.* / Bridgwater, Somerset 3 Apr. 1593, 15*s.* / Stratford 1593 / Leicester 20 June 1593 'more then was gaithered', 24*s.* / Chatsworth, Derbyshire (Cavendish household accounts) 28 June 1593, 20*s.* / Bath 22 Aug. 1593, 13*s.* 9*d.* / Newcastle Sept. 1593, £3. / York Sept. 1593, 53*s.* 4*d.* / Coventry Nov. acct. 1593, 40*s.* / Norwich 18 Oct. 1593, 40*s.* / Southampton 26 Nov. 1593, £1. 6*s.* 8*d.* / Canterbury 1593–4, 20*s.* / Maidstone 1593–4, 20*s.* / Faversham, Kent 1593–4 'at twyse', 30*s.*, 20*s.* / Bath 1593–4, 22*s.* 6*d.* / Gloucester 1593–4, 40*s.* / Leicester 1593–4 'more then was gaythered', 10*s.*/ Ipswich 1593–4, 26*s.* 8*d.* / Bristol 4–10 Aug. 1594, 30*s.* / Southampton Aug. 1594, £2. / Bridgwater, Somerset Oct. 1594, £1. / Rochester 1594, £1. / York Minster 2 Sept. 1594, 20*s.* / Gloucester 1594–5, 30*s.* / Oxford town 1594–5, 20*s.* / Wallingford, Berkshire 1594–5, 2*s.* 6*d.* / Winchester 1594–5, 20*s.* / Maidstone 1594–5, 20*s.* / Canterbury 1594–5, 30*s.* / Folkestone 1594–5, 5*s.* / Lydd, Kent 1594–5, 3*s.* 4*d.*; 13*s.* 4*d.* / Rye, Sussex Mar. 1595, 20*s.* / Bath 1594–5, 18*s.* 4*d.* / Leicester 1594–5, 40*s.* / Dover 23 Aug. 1595, 20*s.* / Exeter 23 Apr. 1595, 20*s.* / Bridgwater, Somerset 29 Apr. 1595, £1. / Ipswich 1594–5, 26*s.* 8*d.* / Norwich 25 June 1595, 30*s.* / Coventry 29 Aug. 1595, 20*s.* / Worcester 1595–6 'to the Quenes plaiers & to other noble mens plaiers' / Gloucester 1595–6 'for their play', 30*s.*; 'in wine and suger' 3*s.* 2*d.* / Exeter 1595–6, 13*s.* 4*d.* / Bridgwater, Somerset June 1596, £1. / Leicester 1595–6 'more than Was gayther', 11*s.* / King's Lynn July 1595, 20*s.* / York City Books Aug. 1595 £3. 6*s.* 8*d.* / Ludlow 1595–6, 20*s.* / Ipswich 1595–6, 26*s.* 8*d.* / Maidstone 1595–6, 20*s.* / Lydd, Kent 1595–6, 20*s.* / Folkestone 1595–6, 6*s.* / Rye, Sussex Apr. 1596, 20*s.* / New Romney, Kent 28 Apr. 1596, 10*s.* / Faversham, Kent 30 Apr. 1596, 20*s.* / York City Books July 1596, 40*s.*; York Minster Accounts 20*s.* / Bristol Aug. 1596 'for playinge in the Guildchalle'[37], £2. / Coventry Dec. acct. 1596, 10*s.*; 40*s.* / Hardwick, Derbyshire (Cavendish household account) 5 Sept. 1596, 20*s.* / Leominster, Herefordshire 12 Oct. 1596, 20*s.* / Worcester 1596–7 'to the Quenes players, and to Certen noble mens players' / Bridgnorth, Shropshire 1596–7, 20*s.* / Shrewsbury 1596–7, 20*s.* / Leicester 1596–7 'more then was gaythered', 30*s.* / Oxford town 1596–7, 10*s.* / Cambridge town 1596–7, 20*s.* / Faversham, Kent 1596–7, 20*s.* / Lydd, Kent 1596–7, 20*s.*; 20*s.* / Folkestone 1596–7, 6*s.* / New Romney, Kent Jan. 1597, 20*s.* / Canterbury Mar. 1597 'We present— Foscew for breiking the peice and drawinge blude uppon one of the Queenes plears'/ Rye, Sussex March 1597 'for a Pottle of wyne bestowed uppon the Queenes players', 16*d.* / Dover 22 Mar. 1597, 12*s.* / Ipswich 19 Apr. 1597, 20*s.* / Dunwich, Suffolk May–July 1597 'and yet much discontented', 6*s.* / Nottingham

---

[37] This, together with a similar note about Derby's playing at the mayoral hall, appears in the Bristol notes of fees paid to visiting companies surprisingly quickly after a Council Order of February 1596 banning such performances. It laid down that 'there shall not be any players in interludes suffred at any tyme hereafter to play in the yeald hall of Bristoll beinge the place of Justice'. Future mayors who permitted such performances were to be fined £5, to be deducted out of the mayoral fees of £40. The Order added 'that noe such players be suffred to playe in this Cittie or within the liberties thereof at any tyme after Sunn sett'. *REED, Bristol*, forthcoming.

1597[38] / Bristol July–Aug. 1597 'in St James weeke', £2 / Bath 1596–7 'at two sundrie times', 31s. 10d. / Coventry Dec. acct. 1597, 20s. / Bristol Nov.–Dec. 1597, £2. / Weymouth, Dorset 1597, 10s., 'bestowed in wine' 2s. 6d.[39] / Worcester 1597–8 'To the Quenes plaiers, & other noble mens plaiers' / Marlborough 1597–8, 20s. / Bridgwater, Somerset 9 Dec. 1597, 20s. / Bath 1597–8, 10s. / Leicester 9 Jan. 1598 'more than was gaythered' 14s. 6d. / Sherborne, Dorset 5 Feb. 1598 'for the use of the churchowse' 2s. [40] / New Romney, Kent 1597–8, 10s. / Dover 22 Apr. 1598, 13s. 4d. / Faversham, Kent 1597–8, £1 / Ipswich 10 June 1598, £1. 6s. 8d. / Norwich 27 June 1598, 20s. / York City Books Aug. 1598 'to William Smyth John garland & John Cowper the Quens players & they to depart this Citty & not to play' 40s. / Shrewsbury 1598–9, 20s. / Reading 1598–9, 20s. / Plymouth 1598–9, 6s. 8d. / Dartmouth 1598–9, 10s. / Oxford town 1598–9, 10s. / Ipswich 1598–9, £1. 6s. 8d. / Dunwich, Suffolk 1598–9, 6s. 8d. / Faversham, Kent 1598–9, 20s. / Lydd, Kent 1598–9, 20s. / Folkestone 1598–9, 6s. / Sherborne, Dorset 21 Jan. 1599, 2s. (receipt) / Winchester 3 Mar. 1599, 20s. / Wallingford, Berkshire 1599–1600, 2s. / Dover 21 Apr. 1599, 10s. / York City Books Sept. 1599, 40s. / Winchester 1599–1600, 20s. / Newark, Nottinghamshire 1599–1600 'the last time they were here', 10s. / Leicester 1600 'more then was geythered', 30s. / Ipswich 20 June 1600, 20s. / Norwich 2 Aug. 1600 'leave to playe for iiijor dayes' / Ipswich 1600–1, 10s. / Hardwick, Derbyshire (Cavendish household account) Sept. 1600, 10s. / Leominster, Herefordshire 1600–1, 20s. / Shrewsbury 1600–1, 10s. / Faversham, Kent 1600–1, 20s. / Folkestone 1600–1, 5s. / Norwich 4 June 1601 'for a benevolence', 40s. / Lydd, Kent 10 July 1601, 20s. / New Romney, Kent 25 July 1601 / Bath 1600–1, 20s. / Coventry Dec. acct. 1601, 30s. / Barnstaple, Devon 1601–2, 15s. / Ipswich 30 May 1602, 20s. / Bath 1602 'Bestowed upon the Quenes men for their Kytchinge bread beare wyne & sugar' 8s., 'paid for their horsemeate' 3s. 2d. / York City Books 27 July 1602, £3. / Leicester 30 Sept. 1602, 40s. / Coventry Nov. acct. 1603, 10s. / Ludlow 4 Sept. 1606, 20s. / Ludlow 1618–19 'to marten Slaughter, the queenes playars', 5s. / Coventry 'to Martyn Slathier one of the Players of the late Queene Elizabeth the 23th of December 1620', 5s. / Coventry Dec. acct. 1623 'to Martin Slathier and others players of the late Queene Elizabeth', 5s.

---

[38] The Nottingham accounts have no payments to players between 1592 and 1614. A bond dated 8 July 1597 exists in the records, though. It was made by a 'bondlace wevar' to 'John Towne one of her majesties plears' for ten shillings as an acquittance. Towne was the player who killed his fellow William Knell in 1587. REED, *Nottinghamshire*, John Coldewey, ed., forthcoming.

[39] The auditors in 1600 disallowed these payments, on the grounds that they were an illegitimate expense. REED, *Dorset*, Rosalind Hays and C. E. McGee, eds., forthcoming.

[40] This was a receipt, not a payment. It is the earliest sign that the professional companies had started to pay for their playing-places instead of using guildhalls and town halls freely. See also Queen Anne's at Bath, 1616–17, note.

13 The Early Boy Companies: Westminster, Merchant Taylors', and Eton Schools; Windsor Chapel, the Chapel Royal Children, and the First Paul's Chapel Children

When the boy companies first started playing professionally for money in the 1570s they had a long pedigree to support them. Choristers and boys from the grammar schools were used to staging plays as part of the educational tradition that exploited playing to improve speech and body language, the art of the orator manifest in 'pronunciation and gesture'. Boys in the choir schools at St Paul's, Westminster, and the Chapel Royal in Windsor were the main stage players, backed intermittently by the non-singing schools such as Paul's and the Merchant Taylors'. These early groups, or rather their teachers and choirmasters, maintained with varying degrees of truth the claim that their play-acting was part of the educational curriculum. That claim, however dubious it became in the 1580s,[1] is what most firmly differentiates the early groups that ran until the government closed the last of them down in 1590 from the two boy companies that reappeared in 1599 and 1600. The educational motive with the early boy companies was a guarantee that the boys were young. In the later companies, when education ceased to be even a pretext, the boys grew into adulthood in their companies.[2]

For all the common factor of education, one distinction has to be made because it separates the academic use of plays from the commercial, and identifies the commercial motive as the context for most of the boy-company plays that have survived. This distinction is between the grammar schools proper and the choir schools. At one period or another all the choir schools offered plays. Some of the grammar schools did, but not many of them, and not regularly. Paul's choir school, for instance, led the early shift from playing for education to playing for money, but Paul's Grammar School, while occasionally offering displays of oratory in the public service (in 1575 and 1579, for instance), never staged plays before the public.[3] Their controllers, the Mercer's Company, stopped William Malin, who was High Master from 1573 to 1581, when he tried to put his boys on show as orators. He had been headmaster of Eton when that school played

---

[1] The commercial impulse certainly began to take over by 1581. Bristol in that year records a boy company calling itself Oxford's which had 9 boy players and was led by one man. For it to be touring strongly suggests that it was no longer part either of a choir or of a school.

[2] See below for the later history of the Blackfriars Boys and Beeston's Boys. On the general question of the boys' ages, see Shen Lin, 'How old were the Children of Paul's?', *TN* 45 (1991), 121–31.

[3] See Anne Lancashire, 'St. Paul's Grammar School before 1580: Theatrical Development Suppressed?', in *The Development of Shakespeare's Theater*, ed. John H. Astington (New York, 1992), 29–56, esp. 43.

at court, and he promoted Paul's School in civic shows until the Mercers stopped him.

Since the ability to construct an eloquent argument and to deliver it in good oratory was the highest aim of the Tudor education system, training children to speak clearly and to use the self-control and artifice of acting by staging plays was an obvious addendum to the syllabus at the higher levels in all schools. For the choristers, the use of song in drama was a rational extension of their musical syllabus. So writing and staging 'academic' drama at schools and at the universities continued throughout the period. It was, however, always subject to the disapproval of the school's financiers, most of whom were members of the livery companies, the supporters of Guildhall who provided the successive Lord Mayors of London. They came from a segment of society that deplored any kind of playing.

The public and, later, the commercial use of plays depended totally on the support and initiative of individual schoolmasters and students. Essentially the difference between the grammar schools and the choir schools seems to lie in the different kinds of authority that the masters of each type of school had. In offering their pupils as performers the choirmasters were much freer than the schoolmasters. They were not hampered by the rigid syllabus of work on the trivium and quadrivium originally laid down by Cardinal Wolsey for Paul's School and followed either as the Paul's or the Winchester syllabus in all the grammar schools. The choir schools produced singers, not scholars, though even at their most commercial they kept up the pretence and, indeed, the necessity of training their boys to study as well as to sing in public.

This position altered in the mid-1570s when two entrepreneurs started making money by offering choirboy plays to the public. Boy groups had been offering plays at court for many years. Between 1564 and 1576 forty-two boy plays in all were presented at court compared to twenty-seven adult company plays. But nineteen of the adult companies' twenty-seven were staged only in the last four of these seasons. The challenge to the boy companies from the adults was growing fast.

To a large extent the growing enthusiasm of London playgoers themselves must have been responsible for the changes that took place. At the Merchant Taylors' school in the city through the 1570s the master, Richard Mulcaster, had a group of boy players trained to a high level. He took them to perform at court on 3 February 1573 and on 2 and 23 February 1574. They appeared again in 1575 and 1576 and finally in 1583. Mulcaster's Boys were renowned. In 1607 Beaumont in *The Knight of the Burning Pestle* made his citizen wife comically show herself to be at least twenty years out of date by asking one of the Blackfriars Boys 'Are you not one of M. Muncasters scholars?'[4] But Mulcaster left the Merchant Taylors' after a quarrel

---

[4] *The Knight of the Burning Pestle* (1613), I. ii. The citizen's wife might not have been so very long out of date, because Mulcaster became High Master at Paul's School in 1596, where he taught Nathan Field, the Blackfriars Boys' best player, who played the lead in the *Knight*. Mulcaster did not have anything to do directly with the revived Paul's Boys from the choir school after 1599, however. Beaumont may have been referring very obliquely to the return of activities at Paul's to schooling after the boy company there closed in 1606.

with his employers in 1586. Early in the 1570s they had expressed their disapproval of his readiness to make the public pay to see his plays. A note in the company archives dated 16 March 1574 shows how offensive the incoming public was to the worshipful masters of the company. It is an early illustration of playgoing's commercial pressures, where the price of a seat buys a social positioning as much as a physical space.

> Whereas at our comon playes and suche lyke exercises whiche be comonly exposed to be seene for money, every lewde persone thinketh himself (for his penny) worthye of the chiefe and most comodious place withoute respecte of any other either for age or estimacion in the comon weale, whiche bringeth the youthe to such an impudente famyliaritie with theire betters that often tymes greite contempte of maisters, parents, and magistrats foloweth thereof, as experience of late in this our comon hall hath sufficiently declared, where by reason of the tumultuous disordered persones repayring hither to see such playes as by our schollers were here late played, the Maisters of this Worshipful Companie and their deare Frends could not have entertaynmente and convenyente place as they ought to have had, by no provision being made, notwithstandinge the spoyle of this howse, the charges of this Mystery, and their juste authoritie which did reasonably require the contrary.[5]

The Company thenceforth banned all plays from the Common Hall. They saw it as Mulcaster's fault (he made no provision for the Maisters and their deare Frends to have convenyente place), and they reckoned, or possibly saw, nothing of the evident profit from such large and popular gatherings of people willing to pay to see the plays.

Other schools did stage plays in public as well as at court, though not so often for money as Mulcaster's. The nearest to London apart from Paul's School and the Merchant Taylors' was Westminster School. It was also the nearest competitor to the choir schools, since it had its own chorister group. Westminster provided several plays at court in the 1560s, including in 1564 Terence's *Heautontimoroumenos* ('The Self-tormentor', a stock school text) and Plautus's *Miles Gloriosus*. John Taylor, its choirmaster, died in 1572, and was replaced by William Elderton, who brought a play by the boys of Eton College to court for Twelfth Night in 1573. Westminster did not reappear at court after 1 January in the following season, 1573–4, when they staged *Truth, Faithfulness, and Mercy*. Civic disapproval may have done its bit in this case too by reducing the school's readiness to appear in public.

The close-down on Mulcaster's commercial exploitation of his boys may have been what prompted the Almoner and master of the Paul's choir school, Sebastian Westcott, to fill the gap by expanding his playmaking activities. He opened a playhouse of his own a year later, in 1575, and the controller of the Chapel Children opened another independent playhouse in the Blackfriars a year after that. Much more than the grammar school, Paul's choristers had been performing plays for the

---

[5] Quoted in *ES* ii. 75. The dismissive 'penny' was an understatement. At Paul's the fee ranged from 2*d.* to 6*d.* See Reavley Gair, *The Children of Paul's: The Story of a Theatre Company, 1553–1608* (Cambridge, 1982), 88–9.

court and visiting dignitaries throughout the century.[6] John Redford, choirmaster and playwright, and after him Westcott, who took over before the beginning of Elizabeth's reign in 1559, were the leading figures in the drama of their time. Westcott remained a Catholic under Elizabeth, and it is not unlikely that his quality as a playmaker helped to keep him in office as a teacher of boys, despite the reservations of Bishop Grindal, from which the earl of Leicester gave him some protection.[7] Paul's Boys appeared in every season at court, eighteen times in all, between 1560 and 1575. That was far more than any other group, boy or adult. Westcott's standing is marked by the fact that the Privy Council intervened when one of his boys, 'being one of his principall plaiers', was stolen in 1575. The theft itself shows the level of profit that was now expected from a company of well-trained boy players. The Council's letter is dated 3 December,[8] which suggests that their action may have been spurred by the need to protect the boy group's annual performances at court. That year it was delayed till 6 January. For Westcott himself the concern was more with keeping his new playhouse in regular use.

The special auditorium for the boy company to show plays that was built at Paul's in 1575 made it only the second commercial playhouse ever built in London, and the first that remained in use for any length of time. It was also unique as the only playhouse ever constructed inside the city for public performances before 1660. Probably that was permitted because it was inside the cathedral precinct, which Guildhall did not presume to control. Some such oversight is more likely than that the Lord Mayor actually believed the old pretext of plays being good for the choristers' schooling. That the playhouse was built for boys to perform in shows how strong they were as competition for the adult companies in the 1570s. It also shows how strongly the commercial incentive was growing. Judging by Westcott's manœuvres it must have been a powerful motive. Mulcaster's difficulties at the Merchant Taylors' and Malin's at Paul's Grammar School were parallelled equally, though in different ways, by Westcott's troubles at the Paul's choir school.

The city's Court of Common Council lodged a complaint against Westcott with the Dean of Paul's on 8 December 1575, on the grounds that he was abusing his children with plays and papistry: 'one Sebastian that wyll not communycate with the Church of England kepethe playes and resorte of the people to great gaine and peryll of the Corruptinge of the Chyldren with papistrie'.[9] The 'great gaine' he got from commerce and his heresy were equally strong grounds for the complaint. But it is not entirely clear just when his commercial motive began to show itself, and when it was transformed into an openly commercial investment with the building of the playhouse.[10] Judging from the city's complaint it had evidently made its mark

---

[6] Gair's book is a detailed history of the Paul's boy company in its two manifestations.

[7] See ES ii. 14 and 15, and Gair, *The Children of Paul's*, 44, 95.

[8] *Acts of the Privy Council of England*, ix. 56.

[9] Quoted by H. N. Hillebrand, *The Child Actors: A Chapter in Elizabethan Stage History* (Urbana, Ill., 1926), 123.

[10] Gair's chapter on the Paul's playhouse, 44–74, concludes from his study of the cathedral docu-

by the end of 1575. Being inside the city made the Paul's playhouse more vulnerable to the city than the other playhouses, the first Blackfriars playhouse which
Farrant opened for his chorister group in 1576, which was in a city 'liberty',
Burbage's Theatre, which he built outside the city's jurisdiction in Shoreditch, and
Savage's Newington Butts theatre, also in the suburbs. Its survival is some sort of
testimony either to Westcott's and his choristers' status or to the protection the
various Deans gave him.

For the educated, St Paul's and the cathedral precinct was the centre of London,
the chief place where gentry met citizens for all kinds of commerce, from buying
trinkets or books to buying whores. What the playhouse sold was about midway in
the Tudor scale of respectability. The boy companies' plays, if we can judge from
the few titles of the plays they staged at court, were 'academic'. They told classical
rather than biblical stories of the kind that advertised the company's respectable
basis in a school. Possibly from their own experience at school or university,
audiences of gentry were used to hearing plays 'recited' by boys, in which familiar
tales were put into new words, the performance depending not on twists of the plot
but on the elegance of the poetry and the clear and graphic diction in which it was
delivered. Since the boys were choristers, songs were a major feature of the performance, often accompanied by dancing. The Paul's repertoire of plays up to
Westcott's death in 1582 included, besides the classical stories, some moralities,
some comedies, and a few plays from history. Titles of plays they performed
between 1575 and 1582 include the classical *Alcmaeon, Cupid and Psyche* and
Iphigenia, plus *A Moral of the Marriage of Mind and Measure, Six Fools*, and *The
King of Scots*, and four plays from classical Roman history, *Meleager, Titus and
Gisippus, Scipio Africanus*, and *The Story of Pompey*.

After Westcott died, his place as Almoner was taken by Thomas Giles. Giles, less
of a playmaker than Westcott, appears to have linked Paul's Boys with the Chapel
Boys, and to have taken on John Lyly as his deputy, to judge by a comment of
Gabriel Harvey in *Pierce's Supererogation*, 1593, that Lyly had 'played the
Vicemaster of Poules, and the Foolemaster of the Theater for naughtes . . .
sometime the fiddle-sticke of Oxford, now the very bable of London',[11] Paul's Vice,
the earl of Oxford's Fool, and now London's chief jester with his bauble-stick. This
merged group presented Lyly's *Campaspe* at court on 1 January 1584. His *Sapho
and Phao* on 3 March was described in the court record as by a joint group of 'her
Majesties Children, and the Children of Paules'. This may have been the same
company as the one man and nine children, called Oxford's players, who got two
shillings each for playing at Bristol in 1581. While the Revels records give them
their old names,[12] the Chamber accounts call the group 'the Erle of Oxforde his
servauntes'.[13] The Oxford's group used Farrant's Blackfriars playhouse until it was

ments that it was in place by 1575. Where exactly it was in the precinct and what was its shape and
capacity are not clear from the surviving documents.

[11] A. B. Grosart (ed.), *The Works of Gabriel Harvey* (3 vols.; London, 1884), ii. 212.
[12] Feuillerat, *Documents relating to the Office of the Revels*, 344.   [13] *MSC* vi. 22.

closed in 1584. Giles became the Paul's choirmaster at about the same time. He took Lyly's boys to Paul's, where he ran the company as a strong commercial enterprise under the Paul's name for the next six years.

Richard Farrant had been made Master of the Windsor Chapel choir in 1564. Before that he had been at the Chapel Royal in London. In November 1570 he became a Gentleman of the Chapel Royal, though he kept his Mastership at Windsor. They were both singing chapels with choirs keeping affiliations with the royal household. Both of them in his time practised playing, and both had been contributors to the Christmas seasons at court since before the time of Henry VIII. The one, at St George's Chapel, Windsor, played at court in the years that Farrant was at Windsor through every season from 1566–7 until 1576–7. The other played less frequently at first. They did a joint performance with Windsor at court in 1567–8, then separate performances in 1570–1, 1571–2, 1572–3, and 1575–6, after Farrant had joined them. On Twelfth Night in 1577 the Windsor boys again played jointly with the other Chapel Children. After that the two groups seem to have merged, presumably to become part of Farrant's semi-detached enterprise at his new playhouse in the Blackfriars. The company was named first in the Privy Council's list of December 1578 ordering the Lord Mayor to permit them to play. This list, which included four adult companies, started with 'the Children of her Majesties Chappell' and ended with 'the Children of Powles'.[14]

From his timing, it seems that Farrant followed both Mulcaster's lead in running his boys for profit at Merchant Taylors', and Westcott's at Paul's in setting up a special place for them to play in. He also had Burbage's and Savage's examples in the northern and southern suburbs. He may have been even more innovatory, since we cannot be sure that the Paul's playhouse was built in 1575. He was certainly ingenious in choosing a 'liberty' for his venture. Removing the boys from the two chapel schools also meant that he dropped his educational duties and made it wholly a profit-making enterprise. He was not the actual Master of the Chapel Children, a post held by William Hunnis from 1566, and he seems to have worked as a self-financing deputy to Hunnis.[15] He took the payments for court performances from the joint *Mutius Scaevola* of 1577 onwards. His death in 1580 brought about the mergers that made Oxford into the patron of the former boys of Paul's and the two Chapels, and put Lyly into place as their playwright and manager.

How long this merger persisted is not entirely clear. The court records variously name Oxford's Boys, the Chapel, and Paul's for the next decade.[16] It was really the one company, operating an almost exclusively commercial programme and keeping no allegiance to its former chorister and schooling pretensions. The owner of Farrant's lease of the Blackfriars repossessed his property in 1584, and that play-house had to close. In 1586 Lyly set up a new deal with Thomas Giles, Westcott's successor at Paul's, to use his playhouse. Giles became choirmaster at Paul's in May

---

[14] *Acts of the Privy Council*, xi. 73.   [15] See *ES* ii. 34.
[16] The different designations are given in the list of court performances below.

1584, and immediately took direct control of the joint company, settling them back at Paul's until the company was closed down in 1590. Hence the court ascription of the plays to Paul's between 1586 and 1590.

Independent though it was of the choir school itself, some hints about the boy-company's working life can be drawn from a letter that Hunnis wrote to the royal household in November 1583 pleading for his choristers to be given more financial backing. As a begging letter it made no mention of any profit they got from their playing, although since it cited Farrant as a current bearer of the costs it should have. Hunnis named his predecessors, Richard Bower and Richard Edwardes, both deceased, before himself as Master, and Farrant as his current colleague. Conceivably Farrant was by now working with the boys independently of the Chapel, and Hunnis only used his name in the letter because officially Farrant was still deputy choirmaster. The letter would then be exclusively about the choir school. It can be read either way. The playing boys were not likely to be treated very differently from the singing boys, and the painful picture of their life that the letter paints would apply to both. Hunnis wrote

First, hir Majestie alloweth for the dyett of xii children of hir sayd Chappell daylie vid. a peece by the daye, and £xl by the yeare for theyre apparrell and all other furniture.

Agayne there is no Fee allowed neyther for the master of the sayd children nor for his usher, and yet nevertheless is he constrayned, over and besydes the ussher still to kepe bothe a man servant to attend upon them and lykewyse a woman servant to wash and kepe them cleane.

Also there is no allowance for the lodginge of the sayd children, such tyme as they attend uppon the Courte, but the master to his greate charge is dryven to hyer chambers both for himself, his usher chilldren and servantes.

Also theare is no allowance for ryding jornies when occasion serveth the master to travell or send into sundry partes within this realme, to take upp and bring such children as be thought meete to be traynnd for the service of hir Majestie.

Also there is no allowance ne other consideracion for those children whose voices be chaunged, whoe onelye do depend upon the charge of the sayd master untill such tyme as he may preferr the same with cloathing and other furniture, unto his no small charge . . .

The burden heerof hath from tyme to tyme so hindred the Masters of the Children, viz. Mr Bower, Mr Edwardes, my sellf and Mr Farrant: that notwithstanding some good helpes otherwyse some of them dyed in so poore case, and so deepelie indebted that they have not left scarcelye wherewith to burye them.[17]

The concern Hunnis expresses for the children after their voices had broken shows, if nothing else, that he was principally concerned with the choristers. The pathetic story of how much it all cost the choirmasters makes Farrant's move into profit-making with plays seem more of an escape from penury than a profiteering venture.

Up to Lyly's arrival, almost nothing can be made of the kind of play the company favoured apart from a hint that, judging by its play-titles from classical history and

[17] *ES* ii. 27–38.

mythology, it had a strongly academic repertoire. Lyly's plays are a different story. In 1585 he was named as Oxford's man at Paul's, in a published letter which warned its recipient to 'take heed and beware of my lord of Oxenfordes man called Lyllie, for if he sees this letter, he will put it in print, or make the boyes in Poules play it uppon a stage'.[18] By then the author of *Euphues* was creating a series of plays so sophisticated in their structure and so discreet in their appeal to the gentry that modern readers have never succeeded in pinning down any close applications to contemporary people or events.[19] The recipient of the letter had little reason to be alarmed over Lyly as a scandalist. It was a reputation that stuck to Lyly and to the company, though. Gabriel Harvey, in *An Advertisement for Papp-Hatchett*, a reply to Lyly's own pamphlet in the Marprelate exchanges of 1589, wrote advising 'all you, that tender the preservation of your good names, were best to please Pap-hatchet, and fee Euphues betimes, for feare lesse he be mooved, or some One of his Apes hired, to make a Playe of you; and then is your credit quite un-done for ever, and ever: Such is the publique reputation of their Playes'.[20] It was a dangerous reputation to have at such a time. Lyly got himself and his boy company into trouble with the government over the Marprelate tracts in 1590, although there is no indication that it was his plays that gave offence. The real problem as it surfaced towards 1589 was the narrowness of the boy companies' appeal at a time when the choice of plays and types of play for playgoers was broadening spectacularly.

Campaspe, probably Lyly's first play for the children, was designed as a show-piece. He launched the final act with a dancer, a tumbler, and a singer each giving a set-piece show of their skills. The play uses a story from the legends of Alexander, but redeploys it, as Lyly did in all of his subsequent plays, into something with a sophisticated local application to courtly interest in the relationship of love and power. Later plays, especially *Endimion*, went even closer to courtly concerns, making delicate ventures into the cult of Elizabeth the virgin queen and circling around the still-current issue of her marriage. The plays are all self-consciously made to appeal to a more or less courtly audience. Lyly asked for 'soft smiling' instead of the 'loude laughing' that people indulged in at the amphitheatre plays.[21] His prologues insisted on the gentle character of his audiences. He introduced a variety of games with cross-dressing and wit-play, some of which found their way into adult plays such as Shakespeare's comedies in the following decade.

There are several ways of explaining what happened at the end of the decade, none of them wholly convincing. A lot has been made of Lyly's entanglement in the anti-Marprelate controversy that the companies, adult and boy, put on stage.

[18] Quoted by G. K. Hunter, *John Lyly: The Humanist as Courtier* (London, 1962), 75.

[19] See e.g. Peter Saccio, *The Court Comedies of John Lyly* (Princeton, 1969); G. K. Hunter, *John Lyly: The Humanist as Courtier*; and *'Campaspe' and 'Sappho and Phao'*, ed. G. K. Hunter and David Bevington (Revels Plays: Manchester, 1991).

[20] *The Works of Gabriel Harvey*, ii. 213.

[21] *Sapho and Phao*, Prologue for the Blackfriars, in *John Lyly: The Complete Works*, ed. R. W. Bond (3 vols.; Oxford, 1892), ii. 371.

Although the attacks by Laneham with the Queen's Men and Lyly with Paul's Boys were effectively pro-government and anti-Puritan they did neither company any good, and brought down a government ban which closed Paul's for nearly ten years. There is nothing in the Privy Council minutes that shows official disapproval, apart from a general instruction dated 12 November 1589 to the Archbishop of Canterbury to appoint a divine to join the Master of the Revels and a nominee of the Mayor of London in checking all playbooks because the players 'take uppon them without judgement or decorum to handle matters of Divinitye and State'.[22] There is no explicit record of Paul's being chosen for any specific punishment, but they did stop playing at their London playhouse, and Lyly's career promptly went into terminal decline. A clamp-down because of their involvement in the Marprelate troubles is certainly a possible immediate cause for the company's closure. But it was also competing with the new large-scale adult company plays like *Tamburlaine*, *Faustus*, *The Jew of Malta*, and *The Spanish Tragedy*. These plays called for a range of skills and a kind of acting that the recitation skills and the singing of the boy companies could not command. Lyly himself complained in 1589 in the prologue to *Midas*, his last play, about new audience tastes: 'Souldiers call for Tragedies, their object is bloud; Courtiers for Commedies, their subject is love: Countriemen for Pastoralles, Shepheards are their Saintes. Trafficke and travell hath woven the nature of all Nations into ours'.

The company certainly closed its doors in 1590 in some disorder. In 1591 the publisher of *Endimion* disingenuously asserted his right to print it on the grounds that 'since the Plaies in Paules were dissolved, there are certaine Commedies come to my handes by chance'. The two amalgamated boy groups separated and tried to make money by touring, itself a mark of their transfer from academic to commercial guidelines. Paul's are recorded at Gloucester between Michaelmas 1590 and 1591, and 'the Children of the Q. Chappell', who had been in East Anglia in 1586–7, were at Leicester in 1591. Either of these groups may have given a private performance of Nashe's *Summer's Last Will and Testament* for Archbishop Whitgift in late 1591 or 1592.[23]

The Paul's closure marks the end of a long process of transition in playmaking and playgoing at the highest levels of society. London playing changed from absolute dominance at court by the boy companies in the 1560s, playing moralities but more often the academically respectable and largely classical stories that fitted their origins, to the boy companies' complete disappearance for a decade through the 1590s. In their place came total dominance at court and in London at large by the series of adult companies that grew up with the Queen's Men after 1583. Those years provide a more graphic instance than any other process of change through the whole Tudor period of the way market forces both reflected and helped to transform urban tastes.

[22] *Acts of the Privy Council of England*, xviii. 24.
[23] A concise summary of the arguments about the date, composition, and conditions of performance of Nashe's play are given in the introduction to Patricia Posluszny's edn. (New York, 1989), 9–13.

WESTMINSTER SCHOOL, 1564–1574[24]

Plays
Heautontimoroumenos, Miles Gloriosus, Paris and Vienna (lost), *Sapientia Solomonis, Truth, Faithfulness, and Mercy* (lost).

Master
John Taylor, William Elderton.

At Court
Jan. 1565 (?*Miles Gloriosus, Heautontimoroumenos*), 17 Jan. 1566 (*Sapientia Solomonis*), 9 Feb. 1567 (Choristers), Christmas 1567–8 (Choristers), 19 Feb. 1572 (Choristers: *Paris and Vienna*), 1 Jan. 1574 (Choristers: *Truth, Faithfulness, and Mercy*).

WINDSOR CHAPEL CHILDREN, 1566–1576

Plays
Ajax and Ulysses (lost), *Mutius Scaevola* (lost), *Quintus Fabius* (lost), *Xerxes* (lost).

Manager
1570–6 Richard Farrant.

At Court
11 Feb. 1567, 2 Mar. 1568, 22 Feb., 27 Dec. 1569, 26 Feb. 1571, 1 Jan. 1572 (*Ajax and Ulysses*), 1 Jan. 1573, 6 Jan. 1574 (*Quintus Fabius*), 6 Jan. (*Xerxes?*), 27 Dec. 1575, 6 Jan. 1577 (with Chapel: *Mutius Scaevola*).

MERCHANT TAYLORS' 1572–1586

Plays
Ariodante and Genevora (lost), *Perseus and Andromeda* (lost), *Timoclia at the Siege of Thebes* (lost).

Manager
Richard Mulcaster.

At Court
3 Feb. 1573, 2 and 23 Feb. 1574 (*Timoclia at the Siege of Thebes, Perseus and Andromeda*), 15 Feb. 1575, 6 Mar. 1576, 12 Feb. 1583 (*Ariodante and Genevora*).

ETON COLLEGE, 1573

Master
Elderton.

At Court
6 Jan. 1573.

[24] Michael Shapiro, *Children of the Revels*: has in App. B (257–60) an accurate list of all boy company performances between 1559 and 1613, and in App. C (261–8) a list of their plays.

CHAPEL CHILDREN, 1575–1590

[Also known in 1580s as Oxford's Boys.]

Plays
Alucius (lost), *The Arraignment of Paris*, *Campaspe* (joint with Paul's), *Damon and Pithias*, *Dido Queen of Carthage*, *A Game of the Cards* (lost), *The King of Scots* (lost), *Loyalty and Beauty* (lost), *Mutius Scaevola* (lost: joint with Windsor Chapel), *Narcissus* (lost), *Sapho and Phao* (joint with Paul's), *Summer's Last Will and Testament*, *The Wars of Cyrus*.

Managers
William Hunnis, Richard Farrant, John Newman, Henry Evans, John Lyly.

London Playhouses
First Blackfriars.

At Court
Christmas 1564–5 (*Damon and Pithias?*), 1 Mar. 1568 (*The King of Scots*), 6 Jan. 1570, 25 Feb. 1571, 6 Jan. 1572 (*Narcissus*), 13 Feb. 1575, 6 Jan. (joint with Windsor Chapel: *Mutius Scaevola*), 27 Dec. 1577, 27 Dec. 1578, 2 Mar. 1579 (*Loyalty and Beauty*), 27 Dec. (*Alucius*), 5 Feb. 1581, 31 Dec., 27 Feb. 1582, 26 Dec. (*A Game of the Cards*), ? 1 Jan. 1584 (Oxford's Boys *Campaspe?*), 6 Jan., 2 Feb., ? 3 Mar. (Oxford's Boys *Sapho and Phao?*), ? 27 Dec. (Oxford's Boys *Agamemnon and Ulysses*), 1 Jan. 1585 (Oxford's Boys), 26 Feb. 1587 (Paul's Boys), 1 Jan. 1588 (Paul's Boys, *Gallathea?*), 2 Feb. (Paul's Boys, *Endimion?*), 27 Dec. (Paul's Boys), 1 Jan. 1589 (Paul's Boys), 12 Jan. (Paul's Boys), 28 Dec. (Paul's Boys), 1 Jan. 1590 (Paul's Boys), 6 Jan. (Paul's Boys: *Midas?*).

Travelling
Norwich 1580–1 'to the Erle of Oxenfordes lades for playeng before Mr maior & his brethren', 40s. / Bristol Sept. 1581 'to my lord of Oxfordes players at thend of their play in the yeld hall before master mayer & master mayer Elect and the Aldremen beyng j man and ix boyes at ij s per piece',[25] 20s. / Norwich 1586–7 'the children of the Queens Chapell', 20s. / Ipswich 3 Sept. 1587 'the Quenes players being the Childeren', 20s. / Fordwich, Kent 1590–1 'to the children players of the Quenes chappell', 13s. 4d. / Lydd, Kent 1590–1 'paid unto the queenes majesties Children of Chappell (players)', 13s. 4d. / Leicester 1590–1 'to the Queenes Majestes playors, beinge an other Companye called the Children of the Chappell'. 26s. 8d.

FIRST PAUL'S CHILDREN, 1575–1582, 1586–1590

Plays
Agamemnon and Ulysses (joint with Chapel: lost), *Alcmaeon* (lost), *Campaspe* (joint with Chapel), *Cupid and Psyche* (lost), *Endimion*, *The History of Error* (lost),

---

[25] Bristol paid the same amount to 'my Lord of Oxfordes players for an Enterlude' nearly two years later, in May 1583. This may also have been the boy-company 'lades', two years older.

Gallathea, Iphigenia (lost), *Love's Metamorphosis* (joint with Chapel), *The Marriage of Mind and Measure* (lost), *Meleager* (lost except for abstract), *Midas, Mother Bombie, The Story of Pompey* (lost), *Prodigality* (lost), *Sapho and Phao* (joint with Chapel), *Scipio Africanus* (lost), *The King of Scots* (lost), *Six Fools* (lost), *Titus and Gisippus* (lost), *Wit and Will* (lost).

Managers
Sebastian Westcott (d. 1582). Thomas Giles.

Boy Players
[ex-choristers named in Westcott's will, 1582] 'Bromehame, Richard Huse, Robert knight, Nicolas Carleton, Bayle, Nasion, and Gregorye Bowringe'; 'Peter Phillipe'.[26]

London Playhouses
Paul's.

At Court
Christmas 1560–1, 1561–2, 2–10 Feb. 1562, Christmas 1562–3, 1564–5, 2 Feb. 1565, Christmas 1565–6 (3 times), Christmas 1566–7 (twice), Christmas 1567–8 (twice: *Wit and Will, Prodigality?*), 1 Jan. 1569, 28 Dec. 1570, 27 Feb. 1571, 28 Dec. (*Iphigenia*), Christmas 1572–3, 27 Dec. 1573 (*Alcmaeon*), 2 Feb. 1575 (*Prodigality?*), 6 Jan. 1576, 1 Jan. 1577 (*The History of Error*), 19 Feb. (*Titus and Gisippus*), 29 Dec. 1577, 1 Jan. 1579 (*The Marriage of Mind and Measure*), 3 Jan. 1580 (*Scipio Africanus*), 6 Jan. 1581 (*Pompey*), 26 Dec., 26 Feb. 1587 [see Chapel Children], 1 Jan. 1588 (*Gallathea?*), 2 Feb. (*Endimion?*), 27 Dec., 1 Jan. 1589, 12 Jan., 28 Dec., 1 Jan. 1590, 6 Jan. (*Midas?*).

Travelling
Gloucester 1590–1 'to the Children of powls', 20s.

[26] Gair, *The Children of Paul's*, 95.

14 *The Lord Admiral's / Prince's / Palatine's Men, 1576–1625*

There is enough continuity of player membership and other kinds of cohesion to identify a single long-running company which might most easily be called the Admiral's Men, even though its first patron had three titles at different times, and the company later ran under two different royal patrons.[1] It began its London-based activities in 1576 and only faded from the London scene in 1625. Its presence in London gives it an eminence and a durability that more than matches the forty-eight-year run of the Chamberlain's-King's Men. It had a variety of existences in its fifty years, of course. It started in 1576 as a company patronized by a lord who was serving or had just served a short stint as deputy to the Lord Chamberlain. The same lord helped to keep the company going as he climbed the status ladder, from Lord Chamberlain and Privy Councillor with a special concern for the playing companies, to Lord Admiral, and later earl of Nottingham. He reconstituted his company in 1594, to make it half of a new duopoly with the Chamberlain's Men. During the first year of James's reign he relinquished its patronage in favour of the heir apparent, Prince Henry. When Henry died in 1613 its patron became his sister's husband, the Elector Palatine, Lord Palsgrave, later king of Bohemia. It took a fire that destroyed the company's playhouse, playbooks, and costumes to bring them low, and even then it was three years before the company finally disintegrated, in the long closure that accompanied James's death.

The Admiral's company is also distinctive because it is the only one whose standard practices and plays in the first years when the companies were fixed in London are known in any detail, thanks to Henslowe's *Diary*, a day-by-day record of the company's transactions through its greatest years. This uniquely valuable record, augmented in 1989 by the discovery of the foundations for the playhouse it used through these years, the Rose, does a little to offset its position as the chief shadow and rival to Shakespeare's company, a position which has led to its being misleadingly judged as a secondary, if not second-rate, enterprise. This second ranking has even been applied to its patron, Charles Howard, whose role as backer of the playing companies in London has been accorded hardly any notice at all.

Charles Howard, the second Lord Effingham, was born in 1536, a grandson of the second of the Tudor dukes of Norfolk. His father was Lord Chamberlain and (under Mary) Lord Admiral before him. He married Queen Elizabeth's cousin and closest friend, Katherine Carey, some time before the first record of a playing

---

[1] Charles Howard was first Lord Effingham, then in 1585 the Lord Admiral, and in 1598 became the earl of Nottingham.

company under his name appears in the records in 1576, when he was forty.[2] The precedent and no doubt the model for his company in the mid-1570s must have been Leicester's Men, although in the cliques on the Privy Council he mostly held to the anti-Leicester faction.[3] He did some naval service for the Privy Council, but his first real duties at court came when he was authorized to deputize for his ailing cousin, the earl of Sussex, as Lord Chamberlain through 1574–5. That service may have been what prompted Howard to start a company of his own. Sussex ran his own company, which performed at court in every year of his chamberlainship, and Howard may have felt the need to provide a similar resource. A company identified as his performed two plays, called *Tooley* and *The Solitary Knight* (both lost), at court in the 1576–7 season, the first after his vice-chamberlainship ended. In the following season they played again, on 5 January 1578. It is quite possible that after his stint as deputy Chamberlain Howard set his company up specifically to perform in the 1576–7 court season, because the first appearance of the company's name in provincial records dates only from the following autumn, in the usual pre-court performance territories, Sussex and East Anglia. A clerk at Bristol in 1577–8 was keen enough on visiting companies to record the titles or 'matter' of their plays, and for Lord Howard's he wrote that 'their matter was the Q. of Ethiopia', presumably Solomon's Queen of Sheba.[4]

Unlike Howard's cousin Sussex, it seems that his own policy when he was finally made Lord Chamberlain at the end of 1583 was, as it had been when he deputized for Sussex in the 1570s, to give his name to a company of players, but not to use his own company at court. His new company was evidently not below standard, since they played at court twice in the 1576–7 season after Sussex took up the reins again, and again in the following year. After that he kept them away from the court until he gave up the chamberlainship to his father-in-law, Henry Carey, and moved on to the Admiralship. They were not at court through the 1584–5 season, but returned in the 1585–6 season, and their attendances grew in frequency thereafter.

When Howard became Lord Admiral in 1585 at the age of forty-nine, his influence at court, his personal prestige, and not the least important, his finances were secured for life. Legalizing piracy made the Admiralty in the years of the wars against Spain a hugely enriching ministry. At the peak of his naval command, in the war of the 1590s, his income from naval commitments and piracy has been estimated to amount to between £12,000 and £15,000 per year.[5] Of more local value to the players was his appointment as Lord Lieutenant of Surrey in July 1585. He had been on the commissions for the peace of the counties of both Middlesex and Surrey since 1580. These posts gave him considerable influence over the magis-

---

[2] The only biography of Howard is Robert W. Kenny's *Elizabeth's Admiral* (Baltimore, Ma., 1970). His genealogy and early career are recounted on 12–28.

[3] The standard account of the Privy Council in this period is by Conyers Read, 'Walsingham and Burghley in Queen Elizabeth's Privy Council', *EHR* 28 (1913), 34–58. See also M. B. Pulman, *The Elizabethan Privy Council in the Fifteen Seventies* (Berkeley, Calif., 1971).

[4] J. T. Murray, *English Dramatic Companies 1558–1642* (2 vols.; London, 1910), ii. 214.

[5] *Elizabeth's Admiral*, 87.

trates who controlled the suburbs of London and their playhouses. He used that influence consistently to help the playing companies.

When Howard's father-in-law, Henry Carey, took over the chamberlainship in 1585, the Admiral's Men were ordered to play at court for the second of that season's presentations, on 27 December 1585, immediately after the Queen's Men's opening performance on St Stephen's Night. They appeared again in a joint performance with Carey's company in the same season, on Twelfth Night 1586. Through the next years they appeared regularly in the travelling records, although they were not called to court in the 1586–7 season. They were playing in London in November 1587, probably making themselves available for another appearance at court, when they suffered a curious mishap. Philip Gawdy, a law student, reported in a letter to his father, dated 16 November, that:

My L. Admyrall his men and players having a devyse in ther playe to tye one of their fellowes to a poste and so to shoote him to deathe, having borrowed their callyvers one of the players handes swerved his peece being charged with bullett missed the fellowe he aymed at and killed a chyld, and a woman great with chyld forthwith, and hurt an other man in the head very soore. How they will answere it I do not study unlesse their profession were better.[6]

There are several puzzles in this story. First, it is difficult to believe that the company could have borrowed a set of firearms to be discharged in a crowded playhouse and neglected to make sure that they were only loaded with blanks. That is a matter of criminal carelessness. Another major mystery is more technical, the close resemblance between the scene described and the shooting of the governor of Babylon in *2 Tamburlaine*, a play which is usually assumed to have been a relatively unpremeditated sequel to *1 Tamburlaine*. The first play, let alone the sequel, is thought not to have struck the stage until late 1587 or 1588. The Admiral's certainly was the company that first performed the two *Tamburlaines* according to the title-page of the first edition in 1590, so Gawdy's story may acknowledge the first performances in London for both *Tamburlaines*. The third puzzle is which London playhouse the play was staged at. The Rose, where Marlowe's plays appeared in later years, was being built in 1587, but there is no evidence that either of the *Tamburlaines* appeared there before 1594. Alleyn and the Admiral's Men were associated with James Burbage at the Theatre in 1591, and are most likely to have been playing there, if not at one of the London inns. The existence of a stage post shows that it was an open amphitheatre, not a city inn.

Whether or not Gawdy's gossip indicates such an early date for the second *Tamburlaine* at the Theatre, the fatal casualness over the loaded firearm may be the reason for the company's non-appearance at court that Christmas. They were high enough in esteem to reappear in the 1588–9 season, when they performed two plays and some 'activities' on 29 December and 11 February. In January 1589 a 'deed of sale' preserved in the Henslowe papers between Edward Alleyn and Richard Jones, both players in the company, indicates that Jones and another player, Robert

[6] I. H. Jeayes (ed.), *The Letters of Philip Gawdy* (London, 1906), 23.

Browne, were off to Germany. They must have been quickly replaced, because the company appeared again at court in the 1589–90 season.

In 1590–1, though, it seems to have merged with, or more likely been confused in the records with, the Strange's Men, who by then were Tilney's most favoured company. This is an awkward part of the broad question about what happened to the Admiral's Men and their Marlowe plays between 1591 and 1594. It is a question that was confused for many years by the theory that the Admiral's and Strange's merged into what Greg and Chambers decided to describe as a single extra-large 'amalgamated' company.[7]

That the Admiral's and Strange's Men were separate companies at the end of 1589 is testified by a letter from the Lord Mayor of London, Sir John Harte, to Burghley, written on 6 November of that year. In it he reports his latest attempt to close the playhouses the day before. He 'sent for suche players as I could here of', who turned out to be 'the L. Admeralles and the L. Straunges players'. Their reactions to his order to stop playing were radically different. 'The L. Admeralles players very dutifullie obeyed, but the others in very Contemptuous manner departing from me, went to the Crosse keys and played that afternoon'.[8] That variation in behaviour by the two companies provides a date when they were clearly not yet merged or amalgamated. Chambers found the chief evidence for his theory of a subsequent amalgamation in two pieces of evidence: the record of court performances, and the theatre plot of 2 The Seven Deadly Sins. Chambers based his theory that the two companies amalgamated in 1590 or 1591 largely on the former. He wrote that in November 1590 'the Admiral's were with Burbadge at the Theatre, and there I conceive the residue of Strange's . . . had joined them. After the quarrel with Burbadge in May 1591, the two companies probably went together to the Rose. The main evidence for such a theory is that, while the Privy Council record of play-warrants include two for the Admiral's men in respect of plays and feats of activity on 27 December 1590 and 16 February 1591, the corresponding Chamber payments are to George Ottewell on behalf of Strange's men'.[9] In other words, the Chamber Accounts show a Strange's man as payee for what the Privy Council records say were two Admiral's Men's plays. The Chamber accounts, dated 7 March 1591, record payment to 'George Ottewell and his companye the Lorde Straunge his players'.[10] The Privy Council records for 5 March 1591 approve an order 'to paie unto the Lord Admyralle's players for shewing and presenting before her Majestie two severall plaies'.[11] The dates given for the performances are the same in both records. The Lord Admiral and the Lord Chamberlain were both present at the Privy Council's meeting at which these payments were approved, held at Greenwich. Chambers attributes the difference in the company names, along with the subsequent success of Strange's at court, to Alleyn's transfer from the Admiral's to Strange's. In other words, neither record is wrong, and the ascription of the same plays to different companies conceals the amalgamation of

---

[7] See Gurr, 'The Chimera of Amalgamation', *TRI* 18 (1993), 85–93.   [8] *ES* iv. 305.
[9] *ES* ii. 120.   [10] *MSC* vi. 27.   [11] *Acts of the Privy Council of England*, xx. 328.

the two. When we consider how much evidence there is from elsewhere for the two companies remaining separate, that seems to put a lot of faith in the accuracy of the Privy Council's scribes.

It is possible to identify some of the players who made up the company patronized by the Lord Admiral up to 1591, when Edward Alleyn left them for Strange's. Besides Alleyn himself and his brother John, James Tunstall was in the company, a loyal second to Alleyn. He had been with him in Worcester's in 1583 when the Queen's Men were created. He moved to Strange's with him in 1591, and stayed on as a new Admiral's Man in 1594.[12] The early company also had Richard Jones, like Tunstall a former Worcester's Man according to a licence in the Leicester records dated 14 January 1583. He stayed with the Admiral's Men outside London up to May 1594, but unlike most of the others he spent the bad years, 1590–3, travelling a long way beyond London, in the Low Countries and Germany. His travels across the Channel were intermittent, and he seems to have kept in touch with the Admiral's. At almost exactly the time that Henslowe's *Diary* shows Alleyn starting to play as one of Strange's Men at the Rose, on 10 February 1592, Howard in his capacity as Lord Admiral issued a passport to four men, specifically naming them his players and servants, and giving them leave to travel as his players through Zeeland, Holland, and Friesland. The paper names Jones along with Robert Browne, John Bradstreet, and Thomas Sackville.[13] The first two had been Admiral's players in 1589, and it seems that all four of them still wore Howard's livery.

It may be making too much of the coincidence to see Howard as judging his company to be too poor after the loss of Alleyn to sustain itself in England, and so speedily dispatching it elsewhere. But there is a distinct implication, that can hardly be read in other terms, in the fact that Howard allowed Alleyn personally to retain his livery while working with another company, and giving other players of his own company a passport to work out of the country. The players that Alleyn had separated from, in fact, split into two groups. One company under Howard's name continued to travel the country outside London, while the other group went across the Channel. Presumably the Lord Admiral thought that so long as a second company travelled under his name outside England it was not breaking the rule about each lord having only one company. Leicester had done the same a few years before. When Jones returned to England in 1594 he joined the new Admiral's Men at the Rose, while Brown and the others stayed on abroad, though they do seem to have retained some contact with the Henslowe enterprises. After 1594 they performed several Rose plays in Germany.

[12] Tunstall was picked out along with Alleyn by Everard Guilpin in *Skialetheia* (1598) as one of the notable figures at the Rose, when he wrote of someone having '*Dunstons* browes and *Allens Cutlacks* gate'. *Cutlack* was an Admiral's play. 'Dunston' was either the fictional saint of *Grim the Collier of Croydon*, or the player Tunstall, whose name Henslowe wrote as 'donstone'. Guilpin's naming of Alleyn suggests it was Tunstall, while his naming of Cutlack suggests Saint Dunston. He was probably offering a minor pun on both names.

[13] Willem Schrickx, *Foreign Envoys and Travelling Players* (Wetteren, 1986), 122, 185–93.

This evidence for one group of the original Admiral's company travelling abroad through these years while another Admiral's company continued to appear in the English towns suggests that it was not difficult to augment the playing membership of a company. There must have been plenty of players-in-waiting in London, a point that gives some credibility to a claim made in the late 1580s that the town was infested with two hundred idle players.[14] The English Admiral's Men are on record as touring in several towns through 1591–3. Earlier than that, the Admiral's company which visited New Romney on 26 June 1590, Faversham, Kent in the same year, and Gloucester at some time in the same financial year 1590–1 (Michaelmas to Michaelmas, October to September) must have been the group including Alleyn, before he left to join Strange's. Subsequent visits to Shrewsbury, York, Newcastle, Ipswich, Bath, the Kentish towns, and other places were by the English Admiral's without Alleyn. Strange's with Alleyn must be the company recorded as performing at Cambridge, Bath, Faversham, and Folkestone in 1591–2, and Canterbury in 1591–2, at Shrewsbury and Coventry in 1592, Coventry in December 1593, and at Faversham and other places in Kent in 1592–3, and elsewhere. They were certainly at Bath and Bristol in August 1593, judging from the Henslowe correspondence, at Norwich in September 1593, and at Coventry in December.

The Admiral's company that was on tour through these years generally received far less in payment than Strange's. It did clearly lose considerably in status and quality without Alleyn and the others, though the loss of Jones and his three fellow-players overseas in early 1592 does not appear to have affected its movements to any great extent. An Admiral's Company is recorded in East Anglia and Kent, Leicester, Shrewsbury, and York in 1592–3, and Kent again in 1593–4. Their status was reflected in their pay. Faversham paid Strange's 20s. in 1592–3 while the Admiral's, on a separate visit, were only paid 10s. Lydd in 1593–4 did rather better by them, with 6s. 8d., calling it 'the Townes benevolence'. As the lesser company, never called to perform at court, they were less highly regarded and less well-rewarded in those years.

Did the English Admiral's Men keep contact of any sort with Alleyn and Strange's? A single record exists to indicate that both companies did play at the same town, possibly in a shared performance: at Ipswich on 7 August 1592, when the payment was twenty shillings. It is a great pity that the guildhall accountants were more concerned with the name on the company's patent than the names of the players or the plays performed. Other apparent alliances by the travelling Admiral's were with Derby's at Shrewsbury after Michaelmas 1591, when the payment was forty shillings, possibly a lump sum for two separate performances, and with Lord Stafford's at Ipswich in 1592–3, when the payment was twenty shillings. The provincial evidence for two playing companies merging for a joint performance is tricky, because there is rarely enough in the records to register whether a single

[14] Letter to Walsingham, *ES* iv. 304. The figure can hardly be a serious estimate of the total number of licensed members of the playing companies then in London, because 200 would comprise more than 10 companies.

payment is for a single performance or just the total sum paid to different companies for different plays.

One other group adds some confusion to the patchy story from the provincial records. Another pair of companies, 'my Lord Admorall & my Lord "Morden" players', were at York in April 1593. This combination went on to Newcastle in May, where they were described as 'my lord admiralles plaiers and my lord morleis plaiers beinge all in one companye'. The new element, Lord Morley's Men, also called Lord Norris's, never played in London, but they frequently appear in provincial records as a separately designated company. Amalgamations by travelling companies were rare, and seem to have been distinctly spasmodic, but Lord Morley's players practised it more than most. Edward Parker, the tenth Lord Morley, had patronized a company for more than ten years by 1593. Its appearances in the provincial records usually link it with another company, which suggests that it may have been a small group, possibly of tumblers or musicians rather than players. But it had very good connections amongst the more prominent companies. On 11 October 1592 it shared a performance with the Queen's Men at Aldeburgh, with payments being made to the two groups separately. It appeared at Southampton in 1592–3, this time jointly with Strange's. Then there is the York visit with the Admiral's in April 1593, and Newcastle the following month. Morley's are on record as allying themselves at different times with three of the four premier London companies on tour in the early 1590s. Given the number of entries for the Admiral's and Strange's working separately that also appear at this time, Morley's Men seem to have been popular partners, though hardly an essential adjunct.

Communication between the different companies of travellers may not have been quite as remote and difficult as is suggested by the sequence of addresses that Alleyn in Bristol in 1593 told his wife to use for her letters. 'Send to me by the cariers of shrowsbery or to west chester or to york to be keptt till my lord stranges players com', he wrote.[15] The players knew their itinerary. If the various mergers of Morley's company are sufficiently tangible evidence, the only possible conclusion is that touring was usually done in separate groups, but that one playing company might join up with another to perform in a town when their visits coincided. On occasion, of course, the civic clerks might have casually put two related performances or two payments into a single entry; but not all of the records of joint performances would fit such a reading very readily. Given the priority of solo touring it seems most likely that these mergers were of a company of players with a team of tumblers or musicians rather than with another playing company. That is probably a gross oversimplification of what was certainly a complex and probably pretty random series of operations. It is inherently unlikely that the travelling groups expected to keep in close touch. The records of companies who were using the same name both visiting the same town only weeks apart is a strong indication that between the travelling groups communication was a lot less than thorough.

[15] *Henslowe's Diary*, 276.

The imprecision of the provincial records, and the likelihood that they did sometimes lump separate visits, performances, and payments into single entries, does not help.

What makes the generally lesser status of the Admiral's Men through these years most remarkable is the possibility that the plays they carried round the country may have included Marlowe's most celebrated early works. In Henslowe's records listing the plays that Strange's performed at the Rose, the absence of any mention of Marlowe's two *Tamburlaine* plays and *Faustus* is a powerful argument that they were out of London through these years, and the obvious place for them was with the travelling Admiral's Men. The *Tamburlaines* were published in 1590 as Admiral's plays. Neither they nor *Faustus* ever appeared with Alleyn in the Strange's repertory at the Rose. They do not turn up in Henslowe's Rose records until after the new Admiral's was playing there in mid-1594. Some of the old Admiral's joined the new Admiral's then, and they must have brought the Marlowe plays with them as part-payment for their share in the new company.

Between his entries for December 1594 and January 1595 Henslowe wrote a list of players in his *Diary*. It is almost certainly a list of the membership of the new Admiral's company, Charles Howard's half of the 1594 duopoly. One column, headed 'E A', for Alleyn, is of the eight sharers. Besides E. A., it names 'J syngr / R Jonnes / T towne / mr slater / Jube / T dowten / donstone'. The other column is of three hired men who in the event became sharers over the next few years: 'same' (Samuel Rowley), 'Charles' (Charles Massey), and 'alen' (Richard Allen).[16]

The new Admiral's was formed around Alleyn, then aged twenty-seven, and its base was the Rose with Henslowe. As we have seen, its status, its playhouse, and possibly its membership had Privy Council backing. Of the earlier Admiral's company members that we know of up to May 1594, apart from Richard Jones and Robert Browne, we have only the names of Alleyn and James Tunstall. Alleyn had been with Strange's while Tunstall most probably led the travelling Admiral's. Jones returned from overseas to the new company. The other members came from several other companies. Besides Alleyn, Tunstall, and Jones, Thomas Downton came with Alleyn from Strange's (now Derby's), while five of the other Strange's sharers went into the other company of the duopoly. John Singer probably came to the new Admiral's from the Queen's, of which he had been a founder member in 1583 and which he was still with in 1588. Richard Allen also appears to have been a Queen's man till 1594. Of the others, Edward Dutton, Edward Juby, Martin Slater, and Thomas Towne, there is no earlier record, despite the familiarity of the names Dutton and Towne in the player lists for the Queen's company. Altogether the variety of companies from which the new sharers came makes both of the new groupings look suspiciously similar to the broad-based selection that made up the Queen's Men eleven years before.

---

[16] *Henslowe's Diary*, 8. Allen has sometimes been thought of as Alleyn's brother, but the birth records name no such sibling. See Mark Eccles, 'Elizabethan Actors i: A–D', *NQ* 236 (1991), 38–9, and Rutter, *Documents of the Rose Playhouse*, 89.

Whether Alleyn himself had very much say in the composition of the new Admiral's company of 1594 is doubtful. Singer's presence from one of the Queen's groups indicates that the two Privy Councillors were doing roughly what Tilney had done with the Queen's in 1583, selecting a few men from each of several different companies. Both Howard and Carey had reason to take the former Strange's Men on, since their patron had died. Sussex's too had lost their patron. The close links between noble families might have played a part in directing the choice of companies from which the players were drawn. Tilney would once again have been the agent with the authority to select the individual talents. Alleyn might have been consulted, but he lacked the power to choose players from other companies for himself. Richard Jones's arrival from overseas may have been fortuitous, though the evidence about communications between companies across the country and abroad made it as feasible to summon him from abroad as it was to summon the old Admiral's from the country. In general the composition of the new Admiral's company looks like Tilney prompted by the patrons and acting with the help of advice from the new company's leading player and prospective financier.

The six years that followed for this half of the duopoly were greatly productive and greatly profitable. Thanks to Henslowe's *Diary*, they are also by a considerable way the most thoroughly and precisely recorded years of any of the London companies. Much of this evidence has been analysed above in Chapter 5. Henslowe's entries about the daily repertory of the new Admiral's are of two kinds, breaking the early history into two blocks of three years each. For the first three years they tell of almost uninterrupted playing except for Lent, a period of uniquely large-scale and rapid commissioning, rehearsing, and staging of new plays. From 15 June 1594 the *Diary* shows them playing for the next fifty-four weeks, except for a five-week break during Lent. Three plays were presented at court in December and January. A summer tour began on 27 June, and playing resumed in London on 25 August. That led to a twenty-seven-week run, up to 28 February 1596, including four court performances. A six-week break for Lent was followed by another London run of fifteen weeks. A summer tour started on 24 July and lasted till 26 October. Another fourteen weeks at the Rose took them to a shorter-than-usual break for Lent 1597, and then another twenty-one weeks, again till late July, when a major disruption was caused over *The Isle of Dogs* and the Privy Council's displeasure. The *Diary* for these first three years records altogether 728 performances of more than 70 plays. Of that 70, as many as 55 appear to have been new titles. Henslowe's records name each day's play and his own share of its takings.[17]

Among the papers in the Dulwich archives is the 'plot' of *Frederick and Basilea*.[18] The play-text itself has not survived, but Henslowe notes a 'ne', presumably a 'new play' performance, on 3 June 1597 for which the plot must have been prepared. It gives a fairly comprehensive list of the new company's players in its first three years. It casts Richard Allen as Prologue and Epilogue and also Frederick, Edward

---

[17] These figures are taken from the *Diary*, 22–37, 47–8, 54–60.
[18] *Diary*, 328–9, and Rutter (ed.), *Documents*, 112–13.

Juby as the king, Alleyn as Sebastian, Martin Slater as Theodore, Thomas Towne as Myronhamec, James Tunstall as governor and friar, Charles Massey as Thamar and a Moor, Samuel Rowley as Heraclius, with walk-on parts taken by Thomas Hunt, Alleyn's former boy 'Pig', 'black Dick', and the gatherers. A boy called 'Dick' played Basilea, 'Griffin' was Athanasia and Leonora was played by 'Will'. Two other boys, including 'E Dutton his boye', were named for other women's parts. It was one of Martin Slater's last contributions to this phase of the Admiral's work, because in July he left to join the new Pembroke's at the neighbouring Swan playhouse. Two other sharers, Richard Jones and Thomas Downton, had already gone that way in February.

There were two major disruptions to Henslowe's and the company's activities at the end of their first three years. One was the departure of the three sharers, Downton, Jones, and Slater to Pembroke's Men at the nearby Swan. The other was the Privy Council's order of July 1597 to pull down all the playhouses. The two matters were very likely connected. The main implication of the story that sits behind the raw details of the Privy Council's order, and its consequences for the new company at the Swan, has been given above.[19] Changes that appear in the *Diary* later in 1597, together with a set of entries about the regrouping of the Admiral's, show some of its effects on Henslowe's relationship with his company at the Rose. Possibly because of the sudden departure and the more gradual return of the Pembroke's players, Henslowe altered the scope of the records in his *Diary* after the summer break that the Pembroke troubles prompted. For the next three years the daily records of plays and takings disappear, and in their place are notes of his contracts with specific players, inventories of stock, and lists of loans and payments made to the players for the purchase of playbooks and apparel. A few lists of daily takings recur, but now on a rather different basis of payment, and without any play-titles. Henslowe was no longer just landlord to the company, taking his rents from the individual performances, and occasionally their money-lender, but their banker and financial manager.

This change must have been in part inspired by Alleyn's withdrawal from the stage and hence from his share as a player in the Admiral's. Most likely his reason for doing so was to take a more active part in his father-in-law's managerial functions. The inventories of company stock, costumes, and properties, and possibly also the list of playbooks, all made in 1598–9, seem to be his. From now on entries of payments in the *Diary* made 'in behalfe of the Company' begin to appear. Financial commitments under the signatures of the company's sharers, Robert Shaw, Thomas Downton, John Singer, and others as acknowledgements of debts recur, along with loans to Shaw for the purchase of plays and apparel. But whether because Henslowe now ran his business in partnership with his son-in-law or because the character of the whole operation had changed in ways that we have no means of diagnosing, the *Diary* suggests that his involvement became much more

---

[19] See Ch. 4.

like that of a manager of a playing company than the owner of a playhouse. This change, from landlord to banker, may have been triggered as much by the problems that followed the short-lived Pembroke's enterprise and its reintegration into the Admiral's as by any direct initiative of Henslowe himself or his son-in-law.

A good part of this shift of role seems to have been called for by the complex manœuvres that followed the reinstatement of the former Pembroke's players. They had bonded themselves to Francis Langley, the Swan's owner, and he wanted compensation. Henslowe took a possessive, even proprietorial stance, calling his side 'my companey' playing 'at my howsse', and bonding the players 'to searve me'. One by one he made the ex-Pembroke's Men, Bird, Downton, Jones, and on their release from prison Spencer and Shaw, all sign bonds 'to playe in my howsse & in no other a bowte London publickeley'.[20] He also had to protect them against Langley, who was pursuing them for their bonds to him. As a financier Henslowe was in a powerful position to set up new terms and controls over the players. It is probably to his credit that he did not take a still more direct role in running the company. That did not come for another fifteen years. And in any case Alleyn was there, no longer just a sharer, to assume the direction of the company.

The Pembroke's company fiasco may have influenced the Privy Council in the next year. On 9 February 1598 it renewed the 'Act for the punyshment of Rogues Vagabonds and Sturdy Beggars', and on 19 February it minuted a renewal of the order about the two companies. This order survives as a letter to the Master of the Revels and to the justices of Middlesex and Surrey, noting that 'Whereas licence hath bin graunted unto two Companies of Stage Players retayned unto us the Lord Admiral and Lord Chamberlain, to use and practise Stage Playes', for Her Majesty's solace, a third company had recently entered without licence, and therefore was to be suppressed.[21] This reads like Howard and George Carey reaffirming the terms of the 1594 deal.

One noteworthy feature of the Admiral's repertory in these years that has been rather underrated is the evident readiness in the company not just to renew old favourites but to admit innovations, new kinds of play. Shakespeare's company's repertoire in some respects seems conservative by comparison with the kind of novelty that the Admiral's were prepared to undertake in these years. They started the new humours comedy, for instance, with Chapman's *Humorous Day's Mirth*. First staged as 'ne' on 11 May 1597, it was repeated on 19 May, 24 May, 31 May, 4 June, and 7 June, and another six times up to the July break. The takings for the first six performances are striking, because the 'ne' performance, which might usually be expected to produce good receipts, brought only £2. 3s., while the next five went on a rising curve, to £2. 15s., £2. 18s., £3. 4s., £3. 6s., and £3. 10s. It was evidently a play whose reputation grew in the course of the month, attracting larger and larger crowds as it went on. This reading of the accounts is confirmed by John Chamberlain, who reported on 11 June in one of his characteristically sharp and

---

[20] *Henslowe's Diary*, 239–40.   [21] *Acts of the Privy Council*, xxviii. 327.

entertaining letters about London affairs to his friend Dudley Carleton, then the English ambassador in Paris, that 'We have here a new play of humors in very great request, and I was drawn alonge to yt by the common applause, but my opinion of yt is (as the fellow sayde of the shearing of hogges) that there was a great crie for so litle wolle'.[22] Whatever his view of the excessive fuss that had drawn him to the play, Chamberlain had clearly helped raise Henslowe's takings into the £3 range.

The 'humours' fashion ran well in both companies through these years. Before Jonson sold *Every Man in his Humour* to the Chamberlain's he sold *The Case is Altered* to Henslowe. In the one company *The Merry Wives of Windsor* made its own use of the idea, while its opposite, *The Two Angry Women of Abingdon*, made much of Nick Proverb's 'humorous mirth'. This interaction is possibly the clearest single indicator of the power and intensity of the commercial incentive in company repertories through the whole period.

Other innovations in the repertory are less easy to identify because so many of the Admiral's plays survive only as titles. None of the company's seven plays known by titles that suggest they were about biblical stories have survived, for instance. This was a substantial element in the repertory, compared with the one such title in the Chamberlain's list.[23] The Chamberlain's title, *Hester and Ahasuerus*, was probably a play they inherited in 1594 from the Queen's Men. How many of the Admiral's biblical plays were from the old stock predating the large plays of the end of the 1580s, and how much their retention in the post-1594 repertory shows them clinging to traditional subjects, it is impossible to say. Henslowe's lists of titles certainly indicate more plays that seem to come from the academic and learned community than from the popular and rural tradition. William Haughton's lost *Ferrex and Porrex*, for instance, was presumably a rewrite of the old academic play that Sidney approved of, *Gorboduc*. Even more titles suggest versions of classical stories. Other plays written for the company between 1594 and 1600 exploit the major fashions set by Marlowe's plays, almost all of which were in the company's own repertoire. Haughton's *Englishmen for My Money* (*A Woman will have her Will*) of 1599, for instance, turns the extravagances of *The Jew of Malta* into xenophobic farce by making its comic villain a Portuguese Barabbas and his daughters' lovers each a gull from a different country. The repertoire of London plays had already become tight and familiar enough to make the exploitation of stock devices in new blends an easy formula for the collaborators to work on.

Without access to a bigger proportion of the plays than we have, it is difficult to identify many distinctly new trends at work through these years. In any case, the hectic pace of the repertory and its new productions makes it extremely unlikely that the participants were particularly conscious of pursuing any trends. It was still less than a decade since *Tamburlaine* and *The Spanish Tragedy* first hit the London stage. It is easier to see innovation in the ways that old materials were being

---

[22] *Letters*, i. 32. The letter is dated 11 June 1597.

[23] Direct comparison of the two repertories is difficult because so little of the Chamberlain's has survived apart from Shakespeare's own plays.

rewritten, as in Munday's two *Huntingdon* plays of 1599–1600. Together they make a lively hotch-potch of the current fashions, implanting political and romantic sub-plots from the pastoral and Arcadian modes of urban theatre into the popular old stories, turning the Robin Hood figures from rural may-games into stage stereo-types mixed incongruously and usually irrelevantly into courtly romance.[24] Such re-mixing of old traditions shows how strongly the new fashions were impressing themselves on London audiences. It was a time of consolidation in the repertory when almost everything being consolidated was itself so new that it had no stock shape to flow into. The one consistency seems to have been variety.

For the first two years of the second period, between August 1597 and late 1599, the company appears to have stayed entirely 'at home'. There were no plague stoppages through the seven summers between early 1596 and March 1603, and the company appears to have enjoyed its new right to remain permanently in London. There was plenty to do there, of course, but it was a rare change. In fact this period was the longest time without travelling to be found in the records for any of the major London companies. Its rival in authority to play in London, the Chamber-lain's Men, undertook even fewer tours in these years, and is also absent from the provincial records from September 1597 until 1600. Through these years neither of the duopoly companies travelled, even though they consistently did so before and after. The only special reason for that which can be clearly identified is the Privy Council's confirmation of the two companies' exclusive access to London's sub-urban playing-places.

At the end of the century a further set of Privy Council orders shows the patrons of the two leading companies working to maintain the terms of the 1594 duopoly. When Henslowe and Alleyn reacted to the transfer of the Chamberlain's Men from Shoreditch to the Bankside in 1599 by planning a move in the opposite direction, Howard went into action to help them. While his cousin, the Chamberlain, took no part in the struggles of his own company to establish their new playhouse on Bankside, Howard gave his backing to his own company and their manager's attempt, as soon as the Globe was under construction, to transfer their playing from the Rose into the now-vacated northern suburbs with a new playhouse, the For-tune. Henslowe and Alleyn took the initiative, of course, but Howard gave their plans a prompt endorsement in writing on 12 January 1600. He wrote to the Middlesex magistrates on their behalf, justifying the new construction by asserting that the Rose was getting beyond repair, and, possibly echoing the players' old grievance at the loss of the city inns for winter playing, that it was 'verie noysome for resorte of people in the wynter tyme'.[25]

Then on 9 March 1600 Lord Willoughby, who lived in the vicinity of the new site (the parish of St Giles without Cripplegate, in Clerkenwell), laid a complaint along with other residents before the Privy Council. The Council ordered the

---

[24] There were at least 5 plays with a Robin Hood figure in the Admiral's repertoire between 1598 and 1601. See Knutson, *The Repertory of Shakespeare's Company, 1594–1613*, 172.

[25] *Henslowe's Diary*, 288.

building to be stopped. Again Howard intervened. His action this time took the form of a reaffirmation of the policy he had operated since 1594. First, he prompted a letter dated 8 April 1600, from the Privy Council to the Justices of Middlesex. It stated that:

Whereas her Majestie (haveinge been well pleased heeretofere at tymes of recreacion with the services of Edward Allen and his Companie, Servantes to me the Earle of Nottingham, whereof, of late he hath made discontynuaunce) hath sondrye tymes signified her pleasuer, that he should revive the same agayne: Forasmuche as he hath bestowed a greate some of money, not onelie for the Title of a plott of grounde, scituat in a verie remote and exempt place neere Golding lane, theare to erect a newe house, but alsoe is in good forwardnes about the frame and woorkmanshipp theareof; the conveniences of which place for that purpose ys testified unto us under the handes of manie of the Inhabitantes of the Libertie of Fynisbury, wheare it is, and recommended by some of the Justices them selves.[26]

It was signed 'Notingham/G Hunsdon/Ro: Cecyll'. Alleyn might have had to jog Howard's elbow to get him to move, but the Admiral's intervention was effective.

The Council followed this letter a month later with a formal order, setting out once again the policy on which the duopoly was based. Dated 22 June 1600, it was modestly and rather misleadingly called an Order 'for the restrainte of the imoderate use and companye of playhowses and players'.[27] A rather tetchy letter also went three days later to the Lord Mayor and the justices of Middlesex and Surrey, affirming how the Council had insisted on restricting the number of playhouses. Self-righteously, the letter adds 'as wee have donne our partes in prescribinge the orders, so unlesse you perfourme yours in lookinge to the due execution of them wee shall loose our labour'.[28]

Things were already happening that began to damage this security for the two companies between 1599 and 1601. The competition for places in London was growing. And it was not just a matter of the competition, since although the two boy companies appear to have drawn some gentry away for a while, the third adult company that now made its presence felt in London and at court was another enterprise backed by Henslowe. Other factors were at work. The two resident adult companies had to face some competition in these years, but it was a complex situation, and its nature needs rather more delicate dissection than is usually given it on the basis of Rosencrantz's claim that the adult companies suffered from the 'innovation' of boy companies.

The so-called Poets' War or Poetomachia had something to do with it, as much by its publicity-seeking as the evidence it offers about the growth of rivalry amongst the multiplying companies now trying to establish themselves in London. Other factors, not least the urge to copy the success of the two established companies, and behind that their rivalry which led to the re-location of their new playhouses, played a part too. When Henslowe set up the third company at the Rose, he did so

[26] *ES* iv. 328–9.   [27] Quoted in full in Ch. 4, 68–9.
[28] *Acts of the Privy Council of England*, xxx. 411.

as a reprisal of sorts, putting it in direct competition with its new rivals and neighbours at the Globe. Henslowe's enterprises had more finance behind them than the Chamberlain's at this time, because of the Blackfriars fiasco and the cost of building the Globe. When the Burbages moved next to the Rose, Henslowe lost no time in moving his main company to the northern suburbs which the Chamberlain's had just vacated. The next step was to apply pressure on the Chamberlain's new Southwark playhouse by reopening the Rose with a third London company. It is in the nature of a duopoly to become competitive. If the duopoly loses its controlling hegemony in the process, that is part of the price of such a competitive situation.

Several different kinds of change were also happening at this time. The two adult companies, for instance, both offloaded a large number of plays to printers in 1599 and 1600. Without doubt this, like the Poetomachia, was partly a self-publicizing activity—certainly that more than profit-making, since booksellers did not yet pay very much for playbooks—and it was very likely also inspired by the growth of competition. More than anything else it reflects the fact that the plays in the two repertories had now become a substantial and evidently durable feature of London life, and their achievements were thought worthy of record and profit in print. Plays like *The Shoemaker's Holiday* and Shakespeare's favourites were given to the press as soon as their first life on stage had been exhausted. Gentry like Sir John Harington, a keen playgoer, had begun to buy play quartos as they appeared. Harington in all bought 90 of the 110 or so plays in quarto that were printed between 1594 and 1610.

There are other indications suggesting that changes of which there is little clear external sign were coming at the turn of century. They affected the Admiral's Men more than the Chamberlain's, and probably more than Worcester's, the new arrival. Perhaps the most significant of these changes was the resurrection of the boy companies in the more costly halls in the city, which began to renew social divisiveness among audiences. Thanks to the surge of plays into print in these years it is possible to detect the beginnings of a shift in social allegiance in the Admiral's company's repertory. Where the Chamberlain's Men maintained their close links with courtly interests, offering wide-spectrum plays that could 'please all', like *Hamlet*, the Admiral's began to develop a new repertory that appealed more narrowly and explicitly to the city and citizens than to the lawyers and gentry.

There is not much evidence in the Chamberlain's repertory of the kind of play that could celebrate a legendary lord mayor, like Dekker's *Shoemaker's Holiday*, or else play to the kind of apprentice aspirations that elevated the image of self-help and citizen generosity mythologized in the Dick Whittington story. This targeting by the Admiral's of audiences in a narrowing segment of society grew stronger as time went on. The so-called 'Elect Nation' plays, stimulated by the surge of nostalgia for Tudor glories that followed Elizabeth's death, became a staple of the repertory at the Fortune. These years saw the start of the repertory tradition that made the post-Restoration historians of the theatre apply to the Fortune and Red Bull the label of 'citizen' playhouses.

One fairly clear symptom of Henslowe's thinking in 1599 can be found in the *Oldcastle* affair. Two years or more previously the Chamberlain's Men's had been embarrassed over their new play *1 Henry IV*, and had to change the name of Oldcastle to Falstaff because the unexpected appointment of Lord Cobham as Lord Chamberlain in Henry Carey's place made him a powerful objector to its ridicule of his Lollard ancestor. In October 1599, with the Globe newly opened on Bankside, Henslowe paid four writers, Munday, Drayton, Richard Hathway, and Robert Wilson, to write the first part of a double play called *Sir John Oldcastle*. It was designed as a reprise, a respectful account of the man as a famous Lollard, rightly cited as a Protestant hero in Foxe's 'Book of Martyrs'. Its Prologue explicitly disavowed the rival company's play: 'It is no pamper'd glutton *we* present, | Nor aged Councellor to youthful sinne'. The Admiral's staged the play at the Rose, just down the lane from the newly-opened Globe, in October and November 1599. Henslowe paid more than usual for the script and for a sequel, including a unique bonus of ten shillings recorded 'as A gefte'.[29] Why the writers should be awarded such a gift for the play is a matter for speculation that relates to the subsequent fashion that the company promoted in their run of Protestant or 'Elect-Nation' plays about Tudor heroes, mostly based on Foxe. Henslowe certainly had the more mundane intention of reminding London of the Chamberlain's Men's old mistake, because once the Admiral's transferred north to the new Fortune he gave the play to Worcester's for them to use at the Rose alongside the Chamberlain's. More than anything else, this play signals the sense of rivalry between the two companies, and Henslowe's concern at the threat to the Rose from the other company's transfer to the Bankside. Whether it also shows a strong sense of the monetary value of Protestant propaganda is more open to question, though the run of plays that followed *Oldcastle* does give some support to the idea that the Admiral's saw itself as representing the traditional order in 1599.[30]

After the release of a number of playbooks to the printers in 1599–1600, the intake of new plays bought for the Admiral's company seems to have dropped off. In 1600 and 1601 only seven new titles appear, compared with the 120 built up in the previous six years. There is no apparent reduction in financial resources to explain either this or the flow of playbooks to the press. Henslowe and Alleyn were paying for the construction of the Fortune, and were also sponsoring other companies, but neither of these distractions affected the company itself or its finances in any direct way. The number of new plays increased a little in the next year, but it still did not reach the earlier levels. Presumably the sharers decided that they now

---

[29] *Diary*, 126. See also Rutter, *Documents*, 170–1.

[30] Rutter, *Documents*, 171. Rutter sees the Chamberlain's as supporters of the Essex faction in 1599, a theory she finds confirmed by the praise of Essex in *Henry V*, while the Admiral's supported the contrary faction of the established order. Some such theory might help to explain why Henslowe did not commission *Oldcastle* until late 1599, when Essex was back in London in disgrace and under arrest.

had a healthy stock to draw on for revivals, and did not need such an urgent and stressful system of constantly introducing new plays into the repertory that had been the practice until then. It has also been suggested that Alleyn, who came out of retirement as a player for these years, was happier performing his old repertoire than introducing new plays.[31] The rate of inflow dropped from one a fortnight to one a month. Henslowe maintained the same process of writing by teamwork, though the number of collaborators on any one play seems to have shrunk a little, and more single-author plays appeared. The records show steady progress, and steady profit, if on a slightly smaller scale, as more companies came to join the London scene.

The next major change came in 1603. The year when Elizabeth died, like the year in which James died, 1625, was made difficult for the playing companies more by the length of the closure for plague than by the official closure to mourn for the dead royalty. No plays were performed in London between March 1603, when the queen died, and the late autumn. That summer the company travelled. At the end of it a letter from Joan Alleyn to her husband dated 21 October says that all the company personnel were back 'at theyr owne houses'[32] in London, along with the other companies, presumably readying themselves for the first court season with the new king. Alleyn was then in Sussex, having made his final retirement from playing during the closure. The Chamberlain's Men had already been taken under James's own patronage. Not until the end of the year were the Admiral's and Worcester's added to this newly prestigious disposition. James's elder son, Henry, became the Admiral's new patron. The third company was allocated at the same time to Queen Anne. The early choice of the Chamberlain's and the rather belated choice in the middle of the Christmas season of the Admiral's for Henry and Worcester's for Anne appears to be an acknowledgement of the companies' relative status, with the Chamberlain's pre-eminent and the Admiral's a little ahead of Worcester's, though how much the priority was fixed by Tilney and how much by James himself it is impossible to establish. Howard does not seem to have had any say in the allocation of the companies to the new patrons. There is no sign of his hand in any of the new dispositions from 1604 onwards, though he lived on through almost the whole of James's reign.

Henslowe's day-by-day records of the Admiral's Men's work stop in March 1603, so the Prince's Men's track from the beginning of 1604 is much less clearly marked. With Alleyn's second retirement and the company only allocated the second of the three royal patrons in status it was, while still one of the select three to be honoured with royal names and liveries, placed distinctly behind its old rival, the Chamberlain's, in royal esteem. It was technically second behind the King's company, ahead of Queen Anne's, but if the court records are any indication, its actual standing was rather lower than the Queen's group at the Red Bull. Its performances at court in the next years were mainly presented in front of the royal

---

[31] Rutter, *Documents*, 194.   [32] *Diary*, 297.

children who were not yet even teenagers. In the initial 1603–4 season the Prince's gave three plays before the prince and two before the king. In 1604–5 they gave seven before the prince, one before the queen, and none before the king. In 1605–6 they gave six before the prince and only one before the king. This allocation had everything to do with the ostensible patronage and consequent status of the company and very little to do with its repertoire of plays.

The company's sharers of 1604 are named in the patent that was eventually issued for them in 1606. They were 'Thomas Downton Thomas Towne william Byrde Edwarde Juby Samuell Rowle humfrey Jeffes Charles Massey and Anthonie Jeffes'. Whether these eight names represent the full list of all the sharers or whether the company had other holders of shares or part-shares not named in the patent we cannot tell. Eight was a smaller total than had operated at the Fortune before, and is fewer than the sharers in the new King's Men. In 1610 a list of his players in Prince Henry's household book adds another six names: 'Edward Colbrande, Wm. Parre, Rychard Pryore, William Stratford, Frauncys Grace, and John Shanke'. William Parr was in the plot of *1 Tamar Cham* drawn up for the Admiral's in 1602, and he must have been in the company when the patent was drawn up. Shank, a clown, had been in Queen Elizabeth's Men and in Pembroke's, and may have joined some time after 1604.

In the absence of any detailed records of the kind the *Diary* shows for earlier years it is not easy to identify the Prince's Men's repertoire of plays after 1604. For playgoers the Fortune remained one of the pre-eminent amphitheatre playhouses, competing with the Red Bull a little to the east, in Clerkenwell, and with the Globe, south of the river.[33] It held itself remote from the affairs of the boy-company playwrights at Paul's and the Blackfriars. The company's continuing allegiance to the city is evidenced by titles such as the lost *Richard Whittington* of 1605. Samuel Rowley's *When You See Me, You Know Me* from the same year reflects some of the nostalgia for Tudor times and the great gifts to the city made by Thomas Gresham that was a feature of James's first years. Similar city-perspectives are latent in Dekker's *The Honest Whore* in 1604 and *The Whore of Babylon* in 1606–7. The company's successes also included *The Roaring Girl*, in which Dekker and Middleton made the most of one of London's more spectacular eccentrics. Too little of the repertory has survived for us to identify any really distinct trends in their choice of plays, but if you add their old staples such as *Faustus* to the new plays the picture runs consistently along lines that can be identified as featuring citizen tastes. In October 1612 the company was picked out by the Middlesex General Session over a complaint that 'certayne lewde Jigges songes and daunces used and accustomed at the playhouse called the Fortune in Goulding lane' were attracting

---

[33] There is an enigmatic reference in the Leicester records for 6 June 1608 to 'the Princes Players of the White Chapple, London'. The Whitechapel playhouse might have been the Boar's Head, but that was some way from the Fortune's parish. Chambers (*ES* ii. 242) thinks the company may have been the new Duke of York's Men, but there is nothing to say that the long-deserted Boar's Head came back into use then.

trouble at the end of their plays.[34] Jigs were a mark of what came to be known as the citizen repertory. The Globe company gave them up at about this time.

Prince Henry died on 7 November 1612. The company managed to hold their position in the royal hierarchy by securing in his place as patron the Elector Palatine, or the lord Palsgrave, later to become the king of Bohemia in exile. He was in London at the time to marry James's daughter, Elizabeth. This marriage was the Protestant survivor of James's grand policy of making peace by distributing his children one to each side of the religious divide in Europe. As Elizabeth's husband, the Elector's status at court was the nearest (in a patrilinear hierarchy) to that of the dead prince. And he was conveniently present at court through the winter of 1612–13, the season of court revels when the company's patronage was reallocated.

The Palatine's (also known as the Palsgrave's) company's new patent was dated 11 January 1613, and names fourteen players: 'Thomas Downton, William Bird, Edward Juby Samuell Rowle, Charles Massey humfrey Jeffes, Franck Grace, William Cartwright, Edward Colbrand, William Parr William Stratford Richard Gunell John Shancke and Richard Price'.[35] The first six names may have been copied from the previous patent, since the same spellings recur. Six of the others appear in Henry's household list of 1610. Towne had died, and Antony Jeffes had left.[36] The company had substantial continuity of membership. Fourteen players would have been enough, with a boy or two, to perform almost any of the plays of this time. Whether the size of the company in the patent means that the number of sharers had been increased, or whether it simply does not bother to differentiate between sharers, part-sharers, and hired men we cannot tell. It was still a strong and substantial group, with a secure base in London, for all that it continued to venture, though rather less frequently than before, into travelling the country.

Summer touring in 1616 revealed an abuse that had become a routine practice for some of the other London-based companies. On 16 July the Lord Chamberlain prompted the Privy Council to send a letter to all the local authorities about duplicates of company licences. Norwich, which copied the letter into its records, supplies the text. As culprits it names two of Queen Anne's Men, one Prince Charles's man, and another man with a boy company, plus three of the Elector Palatine's Men, Thomas Downton, Humphrey Jeffes, and Charles Massey. They were evidently guilty of the not unusual crime of multiplying the number of companies who toured under the one patent. That was a device to improve earnings by spreading the company's resource of playbooks more widely, and had the incidental use, besides maximizing employment for London's hired players, of training larger numbers than the single company in London could manage. Other sharers in the Palatine's company, presumably those not named in the Privy Council's complaint, were on tour at the same time with another full-sized group, though the records are not very specific. Jeffes and Downton were the Palatine's or Palsgrave's players named in a Privy Council summons in the previous year,

[34] *ES* iv. 340–1.   [35] *MSC* i. 3. 176.
[36] Towne's will is transcribed in *Playhouse Wills 1558–1642*, 88. It mentions several of his fellows.

complaining about playing during Lent, so their being named in the Norwich letter may indicate that the Council was using their names in this complaint simply because it thought of them as the leading members of the company. All the London companies of 1616 except the King's were guilty of this use of duplicated licences on tour.

Alleyn's diary for 1618 contains notes of a change that he was planning in his dealings with the company as the owner of its playhouse and its main financial backer. He dined with Parr together with Cartwright and Gunnell, the two youngest sharers, on 22 March 1618, and again in September with five of the company, and with the whole company on 23 October.[37] On 31 October his diary has a note 'after dinner with ye fortune men att selling the lease'. The meetings had been about 'selling' or sealing, putting the seal on, a new tenancy agreement for the Fortune. The lease itself, of the same date, is also in the papers. It was a contract between 'Edward Alleyn of dulwich in the Countie of Surrey esquire to Edward Jubye william Bird alias Bourne Franck Grace Richard Gumnell Charles Massie william Stratford william Cartwright Richard Price william Parre and Richard Fowler Gentlemen'. These ten were now the company sharers, whose collective consent was needed for such a large financial rearrangement. It made the Fortune and its attached taphouse and other properties and grounds over to the company on a 31-year lease at a cost of £200 per annum, a sum reducing to £120 when Alleyn died. The contract was signed by the ten sharers and endorsed by Alleyn. Thomas Downton was one of the three witnesses. He had by this time retired from the stage. Shank had gone to the King's Men. Humphrey Jeffes had recently died, and Fowler's name enters as his replacement. The lease was effectively a transfer of playhouse ownership from Alleyn to the company, roughly in line with the system that the King's Men had run so successfully for the last nineteen years, whereby the sharers became their own landlords or householders. Instead of their weekly rental they paid an annual lump sum for the lease, and in return secured a better grip on their workplace.

This was a promising development, if the precedent of the King's Men was anything to go by. But it also left them more vulnerable than they would have been had Alleyn stayed as their landlord. The King's Men survived the loss of the Globe in 1613 because they had another playhouse, and could call on large reserves of cash and loyalty to rebuild the Globe. When the Fortune burned down on the night of 9 December 1621, Palsgrave's did not have the same resources. The invaluable John Chamberlain summarized the disaster:

On Sunday night here was a great fire at the Fortune in Golding-lane the fayrest play-house in this towne. Yt was quite burnt downe in two howres and all their apparell and play-bookes lost, wherby those poore companions are quite undon.[38]

---

[37] William Young, *The History of Dulwich College* (2 vols.; Edinburgh, 1889), ii. 104: 18 Sept.: 'Dinner att ye marmayd in bred street with mr Edmonds mr bromfeeld Tho: Allen & 5 of ye fortune company'; 23 Oct.: 'I dind with ye company att ye fortune', ii. 111.

[38] *Letters*, ii. 415. It is dated 15 Dec. 1621.

Alleyn's papers have a curt note for 9 December, 'this night att 12 of ye clock ye fortune was burnt'. With everything stored in the one playhouse, the fire took the company's full stock of playbooks and apparel, a loss that the King's Men did not suffer in 1613. The Fortune was rebuilt, like the Globe, more splendidly than before. This was thanks to help from Alleyn, since the company itself could not have sustained such a cost. In fact, Alleyn financed the building of the new Fortune in an extension of the 1618 leasing deal, by cutting in twelve householders plus himself, a device not very different from the way in which the King's householders financed the new Globe in 1614.

But unlike the 1618 leasehold agreement with the company, and the King's Men's arrangements for the Globe and Blackfriars, the householders of the new Fortune included no more than a few of the company's sharers. Only three were Palsgrave's Men: Richard Gunnell, Charles Massey, and Richard Price. That minority holding destroyed the parallel with the King's Men's system, although the three did have a say as well as a share in the new house. But even more than this reduction in the proportion of sharers who were householders, the loss of the playing-stock was a price the company could not easily afford. The Fortune did reopen, probably after an interval of nearly a year for the rebuilding, while the company had to travel and to use temporary accommodation somewhere else in London. But the company's standing was never the same again. They ran on for three more years, until James died in 1625 and the plague forced another long closure. The last years were expensive in a variety of ways. Henry Herbert's *Dramatic Records* list the London companies in 1622. For the Palsgrave's the compiler named 'Frank Grace, Charles Massy, Richard Price, Richard Fowler— Kane, Curtys Grevill'.[39] Three more of the old names are lost from this total. Two names are new, one of whom, Andrew Cane, was to make himself the great clown of the last years, along with Fowler as the great-voiced and great-bodied hero. A lawsuit of 1623 names Richard Clayton and Abraham Peadle, a rope dancer, as other Fortune players along with a Richard Grace and William Stratford.

Thanks to the fire, there was even less continuity in the repertory than in the company's membership. Herbert records thirteen new plays and 'A Masque' bought by the company between July 1623 and November 1624.[40] The titles listed are: *Richard the Third*, *Hardshift for Husbands*, and *A Match or No Match* by Samuel Rowley, *The Hungarian Lion* and *The Way to Content all Women* by Richard Gunnell, the anonymous *Two Kings in a Cottage*, *The Duchess of Suffolk* by Thomas Drewe, *The Whore in Grain*, *Jugurtha*, *Honour in the End*, *The Fair Star of Antwerp*, *The Angel King*, and *The Bristol Merchant* by Ford and Dekker. Of these only *The Duchess of Suffolk* came into print. *Jugurtha* and possibly other titles are of older plays, but most of them must have been new. The authors' names testify to the pressure the company was under to replace its losses. Gunnell was a sharer, and seems to have used the enforced break from playing in the most practical way to

---

[39] *Herbert Dramatic Records*, 63.   [40] Ibid. 24–30.

replenish his company's resources. Samuel Rowley had been a long-serving Fortune player and playwright since his start as a hired man with Charles Massey for
the Admiral's in 1598. Dekker had only recently been released from a long term in
prison for debt, and was still desperately short of money.

One rather mysterious event that took place in the summer of 1621 is a mark both
of the basis for John Chamberlain's reference to the Fortune as 'the fairest playhouse' and of the company's eminence. It also calls in question the general pattern
of their social and political allegiances. On 21 July the Spanish Ambassador, the
notorious Gondomar, made a formal visit with his party to see their play for that
day. It was a well-prepared demonstration of sociability by both ambassador and
company. As Chamberlain again reported it, this time with evident sarcasm, 'the
Spanish ambassador . . . is growne so affable and familiar, that on Monday with his
whole traine, he went to a common play at the Fortune in Golding-lane, and the
players (not to be overcome with courtesie) made him a banket when the play was
don in the garden adjoyning'.[41] Gondomar was good at making extravagant and
spectacular acts of condescension. Why he chose the Palatine's Men for this visit,
though, is perhaps a question of subtler politics than the ordinary populism of
attending a play at a common amphitheatre. The Palatine's / Palsgrave's carried
the name and livery of the man who was leader-in-chief of the forces in Europe
opposed in war to the Catholic might of Spain. King James was reluctant to give aid
to the war across the Channel. In 1621 Gondomar was deeply involved in the
manœuvres to keep James from joining the war party in England and from being
influenced by the flood of popular sentiment that was so anxious to get him to come
to the aid of his son-in-law and the Protestant countries of central Europe. For the
Spanish ambassador to make friends with the Palsgrave's players so publicly was a
much more pointed political act than it would have been had he attended a play at
the Globe with the King's Men.

Another nuance in this complex game of guessing at political motives is the fact
that through its last ten years, from 1615, the Fortune company was never called on
to perform at court. If the records of court performances in front of the royal
individuals who were their patrons is anything to go by, the main reason for this
neglect may have been the Palsgrave's long absences from London. But the view
that the amphitheatres were catering only for citizens was beginning to grow, and
it is certainly true that by 1620 the great majority of court performances were given
by the hall-playhouse companies. Whether that caused or reflected a loss of interest
in court and gentry affairs by the Fortune company is not easy to guess. After 1617
the Red Bull company did not play at court either. The amphitheatre companies'
exclusion does suggest that Gondomar's choice of a playhouse and company to
patronize was publicity-conscious, though it is a moot point whether, with his grip

---

[41] *Letters*, ii. 391. The letter is dated 21 July 1621. In the previous week's letter he had reported a joke
against Gondomar at the Cambridge commencement, where a student entertainment had started with
the offer of music by all possible instruments, barring only the '*fistulum Gondomari*'. The student
responsible was expelled (*Letters*, ii. 387).

on the court secure, he was choosing to expose himself to a section of the London populace otherwise neglected, or whether he was making a public gesture of charming the enemy's people.

Unfortunately the fire of 1622 which burned the company's playbooks meant that very little of their repertory from this time got into print. So there is little evidence to say whether the Palsgrave's company had anything in their plays that might have been seen as support for their patron's political activities. From the list of their titles given above, I suspect that there was none. Still, Alleyn's note in his diary for 26 April 1622 that 'I dind with ye Spanish Embasadore gondomarre'[42] is a tantalizing hint that Gondomar remained attentive to the affairs of Alleyn and his tenant company. Gondomar in fact left his England posting, and the country, in the following month. There is no reason to suspect Alleyn of covert pro-Spanish sympathies. Gondomar's attentiveness towards the players was his own affair, a ploy not at all uncharacteristic of his general mode of behaviour. It is his focusing on this one company and its landlord that is suggestive. The fire and the company's subsequent decline have obscured what might have become an intriguingly complex entanglement of the players in publicizing the different attitudes to state policy over Spain. It hints at the entertaining prospect of the players getting involved in manœuvres that would have anticipated from the other side the King's Men's celebrated intervention in that policy in August 1624 with *A Game at Chess*.

HOWARD'S/ADMIRAL'S/NOTTINGHAM'S PLAYERS, 1576–1603

Plays
(Howard's) *The Queen of Ethiopia* [Bristol 1577 'their matter was the Q. of Ehiopia' 10s.]; (Admiral's) *Alexander and Lodowick* (lost), *Antony and Vallia* (lost), *Friar Bacon and Friar Bungay* (old), *Barnardo and Philameta* (lost), *The Battle of Alcazar*, *Belin Dun* (lost), *The Blind Beggar of Alexandria*, *1 The Blind Beggar of Bednal Green*, *Bourbon* (lost), *1* and *2 Caesar and Pompey* (lost), *Chinon of England* (lost), *Cox of Collumpton* (lost),[43] *Crack Me This Nut* (lost), *Cutlack* (lost), *Diocletian* (lost), *The Disguises* (lost), *Dr Faustus*, *Five Plays in One* (lost), *1 Fortunatus*, *The Four Prentices of London*, *Frederick and Basilea* (plot), *The French Comedy* (lost), *The French Doctor* (lost), *Friar Spendleton* (lost), *Galiaso* (lost), *1* and *2 Godfrey of Boulogne* (lost), *Guido* (lost), *Hardicanute* (lost), *Henry I* (lost), *Henry V* (?old, as *The Famous Victories?*), *1* and *2 Hercules* (lost), *Hoffman*, *An Humorous Day's Mirth*, *Robert Earl of Huntingdon*, *Jeronimo*, *The Jew of Malta* (old), *Julian the Apostate* (lost), *A Knack to Know an Honest Man*, *Long Meg of Westminster* (lost), *Longshanks* (lost), *Look About You*, *The Love of a Grecian Lady* (lost), *The Love of an English*

    [42] William Young, *A History of Dulwich College*, ii. 235.
    [43] Simon Forman saw a play by this title at the Rose on 9 Mar. 1600. His diary has a short summary of its plot (an accurate transcription is given by S. P. Cerasano, 'Philip Henslowe, Simon Forman, and the Theatrical Community of the 1590s', *SQ* 44 (1933), 145–58, 157–8). Henslowe (*Diary*, 126) made payments to Haughton and Day for it in Nov. 1599.

Lady (lost), *The Mack* (lost), *Mahomet* (lost), *The Life and Death of Martin Swart* (lost), *The Massacre at Paris* (old), *The Merchant of Emden* (lost), *Nebuchadnezzar* (lost), *The New World's Tragedy* (lost), *1 Sir John Oldcastle, Old Fortunatus, Orlando Furioso* (old?), *Osric* (lost), *Palamon and Arcite* (lost), *The Paradox* (lost), *Patient Grissil, Philipo and Hippolito* (lost), *Phocas* (lost), *Pythagoras* (lost), *The Queen of Ethiopia* (lost), *The Ranger's Comedy* (lost), *Seleo and Olympio* (lost), *Set at Maw* (lost), *The Seven Days of the Week* (lost), *The Shoemaker's Holiday, The Siege of London* (lost), *The Spanish Tragedy* (old?), *Captain Thomas Stukeley, 1 and 2 Tamar Cham* (plot), *1 and 2 Tamburlaine, Tasso's Melancholy* (lost), *That Will Be Shall Be* (lost), *Three Lords and Three Ladies of London* (old), *Time's Triumph and Fortune's* (lost), *The Tinker of Totnes* (lost), *A Toy to Please Chaste Ladies* (lost), *Troy* (lost), *1 Two Angry Women of Abingdon, Uther Pendragon* (lost), *Vortigern* (the same as *Hengist?*—lost), *The Venetian Comedy* (lost), *Warlamchester* (lost), *The Welshman* (lost), *The Wise Men of Westchester* (? *John a Kent and John a Cumber*), *The Witch of Islington* (lost), *A Woman Hard to Please* (lost), *The Wonder of a Woman* (lost), *The Wounds of Civil War.*

Playing Sharers
In 1590: Edward Alleyn, John Alleyn (d. 1596), John Bradstreet, Robert Browne, Richard Jones, Thomas Sackville, James Tunstall. In 1594: Edward Alleyn, Thomas Downton, Edward Dutton, Richard Jones, Edward Juby, John Singer, Martin Slater, Thomas Towne, James Tunstall. In 1597: William Bird, Richard Cowley, Robert Shaw, Gabriel Spencer, Humphrey Jeffes, Charles Massey [Thomas Towne].[44]

Hired Men
Richard Allen, Thomas Hearne, Thomas Heywood, Humphrey Jeffes, Charles Massey, Samuel Rowley.

Boys
'Pigge', 'Kit' (Beeston?), 'Harry' (Condell?), 'Sander' (Cooke?), Robert Gough, 'Nicke' (Tooley?).

Assistants
Stephen Magett (tireman), William White (propertyman).

London Playhouses
Theatre (to May 1591), Rose (to 1600) Newington Butts, Fortune.

At Court
(as Howard's/Admiral's) 27 Dec. 1576; 17 Feb. 1577, 5 Jan. 1578; 27 Dec. 1585, 6 Jan. 1586 + Hunsdon's; 29 Dec. 1588, 11 Feb. 1589; 28 Dec. 1589 + Paul's; 3 Mar. 1590; 27 Dec. + Strange's (?), 16 Feb. 1591 + Strange's; 28 Dec. 1594, 6 Jan. 1595; 1 Jan. 1596, 4 Jan., 24 Feb.; 27 Dec. 1597, 28 Feb. 1598; 27

---

[44] Towne is named in the Prince's Men in 1605, and his name recurs in the *Diary* up to his death in 1612. Although he does not appear between 1597 and 1604, he is likely to have remained with the Admiral's throughout.

Dec. 1598, 6 Jan. 1599, 18 Feb.; 27 Dec. 1599, 1 Jan. 1600 (*Shoemaker's Holiday*); 28 Dec. 1600, 6 Jan. 1601, 2 Feb.; 27 Dec., 27 Dec. 1602; 6 March 1603, 8 March.

Travelling

(as Howard's/Admiral's) Ipswich 24 Oct. 1577, 13s. 4d. / Kertling, Suffolk 3 Dec. 1577, 5s. / Dover 1577–8 'the Lord Haiwardes players', 13s. 4d. / Faversham, Kent 1577–8, 6s. 8d. / Rye, Sussex July 1578 'the Lord hawardes plaiers', 6s. 8d. / Bristol Sept. 1578, 'their matter was of the Queen of Ethiopia',[45] 10s. / Nottingham 19 Dec. 1578 'my lord haworth plears', 5s. / Norwich 1578–9, 5s. / Ipswich 1578–9, 15s. / Bath June 1578–9 'my L. Charles Haywards plaiers', 3s. 6d. / Coventry Nov. acct. 1579 'the Lord Charles hawardes players', 10s. / Ipswich 8 Oct. 1582 'the Lorde Howards players', 10s. / Folkestone 1584–5, 5s. / Hythe, Kent 1585, 6s. 8d. / Dover 12 June 1585 'my Lord admiralles and my Lord of Hunsdons players', 20s. / Coventry Nov. acct. 1585, 20s. / Leicester 1585–6 'to the Lorde Chamberlens and the Lord Admiralles Playors more then was gathered', 4s. / Ipswich 20 Feb. 1586 'my L. Admyralles players', 20s. / Folkestone 1585–6, 6s. 8d. / Hythe, Kent 1586–7, 7s. / Rye, Sussex July 1586, 10s. / Coventry Nov. acct. 1586, 20s. / Norwich 1586–7, 30s. / Bath June 1586–7, 10s. / Southampton 1586–7, 20s. / Oxford town 1586–7, 20s. / Leicester 1586–7 'more than was gaythered', 4s. / Ipswich 26 May 1587, 10s. / York City Books 1587, 30s. / Coventry Nov. acct. 1587, 20s. / Plymouth 1586–7, 10s. / Exeter 1587, 20s. / Cambridge town 1588–9, 10s. / Marlborough 1589–90 'at St James tide' [25 July], 7s. 4d. / Oxford 1589–90, 6s. 8d. / Winchester 1589–90, 10s. / Maidstone 1589–90, 10s. / Folkestone 1589–90, 6s. 8d. / Lydd, Kent 1589–90, 10s. / Rye, Sussex June 1590, 13s. 4d. / Ipswich 1590, £1; 'the second tyme', 10s. / Bristol Aug. 1590, 30s. / Gloucester 17 Sept. 1590, 20s. / Coventry Dec. acct. 1590, 20s. / Oxford town 1590–1, 10s. / Winchester 1590–1, 20s. / Gloucester 1590–1, 30s. / Southampton 1591, £1. / Canterbury 1590–1 'the Quenes players, and my Lord Admiralls players', 30s. / Faversham, Kent 1590–1 10s. / Rye, Sussex Sept. 1591, 10s. / Bath June 1591–2, 16s. 3d. / Folkestone 1591–2, 3s. 4d. / Shrewsbury 3 Feb. 1592, 10s. / Ipswich 7 Aug. 1592 'unto therll of Darbys players and to the Lorde admirals players', 20s. / Leicester 19 Dec. 1592 'more than was gaythered', 8s. / Faversham, Kent 1592–3, 10s. / Folkestone 1592–3, 3s. 4d. / Rye, Sussex July 1593, 13s. 4d. / Norwich 1592–3, 20s. / Shrewsbury 1592–3, 10s. / Ipswich 1592–3 'the Lord Admyrals & the Lord Staffords', 20s. / York City Books Apr. 1593 'to my Lord Admorall & my Lord [Morden] players', 40s. / Newcastle May 1593 'to my lord admiralles plaiers and my lord morleis plaiers beinge all in one companye', 30s. / Coventry Nov. acct. 1593, 13s. 4d. / Bridgwater, Somerset Sept. 1593, £1. / Lydd, Kent 1593–4 'the Townes benevolence', 6s. 8d. / Bath 1593–4 'the Lord Admiralls, the L Norris players', 16s.; 'more to the same players', 7s. 9d. / Oxford town 1594–5, 10s. / Faversham, Kent 1594–5, 20s. / Maidstone 1594–5, 20s. / Bath 1594–5, 13s.

---

[45] *REED, Bristol*, Mark Pilkinton, ed., forthcoming.

10*d*.[46] / Gloucester 1595–6, 20*s*., 'geven for wine and suger for my Lord Admiralls players', 20*d*. / Ipswich 1595–6, 13*s*. 4*d*. / Oxford town 1595–6, 10*s*. / Bath 1595–6, 14*s*. 2*d*. / Faversham, Kent 21 Feb. 1596, 10*s*. / Dunwich, Suffolk Aug. 1596, 5*s*. / Coventry Dec. acct. 1596, 10*s*. / Ipswich 27 Aug. 1597, 10*s*. / Bristol Sept.–Dec. 1599 'to my Lorde Hawardes players', 30*s*. / Leicester Oct. 1599 'to the Lorde Haywardes playars more then was gaythered', 18*s*. 8*d*. / Coventry 28 Dec. 1599 'the Lord hawardes players', 10*s*. / Canterbury 1599–1600 'in rewarde for a playe which they played before Mr maior and manye of his frendes in the Courte halle', 40*s*. / Bath 1599–1600 'to the Lord heywardes players', 10*s*. / Hardwick, Derbyshire (Cavendish household account) Nov. 1600, 2*s*. / Dunwich, Suffolk 1600–1, 6*s*. / Faversham, Kent 2 Mar. 1602, 20*s*. / Faversham, Kent 1602–3, 10*s*. / York 1603, 20*s*. / Coventry Nov. acct. 1603 'the Lord haywards Players', 5*s*. / Canterbury 1602–3 'to Thomas Downton one of ye Lo. Admiralls Players for a gift bestowed upon him & his company being so appoynted by mr maior & the aldermen becaus it was thought fitt they should not play at all in regard that our late Queene was then ether very sick or dead as they supposed', 30*s*. / York City Books 1603, 20*s*. / Leicester 18 Aug. 1603, 10*s*. / Coventry Nov. acct. 1603 'To the Earle of nottinghams players', 20*s*. / Bath 1603, 10*s*.

PRINCE'S PLAYERS, 1603–1612

See also Admiral's, Palatine's/Palsgrave's.

Plays
The Almanac (lost), *The Honest Whore*, *1* and *2 The Knaves*, *Richard Whittington* (lost), *The Roaring Girl, When You See Me You Know Me, The Whore of Babylon.*

Playing Sharers
[patent 1606:] 'Thomas Downton Thomas Towne William Byrde Edwarde Juby Samuell Rowle humfrey Jeffes Charles Massey and Anthonie Jeffes.' Richard Gunnell, John Shanbrook [with Downton gave bail for Richard Gunnell, 22 March 1612[47]], William Stratford.[48]

London Playhouses
Fortune.

At Court
(As Prince's) five unnamed plays 4 Jan. 1604, 15 Jan., 22 Jan. before the prince, 21 Jan., 20 Feb. before the king; eight unnamed plays 23 Nov. before the queen, 24 Nov., 14 Dec., 19 Dec., 15 Jan. 1605, 22 Jan., 5 Feb., 19 Feb. before the prince; six unnamed plays 1 Dec., 30 Dec. before the prince, 1 Jan. 1606 before the king, 4 Jan. before the prince, 3 Mar., 4 Mar. before the king; six unnamed plays 28 Dec., 13 Jan. 1607, 24 Jan., 30 Jan., 1 Feb., 11 Feb.; four unnamed plays 19 Nov., 30 Dec.,

---

[46] An additional note in the Bath accounts for this period is for 'the charges of twoe prisoners for 14 dayes which were founde with A counterfait licens of my Lord Admiralles'.
[47] Mark Eccles, 'Elizabethan Actors iv: S to End', *NQ* 238 (1993), 165–76, 167.   [48] Ibid. 172.

3 Jan. 1608, 4 Jan. before the king and prince; three unnamed plays up to 5 Apr. 1609 before the king and prince; four unnamed plays 28 Dec., 31 Dec., 7 Jan. 1610, 24 Jan. before the king; four plays 19 Dec., 28 Dec., 14 Jan. 1611, 16 Jan. before the king; 28 Dec. (unnamed) before the king, 29 Dec. (*The Almanac*), 5 Feb. 1612, 29 Feb. before the prince.

Travelling
Maidstone 1604–5, 20s. / Faversham, Kent 1604–5, 10s. / Winchester 1604–5, 20s. / Bath 1605–6, 23s. 8d. / Ipswich 17 Oct. 1606, 26s. 8d. / Bath 1606–7, 20s. / Faversham, Kent 1606–7, 20s. / Maidstone 1606–7, 20s. / Fordwich, Kent 14 Aug. 1607, 10s. / Dover 5 Sept. 1607 £2. / Ipswich Oct. 1608 'in Respecte that they shold not pleye within this towne att all', 40s. / Shrewsbury 1608–9, 45s. / Leicester 6 June 1609 'to the princes players of the White Chapple London', 20s.[49] / Coventry June acct. 1609 'being 20 in nomber', £4. / Leicester 1 Oct. 1609, 50s. / Hereford 1609, 5s. / Bridgnorth, Shropshire 1609–10, 20s. / Winchester 1610–11, 'given to the players of His Excellency Prince Henry', 20s. / Carlisle 1610–11, 20s. / Ipswich 1611–12 'ij companies of pleyers the Quenes & Princes men', 53s. 4d. / Howard of Naworth, Cumberland 12 Aug. 1612, 10s. / Ipswich 1612–13, £1. 6s. 8d. / Barnstaple, Devon 1612–13 'unto the Princes players and unto the Queens players', 40s. / Barnstaple, Devon 1613–14, 15s. / Coventry Nov. acct. 1614 'to the Princes players', 40s. [in same bill as 'the Lord of Albignes players'].

PALATINE'S/PALSGRAVE'S PLAYERS, 1613–1624

Plays
The Angel King (lost), *The Bristol Merchant* (lost), *The Duchess of Suffolk*, *The Fair Star of Antwerp* (lost), *Hardshift for Husbands* (lost), *Honour in the End* (lost), *The Hungarian Lion* (lost), *Jugurtha* (old? lost), *A Match or No Match* (lost), *Richard the Third* (S. Rowley, lost), *Two Kings in a Cottage* (lost), *The Way to Content all Women* (lost), *The Whore in Grain* (lost).

Playing Sharers
[patent 1613:] 'Thomas Downton, William Bird, Edward Juby Samuell Rowle, Charles Massey humfrey Jeffes, Franck Grace, William Cartwright, Edward Colbrand, William Parr William Stratford Richard Gunell John Shank and Richard Price'; [Cambridge 25 Mar. 1616] 'Thomas Dounton, Edward Jubey,[50] William Byrde, Samuel Rowle, Charles Messey, Humphry Jeffe, Franck Grace, Willyam Cartwright, Edward Colebrande, Willyam Parrey, Willyam Stratford, et alii.' [Herbert 1622: 'Frank Grace, Charles Massy, Richard Price, Richard Fowler—

---

[49] This name is an enigma. Prince Henry's Men were at the Fortune in the north of the city, not Whitechapel to the east. Prince Charles's men were at the Curtain, also to the north, although as a new group they might have tried other venues in London. But they were known at this time as the Duke of Albany's players, not the Prince's. So if it is genuine this visit must have been by the Fortune company.
[50] Juby died in 1618. His will is transcribed in *Playhouse Wills 1558–1642*, 113.

Kane, Curtys Grevill.'⁵¹] Andrew Cane, Richard Clayton, Curtis Greville, Abraham Peadle, William Stratford.

Hired Men
Gibbs, Richard Grace.⁵²

London Playhouses
Fortune.

At Court
11 Apr. 1613 (unnamed); 2 unnamed plays before the king, 1 before the prince up to 15 Apr. 1615.

Travelling
Coventry 7 Nov. 1614 'to the Prince his players' [on the same night as 'Prince Charles his players'], 7s. 4d. / Cambridge 25 Mar. 1616 Acta Curiae lists 11 names 'et alij', and orders: 'Dounton et Jubey were Charged themselves & all the rest of their companye presently to departe the universitye & playe noe moore at any tyme hereafter either in Cambridge or the Compasse of five myles' / Hythe, Kent 1616–17 'given to the Players of the Palsgraves cumpany, for that they went oute of the Towne & dyd not play', 20s. / Coventry 13 July 1616 'to the Pallesgraves players', 40s. / Fordwich, Kent 19 Mar. 1617, 7s. / Dover 19 Apr. 1617 'in gold', 11s. / Norwich 4 June 1617 [copy of document of restraint on duplicate warrants mentions Palsgrave's 'Charles Marshall, Humfry Jeffes and William Parr'] / Kendal 30 Aug. 1617, 11s. / Bristol 1617–18 'the Palsgraves Players', £2. / Winchester 1618–19, 10s. / Leominster, Herefordshire 1619–20 'to the King of Bohemya his players', 10s. / Dover 15 Apr. 1620 'to the prince palatine, & King of Bohemia his players', 11s. / Dunkenhalgh, Lancashire (Sir Thomas Walmsley) 2 Dec. 1620, 30s. / Sandwich, Kent Feb. 1621, 11s. / Fordwich, Kent 10 Mar. 1621 'to ye king of Bohemia his players', 3s. 4d. / Dover 24 Mar. 1621, 11s. / Leicester 13 Jan. 1622 'to the Fortune players having the kings Broad seale to their warrant as a gratuitye not playing', 30s. / Dunkenhalgh, Lancashire (Sir Thomas Walmsley) 26 Jan.–1 Feb. 1623 'the prince players 2 nights' / New Romney, Kent 1622–3, 5s. / Kendal 27 Apr. 1623, 10s. / Norwich 31 May 1623 'The Company of the players of the Fortune howse in London doe under their handes protest against william Danyell who hath injuriously gotten their Letters Patentes' / York 1623, 40s. / Dover 17 Apr. 1624, 10s. / Dover 30 Oct. 1624, 11s. / Kendal 1625–6, 10s. / Dover 14 Apr. 1626, 10s. / Kendal 4 Aug. 1626, 10s.

⁵¹ *Herbert Dramatic Records*, 63.
⁵² Brother of Frank, named in his will of Jan. 1624. See *Playhouse Wills 1558–1642*, 131.

15 Strange's/Derby's Men, 1564–1620, and Pembroke's Men, 1591–1601

Too little is known about the involvement in playing of the Lancashire Stanleys, the earls of Derby, and especially about Lord Strange, Ferdinando Stanley, who became the fifth earl of Derby a few months before his death in 1594.[1] The Stanleys were the largest landowners in Lancashire, and they liked plays: most of the major companies made regular visits to perform at their great houses.[2] It was a family packed with historically famous names, which had exercised a peculiar if marginal role in Tudor government. The Stanleys had a long history in the English chronicles, claiming in their ancestry the two Talbots who fought in France against Joan of Arc. They rose high with the first Tudor—one of the more historically precise parts of Shakespeare's *Richard III* was his making the earl of Derby crown Richmond to make him Henry VII at Bosworth—but fell back a little once the Reformation made recusancy into a matter of sedition.

One of the main questions is the Stanleys' religious allegiances. The fourth earl presided over the court that condemned Mary Queen of Scots in 1586, and the Stanleys generally were energetic in the hunting down of recusants. In 1587, after Mary's execution, Lord Strange was praised by the Privy Council for his diligence against Catholics in Lancashire. But it was a strongly Catholic county, and enough members of the Stanleys and their friends were Catholic to call the earl's and his son's faith into question. The fourth earl's wife, Lady Margaret Clifford, was a Catholic, although she separated from and lived apart from her husband from 1567 onwards. Ferdinando Stanley, Lord Strange, was implicated enough with the recusants in the minds of some people, including some Catholics, to be made the figurehead in a Jesuit plot when his father died late in 1593. He did, however, have the tact to reveal the plot to the government's spies.

It is easy to see how Puritans might have associated the Stanley enthusiasm for plays with an enthusiasm for ritual and the rites of the Catholic church. Whether that had anything to do with the strong Stanley tradition of patronizing playing companies there is no way of knowing. It may simply have been one feature among many of the lavish style of living that they enjoyed. Ferdinando, who had a brief stint as the fifth earl, owed his creditors in London more than £6,000 when he died in 1594. The size of this inherited debt did not stop his brother, the sixth earl, from both patronizing a company and writing plays for it.

The fourth earl and his son Ferdinando, Lord Strange, each had their own companies in the 1570s. By 1591 one of them, Lord Strange's Men, had climbed to

---

[1] For a concise account of the Stanleys and their place in playgoing, including Shakespeare's connections, see Peter Thomson, *Shakespeare's Professional Career* (Cambridge, 1992), 23–4, 30–48.
[2] See *REED, Lancashire*, xxvi–viii.

the peak of esteem in the eyes of the Master of the Revels, since he gave them an unprecedented six performances at court for the 1591–2 season. They had acquired Bryan and Pope, both of whom who had been in the Low Countries with the Leicester's group in 1586. Others from either group of Leicester's Men may also have joined Strange's when they lost their title at Leicester's death in 1588. And from early in 1591 they had Edward Alleyn as a player, although for reasons we can only guess at he retained his livery as the Lord Admiral's man while playing with Strange's. His arrival in the company may not have been instrumental in taking them to Henslowe's Rose in February 1592, but he was certainly instrumental in keeping them there when he married Henslowe's step-daughter in October 1592.

The willingness of such an eminent company to move to the Southwark play-house must have been what prompted Henslowe to spend over £100 enlarging the Rose's auditorium and rebuilding the stage and tiring house for the new company at the beginning of 1592. It is impossible to say how much that commitment by Henslowe, which acknowledged the coup he achieved in getting Strange's to work at the Rose, had anything to do with the length of their tenure at the one place. There is no evidence that any of the companies used the same playhouse for any length of time before Henslowe's records start. The five months from February to June 1592 that saw Strange's first stay at the Rose may well have been the longest tenure for one company at one playhouse up to that time. That would have been a good reward for the uniquely large number of their performances at court through the Christmas 1591 season. They were certainly the best company in Tilney's eyes by then.

The story of their rapid rise in status up to late 1591 is not so easy to trace clearly, and probably resulted from a complex of factors besides the acquisition of remnants of Leicester's Men in late 1588 and, later, of the one major figure from the Admiral's Men. Already by the end of 1589 they seem to have been competing on fairly equal terms with the Admiral's. They were, though, characterized by a markedly less docile team temperament, to judge by the incident recorded in a letter from the Lord Mayor of London, Sir John Harte, to Burghley, written on 6 November of that year, where he reported his latest attempt to close the playhouses the day before. He 'sent for suche players as I could here of', who were 'the L. Admeralles and the L. Straunges players'. Their responses to his order to stop playing were radically different. 'The L. Admeralles players very dutifullie obeyed, but the others in very Contemptuous manner departing from me, went to the Crosse keys and played that afternoon'.[3] That variation in behaviour by the two companies may reflect nothing more than Strange's Men's contempt for the may-oralty, or perhaps enough need for cash to make them override his orders. Equally, though, it may indicate a substantial pride in their improving standing, at least in their own eyes.

[3] *ES* iv. 305–6.

Quite what gave them their clout, and the quality to mount their six perform-ances at court in 1591–2 and three in the following year (against two by Pembroke's, and none by any other company), is not at all clear. They had lost some good players in the company changes of May 1591 that brought them Alleyn. Lord Strange himself may have worked to secure their court performances, though he must have done so by interceding with Tilney, since he was not himself a Privy Councillor and had no very close affinity with Henry Carey as Lord Chamberlain. Tilney was related to the Stanleys as well as the Howards, so Strange did have some pull with him.

Tilney's weight in such matters should never be underestimated. It must have been he who prompted the curiously generous note in a Privy Council letter granting the Strange's company leave to return to the Rose. The letter, which is well-informed about their recent movements, is not dated, but most likely was what enabled them to re-open at the Rose for their second run there at the end of 1592. They played at court on 27 and 31 December and 1 January. Henslowe reports them starting at the Rose on 29 December, after their initial performance at court. Tilney, who had vetted their court plays, was in close touch with them. The Privy Council's letter is addressed to the relevant justices, and reads:

Whereas not longe since upon some Consideracions we did restraine the Lord Straunge his servauntes from playinge at the Rose on the banckside, and enjoyned them to plaie three daies at Newington Butts, Now forasmuch as wee are satisfied that by reason of the tediousnes of the waie and that of longe tyme plaies have not there bene used on working daies, And for that a number of poore watermen are therby releeved, Youe shall permitt and suffer them or any other there to exercise them selves in suche sorte as they have don heretofore, And that the Rose maie be at libertie without any restrainte, solonge as yt shalbe free from infection of sicknes.[4]

They had evidently started playing in London at Newington Butts, and with the court's approval wanted to move to their former playhouse closer to London Bridge.

It may have been their high status at court that emboldened them to plead to the Privy Council either then or, more likely, in the difficult year 1593[5] to allow them to reopen at the Rose.[6] A surviving petition from the Thames watermen to the Privy Council asking if the Bankside playhouses could be reopened for the sake of their trade may have been inspired by the same closure. The Strange's letter complains that 'oure Companie is greate, and thearbie our chardge is intollerable, in travellinge the Countrie, and the Contynuance thereof, which wilbe a meane to bringe us to division and seperacion'. This would mean, it goes on, that the company would be unable to perform its usual service before the queen, an argu-ment all too familiar in the Privy Council minutes about playing. It closes with the point that the ban on playing at the Rose would impoverish the poor watermen.

---

[4] *ES* iv. 312–13.   [5] Nearly 11,000 Londoners died from the plague in that year.
[6] The plea does not name the year, but it must have been 1593, because by the following year, the only other possible date, Strange's Men's name had been changed to Derby's.

This reference, allied to the watermen's own petition, is a hint that Henslowe must have been manœuvring backstage to get his Rose back into service. But there is also a new note in this letter, an undercurrent of confidence that the company's services will be admitted as worthy, and that they will be listened to. Something had changed. They knew they were high in Tilney's esteem, they had a valuable patron, and from the letter it appears they had a strong sense that their proper place was in London. It reinforces the point made in Henslowe's letter of August 1593 about Pembroke's Men being 'at home'. They now felt London, not travelling, was their natural place.

It would be putting a lot of weight on a single mention, but Nashe's comment about the fame of Alleyn and *1 Henry VI* in *Pierce Penilesse* might be adduced as the essential evidence for their quality in 1592. Nashe was a keen playgoer and playwright. He composed *Dido* with Marlowe at Cambridge, and *Summer's Last Will and Testament* for a boy company before 1590. His praise of Alleyn applies to Alleyn's time as a member of Strange's, and the comment on 'brave Talbot' as a drawcard is juxtaposed to it. Since 'harey the vj' took so much money in its fifteen performances at the Rose between 3 March and 19 June 1592, Nashe's praise must relate to the company's run in those months. *Pierce Penilesse* was entered in the Stationers' Register on 8 August. The play's hero, Talbot, he says, had in his recreation on the stage 'his bones newe embalmed with the teares of ten thousand spectators at least, (at severall times) who, in the Tragedian that represents his person, imagine they behold him fresh bleeding!'[7] Nobody before Nashe was ever quite so eloquent about the power drama had to move public emotions. He ratifies Tilney's choice of the company to play most often at court.

The membership of Strange's before their arrival at the Rose in 1592 is a complex question, dependent, in large part, on what we think are the precise functions and dates of two play-plots that survive in the Henslowe papers. They appear to belong to the period before Alleyn quarrelled with James Burbage in 1591, because Burbage's son Richard is named in both. Alleyn himself, Will Kemp the clown, and others do not appear, possibly because they had the leading parts and the plot-maker had no need to identify them by name. The players named in the two plots, *2 The Seven Deadly Sins* and *The Dead Men's Fortune*, indicate that, besides the leading tragedian and clown, Strange's included George Bryan, Richard Burbage, Richard Cowley, John Duke, Thomas Goodale, John Holland, Robert Pallant, Augustine Phillips, Thomas Pope, Will Sly, and John Sincler, plus a Harry, Kitt, and Vincent, and several other boys. It was a 'large' company, capable of mounting plays with casts of nearly twenty.

Some of these players left the company in the changes of 1591, probably at Alleyn's break from the Theatre in May. Sincler and Holland reappear with Pembroke's. Richard Burbage, too, was clearly no longer a member of Strange's in the years when Pembroke's was active. And one other absentee is worth some comment. The case has been made more fully elsewhere that the presence of 'harey

---

[7] *Pierce Penilesse* (1592), F3r.

the vj' amongst the Strange's plays at the Rose in 1592, and the listing of Strange's as the first of the companies to play *Titus Andronicus*, before it went to Pembroke's in 1591, makes it very likely that Shakespeare was one of the players in Strange's Men up to the time when Pembroke's was formed.[8] The presence of the later plays of the *Henry VI* sequence together with *The Taming of the Shrew* in Pembroke's does suggest that he left when Richard Burbage left.

There are of course anomalies in this version of such an incompletely evidenced story. It is odd that *Titus* should go to Pembroke's, and then to Sussex's, and finally to the Chamberlain's with the other breakaway players, and that *2 and 3 Henry VI* should also go to Pembroke's, but not *1 Henry VI*. It seems that the eventual reunion of that play with its author had to wait until 1594, when the players who had stayed with Strange's took it with them into the new Chamberlain's. What is most anomalous about this is the recurrence of references to the Stanleys in most of the Shakespeare plays written before 1594. A strong run of figures from the Stanley family goes all through the first Henriad and into *Richard III*, where the earl of Derby crowns Richmond. This appears to suggest that their author was invoking his patron's name throughout the course of their composition, despite the fact that *2 and 3 Henry VI* became Pembroke plays. Other Stanley references may appear in *Love's Labours Lost*, where the King of Navarre is called Ferdinand, and *The Taming of the Shrew*, where Christopher Sly is dressed up as what Charles Nicholl calls 'a mock Lord Strange'.[9] Whether these allusions can all be dated to the time Ferdinando Stanley, Lord Strange, was Shakespeare's patron or to a later time is not as clear as we might wish.

Henslowe's *Diary* supplies the titles of all the plays during the company's first five-month run at the Rose. Some of the playbooks must have belonged to Henslowe, since they remained at the Rose for performance by later companies, and most of them survive only as titles. Alleyn had been with the Admiral's in 1590 when they played the two *Tamburlaines*, but he seems to have lost them when he went to Strange's. He probably also lost *Faustus*, if it was written in 1588, as I believe it was. In their place he got another role that he was to make his own, Barabbas in *The Jew of Malta*. Henslowe may have acquired it from Marlowe when it was first written, in 1589, because it stayed with him when Strange's moved away, and reappeared with Sussex's and then the new Admiral's in 1593–4.[10] He later acquired *The Massacre at Paris*, which followed the same kind of route. Another play that moved from one company to another at the Rose was *Friar Bacon and Friar Bungay*, and another play by Greene, *Orlando Furioso*, may also have been an early Henslowe property. The accusation that Greene originally sold *Orlando* to the Queen's Men and then re-sold the

---

[8] The case for Shakespeare as a Strange's Man is put extensively in E. A. J. Honigmann's *Shakespeare: The 'Lost Years'* (Manchester, 1985), ch. 6.

[9] *A Cup of News* (London, 1984), 206–11.

[10] *The Jew of Malta* is almost the only play we know that was likely to have been staged at the original Rose. Its staging needs must have been in Henslowe's mind in planning the stage of the reconstructed Rose late in 1591.

same play to the Admiral's when the Queen's went on tour is implausible. It was the third play (after *Friar Bacon* and *Muly Mollocco*) staged in the Strange's run in February 1592 at the Rose. If it was in the Admiral's before it appeared with Henslowe at the Rose in 1592, conceivably Alleyn brought it with him to Strange's from his former company. If so, it was the unique case of the kind. Its only appearance in the whole set of performance records in the *Diary* is this one occasion. That, plus the fact that Alleyn's part for Orlando survives in the Henslowe papers, makes the most likely explanation the most innocent one: that Henslowe bought the play from Greene, and gave it to be performed at his playhouse first to the Queen's Men, later to the Admiral's Men, and finally to Strange's, before it was shelved (the part of Orlando has some carping comments about the verse written in Alleyn's own hand). The critic who accused Greene of a double sale was reading the wrong inference from its reappearance with another company at the same playhouse.[11]

Most of the plays that Henslowe records Strange's Men playing in its first season at the Rose have been lost. In their first five months they gave 105 performances from a repertoire of twenty-seven plays. The plays that we have texts of include, besides *Friar Bacon*, *The Jew of Malta* and *Orlando*, *A Knack to Know a Knave*, a 'Jeronymo' which was probably *The Spanish Tragedy*, and 'harey the vj', which was probably Shakespeare's *1 Henry VI*. 'Jeronymo' recurs in the Henslowe lists in later years, but 'harey the vj' does not. The best takings came from *The Jew of Malta* (50 shillings on its first appearance on 26 February, up to £3 in later performances) and 'harey the vj' (£3. 16s. 8d. on its first day, up to 56 shillings on subsequent days). Three others, 'Jeronymo', *Muly Mollocco*, and 'Titus and Vespacia', which most likely was not Shakespeare's *Titus Andronicus*, all took more than £3 on different occasions. In their later stays at the Rose, Strange's added to these titles among others *The Massacre at Paris* on 30 January 1593. Their last three performances at the beginning of February 1593 were *Friar Bacon*, 'harey the vj', and *The Jew of Malta*, which between them brought in £3. 13s. It is likely that the 'iiij plays in one' that they played on 6 March 1592 was *2 The Seven Deadly Sins*, for which the plot survives.[12]

Another play that very likely was written for Strange's at about this time is *Sir Thomas More*. The case for its being written in late 1592 but then suppressed because of the troubles over foreign communities in London is a good one. Unfortunately the surviving manuscript gives information chiefly about the five writers who worked on it, one of whom was probably Shakespeare, with a few indications

[11] The evidence that Henslowe bought plays to be performed by whatever company was renting his playhouse is dubious. No indication exists in the *Diary* that he received any money for giving a company a playbook of his own. But it remains the only likely explanation for the recurrence of some plays performed by different companies at the Rose.

[12] See Roslyn Lander Knutson, 'Henslowe's Naming of Parts: Entries in the *Diary* for *Tamar Cham*, 1592–3, and *Godfrey of Bulloigne*, 1594–5', *NQ* 230 (1983), 157–60. The question of attribution of the *Seven Deadly Sins* plot is examined by Scott McMillin in 'Building Stories: Greg Fleay, and the Plot of *2 Seven Deadly Sins*', *MRDE* 4 (1989), 53–62.

of the company membership it was revised for.[13] One player named in the manuscript is Thomas Goodale, also named in the plot of 2 *The Seven Deadly Sins*. The manuscript of that plot is in the same hand as the scribal hand that wrote the *More* manuscript. Both manuscripts demand a large cast.[14] For all the size of the most obvious questions about this complex multi-authored manuscript, the main point about it as a potential play for Strange's is its manifest sympathy for its hero. That raises once again the question of the company's awareness of its patron's religious allegiance. Hall in his *Chronicle* and, even more strongly, Foxe in his 'Book of Martyrs' were emphatic in their condemnation of More. Antony Munday, chief composer of the manuscript, was a self-proclaimed anti-Catholic who had stayed at a Jesuit seminary in France to spy on its activities. Why he should choose More's life as the subject for his play and why he should choose to give such a sympathetic account from the different sources available to him are questions that must reflect on what he supposed were the religious affiliations of the company's patron. These questions are made more complicated by the likelihood that the manuscript also shows signs of revision in about 1603 for performance by the Admiral's/Prince Henry's company. This was the time when the Prince's was running its 'Elect Nation' plays based on stories from Foxe. That they should think of mounting a pro-More play in the midst of such a trenchantly Protestant repertory in 1603 can only be taken as a mark of a quite extraordinary religious eclecticism.

Strange's did not return to the Rose after their first year there. The long closure that came to the London playhouses because the plague bill climbed above thirty deaths a week in February 1593 took them back on tour. They performed in towns like Bath, Coventry, and Norwich, and in their patron's home county of Lancashire. The company's plea to the Privy Council to allow them back to perform at the Rose must belong to the early part of this long absence from playing in London. The Privy Council's response, which was given in a special licence issued on 6 May 1593, allowed them to play anywhere that was free from plague and outside a seven-mile radius of London. The same order lists the sharers or chief players in the company at this time. They were 'Edward Allen, servaunt to the right honorable the Lord Highe Admiral, William Kemp, Thomas Pope, John Heminges, Augustine Phillips, and Georg Brian, being al one companie, servauntes to our verie good the Lord the Lord Strainge'.[15] Of these, besides Alleyn as an Admiral's man, we can trace Kemp, Pope, and Bryan back to Leicester's in the 1580s. Heminges was previously with the Queen's. To these names we can add Thomas Downton and Richard Cowley, since he carried a letter from Alleyn's wife and her father to

[13] See Scott McMillin, *The Elizabethan Theatre and The Book of Sir Thomas More* (Ithaca, NY, 1987). McMillin dates the MS to 1592–3, made for Strange's, with revisions made for performance by the Admiral's in 1603. A review by Giorgio Melchiori, *MRDE* 4 (1989), 412–17, accepts the attribution to Strange's, but argues that the revisions were also made in 1592–3. This view is renewed in his Revels edition (Manchester, 1991), 33.

[14] For the plays of the Strange's period that demanded large casts, see Gurr, 'The Chimera of Amalgamation', *TRI* 18 (1993), 85–93.

[15] *Acts of the Privy Council of England*, xxiv. 212.

Alleyn that summer. Cowley is named in the *2 Seven Deadly Sins* 'plot'. If the 'plot' did belong to Strange's, Thomas Goodale and Richard Burbage, also named in it, were other members of the company. Goodale had been one of Berkeley's Men in 1581. The fact that his name also appears in the manuscript for *Sir Thomas More* either fixes both plays as Strange's or both men to another company of the time.

In September 1593 Ferdinando Stanley, Lord Strange, succeeded his brother as earl of Derby, and the company took on the new title. It did not last them very long, since the new earl died on 16 April 1594. Their new title did not get them back to court in the bleak season of 1593–4, when the only company to appear was the Queen's, with a single performance. In 1594 Derby's widow took an interest in her husband's players, because they are recorded at Winchester on 16 May 1594 under her name. That, though, was a remnant company trying to re-establish itself after the game of decapitation re-enacted earlier that month by the Lord Admiral and Lord Chamberlain. What the relationship was between the new earl's and his ex-Strange's company and the old earl's Derby's company in this period it is impossible to tell. There is not enough evidence in the provincial records to trace a regular touring route for either company, so from late 1593 onwards the provincial references may be to either group.

After the Lord Admiral had taken Alleyn and Thomas Downton for his company, and Carey five more of the Strange's/Derby's sharers for his,[16] the remnant company did continue for several years in the colours of the sixth earl. He too was a keen playgoer, and a writer of plays. He was said in June 1599 after his marriage broke down to be 'busye in penning comedyes for the common players'.[17] His company did not reappear in London so long as the Admiral's and Chamberlain's men held their duopoly, but they are in the provincial records consistently through those years, at Bath, Coventry, Leicester, Stratford, and other places throughout 1595–9. Whether there truly was only the one earl's company from 1594 onwards is not clear, but in the records set out below they are treated as the one which had been Strange's. Unfortunately nothing about the membership of this re-formed company is known. All the players who were identified as Strange's in the pre-1594 records turn up in the two duopoly companies after that time.

The new Derby's were, however, evidently not found to be greatly inferior as a result of their exile and change of membership. In the Christmas seasons of 1599–1600 and 1600–1 Derby's became the first company to break the duopoly. They were rewarded with two court performances in February 1600 and two more in January 1601. The payee for both of these showings was Robert Browne, the former Admiral's man who until late 1598 had been playing in Germany. Whether his return to England and his taking over the leadership of Derby's preceded or followed the company's return to London is not certain. At some time in this period the Countess of Derby wrote another letter about her errant husband's devotion to

---

[16] For a full account of this change, see Ch. 4.
[17] See Peter Thomson, *Shakespeare's Professional Career* (Cambridge, 1992), 46.

plays, naming Browne as the company's leader.[18] The letter is not dated, but must belong to the period when the company was in London, between 1599 and 1601. Derby's, possibly under pressure from their patron, evidently tried to plant themselves firmly in London in order to break the duopoly's grip. Between a visit to Leicester on 16 October 1599 and one to Norwich on 27 February 1602 there is no record of them in the country. There was no plague, and Browne's most recent travelling experiences were all abroad. London was where they found their best chances. In 1599 Browne was contributing to the cost of converting the Boar's Head Inn at Whitechapel, exactly on the city's eastern boundary, for their playhouse. In 1600, however, Francis Langley, owner of the Swan, joined the enterprise and Browne moved out.

Browne's attempt to find a London foothold for his company was already under heavy competition from Worcester's Men. Through 1601 and 1602 Derby's and Worcester's switched places between the Boar's Head and the now-empty Rose. Derby's got the first foothold at court, but Worcester's had a strong team of older players, and had acquired Will Kemp. Worcester's, its patron a Privy Councillor, unlike Derby's, was finally admitted to be the winner in 1602, in the form of a company made from a merger with another competing group, Oxford's, the two 'being joyned by agrement togeather in on companie', as a Privy Council order of 31 March 1602 put it. The order allocated them the Boar's Head, though they soon left it for the Rose. That ended the Derby company's last intrusion into London. Browne was seriously ill, and the sparseness of records for their appearances in the provinces through the next few years suggests that they soon disintegrated. They played at Norwich in 1602, and at Coventry in 1602 and 1603, but no records have been found for several years after that. They never reappeared at court.

Two plays that came into print with Derby's name on their title-pages from this stay in London give a faint hint of the repertoire with which they tried to challenge the duopoly. *Edward IV*, another play demanding a large cast, was published in 1600, and *The Trial of Chivalry* appeared in 1605. By the standards of 1600, with the return of the boy companies and the rise of their railing comedy, both of their extant plays could be counted rather old-fashioned. The first of them is a history play, with features characteristic of Heywood, chiefly following the 'brave Talbot' taste that gripped London at the beginning of the previous decade in the wake of the Armada. The other, equally set in the heavy-handed drum-and-trumpet mode, is a pseudo-history full of Heywoodish derring-do. What else Derby's had in their repertoire we do not know, nor is there any evidence that they staged any of the plays that their lord was said to be busy penning.

The history of the Pembroke's company is another patchwork full of holes, though some of the patches are distinctly colourful. The only early record of any players wearing the livery of Henry Herbert, the second earl of Pembroke, and from 1586

---

[18] This was her famous plea to Cecil on behalf of Browne and the company, 'for that my Lord taking delite in them, it will kepe him from moer prodigall courses'. See *ES* ii. 127.

the Lord President of Wales, is a single entry by the Canterbury officials as far back as 1575–6. There is no record of any further life in this group, even through the years between 1586 and 1591, when the new large companies were coming into existence. Most of the London companies of this time had longish pedigrees under patrons who kept a standing company. The short-lived yet outstanding Pembroke's of 1591–3 is an almost unique anomaly. Why Herbert, who by 1592 was spending much of his time in Ludlow and the Welsh Marches in his function as Lord President, should have chosen to set up a new company so late in his career (he was fifty-seven in 1591), is one of many questions about the role of the noble patrons who set up new playing companies through these years to which there is no direct answer.

It has been suggested that his wife prompted the establishment of the new company. Mary Herbert, Sidney's sister, became the Earl's third wife in 1586, when she was 25. In 1591 she translated a French play by Garnier and commissioned Daniel to write its sequel.[19] But only one reference connects Mary Herbert directly to her husband's playing company. In 1592 Simon Jewell, a player in Pembroke's with links to the Queen's Men, mentions her as a patron in his will,[20] which J. A. B. Somerset takes to be clear evidence for her sponsorship of Pembroke's.[21] On the other hand, the company is not mentioned as participating in her 'Astraea' entertainment, which was probably held at Ramsbury for Elizabeth's visit on 27–9 August 1592, where, if she was interested in using them, she might have been expected to show their paces.

There are other possible explanations for the creation of this new company and its new patron. I think that one precipitating factor was very likely to have been the quarrel which James Burbage had with Edward Alleyn in May 1591. It took Alleyn and Strange's Men away from Burbage's Theatre and eventually to Henslowe at the Rose. That left Burbage with a vacancy for a playing company, and probably higher expectations than the other companies then camped around London could readily supply. And he had a son, only a year younger than Alleyn, who had been playing in Strange's but who out of family loyalty left Strange's to stand by his father (he was reported in a 1591 lawsuit to have defended his father's interests with a broomstick). So it is conceivable that old Burbage moved to set up a new company led by his son under a new patron. He had himself been wearing Henry Carey's livery in 1584, but could not appeal to him for patronage now because Carey's policy as Chamberlain was not to give his own name to any company. So Burbage may well have arranged to form a new company by applying to Pembroke to sponsor them. What makes that move fairly plausible is Burbage's long life as a Leicester's man and Herbert's long intimacy with Robert Dudley, which has been

[19] For a comment on Mary Sidney's interest in plays, see Ch. 4, n. 38.

[20] See Mary Edmond, 'Pembroke's Men', *RES* (n.s.) 25 (1974), 129–36, and Scott McMillin, 'Simon Jewell and the Queen's Men', *RES* 27 (1976), 174–7.

[21] 'The Lords President, Their Activities and Companies: Evidence from Shropshire', *Elizabethan Theatre*, 10 (1988), 93–111, 109.

described above.[22] Henry Herbert was the obvious choice for a former Leicester's player to turn to as a new patron who was a senior noble, a Privy Councillor, and a playgoer, but who was not currently patronizing any of the major London companies.

It is, of course, also possible that Burbage knew something of Mary Herbert's inclinations, and her own association with the Leicester circle. An appeal to her husband, possibly through her intercession, might have been a way to secure the noblest level of patronage for the new company. Whether Mary Herbert did intervene to add the new company to her already long list of creditable literary patronage it is impossible to say. But Pembroke himself was more often in Ludlow than in London, and his health was declining. That decline might argue against his taking any initiative in setting up a new company for himself, so his wife's intervention cannot be discounted. All we know for certain is that in 1591 or early in 1592 Pembroke chose to change his long-held practice by giving his name and livery as patron to a wholly new London company. It could be added that if we go by the connections of patrons alone, no other great lord would have been a more likely target to be made the patron of a new company sponsored by James Burbage in 1592.

The most tangible evidence, though regrettably also in some ways the biggest puzzle, is the names of the players who composed this new Pembroke's. Much debate has been caused by this question, along with the two matters it relates to, where the recruits for Pembroke's came from and what companies they went to when they broke, partly because some plays of Shakespeare and possibly the playwright himself were involved. Chambers and Dover Wilson thought that Pembroke's was an offshoot of the Strange's–Admiral's amalgamation.[23] David George accepted this, assuming that the other playbooks of the 'amalgamation' reverted to Strange's.[24] This theory does not work. Besides the absence of any real evidence for an amalgamation, it leaves the surviving Admiral's company out of account, and ignores the three companies that, according to its 1594 title-page, acted Shakespeare's *Titus Andronicus* in succession: Strange's, Pembroke's, and Sussex's. Nor is there anything in Henslowe's 1593 letter to Alleyn reporting the Pembroke's break-up that indicates any direct association between them. G. M. Pinciss is doubtful about Pembroke's being a Strange's offshoot on the ground that the 'amalgamated company' split into its two component parts for touring during the plague closure in 1593, and that the numbers involved in travelling make it doubtful that three touring companies could have been formed from the original two. He suggests instead that Pembroke's was made up from one of the two Queen's companies.[25] This is given some support by Simon Jewell's mixed allegiance to Pembroke's and the Queen's. If we call in question Chambers's concept of an 'amalgamation', and add to that doubt David Bradley's argument that the

[22] See Ch. 4.   [23] *ES* ii. 123.
[24] 'Shakespeare and Pembroke's Men', *SQ* 32 (1981), 305–23, 307.
[25] 'The Queen's Men, 1583–1592', *Theatre Survey*, 11 (1970), 50–65.

travelling companies were not reduced in size, none of these theories is very convincing. In the Christmas season at court in 1592–3 only two companies were asked to perform. One was Strange's, based at the Rose. The other, Pembroke's, was most likely at the Theatre, and was very likely led by the son of the Theatre's owner. That would have been a prelude to the new arrangement that the two Privy Councillors set up in 1594.

The only tightly specific evidence about the Pembroke's players and their company finances comes from the will of Simon Jewell, who died in 1592.[26] It may, in fact, not relate solely to the Pembroke's group, but be mixed up with one of the two branches of the Queen's Men of these years. The will, drawn up on 19 August, suggests that the value of a share in the company was then £80, a top price for that decade. It names, besides Mary Herbert as Jewell's benefactor, a 'Smithe' and a 'Cooke' who may be the same men known as players in other contexts, and several others who are less readily identifiable.[27] It makes no mention of a Burbage or a Shakespeare. Jewell may have been a Pembroke's man or he may have been a Queen's man who was helped by Mary Herbert independently of his playing company. Tangible as the will is about Jewell's friends, it does not open a large door on to the company.

The rest of the evidence about the Pembroke's players is intimately bound up with their plays. Four texts of plays that the company had performed according to their title-pages were printed in 1593 and 1594: Marlowe's *Edward II*, Shakespeare's *Titus Andronicus*, and two with some relation to the texts printed as Shakespeare's in the 1623 Folio: *The Taming of the Shrew* and *3 Henry VI*. Their quarto titles are *The Taming of A Shrew*, and *The True Tragedy of Richard Duke of York*. A fifth play, *The Contention of the Houses of York and Lancaster*, which has a relation to *2 Henry VI* closely similar to that of *The True Tragedy* to *3 Henry VI*, has no company name on its title-page, but is almost certainly another Pembroke's play. The two early versions of the *Henry VI* plays contain player's names.[28] The quarto of *Titus* names Pembroke's as the middle one of three companies, after Strange's and before Sussex's. It has been suggested that these three companies performed the play jointly, but in the absence of evidence for amalgamations of this kind I think it unlikely. The second quarto of *Titus* added the Chamberlain's Men's name to the list, which confirms that it describes a succession of companies. The existence of a *1 Henry VI* in the list of Strange's plays, which suggests an early Shakespeare connection, and the existence of *Titus* in Henslowe's record of the Sussex company's repertoire in 1593–4 is a fairly clear indication that the sequence on its title-page records the sequence of its owners and performers.

[26] For speculation about the membership of Pembroke's at large, see Karl P. Wentersdorf, 'The Repertory and Size of Pembroke's Company', *Theatre Annual*, 33 (1977), 74.

[27] The will mentions a 'Mr Smithe' who may be the Queen's Men's William Smith, and 'Mr Cooke' who might be Lionel Cooke. See Ch. 12, n. 26.

[28] See Scott McMillin, 'Casting for Pembroke's Men: The *Henry VI* Quartos and *The Taming of A Shrew*', *SQ* 23 (1972), 141–59, and 71–3 above.

The number of identifiable Pembroke's players who became the new Chamberlain's Servants in 1594 is noted in Chapter 16. Pembroke's name, plus the other circumstantial evidence, strongly supports the view that Richard Burbage, after a period playing with Strange's in 1590 and 1591 that is recorded in the *2 Seven Deadly Sins* plot, separated from them when Alleyn quarrelled with his father, and helped to set up the new Pembroke's as a company to occupy the Theatre when Alleyn and most of Strange's moved to the Rose. When Pembroke's collapsed he may have gone to the Rose with Sussex's for a few months before setting up as the leader of the new Chamberlain's back at his father's Theatre in 1594. It is not, I think, too simple a reading of the fragments to see both Alleyn and Burbage using parental property as the London base for their two companies, not just from 1594 onwards but as early as 1592.

In this farrago of speculative assignments to companies it is impossible not to add the question of Shakespeare's membership. His name does not appear in any of the companies before the Chamberlain's Men some time after 1594, but his plays do. If a company's performance of his plays is anything to go by, they must give clues to his playing allegiances. That puts him in Strange's before 1592, when he might have composed his three pages of *Sir Thomas More*, and Pembroke's after. We can add to those hints a few points from Robert Greene's sour and dying words in his last pamphlet about Shakespeare as an 'upstart crow', which was in the Stationers' Register in late September 1592. Whatever else that notorious jibe implies, it does make a few things clear about what was going on in 1592. Shakespeare was evidently still serving as a player that summer, and his *3 Henry VI* had just mounted the stage when Greene wrote his pamphlet. It was not a Rose play according to Henslowe's *Diary*, so it must have been playing somewhere else in London, most likely at the Theatre. One implication of that could be that Shakespeare had left Strange's along with Richard Burbage, and was now playing alongside him across the water with Pembroke's. It is a possibility. Here we should note what can be drawn from another consequence of Greene's sourness, Henry Chettle's disclaimer.

In the preface 'To the Gentlemen Readers' of his *Kind-Hart's Dreame*, which was entered in the Stationers' Register on 8 December 1592, Chettle made an equally famous and markedly handsome apology to Shakespeare for Greene's jibe. His declaration that since Greene published his attack 'my selfe have seene his demeanor no less civill, than he exelent in the qualitie he professes' is worth noting because it seems to say that Chettle had met the man and had seen him performing some time after Greene's pamphlet appeared. That would have been difficult in London. Strange's was out of town through most of that period, visiting Oxford, Gloucester, Coventry, and later (on 19 December) Leicester. Pembroke's were away too, at King's Lynn and elsewhere. The five performances at court that the two companies shared in that season did not start until St Stephen's Night, 26 December. So either Chettle had seen Shakespeare on stage before Pembroke's left for the country or he remembered him from earlier stage performances with

Strange's and in his memoir added that to a more recent encounter with the poet, now off-stage, who might have remained in London while his fellows went on tour. It is most likely that Shakespeare performed with Pembroke's in mid-1592 in *3 Henry VI* and whatever other plays Chettle saw him in. Whether he left the company before it came back to London for the Christmas season at court, or accompanied it at the start of its long and destructive final tour we do not know. His connections with the earl of Southampton would have started later, at the end of the year.

Shakespeare's place in any of the early companies is uncertain. The case for him belonging to the Queen's has been made as strongly, and on much the same grounds, as for his membership of Pembroke's. But I am almost convinced that Shakespeare was with his plays in Pembroke's Company at the Theatre in 1592 and 1593. My reasons are not just the number of his plays showing evidence that some Pembroke's players were in them (*2* and *3 Henry VI*, in the versions known as *The Contention* and *Richard Duke of York*, and *The Taming of the Shrew* and *Titus*), but the evidence in the quarto and octavo versions of *2* and *3 Henry VI* which indicate that he was on hand when they were staged. Two details of the early staging, one in *The Contention* and one in *Richard Duke of York*, suggest an influence on them that came from a reader closely familiar with their source in Holinshed. In the Folio text of *2 Henry VI* the entry direction at V. ii. reads, '*Enter Richard and Somerset to fight*'. In *The Contention* the stage direction reads, '*enter the Duke of Somerset, and Richard fighting, and Richard kils him under the signe of the Castle in saint Albones*'. Richard then explains the point of the 'alehouse paltry signe', reminding the audience of the prophecy that Somerset would die beside a castle. That point is made in both versions, although in *Contention* Richard makes it more explicit, saying 'Whats here, the signe of the Castle? | Then the prophesie is come to passe'. The players might have taken the hint about a hanging sign from the text, but it would have helped if the author were on hand to confirm the details. The greater emphasis given in the *Contention*'s version is consistent with a writer who remembered the staged version and its use of an ale-house sign.

Another detail in the subsequent play offers quite direct evidence. The Folio entry at II. vi. of *3 Henry VI* simply reports '*Enter Clifford wounded*'. The Pembroke's version has '*Enter Clifford wounded, with an arrow in his necke*'. Holinshed specified the type and the location of Clifford's wound, and the Pembroke's text of the play records that they got it right when it was staged. This replication of visual details from the play's sources, another instance of which appeared in the staging of *Richard III* (Richard's habit of toying with his dagger), makes it almost certain that Shakespeare was on hand when Pembroke's staged the play in 1592–3. These features were not registered in the authorial manuscripts of the plays that were much later used to print the Folio texts.

There is also the point that, for a company of wholly new players, Pembroke's Men became strikingly prominent strikingly quickly in London and at court. Besides performing at least four of Shakespeare's plays and having Marlowe's

Edward II written for them, Pembroke's were good enough in their earliest years to almost match Strange's at court in their very first season, with two performances to the other company's three. Their rise was as sudden as their fall, under the twin pressures of the plague and travelling with a company as large as Strange's in August 1593. Henslowe's report of their breaking and having to sell their playbooks and costumes is factual and unrevealing. Their rapid death, like their rapid rise, is a piece of early theatre history with weighty implications and shadowy information. They fell soon after their peers, Strange's with Alleyn, wrote to the Privy Council for help because of the size of their company and the poor returns from travelling. Pembroke's must have had similar problems. Added to that is the still-open question of James Burbage's part in their rise and his actions when they fell, together with the shifts of company membership that went with their sudden birth and short life.

One factor relating to the patrons may have a bearing on the transfer of players in 1594 from the broken Pembroke's via Sussex's to Carey's new company. After the 1593 break-up, a Pembroke's does reappear in the records as a travelling group. It is noted, for instance, in the Ipswich records on 7 April 1595, and in the same town the following year, and at Bath, Bristol, and Oxford. Pembroke's was also in the Ipswich records for 1592–3, so very likely the 1595 company was the remnant group following its familiar touring path. They had certainly been reduced in status by the losses following the 1593 troubles, whether as a result of their leading players going to Sussex's in 1593 or directly into the Chamberlain's in 1594. And there may have been another reason why they did not get back to London. Henry Carey's son, George, was engaged in hostile wrangles with Pembroke from the autumn of 1593 until 1595, over the possible marriage of Pembroke's fifteen-year-old son, William (later the third earl and dedicatee of the First Folio) to George Carey's daughter. The hot-blooded Henry might have seasoned the family animus against Pembroke in 1594 either by using his office to keep his enemy's playing company out of town or by taking its best players for his new company. That is sheer speculation, but the other evidence for Carey's direct intervention in playing matters does give it a sharp edge.

The patent for Pembroke's Men survived the changes, as the papers usually did when a company 'broke'. For a company to lose its patron's licence altogether the patron usually had to die. So the financial collapse of Pembroke's and the likely departure of some of its members into Sussex's was not a complete demise. Some of the 1593 company were able to continue travelling, which must have been what enabled Francis Langley to bring them back to his new playhouse on Bankside in 1597. A Pembroke's company was in the Welsh Marches in 1593–4, at Bewdley, where they were noted as 'my Lord President his Players', and they returned there in 1598 when their second attempt to fix themselves in London failed. The name had most clout in the patron's own territory. It could not prevail in London, though, once the two other Privy Councillors had given their own companies exclusive access.

The story of the Pembroke's company's attempt to return to work in London in 1597 has been told in Chapter 6. It was a fairly short-lived incursion that settled at the Swan, poached players from its Bankside neighbour, the Rose, and shrank Henslowe's profits for the six months from February 1597 till the end of July, when several of its players were imprisoned for staging *The Isle of Dogs*. Two of them, Humphrey Jeffes and Gabriel Spencer, were among the names of the players in the earlier Pembroke's of 1593, which shows that the original group that 'broke' in that autumn had retained its licence and its identity on tour in the following years. Even after the troubles of 1597 a residual Pembroke's Men still persisted. It used its licence to go back on tour, returning to the patronial territory of Shropshire in 1598 and playing elsewhere in 1599.

What plays they had by this time there is no evidence to tell. The company did rejoin the struggle for a place in London in 1600, opening on 28 October at the Rose once the Admiral's Men had left it for the new Fortune.[29] That was in good time to offer their services to the Master of the Revels for the next season of court plays. The duopoly policy was weakening, but that Christmas it was Derby's, not Pembroke's, who got the chance to join the other two companies at court, and Derby's won again in the following court season. Pembroke's never had another chance, because their patron had died on 9 January 1601. By then Spencer had been killed by Ben Jonson. Jeffes returned to Henslowe.

STRANGE'S PLAYERS, 1564–1594, DERBY'S 1594–1620

Plays
Bendo and Richardo (lost), *Brandimer* (lost), *Clorys and Orgasto* (lost), *Constantine* (lost), *The Comedy of Cosmo* (lost), *Don Horatio* (lost), *Friar Bacon and Friar Bungay*, *Fair Em*, *Henry of Cornwall* (lost), *1 Henry VI*, *The Jealous Comedy* (lost), *Jerusalem* (lost), *The Jew of Malta*, *A Knack to Know a Knave*, *The Looking Glass* (?*A Looking-glass for London and England*), *Machiavel* (lost), *Sir John Mandeville* (lost), *The Massacre at Paris*, *Muly Mollocco* (lost), *Orlando Furioso* (old?), *Pope Joan* (lost), *2 Seven Deadly Sins* (plot), *The Spanish Tragedy*, *1* and *2 Tamar Cham* ('plot', and lost), *The Tanner of Denmark* (lost), *Titus and Vespacia* (lost), *Titus Andronicus*, *Zenobia* (lost).

Playing Sharers
[Edward Alleyn], George Attewell, George Bryan, Richard Cowley, John Heminges, Will Kemp, Augustine Phillips, Thomas Pope.

Hired Men
Richard Burbage? Thomas Goodale? [*2 Seven Deadly Sins* plot].

---

[29] Rutter (ed.), *Documents of the Rose Playhouse*, 195 suggests that the two performances by Pembroke's at the Rose after the Fortune was opened for the Admiral's indicate that Henslowe had a different relation with the Pembroke's company from the one he had operated with the Admiral's since 1597.

London Playhouses
Cross Keys 1589 and 1594; Theatre 1590–1; Rose 1592–3; Newington Butts 1594.

At Court
28 Dec. 1581 (activities), 1 Jan. 1583 (activities), 27 Dec. 1590 with Admiral's (play and activities), 16 Feb. 1591 with Admiral's (play and activities), 27 Dec., 28 Dec., 1 Jan. 1592, 9 Jan., 6 Feb., 8 Feb., 27 Dec., 31 Dec., 1 Jan. 1593, 3 and 5 Feb. 1600, 1 and 6 Jan. 1601.

Travelling
Winchester 1563–4, 7s. 3d. / Southampton 4 Nov. 1563, 10s. / Bristol Nov. 1564, 10s. / Gloucester 1564–5 'to the lord stranges playores', 10s. / Canterbury 1564–5, 10s. / Cambridge town 1565–6 'my lord strange plaiers', 10s. / Ipswich 1566–7, 10s. / Beverley 1566–7, 13s. 4d. / Canterbury 1568–9, 10s. / Dover 1568–9, 11s. 4d. / Bristol Nov. 1569, 10s. / Lydd, Kent 1569–70, 12s. 2d. / New Romney, Kent 1569–70, 3s. / Plymouth 1569–70, 13s. 4d. / Exeter 1576–7, 13s. 4d. / Faversham, Kent 1577–8, 6s. 8d. / Coventry Nov. acct. 1578, 6s. 8d. / Nottingham 7 Dec. 1578, 6s. 8d. / Bath June 1578–9, 5s. 2d. / Ipswich 1578–9, 13s. 4d. / Coventry Nov. acct. 1579, 10s. / Gloucester 1579–80, 5s. / Coventry Nov. acct. 1580, 6s. 8d. / Bristol Nov. 1580, 13s. 4d. / Rye, Sussex Dec. 1580, 10s. / Canterbury 1580–1, 10s. / Lydd 1580–1, 3s. 4d. / Gloucester 1580–1, 13s. 4d. / Bath June 1580–1, 7s. 9d. / Bristol Mar. 1581, 13s. 4d., 'paid for mending of ii fowrmes which were taken out of St Georges Chapple and set in the yeld hall at the play and by the desordre of the people were broken', 2s. 5d. / Nottingham 4 Jan. 1582, 6s. 8d. / Norwich 1581–2, 33s. 4d. / Plymouth 1581–2, 10s. / Barnstaple, Devon 1582–3, 2s. / Liverpool 25 Jan. 1583, 10s. / Bath June 1583, 7s. 9d. / Barnstaple 1583–4, 2s. / Coventry Dec. acct. 1584, 5s. / Beverley 1584–5, 2s. / Coventry Dec. acct. 1588, 5s. / Gloucester 1591–2, 10s. / Cambridge town 1591–2, 20s. / Bath June 1591–2, 17s. / Folkestone 1591–2, 4s. / Faversham, Kent 1591–2, 20s. / Canterbury 13 July 1592, 30s. / Bristol Aug. 1592, 30s. / Bath Aug. 1592, 16s. 3d. / Oxford town 6 Oct. 1592, 6s. 8d. / Coventry Nov. acct. 1592, 20s. / Sudbury, Suffolk 1592–3, 3s. 6d. / Shrewsbury 1592–3 'to my Lord strange and my Lord admyralls players', 40s.[30] / Faversham, Kent 1592–3, 20s. / Rye, Sussex July 1593, 13s. 4d. / Bristol July 1593[31] / Bath Aug. 1593, 12s. 3d. / Norwich 15 Sept. 1593, 20s. / Coventry 2 Dec. 1593, 20s. / Leicester 1593–4 'who did playe', 5s. / Winchester 16 May 1594 'unto the players of the Countess of Derby', 6s. 8d. / Southampton May 1594 'my Lord Morleys players and the Earle of Darbyes', £1. / King's Lynn [Derby's and

---

[30] An 'Admiral's' company received 10s. for playing at Shrewsbury on 3 Feb. 1592. This separate visit was almost certainly by the other group, Strange's as a single company along with Alleyn, the Admiral's solo man. While in Strange's Alleyn was evidently still wearing his Admiral's livery. The 40s. paid for this visit was the same amount as Pembroke's received for its visit in this same year.

[31] Alleyn wrote on 1 Aug. to his wife and her father saying that he had received a letter at Bristol. The company evidently intended to play there, but there is no city record of any payment. A subsequent letter by Henslowe to Alleyn asks about the report of his recent sickness at Bath, where someone else had to take his part. The visit to Bath is in the records.

Morley's not to play] 20 Sept. 1594 / Dunwich, Suffolk 1594–5, 5s. / Canterbury 1595–6, 18s. / Gloucester 1595–6, 30s. / Oxford town 1595–6, 20s. / Bath 1595–6, 14s. 6d. / Dunwich, Suffolk 1595–6, 5s. / Leicester 1595–6 'more than was gaythered', 20s. / Coventry Dec. acct. 1596, 10s. / Bristol July 1596 'which played in the Guildhalle', 30s. / York City Books 30 Sept. 1596 'in reward to my Lord Darbie & Lord Darcies players', 10s. / Ipswich 26 Mar. 1597, 10s. / Bath 1596–7, 13s. 4d. / Bristol April–May 1597, 10s. / Coventry Dec. acct. 1597, 10s. / Kendal 1597–8, 10s. / Leominster, Herefordshire 1597–8, 10s. / Coventry Dec. acct. 1598, 10s.; 'by a warrant from mr Clarke maior', 20s. / Leicester 1598, 10s. / Leicester 16 Oct. 1599, 20s. / Norwich 27 Feb. 1602 'ys graunted to the Earle of Darbye his servuantes to shew theire devises & sportes' / Coventry Dec. acct. 1602, 13s. 4d. / Faversham, Kent 10 Mar. 1602, 10s. / Ipswich 4 June 1602 'for a Reward', 10s. / Norwich 10 June 1602 'It ys this daye ordered & agreed uppon that yf therle of Darby his players shall playe in this Cittie contrary to Mr Maiors Commaundement then they shalbe committed to prison'; 'a letter sent to mr Alcock about the Earle of Darbys men' / Coventry Dec. acct. 1602, 13s. 4d. / Coventry Nov. acct. 1603, 5s. / Coventry Nov. acct. 1604, 5s. / Coventry Nov. acct. 1606, 10s. / Coventry Nov. acct. 1607, 10s. / Barnstaple, Devon 1607–8, 10s. / Coventry 'in december' 1607, 10s. / Kendal 18 Mar. 1609, 5s. / Coventry 24 May 1609, 10s. / Louth 1609 '(not suffering them to playe) att Maday fare', 5s. / Gawthorpe, Lancs. (Household accounts of Richard Shuttleworth) Dec. 1609, 6s. 8d. / Coventry Nov. acct. 1612, 10s. / Gawthorpe, Lancs. 12 Aug. 1612, 26s. 8d. / Gawthorpe, Lancs. (Household accounts of Richard Shuttleworth) 12 Dec. 1612, 7s. 4d. / Gawthorpe, Lancs. (Household accounts of Richard Shuttleworth) Sept. 1613, 20s. / Dunkenhalgh, Lancs. (Household accounts of Thomas Walmesley) 1613, 20s. / Dunkenhalgh, Lancs. (Household accounts of Thomas Walmesley) 21 July 1615, 13s. 4d. / Coventry 14 May 1616, 10s. / Leominster, Herefordshire 1616–17, 5s. / Gawthorpe, Lancs. (Household accounts of Richard Shuttleworth) 18 Mar. 1617, 3s. 4d. / Dunkenhalgh, Lancs. (Household accounts of Thomas Walmesley) 22 Mar. 1617, 13s. 4d. / Dunkenhalgh, Lancs. (Household accounts of Thomas Walmesley) 2 Aug. 1617, 20s. / Leominster, Herefordshire 1619–20, 6s. 8d. / Dunkenhalgh, Lancs. (Household accounts of Thomas Walmesley) 12 Feb. 1620, 10s.

DERBY'S PLAYERS, 1564–1594

See also Strange's.

Travelling

Gloucester 1564–5, Corp. Chamb. acct. 'to the lord stranges playores x s' / Newcastle Apr. 1566 'to my lord of darbyes players whiche was plaid in Mr maiore hous', 20s. / New Romney, Kent 29 Apr. 1568, 2s. 8d. / Coventry 1574, 5s. / Newcastle Nov. 1576, 10s. / Nottingham 30 Aug. 1577, 20s. / Dover 1577–8, 13s. 4d. / Faversham, Kent 1577–8, 6s. 8d. / Coventry Nov. acct. 1578, 6s. 8d., 10s. /

Ipswich 28 May 1578, 10s. / Bristol Monday 26 Oct. 1578, 13s. 4d. / Bath 1579, 4s. / Leicester 1579–80 'more then was gaythered', 4s. 4d. / Gloucester 1579–80, 5s. / Exeter 1579–80, 13s. / Dartmouth 1579–80, 5s. / Exeter Apr. 1580, 13s. 4d. / Faversham, Kent 1579–80, 6s. 8d. / Coventry Nov. acct. 1580, 6s. 8d. / Nottingham 9 Aug. 1580, 10s. / Stratford 1580 / Leicester 1580–1 'more then was gaythered', 14s. / Winchester 1580–1, 8s. 4d. / Exeter 1580–1, 6s. 8d. / Gloucester 1580–1, 14s. 4d. / Bath 10 June acct. 1581, 10s. / Abingdon 1581, 5s. / Winchester 1581–2, 15s. / Norwich 1581–2, 33s. 4d. / Ipswich 1581–2, 20s. / Nottingham 1581–2, 6s. 8d. / Southampton 1582–3, 13s. 4d. / Liverpool 25 Jan. audit 1583, 10s. / Coventry Dec. acct. 1584, 5s. / Gloucester 1591–2, 10s. / Shrewsbury 1591–2, 10s. / Ipswich 7 Aug. 1592 'unto therll of Darbys players and to the Lorde admirals players', 20s. / Southampton 1592–3 'to my L. Morleys players and the Earle of Darbyes', £1. / Coventry 2 Dec. 1593, 20s. / Leicester 1593–4 'who did playe' 5s. / Norwich 15 Sept. 1594, 20s. / King's Lynn Sept. 1594 'upon the Lord of Darbye & the Lord Morley ther players inconsideracion thee shall depart & not playe within this Town', 20s.

PEMBROKE'S PLAYERS, 1591–1601

Plays
Edward II, *The Taming of the Shrew*, *2* and *3 Henry VI*, *Richard III*, *Titus Andronicus* (old), *The Isle of Dogs* (lost).

Playing Sharers
Richard Burbage?, John Holland, William Shakespeare?, John Sinckler, Gabriel Spencer, Humphrey Jeffes; (1597) William Bird, Thomas Downton, Richard Jones, Robert Shaw.

London Playhouses
Theatre?, Swan 1597.

At Court
26 Dec. 1592, 6 Jan. 1593.

Travelling
Canterbury 1575–6, 6s. 8d. / King's Lynn 1592–3, 20s. / Ipswich 1592–3, 13s. 4d. / Leicester 1592 'more than was gaythered', 14s. / Ludlow 1592–3 'to my Lord presidentes players a quarte of whit wine & suger in the new howse', 12d.; 'to them for there play', 20s. / Shrewsbury 1592–3 'to my lorde presidentes players cominge to this towne', 40s. / Bath June–Aug. 1592, 16s.; 'Received of my Lord of Penbrokes plaiers for A bowe that was broken by them', 2s. / Rye, Sussex July 1593, 13s. 4d. / York City Books June 1593, 40s. / Coventry Nov. acct. 1593, 30s. / Bewdley, Worcs. St Andrew's Chapel and Bridge Wardens' Accounts 1593–4 'my Lord President his Players', 20s. / Ipswich 7 Apr. 1595, 10s. / Ipswich 1595–6, 13s. 4d. / Oxford town 1595–6, 10s. / Bath 1596–7, 20s. / Bristol Aug.–Sept. 1597, 'playing twise', £2. / Bristol June–July 1598, 30s. / Dover Oct. 1598, 10s. /

Coventry 12 Dec. 1598, 10s. / Bewdley, Worcs St Andrew's Chapel and Bridge Wardens' Accounts 22 Dec. 1598, 10s. / Leicester 1598–9, 'to the Erle of Penbrucke his players in reward', 8s. 6d. / Norwich 11 Apr. 1599 'This daye the Earle of Penbroke his players have lycens to use theire facultie two dayes and two nightes and {not} to use same after nyne of the Clocke on eyther nighte' / Coventry 4 July 1599, 10s. / Bristol Sept. 1599, 30s. / Bath 1598–9, 14s 2d. / Newcastle Oct. 1599 'to the Earle of Penbroughe players', 53s. 4d. / Marlborough 1599–1600, 8s. / York City Books 18 Jan. 1600, 'my Lord of Penbrokes men shall play before my Lord maiour & aldermen in the common hall on monday next in the afternone & have xl s for reward' / Bristol Mar.–May 1600, 30s. / Leicester 1600 'more then was gathered', 17s. / Hardwick, Derbyshire (Cavendish household account) 15 Feb. 1600, 3s. 4d.

Henry Carey's policies over playing have been described above.[1] He was evidently a supporter of plays and playing throughout his life. He worked closely with his son-in-law, Charles Howard, putting national policy and loyalty to his queen first, only sponsoring a company himself when he was not in authority over playing on the queen's behalf. An early company in the livery of Henry Carey, Lord Hunsdon, is recorded playing between 1564 and 1566, followed by a ten-year gap till 1576, then at York on 8 September 1580 and elsewhere in the following years. It made one appearance at court, on 27 December 1582. After the then Lord Chamberlain, Sussex, died in the following year and the major companies were decapitated to make the Queen's Men, all the patrons of the remaining companies with a foothold in London seem to have backed or been fended off. Carey certainly went along with that. Despite a few records of a 'Chamberlain's Men' between 1585 and 1590, no company of Carey's came to London between 1582 and 1594.

When Sussex died, the office of Chamberlain was transferred first to Charles Howard, Lord Effingham and later Lord Admiral, and then in July 1585 to his father-in-law, Henry Carey. During the time of these two men in the office up to 1594 no players wearing their livery were called to perform at court apart from a single joint appearance by a group called 'the servants of the lo: Admirall and the lo: Chamberlaine', on 6 January 1586.[2] With that one rather ceremonial exception, Howard and his successor never drew on their own companies for court performances until they set up the two new companies. Both men, when in office as Chamberlain, maintained a policy that favoured the Queen's Men against all the others.

In all there seem to have been three companies to which Carey gave his patronage. His first company ran a travelling career for not much more than three years in the 1560s. The second began in 1576 and got to court in the 1582–3 season, where it gave one play along with one each by Derby's, Sussex's, and Leicester's, two boy companies, and a masque. The court records name the play. Its title, *Beauty and Housewifery*, is the only indication we have of the kind of repertory this second company ran. It survived the decapitation process that set up the Queen's Men, though its appearance at court the previous Christmas suggests that its leaders would have been drawn on to make the new company, as Leicester's and Sussex's were. For the next seven years it played exclusively in the country, its last recorded appearance being in Kent in 1589–90. We have to assume that James

---

[1] See Ch. 4.   [2] *ES* iv. 161.

Burbage, who claimed Carey's livery in 1584, was not through these years a playing member of the company, but a London playhouse landlord. He probably retained his former allegiance to Leicester's Men rather than the company whose patron he claimed to serve. He was certainly based permanently in London through these years, so the absence of any sign that Hunsdon's Men came to London must mean that he did not associate himself with the other wearers of Carey's livery. The absence of any record for the company through the next five years from 1590 to 1594 suggests that the membership which Carey put into his company in May 1594 was entirely new.

The Chamberlain's Men, as they are popularly known, came into existence out of an act of policy that has been recounted in full above. Replacements for the old Queen's Men, they comprised five of the ex-Strange's-Derby's sharers, whose patron had died the month before, plus three or four from Pembroke's via Sussex's, and one or two from the Queen's. George Bryan, John Heminges, Will Kemp, Augustine Phillips, and Thomas Pope were drawn from Derby's, Richard Burbage probably came from Sussex's along with John Sincler, John Holland, and possibly William Shakespeare, while the presence of Queen's Men's plays in the subsequent repertory of the Chamberlain's suggests that some of its players, too, may have accompanied their plays into the new grouping.

Tracking the plays that are in Henslowe's list for the company in 1594 is the only way to identify what the new companies were given in playbooks as a resource to get them started. The most intriguing and possibly most revealing list of plays is the one that records joint or alternate performances by the new Admiral's Men and the Chamberlain's for their brief run at the same playhouse in June 1594. The two companies offered seven plays between 3 and 13 June. Inevitably the seven included Henslowe's *The Jew of Malta*, a play that every company who played at the Rose from 1592 had staged. But the others came from elsewhere, almost certainly from the companies where Carey and Howard found the players for their new companies. Besides Alleyn's *Cutlack*, *Titus Andronicus* reappeared, presumably along with some players from Sussex's, who had played it at the Rose earlier that year. Four new plays appear, *Hester and Ahasuerus*, *Belin Dun*, *Hamlet*, and *The Taming of A Shrew*. The last of these had been put into print as a Pembroke's play, like *Titus*. Where the *Hamlet* came from is uncertain. References to a play of that name had been appearing since 1589, which means that it belonged to one of the older companies then appearing in London, most likely the Queen's. It is possible to guess fairly sharply about that from the later history of the seven titles. *Belin Dun*, *Cutlack*, and *The Jew of Malta* appear subsequently in the Admiral's lists with Henslowe. *Titus* and *The Shrew* became part of the Chamberlain's playstock, to judge from their reappearance in the First Folio and the addition of the Chamberlain's name to the three previously-named companies on the 1600 quarto of *Titus*. *Hamlet* and *Hester* may have joined the Chamberlain's too, since they never reappear in the Admiral's lists. Thomas Lodge writes of a *Hamlet* at the Theatre in 1596, which would certainly make it a Chamberlain's play.[3] Possibly the *Hamlet*, like *King Leir*, *The Troublesome Raigne of King John*, and *The Famous Victories of Henry V*, was a Queen's Men's play that passed at this time to the Chamberlain's, all to be rewritten some time later by the company's resident playwright.[4]

The first clear listing of the Chamberlain's personnel did not appear until Jonson supplied the names of the ten 'principall Comoedians' who performed his *Every Man In His Humour* in 1598 to the Folio edition of his plays in 1616. The ten were: 'Will. Shakespeare. Ric. Burbage. Aug. Philips. Joh. Hemings. Hen. Condel. Tho. Pope. Will. Slye. Chr. Beeston. Will. Kempe. Joh. Duke'. To these 'principall' players, not all of whom were the company's sharers, we can add some other names from the play-texts. We know that Richard Cowley, who was with Burbage, Duke, and Sly in the *2 Seven Deadly Sins* plot, was in the company, because he is named as playing Verges against Kemp's Dogberry in the text of *Much Ado about Nothing*. He rose to become a company payee and therefore, presumably, a sharer in 1601. John Sincler, also named in the Strange's *2 Seven Deadly Sins* plot and Pembroke's *3 Henry VI* and *The Shrew*, was in the quarto of *2 Henry IV* as the beadle whom Doll calls 'you thin man in a censer'. He was evidently a distinctly skinny player, and it is possible to trace several parts specially written for him in the post-1594 plays: Nym and Slender in *2 Henry IV*, *Henry V*, and *Merry Wives*, Aguecheek in *Twelfth Night*, possibly Thersites in *Troilus and Cressida*, and probably Robert Faulconbridge, the Bastard's brother, in *King John*, where at I. i. 140–3 he is described in similar terms. In Jonson's plays for the Chamberlain's Men a markedly small player took the part of Shift in *Every Man Out*. Nano the dwarf in *Volpone* has a larger speaking part than the eunuch and hermaphrodite. Sincler may also have been Asinius Bubo in Dekker's *Satiromastix*, and the 'very little man' in *The London Prodigal*, ascribed to the King's Men in 1605. There is nothing in the Shakespeare plays before 1594, particularly *Titus* and *Richard III*, to suggest that any early parts were written for him, for all that his name appears in one of the later *Henry VI* plays. The insertion of his name in the Pembroke texts may indicate that he was a late arrival in that company. The fact that *King John* does have a part for him is no help in fixing the time Sincler joined the company, because its dating is variously ascribed to 1590 or 1595. He was most likely a late arrival in Pembroke's in 1593.

The first listing of the new company's repertoire of plays by its main playwright appeared in 1598, in Francis Meres' *Palladis Tamia*. It includes most of the plays he wrote before 1594. The company appears to have contracted Shakespeare from the outset to write roughly two plays a year, one comedy and one serious play (a

---

[3] *Wits Miserie and the Worlds Madnesse* (1596), 56: 'ye ghost which cried so miserably at ye Theator like an oisterwife, *Hamlet, revenge*'.

[4] Roslyn Lander Knutson, in her careful study of the company's plays, *The Repertory of Shakespeare's Company*, takes a rather more hesitant position over this evidence (9). Her book deals with the plays in the company's repertory between 1594 and 1599 (57–78), 1599 and 1603 (79–102), 1603–8 (103–34), and 1608–13 (135–64). An appendix lists information about publication and stage revivals of all the company's known plays.

tragedy or a history). But he had evidently arrived with a large stock of old plays. We cannot know whether he paid for his share in the company with this stock, or whether it was he who made sure that the new company took on the players who had his playbooks from his own former companies. More likely one of the sponsors of the new company secured that resource for them. If Shakespeare had retained ownership of the older plays while Strange's and Pembroke's were performing them, it would have been a uniquely commercial manœuvre for a playwright of the time. No other player who wrote plays did anything but sell them to the company which performed them, which then became the owners in perpetuity or until they sold them on. That the Chamberlain's acquired so many of Shakespeare's pre-1594 plays is either a tribute to his self-esteem and the high value he put on his own plays, or to his commercial acumen in keeping possession of them for himself and not selling them to the companies. Either that, or his patron or some other agent with influence in the new set-up valued them enough to take them from their various owners for the new company.

Employing Shakespeare for his old plays and as writer and rewriter of others (*King John, Hamlet, King Lear*, the *Henry IV* and *Henry V* plays), gave the company a uniquely sound start. Meres' 'comparative discourse of our English poets with the Greeke, Latine, and Italian poets' gives pride of place as the leading contemporary playwright to the Chamberlain's man:

As Plautus and Seneca are accounted the best for Comedy and Tragedy among the Latines: so Shakespeare among the English is the most excellent in both kinds for the stage. For Comedy, witnes his *Gentlemen of Verona*, his *Errors*, his *Love Labors Lost*, his *Love Labours Wonne*, his *Midsummer Night Dreame*, and his *Merchant of Venice*; For Tragedy, his *Richard the 2, Richard the 3, Henry the 4, King John, Titus Andronicus*, and his *Romeo and Juliet*.

Meres was obsessively keen on making lists, and his assemblage of Shakespearian titles shows him erring on the side of comprehensiveness, unless there was a sequel to *Love's Labours Lost* that has disappeared. But his list of the comedies, histories, and tragedies that were either acquired by the Chamberlain's in 1594 or written for them afterwards appears to be strikingly accurate. The only obvious omissions are the three *Henry VI* plays that led up to *Richard III*, and *The Taming of the Shrew* (which might have been retitled *Love's Labours Won* in Meres' thinking; he must have acquired most of his titles from playbills rather than the printed quartos, since six of the twelve plays named had not yet appeared in print). These, then, were all in the company's repertory in the years 1594 to 1598. The company had clearly made a very good name for itself by then with the work of its resident poet.

Jonson's substantial 1598 list of players and Meres' list of their famous playbooks are deceptive signs of health, though. The company had been in deep trouble since late 1596, when James Burbage's plan to circumvent the new embargo on playing inside the city had gone awry. His lease on the land he had built the Theatre on in 1576 was due to expire in April 1597, and his landlord refused to renew his tenure. Burbage, in any case, was used to the old practice of deserting the open amphitheatres for the roofed city-inns in winter. The Lord Chamberlain's bargain with the Lord Mayor in 1594 to ban the city's inns for playing was firmly in place. Carey himself had to make a special plea to the Mayor to allow the company access to the Cross Keys in its first winter.[5] So Burbage tried to get around the new restrictions by building a roofed playhouse in the liberty of the Blackfriars, for which he bought properties on 4 February 1596. A playhouse had been in use in the building before, for the Chapel Children. Being in a liberty, it was free from the Lord Mayor's control, even though it was inside the city walls. The fourteen years of the older playhouse there, which had closed six years before, spurred Burbage to set up his replacement for the city playing-inns in the same liberty. He bought space a little below and to the west of St Paul's, in an impressive stone building which had once been used for meetings of Parliament but had been converted into tenements in Tudor times. In the summer of 1596 he spent £600 tearing down the tenement partitions and building the Blackfriars playhouse for his son's company. It was in central London, it was designed for a much more upmarket audience than the old Theatre, and for the company it proved a disaster.

On 22 July 1596 Henry Carey died. It is not unlikely that he knew of the plan for a new playhouse, though if he did he could hardly have approved of it since it was a blatant circumvention of his 1594 accord with the Lord Mayor to ban playing inside the city. He may have accepted it, since building in the liberty made it technically not a breach of the accord. But his death immediately made it into a much more hazardous enterprise. Thomas Nashe, writing to an associate of Carey's a few weeks after he died, wrote that the company was already in trouble: 'now the players as if they had writt another Christs tears, ar piteously persecuted by the L. Maior & the aldermen, & however in there old Lords tyme they thought there state setled, it is now so uncertayne they cannot build upon it'.[6] That was a prescient comment, and may show more understanding of the authorities' attitude by Nashe than we can deduce from the external evidence. Carey's death had taken away the company's patron. The Lord Chamberlainship passed to Lord Cobham, who was not their friend, since they had recently put his wife's ancestor, Sir John Oldcastle, on stage, and he had forced them to change the name to Falstaff.[7] The company's patronage passed to Carey's son, George, who later proved to be a good supporter of his father's policy towards helping the players. For the moment, though, he was distinctly hostile, because he lived near the new playhouse in the Blackfriars himself.

In November the leading residents of the Blackfriars presented the Privy Council with a petition objecting to Burbage's plan. It was signed by thirty-one residents, with George Carey's signature coming second after the formidable dowager Lady Russell. Stephen Egerton, the charismatic preacher at the Blackfriars church, to whom Lady Russell was devoted, was another signatory. Cobham, the Lord Chamberlain, was himself a resident in the Blackfriars, but did not need to sign,

---

[5] See above, 66.   [6] *Works*, v. 194.
[7] See Gary Taylor, 'The Fortunes of Oldcastle', *ShS* 38 (1985), 85–100.

because he was already on the Privy Council that was to receive the petition. The petition did, however, put strong emphasis on the disturbance the playhouse would cause him. It started by asserting that the playhouse was 'neere adjoyning' the houses of both the Lord Chamberlain and the new earl of Hunsdon. The Council had no hesitation in acceding to the petition. This put Burbage's entire investment in jeopardy.

A hostile patron and a hostile Lord Chamberlain were only two figures in the throng of troubles the company now faced. They were about to lose their old playhouse, and their financier had tied all his capital up to make a new playhouse in a building they could not use. The bright dawn of 1594, which had secured the exclusive right to play in London for only two companies, and had allocated them specific theatres to play at, was now heavily overcast. It rained the old prejudices that the players must have thought they had mercifully covered themselves against. The Blackfriars petition, for instance, used all the old familiar complaints about the playgoing crowds being full of lewd vagrants, bringing trouble with their noise and the danger of the plague, all of which, though especially the noise from the 'drum-and-trumpet' repertory, would interrupt divine services. It declared that

one Burbage hath lately bought certaine roomes in the same precinct neere adjoyning unto the dwelling houses of the right honorable the Lord Chamberlaine and the Lord of Hunsdon, which romes the said Burbage is now altering and meaneth very shortly to convert and turne the same into a comon playhouse, which will grow to be a very great annoyance and trouble, not only to all the noblemen and gentlemen thereabout inhabiting but allso a generall inconvenience to all the inhabitants of the same precinct, both by reason of the great resort and gathering togeather of all manner of vagrant and lewde persons that, under cullor of resorting to the playes, will come thither and worke all manner of mischeefe, and allso to the great pestring and filling up of the same precinct, yf it should please God to send any visitation of sicknesse as heretofore hath been, for that the same precinct is allready growne very populous; and besides, that the same playhouse is so neere the Church that the noyse of the drummes and trumpetts will greatly disturbe and hinder both the ministers and parishioners in tyme of devine service and sermons.[8]

The petition went on to point out that Burbage was trying to circumvent the Lord Mayor's recent ban on all playing inside the city. It did not add that strictly such a ban could not apply in the liberty. In the face of such weighty opposition and without Carey's backing Burbage had nothing to support him. His investment was frozen. With it went the company's chance of a new playhouse to replace the Theatre and, more substantially, its only source of financial backing. No wonder that, as Nashe wryly and pointedly said, the company's condition was now so uncertain they could not build on it.[9]

In February 1597 James Burbage died, and in April the Theatre was closed. For the next two years it stood in what Everard Guilpin called 'darke silence, and vast

---

[8] *ES* iv. 319–20.
[9] In *Merry Wives*, probably written by early 1597, Shakespeare offered a wry joke about the legal point which lost the company its amphitheatre. See below, 292.

solitude'. The company had to rent the neighbouring Curtain for its perform-ances.[10] Meanwhile the Burbage sons tried to negotiate a renewal of their lease with the Theatre's owner, Giles Allen. The company survived the Lord Chamberlain's hostility because Cobham died only a month after old Burbage, and their patron, George Carey, promptly secured the Chamberlainship. Apart from his objection to their Blackfriars plan, he was generally supportive, and actively reaffirmed the duopoly policy in subsequent years. But it was financially a hard time. Shakespeare wrote two more plays exploiting the re-named Falstaff, while the company raised cash by selling the first of the Oldcastle/Falstaff plays and its most popular other titles to the printers. In these cash-straitened years they sold *Romeo and Juliet*, *Richard II*, *Richard III*, *Loves Labours Lost*, and *1 Henry IV*. Others were to follow when they were short of cash for a different reason, in 1600. Shakespeare's pro-ductivity was at its peak in the years up to *Hamlet*. It did not slow down until the company had been firmly settled at the Globe for three years or more.

The company also made money in these years with their appearances at court and at private houses. A letter survives from Sir Thomas Hoby offering to entertain Cecil at his house in the Strand in December 1595 when 'K. Richard' would 'present him selfe to your vewe', most likely, to judge by the date, in a performance of *Richard II*. *Titus* appears to have been performed at Rutland on 1 January 1596.[11] Like the Admiral's, court records note the company as having two regular payees. For the first Christmas season the two were Will Kemp and William Shakespeare; subsequently it became Thomas Pope and John Heminges. As the years went on Heminges gradually took over all the company's routine financial management. The non-routine management of the difficult playhouse problem remained chiefly a Burbage affair, mainly in the hands of Richard Burbage's older brother, Cuthbert. Company membership remained steady, while its system of management evolved, as did that of its rival across the water.

The two rival companies are remarkable through the whole of this period for their almost-exclusive concentration on playing in London. Between August 1597 and March 1600 the Chamberlain's company appears to have stayed entirely 'at home'. From early 1596 until March 1603 there were no closures for plague, and the company was evidently happy to exploit its new and quasi-unique right to remain in London to the full. This, in fact, was the longest time without travelling to be found in the records for any of the major London companies. The Admiral's Men, its only London rival, is also absent from the records from September 1597 to late 1599. Neither of the duopoly companies travelled nearly as much between

---

[10] Guilpin, a cousin of John Marston, wrote in 1597 about going to plays at either the Rose or the Curtain, in the same book which refers to the Theatre being silenced. Marston's Luscus saw *Romeo and Juliet* at the Curtain in 1598. These were the two suburban playhouses through the middle phase of the duopoly years.

[11] Whether Hoby was referring to Shakespeare's play or to a portrait has been debated. See Gurr (ed.), *Richard II* (Cambridge, 1984), 3. The Rutland reference is intriguing, since the company played at court on 27 Dec. and 11 Jan. If it was the full company that played at Rutland, it was a long way to travel so quickly in a busy winter season. See Knutson, *Repertory*, 60.

1594 and 1603 as they did both before and after. The reason was obviously the Privy Council's grant of exclusive access to the London playing-places, and in the case of the Chamberlain's the pressing need to maximize its income.

Ben Jonson, who did not endear himself to Henslowe when he killed his contracted player Gabriel Spencer in a duel in September 1598, had already left the Rose for Langley's Swan in 1597. On their collapse he started writing for the Chamberlain's Men, probably soon after he was released from the Marshalsea prison for the *Isle of Dogs* affair in October 1597. Borrowing Chapman's humours comedy from the Rose repertory, he gave the Chamberlain's Men *Every Man in his Humour* by 1598,[12] and then *Every Man Out of his Humour* in 1599–1600. How they coped with Jonson's jokes about the other plays in the company's repertoire in *Every Man Out* we do not know. Jonson was firmly independent, keeping himself on Henslowe's payroll while he wrote his humours play for the other company. That suggests they must have valued his services, and may have tried to show themselves complaisant about his derision, or possibly indulged him openly by staging the jibes poker-faced. Webster's sophisticated stage game with the players a few years later in the Induction that he wrote for *The Malcontent* suggests they might have tried the latter.[13] The third possibility is that they cut the jibes out of their script, since on the title-page of the 1600 text Jonson declared that his published text had '*more than hath been Publickely Spoken or Acted*'. A fourth is that the published jibes were a late addition expressing Jonson's scorn for the company he had just left. He certainly put some thinly-disguised satirical portraits of company members into *Poetaster* for the Blackfriars Boys in 1601.[14] Shakespeare's own humour produced *Much Ado about Nothing*, *As You Like It*, and *Twelfth Night* in those years,[15] together with *The Merry Wives of Windsor*,[16] and the completion of his second tetralogy of English history plays, *2 Henry IV* and *Henry V*, plus the first play of a new (though soon discontinued) series about Roman history, *Julius Caesar*.

We have to presume that the Chamberlain's Men's appetite for new plays was as strong as their rival's at the Rose, which means that as many as twenty plays a year from their intake, nearly 90 per cent of their repertory, must have disappeared without trace. Their financial difficulties from 1596 onwards might have restricted their purchase of new plays to something below the Henslowe rate, but the Admiral's Men were having their own financial troubles in 1597 with the competi-

---

[12] Knutson, *Repertory*, 76, notes that Tobie Matthew saw the play on 20 Sept. 1598, two days before Jonson killed Spencer.

[13] Their adoption of the Paul's attack on Jonson in *Satiromastix* in 1601 suggests they were less than wholly complaisant. See below, 342.

[14] See *Ben Jonson*, ix. 558–9, and iv. 193.

[15] It might be argued, as Henk Gras has done, that *Twelfth Night* is in part a response to and defence against Jonson's theory of comedy voiced in *Every Man Out*. See Henk Gras, '*Twelfth Night, Every Man out of his Humour*, and the Middle Temple Revels of 1597–98', *MLR* 84 (1989), 545–64.

[16] We need not take too seriously the story that he wrote *Merry Wives* in 3 weeks in response to the queen's wish to see Falstaff in love. Its aptness for his patron's award of the Garter, normally a Windsor ceremony, in April 1597 is a more likely trigger.

tion from the new company at the neighbouring Swan. Well over half the surviving repertoire of the Chamberlain's in these years was written by Shakespeare, but that cannot represent anything like their complete intake. The main texts surviving from the rest of the company's repertoire at this time are *A Warning for Fair Women*, a dramatization of a domestic murder in London printed in 1599, and *Thomas Lord Cromwell*, a fanciful piece of Tudor pseudo-history based on the hugely popular Protestant martyrology of Foxe's *Acts and Monuments*, the so-called 'Elect-Nation' mode of nostalgia for the Tudors. Printed in 1603, it reads like another imitation of the fashion then beginning to flourish at the Fortune across the river.

Nothing from this period gives quite so direct an indication of the company's popular appeal as did Nashe's reference to 'brave Talbot' with Strange's in 1592. They were certainly noted for *Romeo and Juliet*, and Falstaff was an immediate hit. Nothing in the other company's repertory had a comparable impact. If the Master of the Revels's judgement in choosing companies for the court is a good guide, they were rated rather higher than their rival. Both companies played at court almost every year, the Chamberlain's more often than the Rose company. In the 1594–5 season, each company played three times. In the 1595–6 season, the Chamberlain's played four to the Admiral's three, with one joint evening. In the 1596–7 season, they played six times and the Admiral's did not appear at all. In the 1597–8 season, they played four times to twice by the Admiral's; and in the 1598 season, they each played three times. The 1599–1600 season gave the Chamberlain's three performances, the Admiral's two, and Derby's one. Between 1600 and 1601 they and the Admiral's both played three times, while Derby's played twice, the Blackfriars children twice, and Paul's once. Between 1601 and 1602 they played four times to once by the Admiral's, once by Worcester's, and three times by the Blackfriars children. Between 1602 and 1603 the Chamberlain's and Admiral's launched the season, followed by Paul's Boys and Hertford's, with two more in February by the Admiral's and one more by the Chamberlain's.

Besides these signs of favour, and the private performances, the company also received invitations from the Inns of Court. The Gray's Inn Revels at Christmas 1594 included a performance of *The Comedy of Errors*, and John Manningham noted in his diary a performance of *Twelfth Night* at the Middle Temple on Candlemas, 2 February 1602. More suggestively, John Marston scoffed at the enthusiasm for playgoing among young lawyers in 1597, where his satire says that a question about what is being played today produces a gush of quotations consisting of 'Naught but pure Juliat and her Romio'. Falstaff soon became a famously quotable voice. Tobie Matthew assumed his reader would pick up the reference when he paraphrased Falstaff's honour catechism from *1 Henry IV* in a letter to Dudley Carleton dated 20 September 1598.[17]

---

[17] Knutson, *Repertory*, 61.

The close relations between the company patrons, Howard and Henry Carey, and later the younger Carey, who followed his father onto the Privy Council when he became Lord Chamberlain, were apparently not matched in the companies themselves. The Chamberlain's Men signed up Jonson while he was still in prison for killing the Admiral's Gabriel Spencer. In January 1599 they mounted a lawsuit against another Admiral's writer, Thomas Dekker, and Henslowe had to lend Thomas Downton £3. 10s. to get Dekker free. What the Chamberlain's had him arrested for we do not know. It may have been to recover an advance for a play that Dekker did not deliver, though if it was such a matter Henslowe was unlikely to have taken it very kindly. The Admiral's William Bird also had an enemy in the opposing company. He figures in Henslowe's non-company accounts in a list of loans to him and other players to discharge them from Langley's suits. One of the notes states that in August 1598 he borrowed ten shillings (Henslowe notes 'by my wiffe') 'to folowe sewt agenste Thomas poope'. What this suit against the rival company's player was, and whether it had anything to do with the Langley bonds, we do not know. These entries do suggest that the two companies had some contacts, but not that they were very amicable ones. Of course, friendly relations were less likely to be recorded on paper. Since almost all the players lived either in Shoreditch or on Bankside, and Pope was not a family man, Bird's suit may just have been a matter of unpaid rent.

The repertories of the two companies through these early years show clear signs of the close competition they were engaged in. They copied each other, duplicating specific subjects for their plays and the new fashions each introduced. The Chamberlain's Men had Shakespeare's history plays, so the Admiral's followed suit with a *Richard Crookback* and a *Henry V*. The Admiral's introduced humours comedy, and the Chamberlain's copied them. The Admiral's rubbed in their rival's Oldcastle/Falstaff mistake by taking up the Oldcastle story from Foxe's 'Book of Martyrs', and then developed the idea with a run of plays based on stories from Foxe. The Chamberlain's followed that fashion with *Thomas Lord Cromwell*.[18] Henslowe's records list at least seven plays on biblical subjects, whereas only one (*Hester and Ahasuerus*) can be found in the Chamberlain's list, but that probably only reflects the inadequate records of plays bought by the Chamberlain's company. Henslowe's diary-note about a play concerning Sir Piers of Exton suggests that he visited the rival company's plays and drew ideas about new plays from them.[19] The Admiral's play about two angry wives of the town of Abingdon on the banks of the Thames in Berkshire was matched by the Chamberlain's story about two merry wives of another town by the Thames in Berkshire.[20] This pattern of rivalry and imitation ran consistently from 1594 until Elizabeth died and the companies were reconstituted in 1603.

18 See Knutson, *Repertory*, 48–9, 70.
19 See Gurr, 'Intertextuality in Henslowe', *SQ* 39 (1988), 394–8.
20 See Gurr, 'Intertextuality at Windsor', *SQ* 38 (1987), 189–200.

The Chamberlain's Men's political allegiances are not very evident in their play-texts, apart from the welcome that was so ill-advisedly promised to the earl of Essex in the expectation that he would bring back 'rebellion broachèd on his sword' in the fifth Chorus to *Henry V* in 1599. The same play also has one scene containing that potentially embarrassing figure, Jamy, with his comic Scots accent, accompanying Henry to France. Any keen reader of Holinshed knew that the historical Henry V had a Scottish James with him in France, and not just any Scot but a king, his prisoner the young King James I. The young James was a direct ancestor of the Scottish James VI, who everyone in 1599 expected would eventually become James I of England. To include a Scottish 'Jamy' in the play was an extraordinarily rash joke. Moreover, adding a Scottish accent to the English, Irish, and Welsh spoken in *Henry V* was very peculiar politically, and distinctly awkward dramatically. In the first act of the play the Scots are presented as England's enemies, as any reader of Holinshed would confirm, knowing that almost all the Scots in France fought for the French, not the English. What Jamy was meant to be doing in *Henry V* is a subject for some of the denser explorations of that densest of jungles, Shakespeare's mind. We have to hope that the company was sensitive enough to their new patron's accent and ancestry when the play was chosen for performance at court in 1605 to make them cut that scene out of the text they performed before King James.

Essex did get the company into trouble in 1601, but with a different play by the same author, and for a very different reason. Early in 1601 several of the Essex conspirators approached the company asking them to stage *Richard II* on the afternoon of Saturday 7 February. The coup attempt took place the next morning. Augustine Phillips, summoned to explain to Essex's judges why the company had accepted such a request, pleaded more innocence than Elizabeth herself showed when, a few months later, she told the Keeper of the Tower that she was a King Richard, and that her/his story had been staged forty times in public in London. At the Essex trial, Phillips told the judges that:

Sir Charles Percy Sir Josceline Percy and the Lord Mounteagle with some three more spoke to some players in the presence of this Examinate to have the play of the deposing and killing of King Richard the Second to be played the Saturday next, promising to get them xls. more than their ordinary to play it. Where this Examinate and his fellows were determined to have played some other play, holding that play of King Richard to be so old and so long out of use that they should have small or no company at it.[21]

[21] *ES* ii. 205. The importance of this performance in terms of political power and the place of the stage in the Tudor hegemony has been much debated. Leeds Barroll, 'A New History for Shakespeare and his Time', *SQ* 39 (1988), 441–64, has set out the most sceptical review of the evidence. He concludes that there is no substantial case to be made for the court ever being deeply concerned over the activities of the players at any time, whether over their performance of *Richard II* at the behest of the Essex conspirators, or any other of their intrusions into political and court affairs. They were more concerned, he claims, with Haywood's book about Richard written after Shakespeare's play and subsequently called in by the censors. Haywood was imprisoned for his book, but the players and Shakespeare were never punished. This, I think, rather underestimates the power assigned to the Master of the Revels as theatre censor, and the political weight that backed his labours.

All that can be said about the company's role in that sponsored performance is that the players were unlikely to have known an armed insurrection was imminent, and that they took the forty shillings. Essex's judges accepted their story. The players, who already had to remove their praise of Essex from the text of *Henry V* as soon as he returned disgraced and humiliated from Ireland in the early autumn of 1599, got away lightly.

For all their apparent involvement with Essex, about which there has been a lot of speculation, there is no firm evidence about the political allegiances of the company through these years. Nor is there much about their religious loyalties, unless the smaller number of biblical plays in their repertoire means anything. The core of the company came from Strange's, a company with a Catholic patron, and there are hints of recusancy in the history of some of the leading players, notably Christopher Beeston, who was in the Chamberlain's until he joined Worcester's in 1600.[22] Of course, for a company to make any particular allegiance known, especially recusant sympathies, was impossible. There are a few possible indications of cheekily covert jibes at distinguished enemies such as Lord Cobham (if the Brook/Broome textual confusion in *Merry Wives* is any indication of that kind of game).[23] There is rather more evidence of the kind of fawning to the great that is signalled by the praise of Essex in *Henry V*. Otherwise, apart from the possibility that *The Merry Wives of Windsor* was composed to form part of the celebrations for George Carey's installation as a Knight of the Garter in 1597,[24] the company's post-1594 plays have nothing to compare with such earlier rewritings of source material as the consistent elevation of the Strange's patron's family name, Stanley, through the *Henry VI* plays and *Richard III*.

The oddity of *Henry V*'s use of an alien Scottish 'Jamy' along with the representatives of the English, Welsh, and Irish members of the commonwealth does hint at a peculiarly irreverent attitude to neighbouring royalty in 1599, the more irreverent because it was aimed at the man whom everyone expected to succeed Elizabeth on the English throne. If it was designed to be irreverent, what happened in 1604 suggests a sharp reversal of attitude by the company when Scottish James did come to the English throne and took the company under his patronage. One play that the newly-honoured King's Men produced when they first returned to London after the long closure following Elizabeth's death, not a play written by their home producer, got them into immediate trouble. It seems to have stemmed from a kind of misplaced obsequiousness rather similar to the praise of Essex in 1599. In December 1604 they staged a play about the adventures of King James in Scotland. The Gowry conspiracy of 1600, in which James claimed that the young earl of Gowry and his brother tried to assassinate him when he visited their castle, was represented to the world in a published text for which the full story can only

---

[22] See above, 35.
[23] See *The Merry Wives of Windsor*, ed. H. J. Oliver (New Arden, London, 1971), pp. lii–lviii.
[24] George Carey was actually knighted not at the Garter chapel in Windsor but in London, in April 1597.

have been supplied by James itself. It was, therefore, entirely given to praise of the king and condemnation of his enemies. This is the text the play must have dramatized. It played twice, and attracted large crowds. But it had to portray as its central figure the king himself, and that was outrageous. One of the few specific instructions followed by the Master of the Revels as censor was to cut all references to living people, and especially famous ones. The play upset some of the nobility, who quickly intervened. As the invaluable John Chamberlain reported to his reader in Paris,

the tragedie of Gowrie with all the action and actors hath ben twise represented by the Kings players, with exceeding concourse of all sortes of people, but whether the matter or manner be not well handled, or that yt be thought unfit that princes should be plaide on the stage in theyre life time, I heare that some great counsaillors are much displeased with yt: and so is thought shalbe forbidden.[25]

No text of the play survives, so the suppression was complete. But Tilney as censor must have approved it for staging, and as a play about an event from the new king's earlier career it may even have been designed for higher things altogether. Its staging in December not long before the court season was under way may indicate that the company, and conceivably in the first place Tilney, thought of it as a new play suitable for presentation at court. If so, they miscalculated disastrously. No record of any reproof to Tilney for this or any other of his misjudgements has surfaced.[26] It may be that he himself had second thoughts and belatedly consulted the lords at court about it. John Chamberlain tells of its initial staging at the Globe for only two days, which suggests that it was closed after an unnaturally quick reaction from the court.

Some changes happened in the company's membership before James came to the English throne, together with a small but notable change in the company's playhouse. That change precipitated a more fundamental change in the company's organization, one that had far-reaching effects on all the companies through the last forty years up to the closure. It was a change imposed from outside, a convergence of accidents that fortuitously brought the company great benefit. The membership of the company itself only shifted under incidental pressures such as ageing. The main outside pressures were financial, following from the troubles with the Theatre's lease. In the long run they proved beneficial, because they instigated a new system of management that immeasurably strengthened the company's financial basis. But in the short run the company's difficulties continued up to the new king's accession in 1603 and after.

Of the original sharers, George Bryan dropped out some time after 1596. He is not mentioned in Jonson's *Every Man In* list of leading players, and he turns up in

[25] *Letters*, i. 199. The letter is dated 18 Dec. 1604.

[26] A great deal has also been made of *Measure for Measure* and its use of James's *Basilicon Doron*, seeing it as a play written for the company's new king and patron. It is easy, however, to make too much of such delicate flattery. See Richard Levin, *New Readings vs. Old Plays* (Chicago, 1979), 171–93.

1603 as a groom of the chamber at court, a change of status and work if not of livery. Henry Condell was probably his replacement as a sharer. The First Folio names among the many players who performed Shakespeare's plays a Samuel Cross, who Heywood speaks of in *An Apology for Actors* as being a well-reputed player before Heywood's own time. His presence in the Folio list had Heminges's and Condell's memory to draw on, which may mean that he was an early Chamberlain's man, not a sharer, who withdrew even earlier than Bryan. The largest change in playing membership in these years was the loss of the clown, Will Kemp. He left while the new playhouse was going up, to extend his repertoire of long-distance morris dancing by cavorting in nine days from London to Norwich. He won a bet and wrote a book about it, but the dance-journey divorced him from the Chamberlain's Men for good. He had played Dogberry in *Much Ado*, and the Nurse's man, Peter, in *Romeo and Juliet*.[27] Possibly he also played the great part of Falstaff, but he seems more likely to have been Pistol, and very likely the Host of the Garter in *Merry Wives*.[28] His replacement, Robert Armin from Chandos's Men, was a singer and a wit, a noted solo player. The company's valediction for Kemp and its welcome for Armin was written into the part of Touchstone in *As You Like It*. Kemp in his jigs and other roles (including *A Knack to Know a Knave* with Strange's in 1593) used the persona of the cunning country clown coming to town and making fools of city types, the kind of clown that Tarlton first made famous. Touchstone is the reverse, a court jester who turns himself into a country clown.

As you Like It was almost certainly the first play Shakespeare wrote for the Globe. The enigmatic apology for his playhouse in the Prologue's speech opening *Henry V*, often taken as a mock-apology for the grand new venue, dates from the period early in 1599 when the Globe was still being built. Jaques in *As you Like It* celebrates the new structure. His 'All the world's a stage' speech starts by paraphrasing the new playhouse's motto, *Totus mundus agit histrionem*.[29] In fact, the story of the building of the Globe and its financing was never a matter for celebration, but an even more sordid and desperate affair than most of the other company attempts to insert themselves in London. It shows more clearly than anything how precarious the playing life still was in the late 1590s. The conclusion to the story, fourteen years later, shines in a completely opposite colour. In this otherwise chronological narrative of the company's fortunes it may seem premature to describe the whole story of the first Globe's fourteen years now. But the story

---

[27] Giorgio Melchiori, 'Peter, Balthazar, and Shakespeare's art of doubling', *MLR* 78 (1983), 777–92, argues that the play was originally written in 1593, and that the part of Peter was developed later for Kemp. David Wiles, *Shakespeare's Clown* (Cambridge, 1987), 84–94, counters this view. *Romeo* was current on the stage in 1598.

[28] The evidence is slight, but the man who played Pistol in *Henry V* and the Host of the Garter in *Merry Wives* seems to have had a hand in creating the memorially transcribed manuscripts from which the two quartos were printed, in 1600 and 1602.

[29] The credibility of Malone's story of the new playhouse's motto is secured by several references in plays from 1600 and 1601. See Richard Dutton, '*Hamlet, An Apology for Actors*, and the sign of the Globe', *ShS* 41 (1989), 35–44.

underpins everything that the company did in the great years after the troubles of 1596–9, and gives it its most immediate and strongest context.

By Christmas 1598 the two Burbage sons had been struggling for nearly two years with the hostile landlord of the Theatre's site in the hope of securing a new lease. Giles Allen refused it to them, intending, he said, to pull the playhouse down and use its timbers 'for a better purpose'. The law on the question was difficult. Normally, any construction built on leasehold land reverted to the owner when the lease expired, so Allen had a good case in law. That was the principle that Ford cites so mournfully in *The Merry Wives of Windsor*, probably written in early 1597 when the lease was about to expire and the playhouse to be closed. In II. ii. the disguised Ford, jealous of his wife's loyalty, pretends to Falstaff that he is a forlorn gentleman who loves Mistress Ford, and incites Falstaff to woo her for him. He tells him that his married beloved is a property 'like a fair house built on another man's ground, so that I have lost my edifice by mistaking the place where I erected it'. Such a heavy-handed simile for the lack of sexual favour had a much closer application to the lost Theatre than to Ford's pretended problem. Ford gives the common-law position: the company's promoters had lost their playhouse when the lease expired.

In fact, James Burbage had tried to write in a precaution against this danger when he first took out the lease twenty-one years before. He inserted a proviso into the lease allowing him to dismantle the structure and remove it, should he wish to before the lease expired. Unfortunately by April 1597 it had expired, and then the law of ownership by the landlord came into play. In 1596 Burbage had been too set on the new Blackfriars to remember his old attempt at insurance, and by the next April the chance had gone. In the event, Cuthbert and Richard Burbage did take up the idea that was implicit in their father's proviso, but very belatedly, and illegally. At the end of 1598 they took out a lease on a new plot of land on the Bankside and signed up Peter Streete, a builder, to dismantle the Theatre's framing timbers and re-erect them on the new site as the skeleton for a new playhouse. Conscious of the dubious legal position, they hired Streete and twelve workmen to arrive on the site in the holiday time of 28 December, and to demolish the building as quickly as possible. Then on 20 January 1599, in a single day, before Allen woke up to what they were after, they took the framing timbers across the river to the site where the Globe was to be built. It was risky, because the law as Ford cited it was clearly against such an act. Allen, in fact, when he found what had happened, promptly went to law, accusing Streete of trespass, and started a long legal wrangle with the Burbages to reclaim the value of the building materials they had stolen, which he hopefully estimated at £800.[30]

That figure wildly exaggerates the value of the raw timbers that reappeared when the thatch was off the roof and the lath and plaster in-filling knocked out of the Theatre's frame. The huge 12-inch-square sections of prefabricated oak posts that made the polygonal frame, some of them over thirty feet long and weighing half a

---

[30] The legal documents relating to the Globe are described and quoted by Herbert Berry, *Shakespeare's Playhouses* (New York, 1987), chs. 4 and 6.

ton, were certainly the most expensive single structural item in the old building, but £800 was the price of an entire playhouse when finished, in-filling, thatch, gallery balusters, new plaster, painting, and all. Henslowe and Cholmley paid that amount to build the Rose in 1587. None the less, the cost of building the new playhouse for the Burbages was appallingly high, at about £700 even with the reused timbers, and since their inheritance was buried in their father's Blackfriars project they could not raise even that much cash to pay for it themselves. What they chose to do in order to raise the capital for the company's new playhouse was not necessarily entirely novel—there is some evidence to suggest that the Theatre's neighbour, the Curtain, had secured a similar financial underpinning—but it turned out to be an extraordinarily successful option, and it provided a model for other companies in the next century.

The two Burbages managed to find 50 per cent of the capital for the Globe between them. The rest they raised from other sharers in the company. Five of the sharing players thus joined Richard Burbage and his brother in becoming joint owners of the new structure. Heminges, Kemp, Phillips, Pope, and Shakespeare each provided 10 per cent of the building costs in return for 10 per cent of the equity. This put the playing company, or at least the six sharers who had put up the capital, into a novel position. For the first time they did not have to depend on a landlord or impresario as playhouse-owner, who took rent from them for their tenure, but were themselves owners of their workplace. For the six sharers who now became 'housekeepers' it meant a double income, their share of the daily takings plus a rather larger share of the daily rental. For two years they had paid rent for the Curtain, and had lacked a banker or landlord-impresario like Henslowe who could make them loans for new costumes and playbooks while taking his repayments from the daily takings. Now they still lacked finance, but they would be their own landlords. They could, in fact, become their own financiers. Most important, given that the first secure tenure of a playhouse had only been granted by the Privy Council five years before, they would have total security. In fact they had even better security of tenure than Henslowe's company, since the interests of their landlords now coincided with those of the tenants. In the first and merci- fully plague-free seasons they soon had better financial resources from the co- operative which took their rent and comprised a majority of the company's managing shareholders than they could ever have expected from outside financiers or impresarios.

It was on this basis that the Chamberlain's Men now went forward to build the new playhouse on its old frame. The shareholders' and housekeepers' limited finances in 1599 still meant that it had to be built economically. Giles Allen was pursuing his lawsuit against the Burbages, and twin attacks on the duopoly's grip were already threatened from the flanks with a third adult company and the two revived boy companies. The Chamberlain's was under-resourced compared with its rivals. Henslowe, when the Globe arrived only a few yards away from his Rose, had no hesitation in setting out to make the opposite move and build a new playhouse in the northern suburbs which the Theatre had just left. The cost of building the Fortune was substantial, but Henslowe had the money. Indeed, he still had enough resources at his disposal after the Fortune opened in 1600 to underwrite another company so that it could compete with the Chamberlain's alongside it at the old Rose.

The Chamberlain's had been under strain financially since 1597, and it was telling. When the young Swiss student Thomas Platter, doing the tourist thing and seeing everything London had to offer in the summer of 1599, went to the Globe on 21 September to see *Julius Caesar*, he distinguished the new Bankside playhouse that he chose to visit from its neighbours, the Swan and the Rose, by calling it 'the one with the thatched roof'. The choice of cheap thatch to top off the new Globe, rather than the more costly tiles which Henslowe used for the Fortune, was to prove a false economy fourteen years later. As a new workplace for the company the Globe was a distinctly cut-price job.

None the less, for its first ten years from 1599 until 1608 the Globe did its job superbly. It could only have been a second-best choice as a playhouse in James Burbage's eyes and perhaps those of his sons and the company at first, because it was an open amphitheatre, not the roofed hall like the inns in the city that Burbage had created in 1596. But it held its clientele against the competition of the boys at the hall theatres in the Blackfriars and at St Paul's. The company grew in status there. It was paid to perform at private places, at the Inns of Court, and at noblemen's houses in London and the country. It even flaunted the theft of one of the boy-company plays, *The Malcontent*, as a reprisal for the boys having performed the adults' 'Jeronimo'. Webster's Induction for the Chamberlain's Men's production of *The Malcontent* excuses the theft, and celebrates the repertory's most famous new acquisition by burlesquing Will Sly's playing of Osric in *Hamlet* in the process. From *As You Like It* and *Twelfth Night*, *Hamlet* and *Othello*, to *Antony and Cleopatra* and *Pericles*, the Globe became the sole venue for which Shakespeare's plays were composed. Through those ten years the company was privileged with more invitations to play at court than any other company. In 1603 the new king lost little time in making himself their patron, an accolade unique for an already-established group of players. The company was in its prime. When the queen's brother, King Christian of Denmark, came to London in the summer of 1606 the King's Men was the only group called on to entertain him, giving two plays at Greenwich and one at Hampton Court before he left on 9 August.[31]

The king's accolade was put to good use in 1608. In 1599 the two Burbages had chosen, with what calculation and foresight we cannot tell, to make some extra income from their silent hall playhouse in the Blackfriars by leasing it to a new boy company. Since they chose to do so while the Globe was under construction, their motive was more likely to have been a simple need for cash than anything so

[31] Henry N. Paul, *The Royal Play of Macbeth* (New York, 1950), was the first to suggest that *Macbeth* was written specifically for King Christian's visit. J. Leeds Barroll, *Politics, Plague and Shakespeare's Theater: The Stuart Years*, 147–8, demolishes his case.

ingenious as what it turned into, a device to get the new playhouse into operation by inserting a relatively innocuous company of boy players. In 1608, though, that money-making action brought them a major gain. The Blackfriars boy company had been getting into more and more trouble with the authorities over its deliberately outrageous programme of satires and plays with a political edge. It was also in financial difficulties, not so much because people were not attending its plays as because the programme of boy playing, much more restricted than the men's, being limited to no more than one performance a week, gave it less income.[32] By 1608 the boys' impresario and leaseholder, Henry Evans, had already once tried to surrender his lease back to the Burbages. The long plague-spotted closure that started in the summer of 1608 now caused him to withdraw altogether. The boys moved to another hall playhouse. The Blackfriars at long last, twelve years after James Burbage built it for them, came into the hands of the company's housekeepers.

The plague epidemic delayed its opening with its new occupants for nearly eighteen months, until the end of 1609, but that long break gave the company time to reassess the management system it had first introduced to finance the building of the Globe. Its effectiveness was evident. There was a basic and potentially dangerous difference between a share in a playing company, which depended on the life, status, and co-operation of the members, and so could not be treated as a passive piece of property, as against a share in a playhouse building, which could be inherited or sold outside the company like any ordinary property. The difficulties that emerged from this when segments of the Globe came into non-company hands had yet to start showing. So the company extended the system evolved for the Globe to the Blackfriars. On 9 August 1608 the Burbages divided its title between seven men. Richard and Cuthbert Burbage kept two shares, a smaller proportion than they had of the Globe. Phillips and Pope had both died, Pope at the end of 1603 and Phillips in 1605.[33] Their shares in the Globe had gone to William Sly and Henry Condell. So to Heminges and Shakespeare, the other survivors from the company's original housekeepers, the new contract added Sly and Condell as Blackfriars housekeepers. This made a good majority of King's players. The seventh share went to Thomas Evans, an outside financier. Sly died while the deal was being completed, so at the final count in 1609 the Blackfriars housekeepers were six, four of them players, with Cuthbert Burbage a fifth. There were some subsequent redistributions of the shares, Heminges and Condell taking Sly's portion, and in February 1612 William Ostler was cut in as a seventh housekeeper, but the principle that a large majority of the landlords should be the leading company players retained the vital basis for the arrangement.

[32] The frequency of boy-company performances has been debated, but the epilogue to *Eastward Ho!* is unambiguous in its promise to 'invite you hither once a week'.

[33] Pope's will is transcribed in *Playhouse Wills 1558–1642*, 68–71. He had a share in the Curtain as well as the Globe. Phillips's will is transcribed on 72–4. He was buried at Mortlake, where he had recently purchased a house.

Two things that happened almost together in the late summer of 1608 show more than could anything else the strength of the company's position. They had the Blackfriars playhouse at last, and they determined to use it. The agreement that they signed in August confirms their decision to break the long-standing ban on playing in the city, and to use a hall playhouse that had been barred to them twelve years before. This marked an advance in their status and their confidence; but behind that decision was a potential threat in the coincidental transfer by the king of the whole Blackfriars liberty into the city's control, which was confirmed in September. The company was confident that it could mount plays there daily where previously there had only been weekly performances, and could include their drum-and-trumpet plays where the boys had only offered string instruments and woodwinds. That confidence stood against the fact that they now had to do so under the direct aegis of the Lord Mayor and his long-running opposition to playing of any kind. Hindsight should not blind us to the likelihood that such confidence might easily have proved to be unjustified.

The eighteen-month closure for plague from July 1608 to December 1609 was expensive for all the companies. In the absence of any company accounts, it is the clearest possible sign not only of the company's confidence but of its growing prosperity in the first ten years at the Globe that they now chose to mount the most extravagant system of operation that any theatre management was ever able to run before the subsidized theatres of the late twentieth century came into being. With two playhouses now in their hands they could easily have rented one out to another company. Already more companies had patents to play in London than there were theatres for them to play in. Renting out one playhouse would have secured the King's Men's housekeepers a double income from the two sets of rents. The Privy Council's restriction on playing to just the duopoly was long gone by then and, besides the three adult companies with royal patrons, a fourth, the Duke of York's, was getting started. There were also two boy companies still in need of places to play. There was an ample supply of potential tenants for one of the company's two playhouses. But a higher income was not the sharers' and housekeepers' choice. Instead they chose to revert to the oldest system, even preceding what James Burbage tried for, so expensively, in 1596. They went back to the pre-1594 system where the companies played at the open amphitheatres in the summer and went indoors to play in rooms in the city inns for the winter season. In the previous winter, 1607–8, the weather had been so cold that the Thames froze over from December till February. That was no doubt another incentive to secure an indoor venue for the following winters. The main motive, though, stemmed from their new power. They could afford the self-indulgent and extravagant luxury of buying themselves a new system based largely on nostalgia for the old times.

So from 1609 onwards the Globe was in use for the months from May to September. That was when the summer helped to lengthen the plague bills and drove away the gentry and courtiers who could afford to escape into the country. The court was always out of town through July and August, and the lawyers at the

Inns of Court were on vacation. So the citizens and the poor stayed, and the Globe was kept open for them so long as the summer visits of plague made it possible. From September onwards, when the courtiers and lawyers came back to town, until after the closure for Lent, the company chose to play at the more costly Blackfriars, on the affluent western flank of the city.

To leave one playhouse empty while they used the other was extravagant enough. Their status and their income was by now evidently so healthy and they felt so comfortable that they had no need to rent either playhouse to a second company. There is not a shred of evidence that they were ever tempted to put the Globe or the Blackfriars to any use while the company was playing at the other place.[34] It was a proud, exclusive, and uneconomical choice. What makes this sense of luxury so remarkable is that a famous accident gave them the chance to economize four years later, when they had been given plenty of time to reconsider their own extravagance. Instead they went the other way. Their early false economy of thatching the Globe's galleries in 1599 caught them out in the summer season of 1613. On 29 June a piece of burning wadding from a small cannon fired at a performance of *Henry VIII* from over the stage lodged in the thatch covering the galleries, and the playhouse burned down. That disaster gave them a perfect excuse to forget the Globe and play instead throughout the year at the Blackfriars, which was already beginning to bring in better returns than the much more capacious but lower-priced amphitheatre. Instead they clubbed together again, and raised the money to rebuild the Globe from their own pockets. Not all the housekeepers could meet this exceptional demand. Augustine Phillips's heirs, still holding his housekeeper's share in the old Globe, defaulted, but Heminges and Condell bought the share, dividing its price and the related proportion of the costs of rebuilding a new Globe between them.

It was a very costly act of nostalgia, because the rebuilt Globe was made on a more lavish scale than its predecessor. Its reconstruction appears to have cost at least as much as any of the fourteen playhouses built in London between 1567 and 1629. Presumably Heminges and the other sharers felt that it was a sound investment, given the company's general well-being. Whether they also felt that it was important to maintain the broader appeal and the greater social spread of audiences for their repertoire of plays offered at the Globe, there is no way of telling. Yet the reconstruction of the Globe was unnecessary, and we can only speculate about what led them to do it. I have suggested elsewhere that they may have been reluctant to separate themselves entirely from the popular segment of their clientele by playing only at the Blackfriars, where the poorest seats cost a full day's wage for an artisan.[35] Christopher Beeston's troubles with a mob of apprentices when he took the Red

---

[34] Lionel Cranfield paid 10s. to see a play (presumably paying for his whole party) at the Blackfriars on 10 Jan. 1611 (A. P. Newton (ed.), *Cranfield Papers* (2 vols.; London, 1940–66), i. 232). Simon Forman saw four plays, three of them Shakespeare's, at the Globe in the summer of 1611 (E. K. Chambers, *William Shakespeare* (2 vols.; Oxford, 1930), ii. 337–41). These evidences from playgoing confirm that the company put the new system in place when playing resumed in 1610.

[35] See Gurr, 'Money or Audiences: The Impact of Shakespeare's Globe', *TN* 42 (1988), 3–14.

Bull's company to his new Cockpit hall playhouse in 1616 suggest that abandoning the amphitheatre altogether might have caused trouble.

Whatever it was, 1614 marks a turning-point in the company's history. It re-affirms the extravagant decision they first made in 1608 to run two playhouses for the one company. Their pre-eminence and their royal protection were never in doubt from then until 1642, which makes 1608 the most appropriate point to pause and look at the other developments of the first years under James. Such a turning-point, not the death of its resident poet a few years later, makes it convenient to break the history of the company as the King's Men here. Before the break, though, there is the other complex story of the changing repertory, personnel, and company practices of the Globe's first ten years.

The company celebrated the name of its new/old playhouse in the first plays Shakespeare wrote for it there, *As You Like It* and *Hamlet*. As Claudius said, *Hamlet* was 'loved of the distracted multitude', and it was set explicitly, as Hamlet said, 'in this distracted Globe'. That shows both the new security the company sensed it now had at its new workplace and the more general feeling that companies were no longer itinerant, moving from playhouse to playhouse as they had done till less than a decade past. The Fortune company showed much the same sense of now having a working 'home' by producing plays that exploited their own playhouse name, like *Old Fortunatus* and *Fortune's Tennis*. The Globe and the Fortune were the first and only playhouses to have their names celebrated in the plays written for them.

The story of the company's repertory affairs from the time of their accession to supreme patronage in 1603 up to the great change of 1608 is not easy to set in sequence. *Measure for Measure*, probably written during the 1603 closure, was ready for acting by 1604, and a few other new plays entered the repertoire in James's first year. The new court was far more avaricious for plays than Elizabeth had been, but since the royal patrons were all newcomers the companies were happy to give them plays at court of which most were revivals. The King's Men laid on *As You Like It* in 1603–4, and in 1604–5 *The Merry Wives*, *The Comedy of Errors*, *Henry V*, *The Merchant of Venice*, *Love's Labours Lost*, *Every Man Out*, and *Every Man In*, as well as the more recent *Othello* and *Measure for Measure*. The new royalty had a lot to catch up on. Probably, since the company only staged their more popular plays, all but one of them by Shakespeare or Jonson, the first court seasons were seen as the occasion to advertise the best of their older wares. But the demand for plays at the new court was unprecedentedly high, with eight plays in 1603–4 and another twelve demanded for 1604–5. Since it was usual to offer to the court the latest plays that had proved themselves in the repertory through the preceding months at the Globe, this soon created difficulties.

The company, evidently ready at first to rest on its laurels, ran out of new plays for the second Stuart season. A letter in 1604 to Cecil from Walter Cope, one of his agents, transmits Richard Burbage's justification for offering Queen Anne a revival of the old *Love's Labours Lost*. It also shows some of the pressures the company was under from the new as well as the older hands at court to offer novelty before the Lenten close-down. Cope wrote 'Burbage ys come, and sayes there is no newe playe that the quene hath not seene, but they have revyved an olde one, cawled *Loves Labore Lost*, which for wytt and mirthe he sayes will please her excedingly'.[36] New plays were what the court wanted, and the company evidently had nothing that had worked well enough at the Globe to offer besides what they had already presented. They actually repeated one play, *The Merchant of Venice*, but it stood for new twice, since the first performance was for the king, who demanded a repeat for the prince two nights later, 'Againe commanded By the Kings Majestie', as the Revels account notes.[37] The full list of the plays the company gave at court that season, with six of Shakespeare's old successes and two of his new plays in an unprecedented total of eleven performances, shows where they felt their strength was.

Nevertheless, our current familiarity with what A. C. Bradley called Shakespeare's 'central tragedies' should not be allowed to disguise the continuance in the company's repertoire of the kind of play that the Fortune company was more noted for. Despite the attrition that much of the repertory has suffered, we know that in the years from 1600 to 1608 the Chamberlain's and King's Men ran plays about devils, domestic melodramas, and citizen plays of exactly the kind that the Admiral's and Prince's Men ran at the Fortune as staples of their repertory. Amongst the non-Shakespeare devil plays that the company performed in these years are the romantic comedy *The Merry Devil of Edmonton* (1603 or earlier), which starts with a devil-conjuring induction, and a macabre anti-Papal tragedy of blood and devilry, *The Devil's Charter* (1606). Domestic dramas included *The London Prodigal* (1603–4), *The Yorkshire Tragedy* (1605–6), and *The Miseries of Enforced Marriage* (1606–7), all tragic or moralistic; *The Revenger's Tragedy*; and a broad citizen comedy in the old citizen-romantic tradition, *The Fair Maid of Bristow* (1603–4). *The London Prodigal* was set firmly in the citizen tradition. The name that Beaumont gave his heroine in his splendidly acute parody of citizen tastes and prodigal-son plays for the Blackfriars boy company in 1607, *The Knight of the Burning Pestle*, was Luce, the same as *The London Prodigal*'s heroine. Beaumont made the King's Men's play, printed in 1605 as a text by Shakespeare and the King's, into as prominent a subject for his mockery as the repertory of the Queen's Men at the Red Bull.

The company also kept re-engaging Jonson to write for them. They did take their revenge on him for forcing them to mock their own plays in *Every Man Out* in 1599 by taking a rather dubious dip into the Poetomachia when they supplemented the Paul's Boys' performances of *Satiromastix*, Dekker's attack on Jonson as the self-inflating Horace, by restaging it at the Globe. Jonson first returned to

---

[36] Quoted in *The Third Report of the Royal Commission on Historical Manuscripts* (London, 1872), iii. 3. 148. The 'Burbage' concerned might have been Cuthbert rather than Richard, who had plays to perform. But Richard was the payee at court, and Cuthbert involved himself more in the company's property management than its repertoire.

[37] *MSC* xiii. 9.

them in 1603, after James's accession and the company's elevation into the King's Servants, with his Roman tragedy *Sejanus*. It was not a success on stage,[38] provoking what a contemporary versifier called 'beastly rage',[39] and fascinating though its politics and its applications under the new king were, it cannot have pleased the King's Men. William Fennor defended it when it was published in 1616 by claiming that the gentry had liked it but the mob howled it down ('the multitude . . . screwed their scurvy jawes, and look't awry, | Like hissing snakes adjudging it to die').[40] Jonson's other tragedy, *Catiline*, given to the King's Men in 1611, was disliked even more generally, according to Edmund Gayton, who reported much later that 'the judicious part of the Auditory condemn'd it equally with those that did not understand it'.[41] Jonson persisted by offering the company a comedy, *Volpone*, in 1605, which was far more successful than his tragedy. It stands rather intriguingly as a comic contrary, unnatural children and all, to its stable-mate which the company produced at about the same time, *King Lear*.[42]

Shakespeare's 1605 tragedy is something of an enigma in political terms, though it is also by some way the most explicit indication that the company was concerned with the political issues that interested their royal master. In 1605 James was promoting the union of his two kingdoms, against strong parliamentary opposition in London. To mount a play about 'the division of the kingdom' was a matter that any informed watcher could apply quite directly, if upside down, to the contemporary debate in 1605. To use an old story featuring dukes of Albany and Cornwall made that application unavoidable, since Prince Henry was Duke of Cornwall (as the Prince of Wales still is today) and his younger brother had been made Duke of Albany. Nobody there for the presentation of the play at court on the opening night of the 1606 Christmas season could possibly have missed these applications as an inverted image of the still-disunited kingdoms of England and Scotland. King Lear himself, in any minimally comprehending reaction to the play's events, must have been seen as a clear antithesis to James. He is a ruler who brings his kingdom to disaster through his decision to divide it; James was arguing for the opposite. So in an immediate, if superficial, review of the play, the court's spectators might see the King's Men offering support to their patron through their play's obvious 'application'. What else of political weight there is in the play, and what the significance is of the revisions that appear to have been introduced for the play's revival in 1611 when the union of the kingdoms had died as an issue, are matters

[38] Francis Osborne, writing in the 1650s, claimed to have been at the first performance, where 'I amongst others hissed *Sejanus* off the stage, yet after sat it out, not only patiently but with content and admiration'. *The True Tragicomedy formerly played at Court: A Play by Francis Osborne*, ed. Lois Potter (New York, 1983).

[39] *Ben Jonson*, xi. 317.

[40] *Ben Jonson*, ix. 191. Francis Osborne cannot have been much older than ten in 1603, when he joined in with what Fennor calls 'the multitude'.

[41] Ibid. 241.

[42] The peculiar resemblances between the comedy and the tragedy, especially in their shared images of monsters and monstrosity, are set out by Sidney Musgrove, *Shakespeare and Jonson* (Auckland, 1958), 21–39.

beyond the scope of this book.[43] Whatever political allegiances the King's Men chose to lay before the court (and they had a good year after its first staging to think about whether they should offer *King Lear*), they were not prepared to offer anything like the satirical scoffing at courtiers and Scotsmen that characterized the Blackfriars boy-company's repertory at this time and got them into terminal trouble.

The company's readiness to use older plays at court seems to have had its effect on the relatively smaller number of new plays introduced up to 1608. Shakespeare's own rate of production slowed after James came to the throne, possibly because he felt the company could float safely on his first twenty-eight plays. Besides *King Lear* and *Volpone*, all we know of the company's additions to its repertory in these years are the four domestic dramas noted above, a few plays that copied the other companies, like *Cromwell*, probably the two 'devil' plays, a comedy, a tragedy, and another play of blood, *The Revenger's Tragedy*, printed in 1607, plus the markedly slower inflow of eight new Shakespeares over the eight years from 1601. Shakespeare's exclusive concentration on tragedies (*Othello, Lear, Macbeth, Timon*) and Roman histories (*Antony and Cleopatra, Coriolanus*) at the expense of comedies between 1602–3 (*All's Well* and then *Measure for Measure*) and 1607 (the return to Arcadian romance with *Pericles*), has no easy explanation. Jonson's *Volpone* might have been pushed on the company as a compensation for Shakespeare's own narrowed focus.

However apparently conservative were the texts that survive from this period of the company's repertory, the audiences through these years were certainly broad-spectrum. They included a party put together by the Venetian ambassador to London, Giorgio Giustinian. He took the French ambassador and his wife in his party, together with the chief Secretary to the Florentinian embassy and other dignitaries, to see *Pericles*, the company's newest and most talked-about play, in 1607–8. The whole party commandeered the lords' rooms at the Globe at a cost of over twenty crowns or £5.[44] The Inns of Court and the universities also continued to patronize the company. As part of the credentials for the first quarto of *Hamlet* in 1603 its title-page declared that it had been performed at the universities of Cambridge and Oxford. Jonson made the same claim in his dedication to the first edition of *Volpone* in 1607.[45] The company also continued to dominate performances at court, which grew in number greatly under James. An additional help was

[43] See Gary Taylor and Michael Warren (ed.), *The Division of the Kingdoms* (Oxford, 1983), and Leah Marcus, *Puzzling Shakespeare: Local Reading and its Discontents*, 148–59.

[44] William B. Rye, *England as Seen by Foreigners in the Days of Elizabeth and James I* (London, 1865), 61. Leeds Barroll narrows the possible dates for the visit to May–June 1606, Apr. 1607, or Apr.–July 1608. The last is the most likely. See Barroll, *Politics, Plague and Shakespeare's Theater*, 192–3.

[45] There is something a little over-assertive about these boasts, because Cambridge University banned all public performances of plays at the university as early as 1595. In a parody of their retreat to the suburbs of London, travelling companies sometimes played at Chesterton outside the town instead: see *REED, Cambridge*, ii. 984–6. It is possible that the title-pages were boasting of academic credibility while concealing their marginal locations for performance near the universities, although it is not like Jonson to be so deceitful.

that as the king's company it began to receive from James's own purse some compensation for the plague closures: £30 in 1603, five marks in 1605,[46] and £40 in 1609, the largest amounts being paid after the longest closures.

HUNSDON'S MEN, *c.* 1564–1586
See also Chamberlain's, King's Men.

Plays
Beauty and Housewifery (lost).

London Playhouses
Theatre?

At Court
27 Dec. 1582.

Travelling
Leicester 1564–5 'my lorde of Hundons plears more than was gaytheryd', 5s. / Norwich 1564–5, 20s.; 'with iiiid for brede & Drynke' / Dartmouth 1564–5, 10s. 8d. / Plymouth 1564–5, 13s. 4d. / Beverley 1565 'to the Lord of hunsden his players', 6s. 8d. / Canterbury 1565–6 'my lord off hwnsdens players', 8s. / Lydd 1565–6, 5s. 6d. / Dover 1565–6 'my Lorde of hownesdownes players', 10s. / Gloucester 1565–6 'in rewardes to the lorde hundsons plaiars the makeinge of the scaffolde in the bothall & the drinkinge', 12s. 8d. / Newcastle Apr. 1566 'to my lord of hounsdons palers whiche was plaid in the marchant court', 20s. / Bridgwater, Somerset Mar.–June 1566, 10s. / Bristol June–July 1566, 13s. 4d. / Canterbury 1566–7, 10s. / Norwich Dean and Chapter Receivers' acct. 1575–6 'Servienti domini Hunsdon vocato the lord Hunsdons payer', 5s. / York 8 Sept. 1580 'my lord of hunsdons servauntes beinge players of interludes shall play this after none at the Comon hall at two of the clock in the after none and to have such reward as other players have heretofore had in tymes past' / Norwich Dean and Chapter Receivers' acct. 1581–2, 10s. / Nottingham Jan. 1582, 3s. 4d. / Gloucester 1581–2 'to my lorde Huntesdounes players', 13s. 4d. / Bath June 1582, 10s. 2d. / Ludlow 31 July 1582, 10s. / Doncaster 1582, 10s. / Norwich 1582–3, 20s. / Exeter Apr. 1583, 10s. / Bristol June 1583 'my Lord Hunsdonns and my Lords Morleis players being bothe of one Companeye for a playe in the yelde hall before master Mayor the Aldermen and the reste of the Counsell', 13s. 4d. / Bath June 1583 'the lorde of Hunsdons players in June', 7s. 8d. / Exeter July 1583, 10s. / Dover 12 June 1585 'my Lord admiralles and my Lord of Hunsdons players', 20s. / Leicester 1585–6 'to the Lorde Chamberlens and the Lord Admiralles Playors more then was gathered', 4s. / Coventry 1586 'to the Lord Chamberlayns men', 3s. 4d. / Saffron Walden 1587–8.

THE CHAMBERLAIN'S MEN, 1594–1603
See also Hunsdon's, King's Men.

Plays

All's Well that Ends Well, As You Like It, A Comedy of Errors (old), *Every Man in his Humour, Every Man out of his Humour, The Fair Maid of Bristow, Hamlet, 1* and *2 Henry IV, Henry V, 1, 2* and *3 Henry VI* (old), *Julius Caesar, King John* (old?), *A Larum for London, The London Prodigal, Love's Labours Lost, The Malcontent* (old), *The Merchant of Venice, The Merry Wives of Windsor, A Midsummer Night's Dream, Much Ado About Nothing, Oldcastle* (lost?),[47] *Othello, Richard II, Richard III* (old), *Romeo and Juliet* (old?), *Satiromastix* (old), *The Taming of the Shrew* (old), *Titus Andronicus* (old), *Troilus and Cressida, Twelfth Night, Two Gentlemen of Verona* (old), *A Warning for Fair Women.*

Playing Sharers

George Bryan, Richard Burbage, John Heminges, Will Kemp, Augustine Phillips, Thomas Pope, William Shakespeare, William Sly [1598 *Every Man In*: Will Shakespeare, Richard Burbage, Augustine Phillips, John Heminges, Henry Condell, Thomas Pope, Will Sly, Christopher Beeston, Will Kemp, John Duke].

Hired Men

Alexander Cook,[48] John Lowin [in *Sejanus*. Both were later sharers in King's Men], James Sands [Phillips and Sly both left him money in their wills].

Assistants

Thomas Vincent ['that was a Book-keeper or prompter at the Globe playhouse'[49]].

London Playhouses

Newington Butts, Theatre, Curtain, first Globe.

At Court

26, 27 Dec. 1594, 26 Jan. 1595, 26, 27, 28 Dec.; 6 Jan. 1596, 22 Feb.; 26, 27 Dec.; 1; 6 Jan. 1597, 6, 8 Feb.; 26 Dec.; 1, 6 Jan. 1598, 26 Feb.; 26 Dec.; 1 Jan. 1599, 20 Feb.; 26 Dec.; 6 Jan. 1600, 3 Feb.; 26 Dec., 6 Jan. 1601, 24 Feb.; 26, 27 Dec.; 1 Jan. 1602, 14 Feb.; 26 Dec., 2 Feb. 1603.

Travelling

Marlborough 1593–4, 2s. 8d. / Cambridge town 1594–5, 40s. / Ipswich 1595 'the Lord Chamberlains players', 40s. / Faversham, Kent 'about Lamas' (1 Aug.) 1596 'my Lord Hunsdouns plaiers', 16s. / Dover 1596–7, 13s. 4d. / Marlborough 1596–7, 6s. 4d. / Faversham, Kent 1596–7, 13s. 4d. / Bath 1596–7, 20s. / Rye, Sussex Aug. 1597, 20s. / Bristol Sept. 1597, 30s. / Norwich 8 Mar. 1600 'to Kempe the Lord Chamberleyne his servante', 40s.[50]

---

[47] Roslyn Knutson, *The Repertory of Shakespeare's Company*, 95, suggests that the 'Old Castle' played at a private house in 1600 might have been a play written as the Chamberlain's Company's response to the Admiral's *1 Sir John Oldcastle*. That would fit it to the fashion for plays based on Foxe.

[48] His will is transcribed in *Playhouse Wills 1558–1642*, 94.

[49] John Taylor, *Taylor's Feast* (1638), quoted in Bentley, *The Profession of Player in Shakespeare's Time, 1590–1642*, 81.

[50] This was Kemp's solo visit, after his famous dance in Feb. and Mar. from London to Norwich, not a company performance.

KING'S MEN, 1603–1608
See also Hunsdon's, Chamberlain's Men.

Plays
Antony and Cleopatra, Coriolanus, The Devil's Charter, King Lear, Macbeth, Measure for Measure, The Merry Devil of Edmonton, The Miseries of Enforced Marriage, Pericles, The Revenger's Tragedy, Sejanus, Timon of Athens, Volpone, The Yorkshire Tragedy (Chamberlain's).

Playing Sharers
Richard Burbage, Henry Condell, Richard Cowley, John Heminges, Laurence Fletcher [patent 1603], William Shakespeare, Nicholas Tooley [Augustine Phillips's will of 4 May 1605 names as 'fellows'[51] William Shakespeare, Henry Condell, Christopher Beeston ('my servant'), Robert Armin, Richard Cowley, Alexander Cook, Nicholas Tooley; Richard Burbage, John Heminges and William Sly are also named as executors].

Hired Men and Assistants
Thomas Vincent 'that was a Book-keeper or prompter at the Globe playhouse'.

Apprentices
[Augustine Phillips' will names 'my late apprentice' Samuel Gilborne, and as current apprentice James Sands].

London Playhouses
First Globe.

At Court
Required to attend between 9 and 27 Aug. 1603; performed 2, 26, 27, 28 Dec. 1603 before king, 30 Dec. 1603, 1 Jan. 1604 before prince, 1 Jan., 2, 19 Feb. 1604 before king; 1 Nov. (*Othello*), 4 Nov. (*Merry Wives*), 26 Nov. (*Measure for Measure*), 28 Dec. 1603 (*Comedy of Errors*), 7 Jan. 1605 (*Henry V*), 8 Jan. (*Every Man Out*), 2 Feb. (*Every Man In*), 3 Feb. (not named), 10 and 12 Feb. (*Merchant of Venice*), 11 Feb. (*The Spanish Maze*) before king; ten plays (not named) between Christmas and 24 Mar. 1606; 26 Dec. 1606 (*King Lear*), 29 Dec. (not named), 4, 6, 8 Jan. 1607, 2 Feb. (*The Devil's Charter*), 5, 15, 27 Feb. before king; 26, 27, 28 Dec., 2, 6 (two, unnamed), 7, 9, 17 (two), 26 Jan. 1608, 2, 7 Feb. before king; 12 unnamed plays Christmas 1608–9.

Travelling
Shrewsbury 1602–3, 20s. / Ipswich 1602–3 'for a reward', 26s. 8d. / Coventry Nov. acct. 1603, 40s. / Bridgnorth, Shropshire 1603–4, 40s. / Oxford town 1603–4, 20s. / Bath 1603, 30s. / Barnstaple, Devon 1604–5, 10s. / Fordwich, Kent 6 Oct. 1605, 10s. / Oxford town 9 Oct. 1605, 10s. / Faversham, Kent 1605–6, £1. / Maidstone 1605–6 '& to the Trompetters', £2. 5s. / Saffron Walden 1605–6, 6s. 8d. /

---

[51] G. E. Bentley, *The Profession of Player*, 19, argues that all the 'fellows' named by Phillips must have been fellow-sharers.

Marlborough 1606, 23s. 4d. / Leicester Aug. 1606, 40s. / Dover 30 Aug. 1606, £2. / Dunwich, Suffolk 1606–7, 6s. 8d. / Oxford town 7 Sept. 1607, 20s. / Barnstaple, Devon 1607–8, 20s. / Marlborough 1607–8, 20s. / Coventry 29 Oct. 1608, 20s.

17 The Lesser Elizabethan Competitors: Oxford's, Hertford's, and Chandos's

Throughout Elizabeth's reign companies were struggling to get a secure place in the steep hierarchy of players with noble patrons. That security meant heading for London, both as cause and effect of rising in the hierarchy. In Chapter 10, which examines the early companies, some of these strugglers have been discussed already. A few other companies belong mainly to the last twenty years of Elizabeth's reign, standing below and competing for distinction with the Queen's Men. The strongest five of these competitors, Strange's/Derby's and Pembroke's, the Chamberlain's, the Admiral's, and Worcester's, have four chapters to themselves. This chapter deals with the other companies that at one time or another from 1580, however briefly, found a foothold in London. The first and most intriguing of these, chiefly for the ways in which its eccentric patron intervened in its fortunes, is Oxford's Men.

Francis Meres in *Palladis Tamia*, his 1598 equation of England's writers with the Greeks and Romans, praised the earl of Oxford as a playwright. 'The best for Comedy amongst us bee Edward, Earle of Oxforde' along with Gager of Oxford University, Rowley of Cambridge, plus Richard Edwards and Lyly, Lodge, Gascoigne, Greene, Shakespeare, Nashe, Heywood, Munday, Chapman, Porter, Wilson, Hathway, and Chettle. He does not omit many current writers. The Edward Vere he specifies was the seventeenth earl, Burghley's son-in-law, and father-in-law of both the sixth earl of Derby and of Phillip Herbert, the third earl of Pembroke's younger brother, later the fourth earl. For the last twenty-four years of his life, up to his death in 1604, Oxford was patron of a playing company.

The seventeenth earl was born in 1550, and came to the title in 1562. His ancestors had kept companies of players, the last appearance of the sixteenth earl's company being at Ipswich in 1561–2. The twelve-year-old new earl did not retain his father's group, and the early Oxford's disappears from the records in 1564–5. For the seventeenth earl to acquire one at the age of thirty, in 1580, was natural enough. The actual circumstances in which he did restart an Oxford's company, though, were hardly routine, to judge by the contemporary squib about the Duttons who led the new group. The squib was prefaced by a note alleging that '*The Duttons and theyr fellow-players forsakyng the Erle of Warwycke theyr mayster, becames followers of the Erle of Oxford, and wrot themselves his* COMOEDIANS, *which certayne Gentlemen altered and made* CAMOELIANS.' The verses themselves are an eloquent specimen of the old tradition of flyting. They conclude

> The crest is a lastrylle whose feathers ar blew,
> In signe that these fydlers will never be trew;
> Whereon is placed the horne of a gote,

Because they ar chast, to this is theyr lotte,
For their bravery, indented and parted,
And for their knavery innebulated.

Mantled lowsy, wythe doubled drynke,
Their ancient house is called the Clynke;
Thys Posy they beare over the whole earthe,
Wylt please you to have a fyt of our mirthe?
But reason it is, and heraultes allowe wele,
That fidlers should beare their armes in a towelle.[1]

The Dutton brothers had already passed through Lane's and Clinton's in the 1570s before joining Warwick's in 1575, so the sneer had its point. Whether they actually spent time in the Clink prison in Southwark, a repository for debtors, is more doubtful.

The earl, like other great lords, was conspicuous at court in 1578–9 in the dispute over the queen's Alençon marriage. He refused to participate in a court dance in August 1578 on the grounds that 'he did not want to entertain Frenchmen', but he shared in a court masque with the earl of Surrey and two other lords for the French ambassador a few months later, in the Shrovetide festivities on 3 March 1579. Clearly he felt himself to be a power at court, and he may have decided to set up a company to give himself an even stronger presence. If so, the Duttons seized their chance. These were the years when the great lords were beginning to use their companies for self-advertisement at court in the competitive wrangles that helped to prompt the establishment of the Queen's Men. Possibly Oxford's share in the 'device' for the French in March 1579 helped to spur his ambition as a composer of stage spectacles and the eventual writer of plays that Meres hailed in 1598. He was certainly an independent and very persistent promoter of playing groups, both of men and of boys, for the next twenty years. And with Burghley as his father-in-law he had the kind of leverage that could be used to promote his various companies. The scandals that became attached to his name in 1581–2 did not affect his patronage in any very obvious way.

The Duttons, in any case, were thrustful enough to make their new company prominent in London from the start. They were playing at the city's leading playhouse, the Theatre, in April 1580, as we know from a brawl the players got into there with some Inns-of-Court students. Following a complaint by the Lord Mayor about trouble at the playhouse on 10 April, the Privy Council committed Laurence Dutton and Robert Leveson of the company to the Marshalsea on 13 April.[2] While the justices were examining this 'certaine fraye betwene the servauntes of th'erle of Oxforde and the gentlemen of the Innes of the Courtes', the Council ordered a closure for the plague from 17 April until the end of October (Michaelmas), so the tangle with the law cost them little in terms of playing time. But the affair dragged on. The judges to examine the case were not appointed until 26 May, when the

---

[1] *ES* ii. 98–9.   [2] The papers about the incident are quoted in *ES* iv. 279–80.

Duttons were travelling again, although the matter must have been settled fairly soon after that.

By 21 June the company was at Cambridge, where the vice-chancellor gave them twenty shillings not to play. At the same time he wrote to Oxford's father-in-law excusing himself for doing so, in a letter which shows something of what Oxford was promoting in pursuit of his new enthusiasm. Both Burghley and the Lord Chamberlain, Sussex, had sent letters recommending Oxford's Men. Burghley's letter, dated 9 June, was pointed and succinct.

Where the bearers hereof servauntes to the Right honorable my very good Lord the Erle of Oxford are desierous to repaire to that universitie and there to make shewe of such playes and enterludes as have bene by them heretofore played by them publykely, aswell before the Queens majestie as in the Citie of London, and intend to spend iiij or v. daies there in Cambridg as heretofore they have accustomed to do with other matters and arguments of late yeres, and because they might the rather be permitted so to do without empechment or lett of yow the vicechauncelor or other the heades of howses, have desired my lettre unto yow in their favor.[3]

The wording shows that the players had solicited the letter from Burghley. They could only have got at him through their patron. There is in fact no record of Oxford's company playing at court before the 1583–4 season, so the basis for the claim that they had performed before the queen is dubious. It may have been a formula letter adapted for the specific recipient, without too much concern for the precise truth. Alternatively, it may have been distorted by the long chain of communication, from the company to Oxford to Burghley to Burghley's secretary, during which the plea became more and more generalized. The letter itself is specific, from Burghley to the Cambridge vice-chancellor. How many others Burghley's secretary might have written, and to whom, there is no record. The company must have expected to carry and to need to carry with them a series of such letters to back their requests to each local authority for leave to play.

In his reply to Burghley, the vice-chancellor acknowledged the force of the request that Oxford's Men should be allowed to 'shew their cunninge in certayne playes allready practysed by them before the Queens Majestie'. In defence of his position, however, he pointed out that 'the cause and feare of the pestilence is not yet vanished & gone, this hote tyme of ye yeare'. With the midsummer fair and 'ye commencement tyme at hande, which requireth rather diligence in stodie then dissolutenesse in playes', he felt that he had the right to refuse them leave to play, and paid them 'but xx s towardes their charges'. He had recently, he added defensively, refused permission to Leicester's Men for the same reasons. Evidently Leicester's were not fortunate enough to be carrying a letter from Burghley.

There is no evidence that the Oxford's company appeared regularly in London thereafter. Changes certainly came in 1583, because John Dutton was taken from

---

[3] This letter and the reply are quoted in *REED, Cambridge*, i. 290–1.

them for the Queen's Men. An Oxford's company did play at court in the following season and the one after that. But with the establishment of the Queen's Men Oxford himself had taken up John Lyly and a boy company, and the court records do not make it clear whether the performances in 1583–4 were by the adult company or by the new boy company. In the first year of the Queen's Men, the Queen's played three times at court to twice by an Oxford's group. The Oxford's payee at court was Lyly, which suggests that it was the boy company. In the 1584–5 season the Queen's Men gave five performances and a company of Oxford's boys the only other, while an Oxford's adult company offered a show of tumbling. Given the absolute priority accorded to the Queen's Men among the adult companies from 1583 onwards, and that the only other company to perform in the 1583–4 season was the Chapel Children, it is most likely that the Oxford's company called to play at court in both years was his new boy group.

The story of the Oxford's boys is told in Chapter 13. The adult company kept itself alive in the country, and they were admitted to perform 'activities' at court in the 1584–5 season with John Symons added to their strength. Symons was in Strange's in 1583, and later joined the Queen's. Chambers thinks he was almost exclusively a tumbler, not a player, though the evidence is pretty tenuous.[4] If he was, he may have been drawn into Oxford's after the 1583 reshuffle, while Oxford himself was concentrating on his boy company. Outside London, the adults are recorded extensively around the country for a year or so, in what looks like a regular touring route. It seems to have consisted of a range from Gloucestershire and Somerset to Exeter and other places in Devon, the usual southern circuit including Southampton, Sussex and Kent, Coventry and other places in the Midlands, and East Anglia. York joined the circuit a little later. After the first two years the number of recorded stops shrank sharply and was confined to East Anglia. The company's last recorded appearance was at Maidstone in Kent in 1590, the year before the Oxford's boy company was stopped. A single appearance at Faversham in Kent after five silent years is the only sign of life before they returned to the assault on London at the end of the century.

After his first burst of enthusiasm at the end of the 1570s, there is no sign that Oxford took any direct concern for his adult players. Meres' note of his playwriting might apply to any point in his career. From its context, his writing most probably fits the early 1580s when the Queen's were started at about the time the earl first employed Lyly, rather than the 1590s when Meres wrote his account.

The company renewed its activities after a break of ten years, at the end of the century. It is not recorded around the country at all during the plague-free years between 1597 and 1602, and from its renewal in about 1600 may have concentrated its efforts entirely in London. That gives a strong indication that it was a new company set up in the hope that it might be able to join the duopoly. Two of its plays were registered for printing in 1600 and 1601, *The Weakest Goeth to the Wall*,

---

[4] *ES* ii. 101, 119.

and the lost *History of George Scanderbarge*. The company was evidently at least on the fringes of the metropolis then, since they had access to the London publishers. The text of *The Weakest* that has survived fits it to the mid-1590s, when the old fashion for plays enacting familiar proverbs gained a renewed life.[5]

They succeeded to some extent in their London struggles to get the third foothold by merging with Worcester's at the end of 1601. The combined grouping was then given a Privy Council licence to play at the Boar's Head as London's third official company. At that time Oxford was only two years from his death, and had long lost the ambition he showed in the early 1580s to use his company for advertising himself at court. Worcester was younger, stronger and a much more pushy patron. There is no sign that Oxford sought to renew his company as a separate entity after 1602. The subsequent history of the merged company is told in Chapter 18, under the Worcester's / Queen Anne's title.

Of the other two companies that belong in this category, one gains entry here only because of its two widely separated appearances at court; the other for its presence on the fringes through the 1590s, and its eventual gift of a player to the Chamberlain's Men. Hertford's Men was a marginal company so far as London performances are concerned, but for different reasons it did play twice at court over an interval of eleven years, in two of the more testing seasons for the Master of the Revels, on Twelfth Night, 6 January 1592, and again on Twelfth Night in January 1603.

Viewed from that angle the Hertford's company's history is largely a reflection of the curiously precarious life of its patron. The second company's patron, Lord Chandos, came from a family which traditionally ran a major company with a long and fairly distinguished record of touring. It had a noted clown, who also did one-man acts. The clown, but not the company, ended up in London. Chandos's company never played at court, but it eventually gave Robert Armin to the Chamberlain's.

Chambers rightly called Hertford's 'among the most obscure of the companies'.[6] Its patron, Edward Seymour, the first earl of Hertford, was the eldest son of the Edward Seymour, duke of Somerset, who was executed by Mary for his attempt to secure the throne for Lady Jane Grey and the Protestant Church. Elizabeth created him earl of Hertford at her accession, but he was never firmly in royal favour, because his first wife was Lady Catherine Grey, who according to Henry VIII's notorious will should have been Elizabeth's heir. Such proximity to the royal line was dangerous. After Catherine's death in 1568, the earl married the daughter of the first Lord Howard of Effingham, which made him brother-in-law to Charles Howard, the Lord Admiral. Only three years younger than Howard, he may well have taken a cue from his relative over starting his playing company, because it is first found in the records in Kent in 1581–2.

[5] See Roslyn Knutson, *The Repertory of Shakespeare's Company*, 42.   [6] *ES* ii. 116.

Its subsequent appearances were irregular and infrequent. In its first decade it ranged from Canterbury to Newcastle, though its name appears so infrequently that we have to wonder whether it had a consistent life at all. The records grow more frequent near 1590, and include visits to Newcastle in October 1590, Leicester on 22 November, and Bristol, Marlborough, and Southampton in 1591–2. Through these last years it must have been growing in status, since its first court appearance was on Twelfth Night 1592. That honour, though, may have owed a lot to the three-day visit Elizabeth paid to the earl at his house at Elvetham in Hampshire on 20 September 1591, on her summer progress through Surrey, Sussex, and Hampshire.

This progress, which also took in Edmund Tilney's house in Leatherhead and Southampton's estate at Tichfield, was the climax of Elizabeth's eight-week-long tour, taking most of its final week. To celebrate this honour the earl laid on a series of lavish entertainments, which impressed the queen so much that she told him 'hereafter he should find the rewarde therof in her especiall favour'.[7] Like most such shows, the Elvetham entertainment was expensively mounted, with set speeches, a water show, and a concert of Thomas Morley's music with dances, songs, and masquing. Besides a speech by a poet, who may have been Nicholas Breton, there were enough scenes, set-piece play-acting, and formal speeches to warrant the earl using his players as participants in at least some of the elaborately planned shows. It was either their displays or some intervention by Elizabeth herself with the Master of the Revels to confirm her favour that must explain their sole appearance at court in the exceptional and innovatory Christmas season that followed. In that season Strange's outranked the Queen's by six performances to one, and Hertford's was the only other company to play.[8]

For all the shifts in playing membership of the companies, 1592 was a good time to be in London. The plague was threatening but not yet overwhelming. Strange's had moved to the Rose, and apart from Pembroke's, most likely playing at the Theatre, no other company had the stature to match them. The Queen's was divided and touring, and London had the Curtain available for a third company. There was a good chance for the right group. But Hertford's proved not to be strong enough. They kept on touring the south throughout 1592 and 1593 without ever re-establishing themselves in London after their one court performance, and they then vanish from the records for some years.

The earl's credit did not last long with the queen, because in 1595 he aroused the increasingly paranoid Elizabeth's suspicions again by seeking to have his marriage to Catherine Grey validated. In the wake of Peter Wentworth's pamphlets about the succession issue that was a dangerous venture.[9] By then, in any case, the new

---

[7] See *ES* i. 123–4, iv. 66. An account of the entertainment was printed a month after the show.

[8] Curt Breight, 'Realpolitik and Elizabethan Ceremony: The Earl of Hertford's Entertainment of Elizabeth at Elvetham, 1591', *Renaissance Quarterly*, 45 (1992), 20–48, has a detailed analysis of the show and its political import. He finds no evidence that Elizabeth did show Hertford any favour afterwards.

[9] Wentworth, an MP, was put in the Tower for his presumptuousness, and died there six years later.

duopoly was in force, and that kept the other companies on the margins. Hertford's reappeared at Coventry in 1596–7, came back in the traditional near-London territory of East Anglia through 1601 and 1602, and went to the west in 1602. By then it had acquired the itinerant Martin Slater, formerly of the Admiral's, as its leader. He was the payee for the company's second court appearance in Elizabeth's last season, again on Twelfth Night, in 1603.

Given that Elizabeth's health was the subject of close study at this time, it is of course possible that this final appearance at court by the company may have been a further sign of the earl's ambition to capitalize on his first marriage by reimposing his presence at court once Elizabeth's strength was recognized by everybody to be failing. In a season otherwise dominated by the duopoly (two Chamberlain's performances, three Admiral's, one by Paul's Boys), the arrival of this outsider group which had no regular playing-place in London and very infrequent appearances elsewhere is quite striking. But there is nothing to say why the company received this favour, unless it came from Elizabeth's visits in the preceding December to her two most loyal Privy Councillors and player-patrons, George Carey at Blackfriars and Hertford's brother-in-law, Charles Howard, at Arundel House. Howard might have tried to do his brother-in-law a last favour by putting in a word to secure a place for the company in the court revels, repeating its 1592 success. Hertford himself might have pushed him into it.

After Elizabeth's death, though, and the new order that the royal patrons set up in 1603–4, the company fell back. Hertford's did run on as a touring company for many more years. Their lord did not die until 1621, when he was almost eighty-two, and he seems to have maintained them in his livery for his own occasional entertainment throughout his last years. They played for the earl of Derby at his house in Lancashire in December 1606, and the earl wrote to the Chester authorities asking leave for them to play there before they returned to entertain his household over Christmas. Nothing in the Chester records indicates that the mayor did what he asked.

Giles Brydges, the third Lord Chandos, also entertained Elizabeth on one of her progresses through the home counties, at his house, Sudeley Castle, in September 1592.[10] The usual Arcadian pastoral, his entertainment included speeches by an old shepherd, and an elaborate masque with long speeches which can only have been staged by professional players. That entertainment, though, unlike the Hertford one the previous year, did not lead to a subsequent appearance at court for the company. As a playing group, Chandos's had been in existence since at least 1582, though with no sign of any periods being spent in London as part of its touring circuit. Unlike most of the nobly patronized companies, it seems mainly to have worked as a family accessory. William Brydges, who became the fourth Lord Chandos in 1594, kept the company on until his death in 1602, and his son

[10] *ES* iv. 66.

continued it after that. Whether Armin's transfer to the Chamberlain's Men in 1599 is a mark of the company's proximity to London at that time it is impossible to say. Armin seems to have had a solo act which he took on tour as well as travelling with the company. His reputation may have travelled more widely than his company. Equally, he may have been identified as a possible replacement for Kemp by the Chamberlain's when they met him on their travels.

In 1599, though, when the Chamberlain's took him on, they had not been playing outside London for two years. By that time Armin may have been working and touring independently of the Chandos playing company. There are some hints that through the 1590s he might have used Chandos's livery for a one-man touring act that took him on quite different paths from the company's. Such an act could easily have brought him to London. In any case, the absence of any indications about a London role or performances in London for the Chandos company as a whole excludes them from the stricter purview of this book.

OXFORD'S PLAYERS, 1560–1563, 1580–1602
[United with Worcester's 1602].

Plays
The Weakest Goeth to the Wall, The History of George Scanderbarge (lost).

Playing Sharers
Laurence Dutton, Robert Leveson, John Symons.

London Playhouses
Theatre 1580, Boar's Head 1602.

At Court
1 Jan. 1584, 1 Jan. 1585 (activities).

Travelling Records
Bristol Feb. 1560, 10s. / Bridgwater, Somerset Mar. 1560, 10s. / Norwich 1560–1, 6s. 8d. / Canterbury 1560–1, 5s. / Lydd, Kent 1560–1, 2s. 6d. / Dover 17 May 1561, 10s. / Cambridge town 12 July 1561, 10s. / Southampton 24 Oct. 1561, 10s. / Ipswich 1561–2, 10s. / Barnstaple, Devon 1561–2, 10s. / Faversham, Kent 1561–2, 2s. 4d. / Canterbury 1561–2, 8s. / Cambridge town 1561–2, 10s. / Southampton 5 July 1562, 10s. / Plymouth 1562–3, 13s. 4d. / Exeter 17 Oct. 1563, 13s. 4d. / Leicester 1562–3 'more then was gaythered', 4s. / Cambridge town 1562–3, 10s. / Ipswich 1563, 6s. 8d. / Ludlow 1564–5, 2s. / Cambridge University 21 June 1580 [letter from vice-chancellor to Chancellor] 'it hath pleased your honour to commende unto me and the headdes of the universitye my Lorde of Oxenforde his players . . . consyderinge & ponderinge, that the seede, the cause and the feare of the pestilence is not yet vanished & gone, this hote tyme of ye yeare . . . ye commencment tyme at hande, which requireth rather diligence in stodie then dissolutenesse in playes; and also yat of late wee denyed ye lyke to ye right Honorable ye Lord of Leiceter his servantes . . . I delivered them but xx s towardes

their charges', 20s. / Coventry Nov. acct. 1581, 10s. / Dover 1580–1, 13s. 4d. / Hythe, Kent 1581–2, 5s. / Bristol 1581 'being i man and ix boyes at iis per piece', 20s. / Norwich Dean and Chapter Receivers' acct. 1581–2, 13s. 4d. / Ipswich 1581– 2, 20s. / Gloucester 26 May 1582, 16s. 8d. / Ipswich 27 Oct. 1582, 15s. / Bath June 1582–3, 7s. 11d. / Coventry Nov. acct. 1582, 5s. / Southampton 1582–3, 13s. 4d. / Bristol May 1583, 20s.[11] / Liverpool 25 Jan. 1583 audit, 3s. 4d. / Exeter Apr. 1583, 10s. / Gloucester 26 May 1583, 16s. 8d. / Abingdon 2 June 1583, 20d. / Ticknall Hall, Derbyshire 26 Aug. 1583, 3s. 4d. / Coventry Nov. acct. 1583, 10s. / Glouces- ter 1583–4, 6s. 8d. / Southampton 1583–4, 6s. 8d. / Fordwich, Kent 1583–4, 6s. 8d. / Dover 1583–4, 20s. / Norwich 1583–4 'the Lord of Oxfordes players', 20s. / Ipswich 20 Jan. 1584, 20s. / Gloucester Jan.–May 1584, 6s. 8d. / Exeter 13 May 1584, 13s. 4d. / Bridgwater, Somerset July 1584, 20s. / Southampton 1584, 6s. 8d. / Leicester 11 Aug. 1584, 10s. / Coventry Nov. acct. 1584, 10s. / Ludlow 5 Aug. 1584, 8s. / Faversham, Kent 1584–5 / Dover Apr. 1584–5, 16s. 4d. / Maidstone 1584–5, 10s. / Bath June 1584–5, 7s. 9d. / Gloucester 1584–5, 10s. / Totnes, Devon 1584–5, £1. / Norwich 1584–5 'to thintent they should not playe in this citie', 20s. / Sudbury, Suffolk 17 Apr. 1585, 5s. / Ipswich 4 May 1585, 10s. / Bath June 1584– 5, 10s. / York City Books 30 June 1585, 20s. / Coventry Nov. acct. 1585, 13s. 4d. / Norwich 1585–6, 20s. / Ipswich 1586–7, 10s. / York June 1587, 20s. / Faversham, Kent 1594–5, 3s. 4d.

HERTFORD'S PLAYERS, 1582–1607?

Players
Martin Slater.

At Court
6 Jan. 1592, 6 Jan. 1603.

Travelling Records
Canterbury 1581–2, 10s. / Marlborough 1586–7 'for wyne and sugar', 21s. 4d. / Newcastle Oct. 1590 'to the earle of hardforthes playeres', 40s. / Leicester 1590 'att the hall dore', 6s. 4d., 'by the Appoyntment Aforesaid' [of the mayor and brethren], 20s. / Leicester 22 Nov. 1590, 20s. / Marlborough 1591–2, 15s. / Southampton 1591–2, 20s. / Bath June 1591–2, 20s. / Bristol Aug. 1592, 10s. / Faversham, Kent 1592–3, 10s. / Coventry 1597, 20s. / Faversham, Kent 1600–1, 10s. / Ipswich 1600–1, 13s. 4d. / Norwich 13 May 1601 'leave to plaie . . . for iii daies' / Norwich 17 June 1601 'Whereas my Lord of Hertfordes players were sutors to have leave to plaie at the Signe of the whight horsse in Tomelland but for this daie, it is ordered that no players or playes be made or used in the seid house either now or hereafter' / Bridgwater, Somerset Oct. 1601, 13s. 4d. / Bath 1601–2, 20s. / Ipswich 8 May

---

[11] This payment, to 'my Lord of Oxfordes players for an Enterlude', may have been for the same company of one man and nine boys who had been identified as a special Oxford's group visiting Bristol two years before. It is not clear whether Oxford kept both of his companies, one of adults and one of boys, at this time, nor to which kind of company these records belong.

1602, 13s. 4d. / Norwich 1604–5, 20s. / Coventry Dec. acct. 1605, 'to the Earle of herefordes players', 6s. 8d. / Leicester 1605–6, 10s. / Marlborough 2 June 1606, 17s. / Oxford town 9 July 1606, 10s. / Coventry Nov. acct. 1606, 40s. / Lathom, Lancs. Dec. 1606, Christmas 1606[12] / Coventry 1 Jan. 1607, 10s.

CHANDOS'S PLAYERS, 1577–1610

Playing Sharers
Robert Armin.

London Playhouses
none.

At Court
none.

Travelling Records
Dover 1577–8, 10s. 10d. / Ipswich 1581–2, 6s. 8d. / Ludlow 1581–2, 6s. 8d. / Bath June 1582–3, 9s. 2d. / Gloucester 7 Nov. 1582, 20s. / Norwich 19 Oct. 1583, 10s. / Bath June 1583–4, 5s. / Gloucester 11 Jan. 1584, 10s. / Exeter 15 Mar. 1585, 10s. / Dover 13 Aug. 1586, 5s. / York City Books 1587, 20s. / Coventry Nov. acct. 1587, 10s. / Ipswich 1587–8, 10s. / Norwich 1588–9, 10s. / Gloucester 28 Dec. 1589, 20s. / Rye, Sussex May 1590, 10s. / Ipswich 3 Sept. 1591, 10s. / Norwich 22 Sept. 1591, 10s.; 'a nother Company of his men that cam with lycens presently after saying yat thos that Cam before were counterfetes & not the Lord Shandos men', 20s. / Nottingham 1591–2, 5s. 6d. / Leicester 1591–2 'more then was gaytherd', 6s. 8d. / Coventry Nov. acct. 1592, 10s. / Folkestone 1592–3, 3s. 6d. / Ipswich 1592–3, 10s. / Coventry Nov. acct. 1593, 13s. 4d. / Norwich Oct.–Nov. 1593, 10s. / Bridgwater, Somerset Nov. 1593, £1. / Southampton 28 Nov. 1593, 6s. 8d. / Gloucester 1594–5 'To the Lord Chandois man that brought venison v s. and to my Lordes players', 5s. / Ipswich 1594–5, 10s. / Coventry Dec. acct. 1595, 10s. / Leicester 1595–6 'whoe did not playe att the hall', 5s. / Hardwick, Derbyshire (Cavendish household account) 30 Sept. 1595 'to certayne of the Lord Chaundos men', 5s. / Marlborough 1595–6, 6s. 8d. / Gloucester 1595–6 / Coventry Dec. acct. 1596, 10s. / Norwich 27 Dec. 1596, 10s. / Ipswich 15 Apr. 1597, 6s. 8d. / Bath 1596–7, 10s. / York City Books June 1597, 10s. / Coventry Dec. acct. 1597, 10s. / Leominster, Herefordshire 1597–8, 6s. 8d. / Bath 1597–8, 11s. 9d. / Coventry 4 June 1599, 10s. / Exeter 1599–1600 'mye Lord Saundes players', 10s. / Evesham 1600 (Armin, *Fool upon Fool*, B–C*: 'it hapned that the Lord Shandoyes players came to towne') / Coventry 19 July 1600, 10s.; 'be it had in mind that the lord

---

[12] *REED, Chester*, 219 transcribes a letter from the earl of Derby brought by a company to Chester, and saying 'This Company beinge my Lord of Harforth his men and haveinge beine With mee, Whose retorne and abode for this Christmas tyme I expecte, I ame to desire that if their occutione bee to Come to the Cittie that youe Will permit them to use theire quallitie Lathome my howse this ijth of december 1606'. A footnote adds hopefully, and probably at the players' prompting, 'post Creipt I would request you to lett them have the towne hall to playe in Ile vale'.

Shandoes players were comitted to prisone for their contempt agaynst maister maior & ther Remayned untill they made their submissione' / Bristol Sept. 1600, 10s. / Faversham, Kent 1600–1, 10s. / Ludlow 1600–1, 10s. / York Churchwardens' House Books 14 July 1601 'my Lord Shandoze players shall have Libertie to playe at marmaduke gills howse till sonday next & then to depart & not to play in the night tyme' / Leicester 1601–2, 10s. / Bridgwater, Somerset 2 Apr. 1602, 13s. 4d. / Marlborough 23 Feb. 1603, 10s. / Coventry Nov. acct. 1603, 5s. / Southampton 1603–4, 20s. / Weymouth, Dorset 1604, 5s. / Norwich 15 May 1604, 12s. / Leicester 24 Oct. 1604 'whoe did not playe', 20s., 'in wine & Suger', 19d. / Norwich 1604–5, 20s. / Coventry Nov. acct. 1606, 10s. / Coventry 1 Jan. 1607, 10s. / Coventry Nov. acct. 1607, 6s. 8d. / Canterbury 1607–8 'that played in the Courte Halle', 30s. / Faversham, Kent 1607–8, 10s. / Dunwich, Suffolk 1607–8, 6s. / Coventry Nov. acct. 1608 'to the Lord Candigis players in July', 4s.; 'to the Lord Shandigis players in August', 6s. 8d.[13] / Doncaster 26 Oct. 1608, 10s. / Canterbury 1608–9 'for that they shoulde not playe here by reason that the sicknes was then in this Cytye', 20s. / Coventry Nov. acct. 1609, 5s. / Norwich 15 Aug. 1610 'the Shandoffes men in regard that they did not play', 20s. / Coventry Nov. acct. 1610, 6s. 8d.

[13] R. W. Ingram, *REED, Coventry*, takes this and a later payment in 1609 'to the lord Candishes men' to mean not Lord Chandos's but Lord Cavendish's, a company not known elsewhere. The entry in the Wardens' accounts for Nov. 1610 names 'the Lord Shandowes players'.

The earls of Worcester ran a company or companies from early in Elizabeth's reign. Edward Somerset, the fourth earl, was a rising power in the land from his accession to the title in 1589 at the age of 36. He succeeded Essex as Master of the Horse in 1601, when his company was beginning to compete for the third London foothold. As a Privy Councillor he took an active role in regulating the players. He was a signatory to the Council's warrant of 31 March 1602 ordering the Lord Mayor to accept the Boar's Head as a playing-place for the merged Oxford's and Worcester's, which was designated 'this third Companie'. He also signed the order of April 1604 to the Lord Mayor and the justices of Surrey and Middlesex authorizing the three companies. Thomas Heywood, an early writer for his company and always a loyal client, suggested that it was through Worcester's own generosity that he handed over the patronage of his company to Queen Anne in 1603.[1] Under James he shared responsibility for mounting the great masques and court shows with the Lord Chamberlain. Another of the Herberts, he enjoyed shows of all kinds,[2] and took his playing company with him on his long climb in status at Elizabeth's court.

There are records of a Worcester's company travelling the country from the 1550s. The third earl's company, noted as 'hamond and his fellowes', gave some of the Christmas festivities at Haddon Hall as early as January 1565. A later version of the company and their names is noted at Norwich, in a dispute over playing there in 1583. The city was worried 'for fear of any infeccion as also for that they came from an Infected place', and put a ban on playing.[3] In spite of this prohibition Worcester's played 'in their hoste his hows', presumably an inn. The mayor then ordered 'that their Lord shalbee certyfyed of their contempt & that hensforth the sayd players shall never receive any rewarde of the citty whensoever they shall come agayn And that they shall presently depart owt of this citty & not to play uppon payn of Imprysonment'.[4] The company begged the mayor not to report them to the earl, and he relented. They had a similar run-in with the mayor of Leicester in the same year, though he was much softer, and eventually allowed them to play at their inn. They cannot have known that the mayor of Leicester, and possibly also of Norwich too, had recently received a letter from Tilney, the Master of the Revels, insisting that the mayor must check that his signature authorizing the play for performance was visible at the end of any playscript which the companies proposed staging.[5]

---

[1] See Ch. 6.

[2] Heywood later dedicated his *Apology for Actors* to him.   [3] *REED, Norwich*, 65.

[4] Ibid. 66. The same records give a full account of the trouble the Queen's company had that June, when there was a fight with swords at the entrance to their play, and a man died.

[5] The letter is transcribed in Murray, *English Dramatic Companies*, ii. 320–1.

The Norwich records for 1583 name the players in the company at this time as James Tunstall, Thomas Cook, Edward Browne, William Harrison, '& dyvers others', who we know also included Edward Alleyn and Richard Jones. Several of these men became Admiral's players with Alleyn a few years later. The same names, plus 'Thomas Powlton', the chief troublemaker, appear in the records at Leicester in 1584, along with a William Patterson who appears to have been the younger Somerset's man.[6] Whether this company split up soon after the troubles at Norwich and Leicester or if they stayed together until February 1589, when the third earl died, we do not know. The same five players were certainly named as the Admiral's servants in the course of that year. Since the death of a patron was the usual reason for a company dying, or at least changing its name, the transfer most likely came early in the year, when Worcester died. The new earl Edward Somerset's company evidently had a substantially different membership from his father's company of the earlier 1580s.[7] It is recorded at Coventry in 1589–90, at Newcastle in October 1590 and afterwards at Leicester, and consistently in provincial towns through the 1590s. It may have been led by the William Patterson who was travelling in Edward Somerset's livery in the company of Worcester's Men and was abusive at Leicester in 1584, but no name of any of the 1590s players appears in the provincial records. They did not play in London until the end of the decade.

The court status of Edward Somerset, newly-made Master of the Horse and Privy Councillor, was signalled in 1601 by his company playing at court on 3 January in the 1601–2 season. Three months later the Privy Council accepted Worcester's as a component of the third company with a fixed London base. In a rather tetchy order dated 31 March 1602, the earl and other councillors told the Lord Mayor, in reply to his annual complaint about playing, that:

the servants of our verey good Lord the Earle of Oxford, and of me the Earle of Worcester, beinge joyned by agrement togeather in on Companie (to whom, upon noteice of her Majesties pleasure at the suit of the Earl of Oxford, tolleracion hath ben thaught meete to be graunted, notwithstandinge the restraint of our said former Orders) doe not tye them selfs to one cetaine place and howse, but do chainge there place at there owne disposition, which is as disorderly and offensive as the former offence of many howses. And as the other Companies that are alowed, namely of me the Lord Admirall and the Lord Chamberlaine, be appointed there certaine howses, and one and noe more to each Companie. Soe we doe straightly require that this third Companie be likewise to one place. And because we are informed the house called the Bores head is the place they have especially used and doe best like of, we doe pray and require yow that that said howse, namely the Bores head, may be assigned unto them, and that they be verey straightlie Charged to use and exercise there

[6] Quoted in ES ii. 221–2.

[7] The Leicester records note among the disputants over the licence a 'William Pateson my lord Harbards man' who abused the mayor. The 'lord Harbard' was Worcester's son, Edward Somerset, then Lord Herbert of Chepstow. Evidently William Patterson had a different livery from the Worcester's Men, though he seems to have been playing in their company.

plaies in noe other but that howse, as they will looke to have that tolleracion continued and avoid further displeasure.[8]

This response by the Council to the mayor's annual complaint about playing in London had untypical force. A claim that accepting the third company regularized the situation and cut down the competition was not the sort of answer that Guildhall wanted. Worcester was laying down what he needed for himself. As a Privy Councillor he had the edge on Oxford in enforcing the merger of the two groups, and he was emphatic in setting his innovation out before the mayor as an improvement over the current shifting around of the players that was part of the mayor's complaint. Somerset and Charles Howard were two of the eight signatories of the Council's letter. George Carey was not present that day (he was beginning his final illness, and had become a chronic absentee from the Council), and Oxford was not a Privy Councillor.

What part the companies themselves might have played in negotiating this new deal is not easy to see. Somerset certainly wanted his company to compete with the Chamberlain's and Admiral's on an equal footing. They told him they would prefer to have the Boar's Head as their designated playhouse rather than either of the other possible venues, the Rose or the Curtain. But their own moves suggest that this was a transient opinion. The various shifts of the competing companies in 1601 and 1602 took Worcester's Men from the Rose to the Boar's Head and back again, and within a year or so of their merger with Oxford's to a third playhouse, the Red Bull. At different times they were tenants of Henslowe, Langley, and Robert Browne. Worcester's start at the vacant Rose when the Admiral's left it for the Fortune at the end of 1600 cannot have been their first footing in London, so for their earliest ventures in the city they must have used the Curtain or possibly the Swan. The lease of the Boar's Head that Worcester's took out in late 1601 and that was made official in the council order of March 1602 was only for three months. By 17 August 1602 they were at the Rose, and Browne had replaced them with Derby's Men at the Boar's Head. The combined company's patent as Queen Anne's in March 1604 allocated them to the Curtain. After the Globe and the Fortune there was a range of choice in playhouses. Worcester's took their time choosing the best one, in a way that shows how inferior to the leading pair they thought their alternatives were.

For all this restless shifting and the weight that Edward Somerset had to put behind them, the company that finally got itself the third London place was a substantial group of players, most of whom were long familiar to London playgoers. In 1602 the players who authorized Henslowe's payments for Worcester's at the Rose were Will Kemp, Christopher Beeston, and John Duke, all former Chamberlain's Men. Others in the group who had worked for Henslowe before were Thomas Heywood and Robert Pallant. Two newcomers, who were to become the most famous leading players of the next three decades, were John Lowin and

---

[8] *ES* iv. 334-5.

Richard Perkins. This group formed the core of the new Queen Anne's Men when it got its patent in 1604.

It proved a durable fellowship. The licence re-issued to them in 1609 names as its leader the comedian Thomas Greene, who must have replaced Will Kemp when he died in 1604, together with most of those who started the London company in 1602. They were 'Thomas Greene, Christofer Beeston, Thomas Haywood, Richard Pirkyns, Richard Pallant, Thomas Swinnerton, John Duke, Robert Lee, James Haulte, and Robert Beeston'.[9] Lowin had left to join the King's Men. Most of what we know about the company's repertory relates to this group of 1609.

If Worcester's were at the Curtain in 1601 before contracting to play at the Boar's Head, a Privy Council minute dated 10 May and addressed to the justices of Middlesex about a play staged there must relate to them. The Council was responding to a complaint about the portrayal on stage of events relating to living people, and the portrayal of those people 'under obscure manner', but thinly enough disguised for them to be recognizable. The complaint was 'that certaine players that use to recyte their playes at the Curtaine in Moorfeildes do represent upon the stage in their interludes the persons of some gentlemen of good desert and quallity that are yet alive under obscure manner, but yet in such sorte as all the hearers may take notice both of the matter and the persons that are meant thereby'.[10] Whether it was a play about famous battles of the time, like the one in 1599 when Robert Sidney and Francis Vere were shown on stage, or a more local satire like the lost *Old Joiner of Aldgate* at Paul's,[11] we cannot tell.

Nor is it easy to identify what plays were already in the company's repertoire when they arrived in London in 1600. *How a Man may Choose a Good Wife from a Bad*, which Roslyn Knutson characterizes as an early example of the 'prodigal husband' genre,[12] was printed under their name in 1602, but may have been acquired for their London run. A similar play, Heywood's *The Wise Woman of Hogsdon*, turns up a little later in the Queen Anne's repertory, probably in 1604. His *A Woman Killed with Kindness*, reflecting the same preoccupation with marital and domestic morality, was written for the company once it settled at the Rose in 1602. The company's early repertory is largely known only from Henslowe, who bought twelve plays for them in the seven months that they were under his management. Some of them, like Dekker's *Medicine for a Curst Wife*, had started out as plays intended for the Admiral's. Henslowe was entrepreneurial in his allocation of plays to his two companies. He gave *Oldcastle*, for instance, which had originally been commissioned for the Admiral's in 1599, to Worcester's at the Rose, presumably because playing it next door to the Globe would maximize the contrast and emphasize the embarrassment of the Globe players for their misrepresentation of the martyr Oldcastle as Falstaff.

---

[9] *MSC* i. 3. 270–1.   [10] Quoted in *ES* iv. 332.
[11] See Gurr, *Playgoing in Shakespeare's London*, 144–5.
[12] *The Repertory of Shakespeare's Company*, 84.

Only two of the twelve plays that Henslowe noted as the company's are extant: *A Woman Killed with Kindness* and *Sir Thomas Wyatt*. The former belongs in a fashion rather more characteristic of the Rose and the Fortune than the Globe. The other was an early example of the 'Elect-Nation' history plays that became a strong feature of both the Fortune's and the Red Bull's post-1603 repertoire. Judging by the titles of the rest, which were mostly written by the former Admiral's collaborators Chettle, Day, Dekker, Hathwey, Heywood, Smith, and John Webster, they were of the kind familiar in the Admiral's at the turn of the century. Carol Chillington Rutter[13] suggests that Worcester's staged their plays with more spectacle than the Admiral's, but the evidence for that may simply show the need of a new company to equip itself afresh to work in London. They spent £234. 11s. 6d. in the seven months with Henslowe, a good deal more than the Admiral's did in a similar period. Otherwise, the main divergence that is identifiable in Worcester's from either of the other companies is their chief comedian. The country clown, Will Kemp, after he danced himself 'out of the world' in 1599, had been replaced in the Chamberlain's by the city jester Robert Armin. Worcester's retained Kemp and his jigs, and when he died replaced him with Thomas Greene, a clown of similar qualities, who in the next few years became the most popular clown of the day. The divergence which gradually began to spread between, on the one hand, the companies at the Fortune and the Worcester's company's various venues, and on the other the Chamberlain's at the Globe, may have started with the different kinds of clownage they offered as much as anything. The plays themselves at this time were not substantially different in their species. The clownage and the jigs for which Kemp was famous were indications of a different kind of disposition from what Shakespeare started writing after 1599; but the differences between the Globe's clowns and the others did not show up really strongly for another decade. The rivalry that made the two repertories match each other under the binary system between 1594 and 1600 sustained itself until well after the changes of 1603.

Worcester's, having made their presence known at court for the first time on 3 January 1602, did not appear in the following year, though they seem to have expected a call, since Henslowe notes a purchase on 1 January 1603 of head-tires 'for the corte'.[14] Conceivably they had expected to occupy the Twelfth-Night slot, when the intrusive Hertford's gave their only performance. Worcester's next appearance at court was not until they were Queen Anne's Men. The long London closure for Elizabeth's death and the ensuing plague lasted from March 1603 until April 1604. As compensation for the length of that break, the King's Men received £30 towards their costs. There is no sign that either the Admiral's, becoming the Prince's Men, or Worcester's, becoming Queen Anne's Men, were given anything to match that grant. Indeed, their new patrons were allocated to them some time after the King's, which was announced on 19 May 1603. The other two were clearly regarded as the second and third-best companies, and were not compensated for

---

[13] *Documents of the Rose Playhouse*, 202.   [14] *Henslowe's Diary*, 221.

the closure like the King's Men. That may have been in part simply a consequence of the slower progress in making out their new patents, though it may also reflect James's initial single-mindedness in taking the one company under his own wing and not concerning himself with the others.[15]

Exactly when their new titles were agreed is not known for certain. The Blackfriars Children received their patent from the queen on 4 February 1604. The only surviving record of the Queen's Anne's adult company patent is an undated draft, which allocates them to the Curtain and the Boar's Head. The licence the Privy Council issued for them to play in April 1604 only names the Curtain, so the draft probably dates from earlier, in late 1603. It names 'Thomas Greene, Christopher Beeston, Thomas Hawood, Richard Pyrkins, Robert Pallant, John Duke, Thomas Swynerton, Jeames Hoult, Robert Beeston & Robert Lee, servauntes unto our dearest and welbeloved wyfe the Queene Anna, with the rest of their Associates', and specified 'there now usuall Howsen, called the Curtayne, and the Bores head'.[16] Kemp, who was dead by 1604, is already replaced in this list by Greene. Lowin is absent, having moved to the new King's Men. It is the definitive list of company names for the company's initial period as Queen Anne's Men.[17]

Queen Anne's did not stay long at either the Curtain or the Boar's Head. The Curtain was already the oldest playhouse in London, dating from 1577, and the Boar's Head had limited auditorium capacity, with only a single level of galleries compared to the three of the Fortune and the Globe. The company secured a new playhouse, the Red Bull in Clerkenwell, to the north of the city, in 1604 or 1605. Thomas Swinnerton, a member of the company, acquired a share in the building in 1605 or 1606, 'with a gatherers place thereto belonging', that is, the right to take some of the playhouse takings for his rent.[18] One of the company's plays, *The Travels of the Three English Brothers*, by Day, Rowley, and Wilkins, was credited to the Queen's Men at the Curtain on its title-page in 1607, but it was labelled a Red Bull play in Beaumont's *The Knight of the Burning Pestle*, written for the Blackfriars Boys in the same year. It seems that conceivably from as early as 1604 the Red Bull became their venue. With one large interim, it remained theirs for the rest of their life as Queen Anne's Men through to the death of James in 1625.[19]

---

[15] Chambers, *ES* ii. 230, considers that the patent may never have been completed in 1603. That would explain why a full patent was issued in 1609.

[16] *MSC* i.1. 265.

[17] One other document exists that may add another two names. It is a copy in the Southampton archives for 1606 of the Queen's warrant dated 7 Mar. 1606 that her company was carrying with it on tour (*ES* ii. 235). It names three men, Robert Lee, Martin Statier, and Roger Banfield as the leaders. Lee was certainly one of the company's leaders, but the name Martin Statier, which was almost certainly a mistranscription of the mobile Martin Slater, raises the suspicion that it was a forgery similar to the one recorded with his name and Thomas Swinnerton's by the Norwich authorities in 1616. He was a moveable character, a member of the Admiral's in 1597, leading Hertford's at court in 1603, and in 1608 running the King's Revels Boys. No other record about Banfield exists.

[18] *ES* ii. 445.

[19] George F. Reynolds, *The Staging of Elizabethan Plays at the Red Bull Theater, 1605–1625* (London, 1940), has a priority list for the plays most likely to have been staged at the Red Bull between 1604 and 1620. His careful study deals exclusively with the plays of this company.

If the extra expenditure on visual shows with Henslowe at the Rose in 1603 does not indicate a preference for spectacle over the spoken word, the kind of repertoire they developed with Heywood subsequently through their first decade as the Queen's Men certainly does. It was for this company that he wrote his colourful and firework-spangled *Ages* plays. *The Golden Age* was printed in 1611 as a Red Bull play, and *The Silver Age* followed. By contrast John Webster had much less success with his first non-collaborative writing for the company, if the grudging epistle he published with *The White Devil* in 1613 is to be believed. 'It was acted', he wrote, 'in so dull a time of winter, presented in so open and black a theatre, that it wanted (that which is the only grace and setting out of a tragedy) a full and understanding auditory'. He gave his next play, *The Duchess of Malfi*, to the King's Men at their winter quarters in the roofed Blackfriars.

Other plays exploited the company's strengths better. *Greene's Tu Quoque* for instance, a rewrite of a Middleton comedy, advertised their best drawcard in its title. Heywood's *Four Prentices of London* along with *The Travels of the Three English Brothers* appealed by the titles advertised on their playbills to the citizen and apprentice section of the audience. Other plays of this period were Dekker's *If It be not Good, the Devil is in It*, and *The Honest Lawyer*, both titles offering the kind of paradox that reflects the come-hither element that was increasingly becoming a necessary feature of playbills, and which the paradoxical name *The White Devil* itself exploits. A different sort of come-hither is implied at this time by the number of sneers about the repertory that the Red Bull began to attract. By 1613 there is no doubt that the different playhouses were catering for different tastes, and the Red Bull was seen to be offering the cheapest fare. George Wither scorned the bad verse 'at *Curtaine* or at *Bul*' in the first satire of *Abuses Stript and Whipt* in 1614. On the other hand William Turner in his *Dish of Lenten Stuffe* (1613) voiced his preference for Curtain and Red Bull plays over the Globe's. The Bankside players 'Will teach you idle tricks of love, | but the Bull will play the man'.[20] Turner was praising plays of militant heroics that became known for their noise value and war games as 'drum-and-trumpet' fare over the Fletcherian romances and Shakespearian love-comedies that now prevailed in the King's Men's repertory.

To some extent 1612 can be seen as a high point in the Queen Anne's company's development. That was the year when Heywood's plays triumphed on the Red Bull stage, though it was also when Webster transferred his attention to the King's Men at their hall playhouse. The company had good resources in plays, including Heywood's *Rape of Lucrece*, Webster's *The Devil's Law Case* and, rather surprisingly, a revived Marlowe, *Edward II*.[21] In 1612, too, Greene died, and another

---

[20] *Turners Dish of Lenten stuffe*, in H. E. Rollins (ed.), *A Pepsyian Garland* (Cambridge, 1922), 35.

[21] Marlowe's play was originally written for Pembroke's in 1592. It does not appear in the post-1594 Henslowe records. Beeston might have secured it from Henslowe while the company was playing at the Rose. Henslowe seems to have had all the other Marlowe plays. Alternatively, if it went from Pembroke's with the Shakespeare plays into the Chamberlain's, Beeston might have somehow acquired it and taken it with him when he left them for Worcester's. Its 1622 quarto ascribes it to 'the late Queenes Majesties Servants at the Red Bull', which probably dates its revival to 1619–22.

player took over the company's financial management.[22] This was Christopher Beeston, beginning his long and highly successful career of nearly thirty years as impresario, company manager, and playhouse-owner. Since he built his playhouse in Drury Lane in 1616 to imitate the Blackfriars very largely out of the Queen's Men's income, there is some reason to question how altruistically he handled the company's finances in the years between Greene's death and the building of the Cockpit. The external record of his dealings with the companies he used as tenants at his Cockpit, and the evidence in a lawsuit of 1623 brought against the company by Greene's heirs, say more for his entrepreneurial spirit than his managerial probity. The company's history for the next ten years is interwoven with Beeston's various enterprises.

The evidence set out in the 1623 lawsuit's depositions gives us an outline of the company's finances and general health for the preceding decade. In his will of 1612 Greene left his widow the value of his share in the company, set at £80, plus a credit of £57 that the company owed him. In 1615, after some argument, and the complete failure of the company to pay any of the debt, the widow and her new husband agreed to give the company another £57. 10s. in return for a pension of 1s. 8d. (one-twelfth of a pound) for every playing day in the couple's lifetime. This was revised a year later, when the company had still not paid anything to the widow. The revised agreement required her to lend them another £38 in return for an additional pension of two shillings for her and her son's lifetime. A year later another revision brought in a second son, who was a player in the company and had not been paid his hire. Finally, in 1623, when only three sharers survived from the original company, the long-suffering woman took them to court to get her arrears of payment. Beeston, possibly anticipating this kind of trouble, had taken himself and his profits elsewhere some years before. The surviving players, John Blaney, John Cumber, and Ellis Worth, appealed against Greene's widow to the Court of Chancery. Predictably, the result of it all was that the company broke.

Beeston's part in this story of a company chronically short of the income to pay its legitimate debts appears to have been that of siphoner of their cash. In the 1623 depositions the players claimed that they 'at that tyme and long before and since did put the managing of their whole businesses and affaires belonging unto them joyntly as they were players in trust' into Beeston's hands.[23] The trustful sharers even claimed that Greene's widow had bribed Beeston to set up the agreements she was suing them over. Whatever actually happened, Beeston, having secured either for the company or himself a total of £95 in loans from the widow, had enough cash in his personal possession to build the Cockpit in 1616, while leaving it to the company to pay her pension.

It has to be said that he did try, until the series of troubles with the opening of his new Cockpit overtook him, to do well by his company. He took it from the Red Bull to the Cockpit at the beginning of 1617, a distinct promotion in imitation of the

---

[22] His will is transcribed in *Playhouse Wills 1558–1642*, 90.   [23] *ES* ii. 238.

King's Men at Blackfriars; but, unfortunately, that led them straight into an unexpected crisis. On 4 March, the Shrove Tuesday holiday at the beginning of Lent, a mob of apprentices attacked the new playhouse and left it a shambles. As John Chamberlain reported, 'Though the fellowes defended themselves as well as they could and slew three of them with shot, and hurt divers, yet they entered the house and defaced yt, cutting the players apparell all to pieces, and all other theyre furniture and burnt theyre play bookes and did what other mischeife they could'.[24] There is reason to believe that the apprentices were registering their anger at the company's transfer from the Red Bull, where they could see the plays for a penny, to the much costlier Cockpit. The fact that when they tried to repeat their attack on the following Shrove Tuesday in 1618 they assembled at the Fortune before charging down Drury Lane, and that they also planned to attack the Red Bull, indicates that it was not an indiscrimate attack on playhouses in general. In the event, the Privy Council got word of this second attack and prevented it. But the first attack had cost the company its main resources, its playbooks and apparel, and that strained their finances beyond recovery. They were at their financier's mercy.

Transferring from the Red Bull at Clerkenwell to the Cockpit in Drury Lane near the Inns of Court located the company amongst a new sort of clientele. The city's apprentices still did not have very far to go to reach the Cockpit, but it was at the more affluent West End of the city, and the law students of the Inns had a long history of clashes with apprentices. They could afford the Cockpit's benches, and few apprentices could. Beeston was making a radical switch in his clientele. It would be nice to know whether the plays the company commissioned to make up for their losses in the attack were aimed at the lawyers rather than the apprentices. Beeston did keep a hand on the Red Bull as well as his new hall, probably envious of the King's Servants and their winter and summer playhouses, but he was not so affluent or easygoing as to be able to leave one empty. He switched plays and players between the two venues over the next nine years, but unlike the King's he always kept both of them in full use, summer and winter. Queen Anne's servants returned to the Red Bull while the Cockpit was being repaired.[25] When they started a second time at the Cockpit, Prince Charles's Men moved into the Red Bull in their place. That redisposition lasted for the next two years, until, when Anne died, in 1619, Beeston switched the Prince Charles's Men into the Cockpit, and the re-formed Queen Anne's, now the Revels company, reverted to the Red Bull.

Well before 1619 the company had set up a different kind of double act. While one group led by Greene and then Beeston stayed in London, another, led by Thomas Swinnerton, started to travel the country using a duplicate or 'exemplificacion' of the company's 1609 patent. In 1616 the Norwich authorities

[24] *Letters*, ii. 59–60.
[25] The dates for the company's shifts of venue are not precisely recorded. On 2 Oct. 1617 six of the Queen's, Beeston, Drew, Harrison, Heywood, Perkins, and Worth, sent a petition to Clerkenwell protesting against the continuance of charges for the repair of the highways by the Red Bull. By then they should have been back at the Cockpit, although that would not have exonerated them from back dues for maintaining the roads.

found that Swinnerton and Robert Lee were the only players named in the patent who were actually with the company that arrived in the city on 30 March. It was given leave to play, but on Swinnerton's return on 29 May he took the precaution of not having the patent and its names with him. There is no evidence in the Norwich records that they tipped the Lord Chamberlain off about this duplicity, but a third visit on 20 July, by a company with the same patent but led by Martin Slater, ended the town's patience with the duplication trick. The Lord Chamberlain had to intervene.

In the same year the Chamberlain sent Joseph Moore round the country with a warning against the patent 'exemplificacions' carried by Swinnerton and Martin Slater, in a letter which the Norwich clerks received and copied into their records in 1617.[26] When John Daniell arrived in the next year as 'one of the Company of the Quenes Majesties Players' his dismissal without leave to play was understandable, though he received thirty shillings for going. He was actually running a different company set up at Bristol after Anne's visit there in 1613, which was the cause of other troubles.[27] Robert Lee, Swinnerton's co-leader in 1616, returned with an 'Exemplificacion' on 31 May 1617, and was given leave to play for three days in Whitsun week, just before the Chamberlain's letter arrived. Swinnerton continued his travels using one patent or another into the 1630s.

At Anne's death, according to a list of the players granted black cloth for her funeral, the company sharers had sixteen men counted suitable to walk in the procession. They were Thomas Basse, John Blaney, Christopher Beeston, John Cumber, Thomas Drue, John Edmonds, Thomas Heywood, James Haulte, Robert Lee, Robert Pallant, Richard Perkins, William Robinson, Gregory Sanderson, Martin Slater, Thomas Swinnerton, and Ellis Worth.[28] At least two of these sixteen, Slater and Swinnerton, were travellers with only marginal links to the London company. After the death of its patron, the company divided. Some appear to have left London to travel under the old Queen Anne's licence. Beeston took the Prince Charles's into the Cockpit, making his own final move from playing into management. Perkins, Worth, Cumber, and others went back to the Red Bull, presumably with Beeston's blessing, since he kept his interest in the companies at both venues. At the Red Bull, lacking a patron, they re-formed as the 'Players of the Revels', the first of the Stuart companies not to have a royal patron. With four companies based in London, the royal family was running a little short.

For this last phase of their life the company might more precisely be called the Red Bull company. They were still licensed to play in London, but without a formally identified patron they had no official title. Of the company's players, the name of Robert Lee, the first player named in the funeral list of 1619, appears with a Nicholas Long and 'the rest of their Companie' in a Lord Chamberlain's licence for the company dated 24 February 1620.[29] Lee and Perkins were subsequently named with others as 'Comedians to the late Queene Anne' in a further warrant of

[26] See REED, Norwich, 145, 146, 151–2, and above, 49–50.
[27] See below, 403.   [28] MSC ii. 3. 325.   [29] MSC i. 3. 284.

November 1622. They hung on to their old name when travelling, presumably for the status it still gave them and because it was the name on the only patent they had. They had not been asked to perform at court since 1617, and had to cling to what helps to buoyancy were still in their grasp. A Signet Office warrant dated 8 July 1622, also issued to the 'late comedians of Queen Anne deceased', names Lee and Perkins along with Basse, Blaney, Cumber, Robinson, and Worth.[30] Blaney, Cumber, and Worth were the three surviving Queen Anne's Men whom the widow Greene took to court in 1623.[31]

Some of the plays staged by the company under their new name did appear in print. They include *The Merry Milkmaids*, printed in 1620 as a play of 'the Companie of the Revels', a comedy that remained popular as a neo-Arcadian tragicomedy about courtiers, and which they possibly performed at court in the 1619–20 season. They also had *The Virgin Martyr*, licensed for performance in October 1620 and printed in 1622; Thomas May's *The Heir*, printed in 1622; *Herod and Antipater*, printed in 1622; and *The Two Noble Ladies*, which survives in a manuscript that claims it was acted 'with approbation' at the Red Bull by the Revels Company. The revival of *Edward II* may date from this period too. Later texts ascribed to the company include *The Costly Whore* (1633), and two lost plays, *Gramercy Wit*, which also played at court in the 1621–2 season, and *The Welsh Traveller*. It was this company that suffered a comic mishap when one of its players, Richard Baxter, wounded an apprentice who was sitting on the edge of the Red Bull's stage at a play in March 1622. One of the low paid community of handicraft workers, the apprentice adopted the spirit of the venue and wrote out a formal challenge to Baxter. He threatened to bring along more than a hundred of his fellows 'who are all here present readie to take revenge uppon you unles willingly you will give present satisfaction'.[32] Baxter, acting rather less in accordance with the spirit of the place, passed the letter to the Middlesex magistrates, who ordered the apprentices to keep the peace.

After 1622 there is no record of the company continuing to play in London under its non-name. The last records of their urban existence are, characteristically, first an order to proceed against them for non-payment of their highway bills, dated 2 October 1622, and secondly the widow Greene's lawsuit. The printing of three of their plays in 1622 was probably part of the process of cashing in their assets under pressure from the widow and their lawyers. Cumber died in 1623, soon after testifying in the Greene case. Perkins went into the King's Men. Worth turned up some years later in Prince Charles's (II) company. He married in 1626 and lived in Cripplegate, though there is nothing to say which company he belonged to between 1622 and 1631. Of the others, there is no record of Basse playing anywhere.[33] Baxter later joined the King's Men, while Blaney and Robinson (also known as Robbins) joined Queen Henrietta's at the Cockpit in 1625. Drue moved

---

[30] Ibid.   [31] Lee's will is transcribed in *Playhouse Wills 1558–1642*, 161–2.

[32] *Middlesex County Records*, ed. J. C. Jeaffreson (London, 1887), ii. 175–6.

[33] Basse's will is transcribed in *Playhouse Wills 1558–1642*, 178–9.

across to the Palsgrave's at the Fortune, for whom he wrote *The Duchess of Suffolk*. Heywood started writing for Beeston at the Cockpit. Lee bought a share in the Fortune and probably joined Palsgrave's there. Pallant went with Perkins to the King's. Martin Slater did his usual escape act, appearing at Coventry in 1623 with a group of 'players of the late Queene Elizabeth', and in 1625 at Leicester with a company 'beinge the Kings Playors'. Swinnerton was the one who took the patent and the remnant company into the country.

WORCESTER'S PLAYERS, 1562–1603
See also Queen Anne's Men, Red Bull Company.

Playing Sharers
At Haddon Hall 1565 'hamond and hys fellowes'; at Norwich 1583: 'James Tunstall Thomas Cook Edward Brown Willm Harrison & dyvers others to the number of x players of Interludes & servauntes as they say to the honorable therle of Worcester'.[34] Leicester 6 Feb. 1584: 'Robert Browne, James Tunstall, Edward Allen, william harryson, Thomas Cooke, Richard Johnes, Edward browne, Richard Androwes'; in 1600: Christopher Beeston, Thomas Heywood, Will Kemp.

London Playhouses
Curtain?, Swan?, Boar's Head to 1600, 1602; Rose 1602–3.

Travelling
Bristol June 1562, 10s. / Beverley 1563 'in regardo Lusoribus domini Worceter', 7s. / Leicester 10 Oct. 1563–4 'more then was gathered', 4s. / Bristol June 1563, 10s. / Plymouth 1563–4, 13s. 4d. / Bristol Jan. 1564, 13s. 4d. / Canterbury 1564–5, 5s. / Folkestone 1564–5, 2s. 4d. / Haddon Hall, Derbyshire 13 Jan. 1565 'To hamond and hys fellowes Therle of Worcesters players', 13s. 4d., 2s. / Beverley 1565, 20s., 'for wyne to the same players at Lord Wylloughbys', 12d. / Ipswich 2 Apr. 1565, 6s. 8d. / Leicester 1565–6 'more then was gathered', 3s. 6d. / Bridgwater, Somerset June–Sept. 1566, 3s. 4d. / Dover 1566–7, 10s. / Rye, Sussex Jan.–Apr. 1567 'to the Errle of Worsytors Enterlute players', 6s. 8d. / Southampton 10 Mar. 1567, 10s. / Bristol Nov. 1567 'paid . . . in the yeld hall at the end of their play', 10s. / Gloucester 1567–8 'and their drinkynge', 12s. 6d. / Winchester 1567–8, 5s. 10d. / Plymouth 11 June 1568, 5s. / Canterbury 1568–9, 13s. 4d. / Dover 1568–9, 12s. 7d. / Folkestone 1568–9, 20d. / Fordwich, Kent 1568–9, 6s. / Ipswich 1568–9, 10s. / Gloucester 1568–9, 13s. 4d. / Stratford 1568–9 / Bath June 1568–9, 3s. / Nottingham 11 Aug. 1569 'to the erle of lesyter and to the erle of Worster plears', 20s. / Bristol Sept. 1569, 13s. 4d. / Cambridge town 1569–70, 10s. / Bristol Dec. 1570, 13s. 4d. / Plymouth 1570–1, 6s. 8d. / Barnstaple, Devon 1570–1, 10s. / Gloucester 6 Feb. 1571, 10s. / Bridgwater, Somerset 1571, 13s. 4d. / Beverley 1571, 6s. 8d. / Nottingham 9 Jan. 1572, 6s. 8d. / Leicester 1571–2 'more then was geythered',

---

[34] *REED, Norwich*, 65.

8*d*. / Folkestone 1571–2, 3*s*. 4*d*. / Wollaton Hall, Nottinghamshire (Willoughby household accounts) 31 Dec. 1572 'for playing before my mr and mr Stanhope', 20*s*. / Exeter 1572–3, 13*s*. 4*d*. / Bridgwater, Somerset Oct.–Dec. 1572, 13*s*. 4*d*. / New Romney, Kent 1572–3, 3*s*. / Abingdon 1572–3, 4*s*. 8*d*. / Leicester 1572–3 'more then was geytherid', 4*s*. / Cambridge town 1572–3, 10*s*. / Gloucester 1 Dec. 1573, 10*s*. 'Allsoe spente upon them' 3*s*. 4*d*. / Bristol 18–24 Jan. 1573, 10*s*. / Plymouth 1572–3, 13*s*. 4*d*. / Canterbury 1572–3, 6*s*. 8*d*. / Bath 20 May 1573, 6*s*. 9*d*. / Beverley 1573–4, 5*s*. / Wollaton Hall, Nottinghamshire (Willoughby household accounts) Jan. 1574, 13*s*. 4*d*. / Nottingham 6 Jan. 1574, 6*s*. 8*d*. / Bristol Jan. 1574, 10*s*. / Gloucester 1573–4, 10*s*. / Bristol Dec. 1574 'in the Christmas holidayes', 10*s*. / Nottingham 18 Apr. 1575, 10*s*. / Leicester 1575–6, 10*s*. / Bridgwater, Somerset 5 June 1576 'for there plea in the halle', 10*s*. / Stratford 1576 / Coventry Nov. acct. 1576, 6*s*. 8*d*. / Totnes, Devon 1576–7, 10*s*. / Bath 1576–7, 2*s*. 6*d*. / Stratford 1577 / Southampton 14 June 1577 'being x of them', 10*s*. / Beverley 6 Sept. 1577, 13*s*. 4*d*. / Gloucester 1577–8, 13*s*. 4*d*. / Dover 1577–8, 13*s*. 4*d*. / Newark, Nottinghamshire 1577, 5*s*. / Nottingham 19 Jan. 1578, 5*s*. / Coventry Nov. acct. 1578, 5*s*. / Coventry Nov. acct. 1579, 6*s*. 8*d*. / Abingdon 1580–1, 6*s*. 10*d*. / Plymouth 1580–1 'and for bearinge of Bordes and other fourniture', 15*s*. 9*d*. / Bridgwater, Somerset 19 Sept. 1581, 13*s*. 4*d*. / Southampton 1581, 10*s*. / Nottingham 31 Dec. 1581, 6*s*. 8*d*. / Ipswich 1581–2, 13*s*. 4*d*. / Coventry Nov. acct. 1582, 6*s*. 8*d*. / Bridgwater, Somerset 30 July 1582, 13*s*. 4*d*. / Hythe, Kent 1582–3, 5*s*. / Doncaster 1582–3, 2*s*. / Leicester 6 Mar. 1583 'not to playe', 6*s*. 8*d*.[35] / Norwich 1582 3, 26*s*. 8*d*. / Ipswich 15 June 1583, 15*s*. / Gloucester 22 Dec. 1583, 6*s*. 8*d*. / Maidstone 1583–4, 10*s*. / Leicester 1583–4, 10*s*. / York City Books Mar. 1584, 10*s*. / Coventry Nov. acct. 1584, 13*s*. 4*d*. / Hythe, Kent 1584–5, 5*s*. / Faversham, Kent 1589–90, 6*s*. 8*d*. / Ipswich 20 Mar. 1590, 13*s*. 4*d*. / Newcastle Oct. 1590, 30*s*. / York City Books 24 Oct. 1590, 20*s*. / Coventry Dec. acct. 1590, 10*s*. / Shrewsbury 1590–1 'and my Lord of Darbyes musycyoners', 23*s*. 8*d*. / Leicester 1590–1 'att the hall dore', 6*s*. 8*d*., 'by . . . my mayor and his Bretherne' 33*s*. 4*d*. / Marlborough 1590–1, 3*s*. 4*d*. / Gloucester 1590–1, 10*s*. / Faversham, Kent 1590–1, 10*s*. / Lydd, Kent 1590–1, 10*s*. / Plymouth 1590–1 'to my L Darbyes musysyons and to the Erle of Wosters players', 23*s*. 8*d*. / Norwich 31 Mar. 1591, 20*s*. / Coventry 2 June 1591, 10*s*. / Newcastle Sept. 1591, 40*s*. / Southampton 11 Nov. 1591, 20*s*. / Lydd, Kent 1591–2, 5*s*. / Gloucester 1591–2, 13*s*. 4*d*. / Leicester 1591–2 'for that they did not Playe',

---

[35] The players objected to being stopped from playing. It was a Friday, and they could see no reason for the ban. They met the mayor again two hours later and asked if they could perform 'at there Inn'. He refused permission, so they said they would play regardless. They then went 'with there drum, & Trumppyttes thorowe the Towne'. Two of them, named as 'William Pateson my lord harbardes man' and 'Thomas Powlton my lord of worcesters man', were identified as the most abusive. The players subsequently apologized, begging the mayor not to write to the earl their master. On this sign of their submission, the city's note says 'they are licensed to play this night at there Inn & also they have promysed that appon the stage in the begynning of there play to showe unto the hearers, that they are lycensed to playe by mr mayor & with his good will & that they are sorye for the wordes past'. *REED, Leicestershire*, Alice Hamilton, ed., forthcoming.

10s. / Coventry 1592, 10s. / Norwich 15 Apr. 1592 'Although they played not', 20s. / Bridgwater, Somerset 10 Sept. 1592, 13s. 4d. / Plymouth 1592, 5s. / Lydd, Kent 1592–3 'of benevolence', 6s. 8d. / Rye, Sussex 1592–3, 13s. 4d. / Plymouth 1592–3 'my lord of Wusterdes playters', 5s. / Leicester 1592–3, 20s. / Ipswich 1592–3, 13s. 4d. / York City Books May 1593, 30s. / Newcastle Aug. 1593, £3. / Southampton 18 Oct. 1593 'for yt they should not play', £1. / Maidstone 1593–4, 10s. / Leicester 1593–4 'who did playe', 20s. / Ipswich 10 Mar. 1594, 10s. / Norwich 30 Mar. 1594, 20s. / Bath 1593–4, 11s., 'and given more to the same players' 6s. 10d. / Southampton 7 Sept. 1594, £1. / Rye, Sussex Sept. 1594, 10s. / Lydd, Kent 1594–5, 6s. / Leicester 1594–5, 30s. / York City Books 1 July 1595 'the Earle of worsters players which are late commed to this Cittie and desirous to playe shall xx s given theme forth of the common chamber & so departe from this Cittie & not play' / Rye, Sussex Sept. 1595, 10s. / Ludlow 3 Dec. 1595, 6s. 8d. / Leicester 1 Aug. 1596 'who did not playe att the Hall', 6s. 8d. / Bath 1595–6, 8s. 10d. / Bridgwater, Somerset Feb. 1597, 10s. / Bristol Sept. 1598, 26s. 8d. / York City Books 28 Mar. 1599 'given them and depart & not playe', 30s. / Coventry Nov. acct. 1599, 10s. / Coventry 3 Jan. 1600, 10s. / Leominster, Herefordshire 1600–1, 10s. / Coventry Dec. acct. 1601, 10s. / Barnstaple 1601–2 'to departe the Towne withowt any playnge', 10s. / Coventry Dec. acct. 1602, 10s. / Leicester 1603, 10s., 'one other tyme' 20s. / Coventry Nov. acct. 1603, 20s., 5s. / Coventry Nov. acct. 1611 'to the Lord of Wistes players', 2s. 6d.

QUEEN'S ANNE'S PLAYERS, 1603–1619
See also Worcester's, Red Bull company.

Plays
The Devil's Law Case, *The Four Prentices of London*, *The Golden Age*, *Greene's Tu Quoque*, *The Honest Lawyer*, *How to Learn a Woman to Woo* (lost), *If It be not Good, the Devil is in It*, *The Rape of Lucrece*, *The Silver Age*, *Swetnam the Woman Hater*, *The Travels of the Three English Brothers*, *The White Devil*.

Playing Sharers
[Southampton warrant issued 7 Mar. 1606: 'Wee are well pleased to authorize under our hand and signett the bearers hereof our sworne servauntes Robert Lee, Martin Statier and Roger Barfeld with theyr fellowes and associates being our commedians.']
John Duke, Thomas Greene [Cambridge 1605–6], Christopher Beeston [Norwich 6 May 1615 'Letters Patentes Dated the xth of Aprill Anno Septimo Jacobi . . . Thomas Grene christofer Bretiner Thomas Haywood Richard Pyrkyns Robert Pallant Thomas Swynnerton John Duke Robert Lee James Hoult & Robert Brestiner.']
[Norwich 30 Mar. 1616 'A Patent was this day brought into the Court by Thomas Swynerton made to Thomas Grene, xxofer Beeston, Thomas hayward, Richard Pirkyns, Robert Pallant, Thomas Swynnerton John Duke Robert Lee James Hoult &

Robt Beeston Servants to Quene Anne'] John Danyell [Norwich 1616–17] 'Robert Lee Philip Rossiter william Percy & Nicholas Longe.' [Norwich 1618]
[1619 funeral: Thomas Basse, John Blaney, Christopher Beeston, John Cumber, Thomas Drue, John Edmonds, Thomas Heywood, James Haulte, Robert Lee, Robert Pallant, Richard Perkins, William Robinson, Gregory Sanderson, Martin Slater, Thomas Swinnerton, and Ellis Worth].

London Playhouses
Boar's Head, Curtain 1603–5, Red Bull 1605–17, Cockpit 1617–19.

At Court
2 and 13 Jan. 1604; 30 Dec. (*How to Learn a Woman to Woo*); 27 Dec. 1605; five unnamed plays up to 5 Apr. 1609; 27 Dec.; four unnamed plays 10 Dec. 1610 before the prince, 27 Dec. before the king; 27 Dec. 1611 and 2 Feb. 1612 (*Greene's Tu Quoque*) before the king and queen, with King's Men 12 and 13 Jan. (*The Silver Age* and *Rape of Lucrece*) before the queen and prince, 21 and 23 Jan.; 24 Dec. 1613, 5 Jan. 1614; three unnamed plays up to 25 Apr. 1615; four unnamed plays, 17 Dec. and up to 20 May 1616; three unnamed plays up to 9 Mar. 1617; [no accounts 1617–1621].

Travelling Records
Faversham, Kent 1604–5, 10s. / Dover 2 Nov. 1605, £1. / Faversham, Kent 1605–6, £1. / Bath 1605–6, 20s. / Cambridge town 1606 'Johannes Duke et Thomas Greene both saye that master Maior did give them absolute authoritye to playe in the Towne Hall & did give order to some to buyld theire Stage & take downe the glasse windowes there & did also give them the Key of the Towne Hall', letter signed by Duke and Greene promising not to play within five miles[36] / Leicester 1605, 40s.; 'for lathes and neyles spent at the hawle at such tyme as the Queenes playars were there', 9d., 'for mendinge the Cheyre in the parler at the hall . . . which was broken by the playars', 11d. / Weymouth, Dorset 1605–6, 10s. / Ipswich 25 July 1606, 26s. 8d. / Ludlow 4 Sept. 1606, 20s. / Beverley 2 Oct. 1606, 20s. / Coventry Nov. acct. 1606, 40s. / York City Books 1606, £4. / Ipswich 1606–7, 26s. / Shrewsbury 1606–7, 20s. / Reading 1606–7, 20s. / Oxford town 14 Aug. 1607, 20s. / Bath 1606–7, 10s.; 'given more', 20s. / Coventry Nov. acct. 1607, 20s. / Leicester 1607, 30s. / Bridgwater, Somerset 11 June 1607, 13s. 4d. / York City Books 23 Sept. 1607 'now the Quenes Majesties Players have made suite to this Court that they might be permitted to plaie in this Cittie and have showed licence from her Majestie that they maie be permitted to plaie in all Cittye and Townes Corporate It is agreed by thes presentes that they shalbe permitted to playe in this Citties so as they do not plaie on the Sabaoth daies & on the nightes' / Ipswich Oct. 1607, 26s. 8d. / Dunwich, Suffolk 14 Oct. 1607, 10s. / Oxford town 1607–8, 10s. / Barnstaple, Devon 1607–8, 10s. / Coventry Nov. acct. 1608, 20s. / Manchester 1608–9, 19s. / Shrewsbury 1608–9, 10s. 8d. / Coventry Nov. acct. 1609 'to the

---

[36] *REED, Cambridge*, i. 399 transcribes James's patent for the university, which specified that plays and games were banned within five miles of the town.

Queenes players to Thomas Swinerton' 40s. / Dartmouth 1608–9, 10s. / Dover 1608–9, £1.; 'for wyne given them', 6s. / Folkestone 1608–9, 6s. 8d. / Lydd, Kent 1608–9, 20s. / Faversham, Kent 8 May 1609, 10s. / Canterbury 1608–9, 20s., 'mr Mayor & the Company with hym beinge at the playe by them made at the Checkar and also spent then in beere & byskettes', 8d. / Leicester 6 June 1609, 40s. / Beverley 13 Sept. 1609, 20s. / Leicester 26 Sept. 1609 'one other Companye of ye Queenes playors', 20s. / Norwich 15 Oct. 1609, 30s. / Lydd, Kent 1609–10, 10s. / Maidstone 1609–10, 10s. / New Romney, Kent 7 Apr. 1610, 10s. / Southampton 1609–10, £1. / Ipswich 2 Nov. 1610, £1. 6s. 8d. / Dover 27 Oct. 1610, £1. / Leicester 31 Dec. 1610, 40s. / Southampton 1610–11, 40s. / Norwich 2 Mar. 1611 'to play for one weeke so that they play neither on the saboth day nor in the night nor more then one play on a day' / Ipswich 1611–12 'ij companies of pleyers the Quenes & Princes men', 53s. 4d. / Shrewsbury 1611–12, 20s. / Folkestone 1611–12, 5s. / Maidstone 1611–12, 5s. / Rye, Sussex Apr. 1612, 20s. / Hythe, Kent 10 Apr. 1612, 10s. / Faversham, Kent 18 Apr. 1612, 20s. / Dover 11 Apr. 1612, 13s. 4d. / Lydd, Kent 23 Apr. 1612, 10s. / Southampton 9 May 1612 'unto Thomas Swinarton and his felowes the Queens majesties Comedians or players xl s and is to the end they sholl use no such exercise in this towne', 40s. / Bridgwater, Somerset May 1612, 20s. / Leicester 14 June 1612, 40s. / New Romney, Kent 3 Aug. 1612, 20s. / Dover 29 Aug. 1612, 10s. / Leicester 26 Oct. 1612, 40s. / Barnstaple, Devon 1612–13 'unto the Princes players and unto the Queens players', 40s. / Ipswich 1612–13, £1. 10s. / Manchester 18 Feb. 1613, 20s. / Leicester 16 Mar. 1613, 20s. / Hythe, Kent 3 Apr. 1613, 10s. / Faversham, Kent 15 Apr. 1613, 10s. / Dover 17 Apr. 1613, 10s. / Coventry Nov. acct. 1613, 40s. / Manchester 2 Nov. 1613, 20s. / Leicester 22 Dec. 1613, 40s. / Manchester 1613–14, 20s. / Ipswich 1613–14, 30s. / Wallingford, Berkshire 1613–14, 5s. / Shrewsbury 1613–14, 20s. / Southampton 1613–14, 20s. / Maidstone 1613–14, 10s. / New Romney, Kent 1613–14, 20s. / Oxford town 13 Mar. 1614, 20s. / Sudbury, Suffolk 1613–14, 10s. / Norwich 20 Apr. 1614 'Swynnerson one of the Quenes players in the name of himselfe & the rest of his Company desyred leave to play in the Cytty accordynge to his Majestes Letteres patentes shewed foorth, And mr Maior & Court moved them to play onely on wednesday Thursday & fryday in Easter weke' / Hythe, Kent 30 July 1614, 6s. 6d. / Rye, Sussex Aug. 1614, 10s. / New Romney, Kent 1614–15, 20s. / Fordwich, Kent 27 Aug. 1614, 6s. 8d. / Dover 3 Sept. 1614 'geven of late', 10s. / Sudbury, Suffolk 1614–15, 10s. / Barnstaple, Devon 1614–15 'to the Queenes and Princes players', 25s. 10d. / Southampton 1614–15, 20s. / Manchester 7 Nov. 1614, 20s. / Shrewsbury 1614–15, 20s. / Coventry 15 Apr. 1615, 40s. / Leicester Apr.–May 1615, 40s. / Norwich 6 May 1615 'Thomas Swynnerton produced this day Letters Patentes Dated the xth of Aprill Anno Septimo Jacobi [1609] whereby hee & others are authorised to play as the Quenes men videlicet Thomas Grene christofer Brestiner Thomas Haywood Richard Pyrkyns Robert Pallant Thomas Swynnerton John Duke Robert Lee James Hoult & Robert Brestiner' / Doncaster 1615, 20s. / Leicester 16 Oct. 1615, 40s. / Dunkenhalgh, Lancs. (Household accounts of

Thomas Walmesley) 23 Oct. 1615, 'gyven unto the Queenes players for 2 playes', 30s. / Manchester 26 Oct. 1615, 20s. / Kendal 1 Nov. 1615 [1614?], 10s. / Ludlow 5 Nov. 1615, 40s. / Coventry 14 Nov. 1615, 20s. / Newcastle Dec. 1615, 40s. / Dunwich, Suffolk 1615–16, 5s. / Barnstaple, Devon 1615–16, 20s. / Dover 20 Jan. 1616 'expecially for that they were so earnest that mr Maior the Jurattes and some other gentlemen, that were at the Castle with his Lordshipp to be present at one play', £2. / Southampton 1615–16, 20s. / Nottingham Jan 1616, 20s. / Coventry 17 Feb. 1616, 20s. / Leicester 22 Feb. 1616 'one other Companye of the Queenes playors for a smale gratuytie', 22s., 30s. / Dunwich, Suffolk 1616, 3s. 4d., 'at an other tyme', 2s. / Norwich 30 Mar. 1616 'A Patent was this day brought into the Court by Thomas Swynerton made to Thomas Grene christofer Beeston Thomas Hayward Richard Pirkyns Robert Pallant Richard Pirkyns Thomas Swynerton John Duke Robert Lee James Hoult & Robert Beeston Servantes to Quene Anne & the rest of their associates bearinge Teste xv Aprilis Anno Septimo Jacobi [1609] But the said Swynerton Confesseth that hee himselfe & robert Lee only are here to play the rest are absent he was desired to desist from playing & offered a benevolence in mony which he refused to accept And mr Reason one of the Princes servantes came in at the same tyme affirminge that they had A patent, And theise two Companyes have leave to play ffower dayes this next weke' / Dunkenhalgh, Lancs. (Household accounts of Thomas Walmesley) 20 Apr. 1616, 30s. / Dover 11 May 1616, 11s. 'in gold' / Norwich 29 May 1616, 'Thomas Swynerton came this day into the Court & affirmed himselfeto be one of the players to the Quenes Majestie & bringinge with him no patent desyred to have leave to play here But because the same Company had liberty to play here at Easter last as by an order 30 Marcii 1616 may appeare whereby they were restreyned to the newhall But that restreynt was afterward mittigated & thay had leave to play two of the fower dayes then graunted unto them at Powles howse & the other two at the newhall yet they are agayne returned hether Therefore there ys no leave graunted unto him whereupon yt was sayd unto him yf yow will play yow must doo yt at your perill without our leave his answer was wee will adventure the perill & we meane on monday next to play in the Cytty, yet afterward this howse offered him a gratuitie to desist he was content to accept the same & promised desistance accordingly' / Weymouth, Dorset June–July 1616 'for not plaing here' £1. 10s. / Norwich 20 July 1616, 'This day Martyn Slaughter brought into this Court A Patent Teste 17 Januarii Anno Nono Jacobi [1611] made to Thomas Grene christofer Beeston Thomas Heyward Richard Pirkins Robert Pallant Thomas Swynnerton John Duke Robert Lee James Howlt & Robert Beeston to play &c. This Patent hath ben twise shewed singe Easter, this ys the Third tyme, The said Martyn Slaughter ys not named in the Patent therefore hee hath no leave to play' / Kendal 13 Aug. 1616, 10s. / Ludlow Nov. 1616, 6s. 8d. / Folkestone 1616–17, 5s. / Southampton 1616–17 'to Thomas Swynerton and fellowes being hir Majesties players', £0. (sic) / Oxford town 1616–17 20s. / Norwich 1616–17 'unto John Danyell one of the Company of the Quenes Majesties Players for A gratuitie to the end they might forbeare to play',

30s. / Bath 1616–17[37] / Leominster, Herefordshire 1616–17, 10s. / Nottingham 1616–17, 20s.; 'the Queenes players belonginge to the Courte', 10s. / Leicester 6 Feb. 1617, 20s. / Coventry 24 Feb. 1617 'to the Queenes Majesties players belonging to the Chamber of Bristowe' 40s.[38] / Leicester 1617, 'the Queenes playors' 20s. / Gawthorpe, Lancs. (Household accounts of Sir Richard Shuttleworth) 10 Mar. 1617, 10s. / Fordwich, Kent 14 Mar. 1617, 7s. / Dover 22 Mar. 1617, 11s. / Rye, Sussex Apr. 1617, 20s.[39] / Norwich 31 May 1617 'This day Robert Lee brought into the Court an Exemplificacion of A Patent bearinge Teste xvto Aprilis Anno 7 Jacobi [1609] And the Exemplificacion ys dated Septimo Januarii Anno 9 Jacobi [1611] whereby Lycence ys gyven to Thomas Grene christofer Beeston Thomas Hayward Richard Pirkyns Robert Pallant Thomas Swynnerton John Duke the saide Robert Lee James Howltt & Robert Beeston Servantes to Quene Anne to play &c, they are licenced to play in this Cytty in whitson weeke next, Monday Tuseday & wednesday in Powles howse & no longer'[40] / Fordwich, Kent 16 Sept. 1617, 7s. / Kendal 16 Oct. 1617, 11s. / Coventry 22 Oct. 1617, 20s. / Dover 1 Nov. 1617, 11s. / Coventry 3 Dec. 1617, 20s. / Leicester 16 Dec. 1617, 22s. / Folkestone 1617–18 'in Wyne', 19d. / Sudbury, Suffolk 1617–18, 10s. / Ipswich 1617–18, £1. 6s. 8d. / Nottingham 1617–18, 20s. / Newark, Nottinghamshire 1617–18, 13s. / Carlisle 1617–18, 22s. / Gawthorpe, Lancs. (Household Accounts of Sir Richard Shuttleworth) 10 Mar. 1618, 10s. / Kendal 22 Mar. 1618 'more . . . that was given to the queens players in gold', 11s. / Prescot 5 June 1618 (Court Leet Records) 'wee doe present James dytcheffyeld for makinge a Tusle upon one of the queenes servantes a Player & the said player with others of his Felowes for the lyke upon the said James dytcheffyelld. Pledge for them all Henrye Stanleye Esquier.' / Norwich 29 Aug. 1618, 'Robert Lee Philip Rossiter william Percy & Nicholas Longe . . . lycenced to play Comedyes &c by the space of Fourten dayes in any citty . . . for three dayes, and for further tyme they are not.' / Folkestone 8 Oct. 1618, 4s. / Hythe, Kent 9 Oct. 1618, 10s. / Dover 31 Oct. 1618, 11s. / New Romney, Kent 1618–19, 10s. / Winchester 1618–19, 20s. / Reading 11 Nov. 1618, 22s. / Sudbury, Suffolk 1618–19, 10s. / Leominster, Herefordshire 1618–19, 7s. / Reading 1619–20 'and for a proclamacion to the pursuivant and to the Countess of Rutlandes jester', 27s.

[37] The Queen Anne's visit to Bath marks a shift in policy by this and probably several other towns towards the professional playing companies. The town gave the company nothing, and instead took half a mark, 3s. 4d. or one-sixth of a pound, in rent for allowing the players to use the Town Hall (*REED, Somerset and Bath*, unpublished). From here on the absence of records in town archives may simply indicate that the companies were now free to go their own way without seeking the mayor's leave. The Norwich records are the chief evidence against this, though they show mayoral hostility rather than the direct responsibility for plays that the Tudors laid on local mayors in 1559.

[38] A special company, not the London group. See below, 403.

[39] A note adds 'Not to be Allowed'. Whether this was the mayor banning the performance or an auditor's note refusing to verify the mayor's over-generous payment is not clear. Most likely, to judge by the actions of auditors in other towns, it was the latter.

[40] A subsequent entry dated 7 June allots this time instead to the Lady Elizabeth's players, and orders that 'the said Lee & his Company are comanded to desist as aforesaid accordinge to the Lord Chamberlyns warrant before mencioned'. REED, *Norwich*, 152.

RED BULL (REVELS) COMPANY, 1619–1625

Plays
The Costly Whore, Gramercy Wit (lost), *The Heir, Herod and Antipater, The Merry Milkmaids, Two Noble Ladies, The Virgin Martyr, The Welsh Traveller* (lost).

Players
Thomas Basse, Richard Baxter, John Blaney, Christopher Beeston, John Cumber, Thomas Drue, John Edmonds, Thomas Heywood, James Haulte, Robert Lee, Robert Pallant, Richard Perkins, William Robinson, Gregory Sanderson, Martin Slater, Thomas Swinnerton, Ellis Worth.

Playhouses
Red Bull.

At Court
1620–1 (*The Merry Milkmaids?*); 30 Dec. 1621 *Gramercy Wit*.

Travelling Records
Exeter 1619 'to be stowe one those that wer some tyme the Quens players', £1. 2s. / Carlisle 1619 'upon the late quenes Majesties players', 21s. / Craven, Yorks. 1619, 'Given to 15 men that were players, who belonged to the late Queen, but did not play', 13s. 4d. / Manchester 1619, 20s. / Leicester 1619–20 'to Swynnerton and his Companye of players', £1. / Lydd, Kent 18 Mar. 1620 'to the late Queene Anne her plaiers', 11s. / Dover 18 Mar. 1620 'to the late Quene Anne her players', 11s. / Coventry 29 Mar. 1620 'to Danieel Swynnerton & the Company of Players belonging to the late Queene Ann', 10s. / York City Books 1620 'the late Quenes players', 13s. 4d. / Nottingham Dec. 1620, 13s. 4d. / Manchester 1620–1, 5s. / Lydd, Kent 19 Feb. 1621, 5s. / Sudbury, Suffolk 1621–2 'to the Queens players the La: Elizabeth hir players and the Children of the revells', 28s. / Wallingford, Berkshire 1621–2 'the Kinge and Queenes and princes players', 23s. 4d. / Leicester 21 Dec. 1621 'not playing for a gratuitye', 22s. / Manchester 15 Mar. 1622, 10s. / Faversham, Kent 1621–2, £1. / Norwich 28 June 1622 'players of the late Quene Anne . . . forbidden', 40s. / Leicester 1622 'not playeinge', 20s. / Norwich 24 May 1623 'to william Perry & other of the late Quene Ann her Company of players', 40s. / Nottingham 1623–4, 10s. / Leicester 27 Jan. 1624, 40s. / Dover 20 Mar. 1624 'the players of the late good Quene Anne', 10s. / Coventry Dec. 1624, 12s. 6d. / Leicester 27 Dec. 1624, £1. / Norwich 28 May 1625 'This day Ellis Gest brought into this Court a lycence under the hand & seale of Sir Henry Hobart maister of the Revelles bearinge date the xvith of March Anno xxii Jacobi nuper Regis [1625], whereby the said Ellis & other of his Company are lycensed to play &c to whome was shewed the Letters from the Lords of the Counsell & his Majesties proclamacion And thereupon they were not permitted to play But in regard of the honorable report which this City beareth to the right honorable ye Lord Chamberlyn and Sir Henry Hobart there ys given unto them as a gratuety xxs. A Letter ys to be written to the Lord Chamberlyn

touchinge players.'[41] 20*s.* / Coventry 16 Oct. 1625 'to Martyn Slatier, Robson, & Silvester late servantes to the late queene Anne', 5*s.* / Leicester 1627–8 'Swinnerton and his Companie', £1. / Norwich 19 July 1628 'to Mr Thomas Swynerton A player', 20*s.*

---

[41] Ellis or Elias Guest is a shadowy figure, and his company is even more shadowy. Herbert gave him a licence for playing in 1625, and he appeared at Leicester in company with Thomas Swinnerton in the same year. He is included here on the basis of his link with Swinnerton. Given that Swinnerton was then with the Red Bull company, Guest's licence is likely to have been a copy of theirs. Guest was not a London player. On a later visit to Norwich on 2 July 1628 twelve players besides himself are named in his company, none of whom seem to have been London players. At Norwich in 1629 he was in a company with Moore and Townsend of the Lady Elizabeth's.

When the Paul's Boys were brought back to life in 1599 London playing had been transformed. Regulation of playing was much tighter and quite different from the situation in 1590. First, the Privy Council had finally acceded to the mayor's insistence on banning plays from inside the city. Secondly, it had approved two companies as the only purveyors of royal entertainment in the Christmas season. And the Master of the Revels had backed up the Privy Council policy by tightening his own control, now licensing playhouses as well as performances for public use. The renewed boy companies, and especially Paul's as the first to resurface, offered a challenge to all of these new policies. They had a playhouse in the heart of the city; they threatened to make a not insignificant addition to the number of approved companies; and they would perform in it as a 'private' hall, with the implied freedom this gave them from the Master's control of 'public' performances and public playhouses.

That last point was very possibly a consequence of the first two. Only as a company playing not for the public but privately could they avoid the new regulations that licensed companies and playhouses. How far the much-flaunted distinction between 'public' and 'private' playing was simply a matter of snobbery, and how much it marked the limits of Tilney's control at this time, is not easy to determine. The two terms were used to distinguish the 'public' amphitheatres from the 'private' hall theatres right through into the 1640s. The real question is whether the snobbish air of 'private' exclusiveness that attached to the halls once the King's Men at Blackfriars started catering for a socially superior clientele should be read back into the first uses of the term 'private' in 1600, and, more to the point, whether that snob value was the only reason for insisting that all the boy-performances were 'private'. The fact that the terms only came into use as distinguishing adjectives when the boy companies resurfaced in 1599–1600 suggests that using them was part of the advertising campaign to promote the two new boy companies. The obvious association of the word 'private' with rich men commanding performances for themselves and their friends in private mansions on the Strand and in country houses makes that reading unavoidable.

But the term also indicates an area where the Master of the Revels's jurisdiction had never been expected to reach, and raises the question whether the boy-companies' promoters clung to the term at least partly in order to escape the Master's control and the attendant costs and restrictions. The terms of Tilney's 1581 patent specifying his authority over 'all and every plaier or plaiers with their playmakers either belonging to any noble man or otherwise, bearinge the name or names of usinge the facultie of playmakers or plaiers of Comedies, tragedies,

Enterludes or what other showes soever'[1] was aimed entirely at the professional adult companies. It did not allow for anything in the huge array of non-commercial playmaking activities, which ranged from school performances to family theatricals in great houses, and whose players might be anyone from schoolboys to household servants, and even to members of the noble families themselves. Tilney was given official power over all playing, but his practical scope was never defined. The grey borderline between the patent's real target, professional playing, and the many varieties of amateur playing was soon crossed, when school performances went commercial in the 1580s. But until 1606 and after, when the boy companies were openly commercial, there is not much evidence for the Master ever licensing either the boy company plays or their playing-places.[2]

It would certainly have helped the Paul's choirmasters' intrusion into the London playing scene in 1599 if they had been able to ignore the Master of the Revels and his licensing activities. To a lesser extent than the Blackfriars impresarios, but still conspicuously, they launched the new boy company by acting as if the Master had no control over their procedures at all, and without any of the concern for patrons and patents that dogged the adults. Plays like *Blurt Master Constable*, which advertised itself on its 1602 title-page as 'privately acted by the Children of Paules', were using the term 'private' overtly to deny any need for the Master's licence.[3]

Tilney and the Privy Council proved markedly slower to take note of the new boy companies than they were of the adult companies' attempts to establish a third foothold in London. That itself may reflect Tilney's uncertainty over his position in relation to them. He gave both of them a show at court after their first full year of operation, on 1 January 1601, but did nothing over their adding themselves to the two approved 'public' companies, and I believe did not license them or their plays. They had no patent like the adult companies. The Privy Council took its first note of them in Lent 1601, when a letter was sent to the Lord Mayor 'requiring him not to faile to take order the playes within the cyttie and the liberties, especyally at Powles and in the Blackfriers, may be suppressed during this time of Lent.'[4] Unlike the Blackfriars company, which insisted on being outrageous, Paul's never had much notice taken of it either by the mayor or the Privy Council. For all its presence in the centre of the city, there is no record of any attempt being made to close its playhouse or to control its crowds. That may have a little to do with its uniquely small auditorium capacity, at two hundred bodies or less. It may equally

---

[1] Feuillerat (ed), *Documents relating to the Office of the Revels*, 51.   [2] See above, 57.
[3] In the lawsuit over *The Old Joiner of Aldgate* Pearce declared that he had given the playbook to Doctor Milward of Christchurch in Newgate St. to approve. He makes no mention of having it licensed by Tilney. Milward was an interested party, since he had married the daughter in the case, and Pearce may simply have been clearing it with him rather than inviting him to censor it.
[4] *Acts of the Privy Council of England*, xxxi. 218. These were the two playhouses that the Council might have thought were within the mayor's control, even though the Blackfriars was in a liberty. Their order to the mayor was to uphold civic order, a duty for which he was answerable even in areas outside his strict jurisdiction.

have something to do with its being officially under the control of the dean and chapter. Most obviously, though, unlike its rival at the Blackfriars, the plays that Paul's staged never gave much cause for alarm or offence.

Thomas Giles, the choirmaster who had run the Paul's Boys with Lyly in their last years up to 1590, had begun to fade from the cathedral scene by 1598.[5] On 11 May 1599 a new choirmaster, Edward Pearce, was appointed in his place. The appointment in fact put him in an awkward position, because Giles was supposed to continue in his post and to keep its stipend and housing. Pearce therefore had the post and its work but no income from it and no house until Giles died, which did not happen for another fourteen months. He was placed in a position similar to Richard Farrant's in the 1580s. Marketing the choir as a company of players in the old playhouse, like Farrant before him, was Pearce's obvious answer:[6] he had a straightforward commercial reason, a survival tactic, for restarting commercial playing. This survival tactic also showed in the choice of repertory and other features of their activities. The Paul's ventures always had a concern for respectability that never bothered the Blackfriars companies; unlike most of the other boy groups, they never went on tour, and their role at the cathedral kept them in much closer touch with their local community than the other boy companies.

The launch of the new Paul's was socially pretentious. It had more specific backing from the nobility than any other company or playhouse ever received. Conceivably the new enthusiasm, which led several nobles to start writing plays for public (usually private) showing, marked a new level of respectability for the profession as a consequence of the duopoly's success with its great repertory of the last few years. More likely, though, the nobles were concerned to maintain their own self-respect by writing for boys instead of the professional adults, and still saw the resurrected Paul's as more reputable performers, private or not, than the adults. The opportunities it offered were taken up by writers who included William Stanley, the sixth earl of Derby, and William Percy, Raleigh's friend and close kin to the earls of Northumberland. Stanley is said to have financed the new company, and Percy certainly wrote for it.[7] Rowland Whyte reported on 13 November 1599 that 'My Lord Darby hath put up the plays of the children in Pawles to his great paines and charge'.[8] Between 1599 and 1602 William Percy wrote six plays for the new company. Two survive in editions of 1601 and 1603, the other four in

---

[5] W. Rearley Gair, *The Children of Paul's: The Story of a Theatre Company, 1553–1608* (Cambridge, 1982), 115.

[6] There has been some dispute about the year when Paul's reopened. Michael Shapiro, *Children of the Revels: The Boy Companies of Shakespeare's Time and their Plays* (New York, 1977) 21, suggests that it may have been as early as 1597. I am inclined to see Pearce's appointment in 1599 as the precipitating factor.

[7] An addition by Percy in the MS collection of his plays is headed 'A note to the Master of children of Powles', and offers ways to shorten the plays if they cannot be fitted into the limited time at Paul's, since they are 'not to begin before foure, after prayers, and the gates of Powles shutting at six' (*ES* ii. 21).

[8] *Historical Manuscripts Commission, Report on the manuscripts of Lord de L'Isle and Dudley*, ed. C. L. Kingsford (6 vols.; London, 1925–66), ii. 415.

manuscript.[9] They contain some highly specific stage directions for distinctly spectacular scenic shows, in a few cases specifying one form of staging that he thought was suitable for the Paul's children and an alternative for an adult company. There is, however, no evidence that either Stanley's or Percy's plays were ever staged at the new Paul's.

It was John Marston, a member of the Middle Temple, always a nest for budding playwrights, who gave the new company its first plays. His two books of satires had been publicly burned in June 1599, in the notorious bishops' clamp-down on salacious and seditious verses. Soon afterwards, on 28 September, Henslowe noted a loan of £2 'Lent unto Mr maxton the new poete in earneste of a Boocke called [blank]',[10] which suggests that he had turned to playwriting instead; but at some point that autumn he gave up writing for Henslowe's 'public' venue, and gave *Antonio and Mellida* to Pearce and Paul's. The first known student of the Inns of Court to write for the common stages, it is a nice question whether he felt that it was socially more respectable to write for a boy company, or simply that the more 'gentle' audience at a 'private' playhouse would receive his ambitious plays more warmly than would the nut-crackers in an amphitheatre yard. He was intensely self-conscious about his venture into writing for the theatre, and he insisted on the distinctiveness of the social class for which he was writing. The Prologue to *Antonio and Mellida* is addressed to the 'Select, and most respected Auditours'. It was a point Marston continued to insist on, inserting into his third play for the company a dialogue where a character applauds the company, saying that 'A man shall not be choakte | With the stench of Garlicke, nor be pasted | to the barmy jacket of a Beer-brewer' at Paul's.[11] One wonders whether, for all the company's lordly backing, he was not insisting too much.[12]

Marston certainly knew the players well, if not the audience, while he was writing *Antonio and Mellida*, because the printed text includes the names of two of the boys set to play it.[13] Marston's second play, *Antonio's Revenge*, has thirteen speaking parts, and needs a company seventeen strong. Since boys did not normally practise the doubling of roles, that gives us the size of the company in 1600.

The company did not launch itself into the public eye with Marston's first opus alone, of course. Some plays from 1590 must have been still available, and were put into the early repertory. This recourse to their old staples did not last long, though. A comment two years later in *Jack Drum's Entertainment*, along with Marston's praise of the select audience at Paul's, refers apologetically to its now-abandoned

[9] Chambers, *ES* iii. 464, thinks it possible that they may have been composed originally before the 1590 closure, and revised for 1599.

[10] *Henslowe's Diary*, 124.

[11] *Jack Drum's Entertainment* (1601), V. i.

[12] For a dispute about the question whether the thrust and tone of Marston's plays was parodic, see Anthony J. Caputi, *John Marston, Satirist* (Ithaca, NY, 1961), and R. A. Foakes, 'John Marston's Fantastical Plays: *Antonio and Mellida* and *Antonio's Revenge*', *PQ* 41 (1962), 229–39.

[13] Gair, *The Children of Paul's*, 118–57, gives a detailed account of Marston's Paul's plays and their staging.

habit of reviving old plays, 'mustie fopperies of antiquitie', that 'do not sute the humorous ages backs, | With clothes in fashion'.[14] Humours plays had supplanted the Lyly tradition even at the boys' playhouses. The surviving play that most readily fits Marston's description is Lyly's *Love's Metamorphosis*. More likely, though, that play was revived not by Paul's but by the Blackfriars Children. In the Stationers' Register in November 1600 it was entered as 'wrytten by master John Lylly and playd by the Children of Paules', but that must have been a relic of its earlier life. Its title-page for the 1601 printing corrects this statement, saying that it was 'First playd by the Children of Paules, and now by the Children of the Chapell'.[15] The combined Paul's/Oxford's/Chapel Children playing at Paul's had it in 1590, but it must have been the Blackfriars boys who revived it in 1600. Reavley Gair[16] thinks that the 'mustie' play may have been *The Wisdom of Doctor Dodypoll*, which he relates in style to *Campaspe*. It has a phrase that seems to be a memory of *Julius Caesar*, which would date it after 1599, and it is not otherwise wildly out of step with 1599 writing. Apart from that and Marston's oblique comment on the mistakes with the early repertory, his own plays are the only definite remnants we have from the initial run at Paul's.

That first run shaped the company's future in two distinct ways. Both were direct consequences of Marston's writing, and both took the company sharply off in new directions and away from his darkly Italianate mixtures of romance and revenge. The first was the attention that his extravagantly inventive language and his neologisms produced from Jonson, whose response pulled the company into the Poetomachia and so into direct conflict with the Blackfriars company. The second, which may in some small part have been a reaction to the first, took them into citizen comedy, the mode that Middleton set going for them. While the Blackfriars Boys allied themselves with the gentry, lawyers, courtiers, and satirists, the Paul's company allied itself more and more with the London citizenry. It staged plays about local residents, such as the *Old Joiner of Aldgate*, in 1602.[17] In 1605 a team of three Blackfriars writers, including an unlikely alliance between Marston and Jonson, wrote a burlesque of the first of two Paul's plays which celebrated citizen values, *Westward Ho!*, which they aptly called *Eastward Ho! Westward Ho!* is protective of citizen self-respect to the extent of showing an earl being grossly humiliated in his unsuccessful attempt to seduce a citizen's wife. *Eastward Ho!* is cynical about all values, especially mercantile ones and those of the female citizenry. Once Paul's had veered towards the citizen mode and showed no signs of returning, Marston switched from writing for them to writing for the Blackfriars.

The so-called 'War of the Theatres' seems really to have started with Jonson, whose scathing assaults on the vapid critical opinions of London audiences had first appeared in *Every Man Out* for the Chamberlain's Men. In *Poetaster* for the

[14] *Jack Drum's Entertainment*, V. i.   [15] *ES* iii. 416.   [16] *The Children of Paul's*, 127–8.
[17] The play is now lost, but its story and the circumstances that led Chapman to write it are described from the records of the court case to which it led by C. J. Sisson, *Lost Plays of Shakespeare's Age* (Cambridge, 1936).

Blackfriars Boys he laid about him widely, attacking adult players and his rivals amongst the theatre poets alike.[18] The most vulnerable and the most wickedly quoted of the latter was Marston, and on his behalf Paul's counter-attacked. Whether the Paul's management simply wanted to defend their chief poet against this attack, or whether they engaged in the noisy public controversy on the 'any-publicity-is-good-publicity' principle we cannot be sure. But *Satiromastix*, Dekker's equally caustic counter-attack on Jonson and the insults of *Poetaster*, representing him as a bibulous Horace, was staged first at Paul's and then by the Chamberlain's at the Globe. Giving a play staged in one company's repertoire to another was a unique action. It might have been done to redouble the publicity about the play, or it might have been handed over to the adults to release Paul's from its involvement in the notorious quarrel. The company's subsequent policy, not to run the kind of 'railing' satire that the Blackfriars exploited so whole-heartedly, seems a matter of positive choice, not least since it brought about the departure of Marston to the other boy company. The most common reactions to the Poetomachia, at least those that appeared in print, did not reflect well on the boy companies. John Davies of Hereford wrote reprovingly 'O imps of Phoebus, whie, o why doe yee | Imploy the Pow'r of your Divinity | (Which should but foyle vice from which we should flee!) | Upon impeaching your owne Quality?'[19] This suggests that people felt some animus over a boy company opting to attack another boy company. The choice of new plays dealing with citizen interests was a fresh start. It became a major fashion in the next years, and Paul's was at its centre.[20] The distance from the Blackfriars Boys which that policy took it led to the Blackfriars assault on the Paul's repertory with *Eastward Ho!* By then the Blackfriars Boys were finding their targets everywhere, and built their reputation on it.

The chief agent in the turn to citizen interests was Thomas Middleton. Marston did take up his own version of Middleton's citizen mode so long as he stayed with the company, writing *What You Will* and *Jack Drum's Entertainment* for them in 1601. *What You Will* starts with a discreet acknowledgement of the Poetomachia, and a reminder of *Antonio's Revenge*.[21] It has a comic story using less colourful language than the earlier plays, and including a school scene that reflects and perhaps was designed to advertise the privileged and 'private' status of the boy players. *Jack Drum* is also much less rich in verbal exhibitionism. But these are

[18] The targets of the plays used in the War are not always easily identified. David Bevington, *Tudor Drama and Politics* (Cambridge, Mass., 1968), 262–88, gives a sensitive appraisal of the evidence.

[19] *Wittes Pilgrimage*, n.d. [1605], in *The Complete Works of John Davies of Hereford*, ed. A. B. Grosart (Edinburgh, 1878), ii. 37.

[20] Critics have differed radically in their readings of the 'citizen' comedies, either seeing them as voicing citizen values or as burlesquing them. Like Marston's plays, much of the evidence can be read either way. But I think that some confusion has been caused over this question by the failure to differentiate Paul's plays from Blackfriars plays. See e.g. Alexander Leggat, *Citizen Comedy in the Age of Shakespeare* (Toronto, 1973), 4; Brian Gibbons, *Jacobean City Comedy* (2nd edn. London, 1980), 76–7; and Theodore B. Leinwand, *The City Staged: Jacobean Comedy, 1603–1613* (Madison, Wis., 1986), 14–20.

[21] Gair, *The Children of Paul's*, 139–40.

negative indicators. *Blurt Master Constable* and the story told in Chapman's *The Old Joiner of Aldgate* are much more positive.

The story behind *The Old Joiner of Aldgate* is extraordinary in itself. In 1602 Chapman was employed, so he told the lawyers, to write a play burlesquing, or at least depicting one side of, a distinctly local domestic scandal, a tale about a family dispute that started in 1600 and was still running hotly in a parish barely two hundred yards from the Paul's Churchyard. It concerned a father's financial wrangles with several suitors who were after his daughter, and his attempts to get away without performing the traditional obligation of paying her dowry. A book-binder called John Flaskett, one of the girl's suitors, who had a shop in Paul's yard, paid Chapman to write it and then took the girl's father to see the play at Paul's. The father protested in court that he had not recognized the story as applying to himself. Everyone else saw that the plot, though 'under coulorable & fayned names personated',[22] had a local application. Whether the play was commissioned in order to help settle the dispute, as was claimed, or to show the father the error of his ways, which seems more likely, it fitted the new mode of citizen comedy by confining the personae and the codes of conduct to citizen culture.

Blurt Master Constable, which probably preceded Chapman's play by a year or so, is a stronger candidate for the responsibility of turning the Paul's management's enthusiasm towards its new line. Like Marston's plays, it used the skills of the boys in dances and singing.[23] More to the point, its title located it in London, and although the play itself is not keyed closely to particular London localities it does offer evidence that the company now saw its central position inside London as its best drawcard. Middleton made the same point with *Michaelmas Term* and *The Puritan*. All the extant plays from the next years show this sense of belonging to London and to city audiences, more magnate than apprentice certainly, but far from court affairs and free from the satirical bite that the Blackfriars plays had developed. When Beaumont's foolishly self-satisfied Citizen in *The Knight of the Burning Pestle* complains that the Blackfriars Boys have been producing 'girds at Citizens' for the last seven years at their playhouse he is, however comically and involuntarily, distinguishing the one boy company from the other.

By 1607, though, there was only the one boy company still operating in London. Pearce had been valuable to the company not only as the first instigator of playing in 1599 and as its chief musician and arranger of songs, but for his power to take up boys for singing. After Giles's death as choirmaster he had the power to take up any boy he chose for the choir and therefore for the company. His duties, however, cannot have made it easy for him to run the company on his own, and in 1603 or 1604, probably during the long closure for plague then, he took in another partner. He had already used Thomas Woodford, who secured *The Old Joiner of Aldgate* for the company. His relations with Woodford soured, though, and it was later charged

---

[22] C. J. Sisson, *Lost Plays*, 58.
[23] According to Gair, *The Children of Paul's*, 16, the composer of at least two of the songs in *Blurt* was Pearce.

that on 2 December 1604 he had inflicted some grievous bodily harm on him.[24] Woodford did not stay with the company much beyond that date. Edward Kirkham's is the name in the court payment for the company's two performances in 1605–6.

Kirkham's arrival on the scene is intriguing. The Chamber accounts describe him as 'one of the Masters of the Children of Pawles'.[25] He was actually the Yeoman of the Revels in Tilney's office, and had recently been working as one of the Blackfriars Children's managers. Conceivably he was using his familiarity with company proceedings from his official position to muscle in on the management side of the boy companies whenever there was an opening. Pearce's other duties with the choir probably gave Kirkham the chance to move in with Paul's. He may have brought Marston's *The Fawn* from the Blackfriars with him as a sweetener, since it was in the Blackfriars repertory according to the first of its 1606 printings, 'and since at Poules' in the other. Another possibility is that Kirkham was put in by Tilney to sharpen his grip on the boy groups in the wake of the troubles the Blackfriars company had given him. He may even have acted as a kind of receiver or winder-up for the assets of the dying Paul's company.

Kirkham's arrival certainly did not strengthen the company's position. They played a lost play called *The Abuses* before James and his visiting brother-in-law, Christian of Denmark, at Greenwich on 30 July 1606, but after that Paul's vanishes from theatre history. The decision was taken some time in that year to close down the company's playing activities. The Blackfriars Boys were in serious trouble over their railing plays, and despite the difference in their repertories Paul's may have felt themselves threatened too. Some profit was there to be made by passing the Paul's assets to the other boy company while it was still in being; and some profit was certainly made, because ten of the Paul's playbooks were given to the press in 1607 and 1608, and at least one other, *A Trick to Catch the Old One*, was then taken on by the Blackfriars Boys.

Another possible reason for Pearce's decision to close was the Master of the Revels' tightening control, and especially his control of censorship, which underlines the hazard that the company ran under with one of its last plays, Chapman's *Bussy D'Ambois*. French politics were a muddy field to plough through, as the Blackfriars Boys found two years later, when the French ambassador reacted to Chapman's first *Byron* play and James ordered the company to be suppressed. *Bussy* did not have the political immediacy of the *Byron* plays. Its hero is a malcontent, almost a theatrical cliché after *Hamlet*, whose moral stance exposes the corruptions of the court. Its high moral uplift is an obverse to the mockery of corruption among merchants and lawyers that characterized the comedies of this period, such as *A Trick to Catch the Old One*.

The most likely reason for the company's closure was lack of income. The tiny Paul's playhouse could seat less than half the number at the Blackfriars, and even

---

[24] H. N. Hillebrand, *The Child Actors: A Chapter in Elizabethan Stage History* (Urbana, Ill., 1926), 213.
[25] *MSC* vi. 44.

the Blackfriars was not prospering. Its manager, Henry Evans, had already made an approach to his landlords, the Burbages, in 1605 about surrendering his lease. The boys were not sharers in the profits as the adult players were, but it cost money to keep them fed and housed, however much of the cost Pearce might try to shuffle across to the choir and the school. The fact that they could perform only once a week, whether because of their age and immaturity compared with the adults or because of a traditional constraint that set a limit to 'private' performances, reduced their profitability still further. With managers like Pearce who could turn to other things, their motivation was also a major factor. After seven years Pearce's drive had clearly gone. Woodford had been no help, and Kirkham appears to have had little enthusiasm for much besides taking his winding-up profits.

There were other clouds over the churchyard too. More than any other factor, *The Puritan*, most likely another of Middleton's plays which was staged at Paul's in 1606, brought about the final closure. Its three serving-men, listed in the stage direction that opens the second scene, are 'Nicholas Saint-Tantlings, Simon Saint Mary-Overies, *and* Frailitie *in blacke scurvie mourning coates, and Bookes at their Girdles, as coming from Church*'. They are shown to be hypocritical Puritans. To identify local parishioners in this way was fighting talk. On 14 February 1608 William Crashaw delivered the Paul's-Cross sermon. A major social event, Paul's-Cross sermons were delivered in the open air outside St Paul's on public holidays. They were almost all rated as important enough to be worth publishing. Crashaw's appeared soon after it was delivered, and shows how close by his chief target was. He condemned Pearce roundly and explicitly. His script (with phrases picked out in italics in the printed text) argued that '*hee that teacheth children to play, is not an instructor, but a spoiler and destroyer of children*: they know they have no calling, but are in the State like warts on the hand, or blemishes in the face'. He condemned the play for bringing religion onto the stage. 'Two hypocrites must be brought foorth; and how shall they be described but by these names, *Nicolas S. Antlings, Simon S. Maryoveries?*' *The Puritan* had been registered for printing on 6 August 1607, and would have been ready to Crashaw's hand for his citations. But the guilty script itself was only the preacher's pretext. Crashaw was marshalling the more puritanical elements of the church to have Pearce's playmaking stopped. In the event, by 1608 he was closing the stable door. The company did not appear at court after the Christmas season of 1605–6, and may have closed soon after their Greenwich performance for King Christian at the end of July 1606.

THE SECOND PAUL'S CHILDREN, 1599–1606[26]

Plays
The Abuses (lost), *Antonio and Mellida, Antonio's Revenge, Blurt Master Constable, Bussy D'Ambois, The Family of Love, The Fawn* (old), *Jack Drum's Entertainment,*

---

[26] Michael Shapiro, *Children of the Revels*, in App. B has an accurate list of all boy company performances between 1559 and 1613, and in App. C a list of their plays. The second Paul's are listed on 259–60 and 262–3.

Love's Metamorphosis, A Mad World My Masters, The Maid's Metamorphosis, Michaelmas Term, Northward Ho!, The Old Joiner of Aldgate (lost), *The Phoenix, The Puritan, Satiromastix, A Trick to Catch the Old One, Westward Ho!, What You Will, The Wisdom of Doctor Dodypoll, The Woman Hater.*

Managers
Edward Pearce, Edward Kirkham.

Boy Players
[named in *Antonio and Mellida*] Cole, Norwood. 1605: Henry Burnett, Lightfoot Codbolt, Thomas Codbolt, Nicholas Crosse, John Dawson, Richard Kennedy, John Mansell, Richard Patrick, Thomas Peers, Thomas Waters.

London Playhouses
Paul's.

At Court
1 Jan. 1601; 1 Jan. 1603; 20 Feb. 1604 (*The Phoenix?*); two unnamed plays up to 31 Mar. 1606 before the prince and Duke of York; 30 July (*The Abuses*).

The company of boys that in 1600 found its playhouse in the Blackfriars venture which, four years previously, had been lost by the Chamberlain's Men, had an ironist of sorts behind it. Henry Evans, a scrivener and entrepreneur, had worked with a group of Chapel Children at Farrant's Blackfriars in the 1580s. He was payee at court in December 1584 for the company that was then briefly known as Oxford's Children. His earlier time with the Chapel Children may have prompted him to set up a new company in the new Blackfriars playhouse which he chose to call 'the Children of the Chappell'.[1] He was relying on people's memories to secure him a place in the exclusive neighbourhood that had brought down a ban on the play-house four years earlier, and was using the familiar old name for the players from a royal choir-school to which he had no right. His was a far bolder and riskier venture than Edward Pearce's in reviving Paul's. Pearce gave him the model and the precedent, but he lacked Pearce's resources and backing. He had no playhouse, and no licence to enlist boy-choristers.

None the less he evidently decided that it was an investment capable of bringing him good returns. From the Burbages, short of cash after building the Globe, Evans took a twenty-one-year lease of the Blackfriars playhouse, starting at the end of September (Michaelmas) 1600. In order to obtain his boy players he brought in Nathaniel Giles (no relation of Thomas Giles at Paul's), who had been made Master of the Chapel at Windsor three years before, and so had the authority to take children for his choir. He also brought in Edward Kirkham, Yeoman of the Revels, who was in charge of the Revels Office wardrobe and had access to a large store of theatrical properties. A fourth helper was his son-in-law, Alexander Hawkins, who was soon to prove the value in Elizabethan business practice of relying on family loyalties.

Nathaniel Giles was the vital enabler. He was a music-maker, and it must have been his skills that set up the Blackfriars consort, a group of string and woodwind players who preluded each play with a concert of instrumental music, and who soon became the most celebrated group of musicians in London. Frederic Gerschow, a courtier in the suite of the Duke of Stettin-Pomerania, visiting London in September 1602, reported that the concert before the play ran for as much as an hour in length. As a non-English-speaker he himself was most impressed by the music and the boys' singing.[2] The Blackfriars consort, and the backing it provided

---

[1] That is how they are described on the title-page of Lyly's *Love's Metamorphosis*, printed in 1601, which was probably the first of the company's plays to appear in print.

[2] Quoted (in German) in *ES* ii. 46–7. The full text and a translation is in *Transactions of the Royal Historical Society*, n.s. 6 (1892), 29.

for the boys in their songs and dances, became a major asset and a distinctive and comforting attraction for the gentry attending the new playhouse in its wealthy enclave. That was Giles's lasting contribution to the company and to playmaking at large.

Giles's role as choirmaster authorized to take up choirboys, and the hazards of applying his authority to take up boys for playing, show up in a case that Henry Clifton brought against him in the Star Chamber late in 1601. It came about through a clash of the previous year soon after the company opened, when Giles and Evans upset Clifton. Clifton's son Thomas had been taken by Giles and his 'confederate' Evans in 1600, ostensibly for the choir but actually for the Blackfriars boy company. Clifton's complaint listed several of the boys so taken:

John Chappell, a gramer schole scholler of one Mr. Spykes schole neere Criplegate, london; john Motteram, a gramer scholler in the free schole at Westminster; Nathan Field, a scholler of a gramer schole in London, kepte by one Mr. Monkaster; Alvery Trussell, an apprentice to one Thomas Gyles; one Phillipp Pykman and Thomas Grymes, apprentices to Richard and Georg Chambers; Salomon Pavy, apprentice to one Peerce.[3]

These boys, said Clifton, were 'noe way able or fitt for singing, nor by anie the sayd confederates endevoured to be taught to singe'. Young Thomas Clifton, a thirteen-year-old, had been kidnapped on the way from home to his grammar school at Christ Church, and forced 'to exercyse the base trade of a mercynary enterlude player, to his utter losse of tyme, ruyne and disparagment'. Giles and Evans, Clifton told the Star Chamber, had claimed to have 'aucthoritie sufficient soe to take any noble mans sonne in this land'. After a violent confrontation Clifton secured his son's release.

This was a serious charge against the company managers. In 1602 the Star Chamber censured Evans for 'his unorderlie carriage and behaviour in takinge up of gentlemens children against their wills and to ymploy them for players and for other misdemeanors'.[4] For the company's sake that meant Evans and Giles had to move out of sight. In April Giles went back to his duties at Windsor Chapel, and he does not appear to have helped the Blackfriars any further. He later distanced himself further by becoming a canon at Worcester Cathedral.[5] Evans put his son-in-law into his own place, and brought in three more financiers, Kirkham from the Revels Office, William Rastall, a merchant, and Thomas Kendall, a haberdasher, who between them raised several hundred pounds to underwrite the enterprise. Kendall used his share to make his haberdashery business useful to the players. He was an early theatrical costumier. He supplied costumes and other properties to Oxford for the theatricals that accompanied the king's visit there in June 1605.

The introduction of the new names as controllers and financiers raises a tricky and important question about the company's management. None of the boy companies worked like the 'common players', where the managerial decisions, es-

---

[3] *ES* ii. 43–4.   [4] *ES* ii. 44–5.
[5] His will is transcribed in *Playhouse Wills 1558–1642*, 171–5.

pecially the choice of plays for the repertory, were agreed collectively by the sharers, and only specific tasks such as handling the finances or caring for the apprentices were allocated to individual players. In the boy companies a single controller looked after the boys, hiring and feeding them, and making the decisions about what the repertory should offer. Sebastian Westcott, Richard Mulcaster, Thomas Giles, and Richard Farrant did that for the early boy companies and Edward Pearce did it for the second Paul's Boys. It is less easy to find an equivalent figure working for the Blackfriars Children. Evans started them going, bringing in helpers with specific resources such as Nathaniel Giles and Kirkham.[6] He and Giles set up the Blackfriars musicians, and it was he who later brought in the extra financiers. But whether it was he who ran the repertory, and whether he stayed on in the company taking the daily decisions even when the Star Chamber troubles made him retreat into the background, is not at all clear.

There is actually something rather like a hole at the heart of the Blackfriars company's management. Nobody was ever named as the man who handled its repertory. Jonson arrived on the scene in 1600, and started doing the job that Marston performed for the Paul's Boys, writing their first self-advertising play with *Cynthia's Revels* and taking them into the Poets' War with *Poetaster*. There is plenty of evidence for his directing the boys in the tiring house, but there is none for him taking control of the repertory. And where Pearce at Paul's can be seen changing direction, moving away from Marston towards Middleton and the localized citizen-plays, the man in charge of the Blackfriars repertory took a strong line distinctly his own. The company followed the same line consistently almost from the beginning. Its potent series of 'railing' plays, defying authority throughout, matches Evans's clashes with the Star Chamber and his flouting of Kirkham's Master, Edmund Tilney, in the years following. But whether this strong line with the railing plays was Evans's choice, and whether he was the singular guiding spirit that gave the company its powerful reputation for its first eight spectacular years, we cannot finally be sure.

Tilney took note of the new boy-company that was using an old name in their first Christmas season, inviting them to play at court with a 'showe' on 6 January and a play on 22 February 1601. The Privy Council took note of the resurrected boy companies in Lent 1601, with its letter to the Lord Mayor 'requiring him not to faile to take order the playes within the cyttie and the liberties, especally at Powles and in the Blackfriers, may be suppressed during this time of Lent'.[7] At this time there is nothing to show that Tilney was taking any responsibility for their plays, except to use the company for the Christmas season. When Elizabeth died, a peculiar set of court manœuvres involving the Blackfriars company took place, peculiar enough to suggest strongly that Tilney had still not yet exerted his authority over them. Their later troubles over two unlicensed plays in 1605 and

---

[6] Kirkham had been in the Revels Office since 1581, and Yeoman of the Revels since 1586 (*MSC* xiii. 163). As Yeoman, he had control of all the costumes and properties used for court performances.

[7] *Acts of the Privy Council of England*, xxxi. 346.

1606 seem to indicate that it was not until after the last of these consequences of their free and 'private' performing that the boys did finally come under the Master's control.

The main evidence for this theory is that when Queen Anne gave them her patronage she assigned Samuel Daniel to be their personal Revels Master. That was either an insult to Tilney or, more likely, an acknowledgement that as a 'private' company they had no controller, but that as a royal company they now should have one. Anne ran a court of her own, with its own chamberlain and other officers. In any case this act of royal grace was a distinct favour to the boy company. The long plague-closure of 1603 had been as bad for Evans as for all the other companies, and led him to make the first of several overtures to the Burbages about surrendering his lease of the playhouse. The royal patent, the first issued to a boy company, encouraged him to keep going. It was made out to the company's front names on 4 February 1604.

whereas the Queene our deerest wief hath for her pleasure and recreacion when she shall thinke it fit to have any playes or shewes appoynted her servauntes Edward kirkham Alexander hawkyns Thomas kendall and Robert Payne to provyde and bring uppe a convenient nomber of Children whoe shalbe called children of her Revelles knowe ye that we have appointed and authorized and by theis presentes doe authorize and appoynte the said Edward kirkham Alexander hawkins Thomas kendall and Robert Payne from tyme to tyme to provide keepe and bring uppe . . . and them to practize and exercise in the quality of playinge by the name of Children of the Revelles to the Queene within the Blackfryers in our Cytie of london or in any other convenient place where they shall thinke fit for that purpose. . . . Provided allwaies that noe such Playes or Shewes shalbee presented before the saide Queene our wief by the said Children or by them any where publiquelie acted but by the approbacion and allowaunce of Samuell Danyell whome our pleasure is to appoynt for that purpose.[8]

This patent gave the company a new and imposing name, the Children of the Queen's Revels, and a censor all to themselves. Why Daniel got the job that Tilney was doing for the adult companies must be in part because the company's controllers insisted that their performances were 'private'. It may also have more than a little to do with Queen Anne's own court circle, to which Daniel was the chief poet, and her own interest in what the Blackfriars Boys had to give her.[9] That interest may have helped to push the company still further along its railing path. The evidence why Queen Anne would have been particularly interested in the boy company is inferential, but striking.

On 14 June 1604 the French ambassador, reporting to Paris on English attitudes to the new king, put them into a rhetorical question: 'what must be the state and condition of a prince who the preachers publicly attack from the pulpit, who the comedians of the city bring on the stage, whose wife attends these representations

---

[8] *MSC* i. 3. 267–8.

[9] For a careful study of Anne's court, see Leeds Barroll, 'The Court of the First Stuart Queen', in *The Mental World of the Jacobean Court*, ed. Linda Levy Peck (Cambridge, 1991), 191–208.

in order to enjoy the laugh against her husband?'[10] The only company actually in the city in 1604 with plays that mocked James was the Blackfriars boy company. It was the only company in London with a predominantly satirical repertory. None of the other companies, so far as we know, performed anything that mocked him, and only rarely did they offer railing plays.

We do not know what particular plays the boys may have performed for her that might have prompted the ambassador's report. The most notorious of their plays that have survived and that satirized the influx of Scotsmen who followed the royal family southwards was *Eastward Ho!* in 1605. Its jokes about the new 'thirty pound knights' made James put two of its three authors into prison when a Scots courtier, Sir James Murray, complained about it to the king. The third author fled. Its successor in February of the following year, *The Isle of Gulls*, offered a far more comprehensive mockery of the court. The boys used Scots accents for half the players, according to the testimony of Thomas Edmondes, who wrote that at the beginning of 1606 there was 'much speech of a play in the Black Friars, where in the "Isle of Gulls", from the highest to the lowest, all men's parts were acted of two diverse nations: as I understand sundry were committed to Bridewell'.[11] Neither play had been licensed by Tilney.

Heywood's term for what by 1606 was the characteristic and unique mode of the Blackfriars company was 'railing'. In the course of his extended defence of playing, *An Apology for Actors*, dedicated to his old patron the earl of Worcester and written in 1607 or 1608 although not printed until 1612, he blamed the boy company's playwrights. 'The liberty, which some arrogate to themselves, committing their bitternesse, and liberall invectives against all estates, to the mouthes of Children, supposing their juniority to be a priviledge for any rayling, be it never so violent, I could advise all such, to curbe and limit this presumed liberty.'[12] The boy company's privilege was to presume against the power of the Master of the Revels. But by 1608 Heywood was writing with the advantage of hindsight. Whether it was Evans or the poets who were responsible for giving the juniors their liberal invectives, it is certain that the company in its weekly performances had gained a unique status in London. It needs little hindsight to see the grant by Queen Anne of her patronage as consistent with the generally cynical outlook of their repertory.

In fact between 1605 and 1606 the uncertainty over who should be acting as the government's agent of control over the Blackfriars Boys became a running problem for the Revels Office, because Daniel discredited himself as the Queen's Revels Children's special censor almost straight away with his own *Philotas*. The company performed his hastily completed rhyming play near the end of 1604, giving him his first profits from the new post. By early in 1605, though, more than one noble had taken it to be a work that could be applied all too painfully to the story of the late earl of Essex. That was dangerous, because although James had been merciful to

[10] *ES* i. 325.
[11] Thomas Birch (ed.), *The Court and Times of James I* (2 vols.; London, 1848), i. 60–1.
[12] *An Apology for Actors* (1612), G3v.

the few who had not been executed after the attempted coup of February 1601, and had released the earl of Southampton from imprisonment in 1603, it was still too recent and painful a matter to be re-presented even in the form of a fiction on the public stage. The earl of Devonshire reacted angrily when Daniel tried to defend himself by claiming that he had read part of the manuscript to him. Too many people were still at risk from the Essex troubles, including one of Daniel's patrons, Mountjoy. As it happened, the surviving members of the Essex faction had regrouped themselves, along with the followers of the old Leicester circle, around the court of Queen Anne. Her chamberlain was Robert Sidney and her closest friends were Lucy Harrington, Countess of Bedford, and others who had been members of the Pembroke circle that originally started as a ring around the earl of Leicester. Daniel had been a poet dancing in that circle since 1592.

He may have felt that he was safe writing about Essex for such a tight now-royal coterie. Unfortunately the boys did not perform the play so privately as to free him from the uproar about it amongst the great at the king's court. Daniel lost almost everything with *Philotas*, and the company lost more than just its personal censor. The poet protested to the angry earl that most of the play had been written before the Essex conspiracy, and that he had completed it in all innocence, an attitude he maintained in public for the rest of his life. But the damage was done. *Philotas* lost him the control of the Queen's Revels and the profits it seemed to promise, and it lost the Blackfriars company its right to call itself the Queen's Revels Children. They hung on to what they could of the name, invoking their royal performances by calling themselves 'the Children of the Revels' on the title-pages of *The Fleir* and *The Isle of Gulls* and later plays. That modification to their name, however, was soon to prove more apt than they probably wished it to be. By the end of 1606, like all the other companies, the Blackfriars company was under the orders of the Master of the Revels.

By 1606 the company had an exceptional repertoire based on a special kind of satire. Its plays were designed to appeal quite explicitly to audiences at a higher social and probably critical level than the adult companies and the other boy company. Its target clientele were discontented courtiers and wits, younger sons of gentry, lawyers and Inns of Court students, the kind of aspiring man-about-town gallant or gentleman that Dekker mocked so colourfully as a typical Blackfriars playgoer in *The Gull's Hornbook* of 1606. Starting with Jonson's *Poetaster* in 1601, the company's repertoire included plays by Marston, the first of which was *The Malcontent* in 1604 or possibly earlier, *The Fawn*, and *The Dutch Courtesan*, and others by Chapman (*All Fools* and *Monsieur D'Olive* in 1605 and 1606), by Day (*The Isle of Gulls*, 1606), by Middleton (*The Family of Love* in 1605 or so, and later *Your Five Gallants*), not to mention *Eastward Ho!* in 1605 by Jonson, Marston, and Chapman. Substantial books have been written about this distinctive repertory.[13]

---

[13] The boy company plays were first distinguished as 'coterie' or élite plays written for the boys as compared with the 'popular' plays of the amphitheatre companies by Alfred Harbage in *Shakespeare and*

The company changed in 1606. The change was not so much that they came under Tilney's control, though that may have precipitated it, as an organizational one. Paul's had closed, and the Blackfriars must also have felt threatened. In fact it was a rich time, in plays if not income. The closure of Paul's brought the Blackfriars new resources and new plays. The established poets, Marston, Chapman, Middleton, and Day, continued to write for them. New writers such as Beaumont, Sharpham, and Fletcher joined them. In management Evans was still there as the company's underpinning, although Kirkham, who had his Master, Tilney, on his neck, left to join Paul's as it closed down, and then left playmaking entirely. Which of the managers or boys was imprisoned in Bridewell for *The Isle of Gulls* we do not know. The thirteen-year-olds of 1600 who still played in the company were hardly boys any longer, and may have been taken as fully responsible for their plays, like adult sharers.[14] Giles was finally severed from any residual association by his new commission as choirmaster, issued on 7 November 1606. Its final trenchant diktat expressly forbade him to allow his choristers to be 'used or imployed as Comedians or Stage players or to exercise or acte anye or Stage playes Interludes Comedies or tragedies for that it is not fitt or decent that suche as shoulde singe the praises of god Allmightie shoulde be trayned upp or imployed in suche lascivious and prophane exercises'.[15] With Giles and Kirkham off the scene, the financiers well in the background, and his son-in-law nowhere in sight, Evans was now on his own. That, with the continuity the company maintained in its repertory, is as good evidence as we are ever likely to have that Evans was the moving spirit throughout behind this peculiar and perilous long run of 'railing' plays.

Evans enlisted a new financier in 1606. Robert Keysar was a goldsmith, the commonest type of money-man or money-lender in London. Unlike the other financiers, Rastall and Kendall, he took an active part in the company's management. It was he who wrote the epistle for the publication of *The Knight of the Burning Pestle* in 1613. That brilliantly clever play, first staged in 1607 and mocking citizen frustration and fury over the playhouse where 'this seven yeares there hath beene playes at this house, I have observed it, you have still girds at Citizens',[16] was a disastrous flop on its first performance. Keysar claimed, six years later, when Beaumont had become famous and his name made the play worth resurrecting, that the audience had failed to understand 'the privy mark of Ironie about it'. A seemingly innocent comment, this has caused a lot of dispute about what it really signified.[17] For our purposes, it does show that Keysar, like Henslowe, Beeston, and

the *Rival Traditions* (New York, 1952). The debate continues, not helped by confusion between the Paul's and the Blackfriars repertories.

[14] For the question of how old the 'youths' of the boy companies might have been, see Shen Lin, 'How Old were the Children of Paul's?', *Theatre Notebook*, 45 (1991), 121–31.

[15] *MSC* i. 4 and 5, 362–3.

[16] *The Knight of the Burning Pestle* (1613), Induction.

[17] Harbage, *Shakespeare and the Rival Traditions*, claimed that it was too gentle a satire on citizens for the gentry in the audience. Other critics have suggested that there must have been too many citizens in the audience to appreciate the mockery aimed at them.

presumably Evans, was himself a keen if less-than-acute playgoer and student of plays. To modern audiences and readers, the irony is not at all private.

The company's policy changed only a little after 1606. There were no more plays like *Eastward Ho!* or *The Isle of Gulls*, but *The Knight of the Burning Pestle* shows that they still catered for the sophisticated tastes that derided citizen plays. Comedies like *The Dutch Courtesan*, based on that cynical depiction of 'gallant' male sexuality and a view of women as men's property which much later was to become the staple presumption on which Restoration comedy was based, ran strongly at the Blackfriars. They show very distinctly the clientele that the playwrights expected to flock to that one venue. In Marston's play a lusty gallant satisfies his needs with a foreign courtesan while pursuing a virtuous lady of his own class because she does not share the men's sexual freedom. The readiness of citizen wives to cuckold their husbands, and the gullibility of husbands whose possessiveness calls for them to be robbed of both money and wife, became a predominant Restoration fashion which first began at the Blackfriars. That the Restoration picked up this fashion, rather than any of the others available from this period, reflects the extent to which the young and adolescent Blackfriars Boys after 1600 catered for the sexual cynicisms of a narrow and highly opinionated segment of London's society. That segment was wholly prevalent in the Restoration's two or three small hall-playhouses. In 1606 it was fed only by the Blackfriars Boys.

Besides heroizing the impecunious but sharp-witted young gallant, and deriding gullible citizens, they also continued to stage what has been called anti-court satire; and this taste may be what brought them into their next clash with officialdom early in 1608. On 11 March a signet clerk attending James in Norfolk wrote to Cecil and the Privy Council about two plays, both of which, on different grounds, had offended the king. The letter reports the most direct and personal response James ever recorded over a play.

His majestie was well pleased with that which your lordship advertiseth concerning the committing of the players yt have offended in ye matters of France, and commanded me to signifye to your lordship that for ye others who have offended in ye matter of ye Mynes and other lewd words, which is ye children of ye blackfriars, That though he had signified his mynde to your lordship by my lord of Mountgommery yet I should repeate it again, That his Grace had vowed they should never play more, but should first begg their bred and he wold have his vow performed, And therefore my lord chamberlain by himselfe or your lordships at the table should take order to dissolve them, and to punish the maker besides.[18]

The 'matters of France' are explained in a letter from the French ambassador to Paris dated 29 March. The ambassador reported that all playing at that time was still stopped, not because of the plague but because two offensive plays had been staged, one of which depicted the Byron troubles at the French court. He himself presumably laid the usual complaint about this. The play at issue was almost certainly Chapman's *Conspiracy and Tragedy of Byron*, which appeared in print

---

[18] *CSP Dom. Jac. I*, xxxi. 73.

later in the same year in curtailed form as a play 'acted at the Blackfriars'. Apparently it had a scene where the French king's mistress slaps the queen's face, which is not in the surviving texts.

The clerk's letter to Cecil suggests that the French play was by a different company from the other offending text, on which the French ambassador also reported. It had been acted a day or two before, he reported, and depicted the king and his favourites, and his Scottish silver mine, in a thoroughly contemptuous manner, 'car après luy avoir fair dépiter le ciel sur le vol d'un oyseau, et faict battre un gentilhomme pour avoir rompu ses chiens, ils le dépeignoient ivre pour le moins une fois le jour'.[19] This other offensive play has, perhaps understandably, not survived. It has been suggested on circumstantial evidence that Marston might have been its author. He left playwriting rather suddenly in 1608, and sold his share in the Blackfriars venture to Keysar.

Almost certainly the Blackfriars company was the one guilty of both plays, despite the clerk's assumption that only the personally insulting one belonged to 'ye others'. If the title-page declaration that the Byron play was theirs is correct they must have played both. There is no reason to think the ascription of Chapman's play to them is wrong, so the error must have been the clerk's, and the Blackfriars company was responsible for each of the two offending plays. Conceivably the other was Marston's. There is no doubt which play James found the more offensive. It may have been the personal aim of the insults that focused his mind on the company whom he blamed for the irredeemable offence.

What Tilney did about this trouble there is no direct evidence, but there are some intriguing hints. The circumstantial points are that the king's message was an order to the Lord Chamberlain to 'dissolve' the company, and that the Chamberlain's executive in playing matters was the Master of the Revels. The second point is that Kirkham, Yeoman of the Revels, and serving in some managerial capacity at times with both the Blackfriars and Paul's, now came back to the Blackfriars. He has usually been assumed to have worked for himself in doing so, as he probably was before with the Blackfriars Boys and possibly with the Paul's Boys. This time, though, I suspect that he was doing his Master's bidding, as he may have done when he moved in on Paul's in 1605, so soon before their closure. In July of 1608 he drew up a valuation for the Blackfriars company's 'apparells, properties and goods', precisely the sort of work his Revels-Office work qualified him for. He also, according to a later testimony by Evans, 'delivered up their commission, which he had under the greate seale aucthorising them to plaie, and discharged divers of the partners and poetts'. Taking back the company patent and reorganizing the company's responsible partners was Tilney's work. Kirkham was acting like a government receiver in a bankrupt company. Evans backed out, and in the same month he surrendered his lease of the Blackfriars to the Burbages. The residual company was left with Keysar, who took on new colleagues to replace Evans as

---

[19] 'For after making him curse heaven over the flight of a bird, and have a gentleman beaten for calling off his dogs, they showed him drunk at least once a day'; *ES* ii. 53; my trans.

financier and manager. The clinching evidence that Tilney took a hand in all this through his agent, Kirkham, is that he allowed the new management to give three plays at court the next Christmas, and five the next year, the largest number they ever gave.[20]

The July winding-up ended Evans's role as impresario. The new company was in Keysar's hands as chief manager. Presumably most of the boys in it were the same, but otherwise the company was new, and was treated as new by Tilney. It was still in a very precarious position, not so much because of the Revels Office but because of the financial squeeze that followed the close-down on playing for plague. It had the same plays, if Kirkham's work of receivership did not include taking them, though the 'railing' plays were now a less valuable property than they had been when fresh. But the company needed a new playhouse, which meant more finance. The evidence for what they did in these months during the long plague closure is fragmentary and rather confusing, but it appears that they secured another hall playhouse in the Whitefriars, less than a half-mile to the south-west of their former hall. The Whitefriars had been vacated by another boy company, the King's Revels Children.[21] Nothing much is known about this playhouse, which was built outside the city walls in another liberty, and close to the Inns of Court. It must have been opened in imitation of the Blackfriars. As part of these rearrangements, most of which took place during the long interval of 1608–9, Keysar formed a link with Philip Rosseter, a royal lutenist.

Reformed and re-formed, the one-time Chapel Children and Blackfriars Boys needed a different image. The first success of the new enterprise was returning to play at court, where they gave three performances, including *A Trick to Catch the Old One*, formerly a Paul's play, on 1 January 1609. The first three court plays were staged during what turned into the longest plague closure since 1603, lasting eighteen months in all. In fact, the large number of plays used at court in 1609–10 and the particularly large supply from the Blackfriars company may have been called for because of the disarray that the long closure caused the adult companies. Keysar later claimed that he had spent £500 to keep the boys going through the closure period. That testimony comes from a lawsuit he brought against the King's Men's housekeepers of the Blackfriars playhouse early in 1610. In it he claimed a share in their subsequent profits, on the grounds that when Evans disposed of the lease to the Burbages it had cost him all the work of training 'a companye of the moste exparte and skilful actors within the realme of England to the number of eighteane or twentye persons all or moste of them trayned up in that service, in the raigne of the late Queene Elizabeth for ten yeares togeather and afterwardes

---

[20] They gave 2 in 1604–5, but none in 1605–6. The Chamber accounts (*MSC* vi. 45) note payments made on 30 Mar. 1607 to a '*Thomas Keysar*', presumably a mistake for Robert, for two plays, one on 29 July 1606 before Christian of Denmark, the day before a Paul's play for him, and the other on 1 Jan. 1607. These payments must have been for Blackfriars Boys performances. There were also the two performances in 1608 that outraged James, unrecorded by the officials presumably because not paid for.

[21] See S. P. Cerasano, 'Competition for the King's Men? Alleyn's Blackfriars Venture', *MRDE* 4 (1989), 173–86.

preferred into her Majesties service to be the Chilldren of her Revelles'.[22] His bill, dated 8 February, spoke of that company as now dispersed. He chose to ignore the fact that he had a new patent for the Children of the Queen's Revels dated a little over a month previously. Although the long closure brought in no income other than the £30 for the court performances, it did give time for substantial reorganization, and to find a new place for the regrouped company to play.

There are only a few oblique indications about where the company went after they gave up the Blackfriars in 1608. A reference in 1612 to a play being performed at the 'blacke and white Friers' suggests that the former Blackfriars Boys took over the Whitefriars playhouse. They seem to have done so as part of a merger with the King's Revels Boys, who do not appear in the records subsequently. In 1610 it was still some time before they were to be counted as an adult company and started using amphitheatres.

In the course of the next Christmas season, when they staged five court plays, a new company patent was issued to Rosseter and a few other professional players, on 4 January 1610. The managers named were mostly old hands from the adult companies, 'Robert Daborne Phillippe Rosseter John Tarbock Richard Jones and Robert Browne'. The patent renewed the company's best name once again, the Queen's Revels Children, and designated their playhouse as the Whitefriars.[23] In his managerial role Rosseter took a lease on the Whitefriars playhouse from the King's Revels managers. Given the length of the plague closure through 1608 and 1609, this revival was a feat of some magnitude and ingenuity. The scale of the investment also indicates how confident they now were of good profits from playing.

Who the managers were is one indication of their expectations and their policy. Keysar had sued Daborne, a Cambridge graduate and a playwright, for a debt of £50 in 1608, possibly for an uncompleted commission for plays, but possibly also as part of the financing for the new company.[24] Daborne had money-making ambitions. He was later involved in struggles over his father's tenement property in the Blackfriars, which several people, including Edward Alleyn, tried to make into the 'Porter's Hall' playhouse of 1616.[25] He may have dabbled with the King's Revels Children in the year before he joined the new Queen's Revels Children. He and John Mason, probably the same man who wrote *The Turk* for the King's Revels Children, were jointly charged with robbing a man in the Whitefriars in January 1609. Of the others, Jones and Browne, after early work for the Admiral's, had been running English companies across the Channel through most of the last decade. Tarbock is otherwise unknown. He may have been a front for Keysar, whose name is rather strangely omitted given his control of the enterprise.

[22] *ES* ii. 57.   [23] *MSC* i. 3. 271–2.
[24] Mark Eccles, 'Brief Lives: Tudor and Stuart Authors', Texts and Studies Special Issue, *SP* 79 (1982), 29.
[25] S. P. Ceresano, 'Competition for the King's Men?: Alleyn's Blackfriars Venture', *MRDE* 4 (1989), 173–86.

The boys and something of the company's character changed too. Quite apart from abandoning the satirical and sensationalist 'railing' plays, it now became in composition (if not in management) rather closer to an adult company. Some of the senior boys left during the long closure. William Ostler and John Underwood stayed at their familiar playhouse by joining the King's Men. But Nathan Field, who had been the leading boy in *Cynthia's Revels* in 1601, stayed with the company. His age was now 22. He wrote some commendatory verses for the publication of one of the company's failures, Fletcher's *The Faithful Shepherdess*. In them he emphasized how junior he was, but the very fact of issuing verses in print made them a demonstration of his new maturity. His retention in the company shows how little of the tradition of 'private' and exclusive boy-playing the managers could now retain. Underwood and Ostler going to the King's shows that the best boys wanted full careers as players, so would stay on if it was to their benefit. The possibility of making the whole company a team of 'youths' growing up into adult practices was becoming a possible step forwards. With the King's as an adult company now occupying a 'private' playhouse that had once been allowed exclusively for 'boy' players, there was little reason any longer to retain the full trappings of a boy company.

Some reason there still was, though. Chiefly it lay in the economic fact that a team of boys was easier and cheaper to manage than a company of adults. It also lay in the tradition of boy-company and indoor music and song, for which Philip Rosseter stood large in the company's management team. And there was still at least a remnant of the social appeal that companies of 'youthes' had sustained from their academic origins through the last century.

It was the social ambition attaching to such social climbing with audiences that had caused Fletcher's *Faithful Shepherdess* to flop. The aggrieved epistle that the author attached to his play's publication in 1610 clearly shows both the company's expectations of their audience's taste, and their miscalculation of it. Fletcher's experience seems reminiscent of his collaborator's earlier mishap with *The Knight of the Burning Pestle*. 'It is a pastorall Tragie-comedie,' Fletcher wrote aggressively in his own defence, 'which the people seeing when it was plaid, having ever had a singuler guift in defining, concluded to be a play of country hired Shepheards in gray cloakes, with curtaild dogs in strings, sometimes laughing together, and sometimes killing one another: And missing whitsun ales, creame, wassel and morris-dances, began to be angry.' Morris dancing belonged with country may-games and the traditional festival of spring. Fletcher's pastoral tragi-comedy was based on Guarini's *Il Pastor Fido*, and offered an Arcadian scale of pastoral loves far from the familiar country pleasures the audience expected. It is an ambitious play, depicting four kinds of love, each on a different step up the ladder of purity. Henrietta Maria, a devotee of the pastoral-shepherdess mode which was later to add the queen of France's serio-comic pastoral hamlet to the estate at Versailles, took to the play when the King's Men were clever enough to revive it in 1633. This later success does not mean it was twenty years ahead of its time, but it certainly points up the boy company's mis-estimation of what its audiences would like in 1609 and 1610.

Browne and Jones do not seem to have joined the company's playing strength, but they must have backed the next changes. With Nathan Field it had at least six young men amongst its 'youthes' and 'boyes' by 1610, and the feature of the boy repertory which confined them to performing only once a week was a tradition they had quite literally outgrown. Until this time they had kept at least the pretence of performing only weekly, as we know from the epilogue to *Eastward Ho!*, which ends by farewelling its audience with the hope of continuing to attract them once a week. This lower frequency of performance compared with the professional adults went with school plays and the 'private' tradition of playing, not with commercial practices. It was far more profitable to perform daily, and with the King's Men doing that at the private Blackfriars hall there was now nothing except the dead fiction of the boys' academic origins to stop them. From here on their practices are indistinguishable from those of the adult companies. They became a travelling company, for instance, starting at Leicester in August 1609.

Evidence for the new company's repertory is rather obscure through this early period. Keysar kept several of the old company's plays besides *The Knight of the Burning Pestle*, which he published in 1613 once Beaumont's name had become famous. Chapman's *The Widow's Tears* says on its 1612 title-page that it was 'often presented in the blacke and white Friers', which suggests that it was a pre-1608 playbook that stayed with the company. Chapman's *Revenge of Bussy* was published in 1613 with an ascription to the Whitefriars on its title-page, although the text has signs that it was revised for amphitheatre production, possibly indicating its place in the company's later repertory. No company is likely to have played a sequel without its predecessor, so it seems that the company kept both *Bussy* plays on stage. Jonson's *The Case is Altered*, on the other hand, is assigned on its 1609 title-page to 'the Children of the Blacke-friers', which must relate to the company of the period up to 1608. Similarly, Chapman's *May Day*, printed in 1611 as 'divers times acted at the Blacke Fryars', must belong to the years before the transfer to Whitefriars. *Epicene*, by contrast, entered in the Stationers' Register in September 1610, must have been played only by the reorganized company. Its 1616 edition names Field, but not Ostler or Underwood, among its actors, and its first prologue specifies the Whitefriars.

The 1610 edition of *Epicene* includes two prologues. The second was made necessary by an objection evoked on the play's first staging. The Venetian ambassador, writing on 8 February 1610, reported that Arabella Stuart had taken exception to a reference to the Prince of Moldavia (V. i. 17), with whom her name had been linked on his visit to London in 1607.[26] That indicates a public performance at the new Whitefriars over the Christmas period 1609–10. It is likely that *The Faithful Shepherdess* and other early Fletcher plays also came into the repertory

---

[26] *ES* iii. 370–1.

during the 1608–9 closure, and were staged for the first time when the Whitefriars reopened. Field himself took advantage of the closure to write his first play for the new company, *A Woman is a Weathercock*, which was printed at the end of 1611 as acted 'divers times Privately at the White-Friers, By the Children of her Majesties Revels'. There are too few plays written after the reorganized company opened to show what effects the *Faithful-Shepherdess* fiasco and the *Epicene* trouble might have had on the kind of play they chose to buy in these last years. They do show that the 'railing' fashion had gone for the boy company. *Epicene* itself was not really composed as a satirical-railing play, and *The Faithful Shepherdess* was certainly not.

With travelling, with several adult players, no call to appear at court in the 1610–11 season, and only one in the next, another change in the company's composition and policy was called for. They were alternate to the King's Men at court on 5 January 1612, offering Beaumont and Fletcher's *Cupid's Revenge*. They did better in the 1612–13 season, giving four plays, *Cupid's Revenge* twice, *The Coxcomb* from the same pair of writers, and *The Widow's Tears*. For these plays Rosseter was the company payee. But that was their last recorded appearance under their 'boy company' name. The only other play of this period that might be ascribed to them was by William Barksted, a player with Field in *Epicene*. He appears to have completed Marston's unfinished play of 1608, *The Insatiate Countess*, for them. It was published in 1613 as 'acted at Whitefriars', without naming the company.

By then the remaining 'youths' were part of an adult company, with a new royal patron. Barksted and at least two more of the ex-Blackfriars company's leading players, Field and Giles Carey, joined a new adult company using Henslowe's resources, the Lady Elizabeth's Men, in August 1613.[27] The company regrouped. Predictably, the managers kept the invaluable patent for the Queen's Revels Children and used it to tour with through 1614 and 1615. That was the fall-back position. More ambitiously, Rosseter and three other interested parties in the managerial group took out a patent on 3 June 1615 to build a new hall playhouse in the Blackfriars. This was the 'Porter's Hall', in which the company's writer, Daborne, had property interests. It was clearly designed to replace the Whitefriars, on which Rosseter's lease had expired, although it is not clear whether the revived Revels Children or the Lady Elizabeth's Men were expected to use it.

The one play that they seem to have staged there before the authorities trod the new playhouse project down[28] was Beaumont and Fletcher's *The Scornful Lady*, another play from the boy-company stock.[29] When the playhouse scheme collapsed, Rosseter took to the road with a new company, presumably retrieving the old patent and calling his followers the Queen's Revels. To judge from some of the

---

[27] For a history of this company, see Ch. 22.

[28] The Blackfriars residents had more success in 1615 getting Porter's Hall stopped and demolished than they had with the Burbage playhouse. See S. P. Ceresano, 'Competition for the King's Men? Alleyn's Blackfriars Venture', *MRDE* 4 (1989), 173–86.

[29] Its 1616 title-page claims that it was 'Acted (with great applause) by the children of Her Majesties Revels in the Blacke Fryers'. That, allowing for hazy memories about the company's precise title at different times, dates it to 1608 or earlier.

names mentioned in association with it in the provincial records, it was connected both with Nicholas Long and Robert Lee of Queen Anne's, and with William Perry of a group variously called the King's Revels and the King's Revels Children. It was a marginal, even ghostly company, merging into the other 'young' companies like the 'Children's Revels of Bristow' that sprang up about this time without any specific patron's name to identify them. In one unfortunate winter in 1617–18 three different groups all claiming to be the Queen's Revels Childen came to Leicester. Only the third of the three was accepted as properly licensed. None of these various groupings ever reappeared in London so far as we know, either from the records of court performances or elsewhere. No professional boy company, in fact, ever ran in London on the earlier model again. From 1610 onwards the various companies of 'youthes', including the company known as 'Beeston's Boys' in the late 1630s, were really young adults, following adult-company practices under boy-company management.

Some time after the second Paul's Boys closed down in 1606, and while the Blackfriars Boys were in trouble with the Revels Office, probably early in 1607, a new company calling itself the King's Revels Children appeared in London for a while. It used the new hall-playhouse in the Whitefriars, outside the city's control. There is no patent surviving for the company, and no obvious reason why they chose to operate under such a pretentious title. On 17 November 1608 two men, William Pollard and Richard Gwynn, were imprisoned at Newgate for staging a play at Whitefriars during the plague restraint. Nothing else is known of the two, although they must have been among the chief managers of the company. Little is known about the playhouse, either.

Despite this obscurity, the company is credited with eight or nine plays, all but one produced in the same narrow time-span during 1607 and 1608. The odd case is *Ram Alley*, which R. V. Holdsworth has shown to have distinct signs of borrowings from Jonson's *Epicene*, staged at the end of 1609 at the Whitefriars by the Blackfriars Children; and *The Alchemist*, staged late in 1610 by the King's Men at the Blackfriars, and entered in the Stationers' Register in October.[30] *Ram Alley* was entered a month later, and subsequently printed with the date 1611 on its title-page. Holdsworth reasons that its title-page ascription to 'the Children of the Kings Revels' was a mistake for the Queen's Revels, then at the Whitefriars playhouse which the King's Revels had used during its short life in 1607–8.

The company lost its London playhouse to the reconstituted Blackfriars Boys during the long close-down of 1608 and 1609. Like that company, it evidently had a sufficient number of adult players or near-adult 'youthes' to be able to travel. No names of any of its boys are known for sure. Its history, like that of its plays, is intertwined with the Blackfriars Boys after 1609, when they moved into the Whitefriars playhouse. The Blackfriars company seem to have taken on some of their plays, such as *Cupid's Revenge*, which was performed at court in 1612–13 as by

---

[30] R. V. Holdsworth, 'Ben Jonson and the Date of *Ram Alley*', *NQ* 32 (1985), 482–6.

the Whitefriars Children. Armin's first play, *The Two Maids of Moreclacke*, is put down to them in their 1607–8 run, but may in fact have been given to the other boy company. Another of their plays, Middleton's *The Family of Love*, was originally written for Paul's. The other surviving texts, *Cupid's Whirligig*, *The Dumb Knight*, *Humour out of Breath*, and *The Turk*, follow the generally non-satirical Fletcherian mode of *Cupid's Revenge*, and were presumably all commissioned for the new company in 1607 and 1608. The plays (and probably some of the young players) merged into the new Blackfriars company of 1609–10. More than one set of King's Revels Children is recorded touring the country in later years, though since one of them was led by the notorious inventor of company warrants Martin Slater there is no likelihood that they had any direct links with the original King's Revels Boys.

BLACKFRIARS BOYS, 1600–1613[31]
Known as Queen's Revels Children, Children of the Revels, Chapel Children. See also Lady Elizabeth's.

Plays
All Fools, *Amends for Ladies*, *Bussy D'Ambois* (old), *The Case is Altered* (old), *Conspiracy and Tragedy of Byron*, *Charles Duke of Byron*, *Contention Between Liberality and Prodigality* (old), *The Coxcomb*, *Cupid's Revenge* (old?), *Cynthia's Revels*, *The Dutch Courtesan*, *Eastward Ho!*, *Epicene*, *The Faithful Shepherdess*, *The Fawn*, *The Fleir*, *The Gentleman Usher*, *Sir Giles Goosecap*, *Hieronimo*, *The Insatiate Countess*, *The Isle of Gulls*, *The Knight of the Burning Pestle*, *Law Tricks*, *Love's Metamorphosis* (old), *The Malcontent*, *May-Day*, *Monsieur D'Olive*, *Philotas*, *Poetaster*, *The Revenge of Bussy D'Ambois*, *Sophonisba*, *A Trick to Catch the Old One* (old), *The Viper and her Brood* (lost), *The Widow's Tears*, *A Woman is a Weathercock*, *Your Five Gallants*.

Managers
Nathaniel Giles, Henry Evans, James Robinson, William Rastall, Thomas Kendall, Martin Peerson, Edward Kirkham, Alexander Hawkins, Robert Payne, Samuel Daniel, Robert Keysar, Philip Rosseter, Nicholas Long.

Boy Players
Nathan Field, Salomon Pavy, Thomas Day, John Underwood, Robert Baxter, John Foster (*Cynth Rev*), William Ostler, Thomas Martin (*Poetaster*), Nathan Field, Salomon Pavy, John Chappell, John Mottram, Alvery Trussell, Phillip Pykman, Thomas Grimes (Henry Clifton), Giles Carey, Hugh Attewell, John Smith, William Barksted, William Penn, Richard Allen, John Blaney (*Epicene*). [Exeter 1624: William Perry with 'George Bosegrave Richard Backster Thomas Band James Jones Walter Barrett James Kneller and Edward Tobye'.]

[31] Michael Shapiro, *Children of the Revels*, in App. B supplies an accurate list of all boy-company performances between 1559 and 1613, and in App. C a list of their plays. The Blackfriars Boys are listed on 259–60 and 264–6. The King's Revels Children are listed on 260 and 266. The book does not look at the later Beeston's Boys, who are dealt with here in Ch. 23.

London Playhouses
Second Blackfriars, Whitefriars.

At Court
6 Jan. 1601 (*Cynthia's Revels?*), 22 Feb. (*The Contention between Liberality and Prodigality?*); 6 Jan. 1602, 14 Jan., 14 Feb.; 21 Feb. 1604; 1 Jan. 1605 (*All Fools?*), 3 Jan.; [29 July 1606 (unnamed); 1 Jan. 1607 (unnamed); Mar. 1608?][32] three plays up to Jan. 1609 before the king, including 1 Jan. (*A Trick to Catch the Old One*), and 4 Jan.; [as Children of Queen's Revels] 2 Nov. 1612 (*The Coxcomb?*), 1 Jan. 1613 (*Cupid's Revenge*) before the king; and on 9 Jan. before the prince, Lady Elizabeth, and the Elector Palatine, 27 Feb. (*The Widow's Tears*), up to 24 Nov. (*The Coxcomb*).

Travelling Records
Leicester 21 Aug. 1609 'the Children of the Revells', 20s. / Maidstone Mar. 1610 'the players the Children of the Chappell', 10s. / Norwich 10 Aug. 1611 'Raph Reve came this day into the Court and shewed forth the Kings Majesties Letteres Pattents Comanding all Mayors and others officers to permitt Phillipp Rocester and certaine others named in the said Letteres Pattents to practise and exercise certaine Children in the quallity of playing, which Reeve at the first affirmed that he was Phillipp Rocester one of those that weare named in the letters Pattents but perceiving him selfe discovered confessed his name was Reeve, and for that he could not shew forth any Letters of Deputacion, he was enjoyned to departe the Citty with the rest of his Company and not to play at all upon paine of punishment.' / 20 May 1612 'Nicholas Longe with certen others made request to have leave to play in the Cittie and shewed forth the Kinges Majestes letteres Pattentes made to v particuler persons, gevinge them authoritye to teach & instruct children in the facultye or quallity of playinge for the Queenes Majestes revells. And for that none of those v were here present, but that the said Longe shewed forth a deputacion from Phillip Rosseter one of the said companye made to himself and the rest, and there Commission was onlye to teach and instruct. Therefore by the consent of the Court they had xx s geven them but enjoyned not to play within the Cittye.' / Bristol Michaelmas-Christmas 1612, 'the Queenes Majesties Revellers', £2. / Coventry Nov. acct. 1613 'vnto Two of the Company of the Children of Revells', 20s. / Coventry 7 Oct. 1615 'to the Queenes players called the Revells', 40s. 4d. / Nottingham 1615–16, 10s. / Leicester 1616, 30s.; 22 June 1616, 20s. / Coventry 21 June 1616 'to the Company of the Revells', 40s. / Nottingham 1616–17, 10s. / Leicester 6 Feb. 1617 'to one other Companye of playors called the Chyldren of the Revells', 22s. / Leicester 22 Feb. 1619 'given to a Companye of playors called the Children of the Revells, whoe weare not suffered to playe . . . xs. given to one other Companye of playors called the Children of the Revells whoe were allso not sufferd to playe . . . xs . . . given to one other

[32] See above, 354–5.

Companye of playors called the Children of the Revells whoe had special Lycense to playe £1.'[33] / Norwich 9 June 1619 'This day Nicholas Longe brought a Bill signed under his Majestes hand authorisinge him and others to exercise & practise the youthes and Children of the Revelles of Quene Ann to play &c . . . And because yt ys conceived that the said Patent ys determined[34] by death of the late Quene Ann, therefore mr Maior & this Court doe forbeare to give any allowance to the same, yet the said Longe did boldly affirme that yf he might not have permission they would notwithstanding play yf they could gett a place to play in.' / Leicester 1620, 10s. / Norwich 13 May 1620 'Mr Longe brought his Majesties Patent to play &c Dated in February last, And they have tyme to play till wednesday next.' / Dover Aug. 1620 'to the players called the Children of the Revels who had the kinges licence', 11s. / Sudbury, Suffolk 1621–2 'to the Queens players the La: Elizabeth hir players and the Children of the revells,' 28s. / Leicester 10 Jan. 1622 'for a gratuity', 20s. / Leicester 12 Apr. 1622 'the Queenes Servants and Children of the Revells . . . playd not', 22s. / Leicester 1622–3, 6s. 8d. / Exeter 9 Apr. 1623 [circular from Master of the Revels authorising William Perry and associates, for 'the Children of the Revells of the late Queene Anna . . . George Bosegrave, Richard Backster, Thomas Band, James Jones, Walter Barrett, James Kneller and Edward Tobye, and the rest of their companie not exceedinge the number of twentie', for a year] / Norwich 24 May 1623 'This day William Perry brought into Court an Instrument under his Majesties privie Signet and Signed with his majesties hand authorisinge him with Robert Lee, Philip Rosseter & their Company as Servants to Quene Ann to play &c.' / Leicester 18 Mar. 1624, 10s. / Exeter 31 May 1624 [copy of Herbert's letter] 'Children of the Revells To the Late Quenne Anna . . . I . . . allow and confirme thaforsaid grant Under his Majestie Royall hand and Signett to be and continew Unto the said William Perrie and his associates (videlicett) George Bosegrave Richard Backster Thomas Band James Jones Walter Barrett James Kneller and Edward Tobye and the rest of there companies not Exceeding the number of Twentye . . . for and during the Terme and space of one wholle yeare'. / Dunkenhalgh, Lancs. (Household accounts of Thomas Walmesley) 11 June 1625 'given plaiers being pirrie & his companie', 20s. / Dunkenhalgh, Lancs. (Household accounts of Thomas Walmesley) 12 Nov. 1625 'mr Pirrie the player & his Compny 3 nightes', 40s. / Leicester 8 July 1627 'a Companie of Players Called the Children of the Revells', 13s. 4d. / Dunkenhalgh, Lancs. (Household accounts of Thomas Walmesley) 1626 'Pirrie the plaier & his Companie one night', 20s. / Dunkenhalgh, Lancs. (Household accounts of Thomas Walmesley) Feb. 1630 'Mr. Pyrrie the Player and his Companie. 2. Nyghts' / Dunkenhalgh, Lancs. (Household accounts of Thomas Walmesley) Jan. 1631 'Mr. Pyrrye they Player and his Companie twoo Nights this weeke', May 1631 'given ij players helpinge when the house was on fyre', 2s. / Leicester 1635 'to Mr Perrie,

---

[33] Leicester evidently received visits from Daniel's Bristol Children, and more in this year. The number of 'Revels' companies, boys or not, is a sign of Buc doing the licensing.

[34] i.e., terminated.

a Player, and his Companie to passe by the Towne and not play'. / Leicester 1638–9 'the Children of the Revells', 6s.

KING'S REVELS CHILDREN, 1607–1608

Plays
Cupid's Revenge, Cupid's Whirligig, The Dumb Knight, The Family of Love (old), *Humour out of Breath, Ram-Alley* (?), *Torrismount* (lost), *The Turk, The Two Maids of Moreclacke.*

Manager
[1609: Richard Gwynn, Willam Pollard, Coventry 1627 Nicholas Hanson, Coventry 1635–6 William Daniell] Martin Slater.

London Playhouses
Whitefriars.

At Court
(merged with Blackfriars Boys) Christmas 1609–10 (5 performances).

Travelling Records
Norwich 11 Aug. 1611, 'unto the master of the Children of the Kinges Revelles', 40s. / Norwich 23 May 1612, 20s. / Norwich 1615–16 / Coventry 1615–16 / Leicester 1615–16 / Nottingham Sept. 1619, 20s. / Bristol 1620–1 'to the Kings Children players xls' / Norwich 28 May 1622 'to Nicholas Hanson' / Nottingham 1623–4, 10s. / Leicester 1624–5 'the Kings Playors, called the Children of the Revells', £1. 6s. 8d. / Worcester 1624–5 'to the kinges Revelers', 15s. / Coventry Apr. 1627 'to the Kinges Revells, to Nicholas Hanson one of that Company', 5s. / Leicester 1627–8, 13s. 4d., 10s. / Doncaster July 1631 'Children of the Revells to them that played the Antice tricks, having the Kings privie seale', 5s. / Coventry June 1635 'to William Daniell who brought a Commission for the Revelles. videlicet for himself & 16. more' 10s. / Coventry 5 Dec. 1636 'to William Daniell and others of the Revelles', 10s.

The various crises of 1608 and 1609, when the playhouses had to remain closed for more than a year, produced some basic changes amongst the companies. The boy companies regrouped, running for a while at the one hall playhouse left to them, but they soon turned into young adult companies and took up travelling. The number of adult companies increased as the royal children grew. The King's Men asserted their predominance by taking up two playhouses, one of which gave them the unique privilege of playing in a roofed playhouse in central London, a site more than equivalent to the modern West End. This was the final step to the unquestioned pre-eminence that they enjoyed for the rest of the two Stuart reigns. It was a step upwards that no other company was ever able to match.

By 1608 their security was as complete as was their pre-eminence at court. The king gave them money to help them during the long plague closure, with £40 'for their private practise in the time of infeccion that thereby they mighte be inhabled to performe their service before his Majestie in Christmas hollidaies 1609', paid on 4 January 1609.[1] That kind of insurance was unique to the King's. The reason supplied for giving the grant reaffirmed the duty of the leading playing companies that was first acknowledged by the establishment of the Queen's Men in 1583 and was reaffirmed with the duopoly of 1594. In 1608 the early government concept of companies principally as touring groups which lodged in London whenever they could was finally abandoned. The new concept required a centre in London. Even for the leading company under this new concept two playhouses might have been an indulgence, but they seemed to offer an idealized form of the pattern of London playing that had been developing since before 1583, and were underwritten by the insurance of royal support.

Running the one company at the two playhouses was, none the less, a radical development with a host of pros and cons. There is no evidence that before 1594 the companies ever charged more to see a play indoors at an inn than they charged for a play at an amphitheatre, though they could have done. The difference between the two kinds of venue at that time was simply a matter of convenience, a choice between larger numbers in the amphitheatres or greater comfort in a hall in London's bad weather. The boy companies, with their emphasis on offering 'private' performances as if they were playing to select gentry in great houses, made an explicit appeal to a more select social grouping and pushed the practice and the price up-market. For their successors at the Blackfriars it was no small consideration that they had made up for their less frequent performances and the smaller audience capacity by charging their customers a much higher price for admission. Paul's seems to have started by charging twopence or fourpence for its hall. The

[1] *ES* iv. 175.

boy company at the Blackfriars seems to have started by charging sixpence or more, and the Paul's soon followed suit.[2] This was a basic difference from the old practice of the adults performing at city inns. The early boasts of the boy-company play-wrights about the less common character of the 'private' hall-playhouse audiences with their exclusively 'gentle' clientele reflect the difference in pricing even more than the social snobbery that they also appealed to. The King's Men took on this snobbish separatism when they took on the Blackfriars playhouse. The new play-house carried with it rather more attachments than just the Blackfriars consort of musicians.

The theory first broached by G. E. Bentley, that Shakespeare's last plays are different from those up to *Antony and Cleopatra* because of the new clientele the King's Men could now cater for at the Blackfriars, has long been discredited. Whatever the reason for the changes evident in the last years of his writing it was not the new playhouse. *Pericles*, the first of the 'last plays', made a hit at the Globe in 1607–8 well before the idea of using the two playhouses could have entered the minds of its leading sharers. *Cymbeline* and *The Winter's Tale* were both staged at the Globe in their first years. *Henry VIII* was the play that burned the first Globe down in 1613. For at least the first decade of the company's binary use of the two playhouses there is no sign of any sense that the different audiences expected different kinds of play. Ben Jonson did write *The Alchemist* specifically for the Blackfriars in 1610, setting it, as the first scene says, 'here in the friers'. But it was set there to exploit the Blackfriars neighbourhood, with its puritans, its feather-sellers, and its affluent residents, not directly because of the gentlemanly theatre clientele at the playhouse itself. It plays Jonson's usual games with the audience, though not in such a way as to suggest that he thought its audience was very different from the Globe's customers. The social range of the gulls in the play reflects the range Jonson saw in the audience at Blackfriars.

The Tempest is the first of Shakespeare's plays definitely written for the Blackfriars, and I believe it does show signs that the players expected its audience there to have rather different expectations from the Globe audiences. The opening storm scene with its uproar and confusions was a deliberate shock tactic. It threw an amphitheatre spectacle of noisy running-about at a Blackfriars audience that had just been lulled by the soft harmonies of music and song from the Blackfriars consort of musicians, who stayed at the playhouse when the boy company left.[3] This says more about the new kind of audience than the plays do. It suggests that the audience had an identity different from the Globe's, and that its new caterers were confident that they could satisfy their tastes without surrendering much from the old traditions. With the roofed hall, music was now available, for instance, so they used it. But the old repertory was used too.

---

[2] The Cavendish account book lists the prices that Sir William Cavendish paid to attend plays at Paul's and Blackfriars between 1600 and 1602. At Paul's he paid a minimum of 18*d*., with 3*d*. for his servant. At Blackfriars he paid sums of between 1*s*. and half a crown. *REED, Derbyshire*, forthcoming.

[3] See Gurr, '*The Tempest*'s Tempest at Blackfriars', *ShS* 41 (1989), 91–102.

Along with the higher prices for admission the company did come to change some of its practices, such as introducing off-stage music. In Webster's Induction to *The Malcontent* in 1601 he claimed that he had written the Induction because in its original form at the Blackfriars it was too short. The original play was longer because of the Blackfriars boys' consort of musicians and their preliminary concert. The new music consort brought the largest single alteration to the King's Men's practices when they took over the Blackfriars playhouse. The housekeepers immediately altered the Globe's stage-balcony to make a curtained music-room over its stage so the musicians could play there as well as at the Blackfriars, a clear indication that the difference in pricing between the two venues was not expected to lead to a difference in the plays staged at each place. In the next few years, stage-music and song was what differentiated the King's Men at the Globe from the other amphitheatre companies. Eventually that feature, along with other trends in the repertory that the Blackfriars audiences favoured, was to make the King's Men's repertory even at the Globe quite a different proposition for the playgoer from what could be had at the northern amphitheatres.

The repertory that the company first brought to the Blackfriars was all Globe fare, including *Pericles*. They rebought Jonson's services for the third time, possibly to augment the Blackfriars offerings, as Bentley surmised, since *The Alchemist* was written for it. They also took on Beaumont and Fletcher, all of whose previous plays had been for boy companies. The first of their plays for the King's Men, *Philaster*, I suspect was written for the Globe, not the Blackfriars, since it begins with a group of gentlemen entering and one saying 'Here's nor lords nor ladies', to which another replies that it is very surprising, because they had strict orders from the king himself to attend. That comment would fit an audience of understanders at the Globe more than the gallants seated in the pit at the Blackfriars. *Philaster* is less demanding in its staging than the two authors' previous plays, with a plot mixing romance and politics in a fairly realistic Italianate setting.

Philaster illustrates in various ways the new Fletcherian mode that characterizes the repertory of the subsequent years. It is an adroit rewrite of their earlier play for a boy company, *Cupid's Revenge*, stripped of its gods descending from the sky and most of its Arcadian artifice, and operating entirely in stage realism, without any *dei ex machina*. Its politics are hardly royalist, since the king is a tyrant, and a combination of rebellious lords and a city mob defeat the ruler and his Spanish ally. The next Beaumont and Fletcher play for the King's Men, *The Maid's Tragedy*, was similarly concerned with the wrongs of royal courts. It poses the question of honour against revenge when a gentleman is wronged by the king seducing his lady. One man, persuaded by the king to marry her to disguise his amours, agonizes but chooses to do nothing because the wrongdoer is his king. The woman's brother instead chooses action and takes his revenge, persuading the king's mistress to kill her seducer, and thereafter suffering the guilt of king-killing.[4] Both plays are

---

[4] A possibly fictitious anecdote from the time speaks of them being overheard in a tavern talking about 'killing the king' and being arrested for it.

suffused with Shakespearian situations and language. Like all the fifty-four plays in the 'Beaumont and Fletcher' canon, to which at least five writers contributed a share, they build on the familiar core of the famous Shakespeare plays that ran alongside them in the company's repertory.[5] Shakespeare, and the Beaumont-and-Fletcher rewrites of Shakespearian devices, formed the core of the company's style from this time on.

Perhaps inevitably, with such a weight of great drama in their stocks, reusing old favourites became one of the company's main activities in the second decade of the century. Roslyn Knutson has suggested that the selection of the plays they presented at court in the 1612–13 season shows the consistency of their commercial strategy.[6] Of the eighteen plays they performed, four were new (*The Tempest*, *A King and No King*, *The Captain*, and the lost *Cardenio*), five were in the current repertoire, and nine were revivals from earlier years. Seven were comedies, four tragedies, two were histories, and five tragi-comedies. I suspect that the more settled character of the company at this time meant a rather greater dependence on revivals than in earlier years, and certainly a basic reliance on Shakespeare, who provided eight of the eighteen. His imitators, Beaumont and Fletcher, provided four, Jonson one (*The Alchemist*), and Tourneur, Ford, and Nicholls one each. One Shakespeare (*Much Ado*) and one Beaumont and Fletcher (*Philaster*) appeared twice in the total of twenty King's Men's performances. Fletcher seems to have taken over from Shakespeare as the company's resident poet at about this time, though there must have been some overlap, since they appear to have collaborated in writing *Two Noble Kinsmen*, *Henry VIII*, and probably *Cardenio*. Beaumont left writing for the stage in 1613. Fletcher's subsequent collaborators included Nathan Field, formerly the star of the Blackfriars boy company and later with the Lady Elizabeth's, who joined the King's Men as an actor-writer in 1616 or so. Fletcher also wrote with Ford and most often with Massinger, who took Fletcher's place when he died in 1625. Having Shakespeare as principal writer in the company, whether alive or dead, was a role the King's Men maintained from 1594 until 1642.

Either as a result of the Globe's closure in 1613, or because of the richer audiences, the Blackfriars was already asserting its role by then as the premier playhouse. In 1614 Webster gave his *Duchess of Malfi* to the Blackfriars company. Possibly he was still grieving over the poor treatment *The White Devil* had received at the Red Bull in 1611, and preferred a hall playhouse for his next. The Globe was out of service after its fire from June 1613 until mid-1614, and Webster may have seized the chance to fit his new play into a hall venue. It was a slow process of change, though. On their title-pages the King's Men's plays were ascribed more or less equally to the Globe and the Blackfriars for another ten years. Not until Charles's reign did the Blackfriars command the company's reputation and oust the

---

[5] H. Neville Davies, 'Beaumont and Fletcher's *Hamlet*', in *Shakespeare, Man of the Theater*, ed. Kenneth Muir, Jay L. Halio, and D. J. Palmer (Newark, NJ, 1983), 173–81, analyzes the Shakespearian elements in these plays.
[6] *The Repertory of Shakespeare's Company*, 143.

Globe from its title-pages. But by 1614 it was already bringing in larger revenues to the company. Christopher Beeston offered it the sincerest form of flattery by building his own hall playhouse in 1616, and Alleyn tried to do the same even earlier. Beeston's subsequent troubles confirm the identity of the King's Men by now as the company with the broadest appeal to the different sections of the community, and with a repertory that was not yet designed to appeal exclusively to the richer end of the social spectrum. The company still used some of its old history plays, with the sort of battles that Shakespeare apologised for in *Henry V* as 'four or five most vile and ragged foils | Right ill disposed in brawl ridiculous', a point Jonson insisted on echoing in the Prologue he wrote for the Folio publication of *Every Man in his Humour* in 1616. But they were not more than a minor feature of the repertory by now. The 'drum-and-trumpet' spectacles were seen patronizingly by Jonson and his gentlemen friends as fodder for the undiscriminating playgoers at the Red Bull. The King's Men were beginning to be characterized as the company supplying Beaumont and Fletcher's plays to the gentry.

With such a secure and reputable company, it is not surprising that changes in the company's membership came about more through age than discontent. Burbage was still the leading player, and Heminges the company's controller of finances. Cook and Ostler, by then sharers, died in 1614 and Shakespeare died in 1616, by which time, despite buying a town property in the Blackfriars gatehouse in 1613, he had sold all his shares in the company and the playhouses. The list of the players who performed *The Duchess of Malfi* that was printed in its 1623 quarto comprise Burbage (playing Ferdinand, replaced later by Joseph Taylor), Condell (the Cardinal, later replaced by Richard Robinson), Ostler (Antonio, replaced after his death in December 1614 by Robert Benfield), together with John Lowin as Bosola, John Underwood (Delio and a madman), Nicolas Tooley (Forobosco and a madman), Thomas Pollard (Silvio), Robert Pallant (the doctor, Cariola, and a court officer). Richard Sharpe (the Duchess), and John Thompson (the Cardinal's mistress). Most of these players would have been in the 1614 production, though the evidence is rather smudged.[7] A Robert Pallant was a member of Queen Anne's Men, Lady Elizabeth's, and Prince Charles's at different times between 1603 and 1623, and was a loyal enough Henslowe man to visit him when he was dying in 1616. The Pallant who played Cariola would have been young, and may have been his son. Heminges and Condell both gave up playing for management in the later years, Heminges some time before Condell. Burbage continued on stage up to his death in 1619.

By that year the company's use of the Blackfriars as their 'winter house' had disturbed the neighbourhood for long enough to provoke a petition of complaint.

---

[7] This list is part of the evidence that led T. W. Baldwin, in *The Organisation and Personnel of the Shakespearean Company* (Princeton, NJ, 1927), to chart what he called the acting 'lines' for each player in the company. The theory is not borne out by the company's casting practices, although the expectation that players would take the same parts for each revival of a play in the repertory is not unreasonable.

Whereas the 1596 petition had been directed to the Privy Council and the Lord Chamberlain as a Blackfriars resident, this petition went to the Lord Mayor. Strictly this was right, because James had ceded control of the 'liberty' to the city in 1608; however, that switch now meant that court and city were once again brought into conflict over the public performance of plays. As usual the court won. In January 1619 the officials of the parish sent the mayor a formal complaint with a supporting petition from the residents. The petition had twenty-four signatories, seven women and seventeen men. Its first signatory was the Puritan vicar of St Anne's, who with four churchwardens and sidemen declared 'Wee finde this howse a great annoyance to ye Church'. Two constables as precinct officers also signed it, declaring 'Wee finde this howse a great occasion for ye breach of ye peace'. Two collectors found 'this howse a great hindrance to our poore', and finally two 'Scavengers' found 'this howse a great annoyance for the clensinge of the streetes'. The official complaint itself cited both the 1596 petition and the Privy Council order of June 1600 stating that there should only be two playhouses in London, the Globe and the Fortune. It went on to say that the playgoing crowds and their coaches clogged the city as far as Ludgate, an 'unrulie multitude of people' who came 'almost everie daie in the winter tyme (not forbearinge the tyme of Lent) from one or twoe of the clock till six att night'. The complaint concluded by saying that if they tried to keep out the coaches either by 'Turnpikes, postes, chaines, or otherwise' they would clog up Ludgate and the other nearby streets. The residents' petition was equally eloquent about the 'Coaches, horses and people of all sortes gathered togeather by that occasion, in those narrow and crooked streetes'.[8]

The threat implied in the point about blocking the neighbouring streets by excluding the coaches was clearly meant to leave the city authorities with only one option, to close the playhouse altogether. On 21 January 1619 the city's Common Council duly ordered the players to stop using the Blackfriars playhouse. Their response was to go to their patron. On 27 March James responded by giving them a new licence (not technically a patent), specifying that they were privileged to play so long as the plague bill did not exceed forty 'aswell within their two their now usuall houses called the Globe within our County of Surrey and their private house scituate in the precinctes of the Blackfriers within our City of london'.[9] This time the court did not negotiate, as Howard did in 1584. It assumed the power to privilege its players against the city with none of the delicacy that the Elizabethan ministers showed.

When the same question came up again in 1633, that power was greater, and the company even better protected. On this occasion the parishioners petitioned the Bishop of London. They used the same documents from 1600 and 1619, and re-emphazised the trouble that came from coaches crowding the narrow streets. This time the response, which came from the Privy Council, was a less aggressive but more effective tactic than the 1619 royal licence. It simply called for a valuation of

---

[8] The two petitions are quoted in *MSC* i. 1. 91–4.   [9] *MSC* i. 3. 281–2.

the playhouse. The players put that at £21,000. Even the official valuation was £3,000, towards which the Blackfriars parish could only offer £100. All the Privy Council then had to do was issue another restraint on coach traffic. They ordered playgoers to leave their coaches either at Paul's churchyard on one side or the Fleet conduit on the other, and send them away for the duration of the performance. A contemporary account reported that this order was obeyed for only two or three weeks.[10] The heavy-handed 1619 response compares with the dismissive 1633 reaction as a mark of how government was changing. Authoritarianism grew under James, while Charles promoted a remoteness from city concerns that sometimes led to the use of cynical or quasi-legal devices to fend off what were seen as unimportant pressures.

The licence of 1619 that was issued in response to the Blackfriars petition lists the company as 'theis our welbeloved servantes John Heminges, Richard Burbadge, Henry Condall, John Lowen, Nicholas Tooley, John Underwood, Nathan field, Robert Benfield, Robert Gough, William Ecclestone, Richard Robinson and John Shankes and the rest of their associates'. Burbage had died two weeks before it was issued.[11] His place among the twelve sharing players named in the licence was taken by Joseph Taylor from Prince Charles's Men, who took over his part as Ferdinand in *The Duchess of Malfi*. His name appears instead of Burbage's in the list that the Lord Chamberlain issued on 19 May for the company's liveries. Playing had been stopped for a period by then, because Queen Anne died on 2 March, and her funeral did not take place until 13 May. Since the players were forbidden to perform while the royal body was above ground, the eleven weeks without any playing this year was a much longer stoppage than the usual Lenten break. The closure gave the company an interval to reorganize its resources. This may have been the time when Henry Condell stopped playing, and it is certainly when Joseph Taylor's services were enlisted to replace Burbage. Presumably he and his company were also being held idle in London during the closure.

To the playgoing public Burbage's death was the major loss. Middleton, in his contribution to the flock of elegies, made it much more of an event than Anne's death. He called it and the closure the year's fifth eclipse: 'Death interposing Burbage, and there staying, | Hath made a visible eclipse of playing.'[12] He got away with the implication that it was Burbage's death rather than Anne's that closed the playhouses.

The company's repertory was regularly supplemented with plays from the Beaumont-and-Fletcher factory and other writers, the most substantial of whom in these years was Thomas Middleton. The court papers are deficient for the years up to 1622, and the only plays that the company is recorded as performing there were revivals: *Twelfth Night*, *The Winter's Tale*, and *The Merry Devil of Edmonton* in 1617–18, and *Pericles* on 20 May 1619. These are the only titles surviving from the fourteen or so plays the King's Men now routinely played at court each

[10] See *JCS* i. 31–4.
[11] His will is transcribed in *Playhouse Wills 1558–1642*, 113–14.
[12] BL Egerton MS. 2592, f. 81.

winter.[13] There is no evidence to say whether the company had already begun to depend on its old faithfuls in the repertory. They were still buying new playbooks with some frequency. In the repertory at large the bulk of the playbook stock was still Shakespeare, but it was rapidly being supplemented with Beaumont and Fletcher. By 1620, in addition to Shakespeare's thirty-eight plays, the company had more than twenty-five in the repertory by the Beaumont and Fletcher teams,[14] plus *Hengist*, *Wit at Several Weapons*, *The Widow*, and others by Middleton, two by Field, some plays by Tourneur now lost, and quite a number of others that are also lost.

The trouble the company had in August 1619 over the censorship of *Sir John van Olden Barnavelt* has been described in Chapter 7. The fact that it was thought to be dangerous matter by people in high places marks the company's first step into the complex political manœuvring that culminated in 1624 with the scandal of *A Game at Chess*. It was not a very long step, and it is not easy to see what kind of role it shows the company now taking in the elaborate political games that the company's courtier-patrons were now starting to use it for. There is little tangible evidence to back the idea that *A Game at Chess* was not the first use of the company's capacity to test popular sentiment. Plays were starting to be used for propaganda, but there is no indication that the King's Men went deeper into that exercise than any other of the London groups.

The company's activities from 1621 onwards are recorded far better than for any other period, mainly thanks to the assiduous notes kept by Henry Herbert, the new Master of the Revels. The company's membership remained steady. Heminges continued to be the payee for court performances and presumably the chief financial manager until 1626. In that role, along with Condell who had also given up playing for management, he set up the long job of printing Shakespeare's plays in 1622. A livery allowance of April 1621 shows that Nathan Field, who died in 1620, had been replaced by John Rice. Nicholas Tooley and John Underwood died in 1623 or 1624,[15] and Elliart Swanston, already for some years a leading player in the Lady Elizabeth's at the Cockpit,[16] seems to have been imported as a replacement.

Henry Herbert's work as master of the Revels looms large in the King's Men's great sensation of August 1624, *A Game at Chess*. As we have seen above, the anti-Spanish faction at court must have given strong support to the play's staging, and

---

[13] In 1615–16 they played fourteen, in 1616–17 thirteen, and in 1617–18 fifteen. Figures for the next three years are missing.

[14] In roughly the order of composition or acquisition by the company, these included *Philaster*, *The Maid's Tragedy*, *A King and No King*, *The Coxcomb*, *The Captain*, *Bonduca*, *The Scornful Lady*, *The Honest Man's Fortune*, *Valentinian*, *Wit without Money*, *Monsieur Thomas*, *Love's Pilgrimage*, *The Nice Valour*, *The Mad Lover*, *The Queen of Corinth*, *Thierry and Theodoret*, *The Loyal Subject*, *The Knight of Malta*, *The Humorous Lieutenant*, *Rollo*, *The Little French Lawyer*, *The Custom of the Country*, *The False Marriage*, and *The False One*.

[15] Tooley's will is transcribed in *Playhouse Wills 1558–1642*, 128, and Underwood's 142–5. Underwood had shares in the Globe, Blackfriars, and Curtain.

[16] Sir John Astley's note, transcribed in *Dramatic Records*, 63, reported him in 1622 as among 'The chiefe of them at the Phoenix'.

helped to protect both the company and Herbert from any serious consequences.[17] The story confirms how much closer the company was to the earl of Pembroke, who had received the dedication of the Shakespeare First Folio the year before, than to their royal patron. It is also worth noting the bond of £300 which they had to submit as a token of goodwill while their case was examined. That shows the scale of their resources by this time. The company itself was sure enough of its strength to exploit the fame it brought them. In the prologue to *Rule a Wife and Have a Wife*, staged two months after *A Game at Chess*, October, they strutted unashamed, declaring that 'this day w'are *Spaniards* all againe'.

Their pride in their success may have betrayed them. In December Henry Herbert forced them to give him a written apology over a lost play, *The Spanish Viceroy*. The company had neglected to get Herbert's licence for it, and eleven players had to sign a letter, dated 20 December 1624, apologizing and promising 'that wee will not act any play without your hand or substituts hereafter, nor doe any thinge that may prejudice the authority of your office'.[18] The eleven signatories were Taylor, Lowin, Robinson, Shank, Swanston, Rice, Pollard, William Rowley, Benfield, Sharpe, and George Birch. Will Rowley, writer and player, had been a leading man as a 'fat clown' for ten years in the York's/Prince Charles's Company at the Curtain and Red Bull. He had joined the King's Men by 1623, for the last two years of his life. He probably played the fat bishop in *A Game at Chess*. Birch had joined the King's Men after marrying Richard Cowley's daughter in 1619. He seems to have become a sharer by 1623. Herbert copied the letter into his office book some years later, in 1633, as a reminder of his power to the King's Men. The troubles of 1624 put his position at risk, and he had to flex his muscles.

James's death on 27 March 1625 was followed by the worst plague epidemic of the whole period, killing 35,417 Londoners, over ten per cent of the population. The playhouses were closed from May to September, and Charles indicated that he was continuing his father's favour by giving his new company a hundred marks (£67) at Christmas to compensate for the closure. The way in which Charles took on his father's company for himself so that they kept their title as King's Men may now appear inevitable. His own former company, Prince Charles's of the Red Bull, could not rank with the Blackfriars or the Cockpit companies. Giving the old King's Men his patronage was the first of a number of positive choices by the new king that helped to keep the company under the royal wing.

Fifteen members of the company were granted liveries for James's funeral. A paper of Herbert's dated 27 December 1624 also names twenty-two of the company's assistants, the non-sharers, including its book-keeper, Edward Knight, and its musicians. The two lists together indicate that the company's total manpower was nearly forty men. No other company could maintain such a resource. And they had quality as well as quantity, since Herbert seems to have allowed them to poach the best players from the other London companies.

---

[17] See Ch. 7.   [18] *Herbert Dramatic Records*, 21.

The company also still had the unique asset of the Blackfriars musicians. In Bulstrode Whitelock's memoirs of the 1630s, he tells how they would strike up with his own composition when they saw him in the playhouse.

I composed an Aier myself, with the assistance of Mr. Ives, and called it *Whitelocke's Coranto*; which being cried up, was first played publiquely, by the Blackefryar's Muysicke, who were then esteemed the best of common musitians in London. Whenever I came to that house (as I did sometimes in those dayes), though not often, to see a play, the musitians would presently play Whitelocke's Coranto, and it was so often called for, that they would have it played twice or thrice in an afternoon.[19]

The company's supremacy is really marked by the right it was given to take leading players from other companies to fill its gaps. Besides acquiring Joseph Taylor at Burbage's death, and later adding Will Rowley and Elliart Swanston from Prince Charles's, towards the end of 1623 they acquired Richard Perkins, the long-time star of Queen Anne's Men and the Red Bull. It is almost as if they were strengthening themselves through James's last years in anticipation of the eventual need for a new patron by culling the best players from their rivals. No other company ever had this power. It was unique in the way it marked a kind of official recognition of their status, more useful in practical terms even than their royal title in helping them to maintain their status.

This uniqueness had consequences for the company in the rest of the country. As the professional companies became more and more obviously the beneficiaries of royal privilege, civic opposition to them in the rest of the country intensified. The rules became more lax, so that travelling companies did not always feel obliged to report to the mayor when they arrived in a town. The patronage system had effectively gone as a form of control, being replaced by the Master of the Revels and his annual issue of royal licences to play in London and to travel. One consequence of this for the King's Men was that more and more companies claimed to use the king's name when they identified themselves in the towns they visited. Queen Anne's 'children of Bristol' by 1622 became 'the Kinges players of the chamber of Bristowe', though they still appear to have been 'youths' at least in the 1620s. William Perry ran a company recorded in Nottingham in 1632–3 as 'the kings plaiers of the Chamber of yorke'. Even Martin Slater was claiming at Leicester in 1625 that he was a king's player. One effect of this change for us is that it becomes harder to differentiate the king's companies, and to determine which is the London one. Coventry distinguished 'the kinges players of Blackfriers' from the others in 1636, but Nottingham in the same fiscal year had to identify 'the Kinges Plaieres of Yorke' from 'the Kinges players of the Court' and 'the Kinges players of London'. The first of these was Perry's. The second might have been the King's Revels company, then at Salisbury Court, which would make the King's Men the third of the visitors.

---

[19] Quoted in *JCS* 1: 40.

The 1625 closure brought some other reorganization to the company's membership. Prince Charles's Men disappeared now that their patron had become king, and three of their members, Thomas Hobbs, Anthony Smith, and William Penn, now joined the King's Men. A note dated 23 May 1625 appears to indicate that a share in the company was now rated at £500, which was the 'stock debt' that Thomas Hobbs engaged himself for.[20] Not all such new sharers fitted easily into the company. At some point during the closure one star, Richard Perkins, left to form the new Queen Henrietta's Men with Beeston at the Cockpit. This started an association that in the next years helped to raise the other company to a level that for a while rivalled the King's in esteem. It was the only serious competitor the King's Men ever had. Queen Henrietta's had the second hall playhouse, and an adroit and experienced manager. For all their supreme status, the story of the King's Men in the early years of Charles's reign was not altogether a story of unwavering success.

Several changes took place after playing restarted in 1625. John Fletcher died in that year, and Philip Massinger, a long-time writer in the Beaumont and Fletcher canon, took his place as the company's 'resident' writer. The new patent was headed with the names of Heminges and Condell, but both men were nearing the end of their long careers. Condell died in December 1627, and Heminges in 1630.[21] Heminges remained payee for the company's court performances up to his death. By then he was the company's most substantial backer, owning a quarter of both the Globe and the Blackfriars playhouses. In his last years he lived near the Globe, and his death marks as well as anything the point where the company finally gave the top priority to its more profitable venue, the Blackfriars, and its clientele of court and gentry. The Globe was distinctly the secondary playhouse through the 1630s. In this last period, from 1630, the company's managerial sharers were John Lowin and Joseph Taylor.[22]

Their policy over the company's repertory and its playing-places did not differ greatly from that of their predecessors, though it did submit to some heavy changes in the 1630s. From the outset the new pair retained royal favour. They received £100 in 1630 as a compensation for that year's plague closure, and at the end of 1631 protection once again from the protests of their Blackfriars neighbours about the traffic jams that playgoing caused. In 1633 they fended off another appeal by the Blackfriars residents, and the Lord Chamberlain gave them a unique warrant affirming their supreme status by formally authorizing them to take up players from other companies. They had done this with individuals before, drawing Swanston, Perkins, and others from lesser companies. Now they had explicit official authority to do so.

---

[20] *JCS* i. 18.

[21] Condell died in 1627, in Fulham. His will is transcribed in *Playhouse Wills 1558–1642*, 156–60. Heminges's will is transcribed in *Playhouse Wills 1558–1642*, 164–9.

[22] For an account of the managerial system of these last years, see Rick Bowers, 'John Lowin: Actor-Manager of the King's Company, 1630–42', *Theatre Survey*, 28 (1987), 15–35.

The warrant must have been made out in response to a fairly urgent plea from the company managers, although it is difficult to see what recent deaths or withdrawals from the company's sharer-membership could have prompted it. Addressed to Taylor and Lowin, it stated:

Wheras the late decease, infirmity & sicknes of diverse principall Actors of his Majestes Company of Players hath much decayed & weakened them, soe that they are disabled to doe his Majesty service in their quality, unlesse there bee some speedy order taken to supply & furnish them with a convenient number of new Actors. His Majestye haveing taken notice thereof & signifyed his royall pleasure unto mee therin, Theis are to will & require you & in his Majestes name straitly to charge, commaund & Authorize you & either of you to choose, receave & take into your Company any such Actor or Actors belonging to any of the lycensed Companyes within & about the Citty of London as you shall think fitt & able to doe his Majesty service in that kinde.[23]

It is an odd warrant, because the company membership in this period was fairly stable. Conceivably it was misdated by Malone when he transcribed it, though he was generally meticulous. Had it been dated a decade earlier after the loss of Burbage and Condell, the taking of Taylor and others would appear more justifiable. But the date is firmly transcribed as 1633, and so it has to be fitted into this phase of the company's career. At least in part it may have been evoked by a quarrel with other company impresarios that erupted shortly before the warrant's date, 6 May 1633, although what disabilities any of the sharers were suffering from then is not known. G. E. Bentley suggested that it may have been a retroactive authorization for their acquisition of the young Stephen Hammerton late in 1632.[24] That is a distinct possibility. William Beeston and William Blagrave of the Salisbury Court company petitioned the Lord Chamberlain on 12 November 1632 to get Hammerton back from the Blackfriars. The Chamberlain referred the matter to Henry Herbert, whose note of his recommendations has not survived. He evidently did not accept what the petition asked for. Hammerton, playing women in 1632, had become a celebrated star of the King's company well before 1640.

The company did need new blood in 1632, though as much in writers as in players. A bill which lists the company's offerings at court in the 1630–1 season shows what they saw as their strengths but also the age of the repertory that they felt able to offer at court. They were soon to have their priorities altered. That year the court season ran longer than ever, from Michaelmas on 30 September to a little before Lent, 21 February. It saw in all twenty of the King's Men's plays. One was by Shakespeare, *A Midsummer Night's Dream*.[25] Two were by Jonson, *Volpone* and *Every Man in his Humour*. Other durables included Webster's *Duchess of Malfi*, and *The Merry Devil of Edmonton*. Half the total were from the Beaumont and Fletcher resource. *Rollo* was performed twice, along with *Philaster*, *The Maid's*

---

[23] *MSC* ii. 3. 361.   [24] *JCS* i. 36.

[25] The list also includes an 'Olde Castle', which may have been a reversion to the original *1 Henry IV* of 1596. Roslyn Knutson thinks that it could have been a Chamberlain's play written in 1601 to match the Admiral's *Sir John Oldcastle* of 1600 (*The Repertory of Shakespeare's Company*, 95–7).

Tragedy, *A King and No King*, and six more. Hardly any of the twenty in that season were new. The newest was Arthur Wilson's *The Inconstant Lady*, a play which helped to establish what became the predominant fashion in the hall plays of the 1630s, plays with titles about or appealing to the gentlewomen in the audiences.[26] The company was more and more inclined to rest on its famous repertory. In 1632 Herbert licensed only two new plays for them. Throughout the 1630s that number rarely rose to more than four. They were the first group to find, as many others have since, that they could live off the Shakespeare canon.

By 1632, though, the company's new plays were a blood transfusion from a different kind of source. The story of how Davenant, Carew, and the courtier poets fostered by Henrietta Maria succeeded in their struggle against the more traditional poets of the Blackfriars and Cockpit, Shirley, Massinger, and Ford has been told in Chapter 8. Whether the king's players firmly took sides in that struggle is doubtful. They did choose Davenant as writer ahead of Shirley and Ford, and must, in part, have seen it as a matter of preferred style. Davenant, former protégé of Fulke Greville and an Inns-of-Court resident, won against Ford, also an Inns-of-Court man and for twenty years a part-writer of plays in collaboration with Dekker and others. Davenant's pull was his coterie at court. By their choice of the young Davenant the company showed themselves to be leaves on the stream that carried the hall-playhouse companies closer and closer to the court and further from the country as a whole. As the country hunched more and more tightly into its social and cultural enclaves, so the playing companies reflected that separation.

Lowin and Taylor did try, in their practical decisions, to maintain the long-set traditions of the King's Men. Although the takings at the Blackfriars now ran well in excess of those at the Globe, they clung to the practice of using one playhouse for summer and the other for winter, despite recurrent troubles with their tenure of both playhouses. They suffered the next petition from the Blackfriars residents, a complaint that dragged on from 1631 till 1633. As soon as the Privy Council choked that off the company had to set about renewing its grip on the Globe, which was the start of a long struggle to get the lease renewed for a further nine years beyond the original expiry date in December 1635.[27] The fact that this trouble came to the company only a month or so after the Blackfriars residents' latest attempts to get the Blackfriars closed must have given the sharers a strong incentive to hold on to the Globe. But it could equally well be argued that their continuing faith in the Globe in the 1630s is a measure of how strongly they felt, against the tide, that the binary season and the two playhouses were an essential part of their character as a company.

---

[26] The bill is quoted in full in *JCS* i. 27–8.

[27] The young landlord had signed an extension in the lease when the second Globe was ready to be built in 1614, stretching its term from Dec. 1635 to Dec. 1644. In 1633, however, he tried to cancel the extension on the grounds that he had been a minor when he originally signed it. Probably he wanted to lease it to another company. It took two years of litigation before the company got their extension.

Nevertheless, and probably not entirely of their own will, Lowin and Taylor helped to draw the company further away from its origins and its centre at the Globe towards the court. In 1634 Taylor mounted a production for Queen Henrietta Maria of Fletcher's *The Faithful Shepherdess*, originally played unsuccessfully by a boy company in 1608 or 1610 and not acted on the public stage since. An adroit choice, it fitted the queen's strong interest in pastorals and arcadian love.[28] And now that playwriting had become a sufficiently respectable activity to warrant courtiers writing for the public stage, the company also started taking new plays from the poets who were conspicuously dancing attendance on the queen at court, notably Thomas Carew and William Davenant.

In time the court faction prevailed at the Blackfriars, but the losses were not insignificant. Shirley had an awkward period under attack from the Blackfriars poets when he joined the queen's court circle in 1632 but, more to the point, Massinger had his next play cried down by a claque of courtiers in the Blackfriars audience, and John Ford left the King's to write for Beeston. Courtiers were getting more and more closely involved with playing. When Herbert censored *The Wits*, Endymion Porter took the script for the king to read in January 1634. The king approved it. Herbert had reluctantly to give it a licence as 'corrected by the kinge', and it played at Blackfriars and then at court on 23 January.

The company must have been uncomfortable with some of this attention and the factionality it aroused, but they knew where their allegiance lay. Henrietta Maria herself attended plays at the Blackfriars in 1634, 1636, and 1637, the first royal figure to attend a public (however ostensibly private) playhouse.[29] The King's Men and, specifically, their Blackfriars playhouse had become the centre of courtly attention, attracting the more radical and extravagant poets and plays. Queen Henrietta's Men at the Cockpit were less close to the queen herself than the King's Men, and ran a quieter repertory. The more professional poets, Shirley, Massinger, and John Ford, found it better to write for the Cockpit rather than the Blackfriars. Through their last decade the King's Men followed the new mode of augmenting their old favourites with new offerings by the courtier poets.

In different ways both sides seem to have sensed, for all the newly self-conscious pride in social display, some diminution of quality. The King's Men knew where their chief allegiance lay as the pre-eminent company, and their plays show it. Plays with titles aiming at the ladies in the hall-playhouse audiences appeared in the Blackfriars, Cockpit, and Salisbury-Court plays, most positively at the Blackfriars. Henrietta Maria's tastes showed up strongly in the King's repertory from 1630 onwards, but more rarely in the other halls. Besides *The Faithful Shepherdess*,

---

[28] Shakerley Marmion wrote a poem addressed to Taylor, which said 'When this smooth Pastorall was first brought forth, | The Age twas borne in, did not know its worth. | Since by thy cost, and industry reviv'd, | It hath a new fame, and new birth atchiv'd'. See Gurr, *Playgoing in Shakespeare's London*, 181–2.

[29] *JCS* vi. 34–5.

Taylor presented her with Davenant's play on her favourite fancy, *The Platonic Lovers*, in 1636. The Cockpit, by contrast, stayed more traditional. Theophilus Bird, a player in Queen Henrietta's Men who became Beeston's son-in-law, wrote a prologue in 1639 for Ford's *The Lady's Trial* which deplored the predominant King's repertory:

> *Wit, wit's the word in fashion, that alone*
> *Cryes up the Poet, which though neatly showne,*
> *Is rather censur'd often-times than knowne.*
>
> *He who will venture on a jest, that can*
> *Raile on anothers paine, or idlely scan*
> *Affaires of state, oh hee's the onely man.*
>
> *A goodly approbation, which must bring*
> *Fame with contempt, by such a deadly sting,*
> *The Muses chatter, who were wont to sing.*

One consequence of this factionalism over plays emerged in the depth of the division that now appeared between the two sides and the two playhouses of the company's binary system of playing. For the first two decades when they had a winter and a summer playhouse there is almost no sign of any distinction being made in the repertory between the two seasons. In the 1630s, with royal interest, and with the kind of social cachet for the Blackfriars that made dignitaries such as the Duke of Lennox quarrel in public with Pembroke, the Lord Chamberlain, over the key to a box at the playhouse,[30] the split in audience tastes that started the poets' war of 1630 made itself felt at the Globe. Davenant noted it in a play of 1638.[31] Shirley, back after four years in Dublin in 1640 and writing his first play for the King's Men, also recorded the division he now found between the two audiences. In the 1646 edition of his poems, he printed '*A Prologue at the Globe to his Comedy call'd* The Doubtful Heire, *which should have been presented at the Black-Friers*'. It claims that the play was not designed for Globe tastes, which he will praise for its wit.

> No shewes, no frisk, and what you most delight in
> (Grave understanders) here's no Target fighting
> Upon the Stage, all work for cutlers barrd,
> No Bawd'ry, nor no Ballads; this goes hard.
> The wit is clean, and (what affects you not)
> Without impossibilities the plot;
> No Clown, no squibs, no Divells in't; oh now
> you Squirrels that want nuts, what will ye do?

---

[30] Pembroke demanded the key to his box which Lennox, the King's cousin, had appropriated, in Jan. 1636 at the launch of a new play. The king himself had to mollify them. See Gurr, *Playgoing*, 244. Conceivably Pembroke (Philip Herbert), an extraordinarily eccentric man in an age full of strange behaviour among the great, still expected value from the company for his 1633 warrant allowing them to take players from other companies.

[31] See Gurr, *Playgoing*, 180–1.

This tongue-in-cheek apology is notable in part because it admits that some people used to seeing plays at the Blackfriars would be at the Globe, and that it was the amphitheatre itself which generated the expectation of noise, rough bawdy, and fighting.

Another revelation about the company's position and its policy in this last decade comes from Heywood and Brome's *Late Lancashire Witches*.[32] The company appears once again to have been used by a Pembroke, this time William Herbert's brother and successor, Philip. His aim was to stage a play that gave support to his own manœuvres on the Privy Council against the king's most ardent supporter, Laud. The company may not have taken this Herbert request as seriously as the previous one. The issue was far less populist than the prejudice against Spain exploited in the earlier play, and to judge from the report of the only known witness its preaching was evidently to the not-so-converted. In any case, a play at the Globe now carried less clout than it would have done ten years before. The play precisely matches Shirley's definition of Globe tastes that he laid down in *The Doubtful Heir* six years later. It still proved to be a not unsuccessful piece of knockabout, because the company took it on tour in the following year. Thomas Crosfield, writing in his Oxford diary for July 1635, noted that 'besides ye playes at ye Kinges armes other things were to be seene for money, as . . . 5. The witches of Lancashire over against ye Kings Head, their 1 Meetings 2 Tricks'.[33] There is no official record of the King's Men touring that summer, but by the 1630s companies on tour had long given up the Tudor practice of checking in with the local mayor, so the civic records for this time are extremely patchy. No other company had a play by that name.

In its last years the company continued the policy of running its old repertoire of plays, and making few waves. According to the bill for their twenty-two performances at court from Easter 1636 till Lent 1637[34] they offered two Shakespeare tragedies, *Othello* and *Hamlet*, one Jonson comedy, *Epicene*, nine Beaumont and Fletchers, including *Rollo*, *Philaster*, and *The Maid's Tragedy*, and as new plays from 1636 both parts of the courtier Lodowick Carlell's *Arviragus*, played twice over on successive days, plus William Cartwright's *The Royal Slave*, and a lost play, *The Governor*. A play called *Alfonso*, possibly a revised version of the old *Alphonsus Emperor of Germany* written in the 1590s, was staged for the queen and the prince at Blackfriars on 5 May 1636. The other play was Davenport's *Love and Honour* from 1634. Only four of the twenty plays were new in the repertory, and only five did not date from earlier than 1625.

A story attached to one of these plays, *The Royal Slave*, gives further evidence of the company's closeness to the court. It had been staged originally at Christ Church, Oxford, and the queen asked if the costumes might be passed on to the King's Men so that they could act it for her in London. At Oxford it had been staged with scenery by Inigo Jones of the sort that he supplied for court masques.

---

[32] See Ch. 8.   [33] The MS is in Queen's College Library, MS 390.
[34] Reprinted in *JCS* i. 51–2.

The queen only asked for the costumes, presumably knowing that the players could not use such innovations as perspective shuts at the Blackfriars. The university's chancellor, Archbishop Laud, rather grudgingly agreed to let the players have them, although, as the university's historian reported, 'the Chancellor desired of the King and Queen that neither the Play, or Cloathes, nor Stage, might come into the hands and use of the Common Players abroad, which was graciously granted'.[35]

The summer of 1636 was a bad time for plague, starting a closure that was to last more than sixteen months. The usual royal bounty came to the company for the long lay-off they suffered, although this time it was not a belated grant, but a weekly fee of £1, payable for so long as the king allowed. While the closure lasted it provoked a letter from the new Lord Chamberlain ordering the Stationers' Company to check on its authority to print certain playbooks. Evidently the old practice in times of long closure where unemployed players made money by putting together texts from memory to sell to printers had resurfaced. The letter upholds the rights of the two leading owners, the King's Men and Christopher Beeston. It may, however, also be a response to a dispute over the ownership of some playbooks between the two sets of owners. The King's performance of *Alfonso* for the queen and prince in 1636 possibly had something to do with it. The King's Men presumably seized on this play for the aptness of its subject to the prince without taking enough notice of who owned it. In any case, it is noteworthy as the first record of the companies using officialdom to protect their rights over their playbooks.

The Lord Chamberlain's letter about the plays, dated 10 June 1637, starts by dating the complaint back to the time of his predecessor, William Herbert, third earl of Pembroke, who had passed the office on to his brother more than ten years before, in 1626. That would put it into the time of the Shakespeare First Folio (and incidentally give a belated pay-off for its dedication to the two Herbert brothers). Philip Herbert was seeking precedents for his order. It reads:

Wheras complaint was heeretofore presented to my Deare brother & predecessor by his Majesties servantes the Players, that some of the Company of Printers & Stationers had procured, published & printed diverse of their bookes of Comaedyes, Tragedyes Cronicle Historyes, and the like which they had (for the speciall service of his Majestye & for their owne use) bought and provided at very Deare and high rates. By meanes wherof not onely they themselves had much prejudice, but the bookes much corruption to the injury and disgrace of the Authors, And therupon the Masters and Wardens of the company of printers & stationers were advised by my Brother to take notice therof & to take Order for the stay of any further Impression of any of the Playes or Interludes of his Majestes servantes without their consentes.

---

[35] *JCS* i. 52. Martin Butler, 'Royal Slaves? The Stuart Court and the Theatres', *Renaissance Drama Newsletter Supplement* 2 (Warwick, 1983), takes issue with the assumption that all the playing companies became instruments of royal self-regard in the 1630s. He points out that four of the five companies were never as close to the court as the King's Men, and that even the circle of courtiers around Queen Henrietta who wrote for the Blackfriars could be at odds with Charles. The 'court' was not a simple entity. But the King's Men's share in its interests is not in question.

The immediate concern that prompted the letter follows.

I am informed that some Coppyes of Playes belonging to ye King & Queenes servantes the Players, & purchased by them at Deare rates, haveing beene lately stollen or gotten from them by indirect meanes are now attempted to bee printed & that some of them are at ye Presse & ready to bee printed, which if it should be suffered, would directly tend to their apparent Detriment & great prejudice & to the disenabling of them to doe their Majestes service.

The letter orders the Wardens of the Company of Stationers not to allow any playbook to be printed without first getting 'some Certificate in writeing under the handes of John Lowen & Joseph Taylor for the Kings servantes & of Christopher Bieston for ye Kings & Queenes young Company'.[36] That last reference indicates another possibility, that it was Beeston who inspired the letter. Having dislodged Queen Henrietta's Men from the Cockpit in the course of the closure, he was now setting up a new group of younger players, 'Beeston's Boys', and must have wanted to hold his stock of playbooks for them. That meant keeping them from the old Queen Henrietta's Men who, even without the original playbooks, might have claimed the right to use them if they became available in print. The letter's lack of specificity may indicate how little Philip Herbert actually knew of the real reasons behind the request.

A later pair of documents along similar lines indicates rather more visibly a conflict between the King's Men and the Beeston interests. On 7 August 1641 the new Lord Chamberlain, Essex, wrote to the Stationers identifying the plays not yet in print that belonged to each company and that were to be protected from uncertified printing. The King's Men's list runs to 61 plays, close to half of which are Beaumont and Fletcher plays not yet in print. There are several by Massinger, mostly lost titles, and by Tourneur, Arthur Wilson, and Ford. Besides most of Davenant's and Suckling's plays and others from the 1630s, the list also includes Middleton's *Hengist*, and the *Alfonso* played for the queen and prince in 1636.[37] With the 36 plays in the Shakespeare First Folio and *Pericles*, plus Jonson's 9 and the Beaumont and Fletcher and other plays already in print, the King's were staking a claim altogether to well over 100 plays. That was nearly one-third of the extant texts of the time, and a large proportion of the texts surviving today. Taking the whole gamut of entertainment across the country through the 1630s, it is still a very small iceberg-tip, but there is no doubt where the King's Men stood on it.

Beeston's shake-up of the company using the Cockpit affected the King's Men's membership during the closure. Five of the expelled Queen Henrietta's Men joined the King's: Michael Bowyer, William Robbins, William Allen, Hugh Clark, and Theophilus Bird. Many years later Bird reported that he had paid £200 towards the company stock and signed a bond for the same amount for Bowyer, who preceded him into the company. That, he claimed, was far more than the £50

---

[36] The whole letter is printed in *MSC* ii. 3. 384–5.   [37] The complete list is given below, 387.

which was the normal share price in 1637.[38] The company's sharers then included, besides Taylor and Lowin, Benfield, Pollard, Robinson, Shank, and Swanston.[39] Stephen Hammerton was a young star. Other players, not the leading sharers, are recorded in a list drawn up in May 1636 authorizing them to travel during the closure. The names on that list are 'Wm Pen, thomas Hobbes, Wm Trig, Wm Patrick Richd Baxter, Alexander Gough Wm Hart & Richd Hanley together with Tenne more or theraboutes of their fellowes his Majestes Comaedians & of the peculiar Company of Players in the Blackfryers London'.[40] Eighteen men and boys, plus the eight major sharers, would have meant a large travelling group. Some sharers certainly stayed on in London, or in the 'country houses' nearby, throughout the closure.

That the intake from Queen Henrietta's did not alter the company's policy in any way is indicated most strongly by the staging of *Aglaura* at court in the Christmas season early in 1638. Not only was the company still loyal to its courtier-poets, but it continued to receive rich handouts from them to help the stage spectacle. George Garrard wrote to Strafford on 7 February that:

> Two of the king's Servants, Privy-Chamber Men both, have writ each of them a Play, Sir *John Sutlin* and *Will. Barclay*, which have been acted in Court, and at the *Black Friars*, with much Applause. *Sutlin's* Play cost three or four hundred Pounds setting out, eight or ten Suits of new Cloaths he gave the Players; an unheard of prodigality.[41]

Suckling's 'prodigality' prompted a lot of comment. Aubrey claimed that he had included 'scaenes' in his gift to the players, a further sign of courtly fashion invading the public domain. Poets and companies who lacked that pretension scoffed at poets who paid for their plays to be staged. Richard Brome's epilogue to *The Court Beggar* tells his audience that 'you'l say those Playes are not given to you; you pay as much for your seats at them as at these, though you sit nere the merrier, nor rise the wiser, they are so above common understanding'.[42] The company was firmly bound to its courtier-poets and the tastes of its Blackfriars audiences, and Brome was not of that class.

These practices continued, and the occupation of the Blackfriars by courtly interests went on growing. In 1640 the company staged another play, Habington's *Cleodora, Queen of Aragon*, originally brought to court by the Lord Chamberlain's own servants. Reversing the old tradition of appearing first in public before going to the court, it was taken from the court to the Blackfriars. It was one of the relatively few new plays that the company bought in these last years. In 1638–9 and 1639–40 they performed more than twenty plays at court, mostly old favourites, and sixteen in 1640–1. Massinger remained as resident poet until his death early in

---

[38] Leslie Hotson, *The Commonwealth and Restoration Stage* (Cambridge, Mass., 1928), 31–5.

[39] Shank died in Dec. 1635, after a dispute with his fellows over his playhouse shares. His will is transcribed in *Playhouse Wills 1558–1642*, 186–90.

[40] *MSC* ii. 3. 378–9.

[41] William Knowler, ed. *The Earl of Strafforde's Letters and Dispatches* (2 vols.; London, 1739), ii. 150.

[42] Richard Brome, *Five New Playes* (1653), sig. S8.

1640, when Shirley came back from Dublin to take his place. He gave them five new plays up to April 1642: *The Doubtful Heir*, *The Imposture*, *The Brothers*, *The Cardinal*, and *The Sisters*. These seem to have been almost the only company acquisitions that did not come from courtiers.

There is only one indication that the company was not wholly committed to courtly interests in this last period. In June 1638 Massinger's *The King and the Subject* drew a reproof from Henry Herbert. Charles himself, an avid reader of play-texts, had objected to the Spanish king's announcement in the play that he would use blank charters to raise money. Since Massinger was only re-wording an old device condemned long ago in *Richard II*, the king must have resented its potential application to his own current practice. This is one of the few signs of a less-than-total commitment to the court and their patron that can be found in the company's plays in this period. Being critical of specific court practices did not mean being hostile to the court in general, of course. It rather indicates a close interest in matters that might have prompted discussion and dispute at court.

That there was less than complete loyalty elsewhere in the country by 1641 is entirely apparent. The closedown of court privilege was marked at court that Christmas, when Henry Herbert noted sadly that the only play given was the King's Men's *The Scornful Lady* on Twelfth Night 1642 for Prince Charles, and that the king and queen saw no plays that season.[43] When Parliament finally ordered that 'while these sad Causes and set times of Humiliation doe continue, publike Stage-Playes shall cease, and bee forborne',[44] on 2 September 1642, the company soon disintegrated. The circumstances that brought the closure have been discussed in Chapter 8. Whatever the immediate reasons, it was an edict of Parliament, not of the Privy Council. Parliament had never before intervened over playing. That is the clearest marker of the shift in power, and the demotion of the players' chief protector. The speed with which the King's Men fell apart may be one mark of their proximity to the royal favour. They knew they would go down with the royal family.

Even before the actual closure, with the players knowing how fragile was their condition given the combative role their patron now occupied, the company seems to have started to disintegrate. According to Theophilus Bird, who brought a lawsuit in Chancery in 1655 to defend himself against a suit in common law brought by the heirs of Bowyer, some of the sharers, including Pollard and Bowyer, had sold the company's properties, playbooks, apparel, and hangings as early as 1642.[45] How soon they did this after the September closure is not quite clear from Bird's complaint. Throughout 1642 they could not have been very hopeful, with the country going to war, and they knew that the king's displacement took their power base away. They certainly knew the strength of feeling in the opposition. In the winter of 1641 the Blackfriars residents had renewed their complaint against the

[43] *Herbert Dramatic Records*, 58.   [44] *JCS* ii. 690.
[45] Hotson, *The Commonwealth and Restoration Stage*, 31–4. Bowyer's will is transcribed in *Playhouse Wills 1558–1642*, 203–4.

playhouse, this time along with the adjoining parishes of St Martin's, Ludgate, and St Bride's. The protest this time was not just an objection to the playgoers' coaches creating traffic jams. Simonds D'Ewes in his journal summarized the case made by the petition's presenter, Alderman Pennington, as 'Gods howse not soe neare Divils'.[46] The company folded quickly because the sharers were justified in being pessimistic over their future.

The story of the individual King's players through the closure and into the Restoration is not really a part of this book. They did stay in touch with one another, and evidently hoped to renew their playing activities eventually. Ten of them, Lowin, Taylor, Allen, Benfield, Bird, Clark, Hammerton, Pollard, Robinson, and Swanston, were available to sign the dedication to the 1647 Beaumont and Fletcher Folio. On 28 January 1648, seven of them, Lowin, Benfield, Bird, Clark, Hammerton, Pollard, and Robinson, entered a bond to repay Bowyer's heirs for his share in the company, a remarkable sign of renewed confidence in its future. On 3 February the same men staged *Wit without Money* at the Red Bull. On 5 February a similar group, including Lowin, Taylor, Pollard and two others, Burt and Hart, played *Rollo* at the Cockpit, but were stopped by the army.[47] On 9 February a parliamentary ordinance reverted to Elizabethan thinking by stating that 'Players shall be taken as Rogues', and the Lord Mayor was authorized to pull all the playhouses down. Anyone caught seeing a play would forfeit five shillings to the poor of the parish.[48] These measures set down by Parliament have all the points that the city made as long ago as the 1560s. But now control was in other hands. The players had lost their playhouses, and now they lacked a patron with the capacity to protect them. The Globe had already been pulled down. Allen died in 1647, Robinson in 1648, Benfield in 1649,[49] Hart in 1650, and Swanston, who became a Presbyterian and a jeweller, and who supported Parliament in the war, died in 1651.[50] Taylor died in 1652. Lowin became an innkeeper at Brentford, and died in 1653, the same year as Clark. Hammerton and Pollard were dead before 1655. Only Bird seems to have lived into the Restoration.[51]

THE KING'S MEN, 1608–1642

Plays

Aglaura, Albertus Wallenstein, The Alchemist, Alphonsus Emperor of Germany, Anything for a Quiet Life, 1 and *2 Arviragus and Philicia, A Bad Beginning* (lost), *Sir John Van Olden Barnavelt, The Bashful Lover, Beauty in a Trance, The Beggar's Bush, Believe As You List, The Bloody Brother, Bonduca, Brennoralt, The Broken Heart, The Brothers, The Buck is a Thief, Bussy D'Ambois* (old), *The Captain, Cardenio* (lost), *The Cardinal, Catiline, A Challenge for Beauty, The Chances, The City Madam, The City Match, The Country Captain, The Coxcomb* (old), *The Cruel*

---

[46] Wallace Notestein (ed.), *The Journal of Sir Simonds D'Ewes* (New Haven, Conn., 1923), 412.
[47] As reported by James Wright, *Historia Histrionica* (1699), 6.
[48] Hotson, *The Commonwealth and Restoration Stage*, 32–5.
[49] His will is transcribed in *Playhouse Wills 1558–1642*, 195–7.
[50] Ibid. 205–6.   [51] Ibid. 211–12.

Brother, *The Custom of the Country*, *Cymbeline*, *The Deserving Favourite*, *The Devil is an Ass*, *The Distresses*, *The Double Marriage*, *The Duchess of Malfi*, *The Duke of Milan*, *The Dumb Bawd of Venice*, *The Elder Brother*, *The Emperor of the East*, *Epicene* (old), *The Fair Favourite*, *The Fair Maid of the Inn*, *The Fair One*, *The Faithful Shepherdess*, *The Fatal Dowry*, *A Game at Chess*, *The Goblins*, *The Governor*, *The Guardian*, *Hengist King of Kent*, *Henry VIII*, *The Humorous Lieutenant*, *The Imposture*, *The Inconstant Lady*, *The Island Princess*, *The Just Italian*, *A King and No King*, *The Knight of Malta*, *The Knot of Fools* (lost) *The Late Lancashire Witches*, *The Laws of Candy*, *The Little French Lawyer*, *The Lost Lady*, *Love and Honour*, *The Lover's Melancholy*, *The Lovers' Progress*, *Love's Pilgrimage*, *The Lovesick Maid*, *The Loyal Subject*, *The Mad Lover*, *The Magnetic Lady*, *The Maid in the Mill*, *The Maid's Tragedy*, *More Dissemblers besides Women*, *The New Inn*, *News from Plymouth*, *The Nobleman* (Tourneur: lost), *The Northern Lass*, *The Novella*, *1* and *2 The Passionate Lovers*, *Philaster*, *The Picture*, *The Pilgrim*, *The Platonic Lovers*, *The Prophetess*, *The Queen of Corinth*, *Rollo*, *The Roman Actor*, *Rule a Wife and Have a Wife*, *The Scornful Lady*, *The Sea Voyage*, *The Sisters*, *The Sophy*, *The Spanish Curate*, *The Spanish Maze* (lost), *The Staple of News*, *The Swisser*, *The Tempest*, *Thierry and Theodoret*, *The Twins' Tragedy* (Nicholls: lost), *The Two Noble Kinsmen*, *The Unfortunate Lovers*, *The Unnatural Combat*, *Valentinian*, *The Variety*, *The Widow*, *A Wife for a Month*, *The Wild Goose Chase*, *The Winter's Tale*, *The Witch*, *The Wits*, *The Woman is Too Hard for Him* (lost), *The Woman's Plot* (lost). [Lord Chamberlain's list of King's Men's plays not in print, 7 August 1641. The list is printed in the original sequence, but with standardized titles, and notes to say which texts are not extant.]

The Wild Goose Chase, *Love's Cure*, *The Little French Lawyer*, *Beauty in a Trance* (lost), *The Loyal Subject*, *The Forc'd Lady* (lost), *The Spanish Curate*, *Alexius* (lost), *The Custom of the Country*, *The Unfortunate Lovers*, *The Double Marriage*, *The Fair Favourite*, *A Wife for a Month*, *Valentinian*, *The Island Princess*, *The Goblins*, *The Mad Lover*, *The Spanish Lovers*, *The Pilgrim*, *The Doubtful Heir*, *Hengist*, *The Imposture*, *The Woman's Plot* (lost), *The Country Captain*, *The Woman's Prize*, *Brennoralt*, *The Swisser*, *The Brothers*, *More Dissemblers Besides Women*, *Minerva's Sacrifice* (lost), *The Widow*, *The Judge* (lost), *The Knight of Malta*, *The City Madam*, *The Novella*, *The Corporal* (part ms), *The Lovesick Maid* (lost), *Alphonsus Emperor of Germany*, *The Captain*, *The Nobleman* (lost), *The Humorous Lieutenant*, *The Bashful Lover*, *Bonduca*, *Love and Honour*, *The Inconstant Lady*, *1* and *2 The Passionate Lovers*, *The Chances*, *The Maid in the Mill*, *The Guardian*, *The Bridegroom* (lost), *The Spanish Duke of Lerma* (lost), *The Queen of Corinth*, *The Coxcomb*, *The Prophetess*, *The Noble Gentleman*, *Love's Pilgrimage*, *The Beggars' Bush*, *The Lover's Progress*, *The Honest Man's Fortune*, *News from Plymouth*.

Playing Sharers and Part-Sharers
In 1610: Robert Armin,[52] Richard Burbage, Henry Condell, Alexander Cook, Richard Cowley, John Duke, Lawrence Fletcher, John Heminges, John Lowin,

---

[52] Armin's will is transcribed in *Playhouse Wills 1558–1642*, 96.

William Ostler, William Shakespeare, Nicholas Tooley, John Underwood. In 1619: Robert Benfield, Henry Condell, William Ecclestone, Nathan Field, Robert Gough, Charles Hart, John Heminges, John Honyman, John Lowin, Thomas Pollard, John Rice, Richard Robinson, William Rowley, John Shank, Nicholas Tooley, John Underwood. In 1624: Richard Baxter, George Birch, Henry Condell, William Ecclestone, Alexander Gough, William Hart, Richard Hawley, John Heminges, Thomas Hobbes, John Lowin, William Patrick, William Penn, Richard Perkins, John Rice, William Rowley, John Shank, Eyllaerdt Swanston, Joseph Taylor, Nicholas Tooley, John Underwood. In 1630: Robert Benfield, Curtis Greville, John Honyman,[53] John Lowin, Richard Robinson, John Shank, Richard Sharpe, Antony Smith, Eyllaerdt Swanston, Joseph Taylor.

Hired Men and Assistants
Richard Sharpe, Thomas Holcomb, William Trigg, Nicholas Underhill, Thomas Vincent 'that was a Book-keeper or prompter at the Globe playhouse'.[54] William Tawyer [Folio *Midsummer Night's Dream* names him heading the mechanicals' entry at V. i. 125: '*Tawyer with a Trumpet before them*'. He died in 1625, as a servant to John Heminges.] December 1624: 'Musitions and other necessary attendantes: Edward Knight, William Pattrick, William Chambers, Ambrose Byland, Henry Wilson, Jeffery Collins, William Sanders, Nicholas Underhill, Henry Clay, George Vernon, Roberte Pallant, Thomas Tuckfeild, Roberte Clarke, John Rhodes, William Mago'. George Rickner's and Anthony Knight's names are deleted. A marginal note adds 'Edward Ashborne, Will: Carver, Alexander Bullard, William Toyer, William Gascoyne'. Knight was the book-keeper [he paid Herbert a £2 fee, *Dramatic Records*, 34]. Richard Errington.[55]

Apprentices
[Augustine Phillips's will names 'my late apprentice' Samuel Gilborne, and as current apprentice James Sands] John Rice, Richard Robinson, Stephen Hammerton, Thompson.

London Playhouses
First Globe (to 1613), Blackfriars (from 1609), second Globe (from 1614).

At Court
13 unnamed plays Christmas 1609–10; 15 unnamed plays Christmas 1610 up to 12 Feb. 1611; 31 Oct. (unnamed), 1 Nov. (*Tempest*), 5 Nov. (*Winter's Tale*), 9, 19 Nov., 16 Dec. before prince and York, 26 Dec. (*A King and No King*) before king, 31 Dec. before prince and York, 1 Jan. 1612 (*The Twins' Tragedy*) before king, 12 Jan. with Queen's Men (*The Silver Age*), 13 Jan. with Queen's Men (*The Rape of Lucrece*) before queen and prince, 9 Feb. before royal children, 19, 20 Feb. before prince and

[53] Honyman's will is transcribed in *Playhouse Wills 1558–1642*, 190–1.
[54] John Taylor, *Taylor's Feast* (1638); BL Add. MS 19256, 44, quoted in *JCS* i. 15–16.
[55] A Ludlow note, dated 22 Nov. 1627, quotes a letter from Richard Errington, a player and 'pewterer' of London aged 50. He said he was working as a gatherer for the King's Men on their visit to Ludlow, and that at about 10 p.m., while the play was being performed, he and a local sergeant-at-arms were assaulted by five or six noisily drunken intruders. See *REED, Shropshire*, 111–12.

York, 23 Feb. (*The Nobleman*) before king, 28 Feb., 28 Mar. before royal children, 3 and 16 Apr. before prince and York, 26 Apr. before royal children; 20 plays Christmas 1612–13 up to 20 May (*Maid's Tragedy, A King and No King, Philaster, The Knot of Fools, The Merry Devil of Edmonton, Much Ado, Winter's Tale, Othello, Julius Caesar, Tempest, 'Sir John Falstaff'*,[56] *The Twins' Tragedy, The Nobleman* before prince, Lady Elizabeth and Elector Palatine, *The Alchemist, Cardenio, A Bad Beginning, Much Ado, 1 Henry IV, The Captain* before king); 8 June *Cardenio* before Savoyan ambassador; 1 Nov. 1613 before king, 4 Nov. before prince, 5, 15 Nov. before king, 16 Nov. before prince, 27 Dec., 1, 4 Jan. 1614 before king, 10 Jan. before prince, 2 Feb. before king, 4, 8, 10, 18 Feb. before prince, 6, 8 Mar. before king (all unnamed); eight unnamed plays Christmas 1614–15 up to 19 May 1615; fourteen unnamed plays 1 Nov. 1615–1 Apr. 1616, before king and queen; 12 unnamed plays 1 Nov. 1616–2 Feb. 1617 before king, queen, and prince, 5 Jan. 1617 (*The Mad Lover*); [no records 1617–21]; 5 Nov. 1621 (*The Woman's Plot*), 26 Nov. (*The Woman is Too Hard for Him*), 26 Dec. (*The Island Princess*), 1 Jan. 1622 (*The Pilgrim*), 24 Jan. (*The Wild Goose Chase*), 5 Mar. (*The Coxcomb*), before the king; 9 plays Christmas 1622–3 up to 26 Feb. (four unnamed), 26 Dec. (*The Spanish Curate*), 27 Dec. (*The Beggar's Bush*), 29 Dec. (*The Pilgrim*), 1 Jan. 1623 (*The Alchemist*), 2 Feb. (*Twelfth Night*) before the king; 29 Sept. 1623 (*The Maid in the Mill*) before the king and 1 Nov. before prince, 26 Dec. before king and prince, 28 Dec. (*The Buck is a Thief*) before king and prince, 1 Jan. 1624 (*The Lovers' Progress*) before the prince, 6 Jan. (*More Dissemblers besides Women*) before prince, 18 Jan. (*The Winter's Tale*), before Duchess of Richmond, and three or eight[57] other unnamed plays; 2 Nov. (*Rule a Wife and Have a Wife*) before the 'ladies', 26 Dec. before the prince, 27 Dec. (*Volpone*), 1 Jan. 1625 (*1 Henry IV*) before the prince, 12 Jan. (unnamed) before the king, and possibly 22 Mar.; ten unnamed plays up to 30 May 1626; twelve unnamed plays up to 26 Feb. 1627; ten unnamed plays between 29 Sept. and 31 Jan. 1628, 15 Apr. (*The Dumb Bawd of Venice*), before the king; sixteen unnamed plays between 29 Sept. and 10 Jan. 1629, 6 Apr. (*The Lovesick Maid*) before the king and queen; twelve unnamed plays between Oct. and Feb. 1630; 30 Sept. (*The Inconstant Lady*), 3 Oct. (*Alphonsus, Emperor of Germany*), 17 Oct. (*A Midsummer Night's Dream*), 24 Oct. (*The Custom of the Country*), 5 Nov. (*The Mad Lover*), 7 Nov. and 21 Feb. 1631 (*Rollo*), 19 Nov. (*Volpone*), 28 Nov. (*Beauty in a Trance*), 30 Nov. (*The Beggar's Bush*), 9 Dec. (*The Maid's Tragedy*), 14 Dec. (*Philaster*), 26 Dec. 1632 (*Duchess of Malfi*), 27 Dec. (*The Scornful Lady*), 30 Dec. (*The Chances*), 6 Jan. 1633 (*1 Sir John Oldcastle/1 Henry IV*?), 3 Feb. (*The Fatal Dowry*), 10 Feb. (*A King and No King*), 15 Feb. (*The Merry Devil of Edmonton*), 17 Feb. (*Every Man in his Humour*); eleven plays unnamed 1631–2; twenty-three unnamed plays 3 May 1632–3 Mar. 1633 before king; twenty-two plays 27 Apr. 1633–27 Apr. 1634, 11 unnamed, 16 or 17 Nov. (*Richard III*), 26 Nov. (*Taming of the Shrew*), 28 Nov. (*The Tamer Tamed*), 10 Dec. (*The Loyal Subject*), 1

[56] See Orrell, 'The London Stage in the Florentine Correspondence', *TRI* n.s. 3 (1978), 157–76.
[57] *MSC* vi. 78–80.

Jan. 1634 (*Cymbeline*), 6 Jan. (*The Faithful Shepherdess*), 12 Jan. (*The Guardian*), 16 Jan. (*The Winter's Tale*), 28 Jan. (*The Wits*), 7 Apr. (*Bussy D'Ambois*), 8 Apr. ('The Pastoral'); twenty unnamed plays 13 May 1634–30 Mar. 1635 [9 Nov. (*Catiline*)]; fourteen unnamed plays up to 25 Mar. 1636 [16 Feb. (*2 Arviragus and Philicia*), 18 Feb. (*Epicene*)]; 18 Apr. (*1 Arviragus and Philicia*), 19 Apr. (*2 Arviragus and Philicia*), 21 Apr. (*Epicene*); 17 Nov. (*The Coxcomb*), 19 Nov. (*The Beggar's Bush*), 29 Nov. (*The Maid's Tragedy*), 6 Dec. (*The Loyal Subject*), 8 Dec. (*Othello*), 16 Dec. (*Love's Pilgrimage*), 26 Dec. (*1 Arviragus and Philicia*), 27 Dec. (*2 Arviragus and Philicia*), 1 Jan. 1637 (*Love and Honour*), 5 Jan. (*The Elder Brother*), 10 Jan. (*A King and No King*), 12 Jan. (*The Royal Slave*), 17 Jan. (*Rollo*) 24 Jan. (*Hamlet*), 31 Jan. (*Julius Caesar*), 9 Feb. (*A Wife for a Month*), 16 Feb. (*The Governor*), 21 Feb. (*Philaster*); fourteen plays (12 unnamed) 30 Sept. 1637–3 Feb. 1638 (*Aglaura* and *The Lost Lady*), 2 Mar. 1638 (*The Lost Lady*), 27 Mar. (*Bussy D'Ambois*), 3 Apr. (*Aglaura*), 31 May (*The Unfortunate Lovers*), 29 May (*Oldcastle*), 10 or 26 July (*1 The Passionate Lovers*); 30 Sept. (*The Unfortunate Lovers*), 6 Nov. (*The Merry Devil of Edmonton*), 8 Nov. (*Volpone*), 13 Nov. (*Julius Caesar*), 15 Nov. (*The Merry Wives of Windsor*), 20 Nov. (*The Fair Favourite*), 22 Nov. (*The Chances*), 27 Nov. (*The Northern Lass*), 29 Nov. (*The Custom of the Country*), 6 Dec. (*The Spanish Curate*), 11 Dec. (*The Fair Favourite*), 18 Dec. (*1 The Passionate Lovers*), 20 Dec. (*2 The Passionate Lovers*), 27 Dec. (*2 The Passionate Lovers*), 28 Dec. (*The Northern Lass*), 1 Jan. 1639 (*The Beggar's Bush*), 7 Jan. (*The Spanish Curate*); twenty-one unnamed plays 6 Aug. 1639–11 Feb. 1640; sixteen unnamed plays Nov. 1640–Jan. 1641; 6 Jan. 1642 (*The Scornful Lady*).

Travelling Records

Dunwich, Suffolk 10 Oct. 1608, 5s. / Ipswich 9 May 1609, 26s. 8d. / Hythe, Kent 16 May 1609, 20s. / New Romney, Kent 17 May 1609, 20s. / Dover 6 July 1610, 10s. / Oxford town 1609–10, 20s.[58] / Dunwich, Suffolk Oct. 1610, 10s. / Winchester 1611–12, 20s. / Folkestone 1612–13, 2s. / New Romney, Kent 21 Apr. 1612, 20s. / Oxford town 1612–13, 10s. / Coventry Nov. acct. 1614, 40s. / Nottingham 1614–15, 13s. 4d. / Dunwich, Suffolk 1614–15, 4s. / Norwich Apr. 1615, 13s. 4d. / New Romney, Kent 1615–16, 2s. 8d. / Oxford town 1616–17, 10s. / Marlborough 4 June 1617, 30s. / Marlborough 14 Nov. 1617, 20s. / New Romney, Kent 1617–18, 20s. / Hythe, Kent 21 Aug. 1618, 10s. / Winchester 1617–18, 20s. / Ipswich 1617–18, £1. 6s. 8d. / Exeter May 1618 'paid martyn Slader on his majesties players to forbaer to playe',[59] £2. 4s. / Reading 1618–19, 11s. / Carlisle 1618–19, 30s. / Kendal 21 Oct. 1619, 10s. / Ludlow 1619–20, 2s. 5d. / Leicester 1619–20, £1. / Reading 1619–20, 22s. / Coventry 10 Jan. 1620, 33s. / Reading 3 June 1620, 'paid more', 6s. / Reading Sept. 1620, 22s. / Faversham, Kent 1620–1,

---

[58] Presumably this was the occasion which prompted the don's famous account of the performance of *Othello*. See above, p. 164.

[59] Evidently Slater, after being caught at Norwich in 1616 with a false licence for Queen Anne's, decided to take the king's name in vain for his visit to Devon. He used it again at Leicester in 1625. Later still he used an old Queen Elizabeth's company licence, at Ludlow and Coventry.

£1. / Coventry 9 Aug. 1621 'for Bristow youthes', 15s. / Leicester 1620 'who playd not in the Towne', 20s. / Dunkenhalgh, Lancs. (Household accounts of Thomas Walmesley) 18 Dec. 1620, 20s. / Carlisle 1620–1, 23s., 22s. / Norwich Apr. 1621, 10s. / Nottingham Apr. 1621 'to the Kinges & princesse playeres', 10s. / Kendal 1621–2, 10s. / Fordwich, Kent 2 Aug. 1621, 5s. / Lydd, Kent 30 Oct. 1621, 10s. / Dover 20 Apr. 1622, 11s. / Canterbury 1621–2 'To William Daniell the cheife of the Kinges Players to ridd them out of the Cittie without acting', 20s. / Wallingford, Berkshire 1621–2 'the Kinge and Queenes and princes players', 23s. 4d. / Lydd, Kent 19 Apr. 1622, 10s. / Hythe, Kent 1622–3, 10s. / New Romney, Kent 30 Apr. 1622, 6s. / Leicester 8 June 1622, 10s. / Norwich 15 June 1622 'Forty Shillinges to the kinges players because they should at this tyme forbeare playinge in this Citty' / Coventry 9 Aug. 1622 'to the Kings players for Bristow youths', 15s. / Leicester 26 Aug. 1622, 20s. / Carlisle 13 Sept. 1622, 20s. / Norwich 1622–3 'to Mr Irington & other of his Majestes Company of Players for a gratuitie', 40s. / Nottingham 1623–4 'the Kinges playeres of the Chamber of Bristowe', 10s. / Kendal 22 Feb. 1623, 10s. / Canterbury 24 Apr. 1623 'in regard they should depart the Cittie and not playe', 22s. / Hythe, Kent 7 July 1623, 5s. / Lydd, Kent 9 July 1623, 5s. / New Romney, Kent 9 July, 1623, 5s. / Bridport, Dorset 1623 'to thend they should not playe', 10s. / Leicester 22 Sept. 1623 'who playde not', 22s. / Coventry 26 Sept. 1623 'to the kinges players for bringing xx Bristow youthes in Musick', 15s. / Worcester 1623–4, 20s., 'at another time' 10s. / Ludlow 1623–4, 5s. / Hythe, Kent 1624–5, 2s. / Leicester 1624 'to John Daniell who had a Patent for the Children of Bristoll', 5s. 8d. / Dunkenhalgh, Lancs. (Household accounts of Thomas Walmsley) 16 Dec. 1624, 20s. / Craven, Yorkshire 1624 'to a set of players, going by the name of ye Kings Players, who played 3 times', £3. / Reading 1624–5, 20s. / Carlisle 5 July 1625, £1. / Leicester 15 Oct. 1625 'to one Slator and his Companie being the Kings Playors', £1. / Bridport, Dorset 14 Dec. 1625, 5s. / Kendal 1625–6, 10s. / Gravesend 1625–6, 6s. 8d. / Lydd, Kent 1625–6, 10s. / Hythe, Kent 1626–7, 5s. / Sandwich, Kent 1626–7, £1. / Coventry 16 Nov. 1626, 2s. 6d. / Kendal 23 Nov. 1626, 10s. / Nottingham 1626–7 'of the Chamber of Bristowe', 7s. / Leicester 1626–7, £1. / Reading Apr. 1627 'to forbeare their playeinge', 20s. / Kendal 4 Aug. 1627, 10s. / Carlisle Aug. 1627, £1. 10s. / Ludlow Nov. 1627[60] / Nottingham 1627–8, 10s. / Coventry 9 Jan. 1628, 5s. / Coventry 1 Sept. 1628, 10s. / Dunkenhalgh, Lancs. (Household accounts of Thomas Walmesley) Dec. 1628, 20s. / Canterbury 9 Mar. 1629 'for there forbearing to play in the Citty', 10s. / Nottingham 1629–30, 10s., 'to the kinges players of the Chamber of Bristowe' 10s. / Bristol Mar.–June 1630, £2. / Bristol June–Sept. 1631 'to send them out of this Citty', £2. / Doncaster May 1631, 20s. / Ludlow 1630–1, 2s. 6d. / Worcester 1630–1 'to prevente theire playenge in this Citie for feare of infeccion', 13s. 4d. / Reading 1631–2, £1. / Coventry Dec. acct. 1632 'to Mr. Perry

---

[60] Richard Errington, as the company gatherer, told the parish magistrates of a fracas at the door of their playing-place in Ludlow, a 'howse' in the ward of Oldstreet and Galdford. See *REED*, *Shropshire*, 110–12.

one of the kinges players that came with a Comission', 10s.[61] / Worcester 1632 'to the king's majesty's players, beinge two companies, to prevent their playenge in this city', 20s. / York 1632 / Nottingham 1632–3 'the kings plaiers of the Chamber of yorke Perries Company', 13s. 4d. / York 1633 'To Mr William Perry & others of his Majesties players', 20s. / Fordwich, Kent 1632–3, 5s. / Dover 8 Apr. 1633, 10s. / Norwich 6 July 1633 'that he did forbeare', £3. / Ludlow 1633–4, 5s. / Southampton 27 Mar. 1634 'to begonne out of toune and not to playe',[62] 5s. / Dartmouth 21 Oct. 1633, £1. / Dunwich, Suffolk 1633–4, 5s. / Nottingham 1633–4 'Perries company', 10s. / Norwich 1 Mar. 1634 'This day william Perry brought into this Court his Majesties warrant under his hand & privy signett whereby the said william Perry & his Company are licenced to play &c Dated the last of Aprill Anno Domini 1633' / Norwich 15 Mar. 1634 'william Perry one of the kinges players beinge this day in Court was demanded why hee & his Company did Contynue to play in this City beyond the tyme agreed ypon They sayd they have liberty by their patent to Contynue their playes forty dayes And being desired to forbeare to play any more for the reasons Intimated unto them they haveinge nowe stayd fiften dayes to the great hurt of the poore they would give no answer thereunto but desired eight dayes longer' / King's Lynn March 1634 'To send awaie his majesties Plaiors of his private chamber in Yorke without Actinge heere',[63] 40s. / Dartmouth 5 June 1634, £1. / Norwich 13 Sept. 1634 [Elias Guest], 40s. / Southampton 1634–5 'dismissed without playeng', £1. / Coventry 13 Apr. 1634 'Paid to the kinges players who brought a Commission from Sir Henry Harbert', £2. 0s. 10d. / Newcastle Jan. 1635, 20s. / Oxford 13 July 1635[64] / Nottingham 1635–6 'the Kinges Plaieres of Yorke', 10s.; 'the Kinges playeres of the Court', 10s.; 'the Kinges playeres of London', 10s. / Lydd, Kent 1635–6, 10s., Nov. 1635, 10s. / Windsor 1635–7, 10s. / Gravesend 8 Apr. 1636, 10s. / King's Lynn May 1636 'not to plaie here', 40s. / Norwich 11 May 1636 'This day Richard Wicks & other servantes to his Majestie beinge his Majesties players granted to william Perry & others did bringe in a warrant dated the last of Aprill in the nynth yeare of the kinges Reigne that nowe is [30 April 1633] authorisinge them to play Interludes &c.', 40s. / Bristol June–Sept. 1635 'to one Perry a plaier . . . for yat he should not use his skill heere

---

[61] Not the London company, but one ostensibly based in York: see n. 63.

[62] Southampton banned plays from the town hall on 6 Feb. 1623. The order was strictly obeyed in subsequent years.

[63] The York company of King's players was a distinct group set up by William Perry in 1629. He had earlier appeared with a Revels' Children licence at Leicester on 8 July 1627. He visited Reading with the Red Bull (Revels) company in 1629. He was named in the royal livery list of May 1629, though, and on 18 Sept. was granted a licence 'for making up and keeping a company of players, to present all usual stage plays, by the name of His Majesty's servants for the city of York'. This licence was renewed in Feb. 1633. (JCS i. 24). Perry's was certainly a touring group, most likely the one which appears in the subsequent records for visits to Coventry, Norwich, Leicester, and York. Their existence and their visits to Coventry presumably called out the distinction Coventry made in 1636 between them and 'the kinges players of Blackfriers'. What relation it had to the London company, who besides Perry played in it, and what 'usual stage plays' they performed we cannot tell.

[64] Thomas Crosfield's diary reports The Late Lancashire Witches as on show at an Oxford inn on this date.

in this Citty', £2. / Canterbury Mar. 1636[65] /Coventry Aug. 1636 'to the kinges players of Blackfriers', 20s. / Coventry Nov. acct. 1636, 5s. / Coventry Nov. acct. 1636 'to the kinges players of Blackfriers given at the Councel house in August last', 20s. / Windsor 1636, 10s. / Kendal 1636–7, £1. / Coventry Nov. acct. 1638 'to the Kinges players, and hocus pocus', 20s. / Doncaster 26 June 1641, 10s.

[65] *REED, Kent,* James M. Gibson, ed. The mayor of Canterbury wrote to the Archbishop on 25 Mar. 1636 to complain that he had recently stopped a company from playing after 8 days, for all that it was Lent, and had prompted late nights ('till neere midnight'), proving 'a Nursery for drunkennes' and the seduction of two 'honest mens daughters'. The players had said they would lay a complaint against the mayor for prohibiting them, so he was writing to state the case. The Privy Council replied on 29 Mar. asking for names, and were given those of Weekes and Perry. That a company claiming to be the King's Men should flaunt the Lenten prohibition is perhaps less striking than the evidence that they were prepared to use the king's name against the mayor. It also shows how routine it now was for playing to go on without the local authorities taking any official note of it.

22   The Jacobean royal children's companies:
The Duke of York's/Prince Charles's (I) Company,
and the Lady Elizabeth's Men

The story of the companies that the royal children patronized is one of the less well-documented corners of this large play-room. James, having taken one company for himself and then allocated two more to his son and his wife, may have taken a personal hand in giving his two younger children companies when they were thought to be old enough, but how active the young patrons were in providing for their companies it is impossible to say. At the outset they were too young to have taken any direct part in their companies' activities. Certainly at first the companies were assumed to owe some allegiance to their specific patrons when they performed at court. The two younger royal children, for instance, had special performances laid on for their personal pleasure. For the first years most plays were performed to the king and Prince of Wales. In 1605–6 Paul's Boys provided two plays for the Prince of Wales, just turning 12, along with his young brother, the newly made Duke of York, already the Scottish Duke of Albany, then aged 5. Lady Elizabeth entered the playing scene later. She was aged 11 when she went with her older brother on 22 February 1608 to see lions baited at the Tower. Two years later, on 9 February 1610, she joined her two brothers for the first time to see a play by her younger brother's servants, the Duke of York's Men. The same company performed again for the three royal children on 12 and 20 December 1610 and 15 January 1611. By that time all three of the royal children had their own companies.

The Duke of York's company was set up during the long closure of 1608, when he was seven. It received a patent in 1610. When Prince Henry, the heir apparent, died in November 1612, and the company's patron, the Duke of York and Albany, became heir to the throne in his place, it gradually became known as Prince Charles's company. It is called here Prince Charles's (I) company, following G. E. Bentley's nomenclature, to distinguish it from the company of his son, the later Prince Charles, which was set up when he was newly born in 1631. When Prince Henry died his company, which originated as Worcester's Men and is called here the Prince's, passed under the patronage of the Lady Elizabeth's husband, the Elector Palatine. With a much longer prehistory, and a lengthy tenure at the Fortune, it always remained distinct from the other companies of the royal children.

The companies of the younger two worked closely together for a while between 1614 and 1616, even merging into one group, though they did so for reasons that more probably relate to commercial competition than to any policy choices made on high. An isolated reference by the Master of the Revels to 'the four companys of players' in January 1618[1] suggests that he was maintaining an undeclared policy that restricted the number of companies in London. That policy he was able to maintain, at least in part, by restricting the number of playhouses that he licensed for performance. The consequent lack of any fixed and licensed playing-place for a fifth company must be what forced a merger on the most junior two of the companies in 1614 or 1615. It is an equal chance whether official policy or commercial pressures confined the number of companies to four. Either way, the two that were squeezed most by the limitation were those under the patronage of the younger two royal children. In this chapter it will not be possible to trace their paths wholly independently.

A note in the city of Leicester's records for October 1609 provides confirmation that the Duke of York and Albany's players had been formed. It says that they are 'the right honorable the Lorde Albunye his Playors'. A note at Ipswich of the year before calls them 'the younger Princes players'. Their membership was a useful mix of experience and promise; their chief player, according to the provincial records, was Gilbert Reason, and others included John Garland, William Rowley, and Thomas Hobbes. Garland had been a founder member of the old Queen's Servants twenty-five years before in 1583.[2] Henslowe notes him as being in a travelling company belonging to James's cousin, the Duke of Lennox, in 1605. The name of Will Rowley, who was to stay with the York's / Prince Charles's company till 1623 as player and writer, appears for the first time in this note. Hobbes was also to serve with the company for at least fifteen years. Gilbert Reason, the main payee in the towns the company visited and who led the company for all of its seventeen years, also first appears in the records with this company. The recurrence of his name in the provinces may indicate that his speciality was travelling rather than performing in London. A Norwich record suggests that he separated from the rest of the company in 1617 and was then travelling with a duplicate patent. He was certainly the player who kept the company active and on tour under its original name after the merger of 1615, when the number of London companies was being restricted.[3]

The patent that York's were given after two years of travelling and just after their first appearance at court, under the date 30 March 1610, names seven players: 'John Garland Willyam Rowley Thomas hobbes Robert Dawes Joseph Taylor John Newton and Gilbert Reason alreadye sworne servauntes to our deere sonne the Duke of york and Rothesay'.[4] Taylor left to be a starter member of the Lady Elizabeth's a year later. The experienced Garland may have been the leader at the outset, because a lawsuit of 1612 states that in March 1610 Dawes, Hobbes, Rowley, and Taylor each gave Garland a bond of £200 to secure the company's resources for three years. The five then bought costumes from John Heminges of the King's Men. At Easter 1611, according to a testimony in the lawsuit, Taylor left the company 'by the licence and leave of his said Master the Duke upon some speciall reason'. That reason was presumably to help form the Lady Elizabeth's

---

[1] See Ch. 7.   [2] He died in Sept. 1624. His will is in *Playhouse Wills 1558–1642*, 141–2.
[3] See *JCS* ii. 542.   [4] *MSC* i. 3. 272–4.

Men, who came into existence with a patent just after Easter 1611. Heminges brought the suit for non-payment against Taylor, who alleged that the other four had contrived to lay the blame on him.[5]

The evidence for whatever resources in plays the Duke of York's company may have started with is almost a complete blank. Will Rowley wrote the lost *Hymen's Holiday* for them, and they staged it at court in February 1612. After 7 November of that year, when Prince Henry died, they took on a new name as Prince Charles's Men, and seem to have gained a little in status, at least outside London, as a result. They performed at court in 1612–13 but were not called on in the next season, 1613–14; then in 1614–15 after the merger they gave six plays. By this time Will Rowley seems in many ways to have been more the leader than Gilbert Reason, at least in London. He was payee at court from 1610 to 1614, was called with John Newton as the company's representative to meet the Privy Council in March 1615 over playing in Lent, and was the company's resident playwright. They did a lot of travelling, though apart from Reason it is not certain how many of the players named in the 1610 patent joined the travelling group. There is nothing to say quite when the split happened which kept some in London and turned others into a travelling company, but a split there was.

Nor has the playhouse they used when they played in London ever been clearly identified. Neither the York's nor the Lady Elizabeth's patents allocate them to any specific playhouse in London. There were, though, in reality no halls and only two suburban amphitheatres available for them to use. It is known that the Curtain was in regular use through these years, and in fact it was the only amphitheatre apart from the Swan not already allocated to another company. Since there is positive evidence that the Lady Elizabeth's played at the Swan, I think the Prince's players must have used the Curtain through to 1614. It must therefore be Rowley and the Prince Charles's Curtain playhouse to which Antimo Galli's derisive account of the standing of the theatre and the new Venetian ambassador's antics at it in 1613 relates.

In August of that year Galli, a Florentine, reported to his Italian masters that their favourite enemy, the Venetian ambassador Foscarini, had been walking around London incognito and going to playhouses. Once, Galli wrote gleefully, he had been to the Curtain, which was not far from the ambassadorial house. According to Galli the thirty-six-year-old amphitheatre was 'an infamous place in which no good citizen or gentleman would show his face. And what was worse, in order not to pay a royal or a scudo, to go in one of the little rooms, nor even to sit in the galleries that are there, he insisted on standing in the middle down below among the gang of porters and carters, giving as his excuse that he was hard of hearing— as if he could have understood the language anyway!'[6] This dismissal of the Curtain and its clientele is echoed in the Middlesex magistrates' concern about its cutpurses that dates from the same period. To be playing at the Curtain, with its deeply

---

[5] *ES* ii. 243–4.   [6] Orrell, 'The London Stage in the Florentine Correspondence', 171.

working-class-amphitheatre reputation, was not a good start to a London career for a newish company, however royal its patron.

The company could not under any circumstances have regarded the ageing Curtain as a good theatre, either for social or monetary reasons. Neither the Curtain nor the Swan ever secured official recognition as licensed playhouses, and neither was available for the company to take a housekeeping share in, so they could not even get security of tenure. It may have been their playing-places as much as anything that led the occupants of the Curtain and the Swan to attempt to join forces for London work in late 1614. The two groups continued to travel as separate companies, but from this time onwards their London operations seem to have been run jointly, as a single company. Philip Rosseter of the Lady Elizabeth's gave a hint of their ambition to move out of the suburban amphitheatres with his project to build a hall playhouse in the Blackfriars rivalling the King's Men's. Before that best laid plan went astray, Henslowe's new Hope near the Swan took them in for a while. It is at this point that the history of the second company of the younger royal children, the Lady Elizabeth's, converges on the Prince Charles's and in effect merges with it.

The Lady Elizabeth's company came formally into existence by a patent dated 27 April 1611.[7] Its patron, James's daughter, was then aged fourteen. Her new company gave two plays before her and her brother in the 1611–12 court season, on 10 January 1612. She married the Elector Palatine at the age of sixteen, in February 1613, two months after the older of her brothers died. The Prince Palatine took on the patronage of the former Prince's company, and his wife continued to patronize her own group.

The impetus for creating a company in her name in 1611 must have come from the court. With the younger son gaining his own company at the age of eight, the idea of extending the royal patronage of players to the third royal child was consistent, though it was belated and hardly a feminist decision. It also created a problem of numbers. The Duke of York's was formally patented on 30 March 1610. The Lady Elizabeth's patent a year later made it the sixth company to be officially tolerated in London, after the King's, Queen's, Prince Henry's, and York's, and the Children of the Queen's Revels. It was not a promising position for a new group which did not even have a designated playhouse of its own, at a time when the Revels Office was not licensing more than five playhouses and the King's Men occupied two of them. A merger, or at least some link with a more settled company or impresario, was an immediate priority if the Lady Elizabeth's new company was to build up resources in playbooks and properties quickly enough to hold a firm base in London.

The 1611 patent identified John Townsend and Joseph Moore 'with the rest of theire Companie', and authorized them to use 'such usuall howses as themselves shall provide'. Nothing is known of either man before this patent. They do not

---

[7] *MSC* i. 3. 274–5.

appear in the Henslowe papers before this time, though their names are included with others on a set of bonds for a sum of £500 in the Henslowe papers that date from 29 August 1611. The articles of agreement themselves have not survived, but the names on the bonds are Townsend and Moore, plus William Barksted, Thomas Basse, William Carpenter, Giles Carey, William Ecclestone, Alexander Foster, Robert Hamlen, Thomas Hunt, John Rice, Joseph Taylor, and Francis Wambus. There are enough names in these bonds to constitute a full company, probably in large part the group established for the Lady Elizabeth in 1611. Carey and Barksted had formerly been with the ex-Blackfriars Boys, Rice with the King's Men, and Taylor with the Duke of York's, so it looks as if the new company was not just an old group under a new name, but was collected by a trawl of several London companies in 1610 or 1611. Taylor's excuse for leaving York's, noted above, suggests that this trawl was prompted by an order from on high.

It was done during a precarious time financially for all the companies with the long closure of 1608–9 and the further interruptions in 1610. As usual with such times, they led into years of rapid change and growth. Besides the King's Men's occupancy of the Blackfriars, the Blackfriars Boys restarted at Whitefriars, and the Duke of York's was also working to gain a London foothold. These renewals shook out some players into the new group. It was an expansionist moment; so the Lady Elizabeth's had some reason to be hopeful too.

The first problem for the new company was to find a playhouse. The King's were fixed at the Globe and the Blackfriars. The Prince's Men had the Fortune, and the Queen's Men had the Red Bull. The Blackfriars Boys still occupied the Whitefriars. For the two companies of the younger royal children, that left only the two ageing amphitheatres that the Privy Council never approved for playing, the Curtain and the Swan. York's, I believe, occupied the Curtain. Henslowe at this time had no playhouse free, so the bonds the Lady Elizabeth's laid with him were most likely for loans to help the company purchase plays and other properties, not for a place to play. For a while the Swan played host to the company. Middleton's *A Chaste Maid in Cheapside* was published in 1630 with the claim on its title-page that 'it hath beene often acted at the Swan on the Banke-side by the Lady Elizabeth her Servants', which must date it to the company's early period, 1611–13.

There was something distinctly odd about the Swan, or its omens, because no company ever seems to have used it for long, and *A Chaste Maid* is in fact the only play definitely known to have been staged there. Pembroke's in 1597 had lasted less than six months at the Swan. The Lady Elizabeth's may have been there for longer than that, but by 1613 they too were looking to move elsewhere. In any case, for their first year or so they seem to have used their new patent chiefly for travelling. They played at court for their patron and her brother and then for the king in the winter season of 1611–12, and again in the following season, but are recorded across the country for much of their first two years.

Early in 1613 they underwent a major reorganization. If we can believe the company history that is recounted in the 'Articles of Grievance and Oppression against Philip Henslowe' which members of the company drew up in 1615, Henslowe took on board a merged group of the Lady Elizabeth's and Philip Rosseter's Blackfriars Boys in March 1613. According to the notorious 'Articles',[8] 'In March 1613 hee makes upp a Companie and buies apparrell of one Rosseter to the value of £63, and valued the ould stocke that remayned in his handes at £63' (which the company had more recently valued at only £40). Whether the merger really was Henslowe's own initiative, as the complainants claimed, or one broached by somebody in one of the two companies named is not specified.

It is likely that the merger of 1614 with the first Prince Charles's allowed the Lady Elizabeth's to leave the Swan, since it was empty in that year, on the evidence of a watermen's complaint in midsummer declaring that they were losing custom because the Bankside playhouses were all closed (the Globe was still rebuilding after the 1613 fire). It may be that the new joint company used the ex-Blackfriars Boys' Whitefriars hall for a short time until its lease expired. If so, that would make the Lady Elizabeth's notable as the first adult company to emulate the King's Men's run at the Blackfriars by using a hall playhouse, all of three years before Beeston moved the Red Bull company into his new Cockpit.[9]

The other resources Rosseter brought to the merger included the Queen's Revels Company's playbooks and some of its players, including Nathan Field, who now joined the new Lady Elizabeth's. Field, who had written one play, *A Woman is a Weathercock*, for his own Queen's Revels Boys, wrote another as a kind of apology for his first, and gave it to the Lady Elizabeth's. *Amends for Ladies* shows a degree of sensitivity to the female component in his audiences that might have belonged better in the costly Whitefriars hall than at the Swan. Unfortunately, that delicacy was belied by Henslowe's plan about where to house the company after the Whitefriars vanished. Henslowe replaced his old Bear Garden arena in 1614 with the Hope, a dual-purpose playhouse and bear-baiting arena, and gave it to the Lady Elizabeth's to play in. They did not like sharing it with the bears, and the troubles with Henslowe that followed must have been a factor behind their 'Articles of Grievance'. The grievances chiefly concern his financial mismanagement, and are designed to identify the size of the debt he owed them after they had parted company with him.

Lists of the players who performed two Beaumont and Fletcher plays, *The Coxcomb* and *The Honest Man's Fortune*, most likely date from this phase of the Lady Elizabeth's activities. The *Coxcomb* list is 'Nathan Field, Joseph Taylor, Giles Cary, Emanuel Reade, Richard Allen, Hugh Atawell, Robert Benfeild, and William Barcksted'. *The Honest Man's Fortune* lists 'Nathan Field Robert Benfield,

[8] W. W. Greg (ed.), *The Henslowe Papers* (London, 1907), 93, quoted in *ES* ii. 248–50. For a level-headed appraisal of the 'Articles', see Carson, *A Companion to Henslowe's Diary*, 31–2.

[9] R. A. Foakes, 'Playhouses and Players', in *The Cambridge Companion to English Renaissance Drama*, ed. A. R. Braunmuller and Michael Hattaway (Cambridge, 1990), 31, reckons that this company did more, trying to emulate the King's Men by playing at the Whitefriars indoor playhouse between Michaelmas and Easter, and at the Swan through the warmer months. If so, the expiry of the Whitefriars lease in 1614 made it a distinctly short-lived attempt.

Emanuel Read, Joseph Taylor, Will. Eglestone and Thomas Basse'. Field, who was named as a leading member, and has several warm letters to Henslowe preserved in the papers, is usually thought to have left the company before the 'Articles' were drawn up in 1615. Since he did not join the King's Men until 1616, though, I think that despite the absence of his name from the papers he may have still been with the company when the players drew up their 'Articles'. Field's version of events is several times referred to in the 'Articles'.

Besides Field, Robert Daborne was writing for the company. A series of letters between Daborne and Henslowe from 17 April 1613 to the end of July 1614[10] relate to the plays he was then writing either on his own or in collaboration with Field, Tourneur, and others. Jonson also came in, giving the company *Bartholomew Fair*, staged at the Hope in the autumn of 1614 and at court that Christmas. It may be that, because the Lady Elizabeth's included some former Blackfriars Boys, Jonson was renewing a link with Field and others that he had started back in 1600 when he wrote *Cynthia's Revels* and *Poetaster* for them, and continued with *Epicene* in 1609. His Induction to *Bartholomew Fair* made explicit his contempt for the company's new playhouse, and in that he may well have been deliberately voicing the company's opinion. It is also possible that the play's apparent demand for a larger-than-usual number of players marks its composition at the point of the merger between the Lady Elizabeth's and the remnant company of youths, when they had more players to call on than a travelling group would have.

The provincial records name a few of the other players with the company. One of the payees was Nicholas Long, who had been a boy player at Whitefriars in 1612. In 1614 he is named as the responsible player in the provincial records of the Prince Charles's company on its travels. Moore is also named in 1614 and 1615, and the original pair, Moore and Townsend, are named at Norwich and at Coventry in 1615, in a group identified as seven adults, seven boys, and five horses. It was to prove a durable company, at least for its travelling. Moore and Townsend, along with Alexander Foster and Francis Wambus, are all still named in the company at Norwich in 1621. Intriguingly, Field, although he seems to have led the company in London between 1613 and 1615, never appears in any of their travelling records. Conceivably the 'Articles' were drawn up by the company while they were outside London and Field was staying in the metropolis.

The Coventry document which names fourteen of the travellers is a record of an incident that was triggered by a letter of 28 March 1615 to the Coventry authorities from Lord Chief Justice Coke. Coke had been the city's recorder since 1613, and his letter was chiefly a reminder to the mayor of the ban on Sunday playing. It did in fact go further and order a general ban on playing. The argument was the standard one: 'Theis are to will and require you to suffer no Common players whatsoever to play within your Citie, for that it would lead to the hindrance of devotion, and drawing of the artificers and Common people from their labours'.[11]

---

[10] *Henslowe Papers*, 65, 125.   [11] *REED, Coventry*, 394.

The ban was, interestingly, specific to the Lady Elizabeth's, as if Coke knew they were heading that way. When they got there one of the players voiced his objections loudly. A clothworker, Thomas Barrows, reported that he had called the citizens peevish and deserving to have their throats cut. The Coventry authorities took the names of everyone in the company, and either in reprisal or to take advantage of Coke's letter sent them away without playing and without any fee.

By the time of the quarrel with Henslowe in 1615, and probably some months or even a year before, the company combined with Prince Charles's Men for its London operations. For travelling both companies still used their different patents and ran as separate companies. They probably thought of themselves as separate companies forced to work as one company in London because of the shortage of playhouses. London, of course, treated them as one company. William Rowley and John Newton of Prince Charles's Men are named in a Privy Council roll-call of the responsible players from each company dated 29 March 1615. The Council summoned nobody from the Lady Elizabeth's, which must mean, unless the absence of their travelling group in Coventry was known and was a sufficient reason, that Rowley and Newton were expected to speak for the other company too, and that in London the combined company was now thought of as a single group. Alexander Foster, a Lady Elizabeth's man, was later called 'one of the Princes highnes Players', meaning the Princess Elizabeth's, when he took payment for four Prince Charles's Men's plays at court in 1615–16.[12]

The companies were forced to work together in London chiefly for the lack of more than one playhouse to play in. Rosseter's attempt to build the Porter's Hall playhouse in Blackfriars in 1615 must originally have been designed to solve the playhouse problem as part of this new arrangement. The title-page of the 1611 *Amends for Ladies*, when published in 1616, claimed that both companies had acted it there. A title-page would hardly allow two companies to lay separate claims to it, so it must indicate either a joint performance or a series of performances that started under the Lady Elizabeth's name and then took the name of Prince Charles's after the merger. If, as seems likely, the merger happened late in 1614 before the Porter's Hall playhouse opened, the Hope must have been a necessary expedient for the interim, and Porter's Hall was a late and abortive replacement for the company's short-lived early tenure of the Whitefriars hall.

After the Porter's Hall débâcle, they had to revert to Henslowe's Hope. On 20 March 1616 Alleyn and Henslowe's old partner in the royal bear business, Jacob Meade, signed an agreement with a group of the leading Prince's and Lady Elizabeth's players, Will Rowley, Hugh Attwell, William Barksted, Robert Hamlen, Thomas Hobbes, John Newton, Robert Pallant, William Penn, Anthony Smith, and Joseph Taylor.[13] It was an adjustment of previous financial commitments, whereby the balance of a debt for £400-worth of Alleyn's stock of apparel

[12] *MSC* vi. 61.   [13] *Henslowe Papers*, 90–1.

given to the company would be assessed at £200, which would be recovered by taking one-fourth of the gallery takings at the Hope or any other house they might use. An undated letter from Pallant, Rowley, Attwell, Hamlen, Newton, Smith, and Taylor to Alleyn, which probably belongs to 1616, is an apology for leaving the Hope on Bankside, not because of the intemperate weather but because of the 'more intemperate Mr. Meade', Henslowe's former partner and controller of the bears, who were also players at the Hope.[14] The letter asks Alleyn to find them another playhouse, and to give them a loan to tide them over.

Lack of a playhouse was already a major difficulty in 1615. The Hope could not have pleased the players any more than it did Jonson, who in *Bartholomew Fair* sarcastically called it an apt place for a play about the fair because it was 'was durty as *Smithfield*, and as stinking every whit', thanks to the bears. The Privy Council was holding its line on the number of playhouses it would permit, and there were too many companies for the two-and-a-half amphitheatres (counting the Globe) and the one-and-a-half halls in use, one of which was soon to be banned. The four companies then permitted had too few playhouses open to them so long as the King's kept their two playhouses for their own exclusive use. Beeston's Cockpit, which opened at the beginning of 1617, was much needed. It did not, however, give any direct help to the Lady Elizabeth's and Prince Charles's.

When Henslowe died in January 1616 Alleyn reorganized his main company at the Fortune, and the changes affected the merged company drastically. Besides the Hope, Alleyn had taken a financial interest in the abortive Porter's Hall. Neither venture prospered. His Fortune was safe in the hands of the former Prince's, now the Palsgrave's Men. At Henslowe's death only the Fortune was still in regular use. The Cockpit in 1616 was the third attempt at establishing a new playhouse, and once it became fully useable it released a licensed amphitheatre for another company. So when Beeston was finally able to transfer his company's activities to his new Cockpit, Alleyn and Beeston between them put the reorganized Prince Charles's into the now-vacated Red Bull.

Economies in the number of companies working in London were still necessary, and it was the lesser partner in the merged companies, Lady Elizabeth's, that lost out. Four of its long-standing players, Barksted, Hamlen, Robert Pallant, and Taylor went to a new Prince Charles's at the Red Bull. Two more, Field and Benfield, left for the King's. Basse and Read went to Queen Anne's at the Cockpit. The remainder had to go on their travels. The Lady Elizabeth's company did not return to London until Henry Herbert reported them as playing at the Cockpit in 1622. Joseph Moore became the carrier of a letter of July 1616 from the Lord Chamberlain sent to all the towns which entertained players, complaining about travelling companies using forgeries or duplicates of the official patents.[15] The function of messenger may have been one of the compensations given the Lady Elizabeth's company in that year for its exile from London. Moore

---

[14] *Henslowe Papers*, 93.   [15] The full letter is transcribed in *REED, Norwich*, 151–2.

was the leader of the travelling Lady Elizabeth's when it visited Maldon in Essex in 1619.[16]

Some indications can be seen in the provincial records that additional companies, particularly of young players, were launched in the middle years of this decade. John Daniel led a company of youths called the Children of Bristol, on a licence originally obtained by his namesake, Samuel, as a result of the Queen's visit to Bristol in 1613. This is probably the company recorded at Nottingham in the 1615–16 fiscal year, and again in 1616–17 and 1618–19, when the clerk called it 'the Children of the Kinges Revelles'. Subsequent companies of 'youths' under that name recur in the records into the 1630s. Records at Southampton, Exeter, and Bristol in 1616–17 suggest that Daniel's group ran into trouble in the towns for its players being more than 'children'. This provoked in return a strong letter from Sir Thomas Lake in the king's name to all mayors and magistrates, ordering that his licence be respected. Exeter's mayor replied respectfully that he had turned the company away because, despite its name, it had barely five or six 'youths' in its number. This company seems to have had no direct link with Bristol, though Sir Thomas's steaming letter was duly transcribed into civic records. The company was set up as a travelling group, and got no closer to London than those run by Martin Slater with his various falsified papers.

Prince Charles's company retained a firm grip on London for the next few years. Its members included all of the seven players who wrote the undated letter to Alleyn about leaving the Hope and asking for another playhouse. Four of them, Rowley, Hobbes, Newton, and Taylor, had been in the Prince Charles's from its inception as York's. Taylor had left it for the Lady Elizabeth's, where Barksted and Hamlen had joined him. Pallant was in the Lady Elizabeth's in 1614, and Attwell and Penn joined the same group when it merged with the Queen's Revels in 1613. The basic company in 1616 was made up of the ten men who signed the 1616 agreement with Alleyn and Meade, and it remained a fairly steady grouping from then on. The 1619 text of an Inns-of-Court masque, *The Inner Temple Mask, or Mask of Heroes*, records five of the company taking the speaking parts: Taylor, Rowley, Newton, Attwell, and William Carpenter. Carpenter had been a Lady Elizabeth's man in 1611. After Burbage's death in 1619 Taylor joined the King's Men, and Pallant had become a Queen Anne's man by the time of her death at about the same time. Attwell died in 1621; the others were still Prince Charles's Men in 1625.

The playhouse the company somehow secured for itself in 1617 was the Red Bull. It was a sturdy place, although it had already gained a reputation for volume in speaking and less-than-elegant verse. Who owned and took the rents from the Red Bull has never been clearly identified. The site was originally leased by Aaron Holland from a widow, and it was he who built the playhouse in about 1604.[17] At

[16] Philip Edwards gives an entertaining account of the company's encounter at Maldon with a Dogberry-type in *The Revels History of Drama in English: vol. iv. 1613–1660*, 53.

[17] For a summary of the available evidence, see *JCS* vi. 215–22.

one time Thomas Swinnerton and Martin Slater, both Queen Anne's players, had a part-interest in it, and Christopher Beeston almost certainly had one too. The Prince Charles's Men secured it either through Alleyn or Beeston, who by 1617 was ready to take Queen Anne's company from the Red Bull to his new Cockpit, and must have had some say in who its lease could be reallocated to. Beeston opened his Cockpit in February 1617, but it was wrecked by apprentices on the Shrove-Tuesday holiday following, 4 March, and the company returned to the Red Bull for the three months it took to repair the new hall. So Prince Charles's may not have taken up regular use of the Red Bull until the summer of 1617, although the Public Record Office has a note from the Prince in April 1617 'to the Red Bull with a message to the players', which implies that they had already started playing there.[18] Whether they remained at the Hope until that time or reverted to using the Curtain we cannot be sure. Herbert's diary has two entries for later years that seem to re-locate them at the Curtain. He noted 'A new Play, called, *The Duche Painter and the French Branke*, was allowed to be acted by the Princes Servants at the Curtayne' on 10 June 1622, and in August 1623 he licensed a lost play to 'the Company at the Curtain'.[19] They may have used it occasionally as a fall-back location. Certainly they were at the Red Bull from 1617 until the next shake-up, in 1619. Alleyn's diary has a note about collecting some receipts from a lost play that he called 'ye younger brother' at the Red Bull on 1 October 1617.[20] This must have been part of the repayment for his furnishing the company with apparel in 1616.

The new tenants at the Red Bull came under Beeston's influence. His own company, Queen Anne's Men, had taken their Red-Bull repertory of plays with them to the Cockpit. There is not much evidence for what the Prince Charles's Men offered in its place, apart from the lost *Younger Brother*. The only other play in their repertory for this period known from its title is *The Peaceable King, or the Lord Mendall*, which Herbert licensed in August 1623 as an old play previously licensed by George Buc.[21] The company gave Rowley and Middleton's *A Fair Quarrel* at court in 1616 or early 1617, before they settled at the Bull. Rowley's *All's Lost by Lust* must also have come into their repertory in this period. Herbert names another eleven of their plays from the later period between 1621 and 1625, when they were either at the Cockpit or the Curtain, all of which are now lost. To that later period belongs Dekker's *Witch of Edmonton*, product of an even more frenetic writing stint than usual from that rapid producer. He was released from debtor's prison in 1620, and had a lot of ground and income to make up.

The death of Queen Anne early in 1619 led Beeston to reorganize his interests in companies and their playhouses. The players of the dead queen's company left the Cockpit for their former amphitheatre, and re-formed as the Red Bull or Revels company. Prince Charles's Men ceded them the Red Bull and took their place at the Cockpit with Beeston. Whether this change also brought them Beeston's re-sources of playbooks and costumes must be doubted. Perkins and his fellows in the

---

[18] *MSC* vi. 146–7.   [19] *Herbert Dramatic Records*, 18, 24.
[20] Young, *A History of Dulwich College*, ii. 51.   [21] *Herbert Dramatic Records*, 24–5.

lawsuit, a few years later, alleged that Beeston had taken the dispossessed Queen Anne's company's possessions for himself, but there is no sign that any of the Queen's plays came the way of the Prince Charles's Men. In any case, the Cockpit was a prosperous playhouse to work in, and the company acquired a lot of new plays in the next five years. Besides Rowley's two plays and Dekker's *The Witch of Edmonton* and *The World Tost at Tennis*, they introduced eleven plays now lost. They are William Sampson's *The Widow's Prize*, Brome and Jonson's *A Fault in Friendship*, Dekker and Day's *The Bellman of Paris*, Dekker and Ford's *The Fairy Knight*, Dekker, Ford, Rowley, and Webster's *The Late Murder in Whitechapel*, Barnes's *The Madcap*, plus the anonymous *The Dutch Painter and the French Brawl*, *The Man in the Moon Drinks Claret*, *The Parricide*, *The Peaceable Kingdom*, and *A Vow and a Good One*. All of these except *The World Tost at Tennis* and Rowley's two earlier plays were licensed between 1621 and 1624. Four of them were given at court, *A Fair Quarrel* some time up to 1617, *The Man in the Moon Drinks Claret* on 27 December 1621, *The Witch of Edmonton* two days later, and *A Vow and a Good One* on Twelfth Night 1623.

The infrequency of the Prince Charles's company's appearances at court through these last years, for all they were playing at the Cockpit, may be in part a consequence of a lost play they performed in the 1619–20 season which upset James. What the play was called is not known, since the Revels Office records for this year are missing. What is known comes from a letter by the Venetian ambassador, who was present and who wrote about it to the Doge on 10 January 1620. His letter says baldly that 'the comedians of the prince, in the presence of the king his father, played a drama the other day in which a king with his two sons has one of them put to death, simply upon suspicion that he wished to deprive him of his crown, and the other son actually did deprive him of it afterwards'. James notoriously paranoid about danger to his person, gave this an application that hurt. The ambassador reported, 'This moved the king in an extraordinary manner, both inwardly and outwardly'.[22] He did not go on to say what the outward movement was, but it cannot have been good for the players. The company did not appear at court at all in the following season.

The pattern where companies expected to run undisturbed for a period of no more than three years at one playhouse, a practice starting with Henslowe, according to the Lady Elizabeth's company's complaint, is certainly a feature of the history of this company. It was renewed by Beeston in the summer of 1622, three years after the reorganization that followed Queen Anne's death. He brought in a new company to his Cockpit, and the Prince's had to move back to their oldest amphitheatre, the forty-five-year-old Curtain, where Herbert reports them as playing in June. It was an odd shift in some ways, because the new company that Beeston now brought in to take their place at the Cockpit was called the Lady Elizabeth's Men. It had consistently been a travelling group since the earlier break-

---

[22] *CSP Venetian* 1619–21, 111.

up of 1616, and several names in this new Lady Elizabeth's membership are familiar. It certainly included its original leader, Joseph Moore, whose presence may have been part of a larger resurrection. The player Francis Wambus told the Norwich clerks, one of whom queried Moore's presence in the patent but his physical absence when they visited the town on 22 April 1620, that he had 'not played with them this last yeare, & that the said Moore nowe kepeth an Inn in Chichester'.[23] After that three-year interlude as an innkeeper he evidently returned to the company when it reopened in London in 1622. The new group also took Andrew Cane, who was to become the greatest clown of the last twenty years, from Palsgrave's. They were waiting at the time for the Fortune to be rebuilt after its fire.

There seems to have been some rapid switching of playhouses between the groups in 1622, especially between the Curtain and the Red Bull. These changes were obviously prompted by the fire that destroyed the Fortune in December 1621, and reduced the number of available London playhouses for a longish time. It had to remain out of use until after September 1622. Whatever problems there were that prompted the changes, it was the Red Bull Revels company that seems to have lost most. It may have folded because of the changes of its personnel that went with the return of the Lady Elizabeth's, and its going would have released the Red Bull for a new tenancy.[24] If so, Beeston may well have been the instigator of the new formations. The Prince Charles's and the Lady Elizabeth's did not re-merge, which they might have done, given their former history, if they were in control of the changes. Effectively, if the evidence is read in its simplest form, Beeston brought the re-formed Lady Elizabeth's in from outside London to the Cockpit, the Prince Charles's were sent from the Cockpit to the Red Bull, and the Red Bull company left for the country.

The names of the players in the two companies that ran at the Red Bull and the Cockpit up to the next upheaval, in 1625, offer some confirmation to this reading of the evidence. The Prince Charles's Men listed for James's funeral in May 1625 were William Carpenter, Robert Hamlen, Thomas Hobbes, John Newton, William Penn, William Rowley, Anthony Smith, plus Gilbert Reason from the travelling Lady Elizabeth's. Reason's presence in this list may have something to do with the re-formation of the Lady Elizabeth's, which seems in this period to have kept in two sections as they did some years before, one group travelling, the other based in London. Seven of the Lady Elizabeth's men at the Cockpit in 1622 are named by Herbert. It is an odd list, because although it includes Joseph Moore, it is accompanied by lists giving the names of the other companies at the Fortune and the Red Bull, and the Red Bull list is of the company that had been displaced there by the Prince's Men. So it must precede or at least coincide with the Lady Elizabeth's changeover. The seven names at the Cockpit are 'Christopher Beeston, Joseph More, Eliard Swanson, Andrew Cane, Curtis Grevill, William Shurlock, Anthony

---

[23] *REED, Norwich*, 173.
[24] Bentley, *JCS* i. 207–8, uses a ref. by John Gee in 1624 to the four regularly used playhouses to fix the Prince's at the Red Bull.

Turner'.[25] It must have been this Lady Elizabeth's group which visited Lydd on 24 March 1623, where they are recorded, presumably performing a single play, as 'the players of the late Queene and the princes'.[26] The latter word cannot be the possessive form for 'prince', but an abbreviated spelling of 'princess'. Swanston was a Prince Charles's player in December 1620 according to a note made at Stafford. He joined the King's in 1624. Cane was also in transit, in his case to the Palsgrave's, who were then in difficulty because the Fortune was out of service. He had become a Palsgrave's man by 30 April 1624. The names of the players at the Red Bull in Herbert's list are 'Robert Lee, Richard Perkings, Ellis Woorth, Thomas Basse, John Blany, John Cumber, William Robbins'.[27] These are the former Queen Anne's players who made up the Revels company at the Red Bull until 1622. If the Lydd record is accurate, the touring group was a combination of the Lady Elizabeth's and the Revels company. Herbert must be either a little out-of-date, or registering only part of the personnel changes of this year.

The Cockpit names in Herbert's list apart from Beeston himself are new, so it must have been a newly assembled company when he wrote the list down. Moore's presence indicates that he had already left his tavern and arrived in London to restart this version of the Lady Elizabeth's Men as a new London company. The travelling Lady Elizabeth's who did not join the new group were still led by Foster, Townsend, and Wambus, although the two groups kept their links, because Moore was named at Norwich on 13 March 1622 along with Townsend, Foster, and Wambus.

For the next three years the new company raised the reputation of the Cockpit until it began to rival the Blackfriars, as Heminges and Condell were to acknowledge in their introduction to the Shakespeare First Folio. In those three years Herbert licensed thirteen new plays for them. The extant ones are Massinger's *The Bondman*, Heywood's *The Captives*, Middleton and Rowley's *The Changeling*, Davenport's *The City Night-cap*, Dekker's *Match Me in London*, Massinger's *The Renegado*, Shirley's *The School of Compliment*, Rowley and Middleton's *The Spanish Gipsy*, Dekker and Ford's *The Sun's Darling*, and part of Massinger's *The Parliament of Love*. The lost plays are the anonymous *The Black Lady*, William Bonen's *The Cra . . . Merchant, or, Come to my Country House*, and the anonymous *The Valiant Scholar*. This is a rather better cull than for most companies in such a brief phase of their career. It suggests that Beeston as their impresario was keen on new plays, using Italian or similarly exotic locales, and with a more or less gentlemanly concern for questions of honour and love. It is a repertory standing closer to the Blackfriars than the Fortune or the Red Bull, although it must not be forgotten that Beeston took a number of the Red Bull plays to use at the Cockpit.[28] The Cockpit company appeared at court three times in 1623-4 with new plays, *The Spanish Gipsy*, *The Bondman*, and *The Changeling*, and twice in 1624-5 with old

[25] *Herbert Dramatic Records*, 63.   [26] *MSC* vii. 112.   [27] *Herbert Dramatic Records*, 63.
[28] See Gurr, 'Playing in Amphitheatres and Playing in Hall Theatres', *Elizabethan Theatre*, 13 (1994), 27-62.

favourites, *Cupid's Revenge* and *Greene's Tu Quoque*. Against that number, the King's Men performed eight plays in 1623–4 and six in 1624–5.

The terminus to Jacobean playing came when James died on 27 March 1625. Like Elizabeth's death in March 1603, it coincided with a massive epidemic of plague deaths, the toll rising to 4,000 a week in London through August. The King's Men survived, but otherwise there was a complete shake-up and redistribution of players into new companies. The Lady Elizabeth's vanished, with six of its seven leading players going to other companies. Beeston set up a fresh company at the Cockpit, getting the new Queen Henrietta as its patron. Only Sherlock and Turner from the previous Cockpit occupants, Lady Elizabeth's, joined this new group. Of the other leading Lady Elizabeth's players, Swanston had already joined the King's and 'Courteous' Greville went there after him. Cane had joined the Palsgrave's. Moore returned to travelling, probably rejoining the alternative Lady Elizabeth's led by Gilbert Reason that had been touring since 1615. Its relation to the post-1625 company that united the Lady Elizabeth and her husband the Palsgrave as joint patrons is a matter for the next chapter.

THE DUKE OF ALBANY'S/YORK'S PLAYERS, 1608–1613

Plays
Hymen's Holiday

Sharers
Norwich 18 May 1614: 'John Garland, Willm Rowley Thomas Hobbes & others of the Duke of Yorke his Servants'.

London Playhouses
Curtain (?).

At Court
9 Feb. 1610 (unnamed) before the prince, Duke of York, Lady Elizabeth; three unnamed plays 12 Dec., 20 Dec., 15 Jan. 1611 before the prince, Duke of York, Lady Elizabeth; three unnamed plays 12 Jan. 1612, 28 Jan., 13 Feb., 24 Feb. (*Hymen's Holiday*), before the prince, Duke of York, Lady Elizabeth.

Travelling Records
Ipswich 20 Oct. 1608 'the Younge Princs players', 40s. / Leicester 1 Oct. 1609 'to the right honorable the Lorde Albunye his playors', 40s. / Norwich 3 May 1610 'unto the lord Abnes his men xls . . . in regard that they should not play' / Leicester 1 July 1610 'once more to the Lorde Albunye his playors', 20s. / York City Books July 1610 'to my Lord Albany players which came to this Cittie & plaid not', 10s. / Shrewsbury 1610–11 'which was geven to the Kings, Queens. Princes and other noblemen's players this yere', 20s. / Norwich 18 Apr. 1611 'unto the Lord Abonye his men', 20s. / York City Books Sept. 1611 'Given at Lammas assizes to my Lord Awbenyies players', 20s. / Carlisle 15–27 Aug. 1611 'to my lord Awbeny plaiers', 20s. / Ipswich 1612–13, £1. 6s. 8d. / Leicester 20 Jan. 1614 'to the Lord Awbenyes playors', 13s. 4d. / Coventry Nov. acct. 1614 'to the lord of Albignes

players', 10s. / Norwich 18 May 1614 'John Garland, William Rowley Thomas Hobbes & others of the Duke of Yorke his Servants shewed forth his Majesties Lettres Patents under the great Seale giving them authoritie to play. And the Court apoynted them three dayes this weke & tuseday wednesday Thursday Friday & Satterday the next weke to play, & they thankfully accepted the same'.

PRINCE CHARLES'S (I) 1613–1625

Plays
All's Lost by Lust, The Bellman of Paris (lost), The Dutch Painter and the French Brawl (lost), A Fair Quarrel, The Fairy Knight (lost), A Fault in Friendship (lost), The Late Murder in Whitechapel (lost), The Madcap (lost), The Man in the Moon Drinks Claret (lost), The Parricide (lost), The Peaceable Kingdom (lost), A Vow and a Good One (lost), The Widow's Prize (lost), The Witch of Edmonton, The World Tost at Tennis, The Younger Brother (lost).

Playing Sharers
Robert Dawes, William Eaton, John Newton, Gilbert Reason, William Rowley, Martin Slater,[29] Eyllaerdt Swanston, Joseph Taylor,[30] [Norwich 1616: 'John Garland william Rowley Thomas Hobbes Robert Dawes Joseph Taylor John Newton & Gilbert Reason']. [Letter addressed to all towns, recorded at Bristol April 1618: 'John Daniel gent (the Prince his servant). . . . Martin Slatier John Edmonds & Nathaniell Clay'].

London Playhouses
Curtain 1613, 1622 [Eccles, NQ 1991, 46]; Porter's Hall; Red Bull.

At Court
six unnamed plays up to 17 May 1615 before the prince; four unnamed plays up to 29 Apr. before the prince; fifteen unnamed plays 21 Oct.–13 Jan. 1617, including 28 Dec.; [no accounts 1617–1621]; 27 Dec. 1621 (The Man in the Moon Drinks Claret), 29 Dec. (The Witch of Edmonton); 6 Jan. 1623 (A Vow and a Good One).

Travelling Records
Sudbury, Suffolk 1613–14, 10s. / Maidstone 1613–14, 10s. / Fordwich, Kent 23 Mar. 1614, 6s. 8d. / Dover 16 Apr. 1614, 10s. / Coventry 7 Nov. 1614 'to Prince Charles his players', £4. / Oxford town Oct. 'Allhallows' 1614, 20s. / Leicester 10 Nov. 1614 'to the princes playors', 40s. / Barnstaple, Devon 1614–15 'to the Queenes and Princes players', 25s. 10d. / Southampton 1614–15, 30s. / Nottingham 1614–15, 20s. / Winchester 1614–15, 10s. / Faversham, Kent 1614–15 / New Romney, Kent 1614–15, 20s. / Winchester 1614–15, 20s. / Shrewsbury 20 Sept.

---

[29] Slater and Dawes, as members of Prince Charles's, were arrested for their part in an affray at the door of the Curtain on 27 July 1613. Slater, as usual, did not stay long in the London company, though he was named in the 1618 letter recorded at Bristol. See Mark Eccles, 'Elizabethan Actors iv: S to End', NQ 238 (1993), 165–76, 172.

[30] In 1617 Taylor and Newton of Prince Charles's were bound over to keep the peace. See Eccles, Elizabethan Actors iv: S to End', 173–4.

1615, 20*s*. / Nottingham 1615–16, 20*s*. / New Romney, Kent 1615–16, 10*s*. / Dover 16 Mar. 1616, £2. / Norwich 30 Mar. 1616 'mr Reason one of the Princes servantes came in at the same tyme affirminge that they had A patent, And theise two Companyes have leave to play ffower dayes this next weke' / Dunwich, Suffolk 1615–16, 3*s*. 4*d*. / Rye, Sussex Mar. 1616, 18*s*. / Manchester 22 July 1616, 10*s*. / Southampton Nov. 1615–1616, 30*s*. / Norwich 31 Aug. 1616 'A Patent was this day brought by Joseph Taylor berynge Teste the xxxth of March Anno 8 Jacobi [1611] made to John Garland william Rowley Thomas Hobbes Robert Dawes Joseph Taylor John Newton & Gilbert Reason with the rest of their Company to play &c They are permitted to play but not to sound A Drumme for fower Dayes' / Coventry Nov. acct. 1616, £3, '1 quarter of the pound of refined Suger att the parlor & a quart of sacke', 26*d*. / Barnstaple, Devon 1616–17, 20*s*. / Southampton 1616–17, £1. 2*s*. / Fordwich, Kent 15 Mar. 1617, 7*s*. / Nottingham 1616–17, 10*s*. / Norwich 4 June 1617 'And whereas also Gilberte Reason one of the prince his highnes Playors having likewise separated himselfe from his Company hath also taken forth another exemplification or duplicate of the patent granted to that Company and lives in the same kind & abuse.' / Norwich 1616–17, 10*s*. / Leominster, Herefordshire 1616–17, 10*s*. / Shrewsbury 1616–17 'to the kinges majestes Trompeters and to the princes players', 42*s*. / Nottingham 1616–17, 10*s*. / Coventry 15 May 1617, 40*s*. / Bristol Sept.–Dec. 1617, £2. 4*s*. / Exeter Oct. 1617 'by mr maiors order to dismysse', £1. 2*s*. / Plymouth 1617–18 'towards their charge which came to the Towne and did not play', 30*s*. / Barnstaple, Devon 1617–18 'that they should not playe in Towne', 20*s*. / Sudbury, Suffolk 1617–18, 10*s*. / Winchester 1617–18 'to the players of the Prince of Wales this year', 20*s*. / Bristol Apr. 1618 'grant unto John Daniel gent (the Prince his servant) Aucthoitie to bring upp a Companie of Chilldren and youths in the quallitie of playing Enterludes & Stageplaies. And wee are informed yat notwithstanding his Majesties pleasure therein, that there are some who oppugne and resist the said aucthority in contempt of his Majesties Lettres Patentes. In consideracion whereof and for the further effecting & performance of his Majesties pleasure therein Wee have thought good to grant unto the said John Daniell these our Lettres of Assistance Thereby requiring you and in his Majesties name straightly chardging & commaunding you and every of you not only quietly to permitt and suffer Martin Slatier John Edmonds & Nathaniell Clay . . . to play as aforesaid.' / Faversham, Kent 3 May 1618 'Prince Charles players', 10*s*. / Naworth, Cumberland Aug. 1618, 10*s*. / Kendal 30 Aug. 1618 'to the yonge princes players', 11*s*. / Bristol June–Sept. 1618, £2. 4*s*. / Lydd 10 Oct. 1618, 10*s*. / Reading 30 Nov. 1618, 22*s*. / Ipswich 1618–19 'the Ladye Elizabeth's plaiers & the princes', £2. 13*s*. 4*d*. / Manchester 1619, 10*s*. / Craven, Yorks., Clifford family 28 Sept. 1619 'to a Company of Players being Prince Charles his Servantes, whoe Came hither to Londsbrough & plaied one Play',[31] 11*s*. / Coventry 25 Oct. 1619, 20*s*. / Leicester 1619–20, £1. 13*s*., £1. 11*s*.

[31] This may be the same group as the 'Princes players' who were paid 10*s*. for performing at the house of Lord William Howard of Naworth, Cumberland, in Aug. 1618. They were at Naworth again in Feb. 1621.

/ Kendal 1619–20, 10s. / Dunkenhalgh, Lancs. (Household accounts of Thomas Walmsley) 7 Nov. 1619 'Gyven unto the younge Prince men', 20s. / Sudbury, Suffolk 1619–20 'To the Princes & the Ladie Elizabeths servantes & To the Children of the Revells to every of them Sixe shillinges in all' / Ipswich 1619–20, £1. 6s. 8d. / Leicester 1620 'to the Prince his Players who played not', 20s. / Dover 13 May 1620, 11s. / Lydd 17 May 1620, 11s. / Coventry 12 Aug. 1620, 15s. / Nottingham Dec. 1620, 10s. / Dunkenhalgh, Lancs. (Household accounts of Thomas Walmsley) 2 Dec. 1620, 30s. / Carlisle 20 Dec. 1620, 22s. / Naworth, Cumberland Feb. 1621, 10s. / Manchester 1620–1, 10s. / Ipswich 1620–1, £1. 6s. 8d. / Folkestone 1620–1, 5s. 6d., 5s. / Faversham, Kent 1620–1, 10s. / Fordwich, Kent 9 Feb. 1621, 3s. / Sandwich, Kent Feb. 1621, 22s. / New Romney, Kent 23 Feb. 1621, 10s. / Dover 24 Feb. 1621, 11s. / Lydd, Kent 4 Mar. 1621, 10s. / Coventry 24 Aug. 1621 'to Gilbert Reason one of the Princes Players who brought a Commission wherein himself and others were named', 20s. / Ludlow 27 Sept. 1621, 5s. / Dover 1621–2, 11s. / New Romney, Kent 25 Oct. 1621, 5s. / Barnstaple, Devon 1621–2 'because they should not play within the Towne', 40s. / Wallingford, Berkshire 1621–2 'the Kinge and Queenes and princes players', 23s. 4d. / Norwich 1621–2, 40s. / Leicester 9 Nov. 1621 'who played not', 30s. / Dover 20 Apr. 1622 'geven to the princes players about 3 weekes past', 11s. / Lydd, Kent 3 Apr. 1622, 10s. / New Romney, Kent 4 Apr. 1622, 6s. / Faversham, Kent 3 July 1622, 10s. / Lydd 1622–3, 6s. / Coventry 23 Dec. 1622 'to Gilbert Reason and William Eaton players to the Prince his highnes', 20s. / Stafford 13 Dec. 1622 'Given Mr Sawanston the princes player', 6s. 8d. / Stafford 15 Jan. 1623 'Prince Charles' players', 6s. 8d. / Leicester 1622–3 'that played not', 22s. / Dunkenhalgh, Lancs. (Sir Thomas Walmsley) 26 Jan.–1 Feb. 1623 'the prince players 2 nights' / Carlisle 1622–3, 20s. / New Romney, Kent 19 Mar. 1623, 5s. / Lydd, 24 Mar. 1623 'to the players of the late Queene and the princes', 11s. / Norwich 31 May 1623 'This day Gilbert Reason brought into this Court a Duplicate or exemplificacion of A Patent made to him & others Teste xxx Marcii Anno octavo Regis Jacobi [1610] And the exemplificacion beareth Test xxxi die Maii Anno undecimo Jacobi Regis [1613] whereby they are lycensed to play as servantes to the Prince by the name of Charles Duke of yorke which exemplificacion ys crossed by a warrant from the Lord Chamberlyn dated the xvith of July 1616 . . . Hee & his Company are denyed to play by reason of the want of worke for the poore & in respect of the contagion feared And for many other Causes, but was offered a gratuitie which he refused'. / Hythe, Kent 6 July 1623, 5s. 6d. / New Romney, Kent 6 July 1623, 5s., 'in beere', 6d. / Leicester 27 Oct. 1623, £1. 3s. 4d. / Nottingham 1623–4 'because they should not playe in the Towne', 13s. 4d. / Totnes, Devon 1623–4, 11s. / Dover 17 Apr. 1624, 10s. / Carlisle 5 July 1624, £1. / Dover 30 Oct. 1624, 11s. / Lydd 10 Nov. 1624, 10s. / Faversham, Kent 18 Nov. 1624, 6s. 8d. / New Romney, Kent 1624–5, 5s. / Canterbury 1624–5 'to the princes plaiers. to dept the Cittie and not to play', 11s. / Winchester 1624–5, 20s. / Coventry 24 Dec. 1624, 20s. / Bridport, Dorset 1625?, 10s. / Leicester 1625, £1. / Norwich 29 Jan. 1625 'This day Gilbert Reason brought in & shewed to this Court an Examplificacion of a patent as servantes to the

Prince to play &c . . . xliiijs to be gyven them as a gratuity', 44s. / Worcester 1624–5 'To kinge Charles his servantes when he was Prince', 13s. 4d. / Carlisle 5 Aug. 1626, £1. 10s.

LADY ELIZABETH'S PLAYERS, 1611–1625

Plays
Amends for Ladies, *Bartholomew Fair*, *Chabot*, *A Chaste Maid in Cheapside*, *Cockledemoy* (lost? *ES* iv.180). *The Coxcomb* (old), *Cupid's Revenge* (old), *The Dutch Courtesan* (old), *Eastward Ho!* (old), *Greene's Tu Quoque* (old), *Love Tricks*, *The Proud Maid's Tragedy* (lost), *Raymond Duke of Lyons* (lost), [1622–25] *The Black Lady* (lost), *The Bondman*, *The Captives*, *The Changeling*, *The City Night-cap*, *Come to my Country House* (lost), *Match Me in London* (old), *The Noble Bondman*, *The Parliament of Love* (part only), *The Renegado*, *The School of Compliment*, *The Spanish Contract* (lost), *The Spanish Gipsy*, *The Sun's Darling*, *The Valiant Scholar* (lost).

Playing Sharers
Joseph Moore, John Townsend (1611 patent), [Nathan Field,] Nicholas Long (Norwich 2 Mar. 1614), Robert Finch, Joseph Moore, William Perry, John Townsend, George Bosgrove, Thomas Sewell, James Jones [Coventry letter 1615, *REED, Coventry*, 394, names 'John Townesend / Josephe Moore / William Perry / Robert Fintch / George Bosgrove / Thomas Suell / James Jones / Charles Martyn / hughe haughton / James Kneller / John Hunt / Edward / Raphe / Walter Burrett / .5. Horses in the Company']. 'Alexander Foster, John Townsend Joseph Moore & Fr Wamus' Norwich 23 May 1618. Andrew Cane Norwich 9 Mar. 1636. 'Joseph Moore Ellias Worth Mathew Smyth & others' Norwich 21 Feb. 1637.

Hired Men
Walter Burrett (?)

Boys
Hugh Haughton, John Hunt, James Kneller, Charles Martyn, Edward, Ralph (letter 1615, *REED, Coventry*, 394).

London Playhouses
Swan, Porter's Hall, Hope, Cockpit.

At Court
10 Jan. 1612 (two unnamed) before the prince and Lady Elizabeth, 25 Feb. (*The Proud Maid's Tragedy*) before the king, 11 Mar. (unnamed) before the prince and Lady Elizabeth; probably 20 Oct. (unnamed) before Edward Sackville, 25 Feb. 1613 (*The Dutch Courtesan*) before the prince, Lady Elizabeth, and the Elector Palatine, 1 Mar. (*Raymond Duke of Lyons*) before the prince, Lady Elizabeth, and the Elector Palatine, 12 Dec. (*The Dutch Courtesan*) before the prince, 25 Jan. 1614 (*Eastward Ho!*) before the king; 1 Nov. (*Bartholomew Fair*) before the king; three

unnamed plays before the king in Mar. 1617; [no accounts 1617–1621]; two unnamed plays up to 21 Jan. 1623 before the king; 5 Nov. (*The Spanish Gipsy*), 27
Dec. (*The Bondman*), 4 Jan. 1624 (*The Changeling*) before the prince, and three
unnamed plays before the king: 28 Dec. (*Cupid's Revenge*), 6 Jan. 1625 (*Greene's Tu
Quoque*) before the prince.

Travelling Records
Bath 1610–11, 20*s*. / Ipswich 28 May 1611, £1. 6*s*. 8*d*. / Bath 12 Oct. 1611, 20*s*./
Faversham, Kent Apr. 1612, 20*s*. / Canterbury 11 Apr. 1612, 5*s*. / Dover 9 May
1612, 10*s*. / Coventry Nov. acct. 1612, £4. / Leicester 30 July 1612, 40*s*. / York
City Books 13 Aug. 1612 'wheras the Ladies Elizabeth Players daughter unto the
kinges most excellent Majestie have brought with them his majesties Commission
for to be licensed to playe aswell in such howses or places as are appointed for them
to play within London as in all moote halls skoolehowses towne halles within any
other Citties or townes . . . it is thought good to permitt them to play within this
Cittie in such places as they shall procure or gett so as they do not play on the
sabaoth daies or in the night tyme' / Bristol Dec. 1612–Mar. 1613, £2. / Manchester 1612–13, 10*s*. / Shrewsbury 1612–13, 20*s*. / Newark, Notts. 13 Feb. 1613, 10*s*.
/ Norwich 19 Apr. 1613, 20*s*. / Faversham, Kent 6 June 1613, 10*s*. / Canterbury
4 July 1613, 10*s*. /Dover 12 July 1613, 10*s*. / Leicester 13 Oct. 1613, 40*s*. /
Coventry Nov. acct. 1613 'to the Queenes or the Lady Elizabethes players', £4. /
Shrewsbury 1613–14, 20*s*. / Leominster, Herefordshire 1613–14, 5*s*. / Manchester
1613–14, 10*s*. / Norwich 2 Mar 1614 'Nicholas Longe and other Players Servantes
to the Lady Elizabeth his Majesties Daughter Authorised to play by the Kynges
Majestie under the great Seale Came this day into the Court and beinge
demaunded wherefore their Comeinge was, Sayd they Came not to aske leave to
play But to aske the gratuetie of the Cytty.' / Maidstone 1613–14, 10*s*. / Norwich
21 Mar. 1614 'Whereas Joseph Moore and other Stageplayers servantes to the Lady
Elizabeth Came lately to this Cytty and here attempted to play without leave from
Master Maior, At which their said playes were many outrages & disorders
Commytted As fightynges whereby some were wounded, and throweinge about &
publishinge of sedicious Libelles much tendynge to the disturbance & breach of his
Majesties peace' / Manchester 7 Apr. 1614, 10*s*. / Rye, Sussex May 1614, 11*s*. /
Coventry [misdemeanor 28 Mar. 1615][32] / Nottingham 1614–15, 10*s*. / Norwich 27
May 1615 'An exemplificacion of a Patent brought under the great Seale bearinge
teste 27 Aprilis Anno nono [1612] made to John Townesend & Joseph More sworne
servantes to the Lady Elizabeth and the rest of the Company to play Stage playes
&c . . . They are tollerated to play on monday & tuseday next' / Dunkenhalgh,
Lancs. (Household accounts of Thomas Walmesley) Nov. 1615 'gyven unto the
Ladye Elizabeths men', 20*s*. / Coventry Nov. acct. 1616, 40*s*. / Norwich 5 June

---

[32] 'One of the Company of the Lady Elizabethes players came to this Cittie the 27th of March and
said to Thomas Barrowes Clothworker these wordes . . . you are such people in this towne so peevishe
that you would have your throates cutt and that you were well served you would be fatched upp with
pursevauntes.' *REED, Coventry*, 393–4. The names of all the company are given.

1616 'to desist from playinge within the libertyes of this Cytty', 40s. / Leicester 1 July 1616, 20s. / Nottingham 1616–17, 10s. / Dunkenhalgh, Lancs. (Household accounts of Thomas Walmesley) autumn 1616, 30s. / Leominster, Herefordshire 1616–17, 10s. / Norwich 7 June 1617 'a patent . . . whereby Lycence ys given to John Townesend and Joseph moore sworne Servantes to the Lady Elizabeth with the rest of their company to play &c, They have therefore libertie to play for the tyme formerly given to Lee & his Company videlicet monday Tuseday & wednesday' / Manchester 25 Nov. 1617, 10s. / Exeter Dec. 1617 'by mr maiors order to dismys', £1. 2s. 0d. / Coventry 12 Dec. 1617, 40s. / Carlisle 1617–18 'to me Ladye Elibethe players', 26s. 8d. / Dunkenhalgh, Lancs. (Thomas Walmesley) 19 Jan. 1618, 10s./ Leicester 22 Feb. 1618, 22s. / Hythe, Kent 27 Apr. 1618, 10s. / Folkestone 1617–18, 5s. Dover 16 May 1618, 11s. / Norwich 23 May 1618 'A Lycence . . . whereby Alexander Foster John Townsend Joseph Moore & Francis Wambus servantes to the Lady Elizabeth are lycensed to play in the Citty of London . . . they shall have liberty to play here by the space of the next whole weke & no longer . . . and not to come agayne to play duringe this whole yeare' / Sudbury, Suffolk 1618–19, 10s. / New Romney 1618–19, 10s. / Manchester 31 Oct. 1618, 10s. / Ipswich 1618–19 'the Ladye Elizabeth's plaiers & the princes', £2. 13s. 4d. / Winchester 1618–19, 10s. / Plymouth 1618–19 'being 20 persons which had the Kings hand for playing aswell by night as by day', £3. 6s. / Coventry 4 Jan. 1619, 33s. / Norwich 1 May 1619 / Sudbury, Suffolk 1619–20, 6s. / Reading 1619–20, 33s., 'paid more' 22s. / Leominster, Herefordshire 1619–20, 10s. / Ludlow 16 Jan. 1620, 5s. / Kendal 1619–20 'to the Queens of bohemia players', 10s. / Carlisle 1619–20, 15s. / Norwich 8 Feb. 1620 'till Satterday next' / Norwich 22 Apr. 1620 'the First Fower dayes of May and no longer'[33] / Manchester 1620–1, 10s. / Ludlow 23 Aug. 1620, 5s. / Norwich 1620–1, 40s. / Bristol Sept.–Dec. 1620, £2. / Hythe, Kent 4 Oct. 1620, 10s. / Sandwich, Kent 1620, 22s. / Dunkenhalgh, Lancs. (Household accounts of Thomas Walmesley) 2 Jan. 1621, 40s. / Coventry 5 Jan. 1621, 22s. / Leicester 20 Feb. 1621, 13s. 4d. / Leicester 8 Apr. 1621 'who played not', 13s. 4d. / Nottingham Apr. 1621 'the Kinges & princesse playeres', 10s. / Norwich 2 May 1621 'because none of the said Company but onely the said Towneshend are nowe in Towne . . . this whole Court refuseth to give them any leave to play', 40s. / Manchester 1621, 6s. 6d. / Sudbury, Suffolk 1621–2 'to the Queens players the La: Elizabeth hir players and the Children of the revells', 28s. / Leicester 15 Mar. 1622 'playd not', 15s. / Norwich 11 May 1622 'denyed'; 20 May 1622 'ffourty shillinges . . . for that they will not play' / Lydd, Kent 1622 'at the last faire', 6s. 8d. / New Romney 24 July 1622, 5s. / Barnstaple, Devon 1622–3, 30s. / Coventry 24 Jan. 1623, 13s. 4d. / Leicester 25 Jan. 1623 'that played not', 20s. / Lydd, 24 Mar. 1623 'to the players of the late Queene and the princes', 11s. / Dover 20 Mar.–17 Apr. 1623, 10s. / Norwich 10 May 1623 [patent

---

[33] This entry adds that Wambus, now evidently conscious of Norwich's concern for correct paperwork, declared that Moore, who was named in the patent, was no longer with the company but running an inn in Chichester. Moore had returned to the company by Mar. 1621.

dated 20 Mar. 1621 'whereby John Towneshend Alex Foster Joseph Moore & the said (Francis) wambus servantes to the Lady Elizabeth with the rest of their Company are authorised to play Commodies &c by the space of xiiijen dayes'] 'They have leave for fower dayes onely this next weke & no longer' / Leicester 13 Oct. 1623, 10s. / Coventry Nov. acct. 1624 'in July last', 12s. / Nottingham 1623–4, 10s. / Norwich 24 Apr. 1624 'This day Francis Wambus brought into this Court A Bill signed with his Majesties hand . . . whereupon there was shewed forth unto him the Letters directed from the Lords of his majesties most honorable privie Counsell Dated the 27th of May 1623[34] . . . whereupon the said wambus peremtorily affirmed that he would play in this City & would lay in prison here this Twelvemoneth but he would try whether the kinges Command or the Counselles be the greater . . . the said wambus was accordinge to the Counselles order Comanded to forbeare to play within the liberties of this City And he nevertheles answered that he would make tryall what he might doe by the kinges authority for he said he would play'[35] / Lyme Regis 1624 'to depart the town without playing', 5s. / Leicester 9 July 1624 'to Mr Townesend and his fellowes', 20s. / Gravesend, Kent 1624–5 'to the queene of bohemias players', 6s. 8d. / Hythe, Kent 1624–5, 6s. / Worcester 1624–5, 10s. / Faversham, Kent 1 Apr. 1625 'beeinge here when our Kinge was proclaymed', £1. 2s.

[34] See Ch. 6.   [35] For a more detailed account of this confrontation see Ch. 1.

The grouping of the companies between this chapter and the next in some respects involves a misnomer. As Table 2 in Chapter 8 shows, the division of Caroline audiences between hall and amphitheatre playhouses is a stronger and more consistent way of distinguishing the Caroline companies than the division of the companies themselves. Companies switched between hall and amphitheatre, and between amphitheatre and amphitheatre, almost at three-yearly intervals. So to call any of them a hall company or an amphitheatre company is rather misleading. Moreover, there is rarely sufficient evidence even about their repertories to identify any one company as principally hall-fixated or open-air-playhouse-orientated. But the process which appears to make all the companies interchangeable does not apply to the playhouses. Buildings are more resistant to change than the companies, and the playgoers who went to each playhouse were too. So, since some distinction other than that of the King's Men from the rest has to be made, the next two chapters consider the companies chiefly by the playhouses they were best known at.

Nomenclature is a particular problem in the Caroline period. The final breakdown of the patronage system, which began with James's distribution of the companies to his own family, was completed under Charles, who initially had only himself and his queen for patrons. That is one reason why companies called 'Revels', whether at the Salisbury Court or the Red Bull, began to proliferate. It created a problem not so much in London, where the playhouses more or less identified the companies, but in the rest of the country. There the travels of at least three companies calling themselves 'Revels' groups, and at least three claiming to be 'King's' men, made the identity of any particular visiting group almost impossible for the town clerks to distinguish. And the number of companies travelling on doubtful warrants was increasing. Nottingham in 1635–6 had to try to differentiate between 'the Kinges Plaieres of Yorke', 'the Kinges players of the Court', and 'the Kinges players of London'. Several towns identified them as the King's company at Blackfriars. Occasionally a clerk would put down 'the Court' for a Revels group, and it is an open question whether they intended to identify the Salisbury-Court group or some other company.

The plague closure after James died in March 1625 lasted until the end of November, and caused over 35,000 deaths in London alone. Such a virulent onslaught on the commons was not the best omen for the new reign. Charles had, inevitably, lost his dramatic (Fletcherian) gamble of galloping incognito off to Madrid to marry the Catholic Infanta of Spain two years before, and now was about to marry a French princess instead. Henrietta Maria was a Catholic like the Infanta, but she came from a country which did not inspire the traditional fear and hatred that had shaped English thinking about Spain for the last seventy years. Spain had been the popular enemy ever since an English queen, Mary Tudor, married a Spanish king, who after her death tried to regain the English throne for himself, on the grounds that he had acquired it with his marriage, and launched his Armada to enforce his claim. France was viewed with less animosity. Agincourt was a national victory that could be relished with much more forgiveness towards the enemy than the Armada. But Henrietta Maria was still a Catholic queen who loved plays, and opposition to plays began to merge with opposition to the crown. The fact that royalty imprisoned, impoverished, and cropped the ears of William Prynne in 1633 for writing against plays and women acting in plays was a firm indication of the allegiance that even public and common playgoing was now beginning to command.

With the breakdown of naming by patrons went other modifications to the system of controlling the professional companies. They mark a deeper pattern of change. On the face of it, the controllers could have renewed the royal-patron system almost as a matter of routine. That they did not signifies the deeper shift. At the top end, the King's Men were still pre-eminent enough to acquire the new king as their patron almost automatically. To maintain four companies and their play-houses in London as before might have meant finding only one new patron, supposing that the new king, the Lady Elizabeth, and her husband the Palsgrave would maintain their three companies. The king's own former company, Prince Charles's Men, still had a substantial presence in London at the Cockpit. The fourth patron would then be the new queen, coming as she did from a country with a celebrated theatre tradition and known as she was to be a devotee of theatricals. The royal marriage and the new queen's arrival in London in June was the great event of the first summer of the new reign.

But the new king did not take the initiative that his father had, in taking over the leading groups available in the established playhouses. Only the King's Men survived 1625 unchanged. They got their new patent on 24 June, a week after the king and queen had been welcomed to London. The other three companies all had to reshuffle, starting with the former Prince's Men, now the King of Bohemia's. The new organizations that emerged were set up by the playing groups and their financiers themselves. The Lord Chamberlain and the Master of the Revels had little to do with it. Under Charles the patronage system finally lost its role in the control of playing.

Even the practice of issuing patents for each company under the different royal patrons was not resumed consistently. Not even Queen Henrietta's new company received a patent under Charles. In fact, after the King's Men, none of the other companies except for the new Prince Charles's, set up in 1631 soon after his birth, ever acquired either a patent or a patron. Instead they were issued with annually renewed licences by the Master of the Revels, chiefly for travelling. The Red Bull and Fortune companies of the Caroline years never had a patron, and hence had no official name. The Red Bull and the Salisbury Court companies took the word 'Revels' for their name to affirm who authorized them and their ostensible duty of entertaining the court. Most companies now became known by their playhouses, a change which did not help company identity when the companies switched from one playhouse to another, as happened more or less every three years. The risk of confusing the 'King's Revels' company that was set up to play at the new Salisbury Court hall in 1629 with the 'Revels' company already playing at the Red Bull is one consequence of this new practice.

The Jacobean habit of giving each of the approved companies a royal patron, with the mathematics of the fact that there were only the two Caroline patrons initially and that Prince Charles became a third almost at birth, is one of the more obvious reasons why the practice of giving royal patrons to the four (later five) approved companies died with James. But it was never a simple matter. The Lady Elizabeth and her husband, the titular king of Bohemia, might have kept their two companies running separately under Charles, and their doing so would have kept the four Jacobean royally patronized companies going in an equivalent form as the Caroline four. The fact that neither of these companies did retain their separate identities, and that the companies replacing them had no patents and no patrons' names, reflects several changes in the position of the companies under Charles.

First, it shows the shift in the locus of authority from the great lords of the Privy Council and its agent, the Lord Chamberlain, towards the king himself. Secondly, the prescribed duties of the Master of the Revels were seen as sufficient in themselves to keep the companies in check. Henry Herbert took noticeably more direct control than any of his predecessors. If he had questions about the policy behind his actions he referred them directly to the king. Thirdly, it shows that the personal status of the patrons, whether royal or noble, was no longer seen as having any use as a means of controlling the companies. Patrons had become unnecessary. Once Charles himself had given his name to the King's Men, the others were left under Herbert to organize themselves, reporting directly to the Master of the Revels.

That became the situation under which, during the long plague closure of 1625, the three companies which followed along behind the King's Men had to regroup. Three playhouses were available, and three more or less fresh companies organized themselves to use them. Predictably, the chief agent of this new order was Christopher Beeston. He had the most to gain, since he controlled the only hall playhouse to rival the Blackfriars and also had an interest in one of the two amphitheatres that matched the Globe. In 1626 the Fortune reopened, housing an ostensible merger of the Palsgrave's and Lady Elizabeth's, using their two former patrons' current titles as the King and Queen of Bohemia's Men.[1] That made it

---

[1] G. E. Bentley first identified this group (*JCS* i. 260–9). It was a logical merger of patronage, so far as that was still needed, as well as of players, although up to 1625 the Lady Elizabeth's had much closer links with Prince Charles's Men than with the Palsgrave's. I suspect the available playhouse was the deciding factor.

possible for Beeston to transfer the remnants of the former Prince Charles's Company to the Red Bull. More importantly for his own purposes, these two groupings freed him to cull players from all of the old groups for the new Queen Henrietta's Men at his own prime resort, the Cockpit. It was a private cull that in its way matched the official culls of 1583 and 1594.

In his selection of players Beeston even managed to take Richard Perkins back from the King's Men, where he had gone after a longish stint with the Jacobean 'Revels' Company at the Red Bull. From the company that Beeston expelled from the Cockpit he kept Sherlock and Turner. John Blaney and William Robinson came to him from the residual Queen Anne's Men, more recently the Red Bull Revels company, where they had been sharers with Perkins. Most usefully, he also kept the majority of the plays that the Lady Elizabeth's had been running at the Cockpit. He was a great acquirer of playing resources, and the majority of the plays not already in the hands of the King's Men came to him during these last twenty years of playing. With such resources he could certainly give his new company a rich start.

In the event the new Queen Henrietta's repaid him well. He ran it unchanged for the next ten years, a uniquely long run for the Cockpit. It grew rapidly in esteem. By the court seasons of 1629 and 1630 the Cockpit company was performing almost as many plays before royalty as the King's. And for the new company Beeston acquired the services of the leading new writers. Shirley, who had begun to make his name at the Cockpit before 1625, now became the Cockpit's resident writer. Massinger had given the Cockpit company *The Renegado* in 1624, and over the next decade alternated between the two competing hall companies. First he gave the Cockpit company *A New Way to Pay Old Debts*. He then turned to writing regularly for the King's Men, but two more of his plays went to Beeston when things became difficult with the new courtier poets of the Blackfriars at the beginning of the 1630s. John Ford, a long-serving gentleman poet lodging at the Middle Temple, with a lengthy experience in writing collaborative scripts for the amphitheatres, first wrote one or two of his great solo plays for the King's, and then also joined Beeston when the courtiers took over the Blackfriars repertory.

Besides Massinger and Heywood, now the old guard of playwrights, in the 1630s Beeston also acquired new writers such as Thomas Nabbes and Shakerley Marmion, and even one play from Richard Brome. To older plays by Chapman, Middleton, Davenport, Webster, and Rowley, and Marlowe's perennial *Jew of Malta*, he added all the early Beaumont and Fletchers, originally written for the boys, that had escaped the King's Men. It was a fairly conservative repertory, a hotchpotch. It had a solid basis in the traditional favourites, including Heywood's 1608 Red Bull play *The Rape of Lucrece*, which the Duke of Buckingham saw at the Cockpit shortly before he was assassinated in 1628. Like the King's Men's plays but unlike those in the Fortune and Red Bull repertory, Beeston's choice of new plays showed a strong shift in focus to the concerns of women. Plays like *Love's Cruelty, Love's Mistress, Love's Sacrifice*, and *The Witty Fair One* flaunted their titles on their playbills to draw female audiences. Since respectable women could only attend plays when escorted by a male, such drawcards brought double returns. And London itself became a new kind of subject in the Cockpit comedies. London had been a subject for plays since the late 1590s, but now the old citizen-comedy gave way to locality-plays. The new suburbs of Tottenham Court, Hyde Park, and Covent Garden all supplied titles for plays set there. Perhaps most obviously, though not as distinctly as we might have expected, Beeston's acquisitions also began to reflect his patron Henrietta Maria's interest in pastoral Arcadianism, with plays such as *Arcadia*, *The Shepherd's Holiday*, and *Claracilla*. But he never took that fashion up as strongly as the King's Men.

No patent for the new Cockpit company of 1625 has survived, the first indication that the Jacobean system of patenting had now been dropped. Control was left to the busy hands of the Master of the Revels.[2] Fourteen members of Queen Henrietta's company, including Beeston himself, received allowances for livery on 19 June 1629, so by then the company was well established under its patron's name and officially recognized. Although it did not appear at court until the 1629–30 season, it had certainly been staging plays under its royal title from the first year. Shirley's *The Wedding*, on stage by May 1626, was printed in 1629 as 'by her Majesties Servants'. Performances at the Cockpit in fact restarted after the 1625 plague a little too precipitately for the Middlesex authorities, under whose control Drury Lane lay. On 6 December they issued a special order to 'the howse at the Cockpitt, being next to his Majesties Courte at Whitehall, commaundinge them to surcease all such theire proceedinges, untill his Majesties pleasure be further signified'.[3] The ostensible concern was for crowds spreading plague too near the court in Whitehall, even though the plague deaths that week were down to as few as fifteen.

There were no more major outbreaks of plague after 1626 until 1630, and through these years Perkins and Beeston took the Cockpit company to a level matching the Blackfriars. The exchange of fire between the rival poets of the two companies in 1630 has been looked at already, in Chapter 8. The Cockpit's repertory was safer and less radical than the new courtier poets of the Blackfriars were willing to tolerate. How much the Cockpit poets drew the courtiers' fire because of their conservatism and how much it was their lower social standing that made them vulnerable is not easy to tease out. For Carew and Davenant to link the Cockpit with the Red Bull suggests that some sort of social line was being drawn. But rivalry between coteries and claques in audiences are part of the intimacy that regular playgoing will always acquire. For all its long association with the Red Bull, the

---

[2] How consistent the replacement of patents by annual licences was and how soon the new system started is not entirely clear in the evidence from the travelling records. If patents were no longer necessary, the new system ought to show up in more than just the few references for companies licensed to play in the country by Henry Herbert. But the provincial records were far patchier in recording company visits under Charles. The Elizabethan proclamation of 1559 that required mayors to approve plays no longer applied, and companies now played at inns instead of guildhalls. In Bath in 1616 one company even paid 3s. 4d. to rent a guildhall to play in.

[3] *Middlesex County Records*, ed. J. C. Jeaffreson, iii. 6.

Cockpit's repertory was never remote from the court and court affairs. Its seats were too costly for it to aim at a broad social appeal. Henry Herbert took offence in 1632 over Shirley's *The Ball* for depicting courtiers in a way that the Cockpit audiences were clearly expected to recognize. In his diary he reported:

18 Nov. 1632. In the play of *The Ball*, written by Sherley, and acted by the Queens players, ther were divers personated so naturally, both of lords and others of the court, that I took it ill, and would have forbidden the play, but that Biston promiste many things which I found faulte withall should be left out, and that he would not suffer it to be done by the poett any more, who deserves to be punisht.[4]

Herbert was alert to the games of application going on. A few months later he ordered the portrait of Inigo Jones as 'Vitru Hoop' in Jonson's *A Tale of a Tub* to be deleted from the play in performance.

Possibly as a conciliatory gesture, Herbert complimented Shirley on his next play for the Cockpit, *The Young Admiral*. His note is a prescription about how to write a good play for the time, one that he expected later generations of poets to read. It is an explicit record of authority's position over playwriting in 1633. Beeston would certainly have read it as a programme for his stable of scriptwriters.

1633, July 3. The comedy called *The Yonge Admirall*, being free from oaths, prophaness, or obsceanes, hath given mee much delight and satisfaction in the readinge, and may serve for a patterne to other poetts, not only for the bettring of maners and language, but for the improvement of the quality, which hath received some brushings of late.

When Mr. Sherley hath read this approbation, I know it will encourage him to pursue this beneficial and cleanly way of poetry, and when other poetts heare and see his good success, I am confident they will imitate the original for their own credit, and make such copies in this harmless way, as shall speak them masters in their art, at the first sight, to all judicious spectators. It may be acted this 3 July, 1633.

I have entered this allowance, for direction to my successor, and for example to all poets, that shall write after the date hereof.[5]

The Cockpit's new play, an innocuous drama about romance and valour at court from Spanish sources, provided a model to Herbert, the government's pompous voice, for the necessarily 'harmless way', chiefly harmless through the avoidance of blasphemies, in which plays must now be composed.

Shirley was then scripting two plays a year for Beeston. Ford left the Blackfriars to write for him in 1631, and Massinger came across at about the same time, abandoning the Blackfriars to Davenant and the courtier poets. As the King's Men went into their more witty and courtly mode, the Cockpit became the respectably conservative core of London's theatre world. This is one of several ways in which the centre of gravity shifted under Charles, with a fifth company joining the four that were approved through James's later years. In the 1630s there were three companies at the hall playhouses and two at the amphitheatres. In a sense it was still an equal balance between élite and popular, since the King's Men only used the

---

[4] *Dramatic Records*, 19.   [5] Ibid. 19–20.

Blackfriars for half of their year and the Globe served as a third amphitheatre for the other half, so that the provision of amphitheatre- and hall-playing was mathematically equal. Looking at the ordinary London playgoer in 1633, it may be a distortion to see the two main halls, the Blackfriars and the Cockpit, as the centre of attention. Numerically the amphitheatres catered for five times the audience size that the halls could admit. The survival of so much more printed testimony to the activities of the hall companies, the quartos of the plays from their repertoire, can make us underestimate the strength of the amphitheatres. Herbert's 1633 testimony to Shirley and the Cockpit company was hardly an unbiased act of witness. But his approval of Beeston's work certainly signals the establishment's view. Most playgoers would rather be reassured than provoked. It was the amphitheatre companies remote from the centre who supplied most of the subversion in the last years.

Queen Henrietta's Company gained in status while their patron's profile as a lover of plays strengthened, in 1633 and still more in 1634. Heywood wrote a masque, *Love's Mistress*, which was first staged at the Cockpit before being twice represented at court, with scenes designed by Inigo Jones. The queen may actually have attended the Cockpit for the performance, because she paid to have it re-staged at Denmark House for the king's birthday on 19 November. They both liked it enough to have a third performance immediately afterwards. Heywood wrote a different prologue for all three presentations, in the third making Cupid as prologue hail Henrietta as 'A Presence; that from *Venus* takes all power, | And makes each place she comes in, *Cupids* bower'. If she was the 'State-Lady' who had to enter 'hither at our publike gate', and was addressed by the prologue to the initial performance at the Cockpit, Heywood evidently felt she had made his playhouse the bower of love. Either in courtly honour or in Arcadian pastorals, love was now much more a Cockpit subject than the stories of wars that still ran in the amphitheatres. Prynne's ponderous *Histrio-mastix* in 1633 did little to stem the flow of either.

The patron's influence over her company was also shown in February 1635 when Beeston was constrained to hand over the Cockpit for use by a visiting company of French players. That was in Lent, when English companies would still normally stop playing, and it was by royal command. The dutiful Herbert records that 'the king tould mee his pleasure, and commanded mee to give order that this Frenche company should playe the too sermon daies in the weeke, during their time of playinge in Lent, and in the house of Drury-lane, where the queenes players usually playe'.[6] Beeston's company was high in royal favour. Altogether through these years the Cockpit company was called almost as often to court as the King's Men. In the ten years between 1629 and the long plague closure of 1637 Herbert asked them for sixty-six plays, while the King's Men's gave sixty-seven.

[6] *Dramatic Records*, 60.

Beeston's prejudice against travelling shows in the paucity of evidence for Queen Henrietta's Servants going on tour through its ten years at the Cockpit. His dislike seems to have manifested itself initially with Queen Anne's Men when Swinnerton and Slater took up a duplicate patent to travel, leaving Greene and Beeston to work at the Red Bull. He may have been from the start behind the system where travelling companies used duplicates of the official licence, since in the later years he never travelled himself, and the Cockpit companies did much less travelling than any of the others except the last of the amphitheatre groups.

The plague closure of 1636 brought a sharp check to the orderly progress of the Cockpit company. Beeston, having broken his old habit of running his companies for only three years and allowing Queen Henrietta's to flourish at the Cockpit for ten, found the seemingly endless closure from May 1636 to October 1637 too long, and dismissed them. He replaced them with a company of youngsters who became known as 'Beeston's Boys'. Henry Herbert's notes about the change typically suggest that his role in setting them up was more direct and interventionist than it actually was. He wrote that after the closure 'Mr. Beeston was commanded to make a company of boyes, and began to play at the Cockpit with them the same day'.[7] What he must mean is not that he commanded Beeston to organize a new company and they sprang into being immediately, but that he licensed a company which Beeston had set up already, waiting for the plague ban to end. It was Beeston's choice. He had actually secured his new patent as 'Govvernor of the new Company of the Kinges & Queenes boyes' eight months before, after the first ten months of closure, on 21 February 1637.[8]

Herbert may have been more genuinely active over what happened to the players ejected from the Cockpit than over setting up the new young company. His note adds 'I disposed of Perkins, Sumner, Sherlock and Turner, to Salisbury Court, and joyned them with the best of that company'. The Salisbury Court company, known as the King's Revels, now took Henrietta Maria as their new patron along with the four of her former players from the Cockpit company. It was a fairly large-scale shake-up. Four others from the former Queen Henrietta's, Bowyer, Allen, Robinson, and Clark, went to the King's Men. Two of the younger members, Ezekiel Fenn and Theophilus Bird, a son of Henslowe's Bird, who married Beeston's eldest daughter, stayed at the Cockpit to help form the new Beeston's Boys. Since the central concern here is to track the plays and the repertories which are their context here, rather than the companies and the playhouses, it is appropriate to continue this section with the history of the new occupants of the Cockpit, Beeston's Boys, and look at the other hall-playhouse companies later.

The company that entered the scene in 1637 at the Cockpit to rival the King's at Blackfriars was another group composed largely of youngsters. Beeston's Boys, as

[7] Ibid. 66.   [8] *MSC* ii. 3. 382.

Herbert called them, or the King and Queen's Young Company, first appear in the records on 21 February 1637, in a 'Warrant to sweare Mr Christopher Bieston his Majestes servant in ye place of Govvernor of the new Company of the Kinges & Queenes boyes'.[9] Beeston had been planning this new group for some time. Besides himself and his son William, he took the youngsters Theophilus Bird, Ezekiel Fenn, and John Page from the former Cockpit company, plus the older men Robert Axen and the itinerant George Stutville, who had joined Queen Henrietta's company before the closure. The fencer Edward Gibbs came from the Revels, who were then playing at the Fortune, and Samuel Mannery and John Wright came from the Prince's at the Red Bull. Two boys, William Trigg and Nicholas Burt, came from the King's. The senior helpers to the 'govvernor' did not loom large early on, because a Privy-Council order of 12 May 1637 to keep the theatre closed names the responsible bodies as 'Christopher and Wm Biston Theophilus Bird Ezech: Fenn & Michael Moone'.[10] Altogether, according to a warrant of the Lord Chamberlain's in August 1639, there were at least twelve 'boys' besides the adults in the company. They were named as 'Robert Axon William Trig: John Lacie: John Page, Michaell Moone: Robert Coxe: Edward Davenport: Ezechiell Fenne: Robert Shatterell: Edward Gibbes: John Wright Samuell Manuray'.[11]

The new company's repertory is uniquely well known because of a slightly odd order issued by the Lord Chamberlain on the same day as his warrant for the players, 10 August 1639. It was prompted by William Beeston, who had taken the company over after his father died in October 1638, and is probably the younger Beeston's checklist of the best playbooks he had inherited from his father. Some of them go back more than thirty years, to the first days of Queen Anne's Men and before. The forty-five titles are all recognizable, and almost all the texts are extant. The order reads:

Wheras Wiliam Bieston Gent Govvernor &c of the kinges and Queenes young Company of Players at the Cockpitt in Drury Lane hath represented unto his Majestye that ye severall Playes heerafter mentioned (vizt) Witt without money: The Night Walkers: The Knight of the burning pestill: Fathers owne sonne Cupids Revenge: The Bondman: The Renegado: A new way to pay debts: The great Duke of Florance: The maid of honor: The Traytor: The Example: The young Admirall: the oportunity: A witty fayre one: Loves cruelty The Wedding: the Maids Revenge: The Lady of pleasure: The schoole of complement: The gratefull servant: The Coronation: Hide parke: Philip Chabot Admirall of France: A mad couple well mett: Alls Lost by Lust: The Changeling: A fayre quarrell: The spanish gipsie: The World: The Sunnes Darling: Loves Sacrifice: Tis pitty shee's a Whore: George a greene: Loves Mistress: The Cunning Lovers: the rape of Lucrece: A trick to cheat the Divell: A foole & her maydenhead soone parted King John & Matilda. A Citty night cap: The bloody banquett: Cupids Vagaries: the conceited Duke & Appius & Virginia doe all & every of them properly & of right belong to the sayd House, and consequently that they are all in his propriety: And to the end that any other Companies of Actors in or about London shall not presume to act any of them to ye prejudice of him the said William Bieston and his

---

[9] *MSC* ii. 3. 382.   [10] *MSC* i. 5. 392.   [11] *MSC* ii. 3. 390–1.

Company: his Majesty hath signified his royall pleasure unto me: thereby requireing mee to declare soe much to all other Companyes of Actors heerby concernable: that they are not in any wayes to intermedle with or Act any of th'above mentioned Playes.[12]

In its way this list marks the ultimate step from the commissioning and ownership of plays by company sharers, which still prevailed under Henslowe, to impresario control. That was Christopher Beeston's single most substantial accomplishment in his more than forty years of playing and managing up to his death in 1639.[13] None of the companies who performed at the Cockpit ever took their plays away with them when they left his playhouse. The warrant has a strongly defensive tone, which may be a hint that some of the other companies did not agree with this possessiveness.

The last years of the Boys under their new Beeston were quite as warlike as the protective tone of the note in the warrant might lead us to expect. In May 1640 William Beeston, Stutville, and Moone (or Mohun) were put in the Marshalsea for acting an unlicensed play. It was unlicensed presumably because the players knew it might give offence, as it duly did. Herbert noted that 'the play I calde for, and, forbiddinge the playinge of it, keepe the booke, because it had relation to the passages of the K.s journey into the Northe, and was complayned of by his Majestye to mee, with commande to punishe the offenders'.[14] It was the king who ordered the Lord Chamberlain to protect Beeston's right to his plays in 1639, but his interest in playgoing also made him more quickly alert than his predecessors to any satirical applications. It was most likely this offence that ousted the younger Beeston from his managerial role in 1640.

In his place William Davenant, principal writer for the King's Men and would-be investor in a grand new playhouse, was made the company's new 'governor'. Impresario control was still far from absolute, and government orders still largely directed what happened to the companies. The Lord Chamberlain issued an order dated 27 June 1640 giving control of the Beeston company to Davenant. Directed to the Cockpit company, it stated, 'I doe heerby injoyne & commaund them all, and every of them that are soe authorized to play in the sayd House under the previledge of his or her Majestes servantes; and every one belonging as prentices or servantes to those Actors to play under the sayd previledge that they obey the sayd Mr Davenant & follow his Order & direccions as they will answer the contrary'.[15] Selling playgoing to the general public was not yet an entirely private enterprise. Authority still had the final word in disposing the London companies. It was government control of playing as a quasi-monopoly.

What the financial deals were between Beeston as property-owner of the play-house and Davenant as the new manager of its resident company consequent on this transfer of managerial duties we do not know. As it happened, Davenant did not enjoy his new managerial control for long. He had been less than a year in the

---

[12] Ibid.   [13] His will is transcribed in *Playhouse Wills 1558–1642*, 191–4.
[14] *Herbert Dramatic Records*, 66.   [15] *MSC* ii. 3. 395.

job when his entanglement in the theatrical and more-than-farcical Army Plot got him put in prison. A subsequent list in the Chamberlain's records names the playhouse owner once again as 'Governor of ye Cockpitt Players'.[16] But by then the younger Beeston did not have much time left for the job either.

The Salisbury Court company that opened at the newly built playhouse in Whitefriars in 1629 called itself the King's Revels. It renewed an older habit of the companies at hall playhouses, using a markedly higher proportion of young players than the other companies. Richard Gunnell of the Fortune was the impresario who built the theatre. He set the new King's Revels up as a company whose composition looked back to the Jacobean period, while it also anticipated Beeston's 1637 innovation by comprising a majority of boys or youths. Gunnell already had an adult company at the Fortune, of which he was now the manager.

In its first years the Salisbury Court company ranged itself rather self-consciously behind the King's and Queen's Men as a smaller-scale operation. Salisbury Court had a smaller auditorium-capacity than the other two halls, and the company acknowledged its lower status in a prologue that Shackerley Marmion wrote for the production of his *Holland's Leaguer* there in 1631, where he claimed to be not quite overawed by the 'two great Lawrels' that 'over-top us', the Blackfriars and the Cockpit.[17]

Although no patents were now being issued, and it was a fifth London theatre, it does seem to have been an officially approved enterprise, to judge from a contemporary account which implies that Gunnell's lease of the property from the earl of Dorset had Herbert's approval. George Gresley wrote that the lease was 'unto the master of the revels, to make a playhouse for the children of the revels'.[18] Henry Herbert kept tight control of the London companies. There had been no Revels Children for some years, and the initiative and perhaps the name most likely came from Gunnell. He may have felt at first that another hall playhouse needed the protective guise of a children's company. So far as we can tell, he used a core of five or six experienced players, and made the numbers up with young players. Its starting date can most properly be set by the opening of the new hall-playhouse, in the middle of 1629. The company that visited Carlisle on 29 July 1628, calling itself the 'kings Ravelles', was most likely a remnant company of the old Revels Children, led by the Nicholas Hanson who visited Coventry with a similar group in 1628. Its name may have been taken by Gunnell as an ostensible resurrection of the former London company.

Timothy Reade was the new company's nimble clown. He had been in Queen Henrietta's Men when they staged Shirley's *The Wedding* in 1626, but moved to

[16] *MSC* ii. 3. 326.
[17] *Holland's Leaguer* (1632), Prologue. This was actually written for the Prince's Men who took over the theatre at the end of 1631, and may reflect the nervousness of these new arrivals on the hall-theatre scene.
[18] R. F. Williams (ed.), *The Court and Times of Charles I* (2 vols.; London, 1849), ii. 35.

Salisbury Court when it opened with its young company in 1629. Both of the William Cartwrights, father and son, were also long-time servers at Salisbury Court. Few plays can with reasonable confidence be ascribed to the company in their first two years. Apart from a play by Marmion, *A Fine Companion*, there is only Shirley's *The Changes* which can confidently be allocated to them. Its title-page ascribes it to 'the Company of His Majesties Revels', and sets the play at Salisbury Court. Why Shirley gave this one play to them instead of his usual customer, Beeston, we do not know; but it suggests he had a special commission to help launch the new enterprise.

The King's Revels ran for two fairly quiet years before Gunnell, Alleyn's successor at the Fortune, made the first of a number of curious transfers in this decade between playhouses, switching his two companies between the Salisbury Court youths and the Fortune adults. So in 1631 the newly created Prince Charles's (II) Company, made up largely from the former Bohemia's players who had been playing at the Fortune, moved into the hall, and the King's Revels left the hall for the amphitheatre. It was in some ways a remarkable shift, because the two leading players from the Palsgrave's/Bohemia's company were Richard Fowler, later to gain a reputation as the noisiest and most physical of the amphitheatre tragedians, and Andrew Cane, the amphitheatre's most popular clown and jig-maker. Royal companies evidently needed hall theatres.

The new prince's company played for the usual stint of three years at the Salisbury Court before reverting to another amphitheatre, this time the Red Bull, in 1634. The social division of audiences that is commonly made between the halls and the amphitheatres, with their élite and popular audiences, is complicated by the fact that for three years, from 1631 to 1634, the third and smallest of the three hall-playhouses was occupied by the most apparently strident and downmarket of the amphitheatre companies.

There is regrettably little evidence for what was in the repertory of Prince Charles's (II) company, this newcomer among the royally patronized companies. How many plays from the Bohemia repertory or how many of the drum-and-trumpet plays that the company subsequently ran first at the Red Bull and then at the Fortune were in their list to start with, we can only guess. They did launch their presence at Salisbury Court with *Holland's Leaguer*, a topical tale with a long section about the recent notorious siege of the Southwark brothel of that name. The printed text of 1632 is confusing, probably because it was heavily censored before being released to the press. Its apologetic prologue about being overawed by the two greater halls belongs to this time. It actually had an almost unprecedented run for the period of as much as six days at Salisbury Court. Unfortunately little else survives to say what else the former amphitheatre company chose to run during its three years at this hall.

Only one incident from this period of the Prince Charles's (II) group was recorded. A letter of February 1632 from Thomas Tuke in London to Sir William Armine in Lincolnshire reported the latest city news, including the fact that:

in the space of 9 daies eight died suddenly, the last of which was a Player, who fell down suddenly upon the stage in the play-house in Salsbury court in the sight of all the spectators, wheroff diverse were Lords, come to hear a new play, wherein this man had his part, a lusty young fellow, about 30 years of age. They carried him out into the air, but all done, they could, he so died. This hapned upon fryday last. I say no more but God make us all fit for his kingdome![19]

The records of the company's players are insufficient to identify this spectacular victim.

The switches that came in 1634 were drastic for all three of the companies that now ran behind the King's at Blackfriars and Queen Henrietta's at the Cockpit. The most likely immediate cause of the changes was Gunnell's death at some point in 1634. Both of his playhouses were involved in the changes, along with the Red Bull. The Salisbury Court group, Prince Charles's Men led by Fowler and Cane, went across to play at the Red Bull, where they remained for the next six years. The young King's Revels company who had started the Salisbury Court's career in 1629 now returned there, possibly reflecting a renewal of his old intentions before his death by Gunnell; while the Revels company who had been playing at the Red Bull went to the Fortune, presumably at Gunnell's invitation, since it was now vacated by the King's Revels. What besides the usual three-year turnover prompted these switches we cannot tell. It would help a lot to know just when in this musical chairs Gunnell left the scene. He was still in being in July 1634, when the King's Revels were already back at the hall playhouse. He may have made his new dispositions knowing that he was near death, to redispose his assets. In the redispositions the ambitions of the man who took over as impresario at Salisbury Court, Richard Heton, may have been a factor. His drive showed up more clearly in the next change three years later.

The best evidence about the King's Revels company that returned to the Salisbury Court in 1634 comes from one of its two wardrobe-keepers, Richard Kendall. When the company came to Oxford on its travels in July of that year he talked to a Fellow of Queen's College, Thomas Crosfield, who kept a diary and made notes from their discussion. Kendall described the new arrangement of all five London companies, the King's, the Queen's, the Prince's who were now at the Red Bull, the Fortune company, and the King's Revels. Crosfield noted of Kendall's own company:

The Company of Salisbury Court at ye further end of fleet street against ye Conduit: The cheife whereof are 1. Mr. Gunnell a Papist. 2. Mr. John Yongue. 3. Edward Gibbs a fencer. 4. Timothy Reed. 5. Christofer Goad. 6. Sam. Thompson. 7. Mr. Staffeild. 8. John Robinson. 9. Courteous Grevill. these are ye cheife whereof 7 are called sharers i.e. such as pay wages to ye servants & equally share in the overplus: other servants there are as 2 Close keepers [Richard Kendall Anthony Dover &c.]

[19] Tuke's letters were found by James Knowles in the Somerset Record Office, DD/FJ 25. A selection is to be printed in the *REED* volume for Lincolnshire. I am grateful to Bill Cooke at the *REED* offices for drawing the letters to my attention.

Of all these Companies ye first if they please may come to Oxon, but none without speciall lettres from the Chancellor obteined by meanes of ye Secretary to the ViceChancelour. ... A Crosse mischance happened in this company because of a boy yt quarrelled with a Scholar in ye Taverne. They came furnished with 14 playes. And lodged at ye Kings Armes, where Franklin hath about £3 a day while they stay, i.e. for every play 4 nobles besides ye benefit of seates.[20]

This tells a lot. Of the seven sharers, the recusant Gunnell was still the manager and financier, part-owner of the Salisbury Court playhouse with William Blagrave from the Revels Office. John Young, Timothy Read, and Christopher Goad were Queen Henrietta's Servants in the 1620s and had joined the Revels company when it was first formed in 1629. Edward Gibbs is not known before this entry. In 1639 he was in the Beeston's Boys company. 'Staffeild' is probably George Stutville, who had been with different companies at the Red Bull and the Cockpit, and was a notable leader of Caroline touring groups. He does not seem to have stayed long with any of the London companies. John Robinson stayed longest in the King's Revels group. He married an Elizabeth Gunnell who was most likely a relative and possibly the widow of the company manager. He wrote verses for the publication of the company's *Messallina* in 1640.[21] 'Courteous' or Curtis Greville was in the Fortune company in 1622 and later in the King's. He too had probably been one of the first helpers with the new young company in 1629.

The total of fourteen plays that the company was travelling with is also intriguing, since it appears to be an unnecessarily large repertoire for a company which certainly could not have expected to play every example from its stock at each town it visited. Conceivably it was travelling with its entire stock of playbooks, which may be a sign of doubt about the security of its tenure of a London playhouse. The number of plays is doubly intriguing since the British Library MS Egerton 1994 is a transcription of fourteen plays, including *Edmund Ironside*. It does appear to be a touring company's collection from the third decade of the century, and although its provenance is unknown it may be the stock that the King's Revels took to Oxford.

A list in the Norwich records of the players in the company who visited there in 1635 adds another twenty-one names to the Oxford list. Besides Stutville, Young, Goad, Read, Robinson, and Dover and Kendall the wardrobe keepers, it includes John Barrett, Ellis Bedowe, Thomas Bourne, Antony Bray, the Cartwrights father and son, James Ferret, Henry Field, John Harris, Thomas Jordan, Thomas Loveday, Thomas Lovell, Maivrin, Edward May, Mistale, Thomas Sands, John Stretch, Roger Tosedall, William Wilbraham, George Williams, and Walter Williams.[22] Most of these names occur in no other records anywhere. They certainly include the boys or youths that were still in the group, and the assistants like Dover and Kendall. The only other substantial listing of the company's players

[20] F. S. Boas (ed.), *The Diary of Thomas Crosfield* (London, 1935), 72–3. Boas conjectured that MS Egerton 1994 may be the stock that Crosfield noted in the company's possession.
[21] His will is transcribed in *Playhouse Wills 1558–1642*, 201. Richard Fowler signed as a witness to it.
[22] *REED, Norwich*, 218. The spelling of the names has been standardized.

comes from the cast of *Messallina*, some years later. It has Christopher Goad, Samuel Thompson, John Robinson, William Cartwright senior, Richard Johnson, William Hall, John Barrett, Thomas Jordan, and Mathias Morris, who might be either the Maivrin or the Mistale of the Norwich list. Richard Johnson and William Hall are the only newcomers. Hall, like Cartwright senior, was a Prince Charles's (II) man at Salisbury Court in 1632, and may have shifted companies when the two groups switched playhouses in 1634. Barrett, Jordan and Morris may have been boys, since they took the women's parts in *Messallina*.

For all the names that Kendall gave the highest status to, this was basically a manager's enterprise rather than a company of playing sharers. The first payee for their plays at court in 1631 (though he did not get the money until January 1635)[23] was Gunnell's partner in the playhouse, William Blagrave. Blagrave, like Edward Kirkham before him, worked in the Revels Office as a deputy to Henry Herbert from 1624. Gunnell no doubt valued Blagrave's investment as a further insurance for his new venture, now that the Revels Office licensed and controlled the companies more directly than before. He had changed from player to impresario like Beeston before him. There are distinct similarities between Gunnell's activities in running the Fortune and the Salisbury Court in the 1630s, and Beeston's management of the Cockpit and the Red Bull under James.

Two plays that shifted ground with the King's Revels' first switch from the hall to the amphitheatre in 1631 were Thomas Randolph's earliest attempts at theatre writing, *The Muses' Looking Glass* and *Amyntas*. The first of these was licensed by Herbert when the playhouses reopened in November 1630. With the young William Heminges's first play in March 1633, *The Madcap, or the Coursing of the Hare*, now lost, these plays show how ready Gunnell was early on to try his hand and his hall company on new writers for the new hall. The company's other known play of 1634, after returning to the hall playhouse, was intended to match the new sensation at the Globe, Brome and Heywood's *Late Lancashire Witches*. That story is set out in Chapter 8. Herbert licensed *Doctor Lambe and the Witches* halfway through the month when the King's Men were staging their play, having held it back for his own reasons. He licensed it as 'an ould play, with some new scenes',[24] which were added to make use of the newsworthy Lancashire witches. Gunnell staged it at Salisbury Court rather than the Fortune, where it might have matched the Globe play more exactly. That in its own way may have been a tactful gesture, since Dr Lamb had been killed by a mob after being identified at the Fortune at a play in 1628.

Gunnell died late in 1634 or 1635. There is nothing to say who took over his interest in the Fortune, but Richard Heton took his place at Salisbury Court. This new impresario had never been a player as Gunnell or Beeston were, and had little patience either with players or writers. He took the payment for the company's court performances in the 1635–6 season. In July of the same year he contracted

---

[23] *MSC* ii. 3. 375.　　[24] *Herbert Dramatic Records*, 36.

Richard Brome to write for the company, having staged his *Asparagus Garden* in 1635. It is a symptom of the rising status of managers and impresarios that Brome's contract was with the playhouse manager, not with the company.

Only two of Brome's plays for the Revels company can be identified, so it is not easy to see how his writing may have reflected the company's orientation in its repertory. They seem to have held a middle position, using Brome for his populist subjects and for his affiliation with the almost-legendary Jonson, ready to cash in with a witches-play when occasion called, but also inching upwards into the critical and social sensitivities of the more elevated social levels of playgoing that Randolph exploited in *The Muses' Looking Glass*. Without any confirmation about the provenance of the Egerton manuscript of plays, too few of the fourteen that Kendall reported the company as carrying on tour in 1634 have survived to give any clear sense of their cultural role or position in the 1630s. Prosperous though they were, like the company at their larger neighbour, the Cockpit, they died in the long plague closure and the consequent reshuffles of 1636 and 1637.

Heton proved himself to be a strong-minded impresario. When Beeston severed relations with his long-established Queen Henrietta's company in 1637, Heton took it on at Salisbury Court, and gave it his old stock of Salisbury Court plays. But if he was to operate at a standard approaching the two other hall companies he needed more. That led him to the law. The hard-nosed impresario's wrangles while he fought to get new scripts from his writers by insisting they met the terms of their contracts give the most detail about this phase of the company's life that we have. Heton kept Richard Brome under contract, though Brome would have preferred to move to the new Beeston enterprise. Heton expected him to produce three plays a year, but he only produced four in all, and sold a fifth to Christopher Beeston's son William in 1639.[25] Heton then prosecuted Brome for breach of contract. He was also searching for new writers. Shirley came in from Dublin and sold him a play, *The Gentleman of Venice*, in 1639. Lovelace gave him *The Scholars* at about the same time, and Sharpe sold him *The Noble Stranger*. *The Politician* was printed in 1655 as played by Queen Henrietta's at Salisbury Court. *The Fatal Contract*, by William Heminges, son of John, probably also came to the company in these years.

Brome's more-than-ambivalent feelings about Heton as impresario and the Salisbury-Court company appear in the note for the reader that he attached to the 1640 quarto of *The Antipodes*, the last of his plays for Heton. It says, '*you shal find in this Booke more then was presented upon the* Stage, *and left out of the* Presentation, *for superfluous length (as some of the* Players *pretended) I thoght good al should be inserted according to the allowed* Original; *and as it was, at first, intended for the* Cock-pit Stage'. He adds a plug for '*my most deserving friend Mr.* William Beeston, *unto whom it properly appertained*', pointedly ignoring Heton. But he concedes that '*it was generally applauded, and well acted at* Salisbury Court'.

[25] For a full account of Heton's lawsuit against Brome, see Ann Haaker, 'The Plague, the Theater and the Poet', *Renaissance Drama*, n.s. 1 (1968), 283–306.

Heton's managerial style was autocratic, quite distinct from the collective de-cision-making of the amphitheatre companies and the King's Men, and different from Beeston's, who always kept a velvet glove on his iron hand. It reflects the degree of control that impresarios in effect always had, though they did not often use it so brutally. Heton drew up a paper in 1639 stipulating that he, rather than the company, must be the patent holder, and that he had the right to hire and fire as he thought fit. Whether there was any particular spat that prompted his composition of this remarkable document we do not know. It was a declaration of managerial rights, using the term 'governor' that appeared in the same year on the offical warrant for Beeston's Boys, and insisting on Henry Herbert's backing for his control.

That such of the company as will not be ordered and governed by me as of their governor, or shall not by the Mr of his Majesties Revells and my selfe bee thought fitt Comedians for her Majesties service, I may have power to discharge from the Company, and, with the advice of the Mr of the Revells, to putt new ones in their places; and those who shalbe soe descharged not to have the honor to be her Majesties servants, but only those who shall continew at the aforesaid playhouse.[26]

There is more than a touch of self-protection in this insistence that the manager or 'governor' worked hand in hand with the Master of the Revels. It is an appeal to higher authority, not just to guard against unruly players but against the rising political pressures. Like the two larger hall playhouses, Salisbury Court was heavily dependent on royal favour. Its location in the Whitefriars was convenient for gentle audiences, but its capacity, smaller than either the Blackfriars or the Cockpit, perhaps called for a tighter managerial rein. Heton's self-protective use of Henry Herbert came to an end three years later, after what we have to assume was an era of continuing prosperity, at least for Heton and Herbert. The Queen's company was not called to perform at court at all during its tenure at Salisbury Court.

QUEEN HENRIETTA'S MEN, 1626–1642

Plays
All's Lost by Lust (old), *The Antipodes*, *The Antiquary*, *The Arcadia*, *The Ball*, *The Bird in a Cage*, *Chabot* (old), *The Changeling* (old), *The City Night-cap* (old), *Claracilla*, *The Constant Maid*, *The Coronation*, *Covent Garden*, *The Duke's Mistress*, *The English Traveller*, *The Example*, 1 and 2 *The Fair Maid of the West*, *The Fancies Chaste and Noble*, *The Fatal Contract*, *Fortune by Land and Sea*,[27] *The Gamester*, *The Gentleman of Venice*, *The Grateful Servant*, *The Great Duke of Florence*, *Hannibal and Scipio*, *The Hollander*, *The Honest Whore* (old), *The Humorous Courtier*, *Hyde*

---

[26] *JCS*: vi. 104–5. The document itself is a draft, and there is no guarantee that it came into force. But its drift is like a tidal wave.

[27] This play, by Rowley and Heywood, was printed in 1655 as 'Acted with great Applause by the Queenes Majesties Servants'. Rowley worked with the Prince's, not with Queen Anne's Men, up to 1625, so it seems more likely that this play belongs to Queen Henrietta's Men, for whom Heywood certainly wrote.

Park, *Hymen's Holiday* (old, lost), *If You Know Not Me, You Know Nobody* (old), *The Jew of Malta* (old), *King John and Matilda*, *The Knight of the Burning Pestle* (old), *The Lady of Pleasure*, *Love's Cruelty*, *Love's Mistress*, *Love's Sacrifice*, *A Mad World my Masters* (old), *The Maid of Honour*, *A Maidenhead Well Lost*, *The Maid's Revenge*, *The Martyred Soldier*, *Microcosmus*, *A New Way to Pay Old Debts*, *The Night Walker*, *The Noble Stranger*, *The Opportunity*, *Perkin Warbeck*, *The Politician*, *The Rape of Lucrece* (old), *The Renegado* (old), *The Royal King and the Loyal Subject*, *The Scholars* (lost), *The School of Compliment*, *The Shepherd's Holiday*, *The Spanish Gipsy* (old), *A Tale of a Tub*, *'Tis Pity She's a Whore*, *Tottenham Court*, *The Traitor*, *The Wedding*, *The White Devil* (old), *Wit without Money*, *The Witch of Edmonton* (old), *The Witty Fair One*, *The Young Admiral*.

Playing Sharers
Richard Perkins, William Allen, Robert Axen, John Blaney, Michael Bowyer, John Dobson, Christopher Goad, Timothy Reade, William Reignolds, William Robinson, Edward Shakerley, William Sherlock, John Sumner, Anthony Turner, William Wilbraham, John Young,[28] George Stutville, [travelling only] Richard Errington, Elias Guest.

Apprentices
Theophilus Bird, Hugh Clark, John Page, Edward Rogers.[29]

London Playhouses
Cockpit, Salisbury Court.

At Court
10 unnamed plays Oct. 1629–Feb. 1630; 16 unnamed plays 10 Oct.–20 Feb. 1631; 9 unnamed plays from Oct.; 14 unnamed plays Nov.–Feb. 1633; 7 plays up to 24 Mar. 1634 before the king and queen, including 19 Nov. (*The Young Admiral*), 16 Dec. (*Hymen's Holiday*), 14 Jan. 1634 (*A Tale of a Tub*), 30 Jan. (*The Night Walker*), 6 Feb. (*The Gamester*); 8 unnamed plays up to 10 Feb. 1635 before the queen; 9 plays up to 25 Mar. 1636, including 28 Feb. (*The Knight of the Burning Pestle*); 7 unnamed plays 1638–9.

Travelling Records
Reading 12 Nov. 1630 'Ellys Guest hath licens & company' / Reading 18 July 1631 'Ellis Guest Richard Errington and their company Players shewed their licence under the seale of the mr of the Revells dated the 15th of July 1631 to endure six monethes . . . Desired leave to playe but did not'. / Doncaster 22 Dec. 1632, 10s. / Norwich 22 June 1633 'Elias Gost and his Company of the Quenes players haveinge shewed to mr Maior their patent were desired to forbeare And had Twenty Shillinges as a gratuity given to him', 20s. / Norwich 13 Sept. 1634 'Elias

---

[28] On the evidence of the cast list for *The Renegado*, one of the new company's first plays, Bentley (*JCS* i. 221) suggests that Blaney, Reignolds, and Shakerley had been replaced by Perkins, Sherlock, and Turner by the time that *The Wedding* was staged in May 1626. He sees these newcomers as acquisitions made after the company was started from former Queen Anne's/Revels players.

[29] *JCS* i. 220.

Guest one of the players in the said Lycence [dated 25 June 1634]', 'for that they did forbeare to play', 40s. / Coventry Nov. acct. 1636, 25s.

BEESTON'S BOYS (THE KING AND QUEEN'S YOUNG company), 1637–1642

Plays
All's Lost by Lust (old), *Argalus and Parthenia, The Bloody Banquet, The Bondman* (old), *The Changeling* (old), 1 *The Cid, The City Nightcap* (old), *The Coronation* (old), *The Court Beggar, The Cunning Lovers, Cupid's Revenge* (old), *The Example* (old), *A Fair Quarrel* (old), *The Grateful Servant* (old), *The Great Duke of Florence* (old), *A Jovial Crew, King John and Matilda* (old), *The Lady of Pleasure* (old), *The Lady's Privilege, The Lady's Trial, Love Tricks* (old), *Love's Cruelty* (old), *Love's Sacrifice* (old), *The Maid of Honour* (old), *The Maid's Revenge* (old), *A New Way to Pay Old Debts* (old), *The Rape of Lucrece* (old), *The Renegado* (old), *The Spanish Gipsy* (old), *'Tis Pity She's a Whore* (old), *The Wedding* (old), *Wit in a Constable, Wit without Money, The Young Admiral* (old).

Managers
Christopher Beeston, William Beeston, William Davenant.

Players
Robert Axen, Theophilus Bird, Nicholas Burt, Ezekiel Fenn, Edward Gibbs, Samuel Mannery, John Page, George Stutville, William Trigg, John Wright. [Chamberlain's warrant of August 1639: 'Robert Axon William Trig: John Lacie: John Page, Michaell Moone: Robert Coxe: Edward Davenport: Ezechiell Fenne: Robert Shatterell: Edward Gibbes: John Wright Samuell Manuray'].

London Playhouses
Cockpit.

At Court
7 Feb. 1637 (*Cupid's Revenge*), 14 Feb. (*Wit without Money*).

Travelling
no records.

KING'S REVELS MEN, 1629–1636

[See also Queen Henrietta's.]

Plays
Amyntas, Doctor Lambe and the Witches (old, lost), *Sir Giles Goosecap* (old), *The Lady Mother, The Madcap* (lost), *Messallina, The Muses' Looking Glass, The Proxy* (lost), *The Queen and Concubine, The Rebellion, The Sparagus Garden*.

Playing Sharers
[*Messallina* cast-list] William Cartwright snr, Christopher Goad, William Hall, Richard Johnson, John Robinson. [Crosfield diary:[30] '1. Mr. Gunnell a Papist. 2.

---

[30] *JCS* ii. 688.

Mr. John Yongue. 3. Edward Gibbs a fencer. 4. Timothy Reed. 5. Christofer Goad. 6. Sam Thompson. 7. Mr. Staffeild. 8. John Robinson. 9. Courteous Grevill.']. [Norwich 1635: 'George Stutville, John Yonge Edward May william Wilbraham william Cartwright senior william Cartwright junior christofer Goade Timothy Reade Thomas Bourne John Robynson Thomas Lovell Thomas Sandes Thomas Jorden walter willyams John Barret Thomas Loveday John Harris Antony Dover Richard Kendall Roger Tesedall Elis Bedowe—Mawrice—Misdale John Stretch Henry Field George willans James Ferret & Antony Bray]. [Travellers only: Robert Kempton, William Daniell, Nathaniel Clay, Thomas Holman]. [Nottingham 1632–3: Kompton (probably a mistake for Robert Kempston, listed at Reading in 1630, Norwich in 1632 and at Coventry with John Carr as 'Knipston' in 1631).]

Boys
[*Messallina* cast-list] John Barrett, Thomas Jordan, Mathias Morris.

London Playhouses
Salisbury Court 1629–31, Fortune 1631–4, Salisbury Court 1634–6.

At Court
3 plays in 1631, 3 plays Oct. 1635 and Feb. 1636, including 24 Feb. (*The Proxy*).

Travelling Records
Nottingham 1628–9 'the playeres of the Revelles',[31] 10s. / Nottingham 1629–30 'the kinges plaiors of the Revelles', 12s. / Reading 12 Nov. 1630 'Robert Kimpton Nathaniell Clay Thomas Holman & others named in the license from the Master of the Revells dated the 30th of December 1629 tendred themselves to play in Towne but did not and were here in Lent last'[32] / Nottingham 1630–1 'the kinges playeres of the Revelles', 10s. / Coventry 23 Sept. 1631 'to Robert Knipton & John Carre players of the Revells', 5s. / Norwich 8 Sept. 1632 'Robert Kempston and other of his Company of the Revelles' / Nottingham 1632–3 'Kompton & his assosiates of the Revelles', 10s. / Oxford July 1634 / Nottingham 1633–4 'a Companie of playeres of the Revelles', 6s. 8d. / Norwich 10 Mar. 1635 'This day George Stutvile came up to this Court & did give the names of the rest of his Company videlicet John Yonge Edward May william Wilbraham william Cartwright senior william Cartwright junior christofer Goade Timothy Reade Thomas Bourne John Robynson Thomas Lovell Thomas Sandes Thomas Jorden walter willyams John Barret Thomas Loveday John Harris Antony Dover Richard Kendall Roger Tesedall Elis Bedowe—Mawrice—Misdale John Stretch Henry Field George willans James Ferret & Antony Bray . . . absolutely forbidden to play any longer in

[31] It is not clear exactly which company this name applies to. Now that Henry Herbert was issuing all licences in the king's name, and patrons were no longer supplying their livery to identify their playing servants, the general title 'Revels', and even 'King's', might be applied by the local clerks to whatever company was visiting. This group and the one that came to Nottingham in the following year might have been the Salisbury Court company, or one of the touring children's companies, or the Red Bull Revels company.

[32] This and other Berkshire records are transcribed from the *REED, Berkshire, Buckinghamshire and Oxfordshire*, ed. Alexandra Johnston, forthcoming. An entry for Blandford, Dorset, in 1631 'unto the Children of the Revells, that should have acted a stage play in the hall', 10s., may relate to this company or possibly even to a renewal of the Bristol boy group led by John Daniel in 1616.

this City' / Coventry June 1635 'to William Daniell', 10s. / Norwich 3 Sept. 1635 'A Patent under the hand & seale of Sir Henry Herbert master of the Revelles bearinge date the 28th of November 1634 made to william Danyell william Hart John Townesend Samuell Minion Hugh Haughton Thomas Doughton and the rest of their Company not exceedinge the number of Fiftene persons to play Comedies &c . . . his sute beinge not granted hee had in liew thereof a gratuety of tenn shillinges', 10s. / Nottingham 1635–6 'the Kinges playeres of the Court', 10s. / Leicester 22 Apr. 1636, £1. / Coventry 22 Apr. 1636 'to Richard Erington & William Deniell players of the Revelles', 22s. / Bristol June–Sept 1636 'to the players of his majesties Revells', £1. / Tenterden, Kent 1636–7 'to Stage playes beinge authorized under the kinges Revells', 10s. / Gloucester 1636–7 'payd unto William Daniell one of the Kings Revells because he should not playe beeing in the contagious tyme', £1. 6s. 8d. / Leicester 1637 'ye kinges Revilles', £1. / Coventry 5 Dec. 1637, 10s.

24 The Caroline Amphitheatre Companies: The King and Queen of Bohemia's Men, 1626–1631, Prince Charles's (II) Men, 1631–1642 and The Red Bull Company, 1626–1642

As noted at the beginning of Chapter 23, for all the increasing distinction that playgoers made in Caroline years between the hall-playhouse companies and the amphitheatre companies, grouping them separately by the kind of playhouse they performed in can be misleading. Besides the King's Men straddling the two kinds of venue, the fact that one of the 'citizen' companies switched places with a hall company without any visible sign of discomfort either for their repertory, their acting style, or their playgoers suggests that company loyalty was never as fixed as audience loyalty. The court put its thumb into some of the hall-playhouse activities, but below that level of rich plums the general run of audiences proved more loyal to the playhouses than to individual companies and their repertories. Essentially it was the court itself which made the chief distinction between the hall companies and the amphitheatre or 'citizen' companies. Of the three groups that used the Fortune and the Red Bull between 1625 and 1642 only one was ever called to perform at court, and that promotion more likely came to them because their patron was the young Prince Charles than for any special quality that Herbert found in the amphitheatre players or their plays.

That bias at court in the Caroline period makes the identification of the companies no easier, thanks to the disappearance of the patron system and the convenient clarity of its naming. For that reason, if no other, from 1625 onwards it is simplest to name the companies by their playhouses, although not even that nomenclature is straightforward when the companies shifted playhouse so often, and especially since the companies playing at the two amphitheatres twice exchanged their playhouses.

Membership, playing venues, repertory, and even company names were a fluid set of commodities under Charles. When playing resumed after the long and deep closure of 1625, not much of the Jacobean system of 'foure companyes' was left intact. Four companies did resume playing, but three of them were new. The King's Men, of course, continued, but the Palsgrave's at the Fortune, the Revels players at the Red Bull and the Prince's at the Cockpit all regrouped and secured new names. Beeston plundered several companies for his own new group at the Cockpit. Some of the Palsgrave's players linked up with their patron's wife's players, led by Joseph Moore, to form a joint company at the Fortune. The Red Bull restarted with what was left. The playing companies proved more malleable than their playing venues, so it makes sense to follow the story of the Fortune and the Red Bull companies together through these years. They did share some distinctive features in their activities, hostile to one another though they became at times. Not only was their reputation markedly similar, but they actually exchanged their playhouses twice, in 1634 and 1640. Company make-up and repertories were more fluid than the 'citizen-playhouse' label implies. There were actually two Red Bull companies and two Fortune companies through this sixteen years, and the third of the hall playhouses took a share in this complex game of musical playhouses.

The Fortune, probably because Richard Gunnell was its player-impresario, kept more continuity in its company membership than the Red Bull. Its initial composition was given some continuity by the Palsgrave's, who had played there up to 1625. Their core was augmented with some of the Lady Elizabeth's, which had been at Beeston's Cockpit. This grouping lasted till 1631. Then from 1631 to 1634 the Fortune was occupied by the new Red Bull King's Revels company. This grouping was made up in part from the Bohemia's company previously playing there, and probably had the same plays. The Red Bull company which exchanged places with them in 1631 also had some continuity, with the core of the Revels company which had been at the other amphitheatre since before 1625.

That neither amphitheatre company now had a patron of any kind and was never called to perform at court is a mark of how the court under Charles relegated the amphitheatres below account. That the Fortune company took over the hall at Salisbury Court between 1634 and 1637, and that the former Salisbury Court company, Prince Charles's (II) Company, went to the Red Bull in 1634 is a measure of how content the court now was to rely on the Blackfriars and the Cockpit to provide its entertainment, and mostly to leave the other three companies and their playhouses, either hall or amphitheatre, to themselves. For the first time in the period of these last two chapters the social standing of the playhouses becomes consistently a more powerful influence on status at court than do the companies and their plays.[1]

Judging from the few names which can be identified, the first company to occupy the Fortune in 1625 must have been a merger of the Palsgrave's, at the Fortune up to 1625, and the Lady Elizabeth's, expelled from the Cockpit during the closure, though the evidence is largely circumstantial.[2] William Cartwright, Richard Fowler, Richard Gunnell, and Richard Price were the chief names in what came to be called the King and Queen of Bohemia's company. With three others, including Andrew Cane, these players had signed a bond to play together at the Fortune in April 1624. It is not known who from the queen's pre-1625 group may have joined the new company in 1625. Moore and Townsend continued to appear in provincial

[1] For an exact listing of which Caroline companies performed at which playhouses, and when, see Ch. 8, Table 2.

[2] The Lord Palsgrave, the former Elector Palatine, was crowned King of Bohemia in Nov. 1619, but only occupied his throne for a week. He spent most of his last years on the continent. He died in 1632. His wife had a house in Wiltshire, though she spent most of her life out of the country. Her English residence may explain why her name appears in the provincial records more often than the joint names for the company.

records in a company that still called itself Lady Elizabeth's Men, so they may have carried off the old patent for themselves. That the new company used her name is a hint, if no more, that some of her men may have joined it, but the majority of the company was certainly made up from the Palsgrave's Men.

No new plays survive from this first phase of the company's work at the Fortune. There are records of two affrays at the rebuilt amphitheatre, though, which seem to indicate a less-than-wholly gentle audience. One occurred in May 1626, and a fatal one two years later, on 13 June 1628, when the unpopular charlatan John Lambe was noticed at the Fortune and attacked there by apprentices, who pursued him through the town and eventually stoned him to death.[3] In neither case was the Fortune involved except as the original meeting-place of the people who committed the violence. Little else from the playhouse's first Caroline years has been recorded. Presumably these were the years of running old plays, when the Fortune company began to gain the reputation that identified it for playgoers through the last years as a 'citizen' venue, running drum-and-trumpet plays with wide-mouthed and loud-voiced players.

That was a reputation that linked the Fortune with the Red Bull through these years. A rather weak pun by Henry Rawlins in *The Rebellion*, written for the King's Revels during their stay at the Fortune up to 1634, compared the mouth of their leading player, Richard Fowler, to a fowling-piece or blunderbuss. Fowler's physical presence at the Fortune and the Red Bull became legendary. In a post-Restoration play, *Knavery in all Trades*, a character tells a nostalgic anecdote about Fowler's vigour in battering the metal targets or shields used in battle scenes to make a noise by banging swords on them:

Fowler you know was appointed for the Conquering parts, and it being given out that he was to play the Part of a great Captain and mighty Warriour, drew much Company; the Play began, and ended with his Valour; but at the end of the Fourth Act he laid so heavily about him, that some Mutes who stood for Souldiers, fell down as they were dead e're he had toucht their trembling Targets; so he brandisht his Sword and made his Exit; ne're minding to bring off his dead men; which they perceiving, crauld into the Tyreing house, at which, *Fowler* grew angry and told 'em, Dogs you should have laine there till you had been fetcht off; and so they crauld out again, which gave the People such an occasion of Laughter, they cry'd that again, that again, that again.[4]

Fowler was in the Bohemia company at the Fortune up to its dissolution in about 1631, then in Prince Charles's (II) company which played successively at Salisbury Court, the Red Bull and, in 1640, at the Fortune again.

---

[3] 'Upon Friday the 13. of June, in the yeare of our Lord 1628. hee went to see a Play at the *Fortune*, where the boyes of the towne, and other unruly people having observed him present, after the Play was ended, flocked about him, and (after the manner of common people, who follow a Hubbub, when it is once a foote) began in a confused manner to assault him, and offer violence.' *A Briefe Description of the notorious Life of John Lambe otherwise called Doctor Lambe. Together with his Ignominious Death* (1628), C3v.

[4] *Knavery in All Trades* (1664), III. i.

The Bohemia company seems to have dissolved in 1631, or possibly in 1632 when its nominal patron died. It is more likely that its disappearance coincided with Richard Gunnell's reshuffle of his new venture, the Salisbury Court playhouse, which he had first opened in 1629 with the King's Revels young company. Gunnell was controller of the Fortune, and his new hall-venture was an attempt to repeat Christopher Beeston's transfer from the Red Bull to the Cockpit. Like Beeston, he juggled his resources in players and playbooks to launch the new company. Then after two years using the young company, Gunnell found a patron in the new-born Prince of Wales for a new company of adults to play at his hall playhouse. They came mostly from the Fortune's King and Queen of Bohemia group. Neither patron was then in England to object to the loss of their company.

Prince Charles's (II) Company was in existence by December 1631. A licence was issued to Andrew Cane and others, 'in their new playhowse in Salisbury Court'.[5] Cane, Fowler, and Smith came from the Fortune to the Salisbury Court. A Norwich record of 1635 adds the names of Joseph Moore and Elias Worth to their licence, although by then both players were exclusively involved in touring.[6] This Norwich record is one of several indications that the later London companies kept a second-string group on tour, led by players who themselves never played in London. An entry for May 1632 in the Lord Chamberlain's Warrant book gives eleven names for the new Prince Charles's Men, including Fowler and Cane, and some who had been at the Red Bull.[7] Their transfer to the Salisbury Court hall-playhouse in 1631 may either mean that Gunnell thought his original young-company experiment had not worked, or else that he now felt secure enough to put a new adult company into his fledgling hall.

We have fewer names connected with either the Fortune or the Red Bull than with the more socially advantageous playhouses like the Salisbury Court. Presumably Gunnell's cull of the amphitheatre players for his hall in 1631 was done fairly comprehensively, though not by taking players from other established companies. And the new company's tenure of the hall did not last longer than the average. Within three years the new Prince Charles's was shifted across (or down) to the Red Bull, while the Red Bull company moved over to the Fortune, and the 1631 Fortune company moved to the Salisbury Court.

The Caroline Red Bull company, the Revels players, probably drew its first members from the former Prince Charles's (I) Men who had been working at the Red Bull up to 1625. Like the new Queen Henrietta's Men, there is no record of their ever receiving a patent, though Herbert acknowledged their existence as the Red Bull company in 1627, when he acceded to John Heminges' request to stop them

[5] Public Record Office Signet Book 2/90, C82/2077.
[6] Worth lived on till 1659. His will is transcribed in *Playhouse Wills 1558–1642*: 209–10.
[7] The evidence about companies and their playhouses is rather muddled for this period. It is well sifted by Bentley, *JCS* i. 303–9. See also Ch. 8, Table 2.

playing Shakespeare's plays, presumably obtained from the First Folio.[8] This is a potentially misleading indication of their repertory and their priorities. As a new company they may have been short of plays in 1626 and 1627, which may be one of the reasons why they are so much more on record as a travelling group than the Cockpit company, which shared Beeston's dislike of travelling. It seems that they were able to keep some of the 'drum-and-trumpet' plays that characterized the earlier Red Bull repertory, and in fact all the heavy jokes about its exaggerated acting and noisy plays belong to this last seventeen years of the playhouse's history and the two companies that used it.[9] Marlowe's *Tamburlaine* turned into a Red Bull trademark when it was imported by the Fortune company in 1634,[10] and *Edward II* may have persisted there too after its revival in 1622. *The Two Merry Milkmaids*, first staged at the Red Bull in 1619, was noted as a lastingly popular play at the same playhouse by Edmund Gayton in 1654.[11] Later records treated the Red Bull dismissively as one of the city's two 'citizen' venues, but as a playhouse it was always popular, and it was one of the only two used surreptitiously for playing during the Commonwealth period.

Some confusion about which company was where and playing what in this period is not surprising. *Edmund Ironside*, which survives in manuscript, may have been revived by the Prince Charles's (II) group while they were at Salisbury Court between 1631 and 1634. It contains the names of Gradwell and Stutville, who were in the company at this time. In reality, there is no firm indication of the company's membership for these years, as there was for the core of the Fortune company in Fowler and Cane. The Red Bull company's membership can only be inferred from their continuity between the list of names taken at Reading in 1629 and Crosfield's list of July 1634. The provincial records are little help, since they mainly give the names of the travelling players, not the London groups. Moore and Worth, formerly of the Bohemia company, fit this category in running a sibling company to the Prince Charles's (II) group when they were at the Fortune. It is impossible to tell, though, whether George Stutville was a London player at Salisbury Court or purely a traveller using a duplicate of the now annually issued licence, like Moore and Worth.

In Reading on 30 November 1629 the Red Bull company was identified as 'William Perry and Richard Weekes, his Majesty's servantes, licensed with the rest of their company, John Kerke, Edward Armiger, Hughe Tatterdell, Deavid Ferris, Robert Hint and George Williams, all of the Red Bull company, by the Master of the Revells'.[12] The player John Kirke wrote one of their few plays that survive, *The*

---

[8] 'From Mr. Hemming, in their company's name, to forbid the playing of Shakespeare's plays to the Red Bull Company, this 11 of April, 1627 . . . £5'. *Herbert Dramatic Records*, 64.

[9] See Gurr, *Playgoing in Shakespeare's London*, 183.

[10] Abraham Cowley, in *The Guardian* (1650), C3v, refers to someone roaring 'like *Tamerlin* at the Bull'. That presumably meant the Fortune company before it was supplanted by the Revels company in 1640. [11] *Pleasant Notes upon Don Quixot* (1654), 272.

[12] REED, *Berkshire, Buckinghamshire and Oxfordshire*, forthcoming.

Seven Champions of Christendom, though there is not much evidence to date it to any specific phase or playhouse in the company's variable history. Its title-page ascribes it to both the Red Bull and the Cockpit, which implies that it might have been a Beeston property. The likelihood is that Kirke wrote it for his company in the late 1620s or in the early 1630s. A reference to the Lancashire witches of the summer of 1634 could be seen as fixing its writing to then or later, but that is hardly a feasible basis for dating it, since his company had transferred to the Fortune by July 1634. It uses a popular romance of the 1590s to tell a rollicking story of derring-do, with more provision for action than verse, matching the dismissive comments on drum-and-trumpet plays and '*Red-Bull* wars'[13] that were made in these years. Few other new plays can be ascribed to this company at this playhouse, for all its loyal city following. Few of its players had much note taken of them outside the playhouse either.

In July 1634 Thomas Crosfield's record of what Richard Kendall, the King's Revels assistant, told him about the London companies says that 'The Princes Servants at ye Red-bull in St Johns street' were 'ye cheife Mr Cane a goldsmith, Mr Worth Mr Smith', and 'The Fortune in Golden Lane, ye cheife Mr Wm Cartwright, Edward Armestead, John Buckle, John Kirke'.[14] Kirke's former Red Bull company stayed at the Fortune from 1634 to 1640, while in the same year the former Fortune company, after their three years as Prince Charles's at Salisbury Court, went to the Red Bull. From this point on it is obviously anomalous to call the Revels at the Fortune the Red Bull company, but since they have no other name apart from a spurious or misread entitlement to be called the 'Kings Servants' in the Norwich records for 1635 it seems worth keeping their original playhouse names, and using the Fortune name for the company now at the Red Bull.

Cartwright and Buckle are the new names in Kendall's 1634 list. The absence of Perry and Weekes, chronic travellers, most likely indicates their practice of maintaining a travelling company outside London, and using the London licence for it. The two men were the subject of a complaint from Canterbury in March 1636, where they were called 'the company of the Fortune play house'.[15] It seems that Prince Charles's (II) Servants, in playing at the Red Bull, for all their three previous years at a hall playhouse, became interchangeable with the Red Bull company in more than just the 'citizen' audiences. In fact the Prince Charles's had some players from the old Red Bull company of before 1625.

It was strictly only through this last decade that the players at the Red Bull and those at the Fortune stood apart from the hall-playhouse companies as amphi-theatre groups. Even the one three-year run of the Fortune company at the Salis-bury Court made no waves in the binary division of the playhouses. This overrode the switch of companies, both the annual one by the King's and the three-year transfer of the Prince Charles's, from the one kind to the other. The kind of playhouse was now clearly more influential than the company or its repertory, and

---

[13] *The Two Merry Milkmaids* (1620), Prologue.
[14] *The Diary of Thomas Crosfield*, 72.   [15] *CSP Dom. 1635–6*, 321.

not only in the Revels summonses to court. The two 'citizen' companies of the 1630s were inter-related in past membership and in the thrust of their tradition-based repertories. From 1634 onwards they finally grouped themselves together at a distance from the hall companies. Their history was fairly stable compared with the hall groups. The only change was that at Easter 1640 the Prince Charles's (II) Company exchanged with the Revels company and went to the Fortune, where some of its players had formerly served as Bohemia's Men, while the company of the Revels returned to their old home at the Red Bull.

They did exercise some degree of personal rivalry with each other, despite the double interchange of their playhouses. There is some evidence of acrimony in this last exchange, though little survives to say what it was about. John Tatham wrote a prologue for the Prince's Men while they were still at the Red Bull in *The Fancies Theater*, published in 1640, complaining that you could not rely on the Red Bull company at its old place, the Fortune, 'when *shee's* knowne / An *enemie* to Merit', and making invidious comparisons with the noise of the audiences attending baitings at the Beargarden or Hope. This Bentley sees as the pot calling the kettle noisy. The actual reason for the switch of playhouses cannot have much to do with any such grievance as this between the companies. It must have been a matter of playhouse ownership, an impresario decision. But in the absence of any information about who owned and ran either playhouse at this time there is no way of telling what caused either the quarrel or the switch of venues.

The repertoire of plays that the two amphitheatres became noted for in the last years were chiefly old favourites. The Fortune had Richard Fowler in *The Spanish Tragedy* and the clown, Andrew Cane, to set against the Red Bull's *Tamburlaine* and their clown, Timothy Reade. Both playhouses had a reputation for loud speech laid at the mouths of their players, but perhaps more properly attributable to the open-air venues. That likelihood is affirmed by the fact that the Globe gained a similar reputation with the same players who were performing at the Blackfriars in these years. Edmund Gayton, writing with a characteristic mixture of nostalgia, derision, and imprecision about the citizen playhouses, wrote that the players of the Fortune and Red Bull were 'terrible teare-throats', and that their poets 'made their lines proportionable to their compasse, which were *sesquipedales*, a foot and a halfe'.[16] Thomas Rawlins compared the mouth of the Fortune's leading player, Richard Fowler, to a blunderbuss.[17] Fowler was remembered after the Restoration as the Fortune's master of 'the Conquering parts', which suggests that the drum-and-trumpet plays with their spectacular battles were what created the citizen or amphitheatre tradition that lingered most strongly in people's memories after the closure.[18]

[16] *Pleasant Notes upon Don Quixot*, 24.

[17] *The Rebellion* (1639), V. ii. An amateur player boasts 'Marke if I doe not gape wider than the widest / Mouth'd Fowler of them all'. A blunderbuss was a shotgun fired at birds, a fowling-piece.

[18] *Knavery in All Trades* (1664), quoted in *JCS* ii. 440. The anecdote from which this phrase is taken, quoted above, shows the amphitheatre practice of staging noisy battles by hammering swords on the metal shields or targets of the soldiery.

That, however, was by no means their only identity. They also both gained a reputation for scandal in the last years, at least with the civic authorities. In May 1639 the Fortune players got into trouble, once for staging a scene from an old play, *The Cardinal's Conspiracy*, 'in contempt of the ceremonies of the church'.[19] They set up an altar, a basin, and two candlesticks and bowed to it on the stage. A heavy fine was imposed. Not long after, while Cane was still at the Red Bull, in September 1639, a detailed complaint was laid against the company for some heavy-handed remarks about a notoriously acquisitive alderman of the city, William Abell. The complaint, about a play called *The Whore New Vamped*, tells a lot about the company's current repertoire:

Complaint was this day made that the stage-players of the Red Bull have for many days together acted a scandalous and libellous play in which they have audaciously reproached and in a libel represented and personated not only some of the aldermen of the city and some other persons of quality, but also scandalised and libelled the whole profession of proctors belonging to the Court of Probate, and reflected upon the present government.

Exceptions taken to the play above referred to. In the play called 'The Whore New Vamped,' where there was mention of the new duty on wines, one personating a justice of the peace, says to Cain. 'Sirrah, I'll have you before the alderman;' whereto Cain replies, 'The alderman, the alderman is a base, drunken, sottish knave, I care not for the alderman, I say the alderman is a base, drunken, sottish knave.' Another says, 'How now Sirrah, what alderman do you speak of?' Then Cain says, 'I mean alderman William Abell, the blacksmith in Holborn;' says the other, 'Was he not a Vintner?' Cain answers, 'I know no other.' In another part of the play one speaking of projects and patents that he had got, mentions among others 'a patent of 12d. a piece upon every proctor and proctor's man who was not a knave.' said another, 'Was there ever known any proctor but he was an arrant knave?'[20]

The offence was a local one, and it was the city authorities who took it up. How far such satirical comments were designed as narrowly citizen matters presented to citizen audiences, and how far they might reflect the cynicism of the powerless towards those in power it is never easy to say. The play itself was no broadside on public policies like *A Game at Chess*. The offence was given by the incidental references and asides that tapped a vein of popular cynicism about civic, governmental, and judicial corruption. It might be seen as the flipside of the plays about apprentice heroics, such as the *Four Prentices of London*, which had been popular at the Red Bull nearly forty years before.

The Red Bull and Fortune companies of the last years have had a bad press, which has not been helped by the disappearance of most of their plays. That loss makes it almost impossible to identify any significant political or even cultural position for them. Martin Butler[21] makes as strong a case as can be made that the plays of the last years contained astringent political satire, but the key evidence

---

[19] See *JCS* i. 277. The play is not extant.   [20] *CSP Dom.* 1639, 529–30.
[21] *Theatre and Crisis 1632–1642*, esp. ch. 8.

itself is largely lost or down to hearsay. The conclusion to Kathleen McLuskie's account of the amphitheatre plays, however summary, makes the general point quite firmly:

A good deal of the later public theatre repertory is lost, but in what remains the plots continue to turn on money and sex, and there is little evidence of a coherent counter-culture appealing to a lower-class social group. What is clear is that mockery of the Red Bull and the Fortune provided the élite companies with a means of reinforcing the image of their own superiority, and by implication that of their sophisticated audience.[22]

Given that in this late period politics and religion were inseparable, the little evidence about what was censored in the two lost amphitheatre plays of 1639 and 1640 suggests that there was actually a rather stronger political bias in the amphitheatre companies than this admits. Certainly it was not aligned with courtly interests, nor was it interested in appealing to any anti-establishment bias in the gentry audiences such as we can find in even Brome's last plays for the Cockpit. I do suspect they belong more tightly and intimately with the current politics of the city than any plays before.

THE KING AND QUEEN OF BOHEMIA'S COMPANY, 1626–1631

Players
Richard Gunnell, Andrew Cane, William Cartwright, Richard Fowler, Richard Price [Alexander Foster, Robert Guylman, Joseph Moore, Mathew Smyth, John Townsend, Elias Worth].

Assistants
Thomas Faulkner [described as 'an inhabitant at the Fortune playhouse' in report of affray when a gang of seamen rioted at the playhouse, May 1628.[23]]

London Playhouses
Fortune.

At Court
never.

Travelling Records
Nottingham 1628–9 'the ladie Elizabeths players', 12s. / Leicester 1628–9 'Mr Moore & his Companie being the Ladies Elizabeth her Players', £1. / Norwich 27 June 1629 'This day Elias Guest one of the Company of Joseph Moore Alexander Foster Robert Guylman & John Townshend sworne servantes to the Kinge brought into this Court a warrant . . . & a lycence from the Master of the Revelles dated the eight day of this instant June whereby they are lycenced to play Comedies &c The said Elias affirmed that the residue of his Company are still at Thetford whereupon he did Consent to accept such a gratuety as this Court should thinke fitt

---

[22] *The Revels History of Drama in English: vol. iv. 1613–1660,* 168.
[23] William Young, *A History of Dulwich College,* ii. 261–2.

to give.'[24] 40s. / Leicester 1629–30, £1. / Reading 24 Dec. 1629 'At this Daye Joseph Moore, Alexander Forster, Robert Guilman and John Townesend sworne servantes to his Majestie with the rest of their Company licensed from tyme to tyme to practise the quallitie of playeng, came & tendred their licence to play in the towne hall, dated the 15th of December 1628 . . . xxs was geven to forbeare their playeing at this tyme.'[25] 20s. / Cambridge 12 Feb. 1630 [letter from chancellor to vice-chancellor]: 'This Company of the Queene of Bohemias Players have gott leave from his Majesty to goe abroad this Lent out of London. And because of the likelyhood the Cowrt will bee in Cambredgeshire, it brings them thether Suitors for Intertaynment att the Unyversyty for a day or two . . . I referre them to your acceptance'. [Reply from the vice-chancellor] 'upon view of our charters it appeared we might neither licence them nor connive unto them'. / Norwich 3 Mar. 1630 'This day Joseph Moore and others of his Company brought into this Court a warrant [dated 15 Dec. 1629] whereby they are lycenced to play Comedies &c They have leave to play &c for two dayes next ensuinge.' / Dunkenhalgh, Lancs. (Household accounts of Thomas Walmesley) 19 July 1630 'given a sorte of Players which tearmet them selfes the lady Elizabethes players for playinge one night . . . Mr. Guest they Player and his Companie one night', 20s. / Leicester 1630, £1. / Coventry Dec. acct. 1630 'to Joseph More & others that was sworne servants to the King that the should not play in June last', 20s. / Bristol 1631 'the Palsgraves players', 40s. / Coventry 30 Mar. 1631 'to Joseph More John Townesend & other players to the Ladie Elizabeth', 20s. / Doncaster 18 June 1631, 13s. 4d. / Reading 13 Aug. 1631 'Mr Joseph Moore and the rest of his Company under the name of the lady Elizabeth her highnes servantes shewed their licens to playe &c desiringe liberty to playe in the Towne Hall . . . geven to them to forbeare their plange at this tyme in Readinge', 20s. / Dunkenhalgh, Lancs. (Household accounts of Thomas Walmesley) 16 Feb. 1632 'given the players Gest and his Company nott playinge', 10s.

PRINCE CHARLES'S MEN (II), 1631–1642

Plays

The Cardinal's Conspiracy (lost), *The Changes* (?), *A Fine Companion*, *Holland's Leaguer*, *Edmund Ironside* (old), *The Whore New Vamped* (lost).

[24] Whether the company really was following along after Guest is unclear. The Norwich records do not say that they turned up there subsequently. Although the patent he showed must have been a copy of the authentic document, he had no other known links with the former Lady Elizabeth's. I suspect he conned the Norwich authorities of their 40s. His subsequent appearances in Lancashire at Sir Thomas Walmesley's house in 1630 and 1632 indicate that Guest had a duplicate of the old Lady Elizabeth's licence. The Moore–Townsend group was most likely the more regular of the two. With links to the Salisbury Court and the Fortune they had more to lose than Guest. An entry at Leicester on 6 Mar. 1626 names a company with a Revels patent as comprising 'Ellis Geste, Thomas Swinerton Arthure Grimes and others'. They may have secured a travelling warrant from Henry Herbert at the start of playing in the new reign, but it must have been for travelling only. Guest's name in this group appears at Norwich on 28 May 1625, and recurs there in 1628, then at Leicester's again in 1629, and at Reading in 1630. This group is unlikely to have played in London. The Red Bull 'Revels' company had its own touring group with William Perry, who was also tied to York.

[25] REED, *Berkshire and Buckinghamshire*, forthcoming.

Players
Andrew Cane, William Eaton, Joseph Moore, Matthew Smyth, Gilbert Reason, Elias Worth. [Chamberlain's Account Book 1632: 'Ellis Worth Andrew Kayne Mathew Smyth Richard Fowler William Browne James Sneller Thomas Plumfield Thomas Bond Henry Gradwell & William Hall George Stutville'.[26]].

Apprentices
[cast-list from *Holland's Leaguer*, 1631] Richard Fouch, Richard Godwin, Robert Huyt, Samuel Mannery, Arthur Savill, John Wright.

Hired Men
Richard Honyman.[27]

London Playhouses
Salisbury Court 1631–4, Red Bull 1634–40, Fortune 1640–2.

At Court
3 unnamed plays up to 1 Oct. 1633 before the king; 7 unnamed plays to May 1634; 3 unnamed plays Nov. and Dec. 1637 before the king; 3 unnamed plays Nov. 1639.

Travelling Records
Southampton 7 Sept. 1633 'Payd unto Prinse Charlles Players to rid them out of the towne', £1. / Hythe, Kent 1633–4, £1. / Dover 8 Mar. 1634, 10s. / Coventry Aug. 1634, 40s. / Leicester 10 Aug. 1634, £2. / Southampton 7 Sept. 1634 'to rid them out of ttoune'[28], £1. / Norwich 3 Nov. 1635 'This day Joseph Moore brought an Instrument . . . authorisinge Andrew Kayne Elis worth & others to play Comedies in Salisbury Court & elsewhere within five miles of London And in all other Cities &c.' / Norwich 9 Mar. 1636 'Andrew Kayne to play Comedyes Teste 7 Decembris Anno Septimo Caroli Regis [1631]' . . . 'they desire that mr Maior would appoint an officer whome they will Content for his paynes to see that poore people, Servantes & idle persons may be restrayned' / Kendal 1636, £1. / Dover June 1636, 11s. / Norwich 21 Feb. 1637 'Joseph Moore Ellias Worth Mathew Smyth & others', £3. / Norwich 24 Feb. 1638 'a gratuity of iij li. And so they willingly departed'. / Bridport, Dorset 1639, 10s. / Dover 9 Aug. 1641 'geven the Princes Players for a gratuitie who presently theruppon departed the Toune', £1.

THE RED BULL COMPANY, 1625–1642

Plays
The Cardinal's Conspiracy (lost), *The Knave in Grain, Seven Champions of Christendom, The Valiant Scot.*

Playhouses
Red Bull, Fortune (1634–40), Red Bull (from 1640).

---

[26] *MSC* ii. 3. 358.

[27] Named in John Honyman's will of 1636. See *Playhouse Wills 1558–1642*, 190–1.

[28] Southampton put a ban on players using the town hall for plays on 6 Feb. 1623. For once this order was strictly observed.

Players

Richard Errington, Nicholas Hanson, William Perry (only travelling?[29]). Reading, 10 Nov. 1629: 'William Perrye and Richard weekes his Majesties sworne servant licensed with the rest of their Company John Kerke Edward Armiger hugh Tatterdell deavid Feeris Robert Hint and George Williams, all of the Red Bull company, by the Master of the Revells'.[30]

At Court
never.

Travelling Records

Worcester 1625 'the kings revelers', 15s. / Coventry 21 Dec. 1626, 2s. / Reading 1626–7, 10s. / Coventry Apr. 1628 'to Nicholas Hanson one of that company', 5s. / Carlisle 29 July 1628, £1. / Reading 10 Nov. 1629 / Leicester 1630, £1. / Reading 2 Nov. 1630 'william Perrey & Richard weekes the kinges servantes & their company were here'.[31] / Coventry 20 Dec. 1631 'to the players of the Revells', 10s. / Doncaster 19 Apr. 1632, 10s. / Norwich 6 July 1633 'This day william Perry brought to this Court a Bill signed with his Majesties hand & privy Signett Dated the last day of Aprill in the nynth yeare of his Majesties Reigne [1633] Confirmed by the Master of the Revelles under his seale the 24th of May last to play Comedies &c . . . There is gyvne unto them Thre poundes as a gratuety And thereupon the said william Perry promised to desist', £3. / Norwich 1 Mar. 1634 'william Perry & his Company' . . . 15 Mar. 1634 'william Perry one of the kinges players beinge this day in Court was demanded why hee & his Company did Contynue to play in this City beyond the tyme agreed upon They sayd they have liberty by their patent to Contynue their playes forty dayes . . . they haveinge nowe stayed fiften dayes to the great hurt of the poore they would give no answer thereunto but desired eight dayes longer'.[32] / Bristol June–Sept. 1635 'paide to one Perry a plaier by order of master Mayor for yat hee should not use his skill heere in this Citty', £2. / Norwich 6 June 1635 'This day Richard Weekes and John Shanke[33] brought into the Court a bill signed . . . Dated [30 Apr. 1634]' . . . 'leave to play here till the xviijth of this moneth'. / Norwich 11 May 1636 'This day Richard wicks & other servantes to his Majestie beinge his Majesties players granted to william Perry & others'. / Canterbury 1636.

---

[29] Perry set up a new King's company for travelling in mid-1629, ostensibly based at York. In the next years it is not easy to differentiate the King's travelling company from the King's Revels company of the Red Bull, or the Revels company at Salisbury Court.

[30] The licence was issued on 10 Nov., and the performance was on 30 Nov. *REED, Berkshire, Buckinghamshire and Oxfordshire*, A. F. Johnston, ed., forthcoming.

[31] It seems more likely that their licence was as the King's Men from York at this time.

[32] This abuse prompted another complaint to London about playing. See *REED, Norwich*, 214.

[33] Most likely the son of the King's Men's clown.

Bibliography

Acts of the Privy Council of England, ed. J. R. Dasent (32 vols.; London, 1890–1907 [Vol. VII (1558–70), 1893, to XXXII (1604), 1907; subsequent records published by years to 1631]).

ADAMS, JOHN QUINCEY (ed.), *The Dramatic Records of Sir Henry Herbert, Master of the Revels, 1623–1673* (New Haven, Conn., 1917).

ADAMS, SIMON, 'Faction, Clientage and Party: English Politics 1550–1603', *History Today*, 32: 12 (1982), 33–9.

—— 'Eliza Enthroned? The Court and its Politics', in *The Reign of Elizabeth I*, ed. Christopher Haigh (London, 1984), 55–77.

ALEXANDER, ROBERT, 'Corrections of Bath Dramatic Records 1568–1620 in Printed Texts', *REED Newsletter*, 10 (1985), 2–7.

—— 'Some Dramatic Records from Percy Household Accounts on Microfilm', *REED Newsletter*, 12 (1987), 10–17.

ANDERSON, J. J. (ed.), *REED Newcastle* (Toronto, 1982).

ANGLIN, JAY P. *The Third University: A Survey of Schools and Schoolmasters in the Elizabethan Diocese of London* (Norwood, Penn., 1985).

ASTINGTON, JOHN, 'Descent Machinery in the Playhouses', *MRDE* 2 (1985), 119–33.

—— 'Eye and Hand on Shakespeare's Stage', *Renaissance and Reformation*, 22 (1986), 109–21.

—— 'The Red Lion Playhouse: Two Notes', *SQ* 36 (1985), 456–7.

—— 'Staging at St James's Palace in the Seventeenth Century', *TRI* 11 (1986), 199–213.

AUSTERN, LINDA-PHYLLIS, 'Thomas Ravenscroft: Musical Chronicler of an Elizabethan Theater Company', *Journal of the American Musicological Society*, 38 (1985), 239–63.

BAGLEY, J. J., *The Earls of Derby 1485–1985* (London, 1985).

BALD, R. C., 'Leicester's Men in the Low Countries', *RES* 19 (1943), 395–7.

—— 'Will, My Lord of Leicester's Jesting Player', *NQ* 204 (1959), 112.

BALDWIN, T. W., *Organisation and Personnel of the Shakespearean Company* (Princeton, NJ, 1927).

BARISH, JONAS, *The Anti-Theatrical Prejudice* (Berkeley, Calif., 1981).

BARROLL, J. LEEDS, 'The Chronology of Shakespeare's Jacobean Plays and the Dating of *Antony and Cleopatra*', in *Essays on Shakespeare*, ed. Gordon Ross Brown (Philadelphia, 1965), 115–62.

—— 'A New History for Shakespeare and his Time', *SQ* 39 (1988), 441–64.

—— 'The Court of the First Stuart Queen', in *The Mental World of the Jacobean Court*, ed. Linda Levy Peck (Cambridge, 1991), 191–208.

—— *Politics, Plague and Shakespeare's Theater: The Stuart Years* (New York, 1991).

BARTON, ANNE, 'Harking Back to Elizabeth: Ben Jonson and Caroline Nostalgia', *E.L.H.* 48 (1981), 706–31.

—— *Ben Jonson, Dramatist* (Cambridge, 1984).

BASKERVILL, C. R., *The Elizabethan Jig* (Chicago, Ill., 1929).

BAWCUTT, N. W., 'New Revels Documents of Sir George Buc and Sir Henry Herbert, 1619–1662', *RES* 35 (1984), 316–31.

BAWCUTT, N. W., 'Craven Ord Transcripts of Sir Henry Herbert's Office-Book in the Folger Shakespeare Library', *ELR* 14 (1984), 83–94.

—— 'Evidence and Conjecture in Literary Scholarship: The Case of Sir John Astley Reconsidered', *ELR* 22 (1992), 333–46.

BEAL, PETER, 'Massinger at Bay: Unpublished Verses in a War of the Theatres', *YES* 10 (1980), 190–203.

BECKERMANN, BERNARD, *Shakespeare at the Globe 1599–1609* (New York, 1962).

BENBOW, R. MARK, 'Dutton and Goffe versus Broughton: A Disputed Contract for Plays in the 1570s', *REED Newsletter*, 2 (1981), 3–9.

BENNETT, PAUL E., 'The Word "Goths" in "A Knack to Know a Knave" ', *NQ* 200 (1955), 462–63.

BENTLEY, G. E., *The Jacobean and Caroline Stage* (7 vols.; Oxford, 1940–68).

—— 'Shakespeare and the Blackfriars Theatre', *ShS* 1 (1948), 38–50.

—— *The Profession of Dramatist in Shakespeare's Time, 1590–1642* (Princeton, NJ, 1971).

—— *The Profession of Player in Shakespeare's Time, 1590–1642* (Princeton, NJ, 1984).

BEREK, PETER, 'The "Upstart Crow" ', *SQ* 35 (1984), 205–7.

BERGER, HARRY, Jr., *Imaginary Audition: Shakespeare on Page and Stage* (Berkeley, Calif., 1989).

BERGERON, DAVID M., 'Women as Patrons of English Renaissance Drama', in *Patronage in the Renaissance*, ed. Guy Fitch and Stephen Orgel (Washington DC, 1981).

—— 'Patronage of Dramatists: The Case of Thomas Heywood', *ELR* 18 (1988), 294–304.

BERRY, HERBERT, 'The Player's Apprentice', *Essays in Theatre*, 1 (1983), 73–80.

—— 'The Globe Bewitched and *El Hombre Fiel*', *MRDE* 1 (1984), 211–30.

—— *The Boar's Head Playhouse* (Washington DC, 1986).

—— *Shakespeare's Playhouses* (New York, 1987).

——, and STOKES, JAMES, 'Actors and Town Hall in the Sixteenth Century', *MRDE* 6 (1993), 37–55.

BEVINGTON, DAVID, *From 'Mankind' to Marlowe: Growth of Structure in the Popular Drama of Tudor England* (Cambridge, Mass., 1962).

BILLINGTON, SANDRA, *A Social History of the Fool* (Brighton, 1984).

BINNS, J. W., and DAVIES, H. NEVILLE, 'Christian IV and *The Dutch Courtesan*', *TN* 44 (1990), 118–23.

BIRCH, THOMAS, *The Court and Times of James I* (London, 1849).

—— *The Court and Times of Charles I* (2 vols.; London, 1849).

BLACKSTONE, MARY A., 'Patrons and Elizabethan Dramatic Companies', *Elizabethan Theatre*, 10 (1988), 112–32.

BLISS, LEE, 'Pastiche, burlesque, tragicomedy', in *The Cambridge Companion to English Renaissance Drama*, ed. A. R. Braunmuller and Michael Hattaway (Cambridge, 1990), 237–62.

BOSWELL, JACKSON CAMPBELL, 'Seven Actors in Search of a Biographer', *MRDE* 2 (1985), 51–6.

BOULTON, JEREMY, *Neighbourhood and Society: A London Suburb in the Seventeenth Century* (Cambridge, 1987).

BOWERS, RICK, 'John Lowin: Actor-Manager of the King's Company, 1630–1642', *Theatre Survey*, 28 (1987), 15–35.

—— 'John Lowin's Conclusions upon Dances: Puritan Conclusions of a Godly Player', *Renaissance and Reformation*, 23 (1987), 163–73.

BRADBROOK, MURIEL, *The Rise of the Common Player* (London, 1962).

BRADLEY, DAVID, *From Text to Performance in the Elizabethan Theatre: Preparing the Play for the Stage* (Cambridge, 1992).

BRAUNMULLER, A. R., 'The Arts of the Dramatist', in *The Cambridge Companion to English Renaissance Drama* ed. A. R. Braunmuller and Michael Hattaway (Cambridge, 1990), 53–90.

BREIGHT, CURT, 'Realpolitik and Elizabethan Ceremony: The Earl of Hertford's Entertainment of Elizabeth at Elvetham, 1591', *Renaissance Quarterly*, 45 (1992), 20–48.

BRENNAN, MICHAEL, *Literary Patronage in the English Renaissance: The Pembroke Family* (London, 1988).

BRILEY, JOHN, 'Edward Alleyn and Henslowe's Will', *SQ* 9 (1958), 321–30.

—— 'Mary Sidney: A 20th Century Reappraisal', in *Elizabethan and Modern Studies Presented to Professor Willem Schrickx on the Occasion of His Retirement*, ed. J. P. Vander Motten (Ghent, 1985).

BRISTOL, MICHAEL D., *Carnival and Theater: Plebeian Culture and the Structure of Authority in Renaissance England* (New York, 1985).

BROMBERG, MURRAY, 'Theatrical Wagers: A Sidelight on the Elizabethan Drama', *NQ* 196 (1951), 533–5.

BROMHAM, A. A., and BRUZZI, ZARA, *'The Changeling' and the Years of Crisis, 1619–1624: A Hieroglyph of Britain* (New York, 1990).

BROWNSTEIN, O. L., 'A Record of London Inn Playhouses from c.1565–90', *SQ* 22 (1971), 17–24.

BRUSTER, DOUGLAS, *Drama and the Market in the Age of Shakespeare* (Cambridge, 1992).

BULMAN, JAMES, 'Caroline Drama', in *The Cambridge Companion to English Renaissance Drama*, ed. A. R. Braunmuller and Michael Hattaway (Cambridge, 1990), 353–79.

BURNETT, GILBERT, *The Life of Matthew Hall* (London, 1682).

BURT, RICHARD A., ' "Licensed by Authority": Ben Jonson and the Politics of Early Stuart Theatre', *ELH* 54 (1987), 529–60.

—— *Licensed by Authority: Ben Jonson and the Discourses of Censorship* (Ithaca, NY, 1993).

BUTLER, GUY, 'William Fulbecke: A New Shakespeare Source?', *NQ* 231 (1986), 363–5.

BUTLER, MARTIN, *Theatre and Crisis 1632–1642* (Cambridge, 1984).

—— 'Two Playgoers, and the Closing of the London Theatres, 1642', *TRI* 9 (1984), 93–9.

CARLETON, DUDLEY, *Dudley Carleton to John Chamberlain 1603–1624: Jacobean Letters*, ed. Maurice Lee, Jr. (New Brunswick, NJ, 1972).

CARROLL, D. ALLEN, 'Greene, the Burbages, and Shakespeare', *Renaissance Papers 1980*, 45–51.

CARSON, NEIL, 'John Webster: The Apprentice Years', *Elizabethan Theatre*, 6 (1978), 76–87.

—— *A Companion to Henslowe's Diary* (Cambridge, 1988).

CARTER, PAUL, *The Road to Botany Bay: An Essay in Spatial History* (London, 1987).

CERASANO, S. P., 'Anthony Jeffes, Player and Brewer', *NQ* 229 (1984), 221–5.

—— 'Revising Philip Henslowe's Biography', *NQ* 230 (1985), 66–72, and correction, *NQ* 230 (1985), 506–7.

—— 'The "Business" of Shareholding, the Fortune Playhouses, and Francis Grace's Will', *MRDE* 2 (1985), 231–52.

—— 'Edward Alleyn's Early Years: His Life and Family', *NQ* 232 (1987), 237–43.

—— 'New Renaissance Players' Wills', *MP* 82 (1985), 299–304.

—— 'Competition for the King's Men? Alleyn's Blackfriars Venture', *MRDE* 4 (1989), 173–86.

CERASANO, S. P., 'Philip Henslowe, Simon Forman, and the Theatrical Community of the 1590s', *SQ* 44 (1993), 145–58, 157–8.

CEROVSKI, JOHN S., *Fragmenta Regalia*, ed. Robert Naunton (Washington DC, 1985).

CHAMBERLAIN, JOHN, *The Letters of John Chamberlain*, ed. N. E. McClure (2 vols.; Philadelphia, 1939).

CHAMBERS, E. K., *The Elizabethan Stage* (4 vols.; Oxford, 1923).

—— *William Shakespeare* (2 vols.; Oxford, 1930).

CLARE, JANET, *'Art made tongue-tied by authority': Elizabethan and Jacobean Censorship*, Manchester, 1990.

COGSWELL, THOMAS, 'Thomas Middleton and the Court, 1624: *A Game at Chess* in context', *HLQ* 47 (1984), 273–88.

—— 'England and the Spanish Match', in *Conflict in Early Stuart England*, ed. Richard Cust and Ann Hughes (London, 1989).

COHEN, WALTER, *Drama of a Nation: Public Theater in Renaissance England and Spain* (Ithaca, NY, 1985).

COLETTI, THERESA, ' "Fragmentation and Redemption": Dramatic Records, History, and the Dream of Wholeness', *Envoi*, 3 (1991), 1–13.

COOK, DAVID, and WILSON, F. P., *Dramatic Records in the Declared Accounts of the Treasurer of the Chamber 1558–1642* (Malone Society Collections vi.; Oxford, 1961 (1962)).

COWARD, BARRY, *The Stanleys Lords Stanley and Earls of Derby 1385–1672* (Manchester, 1983).

CUST, RICHARD, and HUGHES, ANN (ed.), *Conflict in Early Stuart England: Studies in Religion and Politics 1603–1642* (London, 1989).

DAVENANT, WILLIAM, *The Shorter Poems*, ed. A. M. Gibbs (Oxford, 1972).

DAVIES, H. NEVILLE, 'Beaumont and Fletcher's Hamlet', in *Shakespeare, Man of the Theater*, ed. Kenneth Muir, Jay L. Halio, and D. J. Palmer (Newark, NJ, 1983), 173–81.

DAVIS, NICHOLAS, 'The Meaning of the word "Interlude": A Discussion', *Medieval English Theatre*, 6 (1984), 6–16.

DEKKER, THOMAS, *The Non-Dramatic Works*, ed. A. B. Grosart (5 vols.; London, 1884–6).

DESSEN, ALAN C., *Elizabethan Stage Conventions and Modern Interpreters* (Cambridge, 1984).

DONNE, JOHN, *The Complete English Poems*, ed. A. J. Smith (Harmondsworth, 1971).

DOUGLAS, AUDREY C., and GREENFIELD, PETER (ed.), *REED, Cumberland/Westmorland/ Gloucestershire* (Toronto, 1986).

DUTTON, RICHARD, '*Hamlet, An Apology for Actors*, and The Sign of the Globe', *ShS* 41 (1989), 35–43.

—— *Mastering the Revels: The Regulation and Censorship of English Renaissance Drama* (Basingstoke, 1991).

—— 'Ben Jonson and the Master of the Revels', in *Theatre and Government under the Early Stuarts*, ed. J. R. Mulryne and Margaret Shewring (Cambridge, 1993), 57–86.

ECCLES, MARK, 'Martin Peerson and the Blackfriars', *ShS* 11 (1958), 100–6.

—— 'Middleton's Comedy *The Almanac, or No Wit, No Help Like a Woman's*', *NQ* 232 (1987), 296–7.

—— 'Elizabethan Actors i: A–D', *NQ* 236 (1991), 38–49.

—— 'Elizabethan Actors ii: E–K', *NQ* 236 (1991), 454–61.

—— 'Elizabethan Actors iii: K–R', *NQ* 237 (1992), 293–303.

—— 'Elizabethan Actors iv: S to End', *NQ* 238 (1993), 165–76.

EDMOND, MARY, 'Pembroke's Men', *RES* n.s. 25 (1974), 129–36.

—— *Rare Sir William Davenant* (Manchester, 1987).

ELLIOTT, JOHN R., 'Entertainments in Tudor and Stuart Corpus', *The Pelican* (1982–3), 45–50.

FEATHER, JOHN, 'Robert Armin and the Chamberlain's Men', *NQ* 19 (1972), 448–50.

FEHRENBACH, ROBERT J., 'When Lord Cobham and Edmund Tilney "Were att Odds": Oldcastle, Falstaff, and the Date of *1 Henry IV*', *Shakespeare Studies*, 18 (1986), 87–102.

FELVER, C. S., *Robert Armin, Shakespeare's Fool* (Kent State, 1961).

FEUILLERAT, ALBERT, *Documents relating to the Office of the Revels in the Time of Queen Elizabeth* (Materialen zur Kunde des alteren Englischen Dramas, xxi.; Louvain, 1908).

FINKELPEARL, PHILIP J., ' "The Comedians' Liberty": Censorship of the Jacobean Stage Reconsidered', *ELR* 16 (1986), 123–38.

FOAKES, R. A., and RICKERT R. T. (ed.), *Henslowe's Diary* (Cambridge, 1961).

FOAKES, R. A. (ed.), *The Henslowe Papers* (2 vols., London, 1978).

—— *Illustrations of the English Stage 1580–1642* (London, 1985).

—— 'Playhouses and Players', in *The Cambridge Companion to English Renaissance Drama* ed. A. R. Braunmuller and Michael Hattaway (Cambridge, 1990), 1–52.

FOTHERINGHAM, RICHARD, 'The Doubling of Roles on the Jacobean Stage', *TRI* 10 (1985), 18–32.

FREEHAFER, JOHN, 'Brome, Suckling and Davenant's Theatre Project of 1639', *Texas Studies in Literature and Language*, 10 (1968), 367–83.

GAIR, W. REAVLEY, *The Children of Paul's: The Story of a Theatre Company, 1553–1608* (Cambridge, 1982).

—— 'Takeover at Blackfriars: Queen's Revels to King's Men', *Elizabethan Theatre*, 10 (1988), 37–54.

GALLOWAY, DAVID (ed.), *REED, Norwich 1540–1642* (Toronto, 1984).

GAW, ALLISON, 'John Sincklo as one of Shakespeare's Actors', *Anglia*, 49 (1925), 289–303.

GEORGE, DAVID, 'Shakespeare and Pembroke's Men', *SQ* 32 (1981), 305–23.

—— 'The Walmesley of Dunkenhalgh Accounts', *REED Newsletter*, 10 (1985), 6–15.

—— 'Blood-Sports and the Evolution of the English Playhouse 1576–1642', *Shakespeare Newsletter*, 190 (1986), 25.

—— (ed.), *REED, Lancashire* (Toronto, 1991).

GERRITSEN, JOHAN, 'De Witt, van Buchell, the Swan and the Globe: Some Notes', in *Essays in Honour of Kristian Smidt*, ed. Peter Bilton *et al.* (Oslo, 1986).

GIBBONS, BRIAN, *Jacobean City Comedy* (1971; 2nd edn. London, 1980).

—— 'Romance and the Heroic Play', in *The Cambridge Companion to English Renaissance Drama*, ed. A. R. Braunmuller and Michael Hattaway, (Cambridge, 1990), 207–36.

GIBSON, COLIN A., 'Another Shot in the War of the Theatres (1630)', *NQ* 232 (1987), 308–9.

GOLDBERG, JONATHAN, *James I and the Politics of Literature* (Baltimore and London, 1983).

GRAVES, R. B., 'Stage Lighting at the Elizabethan and Early Stuart Courts', *TN* 38 (1984), 27–36.

GRAY, H. D., 'The Roles of William Kemp', *MLR* 25 (1930), 261–73.

—— 'The Chamberlain's Men and the "Poetaster" ', *MLR* 42 (1947), 173–9.

GREG, W. W. (ed.), *The Henslowe Papers* (London, 1907).

—— *Two Elizabethan Stage Abridgements* (Oxford, 1923).

—— *Dramatic Documents from the Elizabethan Playhouses* (2 vols., Oxford, 1931).

GRIVELET, MICHEL, 'Note sur Thomas Heywood et le Théâtre sous Charles 1er', *Études Anglaises*, 7 (1954), 101–6.

GURR, ANDREW, 'Who Strutted and Bellowed?', *ShS* 16 (1963), 95–102.

—— *Playgoing in Shakespeare's London* (Cambridge, 1987).

—— 'Intertextuality at Windsor', *SQ* 38 (1987), 189–200.

—— 'Intertextuality in Henslowe', *SQ* 39 (1988), 394–98.

—— 'Money or Audiences: The Impact of Shakespeare's Globe', *TN* 42 (1988), 3–14.

—— 'Singing through the Chatter: Ford and Contemporary Theatrical Fashion', in *John Ford: Critical Re-Visions*, ed. Michael Neill (Cambridge, 1988), 81–96.

—— '*The Tempest's* Tempest at Blackfriars', *ShS* 41 (1989), 91–102.

—— 'Playing in Amphitheatres and Playing in Hall Theatres', *Elizabethan Theatre*, 13 (1994), 27–62.

—— 'Three Reluctant Patrons and Early Shakespeare', *SQ* 44 (1993), 159–74.

—— 'The Chimera of Amalgamation', *TRI* 18 (1993), 85–93.

—— 'The General and the Caviar: Learned Audiences in the Early Theatre', *Studies in the Literary Imagination*, 26 (1993), 7–20.

HAAKER, ANN, 'The Plague, the Theater and the Poet', *RD* n.s. 1 (1968), 283–306.

HAMILTON, ALICE B., 'Research in Progress: Leicester', *REED Newsletter*, 1 (1979), 17–19.

HANNAY, MARGARET P., *Philip's Phoenix: Mary Sidney, Countess of Pembroke* (New York, 1990).

HARBAGE, ALFRED B., 'The Authorship of the Dramatic Arcadia', *MP* 35 (1938), 233–7.

—— *Annals of English Drama, 975–1700* (Philadelphia, 1940; rev. by S. Schoenbaum, 1964, 1970; 3rd edn. by Sylvia S. Wagenheim, New York, 1988).

—— *Shakespeare and the Rival Traditions* (New York, 1952).

HART, A., 'The Length of Elizabethan and Jacobean Plays', *RES* 8 (1932), 139–54.

—— 'The Time Allotted for Representation of Elizabethan and Jacobean Plays', *RES* 8 (1932), 395–413.

HARVEY, GABRIEL, *Foure Letters and Certaine Sermons* (London, 1592).

—— *The Works of Gabriel Harvey*, ed. A. B. Grosart (3 vols., London, 1884).

—— *The Letter-book of Gabriel Harvey A.D. 1573–1580*, ed. E. J. L. Scott (Camden Society, London, 1884).

HATTAWAY, MICHAEL, 'Drama and Society', in *The Cambridge Companion to English Renaissance Drama*, ed. A. R. Braunmuller and Michael Hattaway (Cambridge, 1990), 91–126.

HAY, MILLICENT V., *The Life of Robert Sidney* (Washington DC, 1984).

HAYES, TOM, *The Birth of Popular Culture: Ben Jonson, Maid Marian and Robin Hood* (Pittsburgh, 1992).

HAYNES, ALAN, *The White Bear: Robert Dudley, The Elizabethan Earl of Leicester* (London, 1987).

HAYNES, JONATHAN, 'The Elizabethan Audience on Stage', in *The Theatrical Space*, ed. James Redmond (Themes in Drama 9; Cambridge, 1987), 59–68.

HEINEMANN, MARGOT, *Puritanism and Theatre* (Cambridge, 1980).

—— 'Political Drama', in *The Cambridge Companion to English Renaissance Drama*, ed. A. R. Braunmuller and Michael Hattaway (Cambridge, 1990), 161–206.

—— 'Rebel Lords, Popular Playwrights, and Political Culture: Notes on the Jacobean Patronage of the Earl of Southampton', *YES* 21 (1991), 63–86.

—— 'Drama and Opinion in the 1620s: Middleton and Massinger', in *Theatre and Government under the Early Stuarts*, ed. J. R. Mulryne and Margaret Shewring (Cambridge, 1993), 237–65.

HELGERSON, RICHARD, *Forms of Nationhood: The Elizabethan Writing of England* (Chicago, Ill., 1992).

HEYWOOD, THOMAS, *An Apology for Actors* (London, 1612).

HILLEBRAND, H. N., *The Child Actors: A Chapter in Elizabethan Stage History* (Urbana, 1926).

HISTORICAL MANUSCRIPTS COMMISSION, *Report on the manuscripts of Lord de L'Isle and Dudley* (6 vols.; London, 1925–66).

HOLDSWORTH, R. V., 'Ben Jonson and the Date of *Ram Alley*', *NQ* 230 (1985), 482–6.

HONIGMANN, E. A. J., *Shakespeare: The 'Lost Years'* (Manchester, 1985).

—— and BROCK, SUSAN, *Playhouse Wills 1558–1642: An Edition of Wills by Shakespeare and his Contemporaries in the London Theatre* (Manchester, 1993).

HONNEYMAN, DAVID, 'The Family Origins of Henry Condell', *NQ* 230 (1985), 467–8.

HOSKING, G. L., *The Life and Times of Edward Alleyn* (London, 1952).

HOTINE, MARGARET, 'The Politics of Anti-Semitism: *The Jew of Malta* and *The Merchant of Venice*', *NQ* 236 (1991), 35–7.

HOTSON, LESLIE, *The Commonwealth and Restoration Stage* (Cambridge, Mass., 1928).

HOWARD, JEAN E., 'The New Historicism in Renaissance Studies', *ELR* 16 (1986), 13–43.

HOWARD, SKILES, 'A Re-Examination of Baldwin's Theory of Acting Lines', *Theatre Survey*, 26 (1985), 1–20.

HOWARD-HILL, T. H., 'Political Interpretations of Middleton's *A Game at Chess* (1624)', *YES* 21 (1991), 274–85.

HOWARTH, DAVID, *Lord Arundel and his Circle* (New Haven, Conn., 1985).

HUEBERT, RONALD, 'The Staging of Shirley's *The Lady of Pleasure*', *Elizabethan Theatre*, 9 (1984), 41–59.

HUGHES, CHARLES (ed.), *Shakespeare's Europe: Unpublished Chapters of Fynes Moryson's Itinerary, Being a Survey of the Conditions in Europe at the End of the 16th Century* (6 vols.; London, 1907–36).

HUGHES, P. L., and LARKIN, J. F. (ed.), *Tudor Royal Proclamations* (3 vols.; New Haven, Conn., 1964–9: vol. ii. 1553–1587; vol. iii. 1588–1603).

HUNTER, G. K., *John Lyly: The Humanist as Courtier* (London, 1962).

INGRAM, R. W. (ed.), *REED, Coventry* (Toronto, 1981).

INGRAM, WILLIAM, 'The Theatre at Newington Butts', *SQ* 21 (1970), 385–98.

—— 'The Closing of the Theatres in 1597: A Dissenting View', *MP* 69 (1971–2), 105–15.

—— *A London Life in the Brazen Age* (Cambridge, Mass., 1978).

—— 'Henry Laneman', *TN* 36 (1982), 118–19.

—— 'The Playhouse as an Investment, 1607–1614; Thomas Woodford and Whitefriars', *MRDE* 2 (1985), 209–30.

—— 'Robert Keysar, Playhouse Speculator', *SQ* 37 (1986), 476–85.

—— 'The Early Career of James Burbage', *Elizabethan Theatre*, 10 (1988), 18–36.

—— 'The "Evolution" of the Elizabethan Playing Company', in *The Development of Shakespeare's Theater*, ed. John H. Astington (New York, 1992), 13–28.

—— *The Business of Playing: The Beginnings of the Adult Professional Theater in Elizabethan London* (Ithaca, NY, 1992).

—— 'The Costs of Touring', *MRDE* 6 (1993), 57–62.

IRACE, KATHLEEN M., 'Reconstruction and Adaptation in Q *Henry V*', *SB* 44 (1991), 228–53.

JOHNSTON, ALEXANDRA F. (ed.), *REED, Berkshire and Buckinghamshire* (Toronto), forthcoming.

—— and MARGARET ROGERSON (ed.), *REED, York* (2 vols.; Toronto, 1979).

JONSON, BENJAMIN, *Ben Jonson*, ed. C. H. Herford and P. and E. Simpson (11 vols.; Oxford, 1925–52).

KENNEDY, EDWARD D., 'James I and Chapman's Byron Plays', *JEGP* 64 (1965), 677–90.

KENNY, ROBERT W., *Elizabeth's Admiral* (Baltimore, 1970).

KING, T. J., 'The King's Men on Stage: Actors and Their Parts, 1611–1632', *Elizabethan Theatre*, 9 (1986), 21–40.

—— *Casting Shakespeare's Plays: London Actors and their Roles, 1590–1642* (Cambridge, 1992).

KLAUSNER, DAVID N. (ed.), *REED, Herefordshire/Worcestershire* (Toronto, 1990).

KNAPP, MARGARET, and MICHAL KOBIALKA, 'Shakespeare and the Prince of Purpoole: The 1594 Production of *The Comedy of Errors* at Gray's Inn Hall', *Theatre History Studies*, 4 (1984), 70–81.

KNOWLES, JAMES, 'The Spectacle of the Realm: Civic Consciousness, Rhetoric and Ritual in Early Modern London', in *Theatre and Government under the Early Stuarts*, ed. J. R. Mulryne and Margaret Shewring (Cambridge, 1993), 157–89.

KNUTSON, ROSLYN LANDER, 'Henslowe's Naming of Parts: Entries in the Diary for *Tamar Cham*, 1592–3, and *Godfrey of Bulloigne*, 1594–5', *NQ* 230 (1983), 157–60.

—— 'Play Identifications: *The Wise Men of Westchester* and *John a Kent and John a Cumber*, *Longshanks* and *Edward I*', *HLQ* 47 (1984), 1–11.

—— 'Henslowe's Diary and the Economics of Play Revision for Revival, 1592–1603', *TRI* 10 (1985), 1–18.

—— 'Influence of The Repertory System on the Revival and Revision of *The Spanish Tragedy* and *Dr. Faustus*', *ELR* 18 (1988), 257–74.

—— 'Evidence for the Assignment of Plays to the Repertory of Shakespeare's Company', *MRDE* 4 (1989), 75–89.

—— *The Repertory of Shakespeare's Company, 1594–1613* (Fayetteville, Ark. 1991).

—— 'Telling the Story of Shakespeare's Playhouse World', *ShS* 44 (1992), 145–56.

LAMB, MARY ELLEN, 'The Myth of the Countess of Pembroke: The Dramatic Circle', *YES* 11 (1981), 194–202.

LANCASHIRE, ANNE, 'St. Paul's Grammar School before 1580: Theatrical Development Suppressed?', in *The Development of Shakespeare's Theater*, ed. John H. Astington (New York, 1992), 29–56.

LARKIN, JAMES F., and HUGHES, PAUL L. (ed.), *Stuart Royal Proclamations* (2 vols.; Oxford, 1973–83: vol. i. 1603–1625; vol. ii. 1625–1646).

LAROQUE, FRANÇOIS, *Shakespeare's Festive World: Elizabethan Seasonal Entertainment and the Professional Stage*, trans. Janet Lloyd (Cambridge, 1991).

LAVIN, J. A., 'Shakespeare and the Second Blackfriars', *Elizabethan Theatre*, 3 (1973), 66–81.

LAWRENCE, W. J., 'John Kirke, the Caroline Actor-Dramatist', *SP* 21 (1924), 586–93.

LEGGATT, ALEXANDER, *Citizen Comedy in the Age of Shakespeare* (Toronto, 1973).

—— *Jacobean Public Theatre* (London, 1992).

LEINWAND, THEODORE, *The City Staged: Jacobean Comedy, 1603–1613* (Madison, Wisc., 1986).

LENTON, FRANCIS, *The Young Gallants Whirligig* (London, 1629).

LEVIN, HARRY, 'Two Magian Comedies: *The Tempest* and *The Alchemist*', *ShS* 22 (1971), 47–58.

LIMON, JERZY, *Gentlemen of a Company: English Players in Central and Eastern Europe, 1590–1660* (Cambridge, 1985).

—— 'An Allusion to the Alleged Catholicism of some Jacobean Players in John Gee's *New Shreds from the Old Snare* (1624)', *NQ* 230 (1985), 488–9.

—— *Dangerous Matter: English Drama and Politics in 1623/4* (Cambridge, 1989).

LINDLEY, DAVID, *The Trials of Frances Howard: Fact and Fiction at the Court of King James* (Basingstoke, 1993).

LOADES, DAVID, *The Tudor Court* (London, 1986).

LOFTIS, JOHN, 'English Renaissance Plays from the Spanish Comedia', *ELR* 14 (1984), 230–48.

LOOMIE, ALBERT J. (ed.), *Ceremonies of Charles I: The Note Books of John Finet 1628–1641* (New York, 1987).

LYLY, JOHN, *John Lyly: The Complete Works*, ed. R. W. Bond (3 vols.; Oxford, 1892).

—— '*Campaspe' and 'Sappho and Phao*', ed. G. K. Hunter and David Bevington (Revels Plays: Manchester, 1991).

MACCABE, RICHARD A., 'Elizabethan Satire and the Bishops' Ban of 1599', *YES* 11 (1981), 188–94.

MACCAFFREY, WALLACE, 'Patronage and Politics under the Tudors', in *The Mental World of the Jacobean Court*, ed. Linda Levy Peck (Cambridge, 1991), 21–35.

MACINTYRE, JEAN, 'Conventions of Costume Change in Elizabethan Plays', *Explorations in Renaissance Culture*, 12 (1986), 105–13.

—— ' "One That Hath Two Gowns": Costume Change in Some Elizabethan Plays', *English Studies in Canada*, 13 (1987), 12–22.

MACLEAN, SALLY-BETH, 'Players on Tour: New Evidence From Records of Early English Drama', *Elizabethan Theatre*, 10 (1988), 155–72.

—— 'Leicester and the Evelyns: New Evidence for the Continental Tour of Leicester's Men', *RES* 39 (1988), 487–93.

—— 'The Politics of Patronage: Dramatic Records in Robert Dudley's Household Books', *SQ* 44 (1993), 175–82.

—— 'Tour Routes: "Provincial Wanderings" or Traditional Circuits?', *MRDE* 6 (1993), 1–14.

MCELROY, MARY, and CARTWRIGHT, KENT 'Public Fencing Contests on the Elizabethan Stage', *Journal of Sport History*, 13 (1986), 193–211.

MCGEE, C. E., 'Stuart Kings and Cambridge University Drama: Two Stories by William Whiteway', *NQ* 233 (1988), 494–6.

MCLUSKIE, KATHLEEN E., *Renaissance Dramatists* (New York, 1989).

—— 'The Poets' Royal Exchange: Patronage and Commerce in Early Modern Drama', *YES* 21 (1991), 53–62.

—— *Dekker and Heywood, Professional Dramatists* (Basingstoke, 1994).

MCMILLIN, Scott, 'Casting for Pembroke's Men: The *Henry VI* Quartos and *The Taming of A Shrew*', *SQ* 23 (1972), 141–59.

—— 'Simon Jewell and the Queen's Men', *RES* 27 (1976), 174–7.

—— 'The Queen's Men in 1594: A Study of "Good" and "Bad" Quartos', *ELR* 14 (1984), 55–69.

—— 'Building Stories: Greg, Fleay, and the Plot of 2 *Seven Deadly Sins*', *MRDE* 3 (1988), 53–89.

—— *The Elizabethan Theatre and the 'Book of Sir Thomas More'* (Ithaca, NY, 1987).

McMillin, Scott, 'The Queen's Men and the London Theatre of 1583', *Elizabethan Theatre*, 10 (1988), 1–17.

—— 'Sussex's Men in 1594: The Evidence of *Titus Andronicus* and *The Jew of Malta*', *Theatre Survey*, 32 (1991), 214–23.

McMullan, Gordon, and Hope, Jonathan (ed.), *The Politics of Tragicomedy: Shakespeare and After* (London and New York, 1992).

Maguire, Laurie E., 'John Holland and *John of Bordeaux*', *NQ* 231 (1986), 327–33.

—— 'A Stage Property in *A Larum for London*', *NQ* 231 (1986), 371–3.

Mann, Irene, 'A Lost Version of the *Three Ladies of London*', *PMLA* 59 (1944), 586–9.

Marcus, Leah S., *Puzzling Shakespeare: Local Reading and its Discontents* (Berkeley, Calif., 1988).

Montrose, Louis, 'New Historicisms', in *Redrawing the Boundaries: The Transformation of English and American Literary Studies*, ed. Stephen Greenblatt and Giles Gunn (New York, 1992), 392–418.

Morrill, John, *The Revolt of the Provinces: Conservatives and Radicals in the English Civil War, 1630–1650* (London, 1976).

Morillo, Marvin, 'Shirley's "Preferment" and the Court of Charles I', *SEL* I (1961), 101–7.

Morse, David, *England's Time of Crisis: From Shakespeare to Milton: A Cultural History* (New York, 1989).

Mullaney, Steven, *The Place of the Stage: License, Play, and Power in Renaissance England* (Chicago, Ill., 1988).

Mulryne, J. R., and Shewring, Margaret (ed.), *Theatre and Government under the Early Stuarts* (Cambridge, 1993).

Murray, John Tucker, *English Dramatic Companies 1558–1642* (2 vols.; London, 1910).

Musgrove, S., *Shakespeare and Jonson* (Auckland, 1958).

Nashe, Thomas, *Works*, ed. R. B. McKerrow (5 vols.; London, 1904–10).

—— *Summer's Last Will and Testament*, ed. Patricia Posluszny (New York, 1989).

Nef, J. U., *Cultural Foundations of Industrial Civilizations* (Cambridge, 1958).

Nelson, Alan H. (ed.), *REED, Cambridge* (2 vols.; Toronto, 1989).

Nethercot, Arthur H., *Sir William Davenant* (New York, 1938; revised ed. 1967).

Neuss, Paula, ed. *Aspects of Early English Drama* (Cambridge, 1983).

Nicholl, Charles, *A Cup of News: The Life of Thomas Nashe* (London, 1984).

Nosworthy, J. M., 'A Note on John Heminge', *Library*, 3 (1948), 287–8.

Nungezer, E., *A Dictionary of Actors and Other Persons Associated with the Public Representation of Plays in England before 1642* (New Haven, Conn., 1929).

Orgel, Stephen, 'The Spectacles of State', in *Persons in Groups: Social Behavior as Identity Formation in Medieval and Renaissance Europe*, ed. Richard C. Trexler (New York, 1985), 101–22.

Orrell, John, *The Theatres of Inigo Jones and John Webb* (Cambridge, 1985).

—— *The Human Stage: English Theatre Design, 1567–1640* (Cambridge, 1988).

—— 'The London Stage in the Florentine Correspondence, 1604–1618', *TRI* 3 (1977–8), 155–81.

Osborne, Francis, *The True Tragicomedy Formerly Acted at Court*, ed. John Pitcher and Lois Potter (New York and London, 1983).

Pafford, J. P. H., 'John Clavell, 1606–43, Burglar, Highwayman, Poet, Dramatist, Doctor, Lawyer', *Somerset and Dorset Notes and Queries*, 32 (1986), 549–63.

PALMER, DARYL W., *Hospitable Performances: Dramatic Genre and Cultural Practices in Early Modern England* (West Lafayette, Ind., 1992).

PATTERSON, ANNABEL, *Censorship and Interpretation: The Conditions of Writing and Reading in Early Modern England* (Madison, Wis., 1984).

PAYNE, DEBORAH C., 'Patronage and the Dramatic Marketplace under Charles I and II', *YES* 21 (1991), 137–52.

PECK, LINDA LEVY, *Court Patronage and Corruption in Early Stuart England* (London, 1989).

—— (ed.), *The Mental World of the Jacobean Court* (Cambridge, 1991).

PETTIT, THOMAS, 'The Seasons of the Globe: Two New Studies of Elizabethan Drama and Festival', *Connotations*, 2 (1992), 234–56.

PILKINTON, MARK C., 'The Playhouse in Wine Street, Bristol', *TN* 37 (1983), 14–21.

PINCISS, G. M., 'The Queen's Men, 1583–1592', *Theatre Survey*, 11 (1970), 50–65.

—— 'Thomas Creede and the Repertory of the Queen's Men', *MP* 67 (1970), 321–30.

—— 'Shakespeare, Her Majesty's Players, and Pembroke's Men', *ShS* 27 (1974), 129–36.

PULMAN, M. B., *The Elizabethan Privy Council in the Fifteen Seventies* (Berkeley, Calif., 1971).

RACKIN, PHYLLIS, *Stages of History: Shakespeare's English Chronicles* (Ithaca, NY, 1990).

RAPPAPORT, STEVE, *Worlds within Worlds: Structures of Life in Sixteenth-Century London* (Cambridge, 1989).

RASTALL, RICHARD, 'Female Roles in All-Male Casts', *Medieval English Theatre*, 7 (1985), 25–50.

READ, CONYERS, 'Walsingham and Burghley in Queen Elizabeth's Privy Council', *EHR* 28 (1913), 34–58.

REAY, BARRY, ed. *Popular Culture in Seventeenth-Century England* (London, 1985).

REEVE, L. J., *Charles I and the Road to Personal Rule* (Cambridge, 1989).

The Revels History of Drama in English: vol. iii. *1576–1613*, Leeds J. Barroll, Alexander Leggatt, Richard Hosley, and Alvin Kernan (London, 1975); vol. iv. *1613–1660*, Philip Edwards, Gerald Eades Bentley, Kathleen McLuskie, and Lois Potter (London, 1981).

REYNOLDS, GEORGE F., *The Staging of Elizabethan Plays at the Red Bull Theater, 1605–1625*, London, 1940.

RIEWALD, J. G., 'Some Late Elizabethan and Early Stuart Actors and Musicians', *English Studies*, 40 (1959), 33–41.

—— 'The English Actors in the Low Countries, 1585–c.1650: An Annotated Bibliography', in *Studies in Seventeenth Century English Literature, History and Bibliography*, ed. G. A. M. Janssens and F. G. A. M. Aarts (Amsterdam, 1984), 157–78.

RINGLER, WILLIAM A., Jr., 'The Number of Actors in Shakespeare's Early Plays', in *The Seventeenth-Century Stage*, ed. G. E. Bentley (Toronto, 1968).

ROWAN, D. F., 'Inns, Inn-Yards, and Other Playing Places', *Elizabethan Theatre*, 9, 1–20.

—— 'The Players and Playing Places at Norwich', in *The Development of Shakespeare's Theater*, ed. John H, Astington (New York, 1992), 77–94.

ROZETT, MARTHA, *The Doctrine of Election and the Emergence of Elizabethan Tragedy* (Princeton, NJ, 1984).

RUTTER, CAROL CHILLINGTON (ed.), *Documents of the Rose Playhouse* (Manchester, 1984).

SACCIO, PETER, *The Court Comedies of John Lyly* (Princeton, NJ, 1969).

SAMS, ERIC, 'The Timing of the Shrews', *NQ* 230 (1986), 33–45.

SCHOENBAUM, SAMUEL, *William Shakespeare: A Compact Documentary Life* (Oxford, 1977).

SCHRICKX, WILLEM, *Foreign Envoys and Travelling Players in the Age of Shakespeare and Jonson* (Wetteren, 1986).

SHAPIRO, MICHAEL, *Children of the Revels: The Boy Companies of Shakespeare's Time and their Plays* (New York, 1977).

SHARPE, KEVIN, *Sir Robert Cotton 1558–1631: History and Politics in Early Modern England* (Oxford, 1979).

—— *Criticism and Compliment: the Politics of Literature in the England of Charles I* (Cambridge, 1987).

—— *The Personal Rule of Charles I* (New Haven, Conn. 1992).

SHEN LIN, 'How Old were the Children of Paul's?', *TN* 45 (1991), 121–31.

SISSON, C. J., 'Notes on Early Stuart Stage History', *MLR* 37 (1942), 25–36.

—— 'The Red Bull Company and the Importunate Widow', *ShS* 7 (1954), 57–68.

SMUTS, R. MALCOLM, 'The Political Failure of Stuart Cultural Patronage', in *Patronage in the Renaissance*, ed. G. F. Lytle and Stephen Orgel (Princeton, NJ, 1981).

—— *Court Culture and the Origins of a Royalist Tradition in Early Stuart England* (Philadelphia, 1987).

—— 'Cultural Diversity and Cultural Change at the Court of James I', in *The Mental World of the Jacobean Court*, ed. Linda Levy Peck (Cambridge, 1991), 99–112.

SOMERSET, J. A. B., 'The Lords President, Their Activities and Companies: Evidence from Shropshire', *Elizabethan Theatre*, 10 (1988), 93–111.

—— ' "How Chances it they Travel?": Provincial Playing, Playing Places and the King's Men', *ShS* 47 (1994), pp. 45–60.

—— ed. *REED, Shropshire* (Toronto, 1994).

SOUTHERN, RICHARD, *The Staging of Plays Before Shakespeare* (London, 1973).

STARKEY, DAVID (ed.), *The English Court* (London, 1987).

STEVENS, DAVID, *English Renaissance Theatre History: A Reference Guide* (Boston, 1982).

STOKES, JAMES, and ALEXANDER, ROBERT (ed.), *REED, Somerset and Bath* (Toronto), forthcoming.

STOWE, JOHN, *Annales* (London, 1615).

STREETT, J. B., 'The Durability of Boy Actors', *NQ* 218 (1973), 461–5.

STREITBERGER, W. R., 'On Edmund Tyllney's Biography', *RES* 29 (1978), 11–35.

—— ed. *Jacobean and Caroline Revels Accounts, 1603–1642* (Malone Society Collections xiii.; Oxford, 1986).

TAYLOR, GARY, 'The fortunes of Oldcastle', *ShS* 38 (1985), 85–100.

—— 'William Shakespeare, Richard James, and the House of Cobham', *RES* 38 (1987), 334–54.

THOMSON, PETER, *Shakespeare's Professional Career* (Cambridge, 1992).

TITTLER, ROBERT, *Architecture and Power: The Town Hall and the English Urban Community c.1500–1640* (Oxford, 1991).

TRICOMI, ALBERT H., 'Philip, Earl of Pembroke, and the Analogical Way of Reading Political Tragedy', *JEGP* 85 (1986), 332–45.

—— *Anticourt Drama in England 1603–1642* (Charlottesville, Va., 1989).

UNDERDOWN, DAVID, *Revel, Riot, and Rebellion: Popular Politics and Culture in England 1603–1660* (Oxford, 1985).

VEEVERS, ERICA, *Images of Love and Religion: Queen Henrietta Maria and Court Entertainments* (Cambridge, 1989).

WAGONHEIM, ALFRED HARBAGE, *Annals of English Drama 975–1700*, 19 Revised by S. Schoenbaum, 1964. Third edition revised by Sylvia Stoler Wagonheim, London, 1989. See especially the Index of Dramatic Companies, 348–52.

WALKER, GREG, *Plays of Persuasion: Drama and Politics at the Court of Henry VIII* (Cambridge, 1991).

WALLER, GARY, *The Sidney Family Romance: Mary Wroth, William Herbert, and the Early Modern Construction of Gender* (Detroit, 1993).

WASSON, JOHN (ed.), *REED, Devon* (Toronto, 1986).

—— 'Elizabethan and Jacobean Touring Companies', *TN* 42 (1988), 51–7.

WELLS, STANLEY, TAYLOR, GARY, *et. al.*, *A Textual Companion to the New Oxford Shakespeare* (Oxford, 1987).

WEIMANN, ROBERT, *Shakespeare and the Popular Tradition in the Theater*, ed. and trans. Robert Schwartz (London, 1978).

WENTERSDORF, KARL P., 'The Repertory and Size of Pembroke's Company', *Theatre Annual*, 33 (1977), 48–61.

—— 'The Origin and Personnel of the Pembroke Company', *TRI* 5 (1979), 45–68.

WERSTINE, PAUL, 'Narratives About Printed Shakespearean Texts: "Foul Papers" and "Bad" Quartos', *SQ* 41 (1990), 65–86.

WESTFALL, SUZANNE R., *Patrons and Performance: Early Tudor Household Revels* (Oxford, 1990).

WHITE, BEATRICE, *An Index to 'The Elizabethan Stage' and 'William Shakespeare: A Study of the Facts and Problems' by Sir Edmund Chambers* (Oxford, 1934).

WHITE, HAYDEN, *Tropics of Discourse: Essays in Cultural Criticism* (Baltimore and London, 1979).

WHITE, PAUL WHITFIELD, *Theatre and Reformation: Protestantism, Patronage and Playing in Tudor England* (Cambridge, 1993).

WHITROW, G. J., *Time in History: The Evolution of our General Awareness of Time and Temporal Perspective* (Oxford, 1988).

WICKHAM, GLYNNE, *Early English Stages, 1300–1660* (4 vols.; London, 1959–).

WIKANDER, MATTHEW H., *Princes to Act: Royal Audience and Royal Performance, 1578–1792*, (Baltimore, 1993).

WIKLAND, ERIC, *Elizabethan Players in Sweden 1591–92* (Uppsala; first edn., 1962; second edn. 1991; third edn., 1977).

WILES, DAVID, *Shakespeare's Clown: Actor and Text in the Elizabethan Playhouse* (Cambridge, 1987).

WILLIAMS, CLARE, trans. and ed., *Thomas Platter's Travels in England 1599* (London, 1937).

WILSON, F. P., *The Plague in Shakespeare's London* (Oxford, 1927).

WILSON, RICHARD, ' "A Mingled Yarn": Shakespeare and the Cloth Workers', *Literature and History*, 12 (1986), 164–80.

WORTHEN, W. B., 'Deeper Meanings and Theatrical Technique: The Rhetoric of Performance Criticism', *SQ* 40 (1989), 441–55.

WREN, ROBERT M., 'Salisbury and the Blackfriars Theatre', *TN* 23 (1968), 103–9.

WRIGHT, JAMES, *Historia Histrionica* (London, 1699).

WRIGHT, W. S., 'Edward Alleyn, Actor and Benefactor, 1566–1626', *TN* 20 (1965), 155–60.

YOUNG, ABIGAIL ANN, 'Plays and Players: The Latin Terms for Performance', *REED Newsletter*, 9 (1984), 56–62.

—— 'Plays and Players: The Latin Terms for Performance (Part 2)', *REED Newsletter*, 10 (1985), 9–16.

YOUNG, WILLIAM, *A History of Dulwich College* (2 vols.; Edinburgh, 1889).

Index